Educational Assessment

A Practical Introduction

Educational Assessment
A Practical Introduction

Thomas P. Hogan
University of Scranton

WILEY

John Wiley & Sons, Inc.

Associate Publisher	*Jay O'Callaghan*
Executive Editor	*Christopher Johnson*
Editorial Assistant	*Lindsay Lovier*
Production Editor	*Janine Rosado*
Marketing Manager	*Jeffrey Rucker*
Design Director	*Harry Nolan*
Senior Designer	*Kevin Murphy*
Photo Editor	*Tara Sanford*
Cover Photo	*Getty Images*
Production Management Services	*GGS Book Services*

This book was set in Times Roman by GGS Book Services and printed and bound by R. R. Donnelley and Sons. The cover was printed by Phoenix Color Corp.

This book is printed on acid free paper. ∞

To order books or for customer service please, call 1-800-CALL WILEY (225-5945).

Library of Congress Cataloging in Publication Data:
Hogan, Thomas P.
   Educational assessment : a practical introduction / Thomas P. Hogan.
      p. cm.
   Includes bibliographical references and index.
   ISBN-13: 978-0-471-47248-3 (cloth)
   ISBN-10: 0-471-47248-4 (cloth)
1. Educational tests and measurments.   I. Title.
   LB3051.H682 2007
   371.26—dc22

                                        2005015355

Printed in the United States of America

10 9 8 7 6 5 4 3 2 1

For
Peg
and the Kids
and the Grandkids

Preface

This book provides an introduction to the exciting field of educational assessment. The book is designed for teachers, prospective teachers, and other professionals in education. The most frequent use of *Educational Assessment: A Practical Introduction* will be in the context of a formal, semester-long course at the undergraduate or graduate level. This use dictated such features as the length of the book, the structure of the chapters, and the suggestions for learning activities.

The book's title deliberately incorporates the word "practical" in two senses. *First*, I treat educational assessment as it is practiced today, in the actual world of classrooms, school systems, state departments, and national organizations. This was part of my motivation for preparing the book. I find that too many textbooks on educational assessment treat the field as it existed 20 years ago, criticizing practices that are no longer current or making recommendations that are no longer applicable, and they often fail to cover topics that have assumed great practical importance in recent years.

Second, the book uses a practical approach to pedagogy. This is a textbook, not a reference work. Each chapter begins with a manageable list of learning *objectives* to serve as advance organizers for students. Each chapter concludes with a succinct *summary* and list of *key terms*. The key terms appear in boldface typeface in the text where they are defined, as well as in the Glossary.

Sprinkled throughout the text are four other practical aids to learning. *Key Point Summaries* serve as intermediate summaries at the end of major sections within chapters. *Try This!* exercises appear throughout the main body of each chapter. These are designed to engage students with specific topics they encounter in the text—not just read about them but do something with them. Each Try This! exercise should require only a minute to complete. Toward the end of each chapter are a few points listed in *Practical Advice*. These points arise directly from the topics covered in the chapter. Finally, each chapter concludes with *Exercises* to further engage students in the learning enterprise. These exercises require more work than the Try This! exercises embedded in the text. My rule of thumb was that it should be possible to complete an exercise in 10–20 minutes, thus making it feasible to assign several of these in conjunction with each chapter. Many of the Try This! and end-of-chapter Exercises use Internet resources, which have greatly enriched the array of learning opportunities.

STRUCTURE OF THE BOOK

The book divides conceptually into four areas. Figure 1.1 in Chapter 1 outlines this structure. *First*, Chapters 2–5 cover the basic concepts applicable to all types of assessment: statistical concepts (Chapter 2), reliability (Chapter 3), validity (Chapter 4), and interpretive frameworks (Chapter 5). *Second*, Chapters 6–10 feature the preparation of teacher-made tests. Topics include planning for assessment (Chapter 6), selected-response items

(Chapter 7), and the broad array of constructed-response items, including essays, performances, and portfolios (Chapter 8). Chapter 9 deals with assessment of attitudes, interests, and creativity, and the use of nontest indicators. Chapter 10 addresses the administration and analysis of classroom tests, with a special section on cheating. *Third*, Chapters 11–12 cover standardized tests, with the first of these devoted to achievement tests and the second devoted to other types of standardized tests that are typically encountered in schools. Appendixes A, B, and E serve as important supplements to Chapters 11 and 12. *Fourth*, Chapters 13–15 cover what I refer to as "special applications." This group of chapters might be labeled "other essential stuff," but that is not a very elegant term. The specific topics are grading (Chapter 13), legal issues (Chapter 14), and evaluating one's own teaching (Chapter 15). In general, topical coverage corresponds closely to (or perhaps I should say is dictated by) statements from professional associations about what teachers should know and be able to do regarding educational assessment. Chapter 1 identifies the sources for these statements.

A special word about Chapter 2: A Little Bit of Statistics. One needs a "little bit" (but only a little bit) of statistics to understand and apply the material in Chapters 3–5. I have assumed that students have *not* had a course in statistics. Of course, some students will have had such a course. For them, Chapter 2 can serve as a quick review. Students who have not had systematic exposure to statistics will need to spend more time on this chapter. Chapter 2 is included as an early, stand-alone chapter specifically because I found, after reviewing many syllabi for educational assessment courses, that the majority of instructors handle the topic in this manner. That is, they treat statistics as a separate topic early in the course, regardless of where the material occurs in the text they are using. Instructors can tailor the use of Chapter 2, and the formulas in Appendix C, to the background of their students.

Chapter 14 on the law and Chapter 15 on evaluating one's own teaching are also subject to considerable flexibility in the hands of different instructors. Some instructors will want to cover these two chapters systematically. Other instructors may chose to cover only selected parts of them.

MY ORIENTATION AND BACKGROUND

To help make the myriad choices faced in preparing a book such as this, one must have points of orientation. I have used three points of orientation in preparing the book. The first was simple: It was to be used as a textbook. As identified earlier, the second was the effort to be practical. The third point of orientation was to follow a "best practices" approach. I was not aiming for a "minimal competency" approach. The book does not aspire to be educational assessment for dummies. In the words of contemporary standards-based education, the goal was to bring students to a "proficient" level. This point of orientation dictated that difficult subjects—such as reliability, norms, and the law—be met head on rather than sidestepped. The interests of teachers and prospective teachers are not well served by avoiding or glossing over such topics.

While aspiring to a proficient level of attainment, the book is an introductory treatment, not an advanced treatment of the subject. There are practical limits to what can be accomplished in an introductory course. I have tried to draw the line prudently and, when appropriate, I direct the reader to the professional literature containing more advanced treatments of many topics.

These points of orientation have been informed by my years of practical experience. I have labored in the educational assessment vineyard for a *very* long time. I have been a project director for one of the world's largest publishers of educational assessment materials, working on survey achievement tests, diagnostic tests, and mental ability tests. I have coauthored or authored several editions of one of the nation's most widely used standardized achievement tests, a widely used criterion-referenced basal reader test, a nationally (and internationally) used measure of school attitudes, and numerous other norm-referenced and criterion-referenced tests (even including one in a Native American language). In this regard, I should note that I do not have a proprietary interest in any of the tests featured in this book. I served for 11 years on the Exercise Development Committee of the National Assessment of Educational Progress. My positions have included director of a university testing center and codirector of a statewide assessment center. I have served as consultant on assessment to numerous school systems, as well as to state departments and national organizations. I have also served for 12 years on boards of education. And, of course, across all these experiences, I have been teaching assessment courses in both education and psychology departments. I have tried to distill from these experiences the key concepts and "best practices" in educational assessment that I think will be useful to teachers.

In the end, I hope that students using *Educational Assessment: A Practical Introduction* find it to be a good learning tool. I hope that students attain "proficiency" in the construction of their own tests and in the interpretation of external tests. I hope their proficiency in educational assessment translates into more effective learning for their own students. And, I hope that instructors find the book to be a valuable teaching tool.

Thomas P. Hogan
Scranton, Pennsylvania

Acknowledgments

Accounting for the myriad contributions to preparation of this book is a daunting and humbling task. So many people have done so much to assist me. I am very grateful, especially to the following. To all of my students over many years, for their willingness to suggest ways to present concepts about assessment in effective ways, with special thanks to Kelly Lister, Kim Evalenko, and Katie Barnes for assistance with research and manuscript preparation. To the many publishers that granted permission for reproductions and to their staff who gave helpful advice. To the manuscript reviewers for their helpful insights and commentary, including their tolerant identification of utterly silly errors in early drafts: Barbara Allen, Delta College; Jonathan Brenefur; Robert Carpenter; Irene Chen, University of Houston, Downtown; Ted Coladarci, University of Maine, Orono; M. Ruth Davenport, Eastern Oregon University; Tara Durbin, University of Cincinnati; Pamela Edwards, Mam, Delta College; Bruce Frey, University of Kansas; Christopher Gareis, The College of William & Mary; Marion Godine, University of Houston; Jessica Gomel; Deborah Goodwin, Arkansas State University; Joanna Grymes, Arkansas State University; Thomas Haladyna; Virginia Hamm, Athens State University; Lisa Hass, Arizona State University, Tempe; Mitchell Henke; K.C. Holder, Eastern Oregon University; Jo Ann Holtz, Edinboro University; Diane Hudson, Athens State University; Sarah Huyvaert, Eastern Michigan University; Pat Keig, California State University, Fullerton; Marie Kraska, Auburn University; Mary Kremer, Dominican University; Antony Kunnan, California State University, Los Angeles; Kelly Maples, Clermont College; Cindy Marble, University of Idaho, Moscow; Jan Massmann, Concordia University, Irvine; Nelson Maylone, Eastern Michigan University; Judy Meloy, Castleton State College; Barry Mitchell, Brigham Young University; John Poggio, University of Kansas; Melinda Romero, Arizona State University; Michael Russel; Jonah Schlackman, California State University, Los Angeles; Mindy Sloan; Bob Smith, University of Mobile; Carole Smithwich, Kiebach; Patricia Stinger-Barnes, Carson-Newman College; Laura Thomas, Antioch University; Juan Trujillo, Albany State University; Frankie Williams, Clemson University; Ralph Woodword, Eastern Oregon University; Yuankun Yao, Central Missouri State University.

To Brad Hanson of John Wiley & Sons, Inc., for encouraging me to undertake this project. To Joseph Fusaro and Ivan Shibley of the Education Department at the University of Scranton, to Mike Beck of Beta, Inc., and to Edward M. Hogan of Duchesne Academy for reviews of selected chapters. To attorneys Mary Teresa Hogan Vasquez, Thomas P. Hogan, Jr., and Matthew J. D. Hogan for their trenchant critiques and helpful suggestions regarding technical matters in the chapter on the law. To preservice teacher Margaret E. Hogan for continuing consultation and some rather pointed advice from start to finish. To my colleague John Norcross who served as a sounding board on a host of issues. To my many colleagues in a variety of educational assessment enterprises over the years for their wise counsel and, even more so, for the inspiration I derived from their genuine interest in the welfare of students. Finally, I want to thank my wife, Peg, for moral support throughout the endeavor. With all that help, you'd think the book would be perfect. Alas, that is probably not the case. I must take credit for any imperfections that might have remained in the work.

To the Students

Educational assessment is a crucial topic in education today. In this book, we explore why that is so. We try to provide you with the perspectives and skills you need to be an intelligent user of educational assessment. Our approach is a "best practices" rather than a "minimum competency" approach. We want you to adopt the best practices in the field, not just get by with as little as possible.

There are two main contexts for educational assessment. First, every teacher will conduct assessment. Therefore, we examine how to do a good job assessing your students. Second, everyone today—teachers, students, school administrators, parents, and the public at large—deals with external testing programs. These programs include state assessment programs, achievement batteries, certification exams, and national testing programs, among others. You need to know the origin of these tests and how to interpret results from them.

The subtitle of this book refers to a "practical introduction." The book aims to be practical in two ways. First, it describes educational assessment as it is practiced today. Too many textbooks describe assessment as it existed 20 years ago. That's not very helpful. Second, this book tries to be practical by engaging you, the student, in the material as it is presented. This occurs by way of the Try This! exercises embedded in the text, as well as end-of-chapter exercises. In order for the material to be practical, you must use these features on a regular basis. Doing so will lead to a more meaningful experience for you.

Educational assessment contains a fair number of technical terms and a few moderately difficult concepts. The course will not be a breeze, and we have not tried to oversimplify the material. You need to know these terms and concepts in order to be an intelligent user of educational assessment. The field also includes a host of very specific skills, such as preparing test items and completing report cards. We have tried to maintain the practical orientation for both the concepts and skills within the field. To that end, each chapter concludes with a section entitled Practical Advice.

I hope this book will provide a good learning experience for you. Good luck working through it.

Professor Thomas P. Hogan
University of Scranton
Scranton, Pennsylvania
January 11, 2005

Brief Contents

Detailed Contents

Appendixes

Chapter 1

Introduction: The World of Educational Assessment

OBJECTIVES

- Identify the main areas of concern for an introductory course in educational assessment.
- Outline key points made in guidelines from professional groups on important topics in educational assessment.
- Define the main purposes of educational assessment.
- Identify the main uses of educational assessment.
- Describe each of the seven current trends in educational assessment.
- Define important terms used in educational assessment.

What This Chapter Is About

This chapter provides a broad overview of the world of educational assessment. There are several ways to gain this broad perspective. By taking up each of them we should emerge with a reasonable grasp of the field of educational assessment. Fortunately, there is good overlap among these various ways of introducing the field. We examine the main categories of assessment, guidelines from professional groups, purposes for assessment, users of assessment information, current trends shaping the field, and a host of commonly used assessment terms.

Why This Topic Is Important

This chapter provides an overview of all the topics covered in subsequent chapters. It is important to start with this overview so that we know where we are headed and what the major issues are in this field of educational assessment. This chapter will help us keep perspective about the "big picture" as we move through more detailed topics in other chapters.

THE MAIN AREAS IN EDUCATIONAL ASSESSMENT

Let us begin with the simplest, most direct way of summarizing what educational assessment is all about. What are the main areas we must cover in this book? We can conceptualize the entire field as having four parts. Figure 1.1 outlines these four parts. Let us work

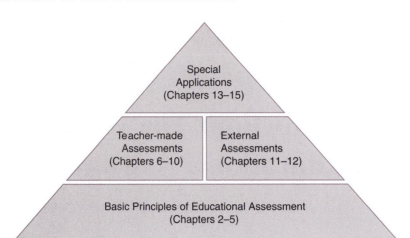

Figure 1.1 Main areas covered by educational assessment.

through this figure in the order in which we will treat the topics. Think of it as a pyramid, with basic principles as the foundation and the first topic to be considered. Teacher-made assessments and external assessments come next. We conclude, at the top of the pyramid, with special applications.

Basic Principles

There are basic principles of assessment that apply to all types of assessment. The concepts incorporated into these basic principles will help us design and evaluate the quality of specific assessments. We identify these basic principles briefly in this chapter and then treat them in more detail in Chapters 3–5, with Chapter 2 providing the necessary statistical background for Chapters 3–5.

The basic principles include reliability, validity, and methods of interpretation. **Reliability** refers to the consistency or stability of measures. We need to assure ourselves that the assessments we make have an adequate degree of consistency. Otherwise, we cannot depend on the measure to draw conclusions or make decisions. **Validity** refers to the extent to which the measure gauges the trait, ability, skill, or attitude we intend to measure. Is the reading test really measuring reading comprehension skill and not reading speed? Is the history test really measuring knowledge of history and not, say, ability to con the teacher with fancy words? Is the inventory of attitude toward mathematics really measuring attitude and not just measuring what the teacher wants to hear? These are all questions about validity. Validity is the most important characteristic of a test—so we want to examine it carefully. A subtopic under the category of validity is the fairness of the assessment. Is the assessment equally valid for all students? For example, does the student with a visual limitation have a fair chance on the reading test? Is the test valid for that student? Is the assessment culturally biased in any way?

The third area for basic principles relates to methods of interpreting student performance. The basic issue is how we make sense out of student performance on a particular assessment. Ned got a score of 37 right out of 50 on the spelling test. What do we make out of that? Abigail got a rating of 5 on her essay. What does that mean? Here we examine methods for norm-referenced interpretation and criterion-referenced interpretation. **Norm-referenced** methods interpret an individual student's performance in the context of other students' performance on the same task. For example, Abigail's score of 5 is the highest in the school—so that's pretty good. **Criterion-referenced** methods interpret a student's performance, not in relation to other students, but in relation to some external criterion or judgment. For example, the teacher may have expected all students in Ned's class to get all the items right on the test—so a score of 37 is quite unacceptable, regardless of how other students scored. Currently, the best example of criterion-referenced interpretation is performance-based reporting in state assessment programs. This is the type of reporting that results in categories of "proficient," "basic," and so on. We will examine a variety of methods for norm-referenced and criterion-referenced interpretation in Chapter 5.

Teacher-made Assessments

The second main area of concern is teacher-made tests or assessments. How does the individual teacher go about developing assessments? We first consider how to plan for assessment and how to approach development of a specific test. Various methods are used to assess student performance. We need to identify each of these methods, examine their strengths and shortcomings, and get some practice in using them. A common way to categorize methods for developing tests is in terms of the response format. The two general categories are selected response and constructed response. In the **selected-response** format, the student selects an answer from among several options. Multiple-choice, true-false, and matching items are examples of the selected-response category. Choosing from alternatives such as Agree/Disagree or Like/Don't Like are other examples of the selected-response format. In the **constructed-response** format, the student constructs a response "from scratch," rather than choosing from among alternatives presented. Free response is another term used to describe this format. Essay questions are the most common application of the constructed-response format. Solving math problems, creating art, and taking oral quizzes are other examples of this format. Figure 1.2 gives examples of

Selected-response Items	Constructed-response Items
14 × 3 = A. 32 B. 42 C. 17 D. Not Given	14 × 3 = _____
Which is a good synonym for the term reliability in educational assessment? A. validity B. teacher-made C. consistency D. criterion-referenced	Describe what "reliability" means in educational assessment.
The selection referred to in a selected-response item is made by the test constructor. [] True [] False	How do selected-response items work?

Figure 1.2 Examples of selected-response and constructed-response items.

parallel selected response and constructed-response items. The examples are deliberately very simple. When the task calls for an extended response, the constructed response is sometimes called a **performance assessment**. For example, a performance assessment may require doing an experiment involving several steps and taking 30 minutes. We say more about performance assessment later in this chapter. We consider how to plan your own assessments in Chapter 6. Then, Chapter 7 treats selected-response items, and Chapter 8 covers constructed-response items.

Try This!

Figure 1.2 gives examples of selected-response (SR) and constructed-response (CR) items. Create your own examples of parallel SR and CR items. Use any topic you wish.

Selected-response Items   *Constructed-response Items*

_____   _____

_____   _____

Externally Prepared Tests

The third major topic is externally prepared tests. This category includes tests and other assessments that teachers use but are prepared by someone else. There are several partially overlapping types of tests in this category. Examples are standardized achievement batteries, such as the *Stanford Achievement Test* and the *Iowa Tests of Basic Skills*; state-mandated tests; national and international testing programs; diagnostic reading and math tests; and tests in specific subjects, such as algebra, American history, and Spanish. Also included in this category are externally prepared tests other than achievement tests. There are tests of mental ability (sometimes called IQ tests) and tests of career interests, as well as many other types of tests. Teachers may see scores from any of these types of tests. Thus, teachers must have some familiarity with them. Further, although teachers are not directly involved in preparing these tests, many teachers will, at some time, serve on committees to select these tests. Chapters 11 and 12 describe these externally prepared tests.

Special Applications

We round out the world of educational assessment with several areas of special application. Each of these areas utilizes all or a significant portion of everything covered under the previously listed topics. The first area of special application is grading. Every teacher needs to assign grades. Usually, grades will be recorded on some type of report card. Therefore, we consider various types of report cards and the special problems encountered when combining assessment information to arrive at a final grade. Chapter 13 treats this topic.

A second area of special application is legal issues related to test usage. Much of this topic revolves around assessing students with special needs or disabilities. Some of the responsibility for such assessment rests with specialists, such as school psychologists. However, with inclusionary practices, many of the students formerly found in special education classrooms are now in regular classrooms. Thus, everyone needs to know the laws related to these situations. In Chapter 14, we identify the main laws related to educational assessment and examine the respective responsibilities of various professionals in applying these laws.

A third area of special application is assessing one's own teaching. We give suggestions for doing this in Chapter 15. Up to this point in the book, we have been examining how to assess students. Now, using the same principles of assessment, we see how we might apply all this material to evaluating our own professional skills.

GUIDELINES FROM PROFESSIONAL GROUPS

Many fields of study provide nearly infinite flexibility in terms of exactly what to cover. That is not so for educational assessment. Several professional groups have summarized the essential points to cover in this field. Thus, statements from these groups provide another useful introduction to the world of educational assessment. Perhaps the most widely referenced document for our concerns is the *Standards for Teacher Competence in Educational Assessment of Students*, developed jointly by the American Federation of Teachers (AFT), the National Council on Measurement in Education (NCME), and the National Education Association (NEA; AFT, NCME, & NEA, 1990). Although now somewhat dated, it is still highly relevant. The *Model Standards for Beginning Teacher Licensing and Development: A Resource for State Dialogue*, developed by the Interstate New Teacher Assessment and Support Consortium (INTASC, 1992), also contains numerous references to expected competencies in assessment. Another useful document is *Classroom Assessment for Student Learning* from the Assessment Training Institute (Stiggins, Arter, Chappuis, & Chappuis, 2004).

The three documents just cited are quite succinct and nontechnical. There are three lengthier, more technical documents that help to define what you should know about educational assessment. The most important of these is the *Standards for Educational and Psychological Testing*, developed jointly by the American Educational Research Association (AERA), the American Psychological Association (APA), and the NCME (AERA, APA, & NCME, 1999). This document, often referred to simply as "the Standards," is a key declaration from three prestigious professional groups about essential characteristics of good assessment. Many of the principles used later in this textbook derive from the Standards. The Standards are especially helpful regarding technical characteristics of tests, such as reliability and validity. The Joint Committee on Standards for Educational Evaluation (2003) provides a useful adjunct to the Standards, especially for classroom assessment applications. Finally, the Joint Committee on Testing Practices (2004), another consortium of professional organizations, has the *Code of Fair Testing Practices in Education*, an important source of guidance, especially on matters of equity and fairness.

All of the sources cited in this section provide guidance regarding expected competencies and "principles of good practice" in educational assessment. Although varying somewhat in emphases and organization, the sources show good agreement. You are encouraged to read the full statements from each source. The following points summarize the main themes in these statements from professional groups. At the end of each point, we note chapters in this book directed specifically at the point.

1. You should carefully articulate your assessment with *learning objectives*. Of course, this implies having clear learning objectives to begin with. Good assessment begins with clear statements of learning goals. Chapter 6 covers this topic.

2. You should have skill in *developing a variety of assessment methods* for your own use. This implies that you become familiar with different assessment methods, know their strengths and weaknesses, and attain skill in their development. Chapters 7–9 treat various methods.

3. You should be familiar with *standardized tests*. This includes the development, use, and interpretation of results from such tests. The results are usually expressed in normed scores, hence you need to be familiar with these types of scores. Chapters 11 and 12 describe these standardized tests; Chapter 5 is also pertinent.

4. You should be conversant with the *technical requirements* for good assessment, especially reliability and validity. This goal includes understanding the special terminology used in these areas. Chapters 3–5 cover these technical requirements, with Chapter 2 providing essential statistical background.

5. You should know how to develop useful *grades and other forms of feedback*. And you should be skillful in communicating this information to students, parents, and other relevant constituencies. Chapter 13 takes up this topic.

6. You should be familiar with and act appropriately regarding *legal and ethical issues* related to assessment. Chapter 14 outlines the relevant material.

PURPOSES OF ASSESSMENT

Another helpful way to introduce the field of educational assessment is to describe its purposes. Educational assessment serves a variety of purposes. Clearly identifying the purpose of a particular assessment helps to determine what type of assessment might be appropriate. In some instances, an assessment will serve several purposes simultaneously. We will identify the main purposes of assessment, treating each distinctly, although the purposes often overlap in practice.

The most common purpose of assessment is to *certify student learning*. This is the primary purpose of most teacher-made tests. For example, end-of-unit tests and final exams are intended mainly to certify student learning. Certification of student learning is also the primary purpose of most statewide assessment programs and standardized tests, such as advanced placement exams and job-related tests. When this purpose is being pursued, the assessment often results in assignment of a grade.

A second purpose of assessment is for *planning*, especially instructional planning. In this application, we are examining student status, not as an end in itself, but to plan for future action. The future action might be setting an appropriate level of instruction or varying the approach to instruction. The term *diagnosis* is often applied to this planning function. For example, we may test students' knowledge of the metric system not to assign a grade but to determine how much time to spend teaching the topic. Or, we might administer a diagnostic reading test to identify areas needing attention in a student's profile of skills.

Terms sometimes used for the distinction between the purposes of certifying current status and planning for future action are **summative evaluation** and **formative evaluation**.

"Big test today, Mom. Got any brain flakes?"

Figure 1.3 Assessment may help to motivate students. (With permission of Cartoon Resource.)

Summative evaluation emphasizes final outcomes. Did Kelly learn the metric system? Did Dan learn how to give a speech? Formative evaluation looks at processes and possible improvements. What difficulties did Kelly seem to experience with the metric system? What were the special strengths and weaknesses of Dan's approach to public speaking? The terms summative evaluation and formative evaluation can be applied usefully to individuals as well as to entire programs. For example, a summative evaluation of the new math program emphasizes student achievement in the program. Formative evaluation of the new math program emphasizes how the program operated and how we might change its operation.

A third purpose of assessment is *prediction*. Although conceptually distinct from the planning function, prediction is closely related to planning from a practical perspective. We may want to predict which students are likely to be successful in advanced math courses or in music instruction. Prediction is one of the primary purposes of college entrance tests, such as the SAT and the ACT.

A fourth purpose of assessment is to provide *feedback*. This purpose is often closely related to the first purpose, certifying student learning. However, this fourth purpose goes beyond certifying to consider the recipients of the information. It is important to provide feedback to students. The information can help guide their learning. Parents and guardians of the students also want feedback about students' progress or lack thereof. School administrators and the public at large also use assessment information as feedback about the overall success of the educational process.

A fifth purpose of assessment is *motivation*. Despite our fondest hopes that students will pursue learning for its own sake, there is little doubt that the prospect of "taking a test" serves as an important motivator for many students. Periodic assessment helps to keep the attention of everyone involved in the educational enterprise: students, teachers, administrators, parents, and so on.

The sixth and final purpose of assessment is *research*. This purpose is the most easily identified and the most restricted. It is, nonetheless, very important. When conducting research on educational issues, we frequently need to use some type of assessment.

KEY POINTS SUMMARY 1.1	*Main Purposes of Educational Assessment*

Certification of learning	Providing feedback
Planning, diagnosis	Motivation
Prediction	Research

Try This!

Think of the last test you took. How would you classify its purpose according to the list in Key Points Summary 1.1? Did it serve more than one purpose?

USERS OF EDUCATIONAL ASSESSMENT

Another convenient way to outline the world of educational assessment is in terms of the main users of assessment. There are five main groups. Each group has a distinctive interest in the field. The first and most obvious group is *teachers*. Teachers are the persons primarily responsible for the day-to-day assessment of achievement in the usual school subjects and other educational outcomes. This group includes regular classroom teachers and specialist teachers—for example, reading specialists—all who work directly with students on a daily basis. Teachers must develop their own assessments: tests, projects, homework assignments, and so on. They are usually responsible for administering externally developed tests, such as statewide competency tests and districtwide achievement batteries. Teachers are also responsible for completing report cards and for communicating with parents in other ways regarding student progress. Finally, teachers often serve on school committees working on development and/or interpretation of assessments.

Second, *school administrators* are users of assessment. This group involves a wide range of individuals from the local to the national levels, including the building principal, the district superintendent, the curriculum director, state-level administrators, and national leaders, for example, in the U.S. Department of Education. All of the individuals in this group have responsibility for students' success but they do not work directly with students on a daily basis. Their responsibilities are reflected in policies, budgeting, planning, and other such matters. Assessment results should help inform such work. Members of this group also design and implement external assessment programs.

A third group consists of *parents and the public at large*. They are primary consumers of assessment information. They do not design or implement assessments on their own. However, they are intensely interested in assessment results, and they expect to receive those results in language they can understand. Parents and guardians, of course, want information about their own children. They receive scores from teacher-made and standardized tests. They receive report cards. Teachers and school administrators must provide help to ensure that such information is interpreted usefully. The public at large uses assessment information to gauge the success of schools, from local to national levels.

KEY POINTS SUMMARY 1.2   *Primary Users of Educational Assessment*

Teachers	Students
School administrators	Researchers
Parents and the public at large	

A fourth group is *students*. Students are not just the "targets" of assessment. They are also consumers of assessment information. Assessment provides feedback to students about their progress. In the upper grades, the results of assessment assume significance in the choice of jobs and postsecondary educational plans, including college entrance and choice of major. In addition, the quality of teacher-made tests is a crucial factor in students' judgments about teachers. Woe betide the teacher who, in students' opinions, gives "unfair" tests. On the other hand, it is high praise from students to give tests that are "hard but fair."

The fifth group of users is *educational researchers*. The conduct of educational research is critically dependent on assessment methods. Good assessment is essential for good research. Consider these questions. Is this new approach to teaching math effective? What is the effect of this school's new policy about homework assignments? Does class size make any difference? Does an increase in student self-esteem lead to an increase in reading skill? Answering these and similar questions almost inevitably requires the use of tests and other assessment techniques. Without good assessment, we won't get useful answers to the questions. Hence, educational researchers spend a good bit of time looking for or developing assessment methods. They also argue a lot about the quality of assessments used in research projects. Many readers of this book will one day conduct their own research. Almost certainly, at the heart of that research will be some type of assessment instrument. You will want to make sure you have a good assessment instrument. The topics discussed in this book will help ensure that outcome.

CURRENT TRENDS AND EMPHASES

We can also gain perspective on the field of educational assessment by identifying current trends and emphases. What are people concerned about today? What assessment topics dominate professional meetings? Where are we headed? Identifying these trends and emphases helps us gain perspective on the entire field—before we consider specific topics in subsequent chapters. However, even before we examine these current trends, it will be helpful to sketch a little bit of the more distant past.

A Little Bit of History

No doubt, assessment has always been a part of the educational enterprise. We find references to what amounted to oral quizzes in the schools of ancient Greece and Rome. The medieval universities featured oral tests of competence in a subject area. The student made a presentation on a topic and was then questioned by professors in an open forum.

Figure 1.4 The humble pencil significantly changed the methods of testing. (PhotoDisc, Inc.)

Vestiges of this practice remain today in the form of the "thesis defense" by candidates for a master's or doctoral degree and some undergraduate honors programs. In the equivalent of today's high school, the Jesuit schools of the early Renaissance period (circa 1600) instituted formal rules for administration of examinations—what we would now call "standardized" administration.

Early American schools had "county examiners," whose primary purpose was to visit a county's schools and quiz the students to determine mastery of the curriculum. The county examiners would then report to the school board about student (and teacher) performance. These examinations, like those in much earlier times, used oral questioning and response.

The modern student puzzles over the near exclusive use of oral examinations in these earlier days. Oral examinations are very rare today. You must recall that writing materials were not widely available for use in the schools until the late 1800s. The pencils and paper ubiquitous in current environments were rarities until almost 1900. Prior to that time, it was simply not feasible to use written tests on a routine basis.[1]

From the mid–1800s to the early 1900s, two significant developments affected the course of educational assessment. First, Horace Mann, sometimes labeled the father of American public schools, advocated for more systematic and rigorous testing in the schools. As the first Secretary of the State Board of Education in Massachusetts and, therefore, very influential in the Boston public schools, Mann had the opportunity to implement his call for reform. And, as perhaps the most influential figure in education at the time, other people listened to his call. Second, in the late 1800s and early 1900s, Edward L. Thorndike was establishing the field of educational psychology at Columbia University's Teacher College, then the premier training ground for future leaders in education.

---

[1] For a brief, fascinating history of the pencil, see Early Office Museum (2004) at www.earlyofficemuseum.com/pencil_history.

Figure 1.5 Horace Mann and Edward L. Thorndike helped shape the early foundations of educational assessment. (Left: © CORBIS; Right: © Teachers College)

Among Thorndike's guiding principles for the new field were that (a) education must be made scientific and (b) in order to be scientific, education variables must be measured accurately.

The foundations of what we now think of as standardized achievement tests were laid in a relatively brief period from about 1910–1930. These developments arose from three sources. The first two were those of Mann and Thorndike, as just mentioned. The third was a concern for test reliability. A number of researchers noted that, as they tried to test students more systematically, the results seemed to depend more on who was administering and scoring the tests than on what students actually knew. Therefore, these researchers attempted to develop more standardized (more scientific) types of tests. As difficult as it may be for the modern student to appreciate, objectively scored tests—for example, multiple-choice tests—were referred to in the literature of the day as "new-type" tests. They were contrasted with "old-type" tests, which used more of a free-response format. These new-type tests gave rise to the first standardized achievement batteries in the 1920s and 1930s. For example, this period saw the publication of the first editions of the *Stanford Achievement Test*, the *Metropolitan Achievement Tests*, and the *California Achievement Test*—all familiar names in today's educational assessment scene. By the 1940s, these tests were widely used in American schools. It is important to note that these types of tests were not developed to accommodate computer scoring. In fact, computers had not yet been invented. The early developers of these tests worried mainly about test reliability—and making education scientific—not about scoring by computer.

Responding to the same scientific impulse as education, the fledgling field of psychology began to produce tests in the early 1900s. The earliest versions, such as the Binet scales for measuring intelligence, targeted individuals. Following the same lines of development as the new-type tests of achievement, the 1920s and 1930s saw measures of intelligence and personality variables converted to group-administered, objectively scored formats. These were the forerunners of the mental ability tests, college entrance tests, career interest inventories, and other such tests that would find ample use in the schools. Tests developed within the field of psychology would also become the mainstays of fields such as school psychology and counseling, which had their primary applications in educational settings.

By 1940, the fields of educational and psychological testing were well established. Various types of tests were used on a routine basis in the schools. Virtually all of the tests familiar to us today were available in some form. Beginning in the 1950s and 1960s, machine scoring and computer analysis of tests became common. These developments made the use of such tests less expensive, more efficient, and seemingly more "scientific." Paralleling these developments was the establishment of a formal theory underpinning the technical characteristics of tests. In today's parlance, we call it **classical test theory** (CTT). It dealt with matters such as the reliability and validity of tests. We use much of this classical test theory in Chapters 3 and 4 of this book.

Standards-based Education

Probably the most important trend currently affecting educational assessment is **standards-based education** (SBE). SBE represents a highly generalized approach to education, with a heavy dose of assessment built into it. SBE incorporates the following five notions. First, there should be a very clear, explicit identification of *learning goals* or objectives. States often express these as "content standards." Nearly all textbooks used in the elementary and secondary schools also list learning objectives. Second, there should be clearly established *performance standards* for these goals. This is where assessment comes in. In other words, having established the goals, you must test to see whether students have attained the goals. These first two propositions are the most important characteristics of SBE. Third, SBE emphasizes setting *high* standards for performance. Minimum competency is not sufficient. Fourth, these high standards are applicable to *all* students, including the socioeconomically disadvantaged, racial/ethnic minorities, and students with various disabilities. Fifth, SBE requires *public reporting* of assessment results.

Try This!

To observe its pervasive influence in modern education, enter the term "standards-based education" in any Internet search engine. See the wide array of applications of this term.

We can trace the development of various strands in this five-part description of SBE over a fairly long period of time. However, clear expressions of the full concept and translation of the concept into practice are rather recent phenomena. We find the clearest expression of the full-blown concept in the **No Child Left Behind (NCLB) Act**.[2] The

---

[2] NCLB is officially known as the No Child Left Behind Act of 2001. However, it was not signed into law until 2002. Thus, its year is sometimes given as 2001, sometimes as 2002.

language of NCLB is rife with references to the five characteristics of SBE just identified. The act is having an enormous impact not only on educational assessment, but also on all aspects of elementary and secondary education in the United States. We will encounter reference to NCLB repeatedly in this book.

Accountability

In many ways, SBE is an outgrowth of the accountability movement in education. From that perspective, we could treat the two notions together. However, the concept of accountability clearly predates SBE; and accountability is a much more general notion. Hence, we treat the two notions separately, although they overlap to a significant degree and, in fact, some references use the two terms almost interchangeably.

Accountability means that schools must demonstrate their outcomes, usually defined in terms of student learning. Of course, schools always had a concern for student learning. But under the title of accountability, the measurement of student learning was to be explicit and it was to be made public. School personnel could no longer hold test results close to the vest. School personnel had to show the public exactly what the product was.

Accountability grew from the educational milieu of the 1960s. This period witnessed a substantial increase in funding for education, especially from the federal government. Much of the legislation that created the funding also required that assessment accompany the new educational programs. The premier example of this movement was the Elementary and Secondary Education Act (ESEA) of 1965. Interestingly, the No Child Left Behind Act is officially a revision of ESEA, illustrating very concretely the historical connection between accountability and standards-based education. Accountability is now so familiar in educational circles that, perhaps, we should not list it as a current trend. It is simply part of the accepted landscape.

Legal Activism

By legal activism we mean the use of laws and the courts to pursue social goals. One can pursue social goals through the public media, through evangelizing, through scholarship, and through various other means. One can also pursue social goals by passing laws and bringing court cases. The legal scholars Monahan and Walker (2002) traced the origins of what they call "sociological jurisprudence" to the early 1900s. However, this movement did not affect education right away. Like the accountability movement, legal activism with respect to educational assessment arose in the 1960s, although for reasons different from those driving the accountability movement.

Legal activism was a prominent tool in the civil rights movement of the 1960s. The original concerns were with discrimination in employment and access to public facilities, including schools. However, the legal activism approach soon turned to matters in the educational assessment arena. Included in the scope of concerns was the fairness of tests for minority students. It became common to bring suit in federal courts about the fairness of tests. It was noted, for example, that certain minority groups failed minimum competency tests at much higher rates than did the majority group, and that, based partly on test results, certain minority groups were assigned to special education classes at substantially higher rates. Did these situations indicate violation of antidiscrimination laws? More recently, the same types of questions have been raised regarding assessment of students with various disabilities. Some of these issues have been resolved through court cases. Other issues have been the subject of specific laws stating that one must (or must not) use tests in certain ways. Thus, prior to the 1960s, there were virtually no laws or court cases related to educational assessment matters. Today, there are numerous laws and a plethora of court cases related to educational assessment. We take up these matters in more detail in Chapter 14.

Concern for Fairness

The fairness of tests and other educational assessment techniques is an important contemporary concern. In fact, concern for fairness or equity has grown substantially in recent years. It is now one of the most frequent topics of discussion in the world of educational assessment. Particular concern is expressed about fairness for racial/ethnic minority groups and students with disabilities. The basic issue is whether a test or an assessment technique is equally fair to all students. The question is essentially one of validity. Recall the discussion of validity earlier in this chapter. Validity deals with whether the test measures what it purports to measure. Now the question for fairness is: Does the test have equal validity for all students? Because fairness is one aspect of validity, we consider it in the chapter on validity (Chapter 4, see especially pp. 87–90.) For now, we simply note that concern for fairness is currently one of the major emphases in educational assessment. To some extent, concern for fairness overlaps legal activism. That is, sometimes the concern for fairness is pursued by legal means. However, the two topics are conceptually distinct, and the concern for fairness is often pursued outside any legal context. Hence, we list the topics as separate, although partially related, trends.

Item Response Theory

In our brief sketch of the history of educational assessment, we noted the emergence of classical test theory (CTT) in the 1950s. For many years, CTT was the principal guide to the development of tests. It also provided the context for discussions of test reliability and validity. Beginning in the 1960s, a new theory of testing emerged: **item response theory** (IRT). It is also sometimes called latent trait theory. IRT is a highly technical, very mathematical approach to the analysis of test items and the construction of tests. We will encounter some of its details in subsequent chapters. For now, we simply note that IRT has become a major influence in the world of educational assessment. Sessions on IRT topics are ubiquitous at professional meetings of testing experts. (Do Exercise 5 at the end of this chapter to confirm this point.) IRT methods are also at the root of many of the newer computer-based tests.

IRT and CTT methods are not antithetical. Both can be applied to a given test. However, IRT methods typically require very large samples. Otherwise, the mathematical procedures do not "settle down." Thus, IRT methods have little applicability to a teacher's own test development. CTT methods do yield some useful approaches and insights for classroom testing. However, the teacher will encounter IRT methods in externally prepared tests: statewide tests, standardized achievement batteries, commercially available computerized tests, and so on. Hence, teachers need at least some acquaintance with IRT.

Performance Assessment

Reference to performance assessment has increased considerably in recent years within the field of educational assessment. As suggested by its title, **performance assessment** refers to an assessment that requires a student to "perform"; that is, to produce or do something. In practice, performance assessment usually implies something about the nature of the task as well as something about the mode of responding. The emphasis for the task is on some holistic or realistic task. The emphasis for the response is on what is called a constructed-response or free-response format. Performance assessment is usually contrasted with a multiple-choice testing format. In this format, the task is usually a simple question or statement, followed by a selected-response format. Because of its emphasis on realistic tasks, at least some types of performance assessments are called **authentic assessments**.

We may view **portfolio assessment** as one type of performance assessment. In portfolio assessment, students collect examples of their work (for example, essays written, speeches given, and experiments conducted). The teacher then evaluates the contents of the portfolio.

In a previous era, most major testing programs relied exclusively on multiple-choice tests. Of course, as noted in our brief historical sketch, in an even earlier era, multiple-choice tests did not exist. They were, at one time, the new-type test. Today, most external testing programs—for example, state assessments—include both multiple-choice items and some type of performance assessment. Some sources contrast "performance assessment" with "standardized tests." This is an inappropriate contrast. Currently, almost all standardized tests include some type of performance assessment, at least as an optional component. We examine performance assessments, including portfolios, in Chapter 8.

State, National, and International Testing Programs

The United States has a strong tradition of local control over education. Each community has its own schools, controlled by a local school board. In some regions of the country, this local control resides at the county level. In other regions, each city or town exercises control—sometimes down to the tiniest village. Traditionally, local control has covered the curriculum and the assessment program. Increasingly in recent years, the real power over schools has migrated to higher levels of government: to the state level and to the national level.

Control over testing programs provides one of the clearest examples of this migration of power. Statewide testing programs have proliferated. The Goals 2000 project, developed under the Clinton administration in the 1990s, nearly resulted in a single national testing program. The No Child Left Behind Act leaves testing in the states' hands, but specifies that all states must test certain subjects in certain grades; and the law specifies what must be done with the test results.[3]

---

[3] States may choose not to participate, but by doing so they forfeit funding connected to the law.

The **National Assessment of Educational Progress** (**NAEP**) bills itself as "the nation's report card." Originated in the 1960s, NAEP tests national samples of students in Grades 4, 8, and 12. Different subjects areas are covered each year. One year may include reading and citizenship. Another year may include mathematics and geography. Reports give scores for groups of students—for example, by state—but not for individual students. States tout or pout about their NAEP results, depending on where they rank and whether their averages have increased or decreased since the last testing. NAEP has grown substantially in its scope and influence since its introduction. The No Child Left Behind Act requires each state to participate in NAEP testing at least every third year.

An international testing program, **Trends in International Mathematics and Science Study** (TIMSS), has attracted increasing attention. TIMSS periodically assesses students in several dozen countries. TIMSS reports focus on comparisons among national averages. Like NAEP, TIMSS does not report scores for individual students. The TIMSS effort, traditionally limited to mathematics and science, is now expanding to the assessment of reading. The new effort is known as the Program for International Student Assessment (PISA). To date, these international testing programs have had little influence on the affairs of local schools. However, the general trend is clear: increasingly higher levels of involvement in educational assessment. Thus, yesterday's teachers learned to interpret locally adopted tests for local students. Today's teachers must learn to interpret statewide and nationwide test results.

Try This!

To get the flavor of state testing programs, NAEP, and TIMSS, check these websites.

For states, go to the appropriate state site as listed in Appendix E.
For NAEP, http://www.nces.ed.gov/nationsreportcard
For TIMSS, http://www.timss.org

Computerization

It is a truism to note that computers have revolutionized modern life. The observation applies aptly to educational assessment. Computers have touched nearly every aspect of educational assessment. There is no sign of the trend abating. Each year brings amazing new developments in the application of computers to assessment methods. Here we highlight some of the major influences.

We can identify three phases in the effects of computers on the world of educational assessment. In the first phase, computers facilitated *processing test data*, especially for large-scale research programs. For example, norming programs for standardized tests became much larger and more sophisticated because the data could be processed by computer. This improved the quality and magnitude of assessment research but had little effect on the individual teacher's use of assessment. This first phase began in the 1950s and continues to the present. It is an important part of the IRT applications described earlier. Routine use of IRT methods would be unthinkable without computers.

The second phase involved computer-based *reporting of test scores*. Computers could easily generate multiple copies of test scores summarized in a variety of ways.

Thus, the availability of assessment information proliferated. Later chapters contain examples of such reports. It would be useful at this point to peek forward at some of these examples to get the flavor of these types of reports. See Figure 5.14 (p. 123), Figure 5.15 (p. 124), Figure 11.2 (p. 252), Figure 11.4 (p. 257), and Figure 13.13 (p. 334).

Evolving from these numerically oriented reports were **narrative reports** that translated the numerical information into ordinary English. Computer-based translation of numerical information into narrative description is an important new development in assessment. Chapter 5 examines how this translation from numbers to words occurs. Some of the figures just cited contain narrative portions.

The third phase in the effects of computers on the world of testing relates to *test administration*. With increasing frequency, traditional paper-and-pencil tests are being administered by computer. In some applications, the old paper-and-pencil test is simply converted to presentation on a computer screen. In a much more sophisticated method, the computer (more exactly, its program) actually selects the items to be presented. It's called **computer-adaptive testing** (CAT). The selection of new items depends on the student's responses to items already presented. Let us illustrate with a simple test of arithmetic computation. The first item is 76 × 4. If you get that wrong, the computer selects an easier item, say, 8 × 6. If you get that wrong, it next presents an even easier item, say, 5 + 8. If you got the first item right, you next get 345 × 15. Get that right and you may next get ½ + ¾ The presentations move back and forth in difficulty until the test concludes with a pretty good fix on your level of arithmetic skill. Figure 1.6 shows an example of the branching routine used. Notice that there are eight items in the "item pool," but an individual student answers only three. Of course, in practice, there would be many more items.

Development of computer-adaptive tests depends critically on the IRT methods described earlier. Large-scale testing programs—such as the SAT, the GRE, and Praxis—are increasingly using these computer-based methods. Such tests are also becoming commonly available for classroom use. For a detailed review of how various computer-based

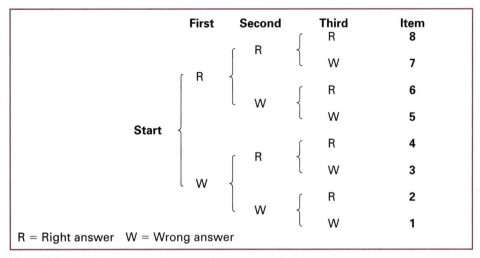

Figure 1.6 Example of the branching used in computer-adaptive testing.

KEY POINTS SUMMARY 1.3	*Current Trends and Emphases in Educational Assessment*
Standards-based education	Item response theory
Accountability	Performance assessment
Legal activism	State, national, and international testing programs
Concern for fairness	Computerization

tests operate, see Parshall, Spray, Kalohn, and Davey (2002). For specifics on computer-adaptive tests, see Sands, Waters, and McBride (1997).

We are beginning to see evidence of even more influence of computers on assessment practices. For example, computers are now being used to score or "grade" essays and other such free-response products; see Chapter 8 (pp. 187–188 for examples). In addition, computers, paired with Internet capabilities, serve as the delivery mechanism for assessments. For example, you can download tests directly (see p. 259 for an example). You can even download forms to help assess your own teaching (see p. 354 for an example). No doubt, tomorrow will bring even more influences of the computer on educational assessment—some that we have not even thought of yet.

Keeping Perspective

In this section, we have identified current trends in the field of educational assessment. The focus has been on changes and newer developments. We must view these changes against a backdrop of stability. Not everything is changing. What we consider important about tests—their reliability and validity—has not changed very much in the past 50 years. Despite increased presentation of tests by computer, the vast majority of classroom assessment still involves paper-and-pencil tests. Although reports of accountability and legal issues about tests fill the public media, the teacher's main concern remains determining whether Johnny knows the metric system or Suzy knows the major periods in American history. The big picture has more stability than change. Thus, while being aware of the changing currents in the field, let's keep our perspective. In this book, we concentrate mostly on this big picture, while reflecting the changes as needed.

SOME MORE TERMINOLOGY

We have already introduced quite a few of the specialized terms used in educational assessment: reliability, selected-response, portfolio, norm-referenced, and so on. In this section, we introduce even more terms. Don't be disheartened. Knowing the terminology of a field is part of professional competence. If you are engaged in sailing, you better know the meaning of starboard, tacking, and coming about—all very peculiar terms. If you perform ballet, you better know the difference between arabesque and pirouette. If you play baseball, you better know the meaning of bunt, steal, and sacrifice fly—more very peculiar terms. So, too, with educational assessment. You need to know the lingo. Of course, we will introduce a considerable variety of specialized terms in subsequent chapters. In this section, we cover some of the most widely used terms.

Measurement, Testing, Assessment

Let us start with the term *assessment* itself, a term incorporated into the book's title. It is closely related to the terms *measurement* and *testing*. Indeed, the entire field has gone by one or another of these names at various times in its history. Today, it is customary to make some distinctions among these three terms. **Measurement** means quantification, usually according to some type of scale. Thus, we measure height with a ruler, weight with a scale, and temperature with a thermometer. The emphasis with the word measurement is on a quantitative index for something. A **test** usually means a process or device with which we measure. Here is a formal definition: "A test is a standardized process or device that yields information about a sample of behavior or cognitive processes in a quantified manner" (Hogan, 2003, p. 43). In an educational context, a test usually means the materials with which we complete a measurement. Examples of tests include final exams, quizzes, essay questions, interest inventories, and so on. The emphasis is on the physical product. Other words commonly used as synonyms for test are scale, inventory, and examination. The term **assessment** implies some use of the test information (for example, drawing a conclusion or making a judgment based on the information). In some contexts, assessment also implies using methods other than formal tests to make such judgments. Yet another related term is *evaluation*. This term clearly implies some judgment: placing a value on something. Thus, its connotation is very similar to that of assessment. All of these terms—measurement, test, assessment, and evaluation—have been used over the years to characterize this field. Preferences have changed from time to time.

Having made these distinctions, we must admit that, in practice, the terms are often used interchangeably with little harm. Thus, someone may ask, "How did you assess that?" Perhaps more precisely, that person means "What test did you use?" Or, someone may say, "We measured that new program last year." More precisely, that person means, "We evaluated that program." The distinctions we have drawn are useful. Some sources describe the distinctions passionately. However, the distinctions are neither universally made nor rigidly used. In the final analysis, regardless of the particular term used, what we are interested in is *information*. We want good information. We want to use it intelligently.

Try This!

Here's a quick way to check on the distinctions (and lack of distinctions) among these words: measure, test, assess, and evaluate: Do a thesaurus search on each word in whatever word processing system you use. How much overlap do you get in the synonyms for each word?

Standardized Testing

Notice that the formal definition of a test given earlier incorporates the word **standardized**. This term, a common one in the field of educational assessment, actually has three different meanings. First, when that term is used in the definition of testing, it refers to *uniform procedures* for administering and scoring. That is, there are definite, clearly specified methods for administering the test. There are rules for scoring the test. It is essential that the test be administered and scored according to these procedures. Second, in other contexts, standardized means that the test has *norms*, for example, national norms based on thousands of cases. In fact, the process of collecting these normative data is often referred to as the standardization program for the test. Clearly, this meaning of the term standardized is different from the first meaning. One can have a test with fixed directions and scoring procedures without having any type of norms for the test. A third meaning, encountered especially in media reporting and public discussions, equates standardized testing with *group administered, machine-scored, multiple-choice tests* of ability and achievement. For example, a newspaper headline may report "Local students improve on standardized tests" or "Cheating on standardized tests alleged." Or, a friend may say, referring to performance on the SAT or the ACT college admissions test, "I don't do very well on standardized tests." This third meaning is obviously much more restrictive than either of the first two. It is important to distinguish among these three meanings of the term "standardized."

Distinctions Among Types of Tests

Let us consider some of the distinctions commonly made among types of tests. One of the most obvious distinctions is between *group-administered* and *individually administered tests*. Group-administered tests can be given to large groups all at once. You have certainly taken some of these and will take more in the future: SAT, ACT, GRE, Praxis, and so on. Most classroom tests qualify as group administered. Individually administered test are given to one person at a time, usually by someone with special training in the administration of that particular test. Examples include intelligence tests (such as the Wechsler tests) and personality tests (such as the Rorschach inkblots). Note that any group-administered test can be administered to a single individual, and this is sometimes done, for example, for make-up testing.

Another useful distinction among types of tests is *speed vs. power* tests. In a speed (or speeded) test, performance depends primarily on how fast a person moves through the test. The actual test items are usually very easy. A reading speed test is a good example. How fast can you read a passage? At what line are you after three minutes? Or, how fast can you complete a page of simple number facts? How many items do you complete in five minutes? In contrast, a power test has items ranging from easy to very difficult. The issue is how many you get right with, more or less, unlimited time. Examples include a 30-item vocabulary test, including some really obscure words, and a 50-item test on American history, each test having a one-hour time limit. Such tests plumb the depths of your knowledge—your power, so to speak, in that area. Giving you an extra 10 minutes on the test will probably make no difference in your score.

A third distinction is between tests attempting to measure *maximum vs. typical performance*. In tests of maximum performance, we want to see you at your very best. Certainly on a final exam, a college admissions tests, a reading speed test, or a teacher certification test, we want to see your best performance. These are tests of maximum performance. On the other hand, on a career interest inventory or test of extroversion, we want to see your typical performance. We don't want to know how interested you can appear to be in a certain occupation if you really try to be interested. We don't want to see how extroverted you can be if you really try. We want to know how extroverted you typically are.

For the sake of completeness in this catalog of distinctions among types of tests, we note here four other distinctions introduced in other parts of this chapter. Recall these distinctions: *criterion-referenced vs. norm-referenced, paper-and-pencil vs. performance, summative vs. formative,* and *selected-response vs. constructed-response.*

High-stakes Testing

Here is one final term in our catalog of common terms: high-stakes testing. This is a relative newcomer in the lexicon of educational assessment. But it is now one of the most frequent references in popular discussions of testing. **High-stakes testing** refers to a situation in which the outcome of a test has exceptionally important consequences for an individual. The concept is old; the term is new. There have always been high-stakes tests. The outcome of a thesis defense in a medieval university was high stakes. Pass and you're Doctor so-and-so. Fail and you're nobody, or worse: You're nobody, who just wasted five years of your life. Bar exams for lawyers, board exams for various professions, the final exam in your chemistry course—all are examples of high-stakes tests. However, contemporary uses of the term "high-stakes" arose in the context of competency exams in the schools instituted in the accountability era. We described this trend earlier in this chapter. One concrete aspect of the trend was the development and application of exams for high school graduation and/or promotion from grade to grade. The use of such exams has proliferated in recent years. Passing such exams obviously has high stakes for the students.

Interestingly, some exams may be high stakes for people other than those actually taking the test. For example, on tests in the NAEP, individual students do not even receive scores. Thus, the tests are not high stakes for the students. However, the students' scores are aggregated for an entire state. A state superintendent of education may be in hot water if the state average is low. Thus, the test is high stakes for the superintendent, but not for the students. In still other cases, the test may be high stakes for both students and school personnel. If Grade 12 students at Lincoln High do poorly on the state competency exam, the students may not get their high school diplomas, the high school teaching staff will take a lot of heat, and the principal's job will be in jeopardy.

Within the past few years, virtually every professional association with any relationship to education has issued a policy statement on high-stakes testing (see Exercise 6 at the end of the chapter). The statements typically emphasize the following points.

- Do not use a single test as the sole basis for making a decision about graduation or promotion. Use multiple measures for making important decisions.
- Ensure that the tests have adequate reliability and validity.
- Ensure that students have had adequate opportunity to learn the material on which they are tested.
- Provide remedial experiences for those who fail the first time.
- Set reasonable standards for passing.
- Ensure that test methods are sensitive to needs of students with disabilities and other subgroups.

This is not an exhaustive list of recommendations from the professional associations, but the list contains many of the important points being emphasized these days. Several of the statements also call for additional research on the consequences of using high-stakes tests.

PRACTICAL ADVICE

1. Make a habit of accessing the websites referenced in the text. Add them to your "Favorites" or "Bookmark" selections. You will find much valuable, practical information in them. Many of them have links to other useful sites.

2. Create a portfolio of references to educational assessment topics you find in the popular media: newspapers, magazines, and so on. As you move through the remainder of this text, you will find it helpful to see what issues come up in the media. For example, the media will make frequent references to standardized tests, state assessment programs, methods of reporting scores, and so on. Having these references should make the topics covered in the text more meaningful.

3. Learn the key terms at the end of this chapter very well. Each key term appears in bold print in the text. Definitions are in the text as well as in the glossary at the end of the book. We will use these terms repeatedly. Thus, it is good to learn them now.

SUMMARY

1. For purposes of an introductory course in educational assessment, the field divides naturally into these four broad areas:

• Basic principles applicable to all types of assessment, including reliability, validity, and methods of interpreting student performance.

• Teacher-made assessments, including planning the test and various types of test items, divided broadly into selected-response and constructed-response formats.

• Externally prepared tests (such as standardized achievement batteries) and specific subject tests, state assessment programs, and tests of abilities and interests.

• Some special areas of application, including grading, legal and ethical issues, and assessing one's own teaching.

2. Guidelines from several professional groups help define what is important to learn in an introductory course on educational assessment. In general, the guidelines confirm the usefulness of the outline in the previous summary point.

3. Assessment serves a variety of purposes. Clearly identifying the purpose of an assessment helps to determine what kind of assessment is appropriate. The purposes include certification of student learning, planning, prediction, providing feedback, motivation, and research.

4. The primary users of educational assessment are teachers, school administrators, parents and the public at large, students, and educational researchers. Each group typically brings a particular interest or perspective to the assessment enterprise.

5. We provided a brief review of the history of educational assessment and then identified these current trends and emphases related to educational assessment:

• Standards-based education emphasizes clear specification of educational objectives and rigorous testing of student accomplishment of those objectives, thus giving testing a prominent role.

• Accountability demands reporting of schools' success, especially as defined by student performance, again giving tests a central role.

• Today, educational assessment, as well as many other aspects of the educational enterprise, are affected by legal activism, that is, the pursuit of social goals by way of laws and the courts. Thus, one must be familiar with laws related to testing and assessment.

• There is great concern today for fairness of tests and other assessment methods, especially fairness to racial/ethnic minorities and students with disabilities.

• Item response theory is a very technical subject that has had a major influence on test development and analysis.

• Performance assessment emphasizes use of holistic, realistic methods, in terms of both test items and responses. It is contrasted with multiple-choice and similar approaches to testing.

• Recent years have witnessed considerable growth in the extent and influence of statewide and national testing programs. International testing programs are also becoming more frequent.

• As is true for nearly every aspect of modern life, computers have had a tremendous impact in the world of assessment. Their influence has been especially noticeable in facilitating the processing of test data, types of reports, and, most recently, the methods for administering tests.

6. To round out the introduction to the field, we defined and made distinctions among the terms measurement, testing, and assessment; differentiated among some classifications of tests; and described high-stakes testing.

KEY TERMS

accountability
assessment
authentic assessment
classical test theory (CTT)
computer-adaptive testing (CAT)
constructed-response (CR) item
criterion-referenced
formative evaluation
high-stakes testing

item response theory (IRT)
measurement
narrative reports
NAEP (National Assessment of
  Educational Progress)
NCLB (No Child Left Behind Act)
norm-referenced
performance assessment
portfolio assessment

reliability
selected-response (SR) item
standardized
standards-based education (SBE)
summative evaluation
test
TIMSS (Trends in International
  Mathematics and Science Study)
validity

EXERCISES

1. To observe the prominent role that tests and other assessment techniques play in educational research, enter "test" as a keyword in an electronic database, such as ERIC (e.g., http://www.eric.ed.gov). Limit the search to one year because you are going to get a huge number of hits. Observe how tests are used in the research for several of the articles your search uncovers.

2. To get the flavor of state assessment programs, check this website: http://www.ccsso.org/projects/Accountability_Systems/. Find the information for your home state. See also the websites in Appendix E for your home state's information. What does your state's assessment program include? Compare it with the assessment system for another state.

3. Go to the NAEP website: http://www.nces.ed.gov/nationsreportcard. Use the NAEP Data Tool, then Search Options. Find the national average and your state's average for reading performance at grade 8.

4. Go to the TIMSS website: http://www.timss.org. Find the TIMSS 1999 International Mathematics Report. Where does the United States rank in mathematics at Grade 8?

5. To demonstrate the dominance of the item response theory (IRT) in current discussions within educational assessment, try this exercise. Go to the program for the annual meeting of the National Council on Measurement in Education at http://www.ncme.org/annual/programs.ace. Do a search for "IRT" and note how frequently this topic comes up in the program.

6. This exercise is a follow-up to the discussion on page 16. Here are websites containing the policy statements on high-stakes testing from several professional associations. Identify important principles within each statement. List at least three common principles.

• For the National Council of Teachers of Mathematics (NCTM) www.nctm.org/about/position_statements/highstakes.htm

• For the International Reading Association (IRA) www.reading.org/positions/high_stakes.html

• For the American Psychological Association (APA) www.apa.org/pubinfo/testing.html

• For the American Educational Research Association (AERA) www.aera.net/about/policy/stakes.htm

• For the National Research Council (NRC) www.nap.edu/html/highstakes/

7. On page 17, we gave a brief description of computer-adaptive tests. To try a simple computer-adaptive test, go to this website: http://edres.org/scripts/cat/catdemo.htm. Click "Let's Get Started," then follow the directions. You do not need to complete the entire test. Just do a few test items and you will get the idea.

8. We identified several documents that outline important competencies in educational assessment (see p. 5). Access one of these documents at the following Internet sites. Examine the document and compare its contents with the list of essential competencies listed in this text on p. 6. What similarities and differences do you find?

• *Standards for Teacher Competence in Educational Assessment of Students* (AFT, NCME, & NEA, 1990) at http://www.unl.edu.buros/artcile3.html

• *Model Standards for Beginning Teacher Licensing and Development: A Resource for State Dialogue* (INTASC, 1992) at http://www.ccsso.org/content/pdfs/corestrd.pdf

Chapter 2

Statistics: Just a Little Bit

OBJECTIVES

- Identify variables of interest to educators. Do so at three levels: the construct, the operational definition, and the raw data.
- Organize raw data in the form of a frequency distribution and display the distribution in a histogram.
- For a set of test scores, determine the three measures of central tendency: mean, median, and mode.
- For a set of test scores, determine two measures of variability: the range and the standard deviation.
- Given the mean and the standard deviation for a set of scores, determine the z-score for a raw score.
- Create a bivariate distribution (scattergram) and provide a reasonable estimate of the correlation coefficient for the data.
- State the cautions applicable to interpreting correlation coefficients.

What This Chapter Is About

This chapter introduces a few elementary notions from statistics. The topics include the idea of a variable, methods for organizing data, measures of central tendency and variability, and the correlation coefficient. These techniques come from what is called descriptive statistics. We do not introduce any notions from inferential statistics. Some readers may have already taken a course in statistics. They may skim this chapter as a refresher. Other readers will need to spend more time learning the material.

Why This Topic Is Important

Chapter 1 identified basic questions asked about any type of assessment. The basic questions involved reliability, validity, and methods of interpreting student performance. Chapters 3–5 take up each of these topics in detail. Each topic uses methods from elementary statistics. Furthermore, analysis of one's own tests (Chapter 10) and assigning grades (Chapter 13) often require use of some simple statistics. Therefore, it is important, before we discuss these topics, to make sure we have some familiarity with the relevant parts of statistics. That is what this chapter aims to accomplish. A course in assessment is not a course in statistics. However, we do need to use a few basic statistics to work competently in the field of assessment.

DIVISIONS OF STATISTICS

The two major divisions of statistics are descriptive statistics and inferential statistics. In many situations, we get quite a bit of data. For example, we may have several test scores for hundreds of students. **Descriptive statistics** help to summarize or describe the data to aid understanding of the data. Most frequently, the data come from a sample of individuals. We are sometimes interested in knowing about the population from which this sample was drawn. **Inferential statistics** help to draw conclusions—inferences—about what is probably true in the population based on what we discovered about the sample. Inferential statistics include such topics as tests of significance, confidence intervals, t-tests, and analysis of variance. In this chapter, we cover only material from descriptive statistics. We do *not* cover the methods of inferential statistics.

USING THE COMPUTER FOR STATISTICS

Examples in this chapter employ some small data sets to illustrate various statistics. In practice, we often have much larger data sets. We use computer software packages to apply statistics to these larger data sets. Commonly used packages include SPSS, SAS, Minitab, and SYSTAT. There are many others. Microsoft's Excel software, oriented more toward other applications, also computes statistics. Understanding the material in this chapter does not require familiarity with any of these statistical packages. However, you may find it helpful to apply one of these packages to data sets introduced here or to data sets you make up yourself.

Try This!

If you are not already familiar with one of the statistical packages listed in the preceding paragraph, find out which of them are available for your use. List where each is available, for example, on your own PC or in a computer lab on campus. Exercises at the end of this chapter will allow you to apply the package.

Software Package   *Where Available*

_____   _____

_____   _____

_____   _____

VARIABLES

How does the field of statistics interface with the field of assessment? To answer this question, we must understand the shades of meaning of the term **variable**. Examples of variables in education are reading comprehension, spelling, scientific literacy, interest in mathematics, artistic ability, verbal intelligence, learning disability, self-esteem, and creative thinking. The individuals we assess *vary* along each of these variables from high to low, more to less, or some similar set of quantifiers. Variables can be described at three

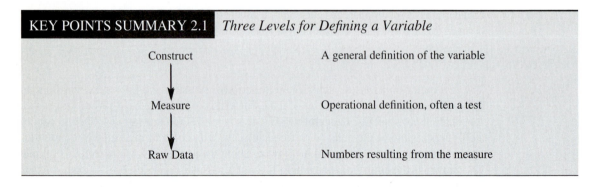

Three Levels for Defining a Variable

Construct	A general definition of the variable
↓	
Measure	Operational definition, often a test
↓	
Raw Data	Numbers resulting from the measure

levels of generality. At the most general level, a variable is a **construct**. Here, we give verbal descriptions and definitions of the variable. For example, intelligence may be defined as the ability to manipulate abstract symbols. Reading comprehension may be described as the ability to extract meaning from the printed word. Interest in math may be defined as positive feelings about the topics in the math text.

At a second level, we *measure* the variable. This is the *operational definition* of the variable. The field of educational assessment deals with these measures and their operational definitions. For example, the *Scranton Reading Test* may be our operational definition of the general construct "reading comprehension." The *North Coast Inventory of School Attitudes* may provide our operational definition of "interest in math." An end-of-unit test in science may provide the operational definition of science achievement. Students' writing of a story may provide the operational definition of writing skill.

At the third level, we get *raw data*. These are the numbers that result from application of the measures. In educational assessment, the raw data are often test scores. Statistics operate on raw data, the most specific level for a variable. Because raw data come from our measures, statistics provide the summaries of the measures (assessments) in which we are interested. Of course, all the while we are most interested in the variable at the level of a construct.

Scores (N = 100)									
73	81	92	78	85	84	84	96	78	89
80	71	80	85	79	79	83	79	86	77
75	83	85	80	83	77	78	72	83	80
81	79	78	75	81	92	80	75	87	84
78	61	83	86	74	73	82	78	78	80
80	87	80	77	82	76	81	81	86	84
77	81	83	81	81	80	71	79	76	80
80	89	78	67	76	84	82	79	81	81
79	82	81	90	79	77	83	73	98	82
78	82	85	75	77	78	70	89	81	75

Figure 2.1 Sample set of raw data: 100 history test scores.

Frequency Distribution		
Interval	F	Cum F
95–99	2	100
90–94	3	98
85–89	12	95
80–84	41	83
75–79	32	42
70–74	8	10
65–69	1	2
60–64	1	1

Figure 2.2 Frequency distribution for scores in Figure 2.1.

ORGANIZATION OF RAW DATA

When confronted with a mass of raw data, we often want to organize it. The most typical way to organize raw data is with a frequency distribution. The **frequency distribution** organizes the data into groups of adjacent score intervals. Figure 2.1 presents a set of raw data, in this case a set of history test scores for 100 students (N = 100). Notice that it is difficult to make much sense out of the raw data just by looking at Figure 2.1. Figure 2.2 organizes the data in the form of a frequency distribution. The frequency distribution in Figure 2.2 shows the intervals into which scores are categorized: the frequency (F), or count of scores falling into each interval; and the cumulative frequency (Cum F), that is, the frequency *at and below* each interval. Notice that the frequency distribution readily reveals such features as the range of scores and the area where scores are concentrated.

A frequency distribution is often converted into graphic form. The most common form for this conversion is the frequency **histogram**. Figure 2.3 presents the histogram for the frequency distribution in Figure 2.2. Each column or bar in the histogram corresponds to one of the intervals in the frequency distribution. The height of each column in the histogram shows the frequency of cases on the interval. Each interval is represented by the

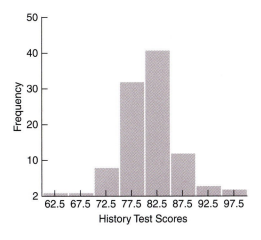

SD = 5.50
Mean = 80.3
N = 100

Figure 2.3 Frequency histogram for history test scores.

midpoint score for that interval. For example, 72.5 on the base of the histogram represents the interval 70–74 in the frequency distribution. That column goes up to a frequency of 8. Carefully compare Figure 2.2 and Figure 2.3. Notice that the histogram gives a nice picture of the frequency distribution. You can "see" how the scores go. They range from the low 60s to the high 90s, with a bulge in the low 80s, very few in the 60s, and so on.

CENTRAL TENDENCY

Although the frequency distribution and histogram are useful summaries of the raw data, it is convenient to have *one index* that best represents the complete set of data. Such an index is called a measure of **central tendency**—the center around which the raw data tend to cluster. There are three commonly used measures of central tendency: mean, median, and mode.

The **mean** is the arithmetic average. We represent it by either M or $\overline{X}$ (read X-bar, or simply "mean"). Its formula is

$$M = \frac{\Sigma X}{N}$$

where

X is a score

N is the number of scores

Σ is the summation sign, saying "add up all these things (Xs)"

Is this the same "average" you learned to calculate in elementary school? Yes, it is.

The **median** is the middle score when scores are arranged in order from low to high. The median divides the array of scores in half. The **mode** is the most frequently occurring score. Figure 2.4 gives examples of the three measures of central tendency for a small data set.

Try This!

Determine the three measures of central tendency for this set of ratings.

Score: 2   5   4   5   3   4   5   2   6

Mean = _____   Median = _____   Mode = _____

Teacher Ratings of Writing Performance

Raw Data: 2, 5, 3, 6, 6, 7, 6, 4, 8, 3, 4

Mean:

$$M = \frac{\Sigma X}{N} = \frac{54}{11} = 4.91$$

Median: 5   Mode: 6

Figure 2.4 Measures of central tendency for a small data set.

VARIABILITY

A measure of central tendency provides a very convenient summary of the data, but it robs us of any sense of **variability**, or scatter, in the data. For example, two sets of data may have the same mean, but in one set all scores are within two points of the mean whereas in the other set the scores are widely scattered. Figure 2.5 provides a good example of these differences in variability. The figure shows two sets of data, each with five cases. Both sets of test scores have a mean of 80. But Set B has much greater variability than Set A. To better describe the raw data, we want an index of variability.

The simplest index of variability is the **range**. This is the distance from the lowest to the highest score. To indicate the range, one may list the lowest and highest scores or the difference between them. For the raw data in Figure 2.1, we may say the range is 61–98 or the range is 37 points. For the scores in Figure 2.5, the range is 8 points (84–76) for Set A, but the range is 40 points (100–60) for Set B.

The most widely used index of variability is the **standard deviation**. It is denoted in various sources by any of these symbols: S, SD, or σ.[1] Its formula is

$$SD = \sqrt{\frac{\Sigma(X-M)^2}{N}}$$

where

    M is the mean

    N is the number of scores

    X is each score taken in turn

    Σ is the summation sign, saying "add up all these things"

The formula gives the formal definition of the standard deviation. When SD is calculated on a sample but is intended as an estimate of SD in a population, the N in the formula is replaced by "$N-1$." For all examples in this chapter, we use N in the denominator. Figure 2.6 illustrates the calculation of the measures of variability for a small data set. Notice how the formula for SD works. It determines the distance of each score (X) from the mean

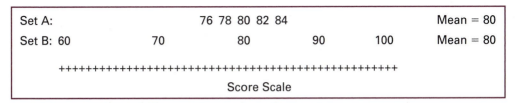

Figure 2.5 Sets of test scores with the same mean but very different variability.

---

[1]The symbol σ, read sigma, is the Greek (lower-case) letter S. In statistics, we use Greek letters to designate measures for an entire population and English letters (e.g., S) to designate measures on samples. Thus, S is the standard deviation for a sample, σ is the standard deviation for the population. The distinction is not rigidly observed in the literature of educational assessment.

Scores	$X - M$	$(X - M)^2$
6	1	1
9	4	16
4	−1	1
5	0	0
5	0	0
1	−4	16
$\Sigma X = 30$		$\Sigma(X - M)^2 = 34$

$$M = \frac{\Sigma X}{N} = \frac{30}{6} = 5 \qquad SD = \sqrt{\frac{\Sigma(X - M)^2}{N}} = \sqrt{\frac{34}{6}} = 2.38$$

$SD = 2.38$ Variance $= SD^2 = 5.66$ Range $= 1 - 9$

Figure 2.6 Measures of variability for a small data set.

(M). The greater these distances, the greater SD will be. The formula squares these distances—that is, $(X - M)^2$—adds them all together, then divides by N, creating a kind of average distance. Finally, the formula takes the square root in order to get the squared values back into the original score system. These operations, especially the squaring and taking of a square root, complicate understanding of the formula, but the basic idea is still clear. The more the scores scatter around the mean, the greater the standard deviation will be. The standard deviation is used heavily in educational assessment. We will observe its use especially in Chapter 5 on methods for interpreting student performance.

An index of variability closely related to the standard deviation is the *variance*, which is simply the standard deviation squared (SD^2). Conversely, SD is the square root of the variance. In some advanced work in statistics the variance is used more than the standard deviation. In educational assessment, the standard deviation is used more frequently, although not exclusively.

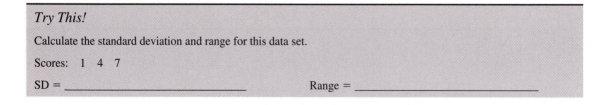

Try This!

Calculate the standard deviation and range for this data set.

Scores: 1   4   7

SD = _____   Range = _____

Except when dealing with very small numbers of cases, such as the examples presented here, we almost always use a computer software package to calculate SD. If you need to compute SD by hand, there is a more convenient formula than the one we just discussed. Appendix C contains the formula and instructions for its use.

There are several other measures of variability. However, the range and standard deviation are clearly the favorites in educational usage, so we will not introduce any of the other measures.

SHAPES OF DISTRIBUTIONS

There is frequent reference in educational assessment to the shape or form of a frequency distribution of test scores. We should be familiar with the terms used to describe these shapes. The reference point, or benchmark distribution, is the **normal curve**, or normal distribution. Its popular name is the "bell curve," although it is only roughly the shape of a bell. The curve, generated by a rather unwieldy formula, is a density function; that is, the area under the curve is filled in, actually packed with data points. Figure 2.7 presents a frequency histogram, similar to the one in Figure 2.3, with the theoretical normal distribution superimposed. Real data do not conform exactly to the theoretical distribution, which is simply a mathematical function. However, the frequency histograms for real data often approximate the normal distribution.

The normal distribution has three characteristics. The distribution in Figure 2.7 manifests these characteristics. The distribution is *unimodal*; that is, it has one mode or "hump." It is *symmetrical* about its central axis, an imaginary line erected perpendicular to the base at the mean. Around this central axis, the left side is the mirror image of the right side of the curve. The curve's "tails" are *asymptotic* to the base; that is, they continue on to infinity, always getting closer to the base but never reaching it. Of course, this is true only in the theoretical normal curve. In practice, the data do stop at some finite point.

Distributions may "depart from normality"; that is, be different from the normal curve, in several ways. The first departure is in terms of **kurtosis**, the "peakedness" of the

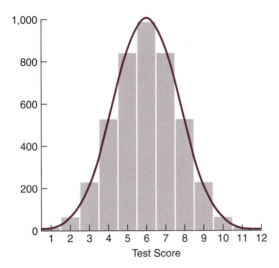

Figure 2.7 Example of normal distribution.

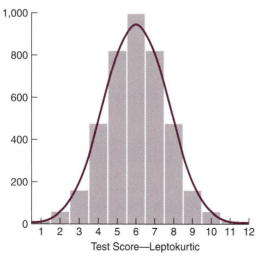
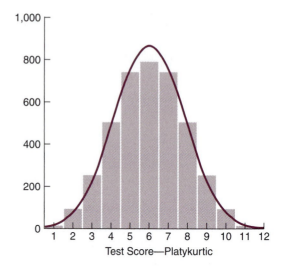

Figure 2.8 Examples of distributions varying in kurtosis.

distribution. Figure 2.8 depicts these departures from normality; that is, departures from normal "peakedness" in two directions. A leptokurtic distribution is more peaked and a platykurtic distribution is flatter than the normal distribution. In other words, the leptokurtic distribution has more data in the middle and "thinner shoulders." The platykurtic distribution has "broader shoulders" and less packing in the middle of the distribution in comparison with the normal distribution.

Another type of departure from normality is in terms of **skewness**, the degree of symmetry for the right and left sides of the curve. *Negative* skewness, or skewness to the left, has a long tail to the left and a bulge in scores to the right. *Positive* skewness, or skewness to the right, has a long tail to the right and a bulge of scores to the left. Figure 2.9 shows

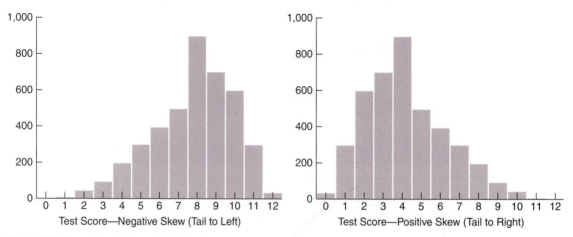

Figure 2.9 Examples of skewed distributions.

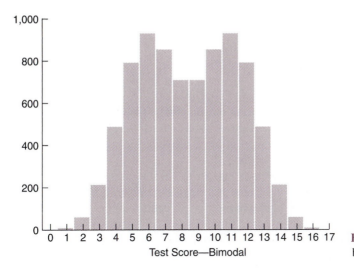

Figure 2.10 Example of a bimodal distribution.

examples of distributions with positive and negative skewness. A final type of departure from normality is in terms of the modality of the distribution. Whereas the normal distribution is unimodal, a distribution may have more than one mode. For example, a *bimodal* distribution has two modes, or humps, as shown in Figure 2.10.

For both skewness and kurtosis, there are technical formulas for defining the degree of departure from the purely normal distribution, although results from these formulas are rarely reported in educational literature. Verbal descriptions, however, are often used for skewness. For example, a report may say that the distribution was "very positively skewed" or showed "slight negative skewness." In contrast, the degree of kurtosis in a distribution is rarely the subject of comment. True bimodality is a rare phenomenon in educational data, except with very small samples. You often hear people report that they have "a bimodal class," but the actual data do not often support that claim. The claim probably arises because the highest and lowest performing students stand out in one's thinking, but they are the tails of the distribution; the majority of students, less noticeable, are in the middle.

Why is the normal curve important in educational testing? Many naturally occurring phenomena tend to be normally distributed. For example, for people of a given sex and age, the following easily measured variables tend to be normally distributed: height, short-term memory span for digits, grip strength, and so on for many other variables. This tendency toward normality is so ubiquitous that when the actual distribution of a variable is unknown, we often assume that it is probably normal. Hence, many tests are built to yield a roughly normal distribution of scores. However, we sometimes deliberately build tests to yield positively or negatively skewed distributions. For example, many diagnostic reading tests yield very negatively skewed distributions (see Figure 2.9) because the tests attempt to spread out scores at the bottom of the distribution. It is also the case that some naturally occurring distributions are distinctly nonnormal. For example, the distributions of people's weight, family income, and city populations are all very positively skewed.

Z-SCORES

A **z-score** or, simply, z is defined as:

$$z = \frac{X - M}{\text{SD}}$$

where X is an individual score or data point, M is the mean, and SD is the standard deviation. The distribution of z-scores has a mean $= 0$ and SD $= 1$. Hence, no matter what the values of the original scores, when converted to z-scores, they always have the same mean and standard deviation.

The z-score is used to "map out" the normal curve in terms of areas under the curve. Figure 2.11 illustrates the use of z-scores to mark areas under the normal curve. Tables in statistics books show what percentage of cases in the normal distribution fall to the left or right of any z-score. Figure 2.11 shows some examples, based on use of these tables. It is customary to refer to areas to the left of a z-score as "below" the point and areas to the right as "above" the point. For example, Figure 2.11 shows that 16% of the cases in the normal distribution fall above a z-score of +1.00. Some types of test norms use z-scores. We will see the role of z-scores in Chapter 5. In fact, if you skip ahead to Figure 5.3 (p. 98), you will see how z-scores relate to a variety of test score systems.

Try This!

Use Figure 2.11. What percentage of the cases in the normal distribution fall below a z-score of +2.0?

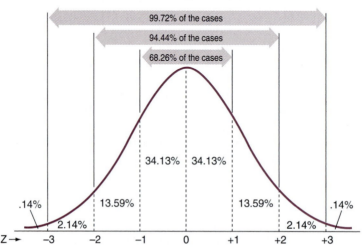

Figure 2.11 Examples of z-scores marking areas under the normal curve.

THE CORRELATION COEFFICIENT AND SCATTERGRAM

All of the statistics examined so far have dealt with only one variable (e.g., a set of test scores) at a time. For example, the mean described the central tendency of a single variable. The standard deviation described the degree of variability for a single variable. Thus, all these methods are called univariate statistics. Sometimes we are interested in the relationship between two variables. Here are examples of questions about the relationship between two variables.

- What is the relationship between performance on a college entrance test and actual performance in college?
- What is the relationship between scores on an essay test and scores on a multiple-choice test in the same subject?
- What is the relationship between performance on a test today and on the same test next week?
- How well do two teachers agree in grading a set of student papers?

All of these questions deal with the relationship between two variables. This calls for bivariate statistics.[2] The primary method for expressing relationships between two variables is the **correlation coefficient**. The correlation coefficient, usually symbolized by r, expresses the degree of agreement between two variables.

The correlation coefficient, r, can range from -1.00, through $.00$, to $+1.00$. We can illustrate the meaning of different values of r by referring to its cousin, the **bivariate distribution**, also known as the **scattergram**. The scattergram is a simple plot of the data points for the two variables being correlated. Consider this example. Two raters grade the essays written by six students. Ratings are on a 6-point scale where 6 is "really terrific" and 1 is "horrible." Table 2.1 shows the grades assigned by the raters. Figure 2.12 shows

Table 2.1 Two Raters Assign Grades to Essays Written by Six Students

Student	Rater A	Rater B
Abby	6	5
Dan	3	3
Meg	2	5
Mike	4	4
Ned	1	2
Tom	4	6

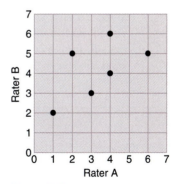

Figure 2.12 Scattergram for scores shown in Table 2.1.

---

[2]Sometimes we are interested in the relationships among *more than* two variables (e.g., among 3, 10, or even 100 variables). The field of *multivariate* statistics deals with these situations. Multivariate statistics go well beyond the scope of this book, although we briefly mention a few such techniques in Chapter 4.

the scattergram for the ratings. Meg's essay got a score of 2 from Rater A and a score of 5 from Rater B. Dan's essay got a score of 3 from both raters. See how the scores for Meg and Dan appear in Figure 2.12.

Try This!

Suppose you have ratings for one more student (Kim) to add to those in Table 2.1. Rater A gave Kim a 2 and Rater B gave Kim a 4. Plot Kim in Figure 2.12.

Figure 2.13 shows several scattergrams with their corresponding correlation coefficients, except for the last row. These examples use the generic designations of X and Y for the variables. The variables might be two different raters, two different tests (e.g., reading and math), height and weight, or any other pair of variables. Let's start with the top row of scattergrams and see the corresponding correlation coefficients. Case A shows what is called a perfect positive correlation: $r = +1.00$. It shows perfect agreement for the two variables. Notice that the higher the score on X, the higher the score on Y. The lower the score on X, the lower the score on Y. Without exception. Perfect agreement. The individual cases (students) go in a perfectly straight line from the lower left corner to the upper right corner of the scattergram.

Case B is just the opposite. It gives a perfect negative correlation: $r = -1.00$. The higher the score on X, the lower the score on Y. Case C shows no relationship between the X and Y scores. The points are scattered randomly, without any pattern. This gives $r = .00$.

Cases A, B, and C show the limiting cases for the correlation coefficient. We rarely see any of these cases in practice. Rather, we usually see intermediate values of r. Look at the second row of scattergrams. Case D shows a strong tendency for X and Y to agree— but not perfect agreement. Case D gives $r = +.90$. Case E shows even less agreement, but still fairly good agreement: $r = +.70$. Case F shows even less agreement, but still a weak tendency toward agreement: $r = .30$.

Try This!

In Figure 2.13, the last row (Cases H and I) shows scattergrams without their corresponding correlation coefficients. Estimate what you think r would be for each of these cases. Check your estimates with someone else's estimates.

H: $r = $ _____   I: $r = $ _____

You do not have to know the formulas for calculating r in order to understand it. In fact, looking at the formulas for calculating r tells you little about how it works. To satisfy the curious student, we have tucked a couple versions of the formula for r into Appendix C. If you need to calculate r, use a software package such as Excel or SPSS rather than trying to calculate it by hand.

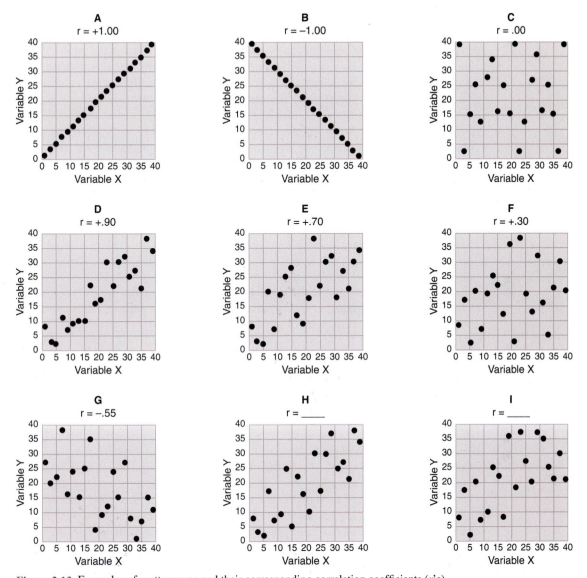

Figure 2.13 Examples of scattergrams and their corresponding correlation coefficients (r's).

Correlation coefficients—such as .75, .32—look like percentages. They are *not* percentages. Do not try to interpret them as percentages. For example, if the correlation between reading and math test scores is $r = .53$, do not say "the correlation is 53%." More advanced treatments of correlations have a way to relate correlations to percentages, but the topic is beyond the scope of this book. We do not need to explain it for our purposes in using correlations in educational assessment. The interested reader may consult such statistics textbooks as Glass and Hopkins (1996) or King and Minium (2003).

The absolute value of the correlation coefficient indicates the *strength* of a relationship. The sign of the correlation coefficient (+ or −) indicates the *direction* of the relationship. For example, $r = -.80$ shows the same strength of relationship as $r = +.80$, although the first indicates a negative relationship and the second a positive relationship. An $r = -.80$ is a stronger correlation than $r = +.50$. Most correlations we encounter in education are positive. Therefore, it is customary to omit the "+" sign before a positive correlation. Thus, when you see "$r = .35$," you may assume it is a positive correlation.

There are actually several different kinds of correlation coefficients. Nearly all of the ones encountered in educational assessment are *Pearson* correlations, named after the famous British mathematician Karl Pearson who invented the first correlation coefficient. Most of the other types of correlation coefficients are variations on the Pearson. More importantly, for practical purposes, you are usually quite safe in interpreting other types of correlations in the same way as you interpret a Pearson correlation; that is, as ranging from -1.00 to $+1.00$. In this book, you can assume a correlation is of the Pearson type unless noted otherwise.

CAUTIONS IN INTERPRETING THE CORRELATION COEFFICIENT

Although the correlation coefficient is messy to compute, it is quite easy to understand. However, proper interpretation requires certain cautions. Let us consider four cautions.

Correlation Does Not Imply Causation

First, correlation does not imply causation. No matter how highly correlated two variables are, we cannot infer any causal direction from the correlation. Note that there are a variety of words implying causation. For example, "leads to," "results in," "affects," and many similar English words or phrases imply causation. We need to be alert to all of them. Consider this example. We find that scores on a reading test and an intelligence test are highly correlated, say, .90. One might be tempted to say that level of intelligence is causing level of reading skill. That is, high intelligence leads to high reading score; low intelligence leads to or results in low reading score. However, it is possible to reverse the argument. The test-taker has to read the intelligence test items. It may be that good readers score high on the intelligence test because they are good readers. Poor reading skill may lead to or result in a low score on the intelligence test because the person cannot read the items. The correlation coefficient by itself does not help to resolve this argument. In the presence of correlations, we must be ever vigilant about avoiding causal implications.

Most Correlations Detect Only Linear Relationships

Second, we must be aware that most correlation coefficients are calculated in such a way that they detect only the linear part of the relationship between two variables. Look at Case A in Figure 2.13. Clearly, the data points fall along a straight line. Look at Case D. One can imagine a straight line fitting these points, although the points will scatter a bit around the line. Suppose, however, that the data points array themselves as in Figure 2.14. This is a curvilinear relationship. The methodology for the Pearson correlation will fit the best possible straight line to this curvilinear situation—and yield a correlation of .00! The correlation of .00 says there is no relationship between these two variables, but there clearly is a

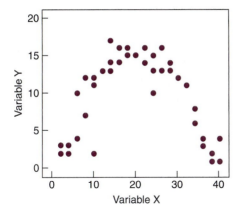

Figure 2.14 Illustration of a curvilinear relationship between two variables.

relationship. It is just not a linear relationship. The data in Figure 2.14 illustrate a very extreme form of a curvilinear relationship. Of course it is possible to have just a slight "bend" in the set of data points. How do we deal with this awkward situation? First, we note that real curvilinear relationships are rare in education. Second, there are some types of correlations that express the degree of curvilinearity in a data set. They are not encountered very frequently. However, if you prepare a scattergram for your data and it shows a curvilinear trend, consult a statistics book (or statistician) about the appropriate correlation coefficient.

The Assumption of Equal Scatter

We referred earlier to fitting a line to the data points in a scattergram. We also referred to the scatter of points around the line. For example, in Figure 2.13, the points do not scatter at all in Cases A and B. The points scatter somewhat in Case D and even more so in Case E. Some uses of the correlation coefficient make an assumption about the degree of scatter up and down the line. Specifically, we expect the same degree of scatter at various places along the line. More importantly, we do not expect the points to cluster tightly around the line in some places but to scatter wildly in other places. Like the matter of linearity, this difficulty usually does not plague us in educational applications. However, we do need to be alert to this assumption of equal scatter.[3]

The Correlation Depends on Variability in the Group

The final caution about interpreting correlation coefficients relates to the degree of variability in the scores being correlated. In general, the greater the variability, the higher the correlation tends to be. The less the variability, the lower the correlation tends to be. Typical names for this phenomenon are "range restriction" and "group heterogeneity."

Observe the situation depicted in Figure 2.15. If we calculate a correlation on all the cases in the bivariate distribution, the correlation is .70 (this is exactly the Example E in

---

[3]The technical name for this assumption is *homoscedasticity*. The term "equal scatter" is a quite suitable alternative.

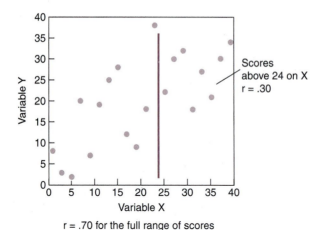

r = .70 for the full range of scores

Figure 2.15 Illustration of the effect of range restriction on the correlation coefficient.

Figure 2.13). If we calculate *r* only on the cases scoring above 24 on the *X* variable (those above the vertical line inserted in the chart), *r* is only .30. The correlation is also only about .30 for cases scoring below 10 on the *X* variable. This does *not* occur because of differences in the size of the groups. It occurs because of differences in the degree of variability in the groups. The standard deviations of both variables in the full range of scores are approximately 10. The standard deviations for both variables for the cases with *X* scores above 24 are approximately 5.

The matters of linearity and equal scatter are not usually problems in educational settings. In contrast, this matter of differential variability has huge and frequent consequences. Various circumstances present us with substantial differences in the degree of variability in groups. Some groups have great ranges. Other groups are much more homogeneous. These differences have a substantial effect on the correlation we observe. We need to be sensitive to this fact.[4]

PRACTICAL ADVICE

1. Become accustomed to thinking in terms of the *variables* of interest to educators. Of course, we are ultimately interested in the whole student. However, from a practical point of view, we are usually working on such variables, as reading comprehension, critical thinking, skill in Spanish, or knowledge of history. Practice identifying such variables.

2. Competence in assessment requires at least minimal knowledge of the simple statistical techniques introduced in this chapter. Be sure you know the meaning of the key terms at the end of this chapter. We will use these terms routinely in subsequent chapters.

3. It is *not* essential to use computer software packages to compute statistics. However, it is very helpful to do so. Try to gain some experience with one of the software packages listed on page 24.

---

[4]For methods to correct correlation coefficients for these differences in variability, see Glass and Hopkins (1996) or Hogan (2003). For more detailed treatment, see Sackett and Yang (2000).

KEY POINTS SUMMARY 2.3	*Cautions in Interpreting Correlation Coefficients*

Do not infer causation from correlation.   Check for equal scatter around the line.

Watch for curvilinear relations.   Group variability can have a major impact on *r*.

SUMMARY

1. A few concepts from elementary descriptive statistics are important for treating the foundation questions in educational assessment: reliability, validity, and interpreting student performance.

2. A variable is a trait or characteristic, such as reading comprehension or interest in math. We represent variables at three levels: the construct, the operational definition, and raw data. We apply statistics to the raw data, although our interest is mainly in the construct. Specific assessments (tests, ratings, etc.) supply the connecting link, the operational definitions.

3. A frequency distribution helps to organize the raw data. It shows the frequency of cases at each score interval. A histogram is a visual display of a frequency distribution.

4. Measures of central tendency help to further summarize the raw data by giving a single index that best represents the entire set of data. The three common measures of central tendency are the mean, median, and mode. The mean is the arithmetic average, the median is the middle score, and the mode is the most frequently occurring score.

5. Measures of variability indicate the degree of scatter in the scores. Commonly used measures of variability are the range, the standard deviation, and the variance. The range tells the distance from lowest to highest score. The standard deviation indicates scatter of all scores around the mean. The variance, used almost exclusively in inferential statistics, is simply the standard deviation squared.

6. The frequency distributions of many naturally occurring phenomena fall in the shape of the normal curve, popularly known as the bell curve. The theoretical normal curve is a symmetrical and unimodal density function, with asymptotic tails.

7. Departures in shape from the normal curve are described in terms of kurtosis, skewness, and bimodality.

8. We use z-scores to describe the position of individual cases in the context of the normal curve. The normal curve can be mapped in terms of z-scores.

9. The correlation coefficient, *r*, describes the degree of relationship between two variables. It ranges from -1.00, through .00, to $+1.00$. The bivariate distribution, or scattergram, provides a graphic display of the relationship between two variables.

10. There are several cautions to be observed when interpreting correlation coefficients. First, the correlation coefficient does not provide a basis for inferring causal direction. Second, the most widely used correlation coefficient, the Pearson, indexes only the degree of linear relationship. Third, we assume an equal scattering of data points around the line that the correlation fits to the data at various places along the line. Finally, and very importantly, the magnitude of the correlation coefficient is critically dependent on the degree of variability in the group used to calculate the correlation.

KEY TERMS

bivariate distribution
central tendency
construct
correlation coefficient
descriptive statistics
frequency distribution
histogram

inferential statistics
kurtosis
mean
median
mode
normal curve
range

scattergram
skewness
standard deviation
variability
variable
z-score

EXERCISES

1. Create a frequency distribution and a histogram for this set of 30 raw scores. Use 5-point intervals, starting with 55–59 as the lowest interval, then 60–64, and so on up to 95–99.

57 79 93 61 77 75 69 82 69 76
89 99 68 94 90 78 72 79 86 62
81 71 85 81 81 64 91 88 83 83

2. Calculate the mean, median, range, and standard deviation for this set of 10 ratings.

4 6 7 3 5 7 4 6 6 8

3. A set of scores has a mean of 50 and standard deviation of 10. For this set of scores, determine the z-scores for the following raw scores:

Raw Score	z-score
40	_____
60	_____
50	_____
52	_____

4. Plot the following pairs of scores in the bivariate distribution:

Student	Math	Reading
Kim	85	80
Kelly	65	65
Rus	80	85
Chris	65	75
Meg	75	75

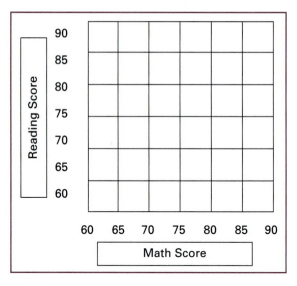

5. What is your estimate of the correlation coefficient for the bivariate distribution you created in Exercise 4?

6. Enter the data from Exercise 4 into a software package, such as Excel, Minitab, or SPSS.

a. Determine the mean and standard deviation for the math and reading scores.

b. Determine the correlation (r) between math and reading scores.

Chapter 3

Reliability: Consistency
of Performance

OBJECTIVES

- Define *reliability* as the term is used in educational assessment.
- Identify the major sources of unreliability.
- Describe the conceptual framework for studying reliability in terms of true score, observed score, and error score.
- For each of these methods of studying reliability, state how the study is conducted and tell what sources of unreliability are covered: test-retest, alternate form, interrater, and internal consistency.
- Explain how the standard error of measurement is used in test score interpretation.
- Tell how reliability is indicated in item response theory.
- Describe the role of reliability for criterion-referenced measures.

What This Chapter Is About

Recall from Chapter 1 that reliability is one of the basic issues for any educational assessment. In this chapter, we first refine our thinking about this matter of reliability. We then examine the main methods used to determine the reliability of assessments. We translate the results of these methods into a practical way to interpret test scores or other assessments.

Why This Topic Is Important

All assessments have some degree of unreliability. They are not perfectly stable and consistent. Further, they vary in degree of reliability. Some are very reliable. Others are quite unreliable. It is crucial that we have methods to study these degrees of variation. We must be sensitive to the degrees of variation and temper our interpretation of assessments accordingly. The methods treated in this chapter should help us to be intelligent consumers of assessment information. In addition, knowledge of these matters will influence how we develop our own assessments of students.

SOME EXAMPLES

To help set the context for our formal study of reliability, let's consider these examples.

1. The sixth grade spelling book includes 240 words. To get a good measure of a student's ability to spell those words, how many words should we include in a test: 5, 10, 15, . . . ?

2. Jack and Jill will take the Praxis exam on Saturday. Jack is feeling "on top of the world" as he enters the testing room. Jill has a head cold and did not sleep very well Friday night. To what extent might these conditions affect the Praxis scores for Jack and Jill? Might their scores differ if they took the test next Saturday rather than this Saturday?

3. You are getting ready to take the on-road part of your first driver's license test. There are three examiners. Do your chances of passing change depending on which examiner you get? Should you trade places in line in order to get the "little bald guy"?

4. Did you ever get on a scale to measure your weight and find that the readings varied by 10 lbs. depending on whether you shifted your weight to your right or left foot? From using such a scale, what would you conclude about your actual weight?

5. A college basketball coach wants to assess the skills of a high school player. The coach views a 30-second video clip of the player from the second game of the season. Will this provide an adequate basis for judging the player's basketball talent? How about 30-second clips from two games? How about 10-minute clips from each of eight games?

RELIABILITY: THE BASIC NOTION

Let's make sure we know what we're talking about—and what we're not talking about. There are four important points to consider.

1. Some Synonyms for Reliability

We can get a good idea of what reliability means by considering some synonyms. The best synonyms for reliability are *consistency* and *stability*. A reliable measure yields consistent information. A reliable measure is stable. Let's apply these synonyms to the scenarios sketched in the last section. Will the college basketball coach get a *consistent, stable* picture of the player's skill from one 30-second clip? Almost certainly not. Any klutz will occasionally make a spectacular play in one 30-second span. On the other hand, even a superstar will occasionally shoot an air-ball or commit a really dumb foul. However, the klutz and the superstar will be easily distinguished in 10-minute clips from eight games.

What about the road examiner for your driver's test? It may be that your chances of passing are much better with the little bald guy. On the other hand, the three examiners may be very *consistent* in how they grade performance. How about the weight scale? Obviously, it is not yielding a *stable, consistent* report about your weight. Finally, what about Jack and Jill at the Praxis exam? It may be that both students would get much the same scores—*consistent* scores—even if their personal circumstances were reversed. Or, it might be that Jack will do a little better and Jill a little worse as a result of their personal circumstances.

As we reflect on these different scenarios and their possible outcomes, it should be clear that we can study the influence of the different factors we have mentioned. In fact, later in this chapter that is exactly what we will do. For now, let's continue to refine our understanding of what reliability is—and is not.

2. Reliability: Not an All-or-None Affair

For most of the measures we use, reliability is not an all-or-none affair. Reliability is a matter of degree. Some indicators or measures are highly reliable (very consistent and stable), but not perfectly so. Some indicators are moderately reliable. We can have some confidence in them, but we must also be somewhat cautious or reserved in using them. Still other indicators have little reliability, but not zero reliability. We need to be very skeptical about these low-reliability measures, but perhaps not dismiss them as entirely meaningless.

Let's return to our scenarios. The single 30-second clip probably does not give the college coach very reliable information. However, it's not meaningless. The combination of 10-minute clips from eight games probably gives a quite reliable, but not perfectly reliable, picture. How about the little bald guy as road examiner? He might be a bit easier (or harsher) than the other two examiners, but probably not wildly so. All three examiners will fail you if you hit a pedestrian on your road test. But they may differ a bit on how they treat your dreaded parallel parking exercise. Obviously, the fluctuating scale is not entirely consistent. On the other hand, if your real weight is 110 lbs., according to a different scale, the fluctuating scale will not register you at 50 lbs. or 200 lbs. no matter how you shift on the scale. And the Praxis exam? It is very possible that Jill's score will be depressed by a few points. But if Jill is a *summa cum laude* student, she'll probably still pass with flying colors. And if Jack hasn't cracked a book in the past four years, he's not likely to do well on the test no matter how great he feels on Saturday morning. In all of these scenarios, we see that reliability is a matter of degree. We will see how to express these degrees of reliability.

3. Reliability Is Not Validity

We need to carefully distinguish between the notions of reliability and the validity of a measure or an indicator. We deal with the topic of validity in more detail in the next chapter. However, we can define it briefly here. The traditional definition of validity is that it deals with the extent to which a test measures what it is intended to measure. More precisely, does the score from a test serve as a useful gauge of what we want to measure? For example, does a reading comprehension test really "get at" comprehension of the text? Does a test of arithmetic problem solving "get at" ability to solve quantitative problems? Does a test of creativity really measure creative thinking?

A test or other indicator of performance can have reasonable reliability while still not being valid or having very limited validity. For example, the test of arithmetic problem solving may be very reliable; that is, yield consistent, stable scores. But it might be more a measure of ability to read the problem (because the statement of the problem is very wordy) than of ability to use quantitative reasoning. The test intended to measure creativity may be more a measure of vocabulary than of creative thinking. As noted earlier, we will explore the methods for studying validity in the next chapter. For now, we want to distinguish carefully between these concepts of validity and reliability.

Before leaving this distinction, we should note that while it is possible to have a test with respectable reliability but lacking validity, the converse is not possible. That is, for a test to have good validity, it must have at least reasonable reliability. In other words, reliability is a necessary but not a sufficient condition for validity. Thus, although validity is the more important property of a test, we need to first ensure adequate reliability. That is why we study reliability before validity.

4. Reliability Deals With Unsystematic Error, Not Systematic Error

Reliability deals with unsystematic error. Noise. Flukes. Chance. Flutter. It does not deal with systematic error or constant error. Systematic or constant error moves test scores in one direction or another. The movement may not be precise and entirely constant, but it is a clear tendency. For example, Dan may be "test savvy." He has a knack for writing clever essays, even when he doesn't know much about the subject matter. Dan will have a tendency to do well on essay tests regardless of the exact selection of essay topics or who scores the essays. Meg's native language is Spanish. She is just learning English. Meg will tend to score low on a test of reading comprehension with English text, regardless of how she feels today. These tendencies for Dan and Meg are not unsystematic errors. They are not captured in our notion of reliability or in the methods of determining reliability described later.

"Before you grade my quiz, you should know about my Theory of Life's Imprecision."

Figure 3.1 Test scores usually have some degree of imprecision or error. (With permission of Cartoon Resource.)

Table 3.1   Major Sources of Unreliability

Test scoring	Who scores the test
Test content	The sample of test items
Test administration conditions	Noise, timing, lighting, etc.
Personal conditions	Temporary ups and downs

WHAT FACTORS AFFECT RELIABILITY: THE SOURCES OF UNRELIABILITY

Before examining how we determine reliability, let us map out the factors that affect reliability. We often call these factors the "sources of unreliability." We need to be alert to situations where any of these sources have a lot of influence. We actually mentioned all of these sources in the scenarios sketched earlier (the coach, Jack and Jill, etc.). However, we will now become more formal in our description of the sources. Table 3.1 lists the major sources of unreliability for the measures we use in educational assessment. Let's examine each source.

Test Scoring

The first potential source of unreliability is test scoring. This usually means who scores the test. Its importance depends on how much judgment is involved in scoring the test or individual items within the test. Recall the example of your on-road driver's license test. Does it make any difference which examiner you get? Is the little bald guy a bit easier (or harsher) than the other examiners? Or suppose you are writing an essay for a contest. The essays will be graded by two English teachers: Ms. Vasquez and Ms. Silbey. Does it make any difference whether your essay is scored by Ms. Vasquez or Ms. Silbey? We usually think about scoring reliability in terms of differences between scorers. But it also refers to differences involving the same scorer at different times. Will Ms. Vasquez give your essay the same score if she scores it in the morning versus the evening?

Scorer reliability is easy to think about for things like essays. But scorer reliability is an issue even for simpler tasks, as long as the scoring calls for some judgment. Consider the examples in Table 3.2. Two different teachers have scored students' responses to

Table 3.2   Responses to Arithmetic Computation Test

Item	Student Response	Scorer 1	Scorer 2
$6 + 1$	7	C	C
$10 - 7$	3	C	C
3×8	26	W	W
$4 + 5$	9	C	W
$27 - 12$	$10 + 5$	C	W
Total Score		4	2
C = correct, W = wrong			

simple arithmetic problems. Scorers 1 and 2 agree that responses to the first two items are correct and that the response to the third item is incorrect. However, for the third item, Scorer 1 credits the reversed "9," noting that the student obviously knows the result of the operation but just has trouble writing it correctly. Scorer 2 insists that the result be expressed correctly. On the fifth item, Scorer 1 generously notes the student's response is technically correct although expressed in a nonstandard form. Scorer 2 dourly finds this nonstandard expression quite unacceptable.

Try This!

How would you score the responses in Table 3.2?

Test Content

The second source of unreliability is test content. To understand this source, think about all the possible test items that might be included in a test. Recall the example with the spelling test. With just two items, you will not get a very reliable indicator of a student's spelling ability. That is, if you pick these two words rather than another two words, you might get a very different picture of the student's spelling ability. If you use 100 words, you'll probably get a very stable (reliable) picture of the student's spelling ability. And, if you use this set of 100 words versus another set of 100 words, you will probably get very consistent (reliable) scores.

Now think of this example. Consider the case of a mathematics test used for placing students in college math courses. The college has 10 slightly different versions of the test to use with incoming students throughout the summer orientation sessions. One version of the test has two items on the Pythagorean theorem while another version has only one such item. A student who is particularly proficient with the theorem may get a slightly higher score on the first version than on the second version. Here is a third example. Consider two students preparing for an essay exam in history. The exam will cover six chapters. The teacher will include on the test four questions from a potentially infinite number she carries around in her head. One student concentrates on the first four chapters and skims the last two. The other student skims the first two chapters and concentrates on the last four. Going into the exam the two students know the same total amount of material for the exam. However, three of the four essay questions come from the last four chapters. How does this variation in content affect the two students' scores? What would happen if three of the four questions came from the first four chapters?

These slight variations in the sampling of items in a test yield unsystematic errors. Individuals' scores increase or decrease, perhaps by only a few points, perhaps by more, not because of real differences in the trait being measured but because of more or less random changes in the particular set of items presented in the test.

Test Administration

A test should have standardized procedures for its administration. This includes such factors as the directions, time limits, and physical arrangements for administration. However, it is impossible to control every conceivable detail of the administration. These details may have some influence on test scores. For example, noise in the hallway outside the testing room or less than ideal lighting conditions might adversely affect scores in a certain administration of the test. If a test has a 30-minute time limit, one administrator may be a little more generous with the limit, giving perhaps 31 minutes while another is a little stingier, giving 29.5 minutes. All of these slight variations in test administration may be sources of unreliable variance in test scores.

Personal Conditions

The temporary conditions of examinees may have unsystematic influences on their test scores. If tested on Monday, Jill may get a somewhat lower score because she has a bit of a head cold. If tested the following Friday, when she's feeling much better, she might garner a few extra points. Ned is in a foul mood on Thursday when he takes an intelligence test. If tested on Saturday, when he has mellowed, his score might be somewhat different. In both of these instances, there is no difference from one day to the next in the person's status on the underlying trait we want to measure, but the temporary personal conditions have influenced the actual scores.

Some books list "temporal fluctuations" as a source of unreliability. We note this just in case you are checking our list against the list in another book. Time itself is not a source of unreliability. Factors that contribute to unreliability are the variations in test administration conditions and/or personal conditions that almost inevitably occur with time. From one perspective, it is fair to list temporal fluctuations as a source of unreliability. However, it is more precise to refer to the changes in administrative and personal conditions as the sources of unreliability.

It is important to note that variations in the factors listed in Table 3.1 do not *automatically* result in unreliability. For example, variations in room lighting or a minor case of the sniffles may not affect test performance. The extent to which these factors affect test scores is an empirical question. We address this empirical question later in this chapter when we discuss methods for determining and expressing test reliability.

A Conceptual Framework

Now that we have listed the major sources of unreliability, let us get formal about how we will treat this nettlesome problem. There are two convenient ways to think about the problem. First, think about the "perfect" test: a perfect set of items, scored perfectly, taken under ideal conditions, and all examinees feeling normal (neither especially "up" nor "down"—just normal). Under these conditions, each examinee should get his or her **true score**. A person's true score is the score unaffected by the sources of unreliability covered

KEY POINTS SUMMARY 3.1	*Major Sources of Unreliability*
Test scoring	Test administration conditions
Test content	Personal conditions

previously. Alternatively, think of each person being tested with a variety of tests, with varying personal and administrative conditions, and scored by a multiplicity of scorers. The average of each person's scores under these multiple conditions should be a good estimate of the person's true score.

We always want to know the person's true score. We yearn to know the true score. Unfortunately, we do not operate under either of these scenarios. We only get one actual, or **observed**, **score**. The observed score is the one we actually obtain from one test administration, under one set of personal and administrative conditions, with one set of test items, and scored in one way by one person (or machine).

In a nutshell, our problem is: We want to know the person's true score, unaffected by sources of unreliability, but we get only an observed score affected by the sources of unreliability. The difference between the true score and the observed score we call error or the **error score**. Error is what results from the sources of unreliability. Thus, another way to think about reliability is to ask: How much error might there be?

Here is a convenient summary of the relationships among true score, observed score, and error score:

Observed score = True score +/− Error score or, more simply, **O = T +/− E**

Of course, by simple algebra we could also write:

True score = Observed score +/− Error score, or **T = O +/− E**

Notice that error may be positive or negative. Sometimes error makes the observed score overshoot the true score, for example, due to some lucky guesses, feeling particularly bright, and so on. Sometimes error makes the observed score undershoot the true score, for example, due to unlucky guesses, some unfortunate decisions about what to study, not feeling well on the day of a test, and so on.

Return to the scenario of the person taking many versions of a test, on different days, under a variety of circumstances, and scored by different people. Let us assume that the person's many different scores distribute themselves as shown in Figure 3.2. We can think of the average, or midpoint, of this distribution of observed scores as the person's true score. Of course, we never get that many observed scores for an individual. Ordinarily, we get only one observed score. However, it is useful to think of the relationship between many possible observed scores and the person's true score in this way. We will return to Figure 3.2 later when we consider the standard error of measurement.

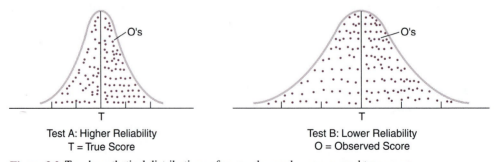

Figure 3.2 Two hypothetical distributions of many observed scores around true scores.

METHODS OF DETERMINING RELIABILITY

There are several standard methods for expressing the reliability of test scores. Each method addresses one or more of the sources of unreliability listed in Table 3.1. In nearly all cases, we express reliability in the form of a correlation coefficient. We introduced the correlation coefficient in Chapter 2. When the correlation is used in this way, we call it a **reliability coefficient**. A reliability coefficient is simply a correlation coefficient, as described in Chapter 2, used for a particular purpose.

Test-Retest Reliability

One method for determining test score reliability involves administering the test to a group of students on two separate occasions, say, one week apart. Then, we determine the correlation between scores on the two occasions. The time interval between the two testing sessions is usually a few days to a few weeks. The resulting correlation is called the **test-retest reliability coefficient**. It is also sometimes called a **stability coefficient**. Table 3.3 shows a set of data for the test-retest method. This method of studying reliability is very easy to understand. However, it is not used very often with educational tests. It is a real nuisance to have students take exactly the same test twice. Further, there is always the worry that some students will learn some of the material in the test between the first and second testing sessions. Nevertheless, the idea of test-retest reliability provides an important perspective. Test-retest reliability is especially important because temporal fluctuations in personal conditions might have a substantial influence on test performance.

Try This!

In Table 3.3, scores for Kelly, Meg, and Chris were a bit lower on Friday than on Monday. But, Russ's score increased considerably. What factors might have caused the increase in Russ's score?

Table 3.3 Array of Data for Determining Test-Retest Reliability

Student	(Test) Score on Monday	(Retest) Score on Friday
Kim	12	13
Kelly	16	14
Meg	8	6
Chris	11	9
Russ	4	10
$r = .63$		

Interrater and Intrarater Reliability

Interrater reliability assesses unsystematic variation due simply to who scores the test. "Who" in this case usually means two different people, although it could mean two different machines or one machine versus one person or any other such combination. Interrater reliability is sometimes called interobserver or interscorer reliability, depending on what the "rater" is actually doing in the testing situation. For example, two persons may score the creativity or observe the degree of hyperactivity of individuals. The shortened names of *scorer reliability, rater reliability*, or *observer reliability* are often used for this type of reliability.

Intrarater reliability refers to the consistency of a single person rating a set of responses. For example, we may study how consistent Ms. Vasquez is when she rates the quality of students' writing on two different days—not when the students write on two different days but when she does the ratings on two different days.

Interrater reliability is easily obtained. A test or other performance for a group of students is scored twice, once by each of two different raters. The interrater reliability coefficient is simply the correlation between the scores obtained by the first and second raters. Table 3.4 shows the ratings assigned by two teachers to stories written by students. The teachers used a rating scale ranging from 1 (low) to 6 (high). The correlation between the two sets of ratings gives the interrater reliability.

Try This!

For the ratings in Table 3.4, notice that Teacher A thought Dan's story was the best. Teacher B thought Dan's essay was no better than Mary's or Ed's and not as good as Matt's. What might account for this difference of opinion?

Intrarater reliability is also easily determined. Simply obtain the correlation between the ratings or scores assigned by the single rater on two different occasions. For example, look at the ratings in Table 3.4. Replace the column headings Teacher A with "first rating" and Teacher B with "second rating." Then, obtain the correlation between the two sets of ratings.

For interrater reliability, it is important that the two (or more) scorers or raters work independently. That is, one scorer should not be influenced by the other scorer or rater. For example, if Scorer B knows what score has been assigned to an essay by Scorer A, then Scorer B might be inclined to assign the same or a similar score, thus inflating the resulting reliability coefficient. Of course, it is conceivable that Scorer B detests Scorer A, and hence deliberately disagrees in assigning scores, thus deflating the reliability coefficient. Whatever the case, influence of one scorer on another contaminates the study of reliability. The scorers should work independently.

In some studies, more than two scorers or raters are used. For example, four teachers might rate the degree of hyperactivity displayed by 10 students in the teachers' respective classes. Ratings are made on a 20-point scale, ranging from "no apparent

Table 3.4 Array of Data for Determining Interrater Reliability

Student	Teacher A	Teacher B
Dan	6	4
Matt	4	5
Meg	2	1
Mary	4	4
Ed	3	4
Tom	1	2

$r = .71$

Table 3.5 Array of Data for Study of Interrater Reliability With More Than Two Raters

	Teacher			
	A	B	C	D
Student	Ratings of Hyperactivity			
1	15	12	13	14
2	8	7	7	6
3	12	18	8	10
4	14	10	14	9
–	–	–	–	–
10	6	4	5	3

hyperactivity" to "extremely hyperactive." Table 3.5 presents the ratings for the students. How shall the interrater agreement be expressed in this situation? It would be possible to compute correlations among all possible combinations of raters (A vs. B, A vs. C, A vs. D, B vs. C, B vs. D, C vs. D), and then average the correlations. In fact, this is sometimes done. However, the more appropriate analysis for this situation is the **intraclass correlation coefficient**, usually abbreviated ICC. There are a surprising number of ways to define and compute an ICC. For our purposes, the important point is that the ICC is interpreted like the familiar Pearson correlation coefficient (r). In treatments of reliability, the ICC's usual application is for determining interrater reliability.

Interrater reliability obviously treats unsystematic errors arising from variation in scorers. It does not treat any other source of error. Interrater reliability information is particularly important when judgment enters the scoring process. Examples of such cases are the scoring of essays, rating artistic productions, judging the quality of participation in a group project, determining the winner of a debate, and appraising severity of attention deficit. All these assessments require someone's judgment. The worry is the extent to which one person's judgment might differ from another person's judgment. Interrater reliability gives an indication of how closely different scorers agree.

Electronic scanners are used to score multiple-choice and other selected-response items. Figure 3.3 shows a relatively small scanner used for such machine scoring. With machine-scored tests, scorer reliability is perfect or nearly so. That is *the* great advantage of such tests. They eliminate interrater differences as a source of unsystematic error. Of course, not even machines are completely reliable. A smudge on the answer sheet might be read as an intended mark once but not another time. However, these differences tend to be miniscule. For practical purposes, we usually say that scoring reliability is not an issue for machine-scored tests. Even so, if you have a really low-budget scoring machine in your school, you might want to check its reliability.

We should also note that multiple-choice, true-false, and other such items that are scored by hand rather than by machine are subject to scoring error. Such error arises from

Figure 3.3 A modern scanner used to score tests electronically reduces scoring error. (Courtesy of NCS Pearson, Inc.)

simple clerical errors in marking and adding up scores. In a typical application, the errors are not large—unless the scorer is very inattentive. Periodic checking of a hand-scoring operation is sensible.

Alternate Form Reliability

Also sometimes referred to as parallel form, or equivalent form, reliability, **alternate form reliability** requires that there be two forms of the test. The two forms should be the same or very similar in terms of number of items, time limits, content specifications, and other such factors. The alternate form reliability study consists of administering both forms of the test to the same examinees. The alternate form reliability is the correlation, usually Pearson, between scores obtained from the two forms. Refer to Table 3.3. Replace the column headings, Test and Retest, with Form 1 and Form 2. That is the basic design for an alternate form reliability study.

The alternate forms of the test may be administered in immediate succession if they are relatively brief and undemanding. Otherwise, an intertest interval similar to that used for test-retest reliability—a few days to a few weeks—may be employed. In the simplest case of alternate form reliability, when the two forms are administered in immediate succession, the method measures only unreliability due to content sampling. For lengthier tests, the alternate forms are usually administered with an intertest interval of a few days to a few weeks. In this case, the method measures unreliability due to content sampling and, as in test-retest reliability, changes in personal conditions and variations in administrative conditions.

Alternate form reliability is not used very frequently for the simple reason that most tests do not have alternate forms. It is hard enough to build one good test, let alone two or more alternate forms of the test. Alternate forms are usually available only for some of the most widely used tests.

Internal Consistency Reliability

Internal consistency reliability is one of the most frequently used methods of expressing test reliability. There are numerous methods for determining a test's internal consistency reliability. We will describe three of the most widely used methods: split-half, Kuder-Richardson, and coefficient alpha. All of these methods, both those we describe here and other methods described elsewhere, attempt to measure the common characteristic of the test's internal consistency.

The internal consistency methods, like the other methods considered thus far, yield a reliability coefficient in the form of a correlation. However, exactly what is happening with the internal consistency methods is less obvious than for the other methods. Once described, the test-retest, interrater, and alternate form methods seem intuitively clear. Not so with the internal consistency methods. We should begin, then, by describing the rationale for these methods, starting with the split-half method.

Split-half Reliability.   Recall the alternate form method from the previous section. Think specifically of the case in which the two forms are administered in immediate succession. Now think of the administration of a single test, but we will score it in halves, as if each half were an alternate form of the test. Then we correlate scores on the two halves of the test. This is like a "mini-alternate forms" measure of reliability. This is essentially what happens with **split-half reliability**.

There are two important expansions on the latter scenario. First, the test is usually *not* split into the first and second halves of the test. The second half of a test often has more difficult items; examinees may be more fatigued toward the end of the test; and, if there is any effect of timing, it is more likely to influence the second half than the first half of the test. So, how shall the test be split in half? One frequently used method is to split the test into odd-numbered and even-numbered items. In this case, the result is sometimes referred to as **odd-even reliability**. Other types of splits may be useful for certain types of test items, but the odd-even split is clearly the most widely used.

Second, the correlation between the two halves of the test does not give the reliability of the full-length test. The correlation gives the reliability of a test half the length of the test one is really interested in. A correction must be applied to the correlation between the two halves of the test to yield the reliability of the full-length test. The appropriate correction is called the **Spearman-Brown correction**. (See Appendix C for the exact formula.) Thus, a test manual may contain a statement like this: "The test's reliability, determined by the odd-even method with the Spearman-Brown correction, was .84." That sounds like a mouthful, but it is not that difficult to understand.

Kuder-Richardson Formulas.   A series of formulas developed by G. Fredrick Kuder and M. W. Richardson (1937) provide other measures of internal consistency. Two of these formulas, numbers 20 and 21, commonly referred to as **KR-20** and **KR-21**, have been widely used. The formulas for KR-20 and KR-21 yield little insight into what aspect of reliability they are measuring. Let us just give a brief narrative description. The matter will become clearer when we examine the third case, coefficient alpha.

Recall the discussion of splitting a test in half. A commonly used method is to split the test into odd and even items. However, many other splits are possible. For example, on a 10-item test, one could use items 1–5 vs. 6–10; or items 1, 2, 5, 6, and 9 vs. 3, 4, 7, 8, and 10; or items 1, 2, 3, 9, 10 vs. 4, 5, 6, 7, and 8. The KR-20 formula yields the average correlation among all possible split-halves for the test. KR-21 is a simplification of KR-20, based on the assumption that all the items are of equal difficulty.

Coefficient Alpha. The Kuder-Richardson formulas require dichotomously scored items, for example, correct-incorrect or yes-no. There is a more general formula that does not have this restriction. Items can have any type of continuous score. For example, items on an attitude scale might be on a five-point scale, ranging from strongly disagree (1) to strongly agree (5). The more general form is **coefficient alpha**, often called **Cronbach's alpha** (see Cronbach, 1951). Do not confuse this alpha with the alpha used in significance tests (e.g., the .05 level). They have nothing to do with one another.

Coefficient alpha is very widely used in contemporary testing. Hogan, Benjamin, and Brezinski (2000) found that 67% of the tests reported in almost 700 journal articles used coefficient alpha. Thus, although coefficient alpha is not easy to understand, it is important to be familiar with it.

What does coefficient alpha indicate? There are several formulas for coefficient alpha. Let us examine one version to see what it does. Assuming that all items are "standardized" (that is, converted to a form so that each has a mean = 0 and SD = 1) then the following formula applies:

$$\alpha = \frac{K(\bar{r}_{ij})}{1 + (K-1)\bar{r}_{ij}}$$

where

K is the number of items

r_{ij} is the correlation between items i and j

the bar over r indicates that it is an average of all such correlations between items i and j.

What is this formula doing? It is certainly not obvious from inspecting the elements in the formula. Recall the rationale for the split-half method. It was like creating alternate miniforms. Now extend this reasoning to individual items. We can think of each item as a miniform of the test. We can then ask how each of these miniforms (items) agrees with all the other miniforms (items) in the test. Then we can sum all this information into a measure of internal consistency reliability. In this formula $\bar{r}_{ij}$ is the average intercorrelation among all the items. It is certainly not a convenient formula to use for practical computing purposes. However, it does give a good idea about what coefficient alpha indicates.

Application of the latter formula provides some practical guidance about how the internal consistency of tests works. Insert sample values for K and $\bar{r}_{ij}$ into the formula and note the consequences. In Table 3.6, we let K take the values 5, 20, and 50, and let $\bar{r}_{ij}$ take the values .10, .25, and .40. Then we calculate α. What do we observe? First, as the number of items increases, reliability increases. Second, as the average interitem correlation increases, reliability increases. Further, when there are relatively few items (say, 5), reliability is very low when interitem correlations are low; when interitem correlations are high, reliability is much higher but still not very high. When there are many items (say, 50), reliability is quite respectable even when interitem correlations are relatively low. Thus, the formula shows that alpha depends on the average correlation among the items. The number of items is also very important. Alpha indicates the extent to which items in the test are measuring the same construct(s) or trait(s). It is sometimes called a measure of *item homogeneity*; that is, the extent to which the items are the same in terms of what they are measuring. Note that individual items are not very reliable by themselves. Hence, the intercorrelations among items will

Table 3.6   Effect of Number of Items (K)
and Average Interitem Correlation ($\bar{r}_{ij}$) on
Coefficient Alpha

K	$\bar{r}_{ij}$	α
5	.10	.36
5	.25	.63
5	.40	.77
20	.10	.69
20	.25	.87
20	.40	.93
50	.10	.85
50	.25	.94
50	.40	.97

seem unusually low. For example, a correlation of .25 is usually considered quite low but it is a respectable level for a correlation among individual items.

In relation to the sources of unreliability outlined in Table 3.1, coefficient alpha relates to unreliability due to content sampling. It does not measure unreliability due to changes in test administration, personal conditions, or scoring. This same generalization applies to all the internal consistency methods of determining reliability.

Try This!

Substitute these values in the formula on page 56: $K = 30$, $\bar{\bar{ij}} = .10$. What is α?

The various measures of internal consistency are *not* appropriate for *speeded tests.* They are entirely inappropriate if the test is primarily a speed test, such as a test of reading rate or clerical speed. Some "power" tests are partly speeded in that some examinees may not finish all items. To the extent that speed does affect scores, the measures of internal consistency will yield inflated estimates of reliability. To deal with this problem, it is possible to split tests in terms of times rather than number of items, but this tends to create a rather artificial testing situation. When speed is a significant factor in determining scores, it is best to simply use other methods for determining reliability.

KEY POINTS SUMMARY 3.2   *Main Methods of Determining Reliability*

Test-retest	Alternate forms
Interscorer	Internal consistency

Three Important Conclusions

As noted previously, it is not easy to see exactly what the formulas for internal consistency measures are doing. However, it is easy to deduce three important conclusions from inspection of the formulas. First, test length is important. The number of test items always enters the formulas. In general, the longer the test, the more reliable it will be. Very short tests are often unreliable. In the limiting case, single items almost always have quite limited reliability. As a general rule, to increase reliability, increase test length. Among widely used, well-developed tests, we find that reliabilities of about .80 require at least 25 items; reliabilities of about .90 usually require at least 45 items.

The second conclusion is not apparent from the simplified formula for coefficient alpha presented here, but it becomes apparent in other versions of formulas for internal consistency reliability. Nevertheless, we can state the conclusion: Reliability is maximized when the percentage of examinees responding correctly in a cognitive ability test or responding in a certain direction (e.g., "yes") in a noncognitive test is near .50. This percentage correct is called the p-value, a topic developed in more detail in Chapter 10. This goal of a p-value near .50 is the reason that standardized tests in the cognitive domain—for example, the SAT or the ACT—often seem so hard. The test developer is trying to maximize reliability. Actually, taking into account the effect of guessing the correct answer, the target p-value for items is usually set somewhat above .50, but still at a difficult level. A common target for the average p-value in standardized tests is .60 or .65. However, when building your own tests, you do not sacrifice much reliability by allowing the average difficulty level (p-value) to rise as high as .85.

The third conclusion is that internal consistency reliability increases as the correlations among items in the test increases. In plain English, the more similar the items, the higher the internal consistency. For example, a test consisting entirely of items about fractions will have higher internal consistency than a test that includes some fractions, some science, some history, and some reading (assuming the two tests have the same total number of items). Thus, to get good internal consistency reliability, create tests that concentrate on one aspect of achievement at a time.

When considering test-retest reliability, we noted that the test-retest method was not used very often with educational tests. For example, you rarely find such information for major achievement batteries. Such batteries require about three hours of testing time. It is very difficult to get groups of students to take exactly the same three-hour test twice! However, for tests in the cognitive realm (e.g., achievement and mental ability tests), test-retest reliability usually tracks closely on internal consistency reliability. The test-retest reliability is usually about .05 lower than the internal consistency reliability for a set of test scores. For example, if the internal consistency reliability for scores on a reading comprehension test is .90, it is likely that the test-retest reliability will be about .85. If the internal consistency reliability for a math computation test is .70, it is likely that the test-retest reliability will be about .65. This is just a very rough generalization. If you really need to know the test-retest reliability, then conduct a separate study for it. Furthermore, this generalization does not hold true for tests in the noncognitive realm, for example, personality tests. For these types of tests, the internal consistency and test-retest reliabilities may be quite different.

THE STANDARD ERROR OF MEASUREMENT

A reliability coefficient provides important information about a test. However, its practical implications for test interpretation are not immediately evident. For practical interpretation, we depend on the **standard error of measurement**, usually abbreviated SEM. The SEM is defined as:

$$\text{SEM} = \text{SD}\sqrt{1 - r}$$

where r is the test's reliability and SD is the test's standard deviation for the group on which the r was determined.

The SEM is the standard deviation of a hypothetically infinite number of obtained scores around the person's true score. Refer to Figure 3.2 (p. 50). Each of these distributions has a standard deviation. This particular kind of standard deviation is called a standard error of measurement. The distribution on the right in Figure 3.2 has a relatively large SEM. The distribution on the left has a relatively small SEM. Observe some of the consequences of the formula for SEM. If test reliability is perfect ($r = 1.00$), SEM = 0; that is, there is no measurement error. What is SEM if the test reliability is .00, that is, completely unreliable? In that case SEM is the SD of the test.

Try This!

Determine SEM for the following cases:

The reliability of the Tri-State Reading Test score is .92; SD is 15. What is SEM?
Suppose the reliability is .70, while SD remains at 15. What is SEM now?

Confidence Bands

The SEM can be used to create a confidence interval, sometimes in testing parlance called a **confidence band**, around the observed score. Since the SEM is a standard deviation of a distribution assumed to be normal, all of the customary relationships within the normal curve apply. Refer to the normal curve in Figure 5.3 of Chapter 5 for a nice picture. For example, in 68% (about two thirds) of the cases, the true score will be within +/− 1 SEM of the observed score. Conversely, in about one third of the cases, the observed score will differ from the true score by at least 1 SEM.

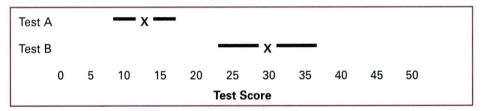

Figure 3.4 Illustration of score report using confidence bands.

Computer-generated score reports often use the confidence band. Figure 3.4 gives an example. The confidence band for Test A ranges from 9 to 17, centered around an observed score of 13. Thus, the confidence band is 13 +/− 3 points. Test B has a band ranging from 24 to 36, centered around an observed score of 30 (i.e., 30 +/− 6 points). Such reports usually give the "band" as +/− 1 SEM—essentially a 68% confidence interval, although it is easy to use a 95% band (+/− 1.96 SEM) or 99% band (+/− 2.58 SEM). In the normal distribution, 95% of the cases fall within +/− 1.96 standard deviation units of the mean and 99% fall within +/− 2.58 standard deviation units of the mean.

Appropriate Units for SEM

The SEM should be expressed in the score units used for interpretation. Test manuals often give the SEM only in raw score units. If interpretation employs normed scores, then the raw score SEM must be converted to the normed score. This can easily be done for normed scores that are linear conversions of raw scores, such as linear standard scores, which we describe in Chapter 5.

Consider the following examples for a 75-item test. Figure 3.5 shows the distribution of scores on this test in terms of raw scores (M = 50, SD = 5), standard scores (M = 500, SD = 100), and percentiles. The test's reliability is .80. Thus, in raw score units, SEM = $5 \sqrt{1 - .80}$ = 2.2. This many raw score units (2.2) equals 44 units in the standard score system, that is, $100\sqrt{1 - .80}$. Obviously, the raw score SEM is not useful if the interpretation is based on standard scores. There is no such simple conversion for percentiles. However, we can estimate the effect of applying +/− 1 SEM in raw score units at various points along the percentile scale. Around the 5th (or 95th) percentile, +/− 2.2 raw score units cover about 10 percentile points. Around the 50th percentile, +/− 2.2 raw score units cover 34 percentile points! This peculiar performance of percentiles at various

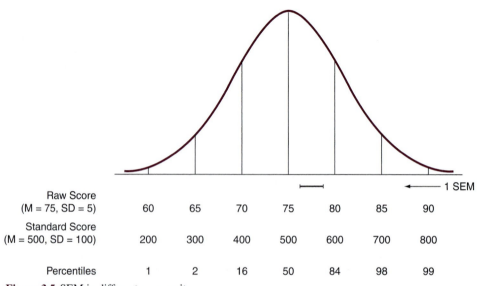

Raw Score (M = 75, SD = 5)	60	65	70	75	80	85	90
Standard Score (M = 500, SD = 100)	200	300	400	500	600	700	800
Percentiles	1	2	16	50	84	98	99

Figure 3.5 SEM in different score units.

points in the distribution (assuming it has a "hump" like the normal distribution) is described further in Chapter 5 (see p. 101).

Some Important Distinctions for the Term "Standard Error"

The term "standard error" has several applications within statistics and testing. The various applications often cause confusion because they sound so much alike. And, in fact, they are all standard deviations—but standard deviations of quite different things. It is important to distinguish the standard error of measurement from two other types of standard errors. First, there is the standard error of the mean. This is an index of the stability of a sample mean drawn from a population. It depends primarily on the number of elements in the sample, usually designated by N. If you had a course in elementary statistics, you certainly encountered the standard error of the mean in connection with t-tests and confidence intervals for means. A second type of standard error is the standard error of estimate, or standard error of prediction. This type of standard error arises when we are predicting status on one variable from status on another variable. It tells us how much we might be "off" in our prediction. Again, if you had a course in elementary statistics, you encountered this standard error of estimate when studying predictions or what we often call "regression." The important point here is that the standard error of measurement applies to individual test scores and not to sample means or predicted scores. To satisfy the curious student, Appendix C gives the formulas for these three standard errors.

Reliability in Item Response Theory (IRT)

Most of what we have described thus far about reliability is formulated within what we call classical test theory (CTT). An increasing number of tests use an alternative theory: item response theory (IRT). For example, computer-adaptive tests use IRT. The concern about reliability is the same for CTT and IRT tests. However, for internal consistency types of reliability, IRT yields a **precision of measurement** index. This is similar to the SEM described earlier. We developed the SEM under classical test theory. One major difference between CTT's standard error of measurement and IRT's precision of measurement index is that the precision index can have different values for different regions of the score scale. The SEM is assumed to be the same throughout the score scale. For example, if the SEM is 5 points on an IQ test, we use SEM = 5 for IQs of 80, 100, 150, and so on. The precision of measurement index in IRT might be smaller in the lower part of the scale and higher in the upper part of the scale for one test; it might be just the opposite for another test. It is important to note that the precision of measurement index in IRT deals only with internal consistency of the test. If the concern is with temporal stability, then the test-retest method of determining reliability should be used regardless of whether the test was developed with CTT or IRT.

It is very unlikely that a teacher or a single school would use IRT methods for developing assessments. IRT methods usually require very large samples. Thus, the individual teacher or school would not ordinarily develop a precision of measurement index. However, the precision index is often available for externally developed tests, for example, state assessments. Hence, the individual teacher should be familiar with this index.

RELIABILITY FOR CRITERION-REFERENCED INTERPRETATION

Recall the distinction between a criterion-referenced test (CRT) and a norm-referenced test (NRT) from Chapter 1. The key difference is in the method of interpretation. One sometimes hears the opinion that reliability is not important for a CRT. This is incorrect. Reliability is important for any type of measurement. However, the methods of determining reliability may have to be different for CRTs, depending on the distribution of scores on the test and the uses for the scores.

The classical approaches to reliability considered in this chapter assume a normal distribution of test scores. At a minimum, there must be a reasonable distribution of scores. Otherwise, the correlation coefficient does not work. Consider the extreme case in a test-retest study where all scores are the same—say, perfect scores—on the retest. The formula for the correlation coefficient will lead to $r = .00$.

What relevance does this concern have for CRTs? First, it should be noted that many CRTs yield distributions of scores that have quite adequate variability. Most end-of-course or end-of-unit tests are good examples. In these cases, conventional approaches to reliability assessment are appropriate. Concern about inadequate variability in test scores *may* be applicable to some mastery testing situations where the score distributions have marked negative skewness; that is, an accumulation of scores at or near a perfect score. The distribution of CRT scores in relation to a "cut-score" may also affect interpretation of the reliability of a CRT. Numerous methods have been developed to express the reliability of CRTs in these special circumstances. We present here two approaches to illustrate variations from the conventional approaches to expressing reliability: proportion agreement and Cohen's kappa statistic. For more extensive treatments of the reliability of CRTs, see Berk (1984), Crocker and Algina (1986), Feldt and Brennan (1989), and Nunnally and Bernstein (1994).

Suppose that in a mastery testing situation we are concerned only with the classification of individuals as "masters" or "nonmasters." Thus, we are not concerned with the full distribution of scores but only with whether individuals exceed some cutoff score, a mastery point. One simple solution is to express the proportion of examinees identified as masters or nonmasters on two administrations of the test. Call this the *proportion agreement* (or % agreement) statistic. The two test administrations are reasonably contemporaneous, as in a test-retest reliability study. It would not be appropriate to use this method with a pre- and posttest (before and after treatment) design where one would expect substantial change from nonmaster to master status between the two testing administrations.

Cohen (1960) presented the **kappa** (κ) statistic to express agreement in classification of individuals between two administrations of a test. This is like test-retest reliability where the only scores are 1 (master) and 0 (nonmaster).

$$\kappa = \frac{(P - P_C)}{(1 - P_C)}$$

where

P = proportion of persons classified in the same category on both occasions; that is, [(master and master) + (nonmaster and nonmaster)]/N

P_c = proportion of persons so classified that would be expected by chance, where chance is determined by use of marginal totals as in the chi-square test

Table 3.7   Examples of the Classification of "Masters" and "Nonmasters" for Two Administrations of a Test

		Case A Second Test				Case B Second Test	
		NM[1]	M			NM	M
First	M	20	30	First	M	10	45
Test	NM	30	20	Test	NM	40	5
% Agreement:			60%				85%
Kappa (κ)			**.20**				**.70**

[1]NM = Nonmaster, M = Master

Table 3.7 provides two sets of data (A and B) involving administration of the same or comparable tests on two occasions. The proportion agreement statistic and Cohen's κ are presented for both data sets. Notice that in the first set of data (A), 60% agreement sounds quite good. However, the data are not very different from a random distribution of the cases with 25 cases in each cell. The kappa statistic (κ) reflects this. Notice how kappa changes for the two cases presented in Table 3.7.

RELIABILITY OF WHAT?

We often refer to "the reliability of a test." This is inappropriate. We should refer to the reliability of a test score. More importantly, we need to think carefully about exactly what "score" we are interpreting. Sometimes, the point of reference is a total score on a test, for example, the total score on a reading test or a history test. However, there are many other points of reference. The application of reliability concepts changes with these changes in points of reference. Sometimes we are most interested in the difference between two scores, for example, the difference between scores in reading and math or the difference in reading scores from Grade 2 to Grade 3. In these cases, the point of reference is the difference, not the individual scores. It is important to note that the reliability of a difference is generally much less than the reliability of either score entering into the difference. That happens because the difference contains error from both individual scores. Appendix C gives the formula for calculating the reliability of a difference. However, short of applying that formula, it is good to be aware that differences between scores are often notoriously unreliable.

Here is another particularly troublesome difficulty. We often have the reliability for a *total* test score, for example, a total math score. However, our attention is drawn to clusters of items or even individual items within the test. These clusters of items or individual items are much less reliable than the total test score. In fact, small clusters of items and individual items usually have very low reliability. The total score on a mathematics test may have a reliability of .90, but this does not transfer to parts of the test. In general, you need to be very wary of the reliability of small clusters of items or individual items. Their reliabilities are often less than .30. You would not consider using a total test with that level of reliability.

SOME CONCLUDING EXAMPLES

Here are a few practical examples of statements about reliability. You might encounter such statements in test manuals or in your own use of tests. Based on the concepts and procedures presented in this chapter, these examples should now make sense to you.

Example 1

- Statement: The Northeast Intelligence Test (NIT) has a test-retest reliability of .95.
- Student score: Chris got a score of 110 on the NIT.
- Comment: The test has very high reliability. It is unlikely that Chris's score would change very much if he retook the test in the near future.

Example 2

- Statement: The standard error of measurement (SEM) on the Texas Reading Scale (TES) is 5 points.
- Student score: Kim's score on the TES is 80.
- Comment: We should think of Kim's true score as probably falling in the range of 75 to 85 and almost certainly within the range of 70 to 90.

Example 3

- Statement: The internal consistency reliability of my 20-item classroom test in math is .70.
- Student scores: Students' scores will be used to assign report card grades.
- Comment: This is not very high reliability. Don't use the scores from this test alone to assign grades. Combine other information with the test scores. In the future, you may want to use a longer test.

Example 4

- Statement: The Southwestern Hyperactivity Scale (SHS) has a test-retest reliability of .65.
- Student score: Ned got a score of 35 on the SHS.
- Comment: The test has rather low reliability. Ned's score might be quite different if he were evaluated with this scale on a different day.

Example 5

- Statement: The interrater reliability of the writing test our school uses is .65.
- Students' scores: Each student's writing sample is scored by only one teacher.
- Comment: The writing scores do not have very good interrater reliability. Be cautious about basing any conclusions on only one writing sample. Use multiple samples and/or multiple raters.

PRACTICAL ADVICE

1. For important decisions, make sure you have very reliable information. Important decisions include such matters as assigning final grades, determining promotions, or selecting students for lengthy special programs. Usually, you want reliability in excess of .90 for such important uses.

2. To increase reliability for important decisions, use multiple sources of information. Each source might have only moderate reliability but the combination of sources will almost certainly have much greater reliability.

3. Normally, an externally prepared test will have reliability information, including the standard error of measurement for a test score. Get accustomed to finding that information and using it. As a general rule, put a band of two times the standard error around each score when interpreting student performance.

4. When using the standard error of measurement (SEM), be sure to have it in the score units used for interpretation. For example, if you are interpreting scores in grade equivalents (GEs), make sure the SEM is in GEs, not raw scores. Also, be exceptionally careful about interpreting percentiles in the middle of the distribution; that is, from about percentiles 35 to 65.

5. In general, to increase the reliability of your tests, increase the number of items in the test.

6. Be wary of short tests—either ones you prepared or those prepared externally. Short tests nearly always have limited reliability. You can use them to draw very tentative conclusions about individual students but, if the conclusions have important consequences, seek more information.

7. The more a test score or grade depends on judgment, the more you need to worry about scorer reliability. Make the criteria for such judgments as specific as possible. If circumstances permit, have more than one person participate in the judgment process.

8. At least occasionally, apply one of the techniques described in this chapter to check the reliability of your own tests or grading procedures. If your school has a software package for grading tests, see if the package yields a reliability coefficient. Many software packages do. Use the information to (a) improve the reliability of your tests and (b) to temper your conclusions. Normally, teachers think all their tests are highly reliable. As a rule, they are not. A little humility, please.

9. Be sure to distinguish, in your own mind and when explaining test scores to others, between reliability and validity. Persons who have not studied these topics (as you have now) often mix up these notions.

SUMMARY

1. We refined our notion of reliability in four ways. We noted some synonyms for reliability. We cautioned that reliability is not an all-or-none affair. We distinguished reliability from validity. We observed that reliability deals with unsystematic error.

2. The major sources of unreliability are test scoring, content, administrative conditions, and personal conditions.

3. A helpful conceptual framework formulates reliability in terms of true score, observed score, and error score.

4. The main methods of determining reliability are test-retest, interrater, alternate form, and internal consistency.

Each deals with a particular source of unreliability and uses the correlation coefficient as the vehicle for expressing the degree of reliability.

5. The standard error of measurement (SEM) translates reliability information into the metric of the test score. The SEM often uses a confidence band around a specific test score. It is important to express the SEM in the score unit actually used for interpretation.

6. We must distinguish the SEM from the standard error of the mean and the standard error of estimate.

7. Item response theory (IRT) uses the precision of measurement index. This index covers only error due to content sampling.

8. The usual methods of determining reliability usually work well for tests interpreted by criterion referencing. Sometimes, more specialized methods are required, especially for highly skewed distributions of scores.

9. When applying the concepts and methods of reliability, it is important to concentrate on exactly what score is being interpreted. Interpretation of differences among scores, small clusters of items, or individual items calls for special caution.

KEY TERMS

alternate form reliability	intrarater reliability	Spearman-Brown correction
coefficient alpha	kappa	split-half reliability
confidence band	KR-20	stability coefficient
Cronbach's alpha	KR-21	standard error of measurement
error score	observed score	(SEM)
internal consistency reliability	odd-even reliability	test-retest reliability coefficient
interrater reliability	precision of measurement	true score
intraclass correlation coefficient (ICC)	reliability coefficient	

EXERCISES

1. Here are the ratings assigned by two different teachers to essays written by 20 students. The teachers used a 9-point system for their ratings, where 9 was high and 1 was low. Use a software package such as SPSS or Excel to determine the correlation between the ratings. This will be the interrater reliability.

Student	1	2	3	4	5	6	7	8	9	10	11	12	13	14	15	16	17	18	19	20
Teacher A	6	9	2	5	9	4	1	3	5	6	8	2	9	4	3	7	5	6	4	5
Teacher B	5	9	1	5	7	4	3	5	3	6	7	3	9	5	6	4	3	6	3	6

2. Determine the standard error of measurement (SEM) for each of these sets of data.

Reliability coefficient	Standard deviation	SEM
.90	100	_____
.60	100	_____
.90	5	_____
.60	5	_____

3. For each of the SEMs in Exercise 2, determine the 95% and 99% confidence bands.

SEM	95% band (multiply SEM by 1.96)	99% band (multiply SEM by 2.58)
_____	_____	_____
_____	_____	_____
_____	_____	_____
_____	_____	_____

4. Access any test review in Buros's *Mental Measurements Yearbook* online or in hard copy. (See Appendix A for a description of this source.) What does the review say about the test's reliability? What type of reliability information is provided for the test? What does the reviewer conclude about the adequacy of the reliability information?

5. Access the website for one of the test publishers listed in Appendix B. Link to one of the publisher's tests. What references are made to the test's reliability?

6. Go to the search engine for a database of educational research articles. Enter "test reliability" as keywords. What references to test reliability do you find?

Chapter 4

Validity: What the Test Measures

OBJECTIVES

- Compare the "standard" and "refined" definitions of test validity.
- Define content validity and show how it is applied to achievement tests.
- Define criterion-related validity and show its typical applications.
- Define construct validity and list some methods used to demonstrate it.
- Define consequential validity and describe its status within the field of assessment.
- Identify how the concept of test fairness fits within the context of test validity.
- Distinguish between test validity and the accuracy of norms.

What This Chapter Is About

In general, validity deals with how well an assessment technique accomplishes its purpose. In this chapter, we refine our thinking about this topic. Then, we examine methods for studying validity. For each method, we identify common applications and special problems using that method. Application of content validity to teacher-made and standardized achievement tests receives special attention. We also examine methods for studying the fairness of tests.

Why This Topic Is Important

Validity is the most important characteristic of a test or other assessment technique. Without good validity, all else is lost. A test may be perfectly reliable and have impeccable norms, but if it is not valid, it is of no use to us. Although validity is the most important technical characteristic of a test, it can also be the most difficult to demonstrate. Therefore, we must study this topic carefully. We cannot make much sense of many other topics in this book without an adequate grasp of validity.

INTRODUCTION

Let us begin with these very practical situations and questions related to test validity.

- Ms. Vasquez is developing a test for a high school biology course. Performance on the test will count for 30% of students' grades. What steps should she take to ensure that she has a good test for this purpose?

- Ivy College uses the *Western Admissions Test* (*WAT*) to select applicants who should be successful in their studies. What type of evidence would help to determine if the *WAT* satisfies its purpose?
- The newly published *Diagnostic Wonder Test* promises to identify children with a mathematics learning disability. How will we know whether the test does so or is simply a cleverly packaged general ability test?
- A school system wants to use an achievement battery that will measure the extent to which students are learning the curriculum specified by the school. How should the school system proceed in reviewing the available achievement tests?

Definition of Validity: Refining Our Thinking

All of the questions just raised relate to the validity of tests. In this chapter, we refine our thinking about this topic and examine methods used to answer the questions. The customary definition of **validity** is the *extent to which a test measures what it purports to measure*. We used this definition in Chapter 1 when discussing the fundamental questions in educational assessment. At a basic level, we are encouraged to ask the question: Is this test or assessment method valid? However, now that we have the opportunity to treat the topic of validity in more detail, we need to refine our thinking. We need to rephrase the question in two ways.

First, it is imprecise to refer to the validity of a test. What we need to establish is the validity of a test score when used for a particular purpose. Even more accurately, we should refer to the *interpretation of a score for a particular purpose or use*. In the scenarios sketched at the beginning of this chapter we always stated a purpose for the test. A score may be appropriately used for one purpose but not for another purpose. We cannot define the validity of a test score in the abstract, but only with respect to a particular use. Thus, we should not ask such questions as: Is the SAT valid? Or, is my final exam valid? Rather, we should ask such questions as: Is the SAT Verbal score valid for predicting GPA at the end of the college freshman year? Or, is my final exam valid for inferring knowledge of the subject matter in order to award a grade?

Second, we note that validity is a *matter of degree*. It is not an all-or-none affair. Some tests may have no validity for a particular purpose. There are probably no assessments that are perfectly valid for a given purpose. Many test scores have some validity. The validity may be very slight, moderate, or considerable. Our concern will be determining the extent of validity. From a practical viewpoint, we want to know if the validity is sufficient to make use of the test or other assessment technique worthwhile. Thus, we further refine our question as: *To what extent* is the SAT Verbal score valid for predicting freshman GPA? To what degree is the final exam valid for awarding a grade based on knowledge of the subject matter?

Construct Underrepresentation and Construct Irrelevant Variance

As we formalize our treatment of validity, two technical terms will aid our thinking. Before introducing these terms, let us consider the overlap between the *construct* we wish to measure and the assessment procedure or test we hope will measure that construct. The **construct** is a trait or characteristic. For example, the construct might be children's self-concept or mathematical reasoning ability. We may have a simple, 20-item questionnaire

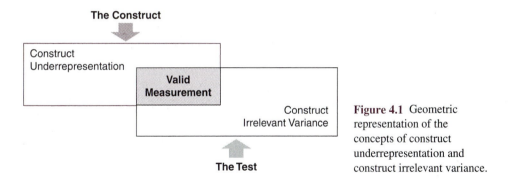

Figure 4.1 Geometric representation of the concepts of construct underrepresentation and construct irrelevant variance.

to measure self-concept or a 50-item multiple-choice test to measure mathematical reasoning. We represent the relationship between the construct and the test by overlapping geometric forms as in Figure 4.1. Overlap between the construct and the test represents validity: measuring what we want to measure. The part of the construct *not* covered by the test we call **construct underrepresentation**. The construct of interest is not fully covered by the test. On the other hand, the test, in addition to measuring part of the construct of interest, may measure some characteristics other than what we want to measure. This "other" measurement we call **construct irrelevant variance**.

Let us first consider some concrete examples, and then examine how these can be represented graphically. Suppose we want to evaluate students' ability in French. We conceptualize this ability as having four components: speaking, listening, reading, and writing. Our test may do an excellent job of covering reading and listening but it gives no information about speaking and writing in French. Thus, the complete construct of "ability in French" is underrepresented by the test, specifically by omission of two components. This analysis assumes that the four components are at least partially independent, not simply different names for the same characteristic. It may also be that, to some extent, the test scores reflect ordinary listening ability; students with a partial deafness may not hear the entire dictated listening test. Sheer auditory ability is not what we want to measure. This aspect of the scores is construct irrelevant variance.

Apply these concepts to the mathematical reasoning test. Mathematical reasoning should be manifested in the ability to solve both conventional and novel problems. However, the test items cover only conventional problems. Thus, the part of the construct related to novel problems is underrepresented. (We assume that reasoning about novel problems is not perfectly correlated with reasoning about conventional problems. If they are perfectly correlated, or nearly so, it does not make any difference which type of problem we use.) Further, the test requires a very high level of reading ability. We do not want this test to be a reading test. That part of the test scores determined by reading ability rather than mathematical reasoning ability is construct irrelevant variance. Haladyna and Downing (2004) used the concept of construct irrelevant variance to describe the possible unwanted influences on high-stakes test performance. For example, to what extent might test anxiety influence such performance? Ordinarily, a high-stakes test is not designed to measure test anxiety, but if test anxiety influences scores on the test, then this is construct irrelevant variance.

We can have an infinite variety of relationships between the construct and the test. The test may cover much of the construct but also have much irrelevant variance. The test may

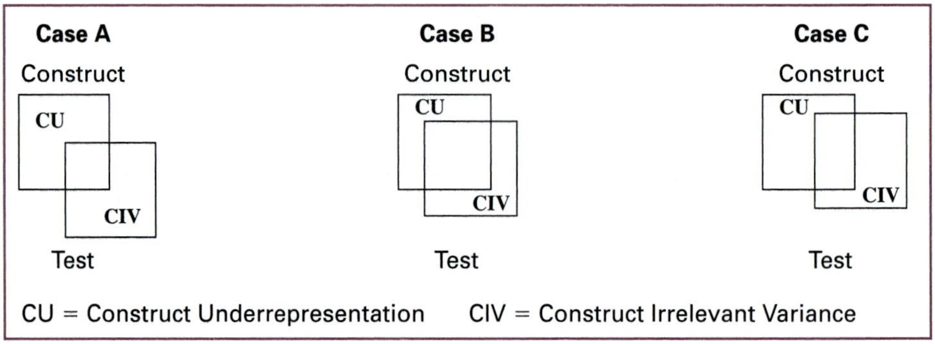

Figure 4.2 Illustrations of varying degrees of construct underrepresentation and construct irrelevant variance.

have little irrelevant variance, but also cover little of the construct. Figure 4.2 shows several different possibilities. Of course, the ideal case is complete overlap of the construct and the test. We do not ordinarily attain that ideal in practice. The notions of construct underrepresentation and construct irrelevant variance will be useful when examining different methods of investigating the validity of tests. Start by thinking of the target for the assessment. Then consider the extent to which a test or an assessment procedure overlaps with this target.

Try This!

Which of the examples in Figure 4.2 shows the highest degree of test validity?
Which example shows the greatest degree of construct irrelevant variance?

Constructs as Targets

The previous section uses the term "constructs." It is a very general term. The professional literature on assessment is filled with references to constructs. So, we should be familiar with that term. However, let us use simpler language. The construct is what we want to get at. Think of it as a target. In the world of educational assessment, relevant constructs or targets include anything that begins with knowledge of . . . , proficiency in . . . , mastery of . . . , and so on. Examples include knowledge of the metric system, proficiency in spelling, and mastery of number facts.

Try This!

List some targets (constructs) for assessment in an area you might teach.

Knowledge of _____

Proficiency in _____

Mastery of _____

Educational assessment also includes behavioral targets. Teachers often rate students' behavior, conduct, and effort on report cards. For example, a report card may contain these targets: cooperates with other students, works hard, pays attention in class. Thus, cooperation, effort, and attentiveness are targets (constructs) for assessment. Other targets relevant for educational assessment are such areas as verbal intelligence, spatial ability, self-esteem, creativity, attitude toward math, and interest in reading. The list could obviously go on and on. In each of these cases, there is a target or construct we want to assess. Validity addresses how well an assessment technique provides useful information about the target.

The Basic Issue

The basic issue is providing *evidence* that the scores on a test are indicative of the trait or construct of interest. This evidence undergirds our interpretation of the test scores. Our treatment of test validity considers the types of evidence that seem to be persuasive regarding this basic issue. The following sections review the types of evidence presented to establish test validity. We also, necessarily, discuss special cautions in interpreting this evidence and introduce the special terms developed for this topic. There is universal agreement that validity is the single most important feature of a test. Good norms, high reliability, and other desirable features are important but they become rather meaningless in the absence of good validity.

Categories of Validity Evidence

We will consider four major categories of validity evidence. The definitive source for listing categories of validity is the *Standards for Educational and Psychological Testing* (AERA, APA, NCME, 1999). Our list differs slightly but not importantly from the list in the Standards. The terminology we adopt here is widely recognized in the field of assessment. Table 4.1 summarizes the major categories we will discuss in this chapter.

Face Validity

When we refer to test validity, we mean some *empirical demonstration* that a test measures what it purports to measure and, more specifically, that scores on the test can be interpreted meaningfully for a particular purpose. We contrast this empirical approach with

Table 4.1   Categories of Validity Evidence

Content
    (including instructional)
Criterion-related
    Concurrent
    Predictive
Construct
Consequential

the notion of face validity. **Face validity** refers to whether a test *looks like* it measures its target construct. Face validity has its advocates and its detractors. The detractors scoff at face validity primarily because it is often used as a substitute for empirical demonstration of validity. It can be alluring and deceptive. A test author may say, "Inspection of items on the *Scranton Creativity Test* clearly indicates that the test measures the major facets of creative thinking." In the absence of any other support, this claim is not helpful. On the other hand, advocates for face validity note that we do work with real people in the real world. We should certainly have empirically demonstrated validity. However, in most circumstances it is also helpful if the test appears to be a valid measure.

We offer the following advice about face validity. Face validity is never a substitute for empirical validity. You cannot simply look at a test and know whether it has any degree of validity. However, face validity may be useful. If two tests have equal empirically established validity, it is usually preferable to use the one with better face validity. When constructing a test, it is prudent to aim for face validity, but never at the expense of empirical validity. Perhaps most importantly, we need to be always aware of the difference between face validity and empirically demonstrated validity.

CONTENT VALIDITY

Content validity deals with the *relationship between the content of a test and some well-defined domain of knowledge or behavior*. For a test to have content validity there must be a good match between the content of the test and the content of the relevant domain. Application of content validity often involves the notion of sampling; that is, the test content covers a representative sampling of all the possible contents of the domain. This is not necessarily the case. The test may cover all material in the domain. However, ordinarily, the domain is too large to make saturation coverage feasible, so we rely on sampling. Content validity has two primary applications: educational achievement tests and employment tests. In each of these areas, there is a well-defined body of content or skills. We want to determine the extent to which the test content matches the content of the relevant area.

Application to Achievement Tests

Content validity is generally considered the most important type of validity for achievement tests. The usual purpose of such tests is to determine the extent of knowledge of some body of material. Table 4.2 lists examples of bodies of material that might be targets for an achievement test.

The process of establishing content validity begins with careful definition of the content to be covered. This process usually results in a **table of specifications** or **blueprint**. Consider some of the entries in Table 4.2. The table of specifications for "high school chemistry" may arise from examination of content in the five most widely used textbooks in this field. The table of specifications for "Chapter 5 in this book" may arise from the list of learning objectives at the beginning of the chapter and the list of key terms at the end of the chapter. "Mathematical concepts covered in Grades 1–3" may be defined by the curriculum guides from several states or the curriculum standards for Lincoln elementary school. Most frequently, written documents serve as the basis for the table of specifications.

Table 4.2   Examples of Bodies of Knowledge as Targets for Achievement Tests

Mathematical concepts covered in Grades 1–3
High school chemistry
First course in educational assessment
Chapter 5 in this book
Geography lessons in Ms. Lister's class last week
Typical elementary school spelling words
Addition, subtraction, multiplication, and division number facts
History of the Civil War
Basic writing skills
Skills in French

Table 4.3 cites statements about the content bases for two standardized achievement tests: the *Praxis Principles of Learning and Teaching* test and the *Stanford Achievement Test*, a multilevel battery for Grades K–12. Notice how references to content define the tests' orientation.

Sometimes the table of specifications is a simple listing of skills, abilities, or knowledge. Such lists often occur in state content standards or basal textbooks. Table 4.4 shows a simple listing of skills for part of Grade 3 mathematics curriculum. In this case, a test should provide coverage of these objectives.

Many applications use a **two-way table** of specifications to represent a content area. The first dimension of the table covers the content topics. The second dimension of the table represents mental processes, such as knowledge of facts, comprehension of concepts, and ability to apply or synthesize material. The most well-known scheme for representing mental processes is **Bloom's taxonomy** in the cognitive domain (Bloom, 1956). Table 4.5 presents only the major categories in Bloom's cognitive taxonomy. The system implies a hierarchy, going from the simplest mental operation (knowledge) to the most complex (evaluation). In its original version, each of these major categories has several subcategories. For example, the first category includes knowledge of specifics, knowledge of universals, knowledge of conventions, and so on. We will explore Bloom's taxonomy

Table 4.3   Statements of Test Purpose Oriented Toward Content Validity

"The [Praxis] Principles of Learning and Teaching test is designed to assess a beginning teacher's knowledge of a variety of job-related criteria. Such knowledge is typically obtained in undergraduate preparation in areas such as educational psychology, human growth and development, classroom management, instructional design and delivery techniques, evaluation and assessment, and other professional preparation" (ETS, 2003, p. 10).

"The *Stanford Achievement Test* Series . . . assesses students' school achievement in reading, mathematics, spelling, language, science, social science, and listening. . . . The test items included in Stanford 10 reflect an extensive review of national and state instructional standards, content-specific criteria, and educational trends as developed by national professional educational organizations" (Harcourt Educational Measurement, 2003, p. 5).

Table 4.4 Example of a Listing of Content Standards for Grade 3 Mathematics

Has mastered basic facts of multiplication
Has mastered regrouping in addition and subtraction for 2-digit numbers
Knows division facts for divisors below 6
Recognizes and correctly applies terms for common solid shapes
Recognizes and correctly applies terms for line, ray, and angle

and several alternatives to it in more detail in Chapter 6. The major categories shown in Table 4.5 are sufficient for discussing test blueprints.

Although the full cognitive taxonomy is sometimes used, people often reduce the six major categories to three. Table 4.6 uses such a reduced Bloom-type system to illustrate a two-way table of specifications for a unit on oil in the earth science curriculum. Entries in the cells of Table 4.6 show the relative weight assigned to each cell in percentage form. For example, approximately 10% of the content deals with facts about the formation of oil. Therefore, about 10% of the test items should deal with such facts; in a 50-item test, this would mean 5 items on this topic. If there were only one item on this topic or as many as 20 items on this topic, the test would have poor content validity to that extent. In terms of marginal totals in Table 4.6, we would expect about 40% of the test items (20 in a 50-item test) to be on "sources of oil."

From a practical perspective, content validity presents two types of questions. First, how do we build content validity into an assessment? For example, how does your instructor ensure content validity of the final exam in this course? How does Ms. Vasquez build content validity into her high school biology test? Second, how do we determine the content validity of an existing test? For example, the history teacher wants to check the content validity of the ABC American History Exam. Or the curriculum director wants to check the content validity of the math tests in the *Stanford Achievement Test*. Let's examine procedures for answering both types of questions.

How to Build Content Validity Into an Assessment

First, start with clear specification of the content to be covered. This often means listing specific learning goals and objectives. Some sources call these content standards. The objectives or standards are often "crossed" with a list of processes or depth indicators, thus yielding a two-way table.

Second, build the assessment to match the table of specifications. Ordinarily, the match calls for an overall balance in relative emphases across specific objectives and

Table 4.5 Major Categories in Bloom's Taxonomy for the Cognitive Domain

1. Knowledge	4. Analysis
2. Comprehension	5. Synthesis
3. Application	6. Evaluation

Table 4.6   Example of a Two-way Table of Content Specifications Based on the Topic of Oil in Earth Science

Content	Process			
	Facts	Concepts	Applications	Total
Oil				
Formation	10	10	0	20
Sources	15	10	15	40
Uses	15	5	20	40
Total	**40**	**25**	**35**	**100**

types of processes. While attempting to get the match between objectives and assessment, try to ensure that your assessment does not call on skills or knowledge other than what you are trying to assess. Also, be aware that in order to get at all of the objectives, you may need more than one assessment technique or test. We take up this topic of building content validity into an assessment in more detail in Chapter 6.

How to Check Content Validity of an Existing Test

The steps needed to check content validity of an existing test parallel those needed to build content validity into a test. The first step is to have a clear definition of the content to be covered. What content is to be covered for the history course in the example given earlier? The answer will probably be a content outline for the teacher's history course or a state's content standards. What content does the curriculum director want covered? The answer will probably be the school district's curriculum guide.

The second step involves matching items in the test to the definition of the content to be covered. Usually this requires examining each item in the test and checking it off against the content outline. At this stage, be cautious about using a summary outline of the test's content. Test manuals often provide such summaries. The summary outline may serve as a rough guide, but direct examination of the actual test items is a better procedure. The matching process allows for two types of mismatch. First, there may be test items that do not match anything in the content outline. Second, there may be elements in the content outline that are not represented in the test.

The matching process requires considerable judgment. As illustrated later (see Table 4.7), items can appear in a variety of formats. How well does the format have to fit in order to be considered a match? Recall, too, the notion of sampling in content validity. A test does not need to cover every detail in a content outline in order to provide a representative sample of the content. In the final analysis, the conclusion about content validity is a judgment call. From a practical viewpoint, the question is not: Is this test content valid? The appropriate question is: Does this test have sufficient content validity to be useful?

In the examples given earlier—involving the history teacher and the curriculum director—we had one person completing the review of content validity. Particularly in the context of high-stakes, statewide testing programs, organizations have developed more elaborate procedures for matching curricular and test content. The current name for these procedures is **alignment analysis**. An alignment analysis is simply a content validity study. It typically involves a panel of individuals (e.g., several teachers and curriculum specialists) matching curricular content and test items. The test might be an off-the-shelf standardized test or a state-prepared test. The matching calls for judgments about coverage of topics and depth of coverage. "Depth" here corresponds to some Bloom-like taxonomy. The alignment analysis concludes with a quantitative index of the degree of match. In some applications, the process extends to matching a state's curriculum (or test) to national and international content standards. For descriptions of several alignment analysis procedures, see Council of Chief State School Officers (2002). The important point for now is that the term alignment analysis signals a content validity study.

Try This!

Go to this Internet site: http://www.ccsso.org/projects/alignment_analysis/Models. Pick one of the models of alignment analysis described there. What type of Bloom-like analysis does the model use?

Instructional Validity

A special application of content validity is the notion of instructional validity, also known as curricular validity. Whereas content validity asks whether the test content fairly matches a well-defined body of content, **instructional validity** asks whether the content has actually been taught. For a test to have instructional validity, there must be evidence that the content was adequately covered in an instructional program. We sometimes call this the **opportunity to learn**. In some contexts, we ask whether the students taking the test have actually been exposed to the material covered in the test.

The concept of instructional validity applies primarily to educational achievement tests. Consider the topic of square roots. This topic may be listed in the school's curriculum guide and in the math textbook used in the school. Therefore, the school's achievement test includes items on square roots. That is good content validity. Suppose, however, that none of the teachers in the school ever cover square roots in class or in homework assignments. Then the square root items do not have good instructional validity. There was no "opportunity to learn" about square roots. Here is another example. A state's standards call for teaching students to write brief stories. The state assessment includes an exercise for writing a brief story. However, in a particular classroom, students never write brief stories. The state assessment has good content validity with respect to the state standards, but the assessment does not have good instructional validity in this classroom.

The notion of instructional validity is not well established as something distinct from content validity. The Standards document does not include the term instructional validity, although it contains brief discussion of the concept of opportunity to learn. In effect, the notion of instructional validity calls for comparing the "well-defined body of content" to what is actually taught rather than to what is supposed to be taught. This is a useful distinction, but it does not introduce an entirely novel type of validity. Nevertheless, the term instructional validity or curricular validity has emerged. It was a prominent concept in one famous court case, *Debra P v. Turlington*, treated in Chapter 14.

Content Validity in Other Areas

The second major application of content validity is to employment tests. The essential notions are the same as for educational achievement tests. For employment tests, the content domain consists of the *knowledge and skills required by a particular job*. When constructing the list of job specifications, it is customary to restrict the list to knowledge and skills, particularly at the entry level. Such factors as motivation and personality traits are not ordinarily included. These other factors might be assessed in the job selection process, but they would be assessed by methods other than the employment tests discussed here. Further, these other methods would be subject to validation through methods other than content validation. The process of developing the list of knowledge and skills required by a job is often called a *job analysis*. After completing the job analysis, we match the test content to the job content. As with achievement tests, we may be matching an existing test with a set of job specifications or we may be constructing a new test to match the job specifications. Schmidt, Ones, and Hunter (1992) and Borman, Hanson, and Hedge (1997) provide reviews of research related to job analysis. Raymond (2001) applies the concept of job analysis to licensure and certification exams.

Try This!

What would you include in a *job analysis* for elementary school teachers? List at least five types of skills or areas of knowledge needed for this job.

Content validity has limited application to other areas—for example, intelligence and personality—because few other areas are susceptible to clear specification of the domains to be covered. What, for example, is the content outline for intelligence or for self-concept? Although we may have simple definitions of these constructs, it is difficult to specify a detailed outline of what they encompass. Hence, content validity does not apply very neatly to them.

Problems With Content Validity

Establishing content validity always seems like a very simple process. Conceptually, it is simple: Specify the content of the domain and then check how well the test matches this content. However, in practice, the process nearly always turns out to be much more complicated. Complications arise from three sources. First, except in a few very simple cases, getting a clear specification of the content domain is often difficult. Consider these examples from Table 4.2. First, we said that the content for "mathematics concepts in Grades 1–3" could be determined by checking the curriculum guides from several states. But state curriculum guides differ somewhat. Suppose we check guides from five states. Three states may include knowledge of metric units in Grades 1–3, but two other states may delay this topic until Grade 4. How shall we handle this? In specifying content for "history of the Civil War," what depth of knowledge do we want: a passing acquaintance with major topics or a thorough grasp of every detail? We can ask a similar question about the knowledge and skills listed in specifications for any assessment.

Table 4.7   Different Test Items Matching a Single Content Category

---

Content Objective: Basic Multiplication Facts
Possible Test Items
1. $5 \times 4 =$ _____
2. $5 \times [\ ] = 20$
3. $5 \times 4 =$ a) 9   b) 20   c) 25   d) 7
4. $5 \times [\ ] = 20$ $[\ ] =$ a) 15   b) 4   c) 5   d) 25
5. Lynn bought 4 pieces of candy at 5 cents each. How much did she spend? _____
6. Lynn bought 4 pieces of candy at 5 cents each. How much did she spend?
                                    a) 9   b) 20   c) 25   d) Not Given
7. Lynn paid 20 cents for 4 pieces of candy. What was the cost per piece? _____

The second difficulty in applying content validity comes in judging how well test items cover elements of the content specifications. Items with a common classification can vary widely in the skills they require. Consider the examples in Table 4.7. Many different items apply to a content category such as "basic multiplication facts." Are all these items equally appropriate? Do they all measure the content category equally well? Probably not. The example of a content category used here—basic multiplication facts—is a simple one. Imagine how much more complicated the situation becomes with a more complex topic, such as knowledge of the Civil War or elementary writing skills. In a listing of test content, all of the items in Table 4.7 might be categorized as "basic multiplication facts." The person judging content validity must examine the actual test items and not rely exclusively on a listing of categories. In the final analysis, content validity requires a judgment, not just checking off boxes in an outline.

Try This!

Write two more test items that apply to the content objective listed in Table 4.7: "basic multiplication facts."

Here is a third difficulty with content validity. It does not refer to actual performance on the test, for example, to students' scores. All other methods of studying validity relate to performance either directly or indirectly. Content validity looks only at the match between curriculum objectives (or job skills) and test items. If actual performance on items spread across the content is highly generalized, it doesn't make much difference how well the items match the content. Consider the example of a content outline covering addition, subtraction, multiplication, and division facts. Suppose that student scores on these four sets of number facts are highly correlated. Students who do well in one area do well in all areas. Students who do poorly in one area do poorly in all areas. In that case, it really doesn't make any difference whether the test consists entirely of multiplication items or is a mixture of the four areas. Nevertheless the all-multiplication test would be judged to have poor content validity. This type of reasoning is widely disregarded in discussions of content validity—although it probably ought not to be.

KEY POINT SUMMARY 4.1 *Problems With Content Validity*

Difficulty in clearly defining some areas
Variety of items for a single topic
Lack of reference to actual performance

CRITERION-RELATED VALIDITY

The essential feature of **criterion-related validity** is establishing the *relationship between performance on the test and on some other criterion* that is taken as an important indicator of the construct of interest. There are three common applications of criterion-related validity and two general contexts for these applications. In all these cases, we are attempting to establish the relationship between performance on the test and standing on some other criterion. The two general contexts for criterion-related validity are predictive validity and concurrent validity. In **predictive validity**, the test aims to predict status on some criterion that will be attained in the future. For example, we may use a kindergarten readiness test to predict success in reading in the first grade. Or, we may use a college entrance exam to predict freshman year GPA. In **concurrent validity**, we check on agreement between test performance and current status on some other variable. For example, we may determine the relationship between performance on a standardized achievement test and a teacher-made test, where both tests are administered at approximately the same time. Or, we may determine the relationship between scores on a test of attention deficit disorder (ADD) and teachers' ratings of classroom attentiveness. The difference between predictive and concurrent validity is strictly one of time for the criterion variable. From all other perspectives, the two concepts are the same.

The three common applications of criterion-related validity involve use of a) an external, realistic criterion defining the construct of interest, b) group contrasts, and c) another test. Fundamentally, these three approaches reduce to the same thing. However, they have some practical differences, so we will treat them separately.

External, Realistic Criterion

In some circumstances, we have an **external criterion** that provides a realistic definition of the construct of interest. The external criterion is what we would really like to have information about. The natural question is: If we really want information for the external criterion, why not get that information rather than rely on the test? There are two possible reasons. First, it may be that we cannot get information on the criterion until some time in the future and we would like to predict, now, what a person's future standing might be on the criterion. Second, it may be that getting information on the criterion is very time-consuming or expensive and we would like to have a simpler method of estimating what the person's standing might be. In either case, we will determine if the test provides useful information about the person's probable standing on the external criterion. Let us consider some examples of this type of criterion-related validity and then examine exactly how the degree of validity is expressed. Table 4.8 lists several instances of using a test to estimate

Table 4.8   Examples of External Criteria Used to Establish Criterion-related Test Validity

Test	Criterion
Readiness test	Success in Grade 1
College admissions test	Freshman year GPA
Creative thinking test	Panel rating of creativity displayed in artistic products
Algebra aptitude test	Grades in algebra course

standing on some external criterion. For example, we may use a college entrance test to predict GPA at the end of freshman year in college. Or, an algebra aptitude test might be used to predict grades in an algebra course. Here, we have some external criterion that defines what we really want to know. We can think of the test we are validating as a potential substitute for the external criterion.

In these situations, we usually express the validity of the test as a correlation coefficient (r_{XY}, the correlation between variables X and Y). Most often, we use the familiar Pearson correlation coefficient, although other types of coefficients may be used, depending on the nature of the scales for the criterion and the test. When the correlation coefficient is used in this way, it is called a **validity coefficient**. Ordinarily, a validity coefficient is simply a correlation coefficient used to express test validity. Hence, everything you have learned about correlation coefficients applies to validity coefficients. Recall also the use of a bivariate distribution (pp. 35–37) showing the relationship between two variables, in this case between the test and the criterion.

Part of the correlation methodology allows us to fit a line to the points in the bivariate distribution. We will not show all the mathematical procedures to fit the line. However, it is easy to see how the line works without knowing all the procedures. Figure 4.3 shows a bivariate distribution with the line of the relationship between X and Y. This line works just like a straight line from high school algebra. It has the form $Y = bX + a$, where b is

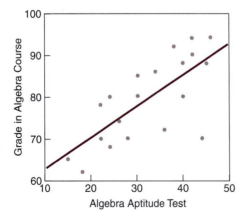

Grade = (.75)(Test X) + 55
$r = .724$

Figure 4.3 The prediction line in a bivariate distribution.

the slope of the line and a is the intercept on the Y-axis.[1] Using this simple formula, we can make predictions about status on the criterion (Y) from scores on the test (X). The box next to the bivariate distribution shows an example of this simple prediction formula.

Using the prediction equation is often puzzling for students. They wonder: If we already have X and Y scores to determine r_{XY}, why do we need to make a prediction about Y? The answer is that we determine r_{XY} in a research study. Then, in another situation, when we do *not* already have the Y scores, we use the information from the research study and our knowledge of the equation to predict Y.

Try This!

Use the equation in the box in Figure 4.3 to make a prediction. What is the predicted grade for a student with a test score of 40? See if you can also make the prediction from a score of 40 just by examining the line in the bivariate distribution.

Contrasted Groups

The second major method for demonstrating criterion-related validity is the **contrasted groups** method. Here the criterion is group membership. We wish to demonstrate that the test differentiates one group from another. Generally, the better the differentiation between groups, the more valid the test. We assume that group membership is a good definition of the criterion. Let us illustrate the method with a few examples.

In the first example, Group A contains 50 students diagnosed as dyslexic. Three school psychologists base the diagnosis on extensive reviews of the cases, so we are confident of the diagnosis. Group B contains 50 students with relatively low reading levels but with no indication of dyslexia. We administer a diagnostic reading test to both groups of students. We want to show that the test sharply distinguishes the dyslexic from the nondyslexic students. If it does, the test could be useful for identifying dyslexia in the future.

In the second example, Group A contains 35 individuals who have completed a course in computer programming with flying colors. Group B contains 35 individuals who did not perform well in the course. We had administered a programmer aptitude test to all 70 individuals at the beginning of the course. We want to establish that the aptitude test clearly distinguishes between those who were successful and those who were unsuccessful in the course. If it does, the test may be useful for selecting people for the computer programming course.

The contrasted group method of studying criterion-related validity may result in little differentiation or considerable differentiation between groups. Figure 4.4 shows examples of two different levels of separation between groups. In this example, the criterion group is the group we want to identify or select.

The perceptive reader will note that the contrasted groups approach can be converted into a form of the external, realistic criterion approach simply by assigning values of 0

---

[1] In algebra, the equation for a straight line is often expressed as $Y = mX + b$, where m is the slope and b is the intercept. In statistics, the equation is usually written as $Y = bX + a$, with b as the slope and a as the intercept. We follow the practice of statistics here.

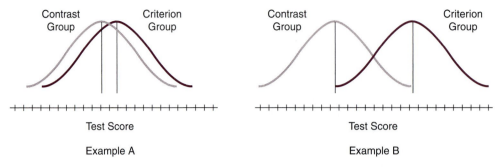

Figure 4.4 Examples of poor and good differentiation in use of the contrasted groups method.

and 1 to membership in the groups. The statistically inclined person can easily make the conversion. However, in practice, the two approaches are usually treated as distinct cases.

Correlations With Other Tests

A third method for establishing criterion-related validity is showing the correlation between the test to be validated and some other test that is known or presumed to be a valid measure of the relevant construct. For simplicity, let us call the test to be validated the "new" test. In this application, the other test becomes the criterion, analogous to the external criterion treated earlier. Upon first encountering this method, one is inclined to ask: If the other test is known or presumed to be valid, why not use it rather than the new test? There are several reasons we might want to establish the validity of the new test. The new test may be shorter or less expensive than the criterion test. For example, we may have a 15-minute test of intelligence that we want to validate against the *Wechsler Intelligence Scale for Children–IV*, which takes about one hour to administer. Or, the new test may have better norms or more efficient scoring procedures. For example, we may wish to show the correlation between a new edition of a test of ADD—enhanced by computer scoring, updated items, and new national norms—and the old edition of the test. Why? Because we may have 20 years of research studies on the old edition. It is a venerable, time-tested measure, richly embedded in the research literature on ADD. We hope our new edition will correlate highly with the old edition. For any of these or similar reasons, we may want to establish the validity of the new test rather than rely on the criterion test.

Using another test to establish criterion-related validity is simple. The correlation (usually Pearson) between the new test and the criterion test expresses the validity. Thus, the methodology is the same as that described earlier for use of an external, realistic criterion. This approach is very widely used in descriptions of test validity (Hogan & Agnello, 2004).

KEY POINTS SUMMARY 4.2   *Three Common Approaches to Criterion-related Validity*

External, realistic criterion
Group contrasts
Another test

Special Considerations for Interpreting Criterion-Related Validity

At first glance, criterion-related validity appears clean and simple. In many ways it is. However, lurking under this veneer of simplicity are several problems and issues that merit special attention. Some of these problems have technical, statistical solutions that go well beyond the scope of this book. However, we will at least alert the reader to the nature of the problems.

Conditions Affecting the Correlation Coefficient

Because the validity coefficient is simply a type of correlation coefficient, conditions affecting correlations are relevant. The most common difficulty in this category is the degree of variability in the group used to determine validity. Greater variability tends to increase the validity coefficient. Less variability tends to decrease it. For example, the validity of a college admissions test for predicting freshman GPA may be established in a multicampus study, including a wide range of abilities. We want to use the test at a single campus where there is a much narrower range of ability. Almost certainly the validity will be less for the single campus. On the other hand, we may conduct the study on a single campus with a narrow range of talent. Surely, the test will have greater predictive validity for schools with a much wider range of ability. The point is to be aware of this effect of group variability when interpreting criterion-related validity.

The Reliability-Validity Relationship

The reliability of both the test and the criterion affect validity. Lower reliability of either the test or the criterion will lower the validity coefficient. This effect is one of the reasons we worry about reliability. Good reliability is a prerequisite for good validity. You can have good reliability without having good validity. You cannot have good validity without good reliability. More advanced treatments of this topic include formulas that yield estimates of the effect of imperfect reliability on validity coefficients (see, e.g., Hogan, 2003; Nunnally & Bernstein, 1994). The important point here is that reliability is a prerequisite for validity. Be especially wary of arguments saying that reliability was not considered important in particular circumstances.

Validity of the Criterion

When discussing criterion-related validity, we tend to focus attention on the test. How well does the test predict or correlate with the criterion? Indeed, the test should be the focus of attention because we are trying to assess the test's validity. However, from another perspective, we need to examine the validity of the criterion, specifically the operational definition of the criterion. Is the operational definition of the criterion appropriate? Consider this example. We want to show that a mental ability test predicts "success in school." We use teacher-assigned grades on a report card as the operational definition of success in school. How good is this operational definition? Teacher-assigned grades provide only one possible definition of success in school. Scores on standardized achievement tests give another definition. Yet another definition is teacher rating of overall success, including class participation. Obviously, we could multiply examples of different ways to define any criterion that might be used for test validation. The important point here is that when considering criterion-related validity of a test, we also need to think about the validity of the operational definition of the criterion.

CONSTRUCT VALIDITY

Among the traditional categories of validity (see Table 4.1), construct validity is, at first, the most difficult to comprehend. The basic notion of construct validity can be described as follows. A test attempts to measure some construct (target). Sometimes this target has no obvious reference points, such as a clearly defined body of content or an external criterion. Nevertheless, a variety of kinds of evidence can be marshaled to support the proposition that the test measures the construct. **Construct validity** encompasses all these methods. In fact, starting from this line of reasoning, construct validity really subsumes content validity and criterion-related validity. The content matching involved in content validity and the test-criterion correlation are simply cases—relatively clear cases—of demonstrating the extent to which the test measures a construct. Any evidence that plausibly supports the proposition that the test measures its target construct is relevant. However, there are certain types of evidence that recur in discussions of construct validity, and we present a few of these types next.

Effect of Experimental Variables

The effect of experimental variables can help to demonstrate the validity of a test. Consider these two examples. We want to establish the validity of the *Scranton Test of Critical Thinking* (*STCT*). We administer the test to a group of 25 students, have them complete a 50-hour course in critical thinking, then we readminister the *STCT*. We would expect the scores to increase. Here is another example. We want to establish the validity of the *Norcross Creativity Test* (*NCT*). We administer the *NCT* to 50 students, give them 10 hours of instruction in techniques for creative thinking, and then readminister the *NCT*. We would expect an increase in NCT scores. (In both of these studies, we should have control groups to rule out the possibility that any increase in scores is simply the result of a practice effect.)

Studying the effects of experimental variables is similar to the contrasted groups method treated earlier under criterion-related validity. In fact, logically they are the same. Contrasted group studies ordinarily employ naturally occurring groups (e.g., dyslexic and nondyslexic students), whereas the groups considered under construct validity are formed specifically to study test validity.

Developmental Changes

Another potential source of information regarding construct validity is developmental changes. We expect children at successively higher ages to have increased mental ability. Showing that a mental ability test reflects these increases helps to establish the validity of the test. We would certainly puzzle over a mental ability test that showed the same scores on average for 8-, 9-, and 10-year-old children. Increases in test scores at successively higher grades help to argue for the validity of achievement tests. We expect performance in reading and mathematics to increase from Grade 3 to Grade 4 to Grade 5. Study of developmental changes, like the study of the effect of experimental variables, may be thought of as a variation on the contrasted groups approach. In this instance, we are contrasting groups at different ages or grades.

Factor Analysis

Factor analysis is a family of statistical techniques that helps to identify the common dimensions underlying performance on many different measures. The techniques are very widely used in the construction and validation of tests. They play a particularly prominent role for personality inventories and intelligence tests. In fact, the development of factor analytic methodology is intimately connected with the classic debates on the nature and measurement of intelligence. One can hardly understand the world of personality testing or intelligence testing without some familiarity with factor analysis.

Here are two examples of how factor analysis might be used. Suppose we have 14 tests that all appear to measure some aspect of mental processing. The tests include verbal material, quantitative reasoning, simple arithmetic, perceptual items, spatial reasoning, and so on. We obtain the correlations among these tests. (These are correlations like those we introduced in Chapter 2.) Some of the correlations may be very high. This suggests that, although the tests may have different titles and even items that look quite different, the tests appear to be measuring the same construct or trait or, in the language of factor analysis, factors. Factor analysis of the 14 tests may indicate that there are four underlying dimensions or traits. As another example, we might have 200 items in a personality questionnaire. We examine the correlations among the items. We may find that responses to all 200 items essentially boil down to three underlying traits: extroversion, diligence, and friendliness. The goal of factor analysis is to discover these underlying traits. Factor analytic techniques can become quite complex. Detailed exploration is certainly beyond the scope of this book. For an excellent semitechnical description of factor analysis, see Bryant and Yarnold (1995). For detailed, technical treatment, see Tabachnick and Fidell (2001).

Response Processes

Study of how examinees go about responding to a test—what we call their response processes—may provide evidence regarding the validity of the test. For example, when studying a test of quantitative reasoning, it may be useful to know that students typically go through several steps to arrive at an answer rather than applying a memorized formula. We could determine that students employed a multistep approach by using a "talk-aloud" administration of the test. For investigating a test purporting to measure creative thinking ability, a talk-aloud administration may help to support the argument that the test measures flexibility in thinking rather than simply extent of vocabulary. Occasionally using the talk-aloud technique with classroom assessments will help the teacher understand how students go about completing the assessment. It is not feasible to do this routinely, but it may be helpful to use with some assessments.

Evidence from response processes does not ordinarily provide strong, highly persuasive evidence regarding test validity. Further, such evidence is not widely used for establishing

KEY POINTS SUMMARY 4.3	*Some Important Ways to Study Construct Validity*
Effect of experimental variables	Factor analysis
Developmental changes	Response processes

validity. However, study of response processes does sometimes provide useful insights about what a test may or may not be measuring.

We have now reviewed several different procedures that help to establish the construct validity of a test. As noted earlier, the list of possible ways to establish construct validity is endless. Any evidence that persuades us that the test is measuring its target construct is relevant and useful.

CONSEQUENTIAL VALIDITY

Consequential validity references the test to the consequences of its uses and interpretations. The concept includes both intended and unintended consequences. What are the consequences, results, or implications of using a test? For example, what are the consequences of systematic use of a high school graduation test? What are the "spin-offs"? Notice that this question is different from the question of whether the test usefully predicts anything: That is a question about criterion-related validity. We might inquire whether the test improves (or detracts from) the quality of instruction in the schools where the test is used. We might also ask about the effect of requiring the test on the high school students who must take it. The last two questions are about consequential validity. Here is another example. Suppose we use a test to identify students for remedial instruction in mathematics. We might ask whether the test adequately covers the content of the mathematics curriculum. That is a question about the content validity of the test. We might also ask whether use of the test leads to educational benefits for the students identified for remedial instruction. That would be a question about consequential validity.

Both the term and the general concept of consequential validity are relatively recent entries in the assessment lexicon. To date, there is not good agreement about where consequences fit. Some authors feel it really is a new type of validity consideration. Other authors feel that consequences are a matter of politics and policymaking: important considerations, but not matters of validity. Further, even if we grant that consequences are a matter of validity, there is no agreement as to how to study the issue or who is responsible for studying it. For example, how would one study the multifarious consequences of using a college admission test or a diagnostic math test? Given the widespread disagreements in the field, we will not present an extended treatment of this topic—as much fun as it would be to do so. Rather, we will content ourselves with the brief description just given. That description at least raises consciousness about the matter of consequences. The interested reader can pursue various opinions on the topic in two special issues of *Educational Measurement: Issues and Practices* (Crocker, 1997; Smith, 1998).

TEST FAIRNESS, TEST BIAS

In the professional literature of educational assessment, the terms test **fairness** and test **bias** generally have the same meaning, although with opposite connotations. A fair test is one that lacks bias. A biased test is one that lacks fairness. We will use both terms—fairness and bias—in our discussion. Clearly, this is one of the hottest topics in all of assessment today. Therefore, we should devote some time to understanding the basic issue and methods for studying it.

Fairness means that a test (or other assessment technique) measures a trait, construct, or target with equivalent validity for different groups. A test is biased (unfair) if it does not measure the trait of interest in the same way across different groups. A simple difference in average performance between groups does not constitute bias. There is bias only if the difference in averages does not correspond to a *real* difference in the underlying trait the test is attempting to measure. Group averages may differ—in fact, they should differ—if the groups really do differ on the ability or trait we are trying to measure. To illustrate this important point, let us examine a few examples. Consider the contrast between students who do and do not study for the final exam in an educational assessment course. Students in Group A study the textbook 20 hours per week and attend all lectures. Students in Group B study the textbook 20 minutes on the night before the exam and have erratic attendance records. On the final exam, the Group A average score is appreciably higher than the Group B average score. That difference does not mean that the exam is biased against Group B. In fact, we would be shocked if the average scores for the two groups were not appreciably different. Why? Because we presume there is a real difference between the groups in the underlying trait of knowledge about the subject matter. Further, if performance on this final exam is intended to be predictive of performance on the Praxis exam, no doubt, it will predict higher scores for persons in Group A than in Group B. This, too, does not indicate that the final exam is biased. Why? Because we presume that people who have studied more will do better on the Praxis exam than people who studied less.

Here is a second example. We want to know if a reading test is fair or is biased against visually handicapped (VH) students. We compare performance of VH and non-VH students on the test. The VH students score lower. Does this mean the test is unfair to VH students? We do not know yet. It may be that VH students really have lower reading skill than do non-VH students. Suppose we present the test in a large-print version and find that the VH students' average score rises to the level of non-VH students. This suggests that the reading test, in its original small-print version, was unfair (biased) for VH students. The result also suggests that the test is fair when presented in a large-print version. Place this example in the context of Figure 4.1. Type size introduces construct irrelevant variance. That is, type size influences scores—but we do not want that to happen.

Finally, consider the case of a test of transportation systems in the United States. Students are expected to know about public transportation systems, as well as other systems. According to the curriculum, knowledge of transportation systems is the target. Rural children may have less knowledge of public transportation because it is generally not used in their environment. Therefore, rural children score lower on the items related to public transportation. Is the test unfair to rural children? No. Knowledge of public transportation systems is precisely part of what we wanted to measure. The solution to this problem is to

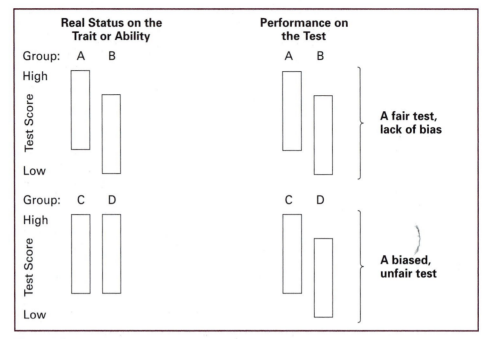

Figure 4.5 Illustration of group performance on a fair test and on a biased test.

teach the rural children about public transportation systems. We would not want to change the test. On the other hand, suppose the items about public transportation systems were intended as a measure of reading ability. If the rural children scored lower on the test, not because of a deficiency in reading skill but because of unfamiliarity with the topic, then we should change the test items to eliminate this unfairness (bias).

Figure 4.5 suggests how to think about these situations. The figure warrants careful study. We compare Groups A and B. In the top portion of the figure, Groups A and B differ in test performance—Group A is higher. However, the groups also differ in terms of real status on the trait. The test is fair; it is not biased. It is simply reflecting real differences between the groups. In the lower portion of the figure, Groups C and D differ in test performance. However, they do not differ in terms of real status on the trait. This indicates test bias. Obviously, to determine test bias, we need information about the groups' real status on the variable as well as information about their test performance.

Do we have methods for studying the fairness (bias) of tests? Yes. There are three broad categories for studying test fairness. They are widely used in the development and analysis of tests. Every student of educational assessment should at least recognize the basic approach for each of these methods.

The first method involves review of test items by panels of judges representing different groups. For example, a panel may include representatives by racial/ethnic group, gender, and types of disabilities. Panel members review each item in a large pool of items intended for use in a test. Panel members try to spot items, or the overall balance of items, that might tilt performance unfavorably for a group. The objective for such reviews is to

KEY POINTS SUMMARY 4.4   *Three Methods of Studying Test Fairness*

Panel review
Differential item functioning
Equivalence of criterion-related validity

have a final set of items with no apparent biases. Such reviews are conducted routinely in the development of many standardized tests. Test manuals contain descriptions of the review process.

One obvious problem with the panel review process is that it relies entirely on human judgment. The panel may tag an item as biased against a group when, in fact, group members have absolutely no problem with the item. Alternatively, the panel may fail to spot an item that is biased against, say, rural children. This difficulty gives rise to the second method for studying test fairness. This second method compares actual performance of different groups on individual test items. There are several techniques for accomplishing this comparison. They are all included under the name **differential item functioning** (DIF). The goal of a DIF analysis is to spot individual items that behave differently in different groups. If such an item surfaces in the test development process, the item is eliminated from the item pool.

DIF procedures compare performance on individual items within relatively narrow bands of total scores. The procedures do not compare groups on total scores. The third procedure for examining test fairness does look at total scores. Specifically, the procedures examine total scores in the context of criterion-related validity. The question becomes whether criterion-related validity of a test is the same for different groups. For example, does the ACT predict freshman year GPA equivalently for right-handed and left-handed students? Or for Hispanic and non-Hispanic students? Notice that the question is not whether the groups differ either in ACT scores or in GPA. The question is about the equivalence of predictive power and precision.

Discussions of test fairness (or test bias) contain a mixture of references to these three methods of studying the issue. Some of the treatments become quite technical. There are three main points for the student of educational assessment to remember. First, simple differences in group averages do not necessarily indicate bias or lack of fairness. The real question has to be about actual differences in the underlying trait. Second, there are methods for studying this matter of test bias. We do not have to rely on armchair analysis or unfounded claims. Third, at root, the question of fairness is one about test validity. It comes back to the questions raised at the beginning of this chapter. What are we trying to measure? Is anything affecting the measure other than what we really want to get at?

Studying Fairness for Classroom Assessments

How does the individual teacher study fairness for classroom assessments? The three methods of studying test fairness just described are used routinely in large-scale testing, for example, state assessments and commercially available tests. However, they are not usually feasible for classroom assessments. The DIF procedures and the study of criterion-related validity typically require large samples of cases. It is unlikely that a single teacher can assemble a panel of diverse individuals to review an end-of-unit test. Nevertheless, fairness is a crucial issue for classroom assessments. This is increasingly true as a diverse mixture of students, including those with various disabilities, appear in regular classrooms.

Perhaps the most important point is for the individual teacher to be sensitized to the issue of fairness and to examine each assessment for potential bias. In effect, each teacher needs to conduct a one-person panel review of assessments. Is there anything about an assessment that will unfairly disadvantage a student or group of students? Is there anything in the mechanics of assessment that calls for skills other than those intended to be measured? Does the math test depend excessively on reading ability? Does the reading assessment depend too much on visual acuity? Does the science assessment depend too much on motor ability in manipulating an apparatus? These are the types of questions a teacher needs to keep in mind when preparing and administering classroom assessments. A key perspective is to keep one's eye on the skills, ability, or knowledge that is the target of instruction.

VALIDITY VS. ACCURACY OF NORMS

There is one final point to round out our discussion of validity. Do not confuse validity with the accuracy of test norms. It is entirely possible to have a test with good validity but also have norms that are well off the mark. When this occurs, some people conclude, erroneously, that the test is not valid. Consider the following scenarios. Tests G and H are both reading tests. Both present paragraphs for students to read followed by a series of questions about the paragraphs. Students in Grade 4 in a perfectly normal school building take both tests. The average grade equivalent score on Test G is 4.6 and on Test H the average is 2.9. Further, the correlation between scores on Tests G and H is .90. Some people might say, "Test H is not valid." That would be an incorrect analysis of the situation. There is apparently something wrong with the norms on Test H, but there is no indication that it is not valid.

Consider this example. Tests K and L are both "IQ" tests used to predict success in high school calculus. Both tests correlate .65 with grades in calculus. Figure 4.6 shows the bivariate distributions. In both instances, the average grade is 90%. On Test K, the aver-

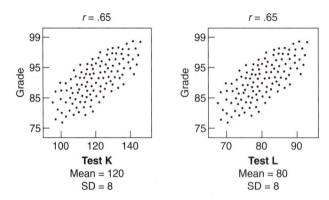

Figure 4.6   Tests with equal validity but different norms.

age IQ is 120, while on Test L the average is 80. The user concludes that Test L is "not valid" because it is difficult to imagine that students with an average IQ of 80 would have an average grade of 90% in calculus. Note, however, that the validity coefficient ($r = .65$) is the same for both tests. They are equally valid for predicting grades in calculus. The problem is with the accuracy of the norms, not with the test's validity. Of course, the converse may also be true. That is, a test may have excellent norms but little or no validity. The point of both examples is the same: Distinguish between the validity of a test and the accuracy of its norms.

PRACTICAL ADVICE

1. For building your own tests, think mainly about content validity. To build content validity into your tests, start with a clear definition of what you want to cover. The most typical approach uses a two-way table. Then, develop test items or assessment techniques to provide a reasonable match to the table of specifications.

2. When judging the content validity of an externally prepared achievement test, start with a clear definition of what is to be covered. Then, match the content of the test to this definition. Examine the actual test items, not just an outline of the test content.

3. When examining studies of criterion-related validity, take into account the variability of the group(s) in a study; and think about the validity of the criterion.

4. When considering test fairness (bias), be sure to distinguish between differences in groups' average scores on a test and group status on the underlying trait. You need information about both issues to make sense of test fairness.

5. When building your own assessments, try to eliminate the influence of any factors not related to what you want to measure.

SUMMARY

1. According to the standard definition, validity is the extent to which a test measures what it purports to measure. The *refined* definition extends this standard definition in two ways. First, it refers to interpretation of scores for a particular purpose. Second, it notes that validity is a matter of degree, not an all-or-none affair.

2. Useful terms for what we want to assess are construct, trait, and target. The notions of *construct underrepresentation* and *construct irrelevant variance* help us to think about the match between what we want to measure and the assessment technique aimed at it.

3. There are four major categories of validity evidence: content, criterion-related, construct, and consequential. Face validity, not one of the formal categories, refers to whether a test *looks like* it is an appropriate measure.

4. Content validity deals with the relationship between the content of a test and some well-defined domain of knowledge or behavior. Content validity is the most important type of validity for achievement tests. Establishing content validity often uses a two-way table of specifications or blueprint. Some version of Bloom's taxonomy often forms the columns in such a table. Alignment analysis describes the matching process for content validity in some state testing programs.

5. Instructional validity refers to the match between test content and what is actually taught; that is, what students have had the "opportunity to learn."

6. Content validity has three types of difficulty: potential difficulty in clearly defining the target, great variation in the items relevant to the content, and lack of reference to actual performance.

7. Criterion-related validity refers to establishing the relationship between performance on the test and on some other criterion that is taken as an important indicator of the construct of interest. Predictive validity and concurrent validity differ only in the time relationship between the test and criterion. There are three common approaches to determining criterion-related validity: having an external, realistic criterion, contrasting groups, and using another test.

8. We examined three issues in criterion-related validity studies: conditions affecting the correlation coefficient, especially the degree of group variability; the fact that reliability of both the test and the criterion limit validity; and the validity of the criterion.

9. Construct validity is a collection of techniques or methods that provide evidence about what a test seems to be measuring. We examined four specific methods: the effect of experimental variables, developmental changes, factor analysis, and the study of response processes.

10. Consequential validity attempts to determine the consequences of using a test or other assessment technique. There is not good agreement about whether this consideration is a type of validity or, if it is, how it can be determined.

11. Test fairness refers to whether a test measures with equal validity for different groups. Test bias is the opposite: measuring differently for different groups. A simple difference in group averages does not necessarily imply bias. The groups may really differ on the trait of interest. We described three methods for studying test fairness: panel review, differential item functioning, and comparison of criterion-related validity for different groups.

12. We noted the difference between validity and the accuracy of norms. Erroneous norms do not imply lack of validity.

KEY TERMS

alignment analysis	construct validity	instructional validity
bias	content validity	opportunity to learn
Bloom's taxonomy	contrasted groups	predictive validity
blueprint	criterion-related validity	table of specifications
concurrent validity	differential item functioning (DIF)	two-way table
consequential validity	external criterion	validity
construct	face validity	validity coefficient
construct irrelevant variance	factor analysis	
construct underrepresentation	fairness	

EXERCISES

1. Create a two-way table of specifications for a unit you teach or plan to teach. Use topics or objectives for the rows. Use Bloom-like categories for the columns. In each cell, enter the percentage of attention devoted to the cell.

2. Think of three tests you took in courses during the last academic term. How would you describe their content validity?

3. Refer to the items in Table 4.7. Rank the items in terms of how difficult you think they would be for students in Grades 3–5. Compare your rankings with someone else's. Do you think all seven items measure the same underlying mathematical ability?

4. Look at the bivariate distribution in Figure 4.3. Use the line of fit to answer these questions. What score on the criterion do you predict for a test score of 45? What score on the criterion do you predict for a test score of 20?

5. A principal purpose of college admissions tests is to predict "success in college." Such success is usually defined as freshman year GPA. List three other possible definitions of "success in college." Compare your list with someone else's list.

6. Consider the 50-item *Hogan Test of Quantitative Reasoning* (*HTQR*) for primary grade students. Recall the method of studying the effect of experimental variables to establish construct validity. Design a study to use this method. Have students experience a 10-hour instructional program to improve their scores on the HTQR. How many students would you use? What would you do in your instructional program? How much score change would you expect on the HTQR?

7. What are some of the consequences of using final exams in high school courses? Are these consequences, overall, good or bad? Should we consider these consequences an aspect of test validity?

Chapter 5

Norms and Criteria:
Interpreting Student Performance

OBJECTIVES

- Describe the basic problem of interpreting student performance.
- Distinguish between norm-referenced and criterion-referenced interpretation.
- Define each of the main methods of normative interpretation (percentiles, standard scores, and developmental norms) and describe the strengths and weaknesses of each.
- Identify the effect that the nature of the norm group has on interpretation of normed scores.
- Describe the strengths and weaknesses of criterion-referenced interpretation.
- Describe a typical procedure for setting performance standards on a test.
- Outline procedures for application of self-referencing on repeated measures.

What This Chapter Is About

This chapter examines methods for interpreting student performance on tests and other types of assessments. These methods of interpretation form part of the technical foundations of assessment. We define the most frequently used norm-referenced methods of interpretation, including the strengths and weaknesses of each. Norm-referenced methods utilize techniques from elementary statistics. We reviewed these techniques in Chapter 2. Then we define criterion-referenced interpretation, including methods for developing performance standards. Finally, self-referenced approaches are described.

Why This Topic Is Important

Intelligent interpretation of student performance is crucial for the use of educational assessment information. Building or choosing good tests, determining reliability and validity, and all the other topics covered in other chapters are important precisely because they should lead to intelligent interpretation and use of the information. This chapter will help sort through many technical terms, such as percentiles, national norms, criterion-referencing, and performance standards. Becoming familiar with all these technical matters should facilitate the interpretation of student performance.

THE BASIC ISSUE

At first glance, you might think that interpreting student performance should be a simple matter. You give a test, score it, and see how students do. However, making sense out of student performance can be a devilishly difficult business. In fact, making sense out of any type of performance for human beings, machines, or organizations ranks as one of life's enduring challenges. Consider the following cases.

- Meg got 16 right out of 20 questions on the math test. Is that good or bad? If Meg is in Grade 6 and the 20 questions were on a college-level calculus test—hooray for Meg. If Meg is a college junior and the 20 questions were simple number facts (e.g., 6 + 7, 3 × 5, etc.)—shame on Meg.

- Dan gets 20 miles per gallon of gas in his vehicle. Is that good or bad? If Dan's vehicle is an 18-wheel tractor trailer, that's terrific. If Dan's vehicle is a motor scooter, that's horrible.

- Jess answered "yes" to 10 items about interest in reading books. Is Jess a bibliophile or a bibliophobe? Obviously, it depends on how many questions there were (12, 50, 100, etc.) and what books were on the list.

- Fran is 5′8″ tall. Is Fran really tall or really short? That's really tall for a Grade 4 student, but really short for an NBA player.

All of these cases illustrate the point that our interpretation of performance or measurements often depends on the context in which we are making the interpretation. This point applies not only to interpretation of educational assessments (such as Meg's math test), but also to many other situations in ordinary life (such as miles per gallon and height). Thus, we need to consider methods that will help to make sense out of how students perform.

NORM-REFERENCED AND CRITERION-REFERENCED INTERPRETATION

Methods of interpreting student performance fall into two broad categories. The first category is **norm-referenced** interpretation. In this method, we make sense out of a student's performance by comparing that performance to the performance of other students on the same test or task. For example, we might note that Meg's score on the math test was the highest ever achieved by a student in her grade. Scores on most standardized tests, like the ACT or the SAT, are usually norm-referenced scores. Your score was compared with scores of other students who took the test, for example, placing you at the 90th percentile or the 25th percentile.

The second broad category of methods for interpreting student performance is **criterion-referenced** interpretation. This type of interpretation involves a judgment about the level of performance regardless of how other students perform. For example, we might conclude that Meg's performance on the number facts test (16 right out of 20) is just horrible—even if that is exactly average performance among college juniors. We might conclude that getting five or more wrong on a 25-item spelling test is unacceptable. It makes no difference how many people got five or more wrong on the spelling test—it's just unacceptable. Most of the classroom tests you take are interpreted in this way. We examine criterion-referenced interpretation in more detail after our treatment of norm-referenced systems of interpretation.

The final section of this chapter discusses what we call "self-referencing on repeated measures" as a method of interpretation. As we will see, this method shares elements of both norm-referencing and criterion-referencing.

Before leaving these introductory remarks about norm-referenced and criterion-referenced interpretation, we note two important distinctions. First, many sources apply the terms norm-referencing and criterion-referencing to tests themselves. Thus, you will read about a norm-referenced test (abbreviated NRT) versus a criterion-referenced test (CRT). This contrast is inappropriate and potentially misleading. It is *not* the test itself that is norm-referenced or criterion-referenced. It is the method of interpreting performance. You cannot look at a test and tell whether it is NRT or CRT. The simplest way to illustrate this point is by noting that we can use both norm-referenced and criterion-referenced interpretation for a given test. For example, we may judge that getting five wrong on a 25-item spelling test is unacceptable: a criterion-referenced interpretation. We may also note that 60% of Grade 8 students got five or more wrong on the test: a norm-referenced interpretation.

When people refer to an NRT, what they really mean is that the usual way to interpret performance on this test is by way of a set of norms. When people refer to a CRT, what they really mean is that criterion-referenced interpretation is the normal way of interpreting performance on this test (and, usually, that there are no norms for the test). Is this nitpicking? No. The distinction between the nature of the test itself and the method of interpreting performance on the test is important.

That brings us to the second point. It is entirely possible, and often desirable, to use both norm-referenced and criterion-referenced interpretation for understanding student performance on a test. Sometimes it is not possible to use both. However, when it is possible to do so, our understanding of student performance is generally enhanced. We will see examples of this point when considering performance standards later in this chapter.

THE RAW SCORE

The most immediate result from a test or other assessment is a **raw score**. Thus, before considering the interpretation of this bit of information, we should pause to think about the raw score itself. Raw scores arise in several different ways. The raw score may be the number of correct answers given to an achievement test. The raw score may be the number of questions answered in a certain direction—for example, "yes" or "agree"—on an interest inventory. The raw score may be the sum of numerically coded responses on a series of attitude items. For example, an attitude scale may have 10 items. Each item calls for a response on a 5-point scale, ranging from strongly disagree (1) to strongly agree (5). The raw score is the sum of the numerical responses to the 10 items. Figure 5.1 gives an example of this type of raw score for a 6-item measure of attitude toward mathematics. In this example, items with negative wording or connotation reverse the scale values for purposes of determining the raw score.

A raw score may also be a number assigned to a product, such as an essay or work of art. For example, a teacher may rate essays on a 6-point scale, where 6 is high and 1 is low. A rating of 4 in this system is a type of raw score. We do not know yet whether a score of 4 is very high, very low, mediocre, or acceptable. Simple counts of behavior may also serve as types of raw scores. For example, an observer counts how many times Frank looks up

	Response					
	Strongly Disagree				Strongly Agree	(Item Score)
Item	1	2	3	4	5	
1. Algebra is great fun.	[ ]	[X]	[ ]	[ ]	[ ]	(2)
2. Geometry is for the birds.	[ ]	[ ]	[ ]	[ ]	[X]	(1)
3. I like computing.	[X]	[ ]	[ ]	[ ]	[ ]	(1)
4. Math is very useful to me.	[ ]	[ ]	[X]	[ ]	[ ]	(3)
5. I love statistics.	[ ]	[X]	[ ]	[ ]	[ ]	(2)
6. Equations give me shivers.	[ ]	[ ]	[ ]	[X]	[ ]	(2)
					Raw Score = 11	

Figure 5.1 Deriving the raw score for an attitude toward math scale.

from his assigned seatwork in a 15-minute period. (Frank is being evaluated for ADD.) Suppose Frank looks up eight times. Is that rather normal? Or does it indicate an unusual amount of inattention? The count of 8 is a raw score, in need of an interpretive context.

Anthropometric and physiological measures may also be thought of as raw scores. Chris is 62 inches tall. Dan's pulse rate is 54 beats per minute. Matt runs a mile in 4 minutes, 32 seconds. All these measures are raw scores. We need some context for interpreting these measures. Is Chris very tall for her age? Is Dan's pulse abnormal? Is Matt running the mile at an Olympic-competition level or is he really slow?

The Correction for Guessing

Scoring procedures for some tests call for a "corrected" or an "adjusted" raw score. The most popular of these adjustments is the **correction for guessing**. This adjustment is applied to some ability and achievement tests that use a multiple-choice format. The theory is that on a multiple-choice test one can get some answers right by wild, blind guessing. More precisely, one should be able to get 1/K of the items correct by guessing, where K is the number of options in the multiple-choice item. In a true-false item, K is 2. In a 100-item test composed of multiple-choice items with four options per item, the expected score from guessing at all items is 25 correct. The correction for guessing formula corrects for this presumed guessing. Appendix C provides the exact formula and examples of its application.

The correction for guessing assumes that a person is guessing randomly among the available options. Of course, sometimes a person can eliminate some of the incorrect options, then guess among the remaining options. Applying a correction for guessing, once rather widely used, has waned in popularity in recent years.

The Special Case of Theta (θ)

Recall the discussion of item response theory (IRT) from Chapter 1 (pp. 14–15). Whereas a test scored in the conventional way yields a raw score that is the sum of responses to all items in the test, a test scored according to IRT is not the simple sum of responses. The

Item Difficulty:	Easy									Moderate							Hard			
Item:	1	2	3	4	5	6	7	8	9	10	11	12	13	14	15	16	17	18	19	20
Kelly	+	+	+	+	×	+	×	+	×	+										
Ned											+	+	+	+	×	+	×	+	+	×

+ = correct response   x = incorrect response

Figure 5.2 Deriving a theta score from different sets of items.

IRT score is a function of the *examinee's responses interacting with the characteristics of the items*. The IRT score is usually called **theta** (θ). Let us consider an example of how theta may arise. It is *crucial* that the items be selected for unidimensionality and scaled for difficulty in a previous research program. Actual scoring of tests according to IRT procedures is complex, requiring sophisticated computer programs. Hence, you will not use these procedures with classroom tests. However, the procedures are widely used with standardized tests, including state assessments. At this point, we can give a rough idea of how IRT methodology yields a theta score.

First, consider the data in Figure 5.2. Items are arranged in order of difficulty from left to right. The lower numbered items are very easy, the higher numbered items are very difficult. For example, if this were a test of arithmetic computation for elementary school students, Item 1 might be 6 + 3 = ___, Item 10 might be 740 − 698 = ___, and Item 20 might be .56 × 1.05. Here we have simply labeled the items as easy, moderate, or hard. In an actual application, exact difficulty values would be used. (The test items need not be arranged in order of difficulty physically, but it is useful to show such an arrangement for our example.) Each "+" in the figure represents a correct response. Kelly is presented with Items 1–10 and gets seven items right. Ned is presented with Items 11–20 and also gets seven items right. Because Ned answered more difficult items, he receives a higher *theta* score, despite the fact that both students got seven items right. Obviously, this procedure will not work unless the items are scaled on difficulty value first.

Try This!

There is an excellent web-based demonstration of the interaction of examinee responses with characteristics of items employing IRT methodology. Go to: http://edres.org/scripts/cat/catdemo.htm. Log on and try your hand at the test. Watch how the "ability estimate" is adjusted after each response. Although scores will be reported as percentiles or some other normed score, these scores are transformations from theta, which is being updated after each response.

There are many specific procedures for scoring tests according to IRT methods. The procedures depend on the particular model used to fit the data. Consideration of these procedures goes well beyond what is appropriate for this book. However, you do not need to know the various procedures in order to have a basic understanding of what theta means.

Theta has some properties of a raw score and some properties of a normed score. It is similar to a raw score because it is a relatively immediate result of student responses. Also like a raw score, it has little meaning by itself. Theta is like a normed score in that it is not a simple summation of responses. It depends not only on whether the answer is correct (or "yes" or other such response), but also on the IRT values of the items to which responses are given. Theta locates the student on a trait or an ability presumed to underlie the total

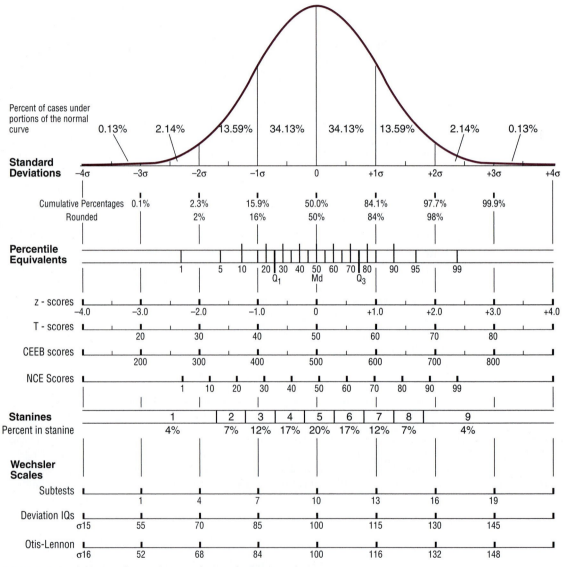

Figure 5.3 Equivalence of several types of norms in the normal curve.

Reprinted from Seashore, H. G. *Test Service Notebook 148: Methods of Expressing Test Scores*. With permission of the publisher, Harcourt Assessment, Inc.

set of items in the test bank. However, the numerical values for the dimension are arbitrary, hence not easily interpreted. Although theta numerical values are arbitrary, they are usually established with 0.00 as a central value and a range of about -4.0 to $+4.0$. Hence, they may look like z-scores (see p. 34). However, they do not refer to a position within a well-defined norm group.

Theta values may be the immediate result of student responses in an IRT environment. However, their practical interpretation ordinarily depends on use of the normed scores presented in this chapter. That is, they are converted to percentiles, standard scores, grade equivalents, and so on. In fact, in a test score report, you may be looking at a percentile or standard score and not even realize that it is a transformation from a theta score rather than from a conventional raw score.

TYPES OF NORMS

This section discusses the types of norms or **normed scores** commonly used with educational tests. There are three major categories of norms: percentile ranks, standard scores, and developmental norms. In this section, we describe each type of norm, then outline the strengths and weaknesses of each. For many tests, several types of norms are available, not just one type. Most of these types of norms are systematically related to one another. Thus, one can convert from one type of norm to another, although this cannot be done for all types of norms. These relationships are important. They are generally conceptualized in the context of the normal curve that was reviewed in Chapter 2. Figure 5.3 displays many of the relationships. *This figure warrants careful study*. Frequent reference will be made to it in subsequent sections of this chapter.

Using the relationships depicted in Figure 5.3 allows us to construct tables converting between various types of scores. Table 5.1 shows such conversions for a few points in the normal distribution. It is convenient to remember at least some of these conversions to aid in interpreting test scores. In this table, the T-score has M = 50 and SD = 10, the SAT scale[1] has M = 500 and SD = 100, the deviation IQ (DIQ) has M = 100 and SD = 15, and the normal curve equivalent (NCE) is designed to match the percentile scale at 1, 50, and 99. Each of these scales is described in more detail later in this chapter.

KEY POINTS SUMMARY 5.1	*The Major Categories of Test Norms*

Percentile ranks
Standard scores
Developmental norms

---

[1] Figure 5.3 shows the SAT scale as the CEEB scale. CEEB stands for College Entrance Examination Board, now known as the College Board, the sponsor of the SAT. The Graduate Record Examination (GRE) also uses this scale.

Table 5.1 Conversions Between Scores Based on Relations in the Normal Curve[a]

z-score	Percentile	T-score	SAT	DIQ	NCE
+3.0	99	80	800	145	99
+2.0	98	70	700	130	93
+1.0	84	60	600	115	71
0.0	50	50	500	100	50
−1.0	16	40	400	85	29
−2.0	2	30	300	70	7
−3.0	1	20	200	55	1

[a] For a more complete version of this table, showing conversions for all percentile points, see Hogan (2003, 2005).

PERCENTILES RANKS AND PERCENTILES

One of the most common types of norms for educational tests is the percentile rank or percentile. There is a technical distinction between these two terms. In practice, the terms percentile and percentile rank are often used interchangeably with no harm. The **percentile rank** (PR) tells the percentage of cases in a norm group falling below a given raw score. Thus, if a raw score of 48 has a PR of 60, this means that 60% of the cases in the norm group scored at or below a raw score of 48. Of course, some cases in the norm group score exactly 48. This score is thought of as an interval from 47.5 to 48.5, with 48.0 being the midpoint of the interval. Hence, in some applications the PR is calculated to include one half of the cases on the raw score interval. A **percentile** (often abbreviated %ile) is a point on a scale below which a specified percent of the cases falls.

We sometimes encounter offshoots of the percentile system. These offshoots include deciles, quintiles, and quartiles. As implied by their Latin roots, these systems divide the distribution into tenths, fifths, and fourths, respectively. Correspondingly, we can think of percentiles as a system that divides the distribution into hundredths. Figure 5.3 illustrates the place of percentile ranks in the normal curve. PRs range from a low of 1 to a high of 99, with 50 being the midpoint, or median.

Try This!

Use Figure 5.3 to provide estimates of the z-scores for these percentile ranks. Then use Table 5.1 to check the estimates.

PR	Estimated z	z from table
50	_____	_____
84	_____	_____
16	_____	_____
99	_____	_____

Raw Score ...	62	64	66	68	70	72	74	76	78	80	82	84	86	88	90	92	94	96	98
Percentile ...	1	1	1	2	3	6	10	18	34	53	71	83	90	92	96	98	98	99	99

Figure 5.4 Raw score to percentile conversion for the history test scores.

Strengths and Weaknesses of Percentile Ranks

Percentile ranks have several attractive features. First, the concept of a percentile rank is simple. It is easy to grasp. It can be quickly explained even to a person with no statistical training. Percentile ranks are also easy to calculate for a norm group. For these reasons, percentile ranks are very widely used.

Percentile ranks have two main drawbacks. First, the layperson frequently confuses the percentile rank with the **percentage-right score** used with many classroom tests. According to the time-honored tradition, in the percentage-right scoring system, 90% is an A, 60% is failing, and so on. Thus, a percentile rank of 72, which is above average performance, may be mistaken for barely passing performance. A percentile rank of 51, which is about average, sounds like horrible performance in the percentage-right system. You must distinguish carefully between percentile ranks and percentage-right scores, especially when interpreting scores to laypersons.

The second major drawback of the percentile rank is the marked inequality of units at various points on the scale. Specifically, percentile ranks are typically "bunched up" in the middle of the distribution and "spread out" at the two extremes of the distribution. At first, this peculiarity sounds like a trivial technicality. However, it has very substantial practical implications. A given raw score difference, say 4 points, will cover many percentile points in the middle of the distribution but only a few percentile points in either tail of the distribution. The phenomenon can be noted in the percentile rank norms for most tests. This difficulty is not a property of percentile ranks but a result of the fact that they are applied to a variable that is bunched up in some parts of the distribution. For example, a normal distribution is bunched up in the middle. The difficulty would not arise in the unusual circumstance where the variable has a rectangular distribution.

Figure 5.4 shows percentile norms for the distribution of test scores in Figure 2.1 in Chapter 2. For compactness, we show the percentiles corresponding to raw scores in two-point intervals. On these norms, going from a raw score of 66 to 70 (4 raw score points) results in negligible movement on the percentile scale, just two points, from a percentile of 1 to 3. However, going from a raw score of 76 to 80 (again, 4 raw score points) corresponds to a percentile difference of 35 points (18–53)! Thus, you need to be very cautious about interpreting differences between percentiles scores in the middle of the distribution.

STANDARD SCORES

Standard scores are another type of norm frequently used with educational tests. Standard scores constitute a family of norms. There are several widely used versions of standard scores and a potentially infinite variety of other versions. We first describe what is common to all standard scores, then identify the properties of specific versions.

A **standard score** system is a conversion of z-scores (see Chapter 2) into a new system with an arbitrarily chosen mean (M) and standard deviation (SD). The new M and SD are usually selected to be nice, memorable numbers like 50 and 10 or 500 and 100. In a few instances, as we shall see, other desirable characteristics are sought.

To convert a raw score into a standard score, first translate the raw score into a z-score. Then multiply the z-score by the new (standard score) SD and add the new (standard score) mean. The steps are outlined in Figure 5.5. The following formula accomplishes these steps:

$$SS = \frac{SD_s}{SD_r}(X - M_r) + M_s$$

where

SS = the desired standard score

SD_s = standard deviation in standard score system

SD_r = standard score in raw score system

M_r = mean in raw score system

M_s = mean in standard score system

X = raw score

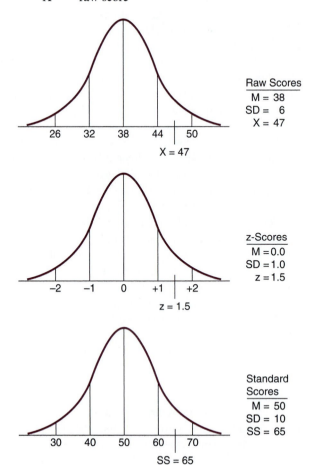

Raw Scores
| M = 38 |
| SD = 6 |
| X = 47 |

X = 47

z-Scores
| M = 0.0 |
| SD = 1.0 |
| z = 1.5 |

z = 1.5

Standard
Scores
| M = 50 |
| SD = 10 |
| SS = 65 |

SS = 65

Figure 5.5 Illustration of converting raw score system to standard score system.

Raw Score: ...	80	81	82	83	84	85	86	87	88	89	90	...
Standard Score: ...	49	51	53	55	57	58	60	62	64	66	68	...

Figure 5.6 Example of raw score to standard score (T-score) conversion.

In ordinary practice, all these steps have already been completed. You simply use a table in the test manual to convert a raw score to a standard score. Figure 5.6 provides an example of such a table. The figure includes only a section of the table, not the full range of scores.

Most standard scores are linear transformations of raw scores. They follow the formula on page 102 and the example in Figure 5.5. However, some standard scores are derived by a nonlinear transformation. In such instances the formula on page 102 does not apply. Nonlinear transformations may be used to yield a distribution of scores that is normal. Hence the result is sometimes referred to as a normalized standard score. For examples in this book, we will assume that standard scores are linear transformations from raw scores.

T-scores

T-scores, sometimes called McCall's T-scores, are standard scores with M = 50 and SD = 10. Thus, the effective range of T-scores is from about 20 (corresponding to −3 z) to about 80 (+ 3 z). T-scores (capital T) should be distinguished from student's t-values (lower case t) used in tests of statistical significance. Many interest inventories and personality tests use T-scores.

SATs and GREs

The SAT I: Reasoning Test (SAT) and the Graduate Record Examination (GRE) utilize a standard score system with M = 500 and SD = 100. These standard score systems apply to the main tests in these series: Verbal and Mathematics for the SAT and Verbal, Quantitative, and Analytic, and the various Subject Tests for GRE.[2] The tests are often combined to yield a total score. For example, a combined Verbal and Mathematics score is often used for the SAT. When this is done, the means are additive but the SDs are not; that is, the mean for the combined or total score is 500 + 500, but the SD for the total score is *not*

KEY POINTS SUMMARY 5.2 *Some Types of Standard Scores*

T-scores	Stanines
SATs and GREs	Normal curve equivalents
Deviation IQs	Multilevel standard (or scaled) scores

[2] Beginning in 2005, the SAT I converts to three tests: Critical Reading, Mathematics, and Writing. In 2003, the GRE converted the Analytical Test to the Analytical Writing Test, scored on a scale of 0–6.

100 + 100. The SD for the total score is less than 200, since the two tests being combined are not perfectly correlated. This phenomenon is not peculiar to the SAT and GRE. It will be true for any combination of tests that are not perfectly correlated.

Deviation IQs

The traditional definition of the IQ (*intelligence quotient*) is IQ = (MA/CA) × 100, where MA is **mental age** (see page 108 for a description of mental age), CA is **chronological age**, and 100 is a multiplier to eliminate the decimal point. For example, Abigail's MA is 10 years, her CA is 8 years, so her IQ is (10/8) × 100 = 125. This is called a **ratio IQ**, since it represents the ratio of MA to CA.

Try This!

Calculate ratio IQs for these cases.

Matt's MA is 78 months (6 years, 6 months). His CA is 84 months (7 years, 0 months). What is his ratio IQ?

Meg's MA is 192 months. Her CA is 124 months. What is her ratio IQ?

Ratio IQs were used with the earliest intelligence tests. The IQs obtained from modern intelligence tests are *not* ratio IQs. They are standard scores with M = 100 and SD usually set at 15 or 16. These standard scores are often referred to as **deviation IQs**. The M = 100 is used in deference to the traditional (ratio) definition of IQ. Ratio IQs on the original Stanford-Binet test yielded a standard deviation of 16 at certain ages. This SD was adopted as *the* SD for the standard scores used with some intelligence tests. Other tests, most notably the Wechsler tests (WAIS, WISC, WPPSI), adopted SD = 15.[3]

Some segments of the educational community strive mightily to shun the term "IQ," while retaining the tradition of using a standard score system with M = 100 and SD = 15 or 16. Hence, what we refer to here as the deviation IQ sometimes surfaces in test manuals and score reports under a variety of other names, for example, school ability index (SAI). Such alternative names are usually easily recognized as standard score systems with the familiar M and SD.

Stanines

Stanines, a contraction of "standard nine," are a standard score system with M = 5 and SD = (approximately) 2. Stanines were constructed to (a) divide the normal distribution into nine units and (b) have the units cover equal distances on the base of the normal curve, except for the units covering the tails of the distribution; that is, Units 1 and 9. When these two conditions are met, the mean will obviously be 5 and the standard devia-

---

[3] The fifth edition of the Stanford-Binet adopted SD = 15.

Table 5.2   Some Widely Used Standard Score Systems

Test	Mean	SD
Wechsler intelligence scales	100	15
Law School Admissions Test (LSAT)	150	10
SAT I: Reasoning Test (SAT)	500	100
Graduate Record Exam (GRE)	500	100
T-scores	50	10

tion will be slightly in excess of 2. Figure 5.3 illustrates these two properties of stanines. See also Figure 5.7. Notice that Units 2–8 cover equal distances on the base of the normal curve. Because the density of the curve varies in different sections, these equal distances cover varying percentages of the cases in the distribution. For example, stanine 2 covers 7% of the cases (from the 4th to the 11th percentile), while stanine 4 covers 17% of the cases (from the 23rd to the 40th percentile).

Try This!

Using Figure 5.3 or Figure 5.7, determine the stanine corresponding to each of these percentiles:

Percentile: 2   36   52   90

Stanine: _____   _____   _____   _____

Stanines are derived by reference to the percentile divisions shown in Figure 5.7. Hence the stanines result in a nonlinear transformation of raw scores (unless the original distribution was already perfectly normal). Stanines are used extensively for reporting scores on standardized achievement tests and some mental ability tests in elementary and secondary schools. They are not used much in other contexts.

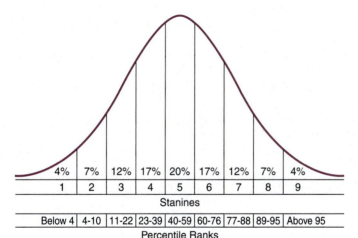

Figure 5.7 The distribution of stanines.

Normal Curve Equivalents

The **normal curve equivalent** (NCE) is a standard score system developed so that the NCEs are equal to percentile ranks at points 1, 50, and 99. Imposing this condition, the NCE system has M = 50 and SD = (approximately) 21. NCEs are used almost exclusively to meet certain federal reporting requirements for achievement testing. Figure 5.3 shows the relationship between NCEs and other norms.

Multilevel Standard Scores

A multilevel test is one that has at least partially distinct tests at different age or grade levels. The primary examples of such tests are achievement batteries and group-administered cognitive ability tests used in elementary and secondary schools. Although one of these tests may have the same name (e.g., *Metropolitan Achievement Tests* or *Otis-Lennon School Ability Test*) across a wide age or grade span, obviously the same items are not used across the entire span. The test is divided into a number of separate levels. One level may be used in Grades 1–2, another level in Grades 3–4, and so on. See Chapters 11 and 12 for examples of such tests.

The raw scores obtained from different levels on such tests are often linked by a system of standard scores that span all levels. These standard scores are sometimes called **scaled scores**. Multilevel standard scores are difficult to interpret. They have a convenient mean and standard deviation (e.g., 500 and 100) at one level, usually for a grade or an age in the middle of the range covered by the entire series, but the mean and standard deviation will differ at other age or grade levels. Thus, a seventh grade student's standard score of 673 on the reading test has no readily interpretable meaning.

Multilevel standard scores can be useful for measuring growth across grade or age levels. The score system is usually developed to approximate an interval scale. However, for ordinary test interpretation, these multilevel standard scores are not very useful.

Strengths and Weaknesses of Standard Scores

Standard scores provide a convenient metric for interpreting test performance in a wide variety of circumstances. Because many traits are presumably normally distributed, the relationship of standard scores to z-scores is helpful. Standard scores avoid the percentile problem of marked inequality of units in various regions of the normal distribution. For this reason, standard scores are more amenable to statistical calculations.

Standard scores do have some drawbacks. First, it must be admitted that only an exceedingly small fraction of the human race has any idea what the normal curve or a z-score is. Hence, relating standard scores to the context of the normal curve and z-scores has little value except for people trained in these matters. Second, in order to make sense of a standard score, one needs to be reminded of the M and SD for the system. Earlier paragraphs cited some of the well-known standard score systems where this problem is minimized, for example, M = 100 and SD = 15 for the deviation IQs on mental ability tests. However, there are many other standard score systems—potentially an infinite variety, since one can choose any values for M and SD. For example, the Law School Admissions Test (LSAT) and the ACT college entrance test each have their distinctive standard score systems. What does a score of 130 on the LSAT mean? What does a score of 26 on the ACT mean? One doesn't have a clue without going to a test manual to look up the M and SD for these standard score systems.

Special note should be made of stanines. They have the merit of simplicity for reporting individual scores. It is easy to explain, for example to parents, that a child's performance is reported on a scale from 1 to 9. Generally, no further explanation is needed about means, standard deviations, and equal distances on the base of the normal curve. This simplicity is an advantage. However, stanines are rather gross for reporting group averages; when averaged, they are usually reported to one decimal place (e.g., 6.4), thereby losing the simplicity of a simple 9-point scale.

NCEs present an unusual situation. They look like percentiles, thereby being easily confused with percentiles. In fact, as noted earlier, NCEs match percentiles at three points in the distribution; but they are notably different at other points in the distribution. Hence, it is important to distinguish between percentiles and NCEs.

DEVELOPMENTAL NORMS

When the trait being measured develops systematically with time, it is feasible to create what we call a **developmental norm**. There are two commonly used developmental norms: **grade equivalents** (GEs) and **age equivalents** (AEs). GEs are used with many achievement tests. AEs are used with some mental ability tests. In this context, the score is called a **mental age** (MA). Developmental norms are meaningful only in the range where the trait being measured is developing or growing with time in the relevant population. In a developmental norm, a raw score is interpreted in terms of the age or grade for which the raw score is typical.

Grade Equivalents

Grade equivalents are developed by administering a test to students in different grade levels. This is done in the norming program. The typical or median performance in each grade is then obtained. The medians are plotted and a curve fitted to the points as in Figure 5.8. Follow the arrows in Figure 5.8 to see how a raw score corresponds to a GE. For example, a raw score (number right) of 40 converts to a GE of 1.6.

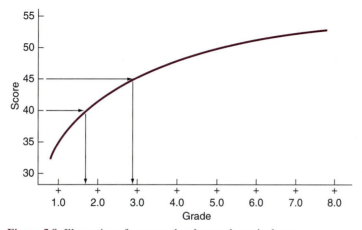

Figure 5.8 Illustration of curve to develop grade equivalents.

Table 5.3 Part of a Raw Score to Grade Equivalent (GE) Conversion Table

Raw Score	...	40	41	42	43	44	45	46	...
GE	...	1.6	1.8	2.0	2.3	2.7	2.9	3.1	...

The GE for a raw score is read from the curve, and a table of raw score-GE conversions is prepared. An example of such a table is shown in Table 5.3.

Try This!

Using Figure 5.8, estimate the GE (grade equivalent) corresponding to these raw scores:

Raw Score	35	50
GE	_____	_____

The convention for GEs is to divide the school year into tenths as shown in Figure 5.9. For example, a GE of 6.3 means the third month of Grade 6. GEs above 12.9 (the last month of Grade 12) are often reported as 12.9+ or with some verbal label, such as post-high school (PHS). The GE scale is not extended to college years.

Mental Age

Mental ages are the primary example of age equivalents. MAs were one of the first types of norms used with tests. They originated with the Binet scales. MAs are determined by finding the typical or median score for examinees at successive age levels. Age groups may be formed by year, half-year, three-month intervals, or any other such grouping of individuals by age. The median score on the test is then determined for each group. The results are plotted and a smooth curve fitted to the points. Similar to the procedure for GEs, in practice, raw scores are converted to mental ages by way of a table prepared from the developmental curve.

Other Developmental Norms

Although mental ages and grade equivalents are the primary examples of developmental norms, brief mention should be made of two other examples. First, there are tests based on *stage theories* of human development. A well-known example of such theories

Sept	Oct	Nov	Dec	Jan	Feb	Mar	Apr	May	June
.0	.1	.2	.3	.4	.5	.6	.7	.8	.9

Figure 5.9 Division of the school year in the grade equivalent system.

is Piaget's theory of cognitive development. Tests based on such theories yield results that place an individual at a certain stage, for example, at Piaget's stage of concrete operations. A second example is anthropometric measurements, such as height and weight. Such measurements are often interpreted in terms of developmental norms. These are essentially age equivalents. For example, a child is reported to be "as tall as the typical 6-year-old." Just as with mental ages, such statements are usually interpreted in relation to the child's chronological age, for example, "Mike is very tall for his age."

Strengths and Weaknesses of Developmental Norms

All developmental norms have some common strengths and weaknesses. On the positive side, developmental norms have a naturalness to their meaning that is quite attractive. To say that a 16-year-old functions mentally like a 3-year-old or that a student in Grade 2 is reading at the Grade 8 level—such statements seem to convey considerable meaning, free from the sterile, statistical jargon of percentile ranks and standard scores. Ideas about normal developmental patterns are deeply imbedded in our thinking about humans. The basic notion of developmental norms is used in many situations. It is noted that Grade 6 students in Japan are doing algebra "usually reserved for Grade 9 students in the United States." Mick is praised for "performing in his first game as a freshman like he was a veteran senior." Age equivalents and grade equivalents simply formalize these natural ways of thinking. They help to accomplish the goal of making raw scores meaningful.

A second advantage of developmental norms is that they provide a basis for measuring growth across multilevel tests. For example, during the elementary school years, a child may take the Primary I level of an achievement test in Grade 1, the Elementary level in Grade 4, and the Intermediate level in Grade 7. Grade equivalents link all these levels of the test.

There are two principal drawbacks to developmental norms. First, they are applicable only to variables that show clear developmental patterns. Hence, they are not ordinarily applicable to such areas as personality traits, attitudes, and vocational interests. It does not mean anything, for example, to say that someone has the extrovertedness of a third-grader. Further, even those variables that do show developmental patterns at some levels do not ordinarily continue their growth patterns indefinitely. Reading ability develops rapidly in the elementary school years but it does not continue to develop indefinitely. There is a useful distinction for purposes of test interpretation between the reading ability of a 5-year-old and a 15-year-old, but not between a 25-year-old and a 35-year-old. This is not an all-or-none affair. Developmental norms do not cease to be useful at a clearly defined point. Rather, they gradually lose their usefulness as the developmental curve (e.g., see Figure 5.8) becomes less steep. When the curve becomes flat, developmental norms become useless.

A second disadvantage of developmental norms is their uncontrolled standard deviations. The SDs are usually not the same at different levels or on different tests. On many tests, the SDs tend to increase systematically with age or grade level. The SDs vary unsystematically between different tests within the same battery even when the norms are based on the same norm group. This may sound like a trivial, technical point. However, it has substantial practical implications. For example, the student in Grade 1.5 who is reading at

GE = 3.5 is practically out of the distribution of Grade 1 students, whereas the student at Grade 7.5 who has a reading GE of 9.5 is not all that unusual. Further, consider the student in Grade 3.5 who has a GE of 4.5 in mathematics computation and a GE of 4.5 in reading. Relative to other students, this student is probably much more advanced in computation than in reading because the SD of GEs is typically smaller for computation than for reading. These differences in SDs for various tests are unsystematic. They may differ from one test series to another.

A third criticism is usually reserved for grade equivalents. It is noted that a student in, say, Grade 3 may get a GE of 6.5 not by knowing the same material as the typical Grade 6 student but by answering perfectly all of the Grade 2, Grade 3, and Grade 4 items, whereas the typical Grade 6 student gets some but not all items right from across a grade span of 2 to 7. This argument, usually mentioned only in connection with grade equivalents, can be applied to any type of normed score. Two students scoring at the 75th percentile or at a standard score of 60 did not necessarily answer the same items correctly. Tests constructed according to item response theory attempt to minimize this problem, but that is a function of the test construction method, not the type of norm used.

EXAMPLES OF NORM TABLES

Now that we have considered each of the major types of norms, it will be useful to observe how test manuals present norms. What does a norm table look like? Actually, norm tables come in an enormous variety. However, there are some standard patterns. After one sees a few examples, it is easy to decipher variations in the patterns. We present here two typical examples of norm tables: one from a test that uses a variety of norms, another from a much simpler case.

Table 5.4 illustrates a norm table for a test that yields a full panoply of norms. You enter the table on the left for a raw score and then read across the table to get a scaled score, grade equivalent, percentile rank, stanine, and NCE. See Figure 5.14 later in this chapter for an example of a score report incorporating many normed scores. Table 5.5 illustrates the much simpler case where a test yields only percentile rank and stanine norms. Again, you enter on the left with a raw score and read across to get the normed scores. In practice, the conversions are often made by a computer, which has the tables built into its programs.

Table 5.4 Portion of a Norm Table for a Test With Several Types of Norms

Raw Score (RS)	Scaled Score (SS)	Grade Equivalent (GE)	Percentile Rank (PR)	Stanine (S)	Normal Curve Equivalent (NCE)
54	705	8.3	82	7	69
53	702	8.1	78	7	66
52	698	7.8	71	6	62

Table 5.5 Portion of Norm Table for a Test With Only Two Types of Norms

Raw Score	Percentile	Stanine
69	91	8
68	89	7
. . .	. . .	. . .
64	79	7
63	77	6

NARRATIVE REPORTS AND NORMS

Recall that the basic purpose of norms is to provide an interpretive context for a raw score. Generally, normative information is quantitative: another set of numbers. Increasingly, however, test scores are being reported in the form of a computer-generated narrative. The user may see no numbers at all, although most reports provide both numbers—the usual kinds of norms—as well as a **narrative report**. How do these narrative reports originate?

The substance for narrative reports always begins with a test score, at least a raw score or theta and most frequently with a normed score. From this beginning, narrative reports range considerably in complexity. At the simplest level, the narrative report may just translate a normed score into a verbal description. For example, a computer may have a table showing the following correspondence between stanines and verbal labels:

Stanines	Verbal Label
7–9	Above Average
4–6	Average
1–3	Below Average

With this table, a profile of an individual's scores on three tests may look like this:

Test	Stanine	Performance Level
Reading	6	Average
Math	3	Below Average
Social Studies	5	Average

The "Stanine" column may not even appear on the report, although the scores are at the root of the report. With a bit more sophistication in programming, the report may read like this: "Jim's performance in both Reading and Social Studies was in the average range, whereas his performance in Math was below average." Narrative reports often incorporate reference to the norm group. For example, "In comparison with other boys in his grade, Jim is at the 60th percentile in mechanical aptitude, which is slightly above average for boys in his grade." Note the use of narrative reporting in Figures 5.14 and 5.15 (pp. 123–124).

Try This!

For use in a narrative report, devise a set of labels that distinguish between various percentile ranks. Labels may be more than single words.

Percentile Group	Verbal Label
Below 25	_____
25–40	_____
40–59	_____

NORM GROUPS

All of the types of norms treated earlier in this chapter are based on **norm groups**. The test is administered to the norm group in what is called a *norming program* or *standardization program*. The value of the norms for a test depends on the nature of the norm group. Interpretation of test scores is affected greatly by the norm group used for deriving norms, regardless of the type of norm derived. Hence, it is important to consider what kinds of norm groups one might encounter. Norm groups for educational tests display enormous variety. We examine here some of the more common types.

National Norms

Some tests aspire to have **national norms**; that is, norms based on a group that is representative of the segment of the national population for whom the test is intended. This segment of the population may be all adults, all children in Grades K–12, all persons applying for admission to college, or all persons who are legally blind. The target group—the population—is ordinarily defined along with the purpose of the test. Table 5.6 shows examples of statements for tests intending to have national norms.

International Norms

In the context of international studies of school achievement, international norms have been developed in recent years. The norms are based on school children drawn from groups of countries—usually limited to economically advanced nations—that have chosen to participate in the studies. Each participating country attempts to provide a nation-

Table 5.6   Sample Statements Claiming Nationally Representative Norms

The WAT norms are based on nationally representative samples of children in the nation's schools from Grades 1–12.

The test norms aim to reflect the nation's population of adults ages 25–80 who are free from any type of physical disability.

Norms on the SLTR Test were derived from samples carefully matched to the 2000 U.S. Census in terms of geographic region, racial/ethnic group, and socioeconomic level.

ally representative sample. These separate samples combine to yield an international norm. See the description of TIMSS on page 266 for an example. Most of the interpretations for these projects are based on comparisons of total scores and percentage of students correctly answering individual items. Hence, there is little use of such norms as percentile ranks or standard scores.

Convenience Norm Groups

Some tests may aspire to have a national norm but make no pretense about actually having such a norm. Rather, they have norms based on one or several **convenience groups** that are "conveniently" available for testing. Often such groups are from a single geographical location; are relatively homogeneous in cultural background; and may be limited in range of age, educational level, and other important variables.

Some tests will present several different norms based on different groups. For example, a self-concept test may present one norm based on 250 Grade 8 students in a northeastern city, another norm based on 150 persons aged 15 to 18 referred for counseling, and another norm based on 200 adults who participated in a consumer attitude survey.

At best, the test user hopes the test manual will contain a frank and careful description of the characteristics of these ad hoc norm groups. Often, even that is not available. Norms based on such convenience groups must be interpreted with the utmost caution. The test user must refrain from assuming that such norms can be used as a fair substitute for a national norm or a clearly defined subgroup norm.

User Norms

Some tests employ what are called **user norms**. These norms are based on whatever groups actually took the test, usually within some specified time. As new groups take the test, the publisher simply adds these cases to the normative database.[4] The percentile rank norms on the SAT and the ACT are user norms. Normative data for the Praxis tests also illustrate user norms. They are based on all students who actually took the test within a recent period of time.

With user norms, there is no a priori attempt to ensure that the group is representative of any well-defined population. User norms are actually a type of convenience norm. As noted earlier for convenience norms, one hopes a detailed description accompanies the user norm.

Subgroup Norms

Some tests provide **subgroup norms**. The subgroups are taken from the total norm group. For example, separate norms may be provided by sex, race, socioeconomic group, occupational group, or geographic region.

---

[4] Hence, this type of norm is usually encountered only in cases where the test publisher scores all or at least a substantial fraction of the tests administered.

Subgroup norms are potentially useful only if there are substantial differences between the subgroups on the variable measured by the test. If the subgroups do not differ on the variable, then the subgroup norms will not differ from the norm based on the total group.

Depending on the purpose of testing, one may prefer to use only a total group norm or only a subgroup norm. In many circumstances, the use of both a total group norm and a subgroup norm will enhance test interpretation. For example, on a test of artistic talent, it may be useful to know that Chris's score is at the 60th percentile on the national norm but at the 30th percentile for students in a third-year art course.

Local Norms

A school uses the *Metropolitan Achievement Tests*. Students' scores in this school are reported in terms of the national norms. In addition, the school prepares a distribution of its own students' scores and interprets each student's score in relation to the scores of other students in this school. This is called a **local norm**. Such norms are almost always expressed as percentiles.

Local norms may be useful for some interpretive purposes. An advantage of local norms is that one certainly knows the characteristics of the norm group, since it is precisely the people in the local situation. Of course, on a local norm, the typical person will be average. This has the potential to be misleading. For example, in the school testing situation mentioned earlier, the typical student in each grade will be "at norm." This is not very informative, since it is true by definition. One cannot determine on a local norm whether the typical individual is above or below average in terms of some external frame of reference.

Figure 5.10 provides an example. In this case, where the local group is somewhat above the national norm, a raw score of "X" is at the 55th percentile on the national norms but at the 45th percentile on the local norm. Much larger differences will be observed when the local group is very much above average or very much below average.

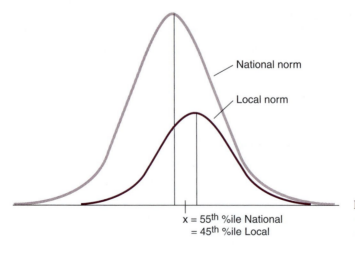

National norm

Local norm

x = 55th %ile National
  = 45th %ile Local

Figure 5.10 Sample comparison of national and local norms.

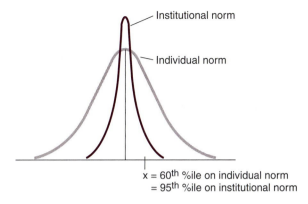

x = 60th %ile on individual norm
= 95th %ile on institutional norm

Figure 5.11 Individual versus institutional norms.

Institutional Norms and School Norms

Some tests, especially achievement tests, provide norms based on institutions as well as norms based on individuals. The **institutional norms** are based on averages for individuals within institutions. For example, a test is administered to all students in 200 school districts. Average scores are determined for each of the 200 districts. A frequency distribution of these averages is obtained and a norm, usually a percentile norm, is developed for the averages. This is an institutional norm. It might be called a school norm, group norm, or some other such designation.

Ordinarily, the distributions of individual scores and group averages will have approximately the same center, but the individual scores will be substantially more varied than the group averages. Hence, a given raw score, except at the middle of the distribution, will be more deviant on the norms for institutions than on the norms for individuals. Above-average scores will be more above average on the institutional norm than on the individual norm and vice versa for below average scores. The differences can be dramatic. Figure 5.11 depicts a comparison of individual and institutional norms. This is only an example. The actual degree of overlap between the two types of norms will vary with different tests and norm groups.

Much confusion may result if one does not distinguish carefully between individual norms and institutional norms. Consider, for example, the statement that "South Park's score is at the 95th percentile on national norms." Many people would interpret this to mean that the typical student at South Park scores better than 95% of students in the country. However, if that 95th percentile is based on school district norms rather than on individual student norms, it may very well be that the typical South Park student scored better than only 60% of the nation's students.

KEY POINTS SUMMARY 5.3   *Major Types of Norm Groups*

National norms   International norms
Convenience norms   User norms
Subgroup norms   Local norms
Institutional norms

The Standardization Group: Determining Its Usefulness

Individuals in the norm group are tested in what is called a norming program, or a **standardization** program. Competent use of educational tests requires not only knowledge of the types of norms—percentiles, standard scores, and so on—but also the ability to judge the usefulness of the norms. Usefulness here means the extent to which the norms provide a meaningful framework for test interpretation. In most instances, this means having a norm that is (a) stable and (b) representative of some well-defined population. Hence, there are two issues: stability and representativeness.

The *stability* of a norm is determined largely by the size of the norm group; that is, the number of cases in the standardization program. This is rarely a problem. It does not take very many cases to achieve statistical stability. Several hundred cases will yield sufficient stability for most practical uses of norms. Consider the norm in a standard score system with M = 100 and SD = 15; with N = 300, the standard error of the mean is less than one point and the 95% confidence interval is $+/-$ 1.7 points. That is good stability. In practice, the norms for many tests are based on thousands of cases.

When considering the number of cases in a norm group, one needs to determine the size of the norm group on which a particular norm is based. The total number of cases aggregated over several norm groups is not the crucial number. For example, a test may boast that its norms are based on nearly 1,000 cases. However, suppose that the actual norms are given separately by gender and by grade over 10 grades. Thus, there are actually 20 norm groups, each with only about 50 cases. The important number here for determining stability is 50, not 1,000.

Stability of the norm is rarely a problem and, in any case, is easily determined. However, stability does not guarantee representativeness. The distinction between stability and representativeness is one of the most important distinctions to learn about norms. It is possible to have very large norm groups, yielding highly stable norms, which are very unrepresentative of the target population for a test.

How shall we determine the *representativeness* of a norm group? The usual procedure for determining the representativeness of a norm group is to compare characteristics of the norm group with characteristics of the intended target population. For example, suppose the target population is Grade 6 students in the United States. We need to examine how the Grade 6 norm group matches the Grade 6 national population. What characteristics are important for this comparison? The correct theoretical answer is that important characteristics are those that are related to the trait we are measuring (e.g., reading comprehension or knowledge of history).

From a practical perspective, we usually look for information on six-to-eight commonly used characteristics. Table 5.7 lists such commonly used characteristics. Most

Table 5.7   Types of Information Helpful in Judging the Usefulness of a Norm Group

Age	Racial/Ethnic groups
Gender	Socioeconomic status
Ability level	Geographic region
Educational level	Size of city

norm groups are described in terms of some combination of these indexes. We look for a good match between the norm group and the target population on these indexes. The more important indexes are those related to what the test is measuring. In fact, a characteristic unrelated to what the test is measuring really does not contribute anything meaningful to the description of the norm group—although it may be important politically.

CRITERION-REFERENCED INTERPRETATION

A 50-item test of basic computational skill is administered to a group of students. The test includes such items as $7 \times 9 =$ ___, $417 + 236 =$ ___, and $2596 - 1688 =$ ___. An individual gets 30 items (60%) right. Such performance may be judged as "unsatisfactory," perhaps by a teacher or a parent. This is an example of **criterion-referenced** interpretation of test performance. In making the judgment that 60% correct was unsatisfactory, there was no reference to any norm group. Thus, criterion-referenced interpretation is contrasted with norm-referenced interpretation. Norm-referenced interpretation was the subject of all earlier parts of this chapter.

Criterion-referenced interpretation requires some well-defined content domain, such as computation, spelling, or skills required by a certain occupation. We often apply criterion-referenced interpretation to scores on professional licensing exams and minimum competency exams for high school graduation. The less well defined the domain, the more difficult criterion-referenced interpretation becomes. The method of testing also becomes important when applying criterion-referenced interpretation. For example, in the computation test mentioned earlier, interpretation of performance may differ substantially depending on whether the test items were free response or multiple choice, whether a calculator was used, and whether a time limit was used. How might the interpretation of "60% correct" change if unlimited time was allowed or if each item had to be completed in 10 seconds? Criterion-referenced interpretation often sounds like a simple idea but it becomes problematic when examined more closely. In many ways, norm-referenced interpretation takes into account or adjusts for different circumstances in testing (multiple choice versus free response, unlimited time versus rigid time limit, etc.). Everyone in the norm group is subject to these conditions. However, there is no norm group for criterion-referenced interpretation. Thus, the person doing the criterion-referenced interpretation must be especially alert to the exact nature of the task and the circumstances surrounding it.

Criterion-referenced interpretation is often applied to classroom examinations. The familiar grading scheme "90% is an A, 80–89% is a B, . . . below 60% is failing" is an example of criterion-referenced interpretation. The content domain may be defined as "what the teacher covered in class" or "everything in Units 1-4 in the textbook." The judgment is that students should have learned all or nearly all of this material. Then the familiar grading scheme is applied. Of course, the grades may be "curved" so that the average score is a "C" and so on. Such "curving" is really a type of norm-referenced interpretation, specifically the application of a local norm.

Performance assessments are often evaluated with what are called rubrics. A *rubric* is an explicit guide describing levels of performance, usually working through the range from unacceptable to highly accomplished. Chapter 8 (pp. 182–185) describes the construction and use of rubrics in detail. For now, we simply note that rubrics illustrate criterion-referenced interpretation. That is, application of a rubric calls for a judgment (usually a teacher's judgment) about the adequacy of performance.

SETTING PERFORMANCE STANDARDS

Contemporary educational practice refers to **performance standards** as a method for interpreting student performance on achievement tests. The term arises in the context of standards-based education. As noted in Chapter 1, standards-based education includes the notions of (a) clear specification of educational objectives, (b) testing for accomplishment of those objectives, (c) setting high standards for performance, and (d) requiring all students to meet the standards.

In educational assessment, setting performance standards is really an application of criterion-referenced interpretation. Scores on the tests are converted to judgment-based categories. Common designations for performance standards are *advanced*, *proficient*, *basic*, and *below basic*. These terms are verbal descriptions about the adequacy of performance on tests. Of course, they are not the only terms that might be used. (See Beck, 2003, for a profusion of other terms applied in the context of educational performance standards.) Nor is it necessary to have four categories. In some applications, there may be only two categories: pass and fail.

Try This!

What alternative terms can you think of for each of the labels listed above?

Advanced _____   Proficient _____   Basic _____   Below Basic _____

Compare your alternatives with another person's.

What is the origin of these labels? In the typical application, these labels result from judgments about the adequacy of test performance. Who makes the judgments? For tests such as state or national assessments, the judgments are made by panels, usually consisting of teachers, administrators, parents, and the lay public. For example, a panel may consist of four teachers, two principals, three parents, and two citizens appointed by the school board.

Exactly how do the panel members make their judgments? There are many methods for making such judgments. Every month seems to bring yet a new method for setting performance standards. See Cizek (2001) for detailed descriptions of a host of such methods and Cizek, Bunch, and Koons (2004) for an excellent introduction. Let us describe one of the more popular methods to illustrate how the process works. We will describe, in a very gen-

---

KEY POINTS SUMMARY 5.4   *Common Terms for Performance Standards*

Advanced	Basic
Proficient	Below Basic

eral way, what is called the Angoff method. Variations on this basic method have been widely used in educational standard setting. Many readers of this book, no doubt, will participate in a standard-setting exercise some time in their professional careers. The process is likely to follow the description given here in a general way, while differing in some details.

Let us work with the four categories identified earlier: advanced, proficient, basic, and below basic. Most of the methods require separate application of the procedure to *each distinction* that is to be made. In our example, that means advanced versus proficient, proficient versus basic, and basic versus below basic. To simplify matters, let us concentrate on one of these distinctions: proficient versus basic. What we need is the test score that separates these two categories. This point is often called the **cut-score**. A cut-score separates two groups. Creation of categories by means of cut-scores is very common in testing, as well as in any decision-making process. Examples are hire or don't hire, buy or don't buy, pass or fail. Where there are more than two categories, there is more than one cut-score. The perceptive reader will note that the number of cut-scores is one less than the number of groups: two groups require just one cut-score, three groups require two cut-scores, and so on.

Of course, there must be preliminary discussion about the purpose of the standard setting, the number of categories to be used, the origin of the tests, and so on. The formal standard setting process begins by having panel members examine the test items. Then, panel members must formulate a concept of the distinction to be made between categories. In our example, it is the distinction between proficient and basic. More specifically, panel members are asked to think about the "minimally proficient" student; that is, a student who just barely exceeds the basic category and just barely makes it into the proficient category. Next, panel members estimate for each item the probability that this minimally proficient student will get the item right. Finally, these probabilities are added for all the items. This yields the cut-score separating the basic group from the proficient group. These cut-scores will be averaged across all panel members.

Figure 5.12 Panel members deliberate about setting performance standards. (© Bob Daemmrich/ The Image Works.)

Item	1	2	3	4	5	6	7	8	9	10
Probability	.95	.95	.90	.90	.90	.80	.75	.70	.50	.25
Sum of probabilities = 7.6										

Figure 5.13 Example of assigning probabilities to items.

Figure 5.13 provides an example of the probabilities assigned by one panel member, Ms. Vasquez, that a "minimally proficient" student would correctly answer each item in a 10-item test. Let us speculate about Ms. Vasquez's thinking as she reviewed the items. She seems to think that Items 1–5 are fairly easy and nearly all proficient students should answer them correctly. Items 6, 7, and 8 are a bit more difficult, in Ms. Vasquez's opinion; most proficient students should get them correct, but there may be some errors. Finally, Ms. Vasquez judges Items 9 and 10 to be quite difficult: You can be proficient and not get these items right.   The sum of the probabilities in Figure 5.13 is 7.6. Thus, a student must score at least 8 to reach the proficient category.

Thus far, our example is a straightforward application of criterion-referenced interpretation of test performance. However, in the actual practice of setting performance standards today, there are several additional steps. First, cut-scores derived as just described are averaged across all panel members. This is simple. Second, after the panel members have established the cut-scores, there is usually discussion about the results. This is like a jury's deliberation. Ms. Vasquez can explain to other panel members why she thought Item 10 was so difficult. Mr. Brier, who pegged Item 10 at .90, can explain why he thought proficient students should answer this item correctly. Third—and here we have a major departure from pure criterion-referenced interpretation—panel members are usually shown the data from actual student performance on the items. The panel may learn, for example, that only 30% of students responded correctly to each of Items 1–3. Or, it may be that only 2% of students received scores of at least 8 on the 10-item test. This type of information, of course, is norm-referenced. Further discussion among panel members follows the introduction of this norm-referenced information. Panel members have the opportunity to revise their judgments. Then, final cut-scores are established.

The entire process, as just described, must be repeated for each cut-score: basic versus below basic, basic versus proficient, and proficient versus advanced (or for whatever other categories are being used). The process must also be repeated for each test or curricular area being covered: reading, mathematics, and so on. Finally, the process must be applied separately for each grade for which interpretation is desired. The definition of proficient, say in arithmetic computation, will surely be different for students in Grades 3 and 10. Thus, a standard-setting process—covering several categories, various curricular areas, and multiple grades—is a formidable undertaking.

In developing the latter example, we used the dividing line (cut-score) between basic and proficient for good reason. The term "proficient" has now been written into federal law, specifically in the No Child Left Behind (NCLB) Act, referred to as a 2001 law but not actually signed into law until 2002. Table 5.8 shows excerpts from the law. The term is also widely used in other educational contexts. Many state testing programs use the term. Several standardized achievement tests provide reports using the term.

Table 5.8 Excerpts Referring to "Proficient" in the No Child Left Behind Act[a]

Standards under this paragraph shall include . . . challenging student academic achievement standards that are aligned with the State's academic content standards, describe two levels of high achievement (**proficient** and advanced) . . . and describe a third level of achievement (basic) to provide complete information about the progress of lower-achieving children toward mastering the **proficient** and advanced levels of achievement.

Each state, using data for the 2001–2002 school year, shall establish the starting point for measuring . . . the percentage of students meeting or exceeding the State's **proficient** level of academic achievement . . .

Each State shall establish statewide annual measurable objectives . . . which . . . shall ensure that all students will meet or exceed the State's **proficient** level of academic achievement. . . .

[T]he school shall be considered to have made adequate yearly progress if the percentage of students in that group who did not meet or exceed the **proficient** level of academic achievement . . . decreased by 10 percent

[a] These are very brief excerpts from a very complex document. You should not try to interpret these brief excerpts without consulting the complete legislation. The excerpts exclude the original outline formatting in the legislation.

This legislation creates a very peculiar situation. There is no universal definition of "proficient." There is no single method for arriving at a definition. The definition rests in the minds of panel members. Even in their minds, its expression may vary depending on the specific method used to set cut-scores. And, it may vary with the selection of panel members. Thus, the definition of "proficient" may vary from state to state, from one subject area to another, and from grade to grade, often with very awkward consequences (see Lane, 2004, for examples). Nevertheless, the term "proficient" has assumed enormous importance in educational circles.

Consider now the traditional system of converting percentages to letter grades: A = 90–100%, B = 80–89%, and so on. Is this essentially the same thing as the elaborate procedure for setting performance standards as just described? For the most part, yes, it is. In this grading system, the instructor has declared that a score of 90% merits the label "A." In turn, the label "A" means superior, excellent, or outstanding performance. Further, it is sometimes the case that, when presented with actual student performance on a test (norm-referenced information), the instructor will make some adjustments in the categories. This is the practice of "curving." The main difference between this old-fashioned system and the new methods of setting performance standards is that the new methods use many panel members rather than a single instructor. Also, note that in the traditional system the instructor creates the test *and* sets the scoring system. In a standard-setting exercise, panel members set the scoring system based on a test created by someone else. Labels from the traditional grading system have become deeply embedded in our culture. For example, quite apart from percentage grades on tests, we may describe someone's performance, say, in a school play, as "A+." Or, we may describe service at a restaurant as meriting "no more than a C+," meaning the service was very mediocre.

We should note that circumstances sometimes dictate that the criterion arises directly from performance on the test. This is a pure example of combining criterion-referenced and norm-referenced interpretation. For example, we may want to select the top 10% of students for some special program. Or we may want to hire the top 25% of applicants for a job. In such cases, the criterion and the norm are one and the same.

SPECIAL SCORES

In addition to the widely used normed scores and performance standard categories already described, there are some special scores constructed for limited areas or specific tests. It is not possible to present a comprehensive list of such scores. We simply alert the reader to their existence. Generally, these special scores follow either a norm-referenced or a criterion-referenced approach to interpretation.

A good example of these special scores is the *lexile* measure, which has gained some popularity for interpreting reading test performance. The lexile bears some resemblance to readability formulas. The lexile attempts to indicate the difficulty level of material that a student is capable of understanding, then relating that level to a broad array of reading materials. The developer of the lexile measure recently announced creation of a quantile score intended to work for mathematics the way the lexile works for reading (MetaMetrics, 2004). In Chapter 11 (p. 256), we will encounter a measure similar to the lexile, illustrating yet another example of the special-score category.

SAMPLE REPORTS

This section includes several formal reports that illustrate the types of scores, both norm-referenced and criterion-referenced, described in earlier sections of this chapter. Full descriptions of the specific tests for these reports appear in Chapter 11. Our purpose at this point is to focus on the types of scores rather than on the specific tests.

Figure 5.14 shows an individual report for Dora Garza on *Stanford Achievement Test, 10th Edition* (SAT10). This report features norm-referenced scores. It contains almost every type of normed score described earlier. The upper part of the report, going from left to right, shows a test name, the number of items on the test (Number Possible), and the Number Correct for this student, that is the student's raw score. Next, a Scaled Score appears; this is a multilevel standard score. Then, the report presents the percentile rank and stanine (PR-S), normal curve equivalent (NCE), and grade equivalent for each test, all based on national norms. For now, we forgo discussion of the "AAC Range." The graph at the right plots the percentile ranks, incorporating the standard error of measurement as described in Chapter 3 (p. 59). Notice that the report also contains the lexile measure along the left side of the report. The number reported here (780L) must be referred to the entire lexile framework for interpretation.

The bottom part of the report in Figure 5.14 shows performance on clusters of items within each area. Check marks indicate whether performance on each cluster is below average, average, or above average. Notice that a code preceding each cluster indicates whether the cluster emphasizes content (C) or processes (P).

Figure 5.15 reports Dora's performance on SAT10 in terms of standards categories: advanced, proficient, basic, or below basic. These categories were established using procedures similar to those described earlier for performance standards. Thus, the report in Figure 5.15 uses a type of criterion-referenced interpretation.

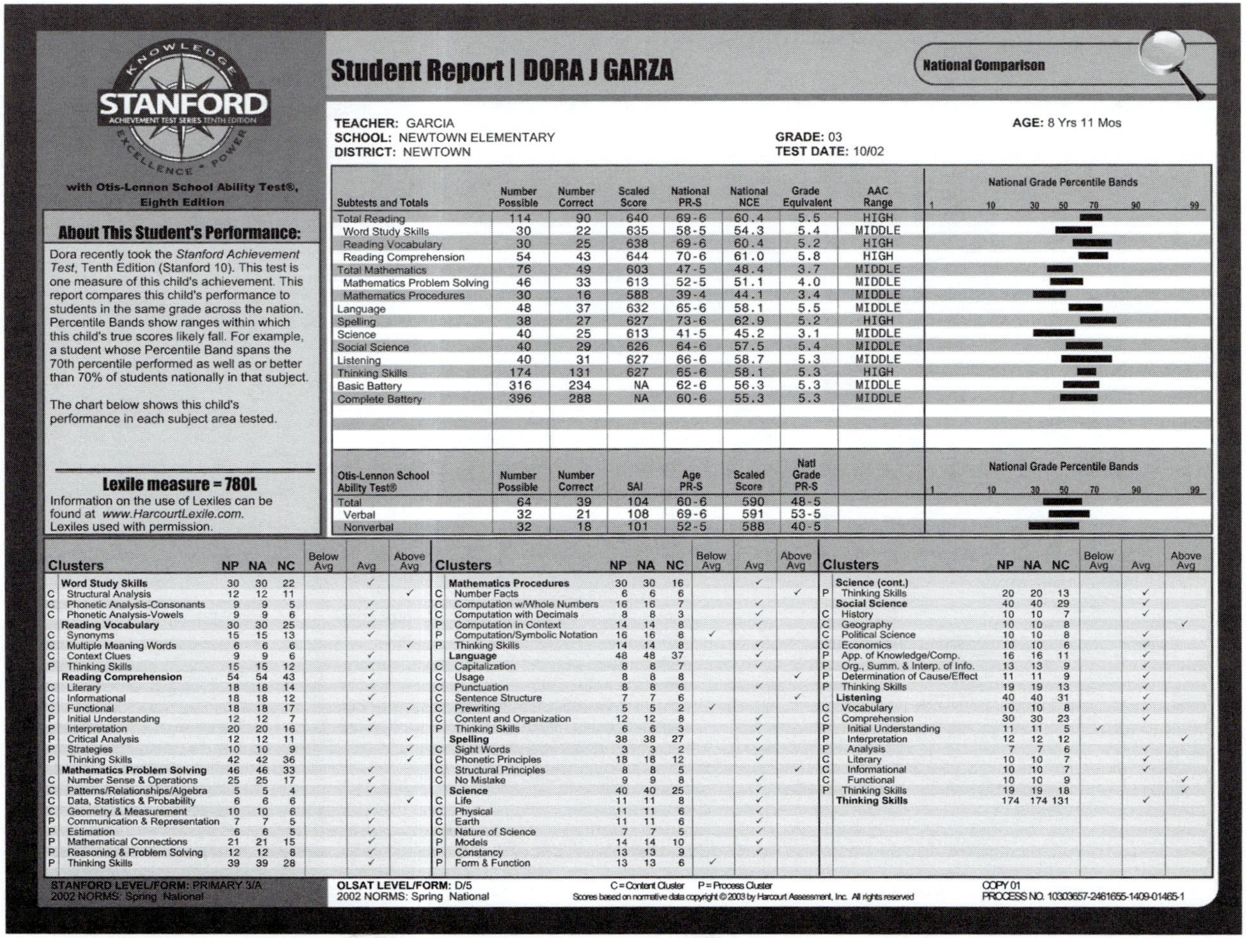

STANFORD ACHIEVEMENT TEST SERIES TENTH EDITION
KNOWLEDGE • POWER • EXCELLENCE

with Otis-Lennon School Ability Test®, Eighth Edition

Student Report | DORA J GARZA

National Comparison

TEACHER: GARCIA
SCHOOL: NEWTOWN ELEMENTARY
DISTRICT: NEWTOWN
GRADE: 03
TEST DATE: 10/02
AGE: 8 Yrs 11 Mos

About This Student's Performance:

Dora recently took the *Stanford Achievement Test*, Tenth Edition (Stanford 10). This test is one measure of this child's achievement. This report compares this child's performance to students in the same grade across the nation. Percentile Bands show ranges within which this child's true scores likely fall. For example, a student whose Percentile Band spans the 70th percentile performed as well as or better than 70% of students nationally in that subject.

The chart below shows this child's performance in each subject area tested.

Lexile measure = 780L

Information on the use of Lexiles can be found at *www.HarcourtLexile.com.* Lexiles used with permission.

Subtests and Totals	Number Possible	Number Correct	Scaled Score	National PR-S	National NCE	Grade Equivalent	AAC Range
Total Reading	114	90	640	69-6	60.4	5.5	HIGH
Word Study Skills	30	22	635	58-5	54.3	5.4	MIDDLE
Reading Vocabulary	30	25	638	69-6	60.4	5.2	HIGH
Reading Comprehension	54	43	644	70-6	61.0	5.8	HIGH
Total Mathematics	76	49	603	47-5	48.4	3.7	MIDDLE
Mathematics Problem Solving	46	33	613	52-5	51.1	4.0	MIDDLE
Mathematics Procedures	30	16	588	39-4	44.1	3.4	MIDDLE
Language	48	37	632	65-6	58.1	5.5	MIDDLE
Spelling	38	27	627	73-6	62.9	5.2	HIGH
Science	40	25	613	41-5	45.2	3.1	MIDDLE
Social Science	40	29	626	64-6	57.5	5.4	MIDDLE
Listening	40	31	627	66-6	58.7	5.3	MIDDLE
Thinking Skills	174	131	627	65-6	58.1	5.3	HIGH
Basic Battery	316	234	NA	62-6	56.3	5.3	MIDDLE
Complete Battery	396	288	NA	60-6	55.3	5.3	MIDDLE

National Grade Percentile Bands: 1 10 30 50 70 90 99

Otis-Lennon School Ability Test®	Number Possible	Number Correct	SAI	Age PR-S	Scaled Score	Natl Grade PR-S
Total	64	39	104	60-6	590	48-5
Verbal	32	21	108	69-6	591	53-5
Nonverbal	32	18	101	52-5	588	40-5

National Grade Percentile Bands: 1 10 30 50 70 90 99

	Clusters	NP	NA	NC	Below Avg	Avg	Above Avg
	Word Study Skills	30	30	22		✓	
C	Structural Analysis	12	12	11			✓
C	Phonetic Analysis-Consonants	9	9	5		✓	
C	Phonetic Analysis-Vowels	9	9	6		✓	
	Reading Vocabulary	30	30	25		✓	
C	Synonyms	15	15	13		✓	
C	Multiple Meaning Words	6	6	6			✓
C	Context Clues	9	9	6		✓	
P	Thinking Skills	15	15	12		✓	
	Reading Comprehension	54	54	43		✓	
C	Literary	18	18	14		✓	
C	Informational	18	18	12		✓	
C	Functional	18	18	17			✓
P	Initial Understanding	12	12	7		✓	
P	Interpretation	20	20	16		✓	
P	Critical Analysis	12	12	11			✓
P	Strategies	10	10	9			✓
P	Thinking Skills	42	42	36			✓
	Mathematics Problem Solving	46	46	33		✓	
C	Number Sense & Operations	25	25	17		✓	
C	Patterns/Relationships/Algebra	5	5	4		✓	
C	Data, Statistics & Probability	6	6	6			✓
C	Geometry & Measurement	10	10	6		✓	
P	Communication & Representation	7	7	5		✓	
P	Estimation	6	6	5		✓	
P	Mathematical Connections	21	21	15		✓	
P	Reasoning & Problem Solving	12	12	8		✓	
P	Thinking Skills	39	39	28		✓	

	Clusters	NP	NA	NC	Below Avg	Avg	Above Avg
	Mathematics Procedures	30	30	16		✓	
C	Number Facts	6	6	6			✓
C	Computation w/Whole Numbers	16	16	7		✓	
C	Computation with Decimals	8	8	3		✓	
P	Computation in Context	14	14	8		✓	
P	Computation/Symbolic Notation	16	16	8	✓		
P	Thinking Skills	14	14	8		✓	
	Language	48	48	37		✓	
C	Capitalization	8	8	7		✓	
C	Usage	8	8	8			✓
C	Punctuation	8	8	6		✓	
C	Sentence Structure	7	7	6			✓
C	Prewriting	5	5	2	✓		
C	Content and Organization	12	12	8		✓	
P	Thinking Skills	6	6	3		✓	
	Spelling	38	38	27		✓	
C	Sight Words	3	3	2		✓	
C	Phonetic Principles	18	18	12		✓	
C	Structural Principles	8	8	5			✓
C	No Mistake	9	9	8		✓	
	Science	40	40	25		✓	
C	Life	11	11	8		✓	
C	Physical	11	11	6		✓	
C	Earth	11	11	6		✓	
C	Nature of Science	7	7	5		✓	
P	Models	14	14	10		✓	
P	Constancy	13	13	9		✓	
P	Form & Function	13	13	6	✓		

	Clusters	NP	NA	NC	Below Avg	Avg	Above Avg
	Science (cont.)						
P	Thinking Skills	20	20	13		✓	
	Social Science	40	40	29		✓	
C	History	10	10	7		✓	
C	Geography	10	10	8			✓
C	Political Science	10	10	8		✓	
C	Economics	10	10	6		✓	
P	App. of Knowledge/Comp.	16	16	11		✓	
P	Org., Summ. & Interp. of Info.	13	13	9		✓	
P	Determination of Cause/Effect	11	11	9		✓	
P	Thinking Skills	19	19	13		✓	
	Listening	40	40	31		✓	
C	Vocabulary	10	10	8		✓	
C	Comprehension	30	30	23		✓	
P	Initial Understanding	11	11	5	✓		
P	Interpretation	12	12	12			✓
P	Analysis	7	7	6		✓	
C	Literary	10	10	7		✓	
C	Informational	10	10	7		✓	
C	Functional	10	10	9			✓
P	Thinking Skills	19	19	18			✓
	Thinking Skills	174	174	131		✓	

STANFORD LEVEL/FORM: PRIMARY 3/A
2002 NORMS: Spring National

OLSAT LEVEL/FORM: D/5
2002 NORMS: Spring National

C=Content Cluster P=Process Cluster

Scores based on normative data copyright © 2003 by Harcourt Assessment, Inc. All rights reserved

COPY 01
PROCESS NO. 10303657-2461655-1409-01465-1

Figure 5.14 Sample report illustrating various normed scores.

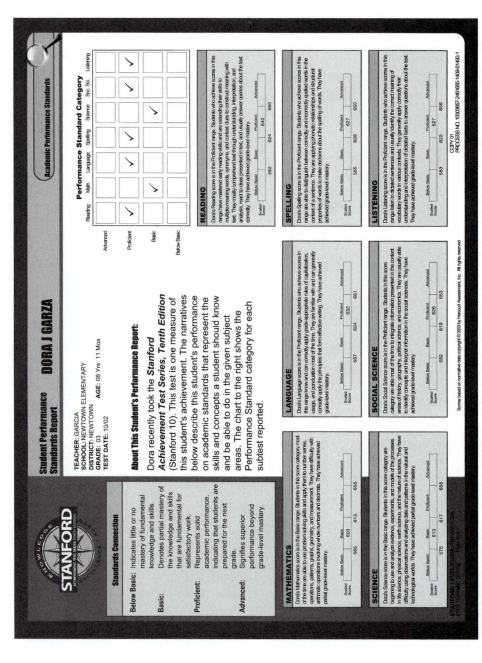

Figure 5.15 Sample report illustrating performance standards categories.

From *Stanford Achievement Test Series—10th Edition.* Copyright © 2003 by Harcourt Assessment, Inc. Reproduced by permission. All rights reserved.

Looking at Dora's Reports

What inferences can we draw about Dora from these reports? In general, Dora performs at an average to somewhat above average level. She is at the 60th percentile on the Complete Battery. On the separate tests, all but one of the stanines are in the 5–6 range. Dora's highest scores are in the verbal areas: spelling and reading. In the cluster report, note the number of checkmarks in the above-average column for the reading clusters. Dora's lowest scores are in mathematics procedures and science. However, her total mathematics performance is almost exactly at the national average, and the difference between her highest and lowest areas is not great. On the Performance Standards report (Figure 5.15), Dora achieves at the proficient level in five areas but at the basic level in two areas (math and science). Notice that her category score is below proficient despite the fact that her normed score for mathematics is almost exactly at the national average. Chapters 11 and 12 contain additional examples of score reports.

SELF-REFERENCING ON REPEATED MEASURES

So far, we have described the two main methods in current use for interpreting student performance: norm-referenced and criterion-referenced. The latter method included the process of setting performance standards. There is a third method for interpreting student performance. This method does not fall clearly into either the norm-referenced or criterion-referenced categories. It shares some features of both categories. We call this method self-referencing on repeated measures. It may be useful for very brief measures that can be repeated frequently. Interpretation depends primarily on tracking an individual student's performance over time. We would like to see change in performance—increases or decreases, depending on the nature of the measure. The method is gaining in popularity, particularly for use with special education students. The method may be especially helpful for the demonstrations of change called for in an individualized education program (IEP; see Chapter 14, pp. 350–353).

Here are some examples. How many words per minute can Kim read? We present Kim with grade-appropriate reading selections for two-minute periods each day. Simply count the words she reads per minute. We would like to see the count increase. How proficient is Tomas with addition and subtraction number facts (e.g., $6 + 7$, $8 - 2$, etc.)? Give him a pageful of number facts and see how many he can complete correctly in 3 minutes. Repeat this procedure every other day. Here, too, we would like to see an increase. Finally, as a third example, recall the example of counting the number of times Frank looks up from his seatwork in a 15-minute period. Repeat this observation every day or perhaps twice per day. We would like to see a decrease in how frequently Frank looks up. Let's say that on the initial measures Kim reads 20 words per minute, Tomas gets 15 correct answers, and Frank looks up 8 times. We want to see these numbers change.

Notice that we are not referencing these scores to any external norm. We are not interested in whether Kim's 20 words per minute is above or below average. Nor are we attempting criterion-referenced interpretation. We are not saying whether Tomas's score of 15 is acceptable or unacceptable. On the other hand, there is criterion-referencing in the sense that the task itself is the criterion, or, more exactly, past performance is the criterion. And there is norm-referencing in the sense that the student's own past performance constitutes the norm.

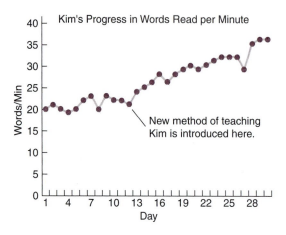

Figure 5.16 Example of graphing a self-referenced measure.

Self-referencing on repeated measures has been particularly popular among a group of school psychologists. Within this group, the measures go by various names: curriculum-based probes, curriculum-based measures, and curriculum-based assessments. There is usually an attempt to relate changes in the measures to changes in instructional (or other) interventions. Figure 5.16 shows a typical display for use of curriculum-based measures, marking introduction of an intervention. See Kramer (1993), Shinn (1989, 1998), and Shapiro (1989) for expanded descriptions of these techniques.

Self-referencing on repeated measures provides an attractive way to interpret student performance. However, it has limited applicability because it requires highly specific behaviors that can be measured in brief periods of time. You are not likely to administer a 30-minute test of reading comprehension every day of the week for three months. You are not likely to have students complete a 40-minute science experiment as an assessment task every other day of the term. And you cannot possibly observe, with any degree of accuracy, the number of times every student in the class looks up from seatwork during a 15-minute period.

Self-referenced measures do not preclude use of a norm-referenced or criterion-referenced interpretation. For example, it would be useful to know that Kim's 20 words per minute places her at the 2nd percentile on such measures or that Frank's looking up 8 times is exactly average for boys in his grade. And, it would be useful to know that a panel of teachers thinks that a score of 15 right on the number facts sheet is terrific. Nevertheless, in each of these cases, we would like to see change.

Finally, we should note that self-referencing on repeated measures has wide applicability as an assessment device beyond measuring student achievement in the usual school subjects. The technique may be used for measuring use of the library (changes in how many books get checked out), school spirit (changes in how many students attend school plays or athletic events), parental interest in the school (how many parents show up for PTA meetings), and so on. All of these applications involve accurate counts taken over a period of time, say, over months or years. See the section on nontest indicators (pp. 212–219) in Chapter 9 for additional examples of such use. Keep the technique in mind for a variety of applications. It does not require a set of norms or judgments about what is high or low. Simply observe change in the measures.

PRACTICAL ADVICE

1. Based on examination of Figure 5.3, develop an understanding of the relationships among the various types of norms.

2. Be particularly careful about interpreting percentiles in the middle of the distribution, say from the 25th–75th percentiles.

3. Whenever interpreting a standard score, be sure you know the mean and standard deviation for the system.

4. Be very cautious about interpreting grade equivalents for individual students, especially in the upper grades.

5. Whenever using a norm, be sure to become familiar with the nature of the norm group. Adjust your interpretation appropriately.

6. Whenever using performance standards, be sure to become familiar with the process used to develop the standard, for example, the group making the judgments and the definitions used by the group.

SUMMARY

1. We need to provide an appropriate context for interpreting student performance on a test or, indeed, any type of raw information. There are two broad categories of methods to help with such interpretation: norm-referenced and criterion-referenced.

2. In norm-referenced interpretation, we interpret a student's performance in relation to the performance of other students on the same test or task. In criterion-referenced interpretation, we interpret student performance in relation to a well-defined body of content or set of skills.

3. There are three main types of norms: percentiles, standard scores, and developmental norms. Each type of norm has its strengths and weaknesses.

4. An important consideration in using a norm is the nature of the norm group. Types of norm groups include na-

tional, international, convenience, user, subgroup, local, and institutional norms.

5. Criterion-referenced interpretation usually requires that someone, often a teacher, make a judgment about what is acceptable, good, or adequate performance.

6. A particular application of criterion-referenced interpretation is setting performance standards. There are many methods for accomplishing this. Most frequently, the standards are established by way of judgments rendered by panel members.

7. Self-referencing on repeated measures uses highly specific behaviors administered frequently, especially to detect changes in performance over time. Such measures often occur in a special education context.

KEY TERMS

age equivalent
chronological age
convenience group
correction for guessing
criterion-referenced
cut-score
developmental norm
deviation IQ
grade equivalent
institutional norm
local norm

mental age (MA)
narrative report
national norm
norm group
normal curve equivalent (NCE)
normed score
norm-referenced
percentage-right score
percentile
percentile rank (PR)
performance standards

ratio IQ
raw score
scaled scores
standardization
standard score
stanine
subgroup norms
theta
T-score
user norms

EXERCISES

1. Using Figure 5.3, make *estimates* for the missing values.

z-score = + 1.0   percentile = _____   NCE = _____   Wechsler Deviation IQ = _____

percentile = 75   z-score = _____   Otis-Lennon = _____   stanine = _____

T-score = 30   percentile = _____   stanine = _____   z-score = _____

2. Using Figure 5.3, *estimate* the percentiles corresponding to the following NCEs

NCE	1	25	40	50	65	80	90	99
Percentile	___	___	___	___	___	___	___	___

3. Using Figure 5.8, what is the estimated GE for a student whose raw score is 50?

4. Again using Figure 5.8, what is the estimated raw score for a student whose grade equivalent is 2.0?

5. Go to the website for the No Child Left Behind Act: http://www.ed.gov/legislation/ESEA02/. Do a word search on "proficient" to see how frequently and in what contexts this term is used in the legislation. The excerpts in Table 5.8 were obtained in this way.

6. Enter the following data into the spreadsheet for a statistical package, such as SPSS, Minitab, or Excel. Run the program to obtain the means and standard deviations for each of the variables. Then, apply the formula on page 102 for standard scores to convert each set of scores to a standard score system with $M = 500$ and SD = 100.

Student	Test 1	Test 2	Quiz 3
Joe	90	88	74
Jim	80	90	90
Sue	76	62	88
Sid	62	80	62
Wanda	78	72	70
Will	79	85	90

7. Here is a 10-item math computation test. How many items should a Grade 4 student get right in order to be classified as "proficient?" How many items should a college freshman get right to be classified as proficient? Compare your answers with someone else's.

$13 + 26 =$ _____ $4(6 + 10) =$ _____

$6 \times 7 =$ _____ $8 \times 4 + 5 =$ _____

$72 \times 18 =$ _____ $2a + (4 \times 3a) =$ _____

$162 - 89 =$ _____ $(a + b)(a + b) =$ _____

$138 + 269 + 85 =$ _____ $(a^2 + b)(a - b^2) =$ _____

8. Refer to Figure 5.14. Examine the report to answer these questions about Dora's performance.

a. On which test did she have the highest raw score (Number Correct)?

b. On which test did she have the highest grade equivalent?

c. Which test shows the greatest difference between percentile rank (PR) and NCE scores?

d. On the Mathematics Procedures test, how close to being in stanine 5 is she? (Refer to Figure 5.7 to help answer this question.)

Chapter 6

Planning for Assessment

OBJECTIVES

- Identify the role of objectives in planning for assessment.
- Outline Bloom's taxonomy and some alternatives to it.
- List major sources for statements of educational objectives.
- List the guidelines for establishing your own instructional objectives.
- Outline the major factors in an overall assessment plan.
- Plan a particular assessment.

What This Chapter Is About

Before you plan a specific assessment, you must have a plan. The plan deals with such matters as the purpose of the assessment, your general approach, and what you will do with the results. This chapter deals with these topics. The first step is to be clear about what you want to assess. That means clearly specifying your objectives. Therefore, we first consider sources and types of educational objectives. Then we outline how to plan for assessment.

Why This Topic Is Important

Conducting assessment is obviously an important element in the total educational picture. Some of this assessment will arise from external sources, for example, use of nationally standardized tests or a state testing program. However, a substantial amount of assessment will originate with the individual teacher. It is, therefore, important to think about how to prepare your own assessments. In this chapter, we examine preliminary planning for assessment. You need to know where you're headed before you charge ahead. The next several chapters go into details about preparing specific assessments.

INTRODUCTION

Reference to "planning for assessment" almost inevitably leads one to think about writing test items. That's the wrong place to start. We need to start with two preliminary steps. First, we need to clearly specify the target for assessment. The target is the content. What do we want students to learn? How do we want them to change as a result of instruction?

Second, we must have an overall plan for assessment. A particular test or exercise will fit into an overall pattern. What do we need to consider about the plan? What purposes will be served? What mix of assessment techniques will be used? What schedule shall we follow? After we examine these topics, we will be ready to prepare particular assessments, which we take up in Chapters 7 and 8.

GENERAL GOALS VS. SPECIFIC OBJECTIVES

Let us begin with a distinction between general goals and specific objectives. Our usage of these terms is not universal. Other sources may use somewhat different terms, but the concepts will be the same. **Goals** are broad statements indicating the general areas to be covered by education. Goals include such areas as reading, mathematics, preparation for college or a job, and citizenship. Goals differ from specific **objectives** in their level of generality. Specific objectives deal with such matters as addition and subtraction facts; knowledge of historical trends; ability to dissect a frog, to analyze a poem, to use a word processor, and so on.

Ordinarily, society determines the goals of education. Society does so through federal and state legislatures, local boards of education, and similar bodies. The individual teacher or school administrator does not choose educational goals. They implement procedures for student attainment of the goals.

At any point in the history of a particular culture, the general goals of education may seem noncontroversial, even obvious. Who in the United States today would quibble with the goals of minimal competency in math? Who does not recognize the importance of reading? However, even a cursory review of other times and other cultures reveals that these goals are by no means universal. At some times in the past, the ability to perform even simple arithmetic calculations was a highly specialized skill, known to relatively few people. They were like today's electricians, possessors of very technical knowledge. In some cultures in the past, and even today, military training was a universal goal. Everyone needed to know how to use weapons, do hand-to-hand combat, and so on. This is certainly not a universal goal in contemporary Western culture.

How do these goals fit into educational assessment? The goals specify broadly what areas will be covered. For example, proficiency in reading and mathematics are broad goals of education in the United States. Therefore, they are covered in national and state assessment programs. For good or bad, society has not adopted proficiency in music as a broad goal. Therefore, it is not covered in national and state assessment programs, except very occasionally or tangentially. The broad goals, however, do not indicate exactly what will be covered in, say, math or reading. That is a matter for specific educational objectives.

TAXONOMIES FOR EDUCATIONAL OBJECTIVES

Before taking up specific educational objectives, we need to examine the topic of educational taxonomies. **Taxonomy** is a rather peculiar term for education. It usually applies to botany: species, phyla, and so on. The term has a very specialized meaning in educational circles. It refers to systems of mental operations. Educational objectives usually refer to specific content. For example, an objective might refer to causes of the Civil War, the use of "ie" versus "ei" in spelling, or the Pythagorean theorem. Educational taxonomies refer

to such matters as memorizing facts, developing generalizations, and knowing the procedures for investigating. These categories in the taxonomies cut across the specific content
objectives.

Education has one classic taxonomy and a host of other, less widely referenced taxonomies. We begin by describing the classic case. Then, we list a few of the alternatives.

Bloom's Taxonomy

The classic case is **Bloom's taxonomy**. In one sense, the reference to "Bloom's taxonomy" is ambiguous. There are actually three taxonomies customarily referred to as Bloom
taxonomies: the cognitive (Bloom, 1956), the affective (Krathwohl, Bloom, & Masia,
1964), and the psychomotor (Harrow, 1972). We should note that, although the taxonomies are almost universally attributed to Benjamin Bloom, the first two (cognitive and
affective) were actually created by several loosely organized committees working over a
20-year period. Bloom and his colleagues were not involved in the creation of the psychomotor taxonomy. Most typically, reference to "Bloom's taxonomy" means the **cognitive domain**. Our subsequent use of the term "Bloom's taxonomy" implies the cognitive
domain. The taxonomies in the affective and psychomotor domains have experienced
much less practical use than the cognitive taxonomy. It is also worth noting that the original motivation for the cognitive and affective taxonomies was to help in writing and classifying items for tests at the college and upper secondary school levels. Perhaps for this
reason, they always seem a bit strained in application to the primary and preprimary
grades.

For practical purposes, the central focus in Bloom's cognitive taxonomy is a sixfold
hierarchy. Table 6.1 lists the six categories. In Bloom's original work, each category had
a series of subcategories. Table 6.1 shows a few examples of these subcategories. For
each category and subcategory, the original work provides explanations and additional
examples. The essential point of the hierarchy is that it goes from the simplest to the most
complex type of mental operation.

Table 6.1 Outline of Bloom's Taxonomy in the Cognitive Domain

Major Category	Example Subcategories
1. Knowledge	Recall, information, knowledge of facts and principles
2. Comprehension	Understanding, interpreting, summarizing
3. Application	Using information and concepts; solving problems
4. Analysis	Organizing, recognizing patterns and connections
5. Synthesis	Putting elements together; written and oral composition
6. Evaluation	Judging value; using standards; appraising

Adapted from Bloom (1956).

Examination of the subcategory descriptors in Table 6.1 suggests the distinctions of interest. The lowest level calls for "mere recall" and simple information. It does include knowledge of general principles as well as just facts. The taxonomy progresses to understanding and interpretation, then to application. Notice that the taxonomy is cumulative. What one interprets at Level 2 is the information learned (recalled) at Level 1. What one applies at Level 3 is material understood at Level 2. The higher levels in the taxonomy call for organization and evaluation—again, of material learned at lower levels. The taxonomy places written and oral composition at the next to highest level. The implication is that composition is not mainly about mechanics (e.g., correct spelling or proper use of voice). Rather, composition is about organizing and synthesizing content.

Try This!

Numerous websites feature summaries and extensions of Bloom's taxonomy. Enter "Bloom's taxonomy" in any Internet search engine. Follow some of the links. Note the many ways in which the taxonomy has been used.

For such a small book, Bloom's cognitive taxonomy has had incredible influence and staying-power. It is among the most widely referenced sources in all of education (Marzano, 2001). It surfaces in nearly all discussions of educational objectives and assessment. Perhaps most remarkable of all, people refer to using Bloom's taxonomy when, in fact, they are not using it. Rather, they are using some rough approximation to the official taxonomy, but still refer to it as Bloom's taxonomy. In some usages, the term "Bloom's taxonomy" has taken on a generic meaning to designate any system that places mental operations in a hierarchy, especially going from "mere recall" to "higher order thinking skills." Later in this chapter, we will describe the practical use of Bloom's cognitive taxonomy in developing test specifications.

The Affective Domain

A taxonomy in the **affective domain** complements the cognitive taxonomy. Although not as widely cited and not nearly so influential as the cognitive taxonomy, the affective taxonomy serves as a continual reminder of the "other side" of education: feelings, interest, attitudes, values, and so on.

Before describing details of the affective taxonomy, let us provide some context for it. First, the affective taxonomy grew out of the same mix of people and concerns as did the cognitive taxonomy. It was the work of a rather loosely organized committee, mostly university professors, with an orientation toward testing. Second, as was true for the cognitive domain, the taxonomy in the affective domain represents a superstructure imposed on an underlying continuum. The taxonomy is usually presented as a series of categories (Table 6.2) and there is a tendency to emphasize the distinctions among the categories. In contrast, the original description of the affective taxonomy continually emphasizes the underlying continuum. That is, there is gradual evolution from lower to higher levels rather than discrete steps. It might be better to think of the labels in the taxonomy as representing regions or phases rather than categories. Third, it is worth noting that the au-

Table 6.2   Outline of Bloom's Taxonomy in the Affective Domain

1.0 Receiving (attending)
    1.1 Awareness
    1.2 Willingness to receive
    1.3 Controlled or selected attention
2.0 Responding
    2.1 Acquiescence in responding
    2.2 Willingness to respond
    2.3 Satisfaction in response
3.0 Valuing
    3.1 Acceptance of a value
    3.2 Preference for a value
    3.3 Commitment (conviction)
4.0 Organization
    4.1 Conceptualization of a value
    4.2 Organization of a value system
5.0 Characterization by a value or value complex
    5.1 Generalized set
    5.2 Characterization

thors of the affective taxonomy "found the affective domain much more difficult to structure [than the cognitive domain], and we are much less satisfied with the result" (Krathwohl et al., 1964, p. v).

Table 6.2 presents an outline of the affective taxonomy. The essential, underlying continuum proceeds from simple consciousness to an "organized and integrated philosophy of life" (Krathwohl et al., 1964, p. 42). The first level emphasizes attention or what we might call simple consciousness. Although the general tenor of the affective domain calls for feelings, interests, attitudes, and so on, there is none of that at this first level. However, one must be aware of things before having any feelings about them, so the starting point is this awareness. This level is not very different from the first level in the cognitive domain: simple knowledge.

The second level in the affective taxonomy calls for responses to the things of which one is aware. Elementary notions of affect, as we usually think of that term, begin to enter the picture at this second level. However, the degree of affect is mild, reaching no further than a form of satisfaction at the upper reaches of this category. However, this region covers such important matters as interest in school subjects (e.g., reading and math). The transition from the second to the third levels is quite important, particularly at the elementary and secondary school levels. The transition reflects the emergence of attitudes and values. At first, the person may not be fully conscious of these emerging attitudes and values. However, consciousness grows and eventually turns into a commitment or conviction. At the lower reaches of the fourth level, the person begins to think about the values and attitudes, and even to think about the nature of values. This type of thinking gradually turns to organizing values and attitudes into some type of system. "Thinking about values" is obviously a type of activity that borders on the cognitive domain.

Try This!

Becky is an avid environmentalist. She just loves studying about ecosystems. She devotes a lot of time to local environmental clean-up projects. Where would you place Becky's affective development in Table 6.2?

Perhaps nowhere is the nature of the underlying continuum in the affective taxonomy more apparent than in the transition from the highest level of Category 4 to the lowest level of Category 5. The taxonomy goes from organizing value systems to integrating all of the value systems. The fifth and highest level is roughly equivalent to what might be called "character" or "philosophy of life." At this level, it is difficult to refer to separate strands, such as reading, science, or civics, because they all merge into a unified whole. We usually think of this level as the work of early adulthood or even mature adulthood.

Figure 6.1 shows practical examples of some different levels in the affective taxonomy, spanning especially the three middle categories. The "interest in . . ." entries fall in the Level 2 region. Most teachers, from the primary grades up to graduate school, try to develop students' interest in a subject area. "Seeing the value in . . ." or being committed to something typifies the Level 3 region. "Relating . . ." actions to a broader perspective and even forming systems of values is more typical of the Level 4 region in the taxonomy. Chapter 9 suggests specific ways to assess these interests and attitudes.

Before leaving the affective taxonomy, we should note that current thinking winces a bit at the cognitive-affective distinction, as a result of the "cognitive revolution" in psychology and education. According to the cognitive revolution, everything is cognitive, even feelings, interests, and attitudes. For example, your *interest* in science results from the way you think about science. When you say you are *depressed*, this results from how you think about your circumstances. Nevertheless, the cognitive-affective distinction has deep roots in ordinary language, so there is value in trying to describe each domain.

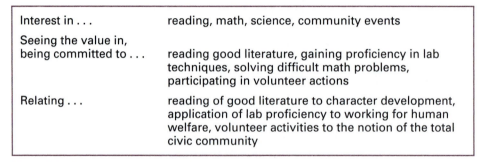

Figure 6.1 Illustrations of successive levels in the affective taxonomy.

The Psychomotor Domain

The taxonomy in the **psychomotor domain** is usually represented as the third part of the complete Bloom system. However, development of the psychomotor taxonomy differed distinctly from development of the cognitive and affective systems in at least three ways. First, although this taxonomy takes its inspiration from Bloom's work, Bloom and his colleagues were not involved in development of the psychomotor taxonomy. It was developed by Anita Harrow (1972). Second, children rather than college and college-bound students served as the reference point for the psychomotor taxonomy. Third, the psychomotor taxonomy did not concern itself with matters of testing and assessment. In contrast, the generation and classification of test items was the primary motivation for the cognitive taxonomy. This flavor carried over to the affective taxonomy. Both the cognitive and affective taxonomies are replete with examples of test items, especially ones appropriate for use at the upper high school and college levels. The psychomotor taxonomy contains no test items.

Table 6.3 provides an outline of the psychomotor taxonomy. The full taxonomy has many additional subdivisions—more than 70 in all. Similar to the underlying structure of the affective taxonomy, Harrow (1972) emphasized that a continuum underlay the psychomotor taxonomy. That is, there was a continuum from simple to complex with the categories being more or less arbitrary divisions along this continuum. The entire structure attempts to outline *movement* in its various manifestations.

The first level in the psychomotor taxonomy covers various reflex movements. These are nonvoluntary movements. They include such simple reflexes as the grasp reflex and more complicated (suprasegmental) ones dealing with posture, the ability to stand erect. The second level (basic-fundamental movements) includes crawling, walking, and running; use of the limbs, especially the arms and legs for other than locomotion; and matters of simple dexterity, for example, the ability to pick up a block or a cup. Most students have mastered all of these movements by the time they come to school, although some children may still struggle with holding a pencil or crayon.

Table 6.3   Outline of Major Divisions in the Psychomotor Taxonomy

---

1.0 Reflex Movements
       Segmental, Intersegmental, and Suprasegmental Reflexes
2.0 Basic-Fundamental Movements
       Locomotor, Nonlocomotor, and Manipulative Movements
3.0 Perceptual Abilities
       Kinesthetic, Visual, Auditory, and Tactile Discrimination,
       and Coordinated Abilities
4.0 Physical Abilities
       Endurance, Strength, Flexibility, Agility
5.0 Skilled Movements
       Simple, Compound, and Complex Adaptive Skill
6.0 Nondiscursive Communication
       Expressive Movement, Interpretive Movement

Adapted from Harrow (1972).

The third level, perceptual abilities, is surely the oddest entry in the psychomotor taxonomy. Most people do not consider perception as a type of movement. The category includes such matters as discrimination of shapes and colors, sounds (e.g., various pitches), and the feel of surfaces (e.g., rough versus smooth). Even more unusual is the fact that smaller subdivisions of this category include aspects of memory, for example, visual and auditory memory.

The fourth level covers basic physical skills, what are often thought of as the components of "physical fitness." In fact, many physical fitness tests cover exactly the subdivisions in this category, especially endurance, strength, and flexibility.

Try This!

To see an example of a physical fitness test (the Fitnessgram), go to: www.cooperinst.org/ftgmain.asp. Check the correspondence between the areas covered by the test and the subcategories at Level 4 in the psychomotor taxonomy.

The fifth category concentrates on physical skills, what we would usually call athletic skills. It includes such areas as tennis, golf, and gymnastics. In the full taxonomy, each of the major subdivisions (simple, compound, and complex) has four more refined subdivisions: beginner, intermediate, advanced, and highly skilled. These subdivisions clearly represent another underlying continuum rather than sharply distinct categories, in this case from rudimentary forms of the skill to professional levels.

The sixth and last category deals with movement as communication. This is obviously movement of a quite different character than that at the preceding levels. The expressive movement subcategory includes such matters as gestures (e.g., an eye roll or a shrug) and facial expressions (e.g., a wry smile or a raised eyebrow) as means of communication. The interpretive movement subcategory includes aesthetic and creative movement, for example, dance. But at this level, the emphasis is not on the physical execution of the dance (which would be at Level 5) but on the creative communication expressed in the dance.

Harrow's psychomotor taxonomy is an interesting historical occurrence. It reminds us of another dimension in the total development of humans. However, beyond making that point, it has not had much practical influence in shaping school curricula. Much more influential, from a practical perspective, have been publications and activities of the American Alliance for Health, Physical Education, Recreation, and Dance (AAHPERD).

Alternative Taxonomies for the Cognitive Domain

Although Bloom's cognitive taxonomy is thoroughly entrenched in the educational literature, some alternatives have emerged. Anderson et al. (2001) reviewed no less than 19 alternative taxonomies. None of these alternatives have attained widespread use. However, we introduce three of them to illustrate that there are different ways to think about these matters. Each of the alternatives begins with a courteous bow to the eminent Bloom system, followed by a critique of its shortcomings. We forgo presentation of the critiques and proceed with description of the alternative systems.

Table 6.4   Summary of Marzano's New Taxonomy[a]

Levels of Mental Processing	Domains of Knowledge		
	Information	Procedures	Psychomotor
1. Retrieval			
2. Comprehension			
3. Analysis			
4. Knowledge Utilization			
5. Metacognition			
6. Self-system Thinking			

[a] After Marzano (2001).

Over many years, Robert Marzano and his colleagues have evolved a system variously known as the dimensions of thinking (Marzano et al., 1988), dimensions of learning (Marzano, Pickering, & McTighe, 1993), and, most recently, simply the New Taxonomy (Marzano, 2001). Table 6.4 outlines Marzano's New Taxonomy in a format designed to facilitate comparison with other models. An important feature of Marzano's system is the distinction between (a) levels of mental processing and (b) domains of knowledge. Levels of mental processing are similar to Bloom's levels, especially in the first four levels. Marzano's top two levels are not represented in the Bloom system. The domains of knowledge correspond to types of memory contents. The information domain includes what is sometimes called declarative knowledge. The "procedures" category refers to knowledge of how to do something. The "psychomotor" domain includes physical execution of an action, for example, dissecting a frog. Thus, in this system, psychomotor means something different than in the psychomotor taxonomy examined earlier.

Stiggins, Rubel, and Quellmalz (1988) presented another alternative to the Bloom system. Their system has five levels, as opposed to Bloom's six levels. The five levels are recall, analyze, compare, infer, and evaluate. The similarities to Bloom's system are obvious. Stiggins and colleagues have made deliberate efforts to show the implications of this system for assessment activities. Although it is not very different from Bloom's original system, we mention this system because it has been very popular for teacher training programs.

A third alternative to the Bloom system came from Anderson et al. (2001). It is explicitly presented as an updating or revision of Bloom's system. The revision is simply called the Taxonomy Table. Like Marzano's system, the Taxonomy Table is a two-dimensional table. Bloom's hierarchy is one-dimensional, ranging only along the dimension from Knowledge to Evaluation. Table 6.5 shows the Taxonomy Table.

The cognitive processes across the top of Table 6.5 are similar to Bloom's processes (see Table 6.1). However, there are some differences. The revision renames "comprehension" as "understand" and "synthesis" as "create." It places "evaluation" at the second highest level rather than at the highest level, with the renamed "create" as the highest level. The revision adds the Knowledge dimension with subdivisions of factual, procedural, and metacognitive knowledge.

Table 6.5 The Taxonomy Table, a Proposed Revision of Bloom's Taxonomy

Knowledge Dimension	The Cognitive Process Dimension					
	1. Remember	2. Understand	3. Apply	4. Analyze	5. Evaluate	6. Create
A. Factual Knowledge						
B. Conceptual Knowledge						
C. Procedural Knowledge						
D. Metacognitive Knowledge						

Adapted from Lorin W. Anderson & David R. Krathwohl, *A Taxonomy for Learning, Teaching, and Assessing*, published by Allyn and Bacon, Boston, MA. Copyright © 2001 by Pearson Education. Reprinted by permission of the publisher.

Notice that both Table 6.4 and Table 6.5 refer to **metacognition**. Roughly speaking, metacognition means your own thinking about your cognitive knowledge and processes. You know something. That's cognition. You know that you know it and perhaps the limitations of how well you know it. That's metacognition. Your metacognitive processes may also direct you to connect this something you know with other things you know.

Try This!

Think of the last test you took in any course. Where would you classify the items in the test in Table 6.5?

The three alternatives to Bloom's system presented here are not the only alternatives. There is an endless profusion of other alternatives, each with its own little twist. Interestingly, some of the alternatives shade off into theories of intelligence. Sternberg's (1994b) triarchic theory of intelligence and Gardner's (1999) theory of multiple intelligences are particularly popular for this purpose.

A Conclusion and a Caution

Use of some type of educational taxonomy has struck a resonant chord with educators. The taxonomies—any of them—seem to make sense. They add an apparently useful dimension to the seemingly sterile list of content objectives. We recommend use of one of the systems. Almost any one of them will do. They are much more alike than they are different.

Nevertheless, let's be cautious about wholehearted acceptance of any of the systems. Researchers' attempts to validate the systems have not been very successful. For reviews

Figure 6.2 The continuum of mental functions probably underlying the various taxonomies.

of research on Bloom's cognitive taxonomy, see Kreitzer and Madaus (1994) and Seddon (1978). For example, research has not been very successful in showing a real difference in the mental operations of comprehension and analysis. In fact, most of the authors of these systems admit that their systems want for solid, empirical verification. Using one of these systems may help us think about what we are trying to accomplish with students. But, let's not assume that a student's mind consists of five or six little boxes corresponding to one of these taxonomies. Students' mental operations seem to be much more general. The human mind probably does not operate in discrete categories. Figure 6.2 shows what is probably a more realistic picture of how the mind functions. No doubt, there are variations from simple to more complex ways of thinking and knowing. They probably shade off into one another along a continuum rather than coming in separate boxes. You can think of a taxonomy as a somewhat arbitrary division along the continuum in Figure 6.2.

Here is another caution about using the taxonomies, especially for classifying test items. A test item's function is partly dependent on how material is taught and learned. One student may correctly answer a question about causes of the Civil War or about the distributive law of multiplication because the student synthesized some material. Another student may correctly answer the same question because the teacher told the student to memorize the material. Be cautious about judging a test item or an assessment exercise independent of its context. Be wary, for example, of statements or classifications that say this item measures "mere recall" while that item measures "deep understanding." Simple inspection of an item or assessment exercise does not reveal what it measures for a particular student or group of students.

The cognitive taxonomies emphasize mental operations. The taxonomies are applied to content-based objectives: what we usually think of as the stuff of education. We turn now to these content-based objectives.

SOURCES OF EDUCATIONAL OBJECTIVES

There are numerous sources of educational objectives. We will examine the major sources from which teachers may draw. In addition, at some time or another, every teacher needs to develop objectives or adapt objectives from one of the standard sources. Therefore, we will offer advice on doing that.

Professional Organizations

Professional organizations for specific content areas often issue lists of educational objectives. In some instances, the lists are quite elaborate, and instructional suggestions accompany the lists. Among the most well-known objectives in this category are those from the

Table 6.6 Examples of Professional Organizations With Lists of Educational Objectives

Area	Organization	Website
Mathematics	National Council of Teachers of Mathematics	www.nctm.org/standards
Reading/Language Arts	National Council of Teachers of English and International Reading Association	http://www.reading.org/resources/issues/reports/learning_standards.html
Social Studies	National Council for the Social Studies	www.ncss.org/standards
Science	National Research Council (and National Academy Press)	www.nap.edu
All	Mid-continent Research for Education and Learning	www.mcrel.org/standards-benchmarks/
	Align to Achieve	www.aligntoachieve.org

National Council of Teachers of Mathematics (NCTM, 2000) and those from the National Council of Teachers of English and International Reading Association (NCTE/IRA, 1996). In other instances, the lists are more general and consist of relatively simple statements, unaccompanied by instructional recommendations. Table 6.6 lists some of the professional organizations issuing objectives.

Two comprehensive sources merit special mention. First, there is the Mid-continent Research for Education and Learning (McREL) center, located in Aurora, Colorado. McREL's "standards-benchmark" project attempts to provide a comprehensive catalog of standards from a host of organizations. The project also summarizes the history of standards-based education. The project's website (see Table 6.6) is a valuable resource for educators working on standards. Second, Align to Achieve (A2A) is an independent, not-for-profit organization that maintains a "standards database" of content standards and benchmarks from states, national organizations, and countries. Both McREL and A2A are valuable sources for educators, parents, and even students.

Try This!

For a content area of interest to you, access a website from Table 6.6 and examine the list of objectives for that area.

Many of the organizations present their objectives at several levels of generality. For example, there may be 10 general areas. Each area has three to five subcategories. Finally, within each category, there are specific objectives. Many of the organizations also divide their objectives by grade level. Most frequently they use groups of grades, for example, Grades 1–3, 4–6, and so on. Table 6.7 shows statements of objectives at the most specific level from the NCTM.

Objectives issued by professional organizations tend to be very influential. Other sources, as reviewed later, usually draw heavily on these statements from professional or-

Table 6.7 Sample Statements of Objectives From the NCTM

From the Geometry strand for Grades 3–5:
- Identify and build a two-dimensional representation of a three-dimensional object.
- Find the distance between points along horizontal and vertical lines of a coordinate system.

From the Data Analysis and Probability strand for Grades 9–12:
- Compute basic statistics and understand the distinction between a statistic and a parameter.
- Recognize how linear transformations of univariate data affect shape, center, and spread.

From National Council of Teachers of Mathematics (2000). *Principles and standards for school mathematics* (pp. 396, 401).

ganizations. Every teacher should be familiar with the objectives issued by the organizations in content areas relevant for the teacher.

States

Every state issues educational objectives for some content areas. As a result of the *No Child Left Behind* (NCLB) Act, states must have objectives at least in reading and mathematics for Grades 3–8. By 2007–2008, science joins the list of required areas in selected grades. Many states go well beyond the minimum requirements, covering additional grades and subject areas.

In the current lingo, states refer to educational objectives as **content standards**. Paralleling the content standards are performance standards. The performance standards describe levels of attainment on the content standards. We described procedures for labeling and developing performance standards in Chapter 5.

State objectives, content standards, and performance standards have assumed enormous importance in recent years. Obviously, it is impractical in this book to cover every state. However, thanks to postings on the Internet, it is relatively easy to access the material for the state relevant for any reader. To examine lists of content standards for a state, go to the state's website in Appendix E.[1] These content standards serve as the basis for state assessments, which we describe in more detail in Chapter 11. Obviously, teachers in the public schools for a given state must be thoroughly familiar with that state's objectives.

Try This!

Access the website for your state from Appendix E. Examine the list of objectives for a grade and content area of interest to you.

---

[1] See also the McREL and Align to Achieve websites listed in Table 6.6.

NAEP and TIMSS

Chapter 1 referred to two major assessment projects: the National Assessment of Educational Progress (NAEP) and the Trends in International Mathematics and Science Study (TIMSS). Each project focuses on assessment. However, to prepare a relevant assessment, the project must start with a clear specification of the content to be covered. The projects often refer to these content specifications as a "framework." The framework is essentially a statement of objectives, often overlaid with some type of Bloom-like taxonomy. Because these projects utilize carefully selected panels of experts to construct the frameworks, the statements tend to influence other groups constructing lists of objectives. Thus, it is prudent to examine these sources.

NAEP covers many different curricular areas. TIMSS, as suggested by its title, covers only math and science. An emerging project, the Program for International Student Assessment (PISA), now covers reading, as well as science and mathematics. All of the projects are limited to only a few grades. None of them delve into the primary grades.

To see the objectives emanating from these projects, check these websites:

- NAEP: http://www.nces.ed.gov/nationsreportcard
- TIMSS: http://www.timss.org
- PISA: http://nces.ed.gov/surveys/pisa

Table 6.8 shows the NAEP framework used in the most recent assessment of geography. Notice that the table uses a content-by-process arrangement, with content listed across the top and a reduced Bloom-like system for cognitive processes down the left. Each content dimension has subcategories (not shown here). Specific objectives fill the cells in the table.

Textbooks

Most textbooks contain lists of objectives. These objectives come at two levels of specificity. First, the textbook has general objectives, written at approximately the same level as those from professional organizations and states. For multigrade basal textbooks, these

Table 6.8   NAEP's General Framework for Geography

	Content Dimension		
Cognitive Dimension	Space and Place	Environment and Society	Spatial Dynamics and Connections
Knowing			
Understanding			
Applying			

From National Assessment Governing Board (2001). *Geography framework for the 1994 and 2001 National Assessment of Educational Progress.* Washington, DC: Author. (Available at www.nagb.org/pubs/gframework2001.pdf.)

KEY POINTS SUMMARY 6.1	*Main Sources of Educational Objectives*
Professional organizations	Textbooks
States	School districts
NAEP and TIMSS	Teacher-prepared objectives

objectives often appear in the "scope and sequence" chart. Second, many textbooks contain very specific objectives for each chapter or section in the book.

School Districts

Some school districts develop their own lists of objectives. As a general rule, in content areas where the state already has objectives, the school district adopts the state objectives. Of course! The state assessment will be based on the state objectives. However, the state usually does not have objectives for all subject areas at all grades. In these cases, a district curriculum committee (or a similar group) may develop district objectives.

Teacher-Prepared Objectives

In some cases, the teacher will simply adopt the objectives from one of the sources described earlier. It depends on the grade level and subject area. A Grade 5 math teacher in the public schools of, say, Texas or Pennsylvania, will almost certainly focus on the state's math objectives. However, in other cases, the teacher will develop a unique set of objectives. The Grade 10 teacher of art in a private school will not focus on any state objectives and may not even use a textbook. What advice can we offer to the teacher developing a unique set of objectives? The next section addresses this question.

GUIDELINES FOR PREPARING YOUR OWN OBJECTIVES

Before planning assessment and, in fact, before teaching, it is very helpful to have a clearly stated set of objectives. Of course, we need objectives for purposes of assessment. The objectives will determine what we assess. More importantly, the objectives help to focus the instructional program. They indicate what to emphasize, how to allocate time, and so on. Every major educational enterprise should begin with a set of objectives in mind. It is best to record the objectives formally. Some might go further and say that any undertaking—for example, a club or a business—should begin with a clear statement of objectives. In formulating a set of educational objectives, there are several guidelines that will prove useful. We suggest the following guidelines.

1. Distinguish carefully between instructional processes and student learning objectives. The goal is to state learning objectives: what students should know or be able to do. When first starting to develop objectives, many people tend to concentrate on processes rather than on outcomes. The processes may describe what a teacher will do or what steps students must take. Here are examples of instructional processes:

- Present the material on historical trends.
- Show students how to dissect a frog.
- Have students give a speech.
- Students will complete homework assignment on a daily news topic.

All of these activities may be important. However, they are not learning outcomes. They are means to an end. What learning should occur as a result of these activities? What should students learn from the dissection demonstration? Should they learn to describe the procedure? Or actually do the procedure? What learning should occur as a result of following daily news? Should students learn the facts of the news? Or learn to critique the news? Or learn to write their own news reports? The focus of an instructional objective must be on what students are supposed to learn, not on the means for accomplishing that learning.

2. Try to strike the right balance between generality and specificity in the statement of the objective. This guideline is difficult to achieve. It takes practice to get it right. An overly general statement gives insufficient guidance for instructional purposes. It is also difficult to assess. Here are examples of objectives that are too general:

- To be a good reader
- To know algebra
- To enjoy science

On the other hand, overly specific statements become unmanageable. The teacher becomes overwhelmed with the number of such statements. Record keeping becomes impossible. For example, making separate statements about each addition number fact ($2+2$, $2+3$, $2+4$, etc.) is silly. Making separate statements about every principle in science, every fact or trend in history, or every word analysis skill is not helpful.

The total number of objectives pursued in one content area for one group of students during one marking period should be manageable. Perhaps a handful to a couple dozen objectives might be right. Does that sound vague? It is—deliberately so. There is no magic number. However, it gives some idea of what people have found reasonable.

3. Use specific, action-oriented words to describe the objective. Words such as list, identify, outline, perform, and complete are useful. Words such as understand, know, and comprehend are less desirable. Figure 6.3 contains a list of action words you may find helpful. Of course, the English language contains thousands of action words; these are only examples. Specific, action-oriented words will help focus your instruction. They will also facilitate preparing assessments.

Try This!

Try to add two more action-oriented verbs to the list in Figure 6.3.

Analyze	Estimate	Recommend
Calculate	Evaluate	Relate
Classify	Explain	Show
Compare	Identify	Solve
Compose	Illustrate	Specify
Contrast	Indicate	Spell
Describe	List	State
Differentiate	Name	Summarize
Distinguish	Point to	Translate
Draw	Predict	Write

Figure 6.3 Examples of action-oriented verbs for use in objectives.

4. Articulate your objectives with external sources when appropriate. Application of this suggestion will vary considerably with subject areas and grade levels. For some subjects and grades, external sources (e.g., state standards) will largely dictate the objectives. In other cases, external sources will supply some useful guidance but will not completely determine the objectives. In still other cases, no external sources are relevant. The individual teacher, with advice from local curriculum specialists and school administrators, needs to sort this out.

5. Never omit an objective because it seems difficult or impossible to assess. We will eventually use the objectives as a basis for assessment. Proceed to state the objective. Include it in the instructional program. It is no less important because its assessment seems elusive. Chances are that after awhile you will figure out some relevant assessment.

6. Be realistic. We want students to learn everything and to do so at a high level of proficiency. These are admirable goals. They are also recipes for frustration, for both teachers and students. Be realistic when establishing the number of objectives and the desired levels of proficiency. Knowing what is realistic requires experience with the content and students. This experience may lead to revisions in the statement of objectives. This guideline is not an invitation to set low standards. It is just what it says: Be realistic.

Remember this guideline when examining objectives from external sources. Some external sources issue objectives that are aspirations rather than realistic targets. Some sources develop objectives that sound great for purposes of public relations but are quite unrealistic for actual student accomplishment.

7. Periodically review your objectives. As you pursue them in your instructional program, you will almost certainly find ways to sharpen the statements, add new ones, and delete old (or poorly expressed) objectives. Developing the initial list of objectives will require significant time. Thereafter, only a little time is needed to revise—but it does take some time.

8. Share the statements of objectives with students, parents, and colleagues. The objectives will help focus students' attention. This may not be helpful in the primary and preprimary grades. However, it is certainly helpful beginning in the middle grades. Parents, at all

| KEY POINTS SUMMARY 6.2 | *Guidelines for Preparing Your Own Objectives* |

Distinguish between processes and objectives.

Strike the right balance between generality and specificity.

Use specific, action-oriented words.

Articulate your objectives with external sources.

Never omit an objective because it seems difficult or impossible to assess.

Be realistic.

Periodically review your objectives.

Share the statements of objectives with students, parents, and colleagues.

levels, may lend a hand in moving toward accomplishment of the objectives, for example, by helping with homework assignments. In any case, parents will appreciate knowing the objectives. Colleagues may have helpful suggestions about your objectives. Colleagues may also have some objectives that overlap with yours.

For additional discussion of the process of preparing instructional objectives, you should consult two classic references. The first is Mager's (1984) *Preparing Instructional Objectives*. The second is Gronlund's (2000) *How to Write and Use Instructional Objectives*. Both are rather short books—each about 125 pages. Both have been extensively used by educators for many years. Both contain much practical advice and numerous examples related to preparing instructional objectives.

THE OVERALL ASSESSMENT PLAN

Before you prepare a specific test or assessment, prepare an overall assessment plan. The plan deals with such matters as the frequency of assessment, the general approach, and so on. Prepare this plan early in the year or marking period. The plan should cover the following points.

First, indicate the *purposes* of different elements in the plan. See Chapter 1 for a review of the various purposes of assessment. Some assessments may aim primarily at grading students. These elements will enter into students' grades at the end of the period or year. Other elements may not aim at grading. They may be strictly motivational. Or, they may be strictly formative; that is, to give you information about how to proceed with instruction. Some of the activities may be designed mainly to promote student self-assessment. Clearly identify the purpose for each element in the plan.

Second, decide on the *frequency* of assessments. Of course, this book is about assessment, so we are preoccupied with this topic. But, frankly, most of a teacher's time is devoted to activities other than assessment. Nevertheless, assessment must fit into the picture periodically. So, schedule it. As a general rule, more frequent is better than less frequent for two reasons. First, more frequent assessment will enhance reliability. Second, there is evidence that more frequent assessment promotes student learning (Black & William, 1998a, 1998b). Of course, the definition of "more frequent" requires prudence. One reason for more frequent assessment is that, as a practical matter, assessment does capture students' attention. Periodic assessment helps to keep students on task.

Third, consider the *schedule* for assessments. This point takes into account several practical matters. Do not schedule one of your own assessments at the same time as an external assessment (e.g., a state-mandated test). Do not schedule your assessment on the day before or after a major holiday. Some parents pull their children out of school on those days for family vacations. Students have little or no control over such family plans. Be sure to leave enough time to complete instruction on a topic before assessing students' grasp of the material. The last minute rush to cover a ton of material does not promote student learning, and it irritates the daylights out of students. If you are testing at the end of a marking period, be sure to allow sufficient time to score the test, enter the scores in your gradebook, and determine the grade for the report card. It always takes longer than you think it will!

Fourth, plan for the *right mix of types of assessments*. The types include objective (selected-response) and performance (constructed-response) assessments. We explore each of these types in detail in the next two chapters. Thus, to some extent, you cannot do this type of planning yet. However, we outlined these types of assessments generally in Chapter 1. Objective assessments include such items as multiple choice, true-false, and matching. Performance assessments include essays, projects, portfolios, and so on. Your overall plan should probably include a mixture of these types of assessments.

Fifth, for important assessments that will affect students' grades, plan to *revise your assessments periodically*. Using exactly the same assessment repeatedly is an invitation to cheating, at least from the middle grades upward. We will examine the matter of cheating in more detail in Chapter 10. For now, we simply note the importance of periodic revision.

Finally, decide about use of *textbook-based tests*. These days, almost all textbooks come with a set of test items. Sometimes these are built into the text. In other cases, the test items are supplied only to the teacher. Decide to what extent you will use these materials. To make this decision, you need to examine the test items or other assessments. Do not assume that they are valid just because they come with the text. Very often the items are not prepared by the persons who developed the text. Even if the authors of the text developed the items, the items may not be any good. You need to examine the test items on your own to make a judgment. Of course, they may be excellent, in which case you save a lot of time by using them.

"Class, I've got a lot of material to cover, so to save time I won't be using vowels today. Nw lts bgn, pls trn t pg 122."

Figure 6.4 Finish instruction before you test.

(With permission of Randy Glasbergen. Copyright 1997 Randy Glasbergen.)

PLANNING A SPECIFIC ASSESSMENT

With an overall plan in mind, you can plan for a specific assessment. As noted earlier, the next two chapters provide detailed advice on preparing objective items and performance assessments. However, there are several general guidelines that transcend the specific item types.

The first crucial step is to *prepare the test **blueprint***. Blueprint is the semitechnical term for the outline of intended test content. Another name for it is the **table of specifications**. The blueprint reflects the learning objectives. If you have developed a good set of objectives, preparing the blueprint is easy.

Some teachers use a one-way blueprint. This is a simple listing of the learning objectives. Table 6.9 shows a one-way blueprint for a unit on geometry and measurement. The left side of the table lists an abbreviated statement of objectives. Next to each objective is the percentage of the test content, reflecting emphases in the unit.

Some teachers prefer a two-way blueprint. The two-way blueprint uses a list of content objectives crossed with some form of taxonomy. Table 6.10 shows a two-way blueprint, using a reduced Bloom-like set of processes. Entries in the body of the table show the percentage of test content devoted to each cell.

Second, decide the *length of the assessment*. For objective items (e.g., multiple choice), length is defined in terms of number of items. Will the test contain 20 items? 40 items? 60 items? In general, the more items, the more reliable the test will be. Of course, there are practical limits. The test must ordinarily occur within one class period. Let's work with a 40-minute period. Allow about 5 minutes for distributing materials, another 5 minutes for collecting materials. That leaves about 30 minutes for actually completing the test.

How many objective items can students complete in 30 minutes? The usual rule of thumb is one item per minute. Of course, there is variation around this rule, depending on the nature of the items. Some very simple items require only one minute for every two items. Other items—for example, those requiring reading a passage or doing calculations—may require more than one minute per item. Experience will provide guidance. In advance of experience, use the one-item-per-minute rule.

How many constructed-response items can students complete in 30 minutes? It is difficult to give a rule here. In most instances, constructed-response items will require more time per item than will selected-response items. Even short essays may require 5 to 10 minutes per item. At that rate, students will complete only 3 to 6 items in a 30-minute period. Some-

Table 6.9   A One-Way Test Blueprint for a Unit on Geometry and Measurement

Objective	% of Test Content
Plane shapes	10
Comparing lengths	25
Using a ruler	20
Nonstandard measures	20
Metric units	10
Everyday problems	15

Table 6.10 A Two-Way Test Blueprint for a Unit on Geometry and Measurement

Objective	% of Test Content		
	Facts	Principles	Applications
Plane shapes	10	—	—
Comparing lengths	10	15	—
Using a ruler	5	5	5
Nonstandard measures	—	10	10
Metric units	5	—	10
Everyday problems	—		15

times one constructed-response item will require 30 minutes. That is not a recommended type of item. Generally, it will provide very little content reliability. In addition, one misunderstanding on the student's part can spell disaster. The teacher must plan carefully to adjust the number of constructed-response items to the testing time available.

Try This!

Think of the last test you took in any course. If it had objective-type items, how many were there and how long did it take to complete them? If it had essay items, how many were there and how long did it take to complete them?

To get reliable information, you need a test of adequate length. That doesn't mean the test needs to occur all at once. Four 10-item quizzes are equivalent to one 40-item test. Four short essays distributed over two weeks are equivalent to one period-length essay exam. Thus, seeking the right length becomes integrated with the matter of frequency of assessment.

Third, allow sufficient *time to prepare* the assessment. Last-minute planning is a recipe for a botched job. This guideline is particularly important for novice teachers. The first year or two of teaching (or teaching a new subject area) will require extra time. After some experience, specific tests and other assignments can be recycled with some revision.

Fourth, decide in advance *how to score* the assessment. This is relatively easy for objective items. The score is the number correct. It is much more complex for performance assessments. In Chapter 8 we examine methods for scoring performance assessments. Select one of these methods at the time the assessment is prepared. The scoring method may influence how the assessment is presented to students.

Finally, decide in advance the *method for providing feedback*. Will students simply see their grade? Will you return the entire test and go over the results? Will you show the distribution of scores for the class? It is best to decide these matters at the time the assessment is prepared. Research suggests two general rules for providing feedback (Black & William, 1998a, 1998b). First, the sooner it is provided, the better. Second, the feedback should be tied as closely as possible to the learning objectives. Thus, the test blueprint is important not only when preparing the assessment but also when providing feedback.

KEY POINTS SUMMARY 6.3

Factors to Consider for an Overall Assessment Plan	*Factors to Consider for a Single Assessment*
Indicate the purposes of the assessments.	Prepare a test blueprint.
Decide on the frequency of assessments.	Decide on length.
Consider the schedule for assessments.	Allow time for preparing.
Plan for the right mix of types of assessments.	Plan for scoring.
Revise your assessments periodically.	Consider method of feedback.
Decide about use of textbook-based tests.	

PRACTICAL ADVICE

1. Get your instructional objectives clearly identified. Where appropriate, consult the objectives from relevant professional organizations, your state, or textbook. Where these sources are not relevant, use the guidelines on pages 143–146 to construct your own objectives.

2. When using an externally prepared assessment, be sure to check how the assessment aligns with the relevant objectives. These objectives may be your own or those from another source.

3. Construct an overall plan for assessment. The plan should reflect the guidelines on pages 146–147. Prepare this plan early in the year or marking period.

4. When planning your own assessment, remember to use what you learned in Chapters 3–5 about reliability, validity, and interpreting student performance. Most importantly, become proficient in preparing a test blueprint.

5. At least some of your assessments will be used to assign grades to students. Therefore, as part of your preliminary planning, you may want to peek at Chapter 13. Points made in Chapter 13 are relevant for your planning.

SUMMARY

1. Good planning for assessment starts with clear specification of objectives. We distinguish between the general goals of education, which are established by society, and specific learning objectives. Assessments aim at these specific objectives, within the framework of the general goals.

2. Many discussions of objectives incorporate a consideration of an educational taxonomy. A cognitive taxonomy usually focuses on mental operations, ranging from simple mental functions like recall to more complex forms of thinking. Bloom's cognitive taxonomy is the classic case. There are many alternatives. The taxonomies help us think about the range of objectives we pursue. However, we should not take any taxonomy too literally.

3. In addition to cognitive taxonomies, there are oft-cited taxonomies in the affective and psychomotor domains. They are not as widely used as the cognitive taxonomies, but they are useful reminders about other areas of student development.

4. There are several sources for specific educational objectives. Chief among them are professional organizations, states, large assessment projects such as NAEP and TIMSS, textbooks, and individual school districts. Teachers also prepare their own objectives.

5. We offered eight suggestions for preparing your own objectives. See the Key Points Summary 6.2 on page 146 for a list of suggestions.

6. Before preparing a particular assessment, prepare an overall assessment plan for the year or marking period. The plan should address these issues: purposes, frequency, schedule, mix of types of assessments, periodic revision, and possible use of textbook-based tests.

7. Considerations for preparing a particular assessment include making the test blueprint, deciding on appropriate length, allowing time to prepare, planning for scoring, and considering the method of feedback to students.

KEY TERMS

affective domain	cognitive domain	metacognition	table of specifications
Bloom's taxonomy	content standards	objectives	taxonomy
blueprint	goals	psychomotor domain	

EXERCISES

1. Look at Figure 6.2. What divisions would you make along this continuum to indicate levels of thinking?

2. Compare the six categories in Bloom's cognitive taxonomy (Table 6.1) with the levels of mental processing in Table 6.4 and the cognitive process dimension in Table 6.5. What similarities and differences do you observe?

3. Access the website for one of the professional organizations listed in Table 6.6. Examine the objectives listed for one grade.

   a. What structure is used to present the objectives?

   b. For the objectives stated, can you determine appropriate assessments?

   c. Does the source list any expectations for student performance?

4. Select a content area and grade you might teach, for example, math in Grade 2 or American history in Grade 10. Create an *overall assessment plan* for a marking period. The plan should cover these elements:

   a. Purposes of various assessments

   b. Frequency of assessments

   c. Schedule for assessments

   d. Mix of types of assessments

   e. Periodic revisions

   f. Possible use of textbook-based assessment materials

5. Select a content area and grade you might teach, for example, math in Grade 2 or American history in Grade 10. Create a *plan for a specific assessment*, for example, a single test or performance assessment. List your decisions on these matters:

   a. What the test blueprint will look like

   b. Length of the assessment

   c. How much time you need to prepare it

   d. How you will score it

   e. The method of feedback to students.

6. For the content area selected for Exercise 4 or 5, list at least two affective or noncognitive objectives you might pursue for that area. Reference to Table 6.2 and Figure 6.1 might be helpful in completing this exercise.

7. Access the website for your state, as given in Appendix E. Pick a content area and grade level (e.g., math, Grade 5). Examine the objectives.

   a. Do the objectives seem clear to you?

   b. Can you determine appropriate assessments for the objectives?

   c. Does the site cross-reference the objectives to state test items?

   d. Does the range of objectives seem realistic?

8. Access the website for NAEP (www.nces.gov/nationsreportcard). Pick one content area. Examine the content outline (often called the framework) for that area.

   a. What structure is used for the outline?

   b. Is there a Bloom-like dimension?

   c. How does the content outline cross-reference to assessment items?

Chapter 7

Selected-Response Items:
Multiple Choice, True-False,
and Matching

OBJECTIVES

- Identify common terms used to describe selected-response and constructed-response items.
- Compare the advantages and disadvantages of selected-response and constructed-response items.
- List the main types of selected-response items.
- Use the recommendations for constructing the following types of selected-response items:
  - Multiple choice
  - True-false
  - Matching
- Show how to analyze the effect of guessing on selected-response items.

What This Chapter Is About

This chapter covers what we call selected-response items. It introduces the terms commonly used to describe various types of test items and discusses the distinction between selected-response and constructed-response items, including alternative terms. Most of the chapter deals with recommendations for constructing objective, selected-response items, including multiple-choice, true-false, and matching items. The chapter identifies advantages and disadvantages of various selected-response items.

Why This Topic Is Important

At some time, almost every teacher will develop objective, selected-response items. It takes skill and practice to do a good job developing them. In addition, at one time or another, most teachers will evaluate the quality of selected-response items in existing tests (e.g., in state assessments). Therefore, it is important to learn what experts have to say about this skill. Also, in the world of educational assessment, every teacher will hear about the advantages and disadvantages of selected-response and constructed-response items. It is important to become familiar with what research has to say about this topic.

TYPES OF TEST ITEMS: CATEGORIES AND TERMS

Any test or assessment may be thought of as a set of items. In the world of educational assessment, an **item** is simply the task to which a student responds or on which an observation is made. The task may be a simple question—such as, "How much is 4×7"—or a command—such as, "Spell reliability." The task may be more complicated—for example, "Write an essay on the causes of the U.S. Civil War," or "Perform an experiment to show the effect of heat on the expansion of a gas."

It is customary to categorize test items into two broad groups. The most formal titles for the groups are selected-response and constructed-response items. These terms are nicely descriptive, although they relate only to the method of responding. The **selected-response (SR) item** presents the student with several alternatives. The student selects an answer from among the alternatives presented. The **constructed-response (CR) item** does not present any alternative answers. Rather, the student constructs a response "from scratch," although directions for the item should indicate something about what is expected (e.g., write an essay, give a speech, or perform an experiment).

There are some other terms for the selected-response and constructed-response categories. A common alternative term for selected-response is "objective." An **objective item** is one that can be scored objectively; that is, by a clerk or a machine. In this usage, the term "objective" does not imply that the content of the item is objective. The term refers only to the scoring of the item. Some sources use the term **multiple-choice (MC) item** for all types of selected-response items. Other sources distinguish among various types of multiple-choice items. True-false and matching items are two subcategories under multiple-choice items. We examine these distinctions later in this chapter.

A common alternate term for constructed response is free response. In a **free-response item**, the student is free to respond in whatever way seems appropriate. Of course, the item must give some indication about how to proceed. Especially in the older professional literature, the contrast for objective items was **essay items**. As described more fully in the next chapter, the term "essay" can have two rather different meanings. In one use, the essay serves primarily to assess writing skill. In another use, the essay serves to assess knowledge of a topic (e.g., a period of history or a literary genre). Yet another term used as a contrast for objective items is **performance assessment**. In its ordinary use within education, performance assessment implies doing something, especially something that results in an observable product. For example, a performance assessment might involve completing a science experiment, delivering a speech, or writing a poem.

This chapter concentrates exclusively on objective, selected-response items. There are several subcategories. We will examine each. For each one, we give examples and offer suggestions for writing the item. The next chapter deals with constructed-response items.

KEY POINTS SUMMARY 7.1	*Terms for Types of Test Items*

Selected response (SR), objective, multiple choice

Constructed response (CR), free response, essay, performance

COMPARISON OF SELECTED-RESPONSE AND CONSTRUCTED-RESPONSE ITEMS

One of the most persistent, nagging issues in educational assessment concerns the relative merits of SR and CR approaches to assessment. The topic receives attention in almost any discussion of assessment from the classroom to the state, national, and international levels. Therefore, before beginning treatment of SR items in this chapter and then CR items in the next chapter, let us face this issue squarely. What can we say about the relative merits of SR and CR items? Facing the question now should help to clarify points we will make regarding uses of SR and CR items. SR and CR items may be compared along several dimensions. On some dimensions, the differences are quite clear. On other dimensions, the differences are less clear.

Reliability.   Tests composed of SR items are generally more reliable than tests composed of CR items. There are two reasons for this result. First, scorer reliability is usually a significant problem for CR items. For example, scores assigned to essays may vary noticeably from one rater to another. In contrast, scorer reliability is nearly perfect for SR items. Different teachers scoring a 30-item multiple-choice test will usually arrive at exactly the same scores. Second, the SR format usually allows more coverage per unit of testing time than does the CR format. For example, in a 30-minute period, a test may include 40 SR items. In contrast, the 30-minute period might allow only three CR items (say, essays). Recall from Chapter 3 on reliability: In general, the more items, the greater the reliability.

Time to Prepare.   CR items generally require less time to prepare than do SR items, per unit of testing time. Using the example just mentioned, it would require several hours, perhaps as much as 10 hours, to prepare 40 SR items. (This time may be reduced substantially if the SR items are drawn from an existing item bank, such as one accompanying a textbook.) It may require only 10 minutes to prepare three CR items. This difference in time can be deceptive. Part of preparing CR items involves developing scoring criteria. (We explore this topic in detail in the next chapter.) This requires careful thought—which requires time. On the other hand, carefully prepared scoring criteria may not be needed for some purposes. See the following discussion of flexibility on this point.

Time to Score.   In terms of scoring time, the advantage clearly goes to the SR format. Scoring CR items generally requires a substantial investment of time. Time to score SR items is usually minimal.

Flexibility.   Flexibility refers to ease of adapting the format to a wide variety of purposes and circumstances. CR items generally have greater flexibility or adaptability than do SR items. For example, if a teacher simply wants a quick assessment of students' general understanding of or interest in a topic, the CR approach will be more convenient to use. If a teacher is uncertain about exactly how to assess certain objectives, CR items may offer better possibilities.

Cost.   It is easy to compare the costs of SR and CR tests for external testing programs. Clearly for such programs, CR testing is more expensive, often dramatically so, due to the cost of human scoring. Calculating costs of SR testing and CR testing at the classroom level is difficult. How do we allocate costs for the teacher's time? If we do not ascribe any cost for a teacher's time, then SR testing and CR testing are approximately equal in cost. If we do ascribe cost for the teacher's time, then we have to "amortize" the time for preparing SR items over possible multiple uses of those items. Time for scoring CR items accumulates with each testing. Similar to the costs for CR items in external testing programs, costs for CR items in classroom testing can be substantial if we ascribe costs to teacher time.

Student Reactions.   There are two questions in this category. First, do students prefer SR or CR items? Second, do students study differently for SR versus CR tests? Researchers have attacked both questions. Unfortunately, the answers are not clear. Some studies suggest that students prefer SR items. Other studies suggest the opposite. The real answer is probably: It depends. That is, it depends on which particular test is referenced, how well developed it is, and what its purpose is. Regarding the effect of using one type of test or the other, the research is similarly mixed. Some studies suggest a differential effect. Other studies contradict this result. Altogether, this matter of student reactions needs considerably more research before we have clear answers. Meanwhile, beware of broad pronouncements that either type of item has a clear effect in terms of student preferences or study habits. For some of the research on these matters, see Bennett and Ward (1993), Hogan (1981), Mehrens (2002), and Snow (1993).

Validity.   As with most topics in educational assessment, validity is the key issue for the comparison of SR and CR items. Here we ask two related questions. Do CR and SR items measure anything different? If so, what is the difference? Let's begin by illustrating how to study such questions. A typical study investigating the comparative validity of SR and CR items would involve administering a test of each type to the same students. Suppose we examine students' knowledge of American history. Compose one test entirely of essays on American history. Compose another test entirely of MC items. Administer both tests to the students and determine the correlation between their scores.

There have been many studies such as the one just described, covering a wide range of subject matter and types of students. The most typical result is that the CR and SR scores are almost perfectly correlated (after making the appropriate correction for less-than-perfect reliability in the measures). In most instances, the correlation between CR and SR tests is about the same as the correlation between two different versions of a CR test or two different versions of an SR test. Other designs for studying the comparative validity of SR and CR tests tend to yield similar results. For summaries of the research on SR versus CR items, see Hogan (1981), Rodriguez (2002, 2003), and Traub (1993). Rodriguez (2002, p. 214) gives this succinct answer: "Do multiple-choice (MC) items and constructed-response (CR) items measure the same cognitive behavior? The quick answer is: They do if we write them to do so."

These results seem very surprising. Most people think that CR and SR items "get at" different kinds of understanding or mental processes. Reference is often made to the difference between recall (tapped by CR items) and recognition (tapped by SR items). In fact, the presumed superiority of CR items to measure higher mental processes is repeated like a mantra in many educational circles. According to the results of the many research studies on this matter, for testing knowledge in typical school subjects, the SR and CR formats seem to function equivalently. In an earlier chapter, we referred to the lack of solid evidence in favor of the distinctions made in taxonomies of mental processes (see p. 138). That finding may be related to the lack of difference between measures resulting from SR and CR items. Perhaps there are no major differences in mental processes for the two types of items to measure, despite the face validity of the taxonomies.

There are several qualifications to add to the generalization about the approximate equivalence of SR and CR items. First, some studies or parts of studies have detected minor differences in the measurements provided by CR and SR items. However, the differences tend to be quite small. Second, where differences are detected, the origin or explanation for the differences is not clear. That is, it is not possible to say that either the CR or the SR format is superior because the difference results from a particular factor. Third, there is some evidence that less able students may be disadvantaged by the more complex structure and more ambiguous demands of some CR items (Snow, 1993). Also, boys may be disadvantaged when responses to CR items depend, irrelevantly, on writing skill (Bennett, 1993; Ryan & DeMark, 2002). Fifth, the generalization about approximate equivalence of SR and CR items does not apply to the measurement of pure writing skill; this skill requires separate attention in the discussion. Finally, it is likely that what is being measured with either the SR or the CR item depends on the instructional program. For example, an essay (CR) question may ask students about causes of the U.S. Civil War. One teacher may have given students a list of exactly four causes and told them to memorize the list. Another teacher may have only generally discussed the causes. The essay question probably functions somewhat differently for these two groups of students.

Conclusions.   From all of the foregoing discussion, what can we conclude? We can make several points. First and perhaps foremost, the teacher should develop skill in the use of both SR and CR items. Both types will be useful in one context or another. Second, when using either type of item, the teacher should be aware of the relative strengths and weaknesses of each type. Third, the teacher should not gullibly accept the rhetoric about one type of item measuring one (or a few) mental processes and the other type of item measuring other mental processes. The research does not support that distinction. Fourth, to cover all bets, it may be best to use a combination of CR and SR items. They may be mixed in a single assessment or used at different times during a marking period.

KEY POINTS SUMMARY 7.2	*Bases for Comparing SR and CR Items*
Reliability	Cost
Time to prepare	Student reactions
Time to score	Validity
Flexibility	

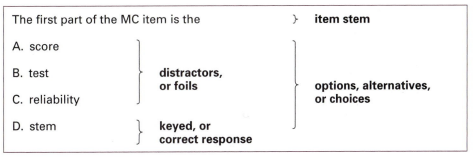

Figure 7.1 Terms for parts of a multiple-choice item.

MULTIPLE-CHOICE ITEMS

Among selected-response items, the multiple-choice (MC) item is easily the most widely used. It is the most popular format for all types of standardized tests as well as for many teacher-made tests. Because of its popularity, the terminology applicable to MC items often carries over to other types of items. Further, the MC item has been the subject of a considerable amount of research. For all these reasons, it is a good one to treat first.

Figure 7.1 identifies the terms used to describe parts of the MC item. The first part is the **item stem**. It can be a question or an incomplete statement. In Figure 7.1, the item stem is an incomplete statement. However, it could easily be a question: What is the first part of an MC item? The essence of the MC item is the set of **alternatives** following the item stem. These are the "multiple choices" from which the student selects. One of the alternatives is the correct, or "keyed," response. That is, the answer key shows this as the correct or preferred response. The other alternatives are called **distractors**,[1] or **foils**, a quaint, old-fashioned term. Obviously, these are the incorrect or nonpreferred answers. Figure 7.2 includes a variety of MC items, illustrating minor variations in the format of the stem and alternatives.

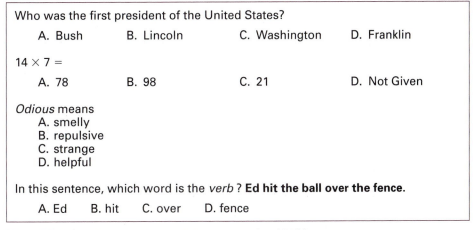

Figure 7.2 Examples of simple, stand-alone, conventional MC items.

---

[1] Dictionaries generally give "distracter" as the correct spelling of this word. For some reason, the testing literature prefers "distractor." We will follow that tradition and disregard the repeated spell-check warnings.

Most MC items fall into the category variously described as simple, stand-alone, or conventional MC items. In this category, each item (stem and alternatives) stands on its own. The examples in Figure 7.2 illustrate this conventional category. For some items, the item stem can be very short, (e.g., *14 × 7 = ___* or *Odious* means ___). More typically, the stem is a brief question or an incomplete statement; the stem may also be longer (e.g., several sentences).

Sometimes MC items come in a group, centered on a single stimulus, such as a paragraph, poem, chart, map, or other object. Then, each item stem uses that object. Various sources call the group of items a testlet, an item set, context-dependent items, or an interpretive exercise. The most common application for this type of item is a reading comprehension exercise. The test presents a paragraph (or other reading passage, even an entire book). The student answers a set of questions about the passage. A typical reading comprehension test will have several paragraphs, each followed by several items. However, the same technique may be used with a wide variety of other applications. Figure 7.3 shows an application with a poem. Figure 7.4 uses a chart as the item stem, followed by three items based on the chart.

Most MC items have either four or five alternatives. There can be as few as two alternatives or as many as the item writer wishes, but it is rare to have more than five alternatives. In the typical application, there is one right answer. However, there are some (rarely used) other possibilities. For example, the student may mark a first choice, a second choice, and so on for as many alternatives as there are. Then, points are awarded for how closely the student's choices match a preferred pattern of answers. Or the student may cross off answers that are certainly wrong (e.g., two of the four choices), leaving unmarked those of uncertain status. We do not recommend such variations for routine use by the novice item writer. They are better left to people with much experience in item writing and for research applications.

In addition to the two types of MC items presented here—the conventional and the item set—there are numerous other variations. We will not list them. Some of them are interesting, but none of them are widely used. Especially for the novice item writer, the two

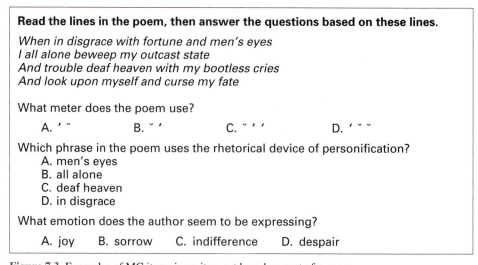

Figure 7.3 Examples of MC items in an item set based on part of a poem.

Use this chart to answer the questions below it.

State	Population 2000 (in millions)	Population Change % (1990–2000)	Land Area Square Miles (in 1000s)
California	34	14	156
New York	19	6	47
Pennsylvania	12	3	45
Texas	21	23	262

Which of these states showed the greatest change in population from 1990 to 2000?

   A. California   B. New York   C. Pennsylvania   D. Texas

Which of these states has the greatest population density?

   A. California   B. New York   C. Pennsylvania   D. Texas

If populations continue to increase at the rate shown for 1990–2000, which would be a good estimate of the population (in millions) for Pennsylvania in 2010?

   A. 9   B. 13   C. 15   D. 36

Figure 7.4 Examples of MC items in an item set based on a table of information.

types we have presented are quite sufficient. The student interested in other variations may consult Gronlund (1993) and Haladyna (2004).

Try This!

Here is another item stem for Figure 7.4.

Write four options to make an MC item.

Stem: Which is the best estimate of the population of Texas in 1990?

Options: A. _____   B. _____   C. _____   D. _____

SUGGESTIONS FOR WRITING MC ITEMS

Every educational assessment textbook includes a list of recommendations for writing MC items. They come under such titles as rules, guidelines, suggestions, or "do and don't" lists. For simplicity, we will call them rules, although they should not be adhered to rigidly. The rules have accumulated over time from test writers' experiences, wisdom, and common sense, and—to a certain extent—research on the effects of various formats.

Professor Thomas Haladyna and his colleagues have provided a great service by compiling all these rules and summarizing the research related to them. Their first sum-

Table 7.1   Haladyna's Taxonomy of Multiple-Choice Item-Writing Guidelines

Content concerns

1. **Every item should reflect specific content and a single specific mental behavior, as called for in test specifications (two-way grid, test blueprint).**
2. **Base each item on important content to learn; avoid trivial content.**
3. **Use novel material to test higher level learning. Paraphrase textbook language or language used during instruction when used in a test item to avoid testing for simply recall.**
4. Keep the content of each item independent from content of other items on the test.
5. Avoid over specific and over general content when writing MC items.
6. **Avoid opinion-based items.**
7. **Avoid trick items.**
8. **Keep vocabulary simple for the group of students being tested.**

Formatting concerns

9. Use the question, completion, and best answer versions of the conventional MC, the alternate choice, true-false (TF), multiple true-false (MTF), matching, and the context-dependent item and item set formats, but AVOID the complex MC (Type K) format.
10. Format the item vertically instead of horizontally.

Style concerns

11. Edit and proof items.
12. **Use correct grammar, punctuation, capitalization, and spelling.**
13. **Minimize the amount of reading in each item.**

Writing the stem

14. **Ensure that the directions in the stem are very clear.**
15. **Include the central idea in the stem instead of in the choices.**

(continued)

maries, based on analysis of 46 textbooks and 93 empirical studies, appeared in two articles in 1989 (Haladyna & Downing, 1989a, 1989b). These articles were followed by a book-length treatment of the topic in 1994, updated with revised editions in 1999 and 2004 (Haladyna, 1994, 1999b, 2004). Haladyna, Downing, and Rodriguez (2002) produced a refined list of guidelines based on a new analysis of 27 textbooks and 27 research studies published since the 1989 summaries. We could hardly do better than to present their excellent summary of recommendations for writing MC items. We mention the other references because the list of rules has changed somewhat through the different publications. The reader may encounter citations to these other works and wonder why one list differs from the one presented next.

Table 7.1 presents Haladyna's 2002 summary. There are 31 "rules," 36 if you count the subpoints contained in Rule 28. Rules appearing in boldface type were favorably endorsed in more than half of the 27 textbooks analyzed. Most of the rules are self-explanatory. Thus, we need not comment on each one. Some are just plain common sense, such as Rule 11.

Table 7.1 (continued)

16. **Avoid window dressing (excessive verbiage).**
17. **Word the stem positively, avoid negatives such as NOT or EXCEPT. If negative words are used, use the word cautiously and always ensure that the word appears capitalized and boldface.**

Wording the choices

18. **Develop as many effective choices as you can, but research suggests three is adequate.**
19. **Make sure that only one of these choices is the right answer.**
20. **Vary the location of the right answer according to the number of choices.**
21. **Place choices in logical or numerical order.**
22. Keep choices independent; choices should not be overlapping.
23. **Keep choices homogeneous in content and grammatical structure.**
24. **Keep the length of choices about equal.**
25. None-of-the-above should be used carefully.
26. **Avoid All-of-the-above.**
27. **Phrase choices positively; avoid negatives such as NOT.**
28. **Avoid giving clues to the right answer, such as**
    a. **Specific determiners including always, never, completely, and absolutely.**
    b. **Clang associations, choices identical to or resembling words in the stem.**
    c. **Grammatical inconsistencies that cue the test-taker to the correct choice.**
    d. **Conspicuous correct choice.**
    e. **Pairs or triplets of options that clue the test-taker to the correct choice.**
    f. **Blatantly absurd, ridiculous options.**
29. **Make all distractors plausible.**
30. **Use typical errors of students to write your distractors.**
31. Use humor if it is compatible with the teacher and the learning environment.

Note: Entries in boldface were endorsed in more than 50% of the textbooks analyzed.

From Haladyna, T. M., Downing, S. M., & Rodriguez, M. C. (2002). A review of multiple-choice item-writing guidelines for classroom assessment. *Applied Measurement in Education, 15*, 309–334. With permission of the authors and publisher, Lawrence Erlbaum Associates.

This rule should really end with double exclamation points, as in: Edit and proof!! It is amazing how many errors simple proofreading will catch. Some of the rules partially overlap, such as Rules 8, 13, and 16. All three of these say: Keep it simple. We will comment on the more important rules as well as on the less obvious ones. The reader is encouraged to look through the entire list of rules in Table 7.1. For more detailed coverage, the reader should consult the full 2002 article or the 2004 book referenced earlier.

Content Concerns: Rules 1–8

The first group of recommendations concerns the content of the items. The essence of these recommendations is *to make sure each item covers meaningful content*. Of course, what is meaningful is a matter of judgment by the person(s) preparing the items. What is trivial or important depends very much on a teacher's specific objectives. What may be trivial in one context may be crucial in another context. Consider the first item on meter in a poem in Figure 7.3. This item may be crucial if the teacher covers types of meter, but the item would be irrelevant if meter is not an instructional objective. The content should arise from the table of specifications for the test. Notice the reference to the test blueprint in Rule 1. We covered preparation of such blueprints in the previous chapter.

Formatting Concerns: Rules 9–10

The section on formatting concerns contains only two rules. They are very different in scope. Rule 9 actually contains a host of comments, essentially approving use of several of the formats introduced in this chapter as examples of MC items. Rule 9 also recommends against using the "complex MC" item. This type of item presents a number of conditions in the item stem. Then, the alternatives are combinations of the conditions (e.g., I & II, I & III, II & IV). Rule 10 deals with the arrangement of the choices. The rule recommends starting each choice on a new line rather than listing options horizontally across the page. In Figure 7.3, the first and third items use the horizontal format for the options. The second item uses the vertical format. Research suggests that the spatial arrangement of options does not make any difference. For classroom tests, perhaps the more important suggestion is: Make the appearance neat and easy to follow.

Style Concerns: Rules 11–13

The style concerns are mostly matters of common sense. As noted earlier: Edit and proof!! Use correct English. Keep the reading simple unless, of course, you are testing reading skill. Notice that Rule 13 is similar to Rule 16. Consider the example in Figure 7.5.

In the first version of the item (I), the opening phrase is not needed. The second version (II) is much simpler and appears to get at the student's knowledge of the rule without requiring the reading of some rather long words.

Figure 7.6 presents a more egregious example of excessive wording. If the intent of the item is to determine whether a student can find the perimeter of a rectangle, version II does so with a minimum of verbiage. In fact, a student with a reading difficulty may struggle with version I not because of inability to find perimeter but because of the reading demands in version I. Notice the difference between versions II and III in Figure 7.6. If the intent is to determine whether the student knows the *concept* of perimeter, then version II is probably preferable. If the intent is to determine if the student knows the *term* "perimeter," then version III is preferable.

There is one exception to the rules about keeping the wording simple and avoiding "window dressing." If you are deliberately trying to teach students to disregard irrelevant

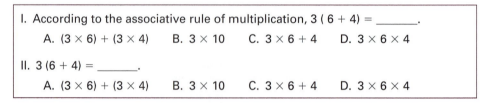

I. According to the associative rule of multiplication, 3 (6 + 4) = _____.
      A. (3 × 6) + (3 × 4)   B. 3 × 10   C. 3 × 6 + 4   D. 3 × 6 × 4

II. 3 (6 + 4) = _____.
      A. (3 × 6) + (3 × 4)   B. 3 × 10   C. 3 × 6 + 4   D. 3 × 6 × 4

Figure 7.5 An MC item with excessive wording.

I. Tracy, Juaquine, and Rus are constructing a fence around a rectangular plot with dimensions 14 feet by 26 feet. How many feet of fencing will be required to complete the project?

   A. 14 + 26   B. 2 (14 + 26)   C. 14 × 26   D. 2 × 14 × 26

II. What is the distance around a 14′ × 26′ rectangle?

   A. 14 + 26   B. 2 (14 + 26)   C. 14 × 26   D. 2 × 14 × 26

III. What is the perimeter around a 14′ × 26′ rectangle?

   A. 14 + 26   B. 2 (14 + 26)   C. 14 × 26   D. 2 × 14 × 26

Figure 7.6 Keeping the wording simple for an MC item.

information, then your item *should* include information not needed to answer the question. In that case, some of the incorrect options should incorporate the irrelevant information. In fact, the options may ask the students to identify the information *not* needed to answer the question. Figure 7.7 shows an example that does precisely this. In version I, students indicate the solution sentence, with some options incorporating the irrelevant information. In version II, students identify the irrelevant information.

Writing the Stem: Rules 14–17

Of the four rules in this category, two are particularly important. As per Rule 15, experienced item writers try to get the "meat" of the item into the stem, thus allowing the choices to be relatively short. This helps to focus the item on the intended content. It also tends to reduce ambiguity and the amount of unnecessary reading. Consider the item stems in Figure 7.8. The first one (I) has too little in the stem. The stem could be followed by an almost infinite variety of statements. The second one (II) places the central idea in

I. We are putting a fence around a rectangular field that is 14 feet by 26 feet. Fencing costs $1.69 per foot. How many feet of fencing will we need?

   A. 14 + 26 + 1.69
   B. 2 (14 + 26)
   C. 14 × 26 × 1.69
   D. 2 × 14 × 26

II. We are putting a fence around a rectangular field that is 14 feet by 26 feet. Fencing costs $1.69 per foot. How many feet of fencing will we need?

Which piece of information is NOT needed to answer the question?

   A. 14 feet
   B. 16 feet
   C. $1.69 per foot

Figure 7.7 Using irrelevant information as part of the item.

I. In a triangle—

    A. The sides are equal in length

    B. The angles are equal

    C. The angles sum to 180°

    D. The sides are always unequal in length

II. The angles in a triangle sum to _____

    A. 180°   B. 90°   C. 360°   D. 100°

Figure 7.8 Getting the central idea into the item stem.

the stem. The central idea in this item is the sum of angles in a triangle. The second stem allows for relatively brief, efficient choices. Novice item writers seem to have particular difficulty with this rule. They tend to write short stems and pack too much into the options. It takes practice to get the main item into the stem.

The second important rule (17) in this section is to avoid use of negatives in the item stem. When the examinee is trying to figure out the correct answer, the inclusion of "not" in the stem often requires thinking in terms of double negatives. That becomes a logic test rather than a test of knowledge in the subject matter of interest. Or, the student may miss the "not" when reading the item and get the whole intent of the item backwards. It is sometimes possible to write a good, simple item using "not." When that is the case, the rule sensibly recommends putting NOT in uppercase bold letters.

Writing the Choices: Rules 18–31

This section contains the largest number of rules. The first (18) is a curious one. It recommends using three options. The rationale for this is that, in most instances, you cannot think of more than two good incorrect responses. In contrast, all major test developers routinely use four or five options. Make of this discrepancy between Rule 18 and ordinary professional practice whatever you wish. The number of options depends on the content tested. Sometimes it is easy to make up good options. Sometimes it is difficult to think of more than two or three meaningful options. For simplicity of format, it is probably best to use the same number of options for all MC items in a section of a test.

Try This!

Look at the four options in Figure 7.6. Which option might be eliminated as relatively useless, leaving only three options?

Rule 20 might be made a bit more specific. Make sure the correct answer occurs in each position about equally often. The most typical way to accomplish this is to randomly assign the correct answer position. Interestingly, one study found a noticeable tendency for item writers to place the correct answer in a middle position among the available slots (Attali & Bar-Hillel, 2003). Of course, if students detect this pattern, or any other pattern, the validity of the test will be compromised. That is, to some extent the test will be measuring testwiseness rather than knowledge of the subject matter.

Rules 23 and 24 both relate to the external appearance of the choices. All the choices should have similar appearance and flow nicely from the item stem. It is especially important to ensure that the correct answer is not easily spotted just by its appearance or its compatibility with the stem. We will say more on this point in connection with Rule 28.

Students often wonder about such options as None of the Above (NOTA) and All of the Above (AOTA). Rule 25 says to use NOTA carefully. What does that mean? In practice, it means limiting this option to situations having a crystal-clear correct answer, such as arithmetic computation items or similar areas. In those situations, NOTA may be useful because it helps to reduce the effect of guessing. Otherwise, do not use NOTA. This rule includes variations in wording, such as Not Given and Not Here. If you do use NOTA as an option, make sure it is sometimes the correct answer.

Rule 26 says to avoid AOTA at all times. Of course, every student knows why: If the student can find two options that are acceptable, then the correct answer must be AOTA—even if the student has no clue about the other options. Consider the example in Figure 7.9. Few people (outside of New Hampshire) know that New Hampshire has a small border on the Atlantic Ocean. However, many people know that Florida and New Jersey have Atlantic coastal borders. Therefore, the answer must be AOTA—despite uncertainty about New Hampshire.

Rule 28 is a whopper. It actually contains six rules. However, the key idea is in the opening statement: *Avoid giving clues to the right answer.* Here is a useful question for the item writer: Could a person who knows nothing about this topic pick out the right answer just by carefully examining the item? Look at the first example in Figure 7.10. The only option that follows the stem with grammatical correctness is option D. A person who knows nothing about this topic (but does know about subject–verb agreement) would get this item correct. In the second example in Figure 7.10, the stem's wording easily gives away the correct answer (A).

Rule 30 suggests using students' common errors for distractors. This is useful not only to help in creating options but also because it may yield useful diagnostic information. That is, it may help the teacher determine students' misunderstandings. Notice the options for the second item in Figure 7.2. The first option results from a failure to "carry." The third option results from using the wrong operation, addition rather than multiplication.

Rule 31 on the use of humor is a bit odd for several reasons. First, it obviously does not fit into the category of Wording the Choices. The rule relates to the item as a whole, not just to the choices. Second, the rule is not endorsed by *any* of the textbooks analyzed by Haladyna and his colleagues. Nevertheless, it appears as one of the rules. Third, it is interesting that the authors have reversed themselves from their earlier (1989) list where

---

Which of these states borders on the Atlantic Ocean?

   A. Florida

   B. New Jersey

   C. New Hampshire

   D. All of the Above

Figure 7.9 An example of using All of the Above as an option.

Many studies of test reliability

    A. uses the method of criterion-referenced interpretation

    B. is based on incorrect assumptions

    C. yields surprisingly high results

    D. depend on use of the correlation coefficient

The consequential validity of a test refers to the _____ that may follow from using the test.

    A. consequences B. reliability C. face validity D. criterion-referencing

---

Figure 7.10 Examples of items with clues to the right answer.

the use of humor was strictly abjured. Certainly we would never expect to encounter a "funny" item in a high-stakes test, such as the SAT, Praxis, or a state minimum competency test. What about a classroom quiz? It probably depends on the teacher's personal style and relationship with students. A bit of humor might fit for some teachers, perhaps not for others. If a "fun" item is included in a test, it is probably best not to count it in the test score. For example, Mr. Atwadder (Figure 7.13) probably should not score his square root item. Presumably Mr. Atwadder would not use option C for all of his items.

Similarity of Options

Similarity of options is one other matter to consider that is not covered by any of the rules in Table 7.1. In fact, this is not a rule but rather an important point about constructing MC items. The difficulty level of an MC item depends partly on the similarity of the options. Consider the examples in Figure 7.11. In each example, version I has options that are distinctly different. Version II has options that are more similar. The degree of difference among options may be defined in a variety of ways: conceptual, numerical, chronological, and so on. For each topic in Figure 7.11, which is the better item? The answer depends on the teacher's expectations. For

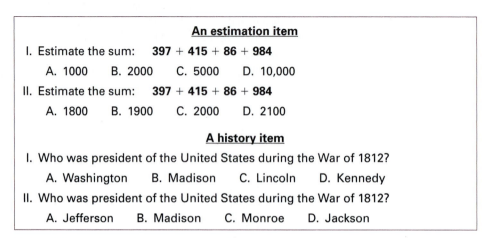

Figure 7.11 Similarity of options makes a difference.

the estimation item, the teacher may be satisfied with only the grossest estimate or the teacher may want a much more refined estimate. In the example of presidents, the teacher may want students to demonstrate a very refined knowledge of the period or only a very general knowledge of the period. The point to remember is that how a test item functions depends on all the characteristics of the item, including the degree of similarity among the options.

A Brief Summary

We are loath to present yet another list of rules for writing MC items. However, for the sake of simplicity, we suggest that the following points cover most of the numerous extant rules.

1. Get the content right.
2. Keep things simple, concentrating on what you really want to test.
3. Don't give clues to the right answer.
4. Disregard all other rules when it seems to make sense to do so.

The fourth point reminds us that the rules for item writing are not to be applied rigidly. They are helpful guidelines. Preparation of good items calls for some finesse and ingenuity, not just application of rules.

TRUE-FALSE ITEMS

The venerable true-false (TF) item is essentially a MC item with only two options: true and false. As such, it is subject to all the rules for good item writing listed earlier for MC items. For example: Cover important content, edit and proofread the items, and make sure about the correct answer.

Much of our knowledge reduces to the truth or falsity of propositions, at least when they are carefully worded. That is probably the main reason for the traditional popularity of this item format. There is also a good technical reason for the use of TF items. You can include more TF items *per unit of testing time* than any other type of item. For studies of the time requirements and reliability of TF items, especially in comparison with MC items, see Ebel and Frisbie (1991) and Frisbie (1973, 1974). In 30 minutes you may be able to cover 60 TF items but only 40 conventional MC items or only 5 short essays. Conventional MC items almost inevitably require more reading time than do TF items. Essays, of course, require much more response time. Thus, the TF format allows for covering a greater variety of topics in a given time. Figure 7.12 contains sample TF items for a unit on the Lewis and

---

Here are sample TF items for a unit on the Lewis and Clark expedition.

Mark T if the statement is true or mostly true. Mark F if the statement is false or mostly false.

T   F   The westward journey ended along the Columbia River.

T   F   Most of the journey was along the Mississippi River.

T   F   The first winter was spent with the Mandan Tribe.

T   F   Sacajawea joined the expedition at St. Louis.

Figure 7.12 Sample true-false items.

Clark expedition. Notice that the statements tend to be short. Therefore, it is possible to cover many elements of the unit in a relatively brief amount of testing time.

Try This!

Try This!
Add one more true-false item to those in Figure 7.12.

T   F   _____

The TF format has three main drawbacks. *First*, the format invites testing trivial content. The antidote for this first difficulty is, quite simply, to think carefully about the item content. As noted previously, what may be trivial in one context may be crucial in another context. The *second* difficulty is that the TF format has a special knack for inviting controversy from students. It takes only one counterexample or minor difference in interpretation to show that a statement that is almost always true (or false) is not *always* true (or false). Students delight in finding such counterexamples or variations in interpretation. To deal with this difficulty, some item writers include directions saying that T means True or Mostly True and F means False or Mostly False.

The *third* drawback for the TF item is that, one must admit, it has a terrible public image. It is a favorite target for cartoonists and comedians, as well as students. This seems to result partly from the first drawback (a tendency to test trivial content) but more so from people's opinion about guessing. People believe it is easy to get a good score on a TF test merely by guessing. It is *not* easy to get a good score on a TF or any MC test just by guessing, provided there are enough items in the test. We show how to analyze the effect of guessing later in this chapter. Nevertheless, people's belief on this point is strongly held and often expressed.

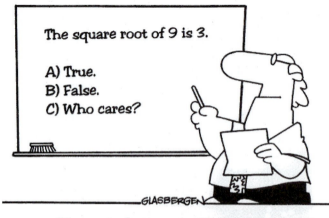

Many students actually look forward to Mr. Atwadder's math tests.

Figure 7.13 Mr. Atwadder's unorthodox approach to true-false items. (With permission of Randy Glasberger.)

Here are suggestions for writing TF items. Remember, too, that the rules in Table 7.1 apply to TF items.

1. Perhaps more so than for any other type of item, be sure to cover important content.

2. Use an approximately equal number of True and False statements.

3. Avoid use of NOT (or other negatives) in the statement. For the TF format, including NOT in the statement almost inevitably requires thinking in terms of double negatives. Then, the test becomes a test of logic rather than of the content you want to cover. (Of course, you can use NOT in the statements if it's a logic test.)

4. Because of the TF format's poor public image, it is probably best when using TF items to also use other types of items in the test. For example, a test might include 25 TF items, 10 MC items, and 2 short essays; or 10 TF items, 10 MC items, and 3 short essays.

5. Because guessing has a greater effect on TF items than on other types of items, be sure to use a sufficient number of items. What constitutes a "sufficient" number of items? The answer depends on the purpose of the assessment. The important point here is that when using TF items, lean toward using more rather than fewer items.

Other Binary Choice Formats

A binary choice item is one that has just two options. The TF item is the most popular binary choice item. However, there are others, indeed a potentially endless list. An obvious example is a Yes-No format. Other examples might suggest themselves for particular content areas. For example, in mathematics a binary choice is $=$ or $\neq$; another is $\leq$ or $\geq$. A common classification of literary works is fiction and nonfiction. Any such binary choice can be converted into an item. All these binary items have the same strengths and drawbacks as listed for TF items. And the same suggestions for item writing apply to them. Figure 7.14 shows binary choice items to test spelling of "ie/ei" words. Figure 7.15 shows binary items based on equalities.

MATCHING ITEMS

The matching exercise is actually a series of multiple-choice items. As with the conventional MC format, there are several alternative answers. However, there are also several stems grouped together. Figure 7.16 shows an example of a matching exercise. This example is for Items 31–34 embedded in a test. Each of Items 31–34 could serve as a stand-alone MC item with options A–E as the choices. Here, each president serves as an item stem. The list of wars provides the options.

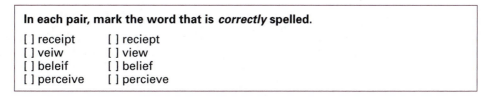

In each pair, mark the word that is *correctly* spelled.

[ ] receipt   [ ] reciept
[ ] veiw   [ ] view
[ ] beleif   [ ] belief
[ ] perceive   [ ] percieve

Figure 7.14 Example of binary item to test spelling.

In each pair, mark whether the expressions are equal ($=$) or unequal ($\neq$).			
36 + 46	=	$\neq$	**46 + 36**
49 − 18	=	$\neq$	**18 − 49**
26 × 3	=	$\neq$	**3 × 26**
98 / 4	=	$\neq$	**4 / 98**

Figure 7.15 Example of binary item to test equalities.

The matching exercise is a very efficient way to cover a lot of factual information. Obviously, the format concentrates on associations and making distinctions among similar items in a list. Much of our knowledge base involves associations in our memory banks. Think of the difficulties someone has when these associations break down (e.g., following brain injury or onset of Alzheimer's disease). Associations are important. Making appropriate distinctions among similar items is important. For this type of knowledge, the matching exercise may provide a very useful testing mechanism.

Here are suggestions for preparing matching exercises. Most of the suggestions are made so that the entire matching exercise is an efficient test of knowledge rather than a test of perceptual speed, short-term memory, or some other ability irrelevant to the test.

1. Don't make the lists too long. The student should be able to scan both lists quickly to find correct associations. If the lists are too long, the student has to waste time simply scanning up and down. If there are many associations to be covered, break them up into separate blocks of items. Note that use of a machine-scorable answer sheet imposes one practical limit on the number of options in a matching exercise. Most answer sheets allow a maximum of five choices. This fact, combined with the next recommendation, suggests having three-to-four elements as stems and four-to-five elements as options.

2. It's a good idea to have at least one more element in the list of options than in the list of stems. This helps to ensure that the last selection made involves some knowledge rather than sheer elimination.

3. Try to arrange one of the lists, either stems or options, in some natural order. The order can be alphabetical, chronological, or numerical. Other orders might suggest themselves for particular types of content. The intent of this recommendation is to make scanning the lists easier for the student.

Match the president with the war occurring while he was in office.	
President	**War**
31. Abraham Lincoln	A. Civil
32. Harry Truman	B. Persian Gulf
33. Lyndon Johnson	C. World War I
34. George Bush	D. World War II
	E. Vietnam

Figure 7.16 Example of a matching exercise.

4. Each list should be internally consistent. That is, it should contain only one type of element. For example, in Figure 7.16 you would not want a mixture of presidents and years in the left column nor a list of wars and social trends in the right column.

5. It is permissible to allow the options to be used more than once. If that is intended, the directions should clearly state it.

ALLOWING STUDENT COMMENTS

One of the great fears about all selected-response items is that a student will see something in the item that the item writer did not intend—and then get the answer wrong. Anecdotes about such occurrences abound. To deal with this difficulty, some item writers allow students to comment on the items. For example, the student may provide a rationale for the answer selected. The teacher can then evaluate the legitimacy of the rationale. Essentially, this turns the selected-response item into a constructed-response item if the student chooses to comment. Of course, this type of variation is not used for standardized tests. On those tests, you just mark an answer—and hope it's right. However, teacher-made tests permit more flexibility. A teacher may use this "comment-if-you-wish" technique. However, one must be cautious. This type of variation may compromise the efficiency and objectivity of the selected-response item. But, it is worth considering.

DEVELOPING ITEM-WRITING SKILL

Item writing is a skill. Like any skill—say, playing the piano or riding a bike—it takes practice to be good at it. You will not develop skill in playing the piano or in writing test items just by reading about it. Also, like any other skill, some people get to be very good at it while other people continue to struggle. Following the guidelines covered in this chapter will help you be successful. But you need to practice. You also need feedback. You need people to critique your work. You will not be your own best critic. You will probably think that all items you write are great. They won't be. Some of them will be awful: ambiguous, no correct answer, poor sentence structure, and so on. You need to get feedback from other professionals. And you need to accept the feedback. If someone tells you an item is rotten, don't argue about it. Change it. Also, be willing to offer constructive criticism of other people's items when you are asked to do so. The exercises at the end of this chapter will help to develop this skill.

KEY POINTS SUMMARY 7.3	*Major Types of SR Items*
Multiple choice	Other binary items
True-False	Matching

LUCKY GUESSING

A common criticism of all selected-response items is that it is easy to get a good score just by lucky guessing. For tests with decent length, this criticism is silly. It is a simple matter to show why this is so. Recall from high school algebra the binomial formula. Consider a four-choice item. The probability of getting one such item right by sheer guessing is $\frac{1}{4}$, or .25. The probability of getting two such items correct is $(.25)^2 = .0625$, three such items correct is $(.25)^3 = .016$, and so on. Suppose the test has 20 items. Using the binomial formula, you can work out the probability of getting any score just by guessing. What is the probability of getting at least 70% correct by guessing; that is, 14 or more right? The chances are 3 in 100,000. The chances of getting a good score (90% or better) by guessing on the 20-item test are less than 1 in a billion. The most likely score on this 20-item test based on guessing is 25%—hardly an enviable score.

Even on a true-false test of any decent length, it is exceedingly unlikely that a student will get a good score just by guessing. Use the same analysis as just outlined. The probability of getting one item right by guessing is $\frac{1}{2}$, or .50. The probability of getting two items right is $(.50)^2 = .25$, three items right is $(.50)^3 = .125$, and so on. On a 20-item test, the probability of getting a good score (90% or better) is 2 in 10,000. Not very good odds. Of course, on a 5-item TF test, one might get a respectable score by guessing. However, as we have emphasized repeatedly, do not use very short tests. Recall, too, the correction for guessing introduced in Chapter 3. If the correction for guessing is applied, a person's expected score from guessing at all items is 0.

Try This!

Suppose a multiple-choice item has 10 options. What is the probability of correctly guessing the answer to two such items?

PRACTICAL ADVICE

1. Become familiar with the recommendations for writing various types of selected response items. Practical advice about these matters is scattered throughout the chapter. Table 7.1 serves as a convenient checklist.

2. Gain experience in writing selected-response items. In other words, practice.

3. Have other people critique your items. This is especially important when you first start to write items. Be accepting of criticism. Don't be overly defensive.

SUMMARY

1. The two broad categories of test items are selected response (SR) and constructed response (CR). The professional literature contains several alternative terms for each of these broad categories. This chapter concentrates on SR items. The next chapter deals with CR items.

2. We compared SR and CR items in terms of reliability, time to prepare and score, flexibility, cost, student reactions, and validity. The most important point was that SR and CR tests seem to measure with approximately equivalent validity. This is surprising, but the research has been remarkably consistent on the point. However, we noted several qualifications to this generalization.

3. The multiple-choice (MC) item, the most general type of SR item, consists of an item stem and several alternatives, or choices. Two common types of MC items are the conventional, stand-alone item and the item set. Most MC items have four or five alternatives, one of which is scored as the correct answer.

4. We examined 31 rules or guidelines for writing MC items. The guidelines, compiled by Haladyna and his colleagues, were based on analysis of textbooks and research on the effects of item-writing variations. We worked through these rules in detail. Most of the rules reduced to these four points: Get the content right. Keep it simple. Don't give clues to the right answer. Finally, disregard all other rules when it seems sensible to do so.

5. The true-false (TF) item is a special case of an MC item, one where the choices are limited to true or false.

TF items are subject to most of the item-writing rules for MC items. In addition, TF items have a few special rules. There are also some other types of binary choice items.

6. The matching item is also a special form of the MC item. Its distinctive characteristic is having several related stems. Most of the rules for MC item writing also apply to matching items. In addition, there are a few special rules for matching items.

7. Developing skill in item writing takes practice. Just reading about item writing is not sufficient. Feedback on item writing is also necessary.

8. Guessing can affect scores on tests composed of SR items. However, provided there are a sufficient number of items, it is very unlikely that a student will get a decent score on the SR test.

KEY TERMS

alternatives	foils	multiple-choice (MC) item
constructed-response (CR) item	free-response item	objective item
distractors	item	performance assessment
essay items	item stem	selected-response (SR) item

EXERCISES

1. For each selected-response type of item (multiple choice, true-false, matching), write five items based on the content of this chapter or on an area you will be teaching.

2. Have at least two other people critique the items prepared for the first exercise. Revise your items based on the critiques.

3. Pick three of the recommendations for writing MC items in Table 7.1. For each recommendation, write an MC item that violates the recommendation.

4. Choose a particular topic in this chapter (e.g., terminology or rules for item writing). Prepare two MC and two TF items that aim to provide *equivalent* measures of knowledge of the topic.

5. Choose an area you teach or plan to teach. Write four MC items that meet the following two conditions: (1) The items are sufficiently similar that they are measur-

ing the same content and depth of knowledge. (2) They are sufficiently different that they could be used on different occasions (e.g., in different sections of a course) without one item giving away the answer to another item.

6. Here is a simple story that might be read by students in Grade 2. Write three multiple-choice items based on the story.

> Mary and her sisters, Meg and Kelly, went to the mall. Meg wanted to buy a present for a friend. The bookstore was having a sale so they went in there. They found three books they really liked. They could not decide which one to buy. Meg wanted to buy all of them. She did not have enough money. She borrowed some money from Mary.

7. Use this table and the charts to develop sets of multiple-choice items. Make some of the items very simple and other items quite difficult.

State	Pop 1990	Pop 2000	% Change
California	29.8	33.9	13.8%
Florida	12.9	16	24.0%
Nevada	1.2	2	66.7%
New York	18	19	5.6%

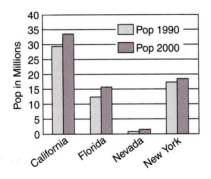

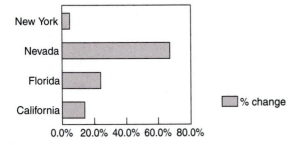

8. This is for the quantitatively inclined student. Use the binomial formula to work out the probabilities of getting certain scores on a multiple-choice test by sheer guessing at all answers. The test has 20 items. Each item has five choices.

  a. What is the probability of getting all 20 items right?

  b. What is the probability of getting at least 80% right? Note that this is equivalent to asking: What is the probability of getting 16 or 17 or 18 or 19 or 20 right?

  c. What is the most likely score?

Chapter 8

Constructed-Response Items: Essays, Performances, and Portfolios

OBJECTIVES

- Describe the general nature of constructed-response items.
- Identify the various terms used to describe constructed-response items.
- Describe the two key problems encountered when using constructed-response items.
- Give suggestions for appropriate use of completion items.
- Describe the main methods for scoring essays and performance tasks.
- List the suggestions for preparing essays and performance tasks for assessment.
- List the suggestions for completing the scoring of essays and performance tasks.
- Give examples of using brief constructed-response questions for formative evaluation.
- Identify the special issues related to using portfolios for assessment.

What This Chapter Is About

This chapter covers the broad category of constructed-response items. These items range from simple fill-in items to very complex projects and portfolios. We present the features and uses of these various types of items. A key issue is how to score them. We describe and give examples of the main methods available for scoring such items. Throughout the chapter, we note the strengths and weaknesses of the constructed-response approach to assessment.

Why This Topic Is Important

Every teacher will employ some types of constructed-response items for assessment. It is important to become familiar with the variety of approaches these items offer. It is also important to become sensitive to the special problems these items present and how to deal with these problems. Quite apart from their own use of these types of items, teachers will hear about the use of these items and the scoring methods in the context of large-scale testing programs. This adds to the importance of being familiar with these topics.

GENERAL NATURE OF CONSTRUCTED-RESPONSE ITEMS

As suggested by its title, the principal feature of the constructed-response (CR) item is that the student must develop the response "from scratch." In contrast, the selected-response (SR) item, described in the previous chapter, presents alternatives from which the student chooses an answer. CR items range tremendously from very simple one-word answers to very complex, extended responses, such as writing a term paper or performing an experiment. SR items fall into a few clear-cut categories: true-false, matching, and multiple choice. CR items do not fall into such clear-cut categories. They fall along a continuum from very simple to very extended responses. Figure 8.1 shows such a continuum. On the left side of the continuum are such simple tasks as computations (e.g., number facts), spelling single words, fill-in-the-blank items, and simple lists, such as a list of state capitals. On the right side of the figure are extended responses, such as writing a term paper, creating a painting, giving a speech, or developing a portfolio. In the middle of the continuum, we find intermediate level responses, such as writing paragraph-length compositions, solving math word problems, creating a sketch, or doing a relatively routine science demonstration. For ease of presentation, we will create some categories for CR items. However, we should remember that our categories are somewhat artificial.

Some Other Terms

The term "constructed response" is a rather technical term. Official sources, such as the *Standards for Educational and Psychological Testing* (AERA, APA, & NCME, 1999), use this term. Many journal articles also use it. However, more popular literature uses other terms to describe CR items. Let us introduce some of these other terms. A common alternative to constructed response is **free response**. This is a good descriptor. The student is free to develop a response rather than just picking from a set of alternatives.

Older literature uses the term **essay item** as the main contrast with SR items. That is, anything other than a multiple-choice (MC) item was an essay item. In contemporary usage, the term "essay" has a more restrictive meaning. It implies writing something, ranging from a few sentences to a few pages. Later in this chapter, we adopt this usage. However, be aware that in older professional literature, the term "essay" has a much broader connotation, including various types of performances.

In current educational parlance, the main term of contrast with SR items is **performance assessment** or performance testing. A performance test implies doing something—other than marking bubbles on an answer sheet. Contemporary use of the term

Figure 8.1 The continuum of constructed-response items.

performance assessment often includes essays, whether written to demonstrate writing skill or content knowledge. Examples of performance tasks used for assessment are science projects, artistic products, public speaking, and a host of other tasks. Of course, none of these activities are tests until we figure out how to score them. We take up that matter in a moment.

Another term encountered in the contrast with SR testing is **authentic assessment**. Authentic assessment implies using realistic, everyday situations as test material. The term actually applies to the nature of the material rather than to the format of the response. Nevertheless, the term is often used as a contrast with multiple-choice methodology. The implication is that the MC format is not authentic or realistic. It must be admitted that some test materials presented as "authentic" are really quite foreign to the everyday experiences of students. See Montgomery (2001) for a useful description of authentic assessment at the elementary school level.

At a very general level, the CR items described in this chapter are sometimes referred to simply as **alternative assessment**. This is not a very useful term. Alternative to what? The implication is that it is an alternative to SR testing. However, review of the history of testing shows that multiple-choice testing was, at one time, the alternative assessment. A brief history lesson: For many years, virtually all testing called for an oral response (writing materials were not routinely available). As writing materials became common, virtually all testing was in essay form. The earliest forms of the SAT were all essay. As people became dissatisfied with essay testing, multiple-choice (and other selected-response) items became dominant. Multiple-choice tests were referred to as "the new-type" tests. Today, essays and performance assessments have made a comeback. Thus, in current literature, the term "alternative" assessment is roughly equivalent to constructed-response methodology. However, in some contexts, the term "alternative" assessment may have a quite different meaning. It may apply to modifications in testing conditions for students with disabilities or limited English language proficiency. In this usage, alternative assessment may mean providing accommodations, such as extended time (but otherwise the same test) or a given test in a different language. Thus, the term "alternative assessment," although frequently encountered, has ambiguous meaning.

Two Key Challenges for Constructed-Response Items

Use of any constructed-response format presents two key challenges. The first is scoring reliability. The second is adequacy of content coverage. Let's consider these two issues before examining specific methods.

Scoring Reliability

Scoring selected-response items is easy because each item has (or should have) one correct answer. You just add up the number of correct answers. Quite literally, a machine can do it. This is not so with constructed-response items. The essence of the CR item, from its simplest to its most complex form, is that it allows for variation in responses. Thus, evaluating responses calls for human judgment. Such judgments may vary from one person to another. This is the problem of *interrater reliability*. One teacher may look at an essay and give it a grade of "A." Another teacher may give the same essay a grade of "C." Judg-

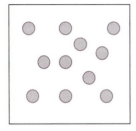

Coverage by SR Items

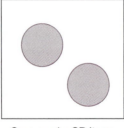

Coverage by CR Items

Figure 8.2 Illustration of differences in content sampling for SR and CR items.

ments may even vary for the same person from one time to another. This is the problem of *intrarater reliability.* Feeling cheery on Saturday, a teacher may give a grade of "A" to a project. Forgetting that it was already graded and now in a dour mood late Sunday night, the teacher may give the same project a "B−." With any type of constructed-response item, we must try to minimize the problems of interrater and intrarater reliability. We described these types of reliability in Chapter 3.

Content Sampling

The second key challenge for constructed-response items relates to adequacy of content sampling. Most CR items require more time to complete than do selected-response items. For a fixed amount of testing time, you usually have many fewer CR items. Figure 8.2 illustrates the problem. The target is a body of content, including knowledge and skills. Many SR items scatter evenly around the target. Fewer CR items allow for gaps in coverage. Each CR item may be somewhat more complex than an SR item, as illustrated by the larger circles in the figure. However, they still present more of a problem for even content coverage. For example, for 30 minutes of testing time, you may have 45 multiple-choice items but only three essays. In 30 minutes, you may get 60 true-false items but only two experiments. When you are trying to cover many learning objectives in a test blueprint, this difference in time requirement presents a problem. If a student misunderstands one multiple-choice item, that does not do much harm among 45 items. If a student misunderstands one of the three essay questions, that will have a substantial impact on the student's total score.

Are there solutions to these two special challenges? Yes. We will consider them as we present specific applications of constructed-response items in the following sections.

Try This!

Think about your own experience, specifically about the last test you took. What kinds of items were on the test? How long did it take for you to complete each type of item?

COMPLETION ITEMS

The simplest form of a constructed-response item is the **completion item**. This item presents a statement or question calling for a very brief response. The student supplies the re-

---

- $7 \times 6 = $ _____
- $\begin{array}{r} 386 \\ \times\ 48 \\ \hline \end{array}$
- (Dictated) Spell: believe
- The capital of New York State is _____
- Who wrote *Romeo and Juliet*? _____

Figure 8.3 Examples of completion items.

sponse. The response is often one word or number. In one version of this item, a word is missing in a sentence. The student inserts the missing word. In this form, the item is called a fill-in-the-blank item. The completion item is obviously very simple. Some sources classify it with SR items. However, it clearly calls for construction of a response, hence it should be classified with CR items.

Completion items find their most typical application with simple skills and knowledge. They are especially appropriate for objectives calling for quick and accurate recall, such as number facts, spelling, and simple associations (e.g., states and their capitals, countries and their continents, authors and their writings). Figure 8.3 shows examples of such simple completion items.

Another form of the completion item involves deleting a word from a sentence and having the student supply the missing word. As noted earlier, this is sometimes called a fill-in-the-blank item. Figure 8.4 shows examples of such items based on the first paragraph in this section.

How do completion items fare in terms of the two key challenges of scoring reliability and content sampling? Because completion items are usually very simple, they do not suffer from the problem of content sampling as much as other CR items do. You can cover a lot of material in a given amount of time with completion items.

The scoring of completion items does require some judgment. Thus, scoring reliability is an issue. Usually, the problem is not as severe as for more complex CR items. However, judgment will come into play. The teacher has to decide how to handle minor variations from the intended response. Because students construct responses "from scratch," unexpected variety will occur. When variations occur, different scorers (teachers) may reach different conclusions. Consider the examples in Figure 8.5. What will we do with the "other answers" in these examples? Is the evident spelling error (Albane) for the first item a fatal error? Does the student really confuse the country (Albania) with the capital (Albany), or is this also a spelling error?

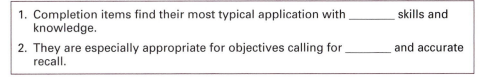

1. Completion items find their most typical application with _____ skills and knowledge.
2. They are especially appropriate for objectives calling for _____ and accurate recall.

Figure 8.4 Examples of fill-in-the-blank items.

Item	Intended Answer	Clearly Incorrect	Other Answers
What is the capital of New York State?	Albany	Buffalo	Albane; Albania
Spell "color," as in What color is your shirt?	color	coller	colour; color's
Complete the series: 2, 4, 6, ___	8	7	8, 10, 12; +2

Figure 8.5 Examples of variations in answers to simple completion items.

Try This!

Score each of the "Other Answers" in Figure 8.5 as either correct or incorrect. Compare your results with someone else's.

The fill-in-the-blank type of item presents even more difficulties in terms of scoring. Consider the synonyms that might be used for the missing words in Figure 8.4. Differing judgments about the acceptability of synonyms introduces unreliability. Perhaps equally harmful, disputes with students about what is acceptable can be demoralizing. For these reasons, most authorities do not recommend using fill-in-the-blank types of items, especially when a sentence is lifted directly from a textbook. A special version of the fill-in-the-blank item is the cloze technique sometimes used to measure reading comprehension or speed. For examples of the cloze technique, see page 255.

It should be evident that any of these completion items could easily be converted into multiple-choice items. Many sources recommend this course of action. However, some teachers might like to insist on the immediate free recall of some basic information. If that is the case, the teacher should be prepared to deal with variations such as those we have described here.

ESSAYS

The essay item constitutes the second major category of constructed-response item. As noted earlier, the essay may be used primarily as a measure of writing skill or as a measure of content knowledge. As a measure of writing skill, the term "essay" is rather generic. It includes stories, news reports, letters, and other such forms of writing, as well as the more traditional essay. Nearly all teachers responsible for the development of writing skills will use some form of essay as an assessment tool. It is now common for stan-

Look at the cartoon on page 191. Write a story about the cartoon.

Write a letter to your newspaper, complaining about a local problem.

Write an essay describing a problem at your school and what should be done about it.

Compare the written and the movie versions of *The Hobbit*.

Figure 8.6 Examples of essay items used to measure writing skill.

Describe and evaluate the complaints made in the Declaration of Independence.

Compare selected-response and constructed-response test items.

Analyze the imagery in the XXIII Psalm (The Lord is my shepherd . . .).

Describe the major features of the human brain.

Figure 8.7 Examples of essay items used to measure content knowledge.

dardized tests to provide an essay portion as a measure of writing skill. Figure 8.6 gives examples of essay-type items used to measure writing skill.

As a measure of content knowledge, the essay attempts to elicit the student's understanding of a particular topic. It may call for simple memorization or for understanding, analysis, and evaluation. The essay may be short, perhaps only a paragraph. Or, it may be quite long, such as the traditional term paper requiring library research and appropriate citations. When essays are part of a formal test, it is not unusual to require several essays. For example, a common pattern from the middle grades upward is a test with some multiple-choice items and three or four short essays. Figure 8.7 gives examples of essay questions used to measure content knowledge. The essay topic itself may not distinguish between the targets of writing skill and content knowledge. That distinction may come only in how the essay is scored.

How do essays fare in terms of the issues of scoring reliability and content sampling? We will delay answering that question until after we have introduced performance tasks in the next section.

PERFORMANCE TASKS

Performance tasks provide a common means of assessment. As suggested by the title, they ask the student to do something. The implication is that this "something" is more than answering a simple question in a selected-response format or even writing an essay. Performance tasks have such wide applicability that they nearly defy simple definition. However, it is easy to list examples. Figure 8.8 lists a variety of performance tasks that might be used for assessment.

Try This!

For an area you plan to teach, add two more performance tasks to the list in Figure 8.8.

Demonstrate dissection of a frog	Translate this into Spanish
Present a musical performance	Give a 5-minute speech
Write a news story	Present a lesson to the class
Draw a map of the world	Solve a novel math problem
Write a poem	Write 5 multiple-choice items
Build a bridge from toothpicks	Use a compass to bisect a line

Figure 8.8 Examples of performance-type items.

An interesting feature of performance tasks is that they are usually interchangeable with ordinary instructional activities. Consider almost any of the entries in Figure 8.8. One day it might be used as part of an instructional program. Another day, it might be used for assessment purposes. The key difference is that, when used for assessment purposes, you have to figure out how to evaluate the quality of student responses.

Some sources contrast performance assessment (and essays) with norm-referenced assessment or standardized tests. Both contrasts are inappropriate. Performance assessments (and essays) can be norm-referenced in interpretation. In fact, many performance assessments do have norms. In addition, many performance assessments are administered with highly standardized conditions. That is, they are standardized tests. These points are evident in the use of essays or performance assessments in many statewide assessment programs, in the Advanced Placement exams, the SATs, and many standardized achievement batteries. On the other hand, many multiple-choice tests (including nearly all teacher-made tests) do not have norms. And, any selected-response test can be administered in a nonstandardized manner. Performance assessments *are* appropriately contrasted with selected-response methods of assessment. Muddled language on these matters leads to muddled thinking. Muddled thinking, in educational assessment, as in most of life, is not helpful.

METHODS OF SCORING AND SCORING RUBRICS

In this section we describe methods for scoring essays and performance tasks. Most of the methods originated in the context of scoring essays. As noted earlier, the essay is just one type of performance task. The methods were later transferred to scoring any type of performance task. However, specific terms related to scoring performance tasks still retain the flavor associated with scoring essays. In the following presentation, we will refer to "responses" to cover essays, projects, and other performance items. The responses are what students prepare in response to the essay question or performance task. These are precisely the constructed responses involved in this type of assessment. We will also refer to the "rater." This is the person scoring the response. In a classroom situation, the rater is the teacher. In external testing programs (e.g., a state assessment program), the rater is hired and trained to score. Usually, there are two or more raters for each response in these external assessment programs.

The first method is **holistic scoring**. In holistic scoring the rater forms a single, overall, holistic judgment. The score assigned to the response reflects this overall judgment. The score scale may contain any number of points (e.g., 1–4, 1–10, or 1–100). The review of the response, for example, reading the essay or viewing the artwork—is typically done rapidly. In large-scale testing programs, the rater makes no notes, corrections, or comments directly on the response. The rater will record scores on a special form. In classroom applications, the teacher may make notes on the paper and records the score directly on the paper.

In external testing programs, considerable effort is expended in developing "anchor points" for values on the holistic scale and in training raters to use these anchor points consistently. Anchor points have two manifestations. First, there are brief descriptions of key characteristics for each point on the scale. Second, there are sample responses illustrating each point. Raters practice using these anchor points in rendering judgments. In the typical classroom application, the teacher will not go to these lengths. However, the teacher should model these practices to the extent possible. For example, if using a

4-point scale, the teacher should have a pretty good idea of what a "4" means and how it differs from a "3."

Exactly what is rated in the overall, holistic judgment? That depends on the specific application. What knowledge or skills do you want to assess? You may want to assess the overall quality of writing skill or how pleasing a piece of artwork is. You may want to assess the depth of knowledge of history revealed in the response. Or, you may want to assess the careful application of scientific reasoning or the steps in a mathematical process. The key characteristics of quality are incorporated into descriptions of the anchor points mentioned earlier. These key characteristics, along with the scale points, are called the scoring **rubrics**.[1] While on the matter of terminology used in performance assessment, we note that the task presented to the student is often called the **prompt** or **exercise**. Both terms mean the same as the test item.

Most external testing programs use either a 4-point or a 6-point scale. Using an even number of scale points helps to avoid piling up cases in a nondescript middle category. That is, it forces the rater, at a minimum, to go a little above or a little below a midpoint. However, it is not necessary to use an even number of scale points.

Figure 8.9 shows the scoring rubrics for a 6-point holistic scale used to rate the quality of writing for elementary school students. Figure 8.10 shows a 4-point holistic scale

Prompt: Look at the cartoon on page 191. Write a story about what is happening and what might happen next. (Allow 20 minutes for writing.)	
6	Story has beginning, middle, and end. Has a theme or story line. Sentences are well formed, with virtually no errors in mechanics. At least some use of unusually apt words.
5	Clear story line. Organization is evident. Most sentences are well formed. Only occasional errors in mechanics (grammar, punctuation, capitalization, and spelling).
4	Story line clearly perceptible but somewhat jumbled. Some errors in mechanics are very noticeable but do not interfere with meaning.
3	Story line present but not well organized. Frequent errors in mechanics, often interfering with meaning or very distracting.
2	Barely perceptible story line. Mainly just comments on features of the picture. Little production. Clear errors in mechanics.
1	Very little production. Incomplete sentences with little meaning. Clear errors in mechanics. Difficult to make sense out of what was written.
0	No basis for rating. Illegible or off topic.

Figure 8.9 Example of six-point holistic scoring rubric for writing a story.

---

[1]Rubrics comes from the Latin *rubrica*, meaning red. It's the same root word as for ruby. In ancient liturgical documents, directions to the person performing the ceremony were often written in red. Modern liturgical documents continue the practice. Thus, red notes (rubrics) are directions on how to proceed. The term is an apt one for what a rater is supposed to do.

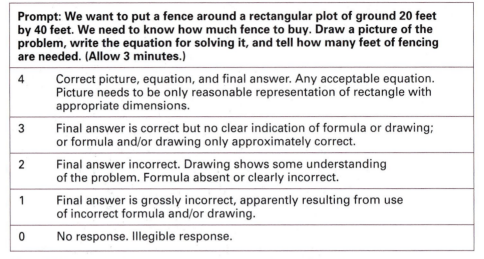

	Prompt: We want to put a fence around a rectangular plot of ground 20 feet by 40 feet. We need to know how much fence to buy. Draw a picture of the problem, write the equation for solving it, and tell how many feet of fencing are needed. (Allow 3 minutes.)
4	Correct picture, equation, and final answer. Any acceptable equation. Picture needs to be only reasonable representation of rectangle with appropriate dimensions.
3	Final answer is correct but no clear indication of formula or drawing; or formula and/or drawing only approximately correct.
2	Final answer incorrect. Drawing shows some understanding of the problem. Formula absent or clearly incorrect.
1	Final answer is grossly incorrect, apparently resulting from use of incorrect formula and/or drawing.
0	No response. Illegible response.

Figure 8.10 Example of 4-point holistic scoring rubric for a math problem.

used to rate completion of a math problem. Notice that both examples provide a category for responses that do not fit the scale. This category is usually labeled "0," although this should not be thought of as a point value one less than "1" on the scale.

It is not unusual to encounter very generic scoring rubrics. Figure 8.11 provides an example. They sometimes accompany textbook materials or collections of what a publisher advertises as criterion-referenced test kits. Many of them amount to little more than: correct, partially correct, and incorrect. These generic scoring rubrics are not very helpful.

Try This!

The following website is a "rubric bank": http://intranet.cps.k12.il.us/assessments/ideas_and_ rubrics/rubric_bank/rubric_bank.html It contains many scoring rubrics from states, school systems, and other sources. Access the site. Find a scoring rubric for an area you plan to teach.

A second method for scoring essays and performance tasks is **analytic scoring**. This method involves assigning separate scores to separate characteristics of the response. What are the separate characteristics? That depends on what characteristics are considered important and reasonably distinguishable. For example, in the story-writing prompt used

3	Correct or acceptable response.
2	Partially acceptable response.
1	Response is present but clearly incorrect.
0	No response. Illegible response.

Figure 8.11 Example of a generic scoring rubric.

Skill	Poor				Excellent
Use of voice	1	2	3	4	5
Organization	1	2	3	4	5
Posture	1	2	3	4	5
Pace	1	2	3	4	5
Clear message	1	2	3	4	5

Figure 8.12 Sample form for analytic scoring of public speaking skill.

in Figure 8.9, separate scores might be assigned for organization, mechanics, and word usage (diction). Some sources use what are called the "big five" characteristics of writing: content, style, mechanics, creativity, and organization (Shermis & Daniels, 2003). In a math exercise, separate scores might be assigned for properly conceptualizing the problem and for the computations involved.

A crucial assumption for analytic scoring is that there are reasonably distinct skills or levels of knowledge involved in the task. If the skills or levels of knowledge are highly correlated, it does not make much sense to assign separate scores. To the extent that distinct skills or levels of knowledge are involved, analytic scoring is helpful. Forms used to assess public speaking skill provide a useful example of analytic scoring. Figure 8.12 shows such a form. Figure 8.13 shows an example of a form for analytic rating of writing skill.

The form in Figure 8.12 helps to illustrate the question about the distinctness of skills used in analytic ratings. Does "use of voice" actually include two separate skills: volume and pronunciation? Is "organization" really distinct from "clear message"? Such questions apply to any type of analytic rating scheme. To some extent, the questions call for knowledge of the area being rated. To some extent, the questions call for empirical analysis of the separation of skills. Unfortunately, for most applications in ordinary classroom situations, no such empirical analysis is available. Hence, the teacher must rely on good knowledge of the area, seasoned with common sense.

Try This!

Create an analytic rating scale for the prompt used in Figure 8.10. What different skills or abilities should be rated? How many points will you use for each area?

Skill	Low					High
Content	1	2	3	4	5	6
Organization	1	2	3	4	5	6
Creativity	1	2	3	4	5	6
Style	1	2	3	4	5	6
Mechanics	1	2	3	4	5	6

Figure 8.13 Sample form for analytic scoring of the "big five" traits of writing.

The big disadvantage of analytic scoring, in comparison with holistic scoring, is the extra time required. For each new score in the analytic scheme, more time is required. Further, in formal applications of analytic scoring, each score should be assigned by a different rater. Hence, analytic scoring can be very expensive. For this reason, it is not used nearly as much as holistic scoring.

A third method for scoring essays and performance tasks is **primary trait scoring**. The basic notion in primary trait scoring is that each piece of writing or other product has a primary purpose. If the purpose is accomplished, the product is successful, even if flawed in its peripheral aspects. Consider the case of a letter written to order a DVD. If the DVD company can fill the order based on the letter, the letter is successful. We disregard the fact that the letter may be filled with spelling errors, incomplete sentences, and so on. On the other hand, a letter impeccably written in terms of sentence structure and spelling but failing to say where to send the DVD would be considered unacceptable. It would not fulfill the primary purpose of the letter. Primary trait scoring developed within the National Assessment of Educational Progress (NAEP; see p. 266). The method went on to gain some use in statewide assessment programs. However, at present it is used sparingly.

A fourth method for scoring essays and performance tasks is the **point system**. In this system, the rater looks for key points in the response. The final score is simply the sum of these points. For example, a history teacher may expect a response to cover eight points. The teacher simply checks off these points while reading the essay response. A point system might be used to score responses to a science project. The teacher may assign five points, one for correctly completing each of five steps in the project. The point system is not widely used in formal external assessments of achievement (e.g., statewide or national programs). However, it is widely used by teachers in classroom assessment.

Automated Scoring

Automated scoring is the technical term for the process of having a computer simulate human judgment of a constructed response. Do not confuse this process with simple machine scoring of selected-response items. Automated scoring applies to a response such as an essay. Some large-scale testing programs now use these systems routinely. Some of the systems are now becoming available for classroom use.

Here is what happens with automated scoring. You start with the human ratings of a constructed response. For example, start with human ratings of the quality of an essay. Researchers try to figure out what elements of the writing seem important to the raters. Then, the researchers quantify these characteristics and write a computer program to capture the characteristics. For example, research may show that human ratings differ depending on sentence length, number of unusual words, and absence of spelling errors.

KEY POINTS SUMMARY 8.1 *Methods of Scoring Essays and Performance Tasks*

Holistic	Primary trait
Analytic	Point system

Researchers build a computer program to capture these elements. Of course, many such elements may enter the program. Once prepared, the program "scores" the essays as if it were a human rater. Automated scoring programs have been developed for such diverse areas as architecture and medicine. The largest area of application is writing skill.

Automated scoring will continue to develop in a variety of areas. Practical applications will occur primarily in large-scale testing programs. However, some of the applications are now becoming available for routine use in classrooms. Readers interested in exploring this fascinating topic in more detail may consult Burstein, Kukich, Wolff, Lu, and Chodorow (1998); Page and Petersen (1995); Williamson, Bejar, and Sax (2004); and Yang, Buckendahl, Juszkiewicz, and Bhola (2002). Shermis and Daniels (2003) provide an excellent collection of chapters on this topic. To see an example of one of these scoring systems in operation, do Exercise 10 at the end of this chapter.

SPECIAL ISSUES FOR PERFORMANCE ASSESSMENTS

Use of performance tasks presents some special issues for assessment beyond those related to scoring them. We take up these special issues in this section.

Differing Applicability

All curricular areas can use performance assessments. In most curricular areas, we recommend using a mixture of performance assessments (or essay-type exercises) and selected-response items. However, performance assessments come more naturally to some areas than to other areas. Similarly, SR items adapt more easily to some areas than to others. Let's consider a few examples.

Many of the objectives in physical education call for use of performance assessments. It may be useful to know if a student can answer questions about the correct way to do sit-ups, but what you really want to know is whether the student can do 10 sit-ups in a minute. This is true for many objectives related to physical fitness. Writing, public speaking, art, music, and shop (woodworking, engines, etc.) are other areas for which performance assessments are particularly appropriate. Selected-response items seem to work particularly well in areas such as reading, mathematics, social studies, and science. We refer here to tilting in one direction or another, not to absolute preferences. To repeat an earlier point: We recommend a combination of approaches.

Collaborative Work on Performance Tasks

It would be rare for a teacher to have students work collaboratively on a multiple-choice test. However, it is not rare for a teacher to have students work collaboratively on a performance task. Students, in small groups, may work on a science project or a class presentation on some topic. Do such collaborative projects present any unique problems for assessment? Yes and no. We should note that the project may be used strictly for instructional purposes without any assessment implications. If the teacher uses the project for assessment, everything we said about rating the quality of the work earlier in this chapter still applies. For example, the teacher can use holistic or analytic ratings. However, there is one additional concern: how to apply the results to individual members of the group.

There are two options. First, all members of the group may receive the same grade. This is the most common procedure. Its obvious drawback is that one or more members of the group may, in fact, have contributed little to the project. The second option is to assign grades to members individually. This is usually difficult to do because the teacher may not have good information about the relative contributions of group members. What is our advice on this matter? Probably the single most important point is this: Make the basis for grading explicit to the students in advance of their work. If all group members will get the same grade, let them know that. If you will assign separate grades to different students, let them know that; and let them know the basis for the differentiation.

Essays and Performance Tasks Completed Outside the Classroom

A teacher would virtually never give a multiple-choice test for completion at home. However, it is not unusual to see essay or performance tasks assigned for completion outside the classroom. The essay task might be a book report or a term paper. The performance task might be a science project.

Beware! Any project completed beyond the immediate supervision of the teacher is open to abuse. Downloading all or substantial portions of a report from Internet sites is common. So, too, is getting unauthorized help from parents, siblings, or other students. Of course, what we are talking about is academic dishonesty. We take up the matter of academic dishonesty more formally in Chapter 10. For now, while considering performance assessment, we simply note that completing such assessments outside the classroom presents a special problem.

BRIEF CRs FOR FORMATIVE EVALUATION

Recall from Chapter 1 the distinction between summative evaluation and formative evaluation. The summative variety calls for a final judgment of quality. Assigning grades is often the purpose of summative evaluation. Formative evaluation, in contrast, provides information to guide instruction in a more immediate manner and without reference to grading. Brief constructed-response items can be especially helpful for formative evaluation. They can be developed quickly. They need not be formally scored or recorded. The teacher simply reviews the responses "to see how things are going."

Some authors call these brief CRs "classroom assessment techniques." This term is too broad. Virtually everything we have covered so far is a classroom assessment technique. Nevertheless, the term has gained some currency, so we adopt it here. Thomas Angelo and Patricia Cross popularized the term "classroom assessment techniques." Their focus of attention was college teachers. However, the techniques are equally applicable below the college level, at least down to the middle grades. We have provided a few examples of the techniques here. For a collection of 50 classroom assessment techniques, see Angelo and Cross (1993).

Let us illustrate this group of techniques. At the end of a lesson (it might be one class period or several), have students write a *one-sentence summary* of what was covered. Or, ask students to identify the *three most important points* about the topic. Or, have students formulate *one question* they have about the topic. In each case, the administration is easy. Just have students record answers on a sheet of paper. Many of the techniques work well with 3 x 5 index cards. Give about three minutes, perhaps less, to answer. Then, collect

Technique	Brief Description
	After a class period or unit, have students:
One-sentence summary	Write a one-sentence summary of the topic/lesson
Three important points	Identify the three most important points
One question	Write one question they have about the topic
Student-generated test items	Prepare a test question appropriate for the topic
Muddiest point	Identify the muddiest (most confusing) point
Empty outline	Complete a partial outline

Figure 8.14 Examples of classroom assessment techniques.

Adapted from Angelo and Cross (1993).

the papers or cards. Let students know their responses will not be graded, lest panic break out in the classroom. Figure 8.14 lists examples of classroom assessment techniques.

Analysis of responses is equally simple. Do not assign grades. There's no need for a scoring rubric! This is the antithesis of high-stakes testing. Simply review the responses to see if students are "getting it." Responses may reveal gross misunderstanding or minor confusions. Responses may also suggest follow-up activities. Because the teacher need not worry about fairness in grading, reviewing responses to one of these classroom assessment techniques should take no more than five minutes for a class of 30 students. Figure 8.15 shows a few cards with one-sentence summaries written by students after listening to

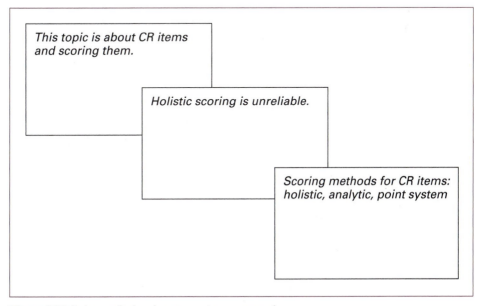

This topic is about CR items and scoring them.

Holistic scoring is unreliable.

Scoring methods for CR items: holistic, analytic, point system

Figure 8.15 Index cards showing one-sentence summaries.

a lecture on part of this chapter. The second card suggests less than complete understanding of the topic. Note that the techniques capitalize on the fact that CRs are easy to develop but the techniques avoid the problem of how to score them reliably. It is hard to imagine investing the time to develop selected-response items for the formative purpose outlined here.

An incidental benefit of these simple techniques is that they help students stay engaged with the material. It does something to capture their attention. It gives them something to do, which is usually beneficial.

Try This!

Write a one-sentence summary of this section on brief CRs. Compare your summary with another student's.

SUGGESTIONS FOR PREPARING CONSTRUCTED-RESPONSE ITEMS

As noted in the previous chapter, textbooks and articles contain numerous suggestions for writing selected-response items. Suggestions for writing constructed-response items are more limited. Perhaps the very open-ended nature of these items makes it more difficult to formulate specific advice. Interestingly, the first bit of advice that most experienced test developers give is to use SR items whenever possible. Having said that, we can offer the following advice about preparing CR items. Relative emphasis of the suggestions varies with the complexity of the task. That is, some bits of advice weigh more heavily for complex performance assessments than for completion items or short essays.

1. Align the tasks with learning objectives. The first bit of advice is simply a reminder to start with a test blueprint. The test blueprint outlines the learning objectives. Then, devise the constructed-response items (essays or performance tasks) to cover parts of the blueprint. For example, the learning objective may be this: Students will be able to construct a story that has a clear organization. Then, for this objective, the scoring will concentrate on whether the story has a recognizable beginning, middle, and end.

2. Make sure the task is clear. With selected-response items, the student's task is clarified by looking at the possible responses. The constructed-response item lacks such guidance. Hence, we need greater care in formulating and clarifying the directions for these items. You may want to suggest the approximate amount of time needed to construct a reasonable response for an essay question. You may want to indicate what an acceptable science project might look like. Peppermint Patty's science project (see Figure 8.16) may not be quite what you had in mind. It may be helpful to students to know what scoring criteria you will use.

3. Minimize the influence of irrelevant skills. Focus the task on what you really want to evaluate. Try to devise the task in such a way that irrelevant skills will not contaminate the response. Be especially alert to excessive reading demands in the directions for performance assessments, unless you are trying to measure reading skill. It is not unusual to encounter a performance assessment for science or math, where the real task is to

Figure 8.16 Peppermint Patty's teacher may need to be more explicit about expectations for the science project. (PEANUTS © by Charles Schultz; reprinted by permission of United Features Syndicate, Inc.)

understand the rather complicated directions. Similarly, be careful about requiring extensive writing, unless you are trying to measure writing skill. For example, a teacher may ask for a written report about a science project where the instructional objective is to develop an understanding of a scientific principle. In that case, it is important that writing skill not be the main basis for the assessment.

4. Be specific about the scoring system at the time the item is prepared. A common practice for the constructed-response format is to prepare the item, administer it, and assume that the method of scoring will become clear later. That strategy is an invitation to disaster. The way the item will be scored should be clear before the item is administered. This suggestion applies regardless of the generality of the response. It is equally important in scoring fill-in-the-blank items and in scoring lengthy essays or performance assessments.

5. Use a sufficient number of items. There is a tendency with constructed-response items to consume all of the available testing time with just a few items, perhaps only one item. The reliability and validity of the assessment are generally better served by including more items. If there is only one item and, for some reason, a student misunderstands it or "makes a wrong turn" with it, there is no way to counterbalance the situation with responses to other items. Although the CR format usually allows for fewer items than the SR format, you should lean toward more rather than fewer items when using CR items.

Try This!

Look at the essay items in Figure 8.7. For each one, indicate how much time you would allow for high school students to answer it.

6. Avoid optional items. When administering a multiple-choice test, rarely would a teacher allow the students to pick the questions they want to answer. However, it is not unusual to encounter an essay test with directions such as "Answer three of the following five questions." This procedure is *not* recommended. It complicates making consistent, reliable judgments. In an extreme form, it would be like having every student answer a different question. Although no teacher would go to that extreme, using optional items leans in that direction. It is not a good idea.

KEY POINTS SUMMARY 8.2   *Preparing CR Items*

1. Align the tasks with learning objectives.
2. Make sure the task is clear.
3. Minimize the influence of irrelevant skills.

4. Be specific about the scoring system.
5. Use a sufficient number of items.
6. Avoid optional items.

SUGGESTIONS FOR COMPLETING THE SCORING

An earlier section described procedures for scoring essays and performance tasks. Regardless of the procedure selected (e.g., holistic or analytic), there are suggestions for actual application of the scoring procedure. We have five suggestions.

1. Score anonymously.   Try to score essays or performance tasks without knowing the student's name. Knowing who the student is may unfairly influence your judgment of the actual response. If you know that Betty Bright wrote the essay, you may be inclined to rate it highly—regardless of the actual quality of the response. In contrast, you may not give Dolly Dull the benefit of the doubt on a close call. It's better that you not know whether you are scoring Betty's or Dolly's paper.

2. Score one item at a time.   Suppose you have three essays (or tasks) to score. Call them X, Y, and Z. It is best to score all the Xs first, then all the Ys, and then all the Zs. This procedure should promote consistency in scoring each item. It should also reduce the chances that performance on one item will influence your judgment about performance on another item. Admittedly, following this procedure is a nuisance. Nevertheless, it is good practice.

3. Focus on the learning objectives.   This suggestion parallels the third suggestion made earlier about developing essays and performance tasks. There we recommended devising tasks to minimize the influence of irrelevant skills. Now that you are actually scoring the items, make sure you continue to focus on what you want to assess. Disregard irrelevant skills. Of particular importance is how to handle such factors as elegance of expression, penmanship, neatness, and so on (when these are not the skills you are assessing). From a practical viewpoint, it is difficult to disregard these matters. They can be really irritating. Here is a good compromise position. Comment on these irrelevancies (Watch your spelling! Very neat paper!, etc.), but do not let them influence the score you assign.

4. Periodically recalibrate yourself.   You are the measuring stick when rating essays and performance tasks. You will not be entirely consistent as you proceed. You will expand and contract a bit with time. You may be more lenient with earlier papers, more severe with later papers. Or the opposite. If you score three essays for each of 60 students, you will be at the task for several hours, perhaps several days.

There are a number of ways to improve your consistency. After scoring, say, 20 essays or tasks, return to a few of the earlier ones and reevaluate them. After scoring all of the material, skim through the entire batch. See if you have been consistent in applying your standards. It may also be helpful to preview a sampling of the entire batch before assigning any scores. This practice helps you to keep the range of responses in view. If your scoring extends over several sessions, start each session by again previewing a sampling of the responses. This will take only about five minutes and it should aid your consistency.

Also, set a sensible schedule for scoring very extended responses, such as term papers or substantial science projects. The scoring may require several days. This might constitute an entirely separate suggestion, but we include it here because it relates primarily to scoring consistency. Beyond our concern about good assessment, the suggestion also relates to maintaining your sanity.

5. Multiple Raters?   Most authorities conclude their recommendations on scoring essays and performance tasks by suggesting use of more than one rater if the test is quite important. Theoretically, this is a fine suggestion. External testing programs usually do this. However, for ordinary classroom application, the suggestion is quite unrealistic. Can you imagine Ms. Evalenko, the Grade 9 social studies teacher, asking Ms. Barnes, the Grade 10 social studies teacher, to grade 180 essays (three essays for each of 60 students)? Instant unpopularity for Ms. Evalenko! The more practical suggestion for this matter is one we have made repeatedly in this book: Use multiple measures. Use several different tests. Use essays, performance tasks, completion items, and multiple-choice items in combination for any important conclusions, such as final grades.

PORTFOLIO ASSESSMENT

A **portfolio** is a collection of a person's work or other "stuff." The most common use of the term applies to artists. The artist's portfolio is a collection of his or her paintings, sketches, and so on. The financial world also uses the term for a collection of stocks, bonds, and other investments. In educational circles, a portfolio means a collection of a student's work in a subject area. For example, a student may have a science portfolio containing material on completed science projects or a writing portfolio of completed stories, poems, and reports. Figure 8.17 lists examples of areas in which students might develop a portfolio. Numerous sources provide examples of portfolios in language arts. Excellent examples are Barr, Craig, Fisette, and Syverson (1999); Barr and Syverson (1999); and Farr and Tone (1994). To place portfolio assessment in the context of the language arts in general, see Farr and Beck (2003); Frey and Hiebert (2003); and Simmons and Carroll (2003). Barton and Collins (1997) provide a very nice collection of examples from diverse

KEY POINTS SUMMARY 8.3	*Scoring CR Items*
1. Score anonymously.	4. Periodically recalibrate yourself.
2. Score one at a time.	5. Multiple raters?
3. Focus on the learning objectives.	

All drafts, notes, and background research on preparation of an essay or a story

All weekly writing assignments for an English course, including teacher notes

All science projects completed during a term

Types of geometry problems dealt with in a chapter, with notes on solutions

Preliminary sketches, final products, and self-reflections on art projects for a term

Figure 8.17 Examples of topics for portfolios.

curricular areas (writing, math, science, and social studies) and various grades. As we shall see in Chapter 15, a teacher may also have a portfolio containing evidence about teaching activities.

Try This!

Pick an area you teach or plan to teach. Identify a type of portfolio that may be appropriate for that area. List at least five entries you think might appear in the portfolio.

———————   ———————   ———————   ———————   ———————

Special Characteristics of Portfolios

In the context of assessment, the portfolio clearly falls within the realm of constructed-response assessment, hence its treatment in this chapter. However, portfolios have some very special characteristics that set them apart, to some extent, from other types of CR items. To place portfolios in the appropriate context, we should examine these special characteristics. Then we will discuss principles for evaluating portfolios.

Multiple Entries.   The most evident feature of a portfolio is that it has multiple entries. Figures 8.18 and 8.19 show examples of the entries in two different portfolios. These are simplified examples. Any portfolio may contain numerous other items. In previous sections of this chapter, we examined individual constructed-response items (e.g., an essay on world history, a story, or a simple completion item). The portfolio is an entity unto itself, with many entries. Any single entry could be used for assessment purposes, but a special feature of the portfolio is the relationship among the various entries.

Self-reflection.   Nearly all writers emphasize that self-reflection by the student is a critical component of portfolio construction and usage (see, e.g., Farr & Tone, 1994; Sunstein & Lovell, 2000). That is, the student does not just "put stuff" into the portfolio but must also think about the entries and the connections among the entries. These self-reflections may be made explicit and become part of the portfolio; for example, the student may enter notes about her sketches of the human figure, as in Figure 8.19. Notice that the very first entry in Figure 8.18 is a type of self-reflection simply on what to write. The

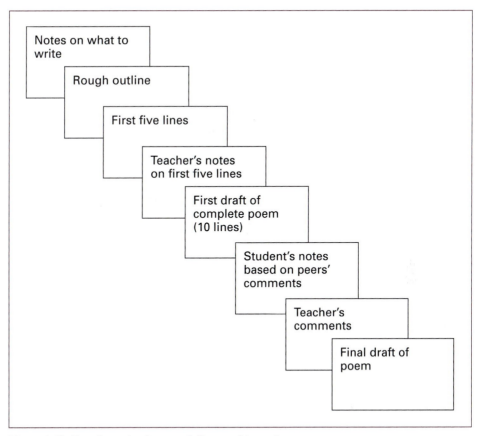

Figure 8.18 Sample entries for a portfolio on writing a short poem.

teacher may provide some simple forms to help with the self-reflection process. For example, Figure 8.20 shows a simple form for students to record their thoughts about a succession of writing projects. In this case, students write a story, a letter, and a description of something. The projects may span several weeks. For each writing project, students will spend some time making notes about what they liked about the project, their self-assessment of how well they did, and what they should do to make their writing better. Alternatively, the teacher may simply provide opportunities for students to discuss their entries.

On-going.   The portfolio is on-going (within some finite term defined by the school calendar). That is, it is not simply a matter of gathering up a lot of material at the end of a school term and filing the material. Rather, the portfolio grows during an entire term, year, or, perhaps, from the beginning to the end of some project. As noted earlier, any single entry could be evaluated by itself. For example, the "final human figure in charcoal" in Figure 8.19 could be rated with an analytic scale. However, as one entry in the

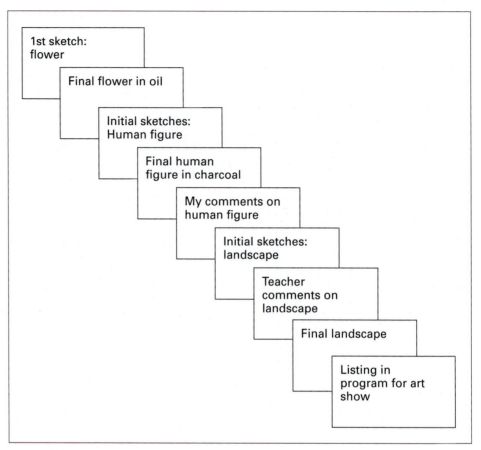

Figure 8.19 Sample entries for an art portfolio.

portfolio, this entry has a relationship to the initial sketches and "my comments" on the entry.

Student Involvement.   Student involvement is encouraged. That is, the teacher is not the sole determiner of what goes into the portfolio or how it will be used. The student decides what will enter the portfolio. The self-reflection process mentioned earlier is also an important part of this student involvement. This is a particularly important contrast with other types of constructed-response assessment tasks. For example, when using a typical assignment to evaluate student writing skill, we simply want the student to write a story or essay, which the teacher will then evaluate. The student does not have any choice in the matter. In contrast, the student exercises considerable control over what will enter the student's portfolio.

Communication to Multiple Audiences.   The portfolio may serve as an effective communication device, especially for external audiences. The portfolio may be espe-

---

My Writing Record

Project

Story   What I liked about this _____

_____

How was my writing _____

_____

What to do better _____

_____

Letter   What I liked about this _____

_____

How was my writing _____

_____

What to do better _____

_____

Description What I liked about this _____

_____

How was my writing _____

_____

What to do better _____

_____

Figure 8.20 Example of a simple form for encouraging self-reflection on writing.

cially helpful in describing exactly what the student is doing in school and what progress is being made. A single test score, while helpful for some purposes, may not convey much about exactly what a student is accomplishing. However, the contents of a portfolio may be revealing. Primary among the external audiences are parents. In some applications, the external audience may include community members and school administrators.

KEY POINTS SUMMARY 8.4   *Special Characteristics of Portfolios*

Multiple entries   Student involvement

Self-reflection   Communication to multiple audiences

On-going

Some Cautions

Most authors who advocate use of portfolios agree on certain cautions about their use. In fact, among those with extensive experience in using portfolios, there is remarkable agreement about these matters.

Go Slowly.   Portfolio entries can accumulate rapidly. The amount of material in portfolios can become overwhelming. Simply finding space to store the portfolios can become a problem. Therefore, all advocates of portfolios recommend that a teacher start slowly when beginning to use portfolios. Perhaps start with one project, say, a writing project with its multiple drafts, self-reflections, notes on student-teacher conferences, and so on. Do not try to begin with portfolios in several different subject areas for entire classes. See Lescher (1995) and Seidel et al. (1997) for specific guidance on this matter.

Clarify Purpose.   Portfolios may serve several different purposes. It is important to identify the particular purpose before launching a portfolio project. A common distinction is between a "showcase" portfolio and a "working" portfolio. The showcase portfolio contains only the student's best work. As suggested by its title, it is meant to impress people. In contrast, the working portfolio is meant to show work in progress. It may contain working drafts, rough starts, even criticisms of entries. It is important to have a clear purpose for the portfolio in order to know what kinds of entries will be appropriate.

Authors differ regarding adoption of the purposes. Farr and Tone (1994) explicitly recommend against the use of showcase portfolios. They feel that such a purpose interferes with effective instructional use of the portfolio. Therefore, they emphasize use of a working portfolio. Benson and Barnett (1999) advocate use of showcase portfolios, especially for purposes of conferences. Other authors—for example, Frey and Hiebert (2003) and Jenkins (1996)—simply distinguish among various purposes and recommend that teachers clearly identify a particular purpose before beginning to use portfolios. Of course, once a teacher identifies a purpose, it is important that students understand the purpose, too.

Use for Assessment.   In what way should portfolios be used for assessment? Opinions diverge noticeably on this question. To treat the question, we should recall the distinction between formative and summative from Chapter 1 (p. 6). Summative aims at final conclusions regarding students' status, usually with regard to some body of content. Summative provides the basis for assigning grades or evaluating the effectiveness of a program. Formative, on the other hand, aims primarily at guiding instruction. It may deal with matters of the best next step for this student or the exact pace of instruction.

Many authors recommend *against* the use of portfolios for any type of summative. Hebert (2001) calls the use of portfolios as a substitute for any type of standardized assessment "misguided" (p. xii). Farr and Tone (1994) state explicitly: "Given a choice, it would be a mistake, we believe, for the teacher to grade portfolios" (p. 42). Shaklee, Barbour, Ambrose, and Hansford (1997) note that portfolios are not useful for what they call "macrolevel accountability" (p. 138). The emphasis for all these authors is primarily on the use of the portfolio as an instructional device. To the extent the portfolio is used for any assessment purpose, it is strictly formative assessment and that only in a very mild way.

On the other hand, many sources describe procedures for using portfolios for summative. For example, Hewitt (1995), Dodd (1997), and Jones (1997) describe the routine use of rubrics and holistic scoring of portfolios in much the same manner as we described these procedures earlier. Even Farr and Tone (1994), after recommending against the use of such procedures, go on to describe these summative procedures, admitting that it is sometimes necessary to use them. The application of portfolios for summative does not have an impressive track record. Perhaps the classic application was in the Vermont statewide assessment. Koretz, Stecher, Klein, and McCaffrey (1994) describe the results: There were very substantial problems of reliability, validity, and practicality. Williams (2000) also found that the unstandardized nature of portfolio assessment allowed for the operation of biases. This final caution is a good introduction to the next section.

Principles for Evaluating Portfolios

We need to distinguish between the use of portfolios for assessment purposes and for instructional purposes. A teacher may use portfolios strictly for instructional purposes. Or a teacher may use portfolios only for formative assessment. On the other hand, a teacher may wish to use portfolios for a formal, summative assessment. If that is the case, the principles outlined in this section apply.

Recall that at the beginning of our treatment of portfolios, we identified the portfolio as a type of constructed response. As is true for most constructed-response items, the principal task in using portfolios for assessment purposes is to devise a scoring system. In this regard, using portfolios for assessment is much like using performance tasks: A scoring scheme is crucial. However, the portfolio presents some unique challenges beyond those for performance tasks. These unique challenges arise precisely because the portfolio is a collection rather than a single response.

There are three main questions. First, from the assortment of materials in the portfolio, what will be evaluated? Second, who will do the selection? Third, who will do the judging or rating? Let us consider the possible answers to each of these questions.

The collection of materials in a portfolio offers several choices for what will be evaluated. There are three main alternatives. First, one can evaluate just the *best*. "The best" might be the single best entry or the three best entries or some other number of best entries. The essential point is that the evaluation concentrates on the best. A second alternative is to evaluate the most *typical*. Again, "the most typical" might be a single entry, three entries, or some other number. The third alternative is to judge *progress* from the beginning to the end of the entries. Obviously, this approach entails two types of selections: earlier entries and later entries. Once again, "earlier" and "later" may each be defined by single entries or several entries.

Second decision: Who will select the materials from the portfolio? Note that this question must be answered regardless of what choice is made regarding what will be evaluated. The choices here are the student or the teacher. If the portfolio is being used mainly for instructional purposes, there may be a preference for having the student make the selection. It may be instructive, to both student and teacher, to see what selections the student makes. However, if the material is used mainly for summative assessment purposes, it might be best to have the teacher make the selection.

Third decision: Who will do the rating of quality? This decision is similar to the second one. The choices are also the same: student or teacher. Further, the rationale for making a choice is similar for this question and the second question. That is, if the primary application is instructional, it may be useful to have the student complete the rating. In effect, the student's ratings become part of the self-reflection process. For summative assessment purposes, the rating should almost certainly be done by the teacher.

Try This!

Use the entries in Figure 8.19. Make decisions on how to evaluate the portfolio. What entries or combination of entries will be evaluated? Who will make the selections? Who will do the ratings?

After decisions are made on the three issues just described, actual rating occurs according to one of the scoring schemes described earlier for essays and performance assessments. For example, a holistic rating can be made based on (a) the best entry, (b) selected by the student, with (c) the teacher making the rating. Or, an analytic rating may be applied to (a) three typical entries, (b) selected by the student, and (c) rated by the student. Thus, the rating systems available for use are the same for portfolios as for other performance assessments. We should note that some sources recommend including scores from ordinary tests in the portfolio. Tests might be regular classroom tests or externally standardized tests. Obviously, these tests have already been scored and need not be rated.

One of the principal drawbacks of portfolios is the amount of paperwork they entail. This difficulty is not peculiar to their use for assessment purposes. Any use of portfolios generates paperwork, potentially a very large amount. The teacher needs to manage this problem, regardless of the use of the portfolio. For at least some types of work, an electronic portfolio helps with this management. The electronic portfolio does not introduce any new assessment issues. That is, when using electronic portfolios, the same types of decisions must be made about what to evaluate, who makes the selection, and who assigns ratings. However, the electronic portfolio may reduce the amount of paperwork involved.

PRACTICAL ADVICE

1. It seems sensible to use both selected-response and constructed-response items. In many circumstances, this means using a mixture of multiple-choice and essay or performance items. The mixture may be within one assessment or it might result from a number of different assessments. The main point is: Become proficient in using both SR and CR items in your overall assessment plan.

KEY POINTS SUMMARY 8.5   *Choices to Make in Evaluating Portfolios*

What to evaluate: Best, Typical, or Progress
Who selects: Student or Teacher
Who rates: Student or Teacher

2. When using CR assessments, be sure to devise the scoring system (rubric) in advance; that is, before administering the assessment. Even for simple completion items, know how you will treat variations in responses. For performance assessments, choose one of the scoring methods described in this chapter and apply it consistently.

3. For the more time-consuming CR items, be sure to provide adequate content coverage. Usually, this means testing on several different occasions because any one occasion does not allow sufficient time.

4. Make sure your performance assessment is getting at what you want to assess and is not overly dependent on extraneous skills. Be especially careful about giving complicated directions. If the assessment is completed outside the classroom, make sure the student, not someone else, completes the work.

5. If you are just beginning to use portfolios for assessment, start prudently. Be careful that you (and your students) do not become buried in paper.

SUMMARY

1. The essence of the constructed-response item is that it calls for the student to produce a response more or less "from scratch." In contrast, the selected-response item calls for the student to choose an answer from given alternatives. CR items range from simple completion or fill-in-the-blank items to written essays and a variety of performance tasks.

2. We encounter a considerable variety of terms for constructed-response items. Among these terms are free-response items, essay tests, performance assessments, authentic assessments, and alternative assessments. Some sources inappropriately contrast constructed-response items with norm-referencing or standardized testing.

3. The two key challenges in using constructed-response items are scoring reliability and adequacy of content sampling.

4. Completion items are appropriate for some simple skills and facts. Although simple in appearance, they still present some problems for scoring. Fill-in-the-blank items are not generally recommended.

5. Essay-type items have wide applicability. They are the principal means for assessing writing skill. They are also widely used as measures of content knowledge, especially in the social sciences, literature, and similar fields.

6. Performance tasks imply doing something (other than answering a selected-response item or writing an essay). As a basis for assessment, performance tasks also have wide applicability. They provide an especially good fit for areas such as the sciences, fine arts, public speaking, physical education, and some aspects of mathematics.

7. We described four main methods for scoring essays and performance tasks: holistic, analytic, primary trait, and a point system. Especially for holistic and analytic methods, the specification of points on the scale, often accompanied by sample responses, constitutes the scoring rubric.

8. We provided six suggestions for the development of essay questions and performance tasks. The suggestions concentrate on making the task clear to the student and ensuring adequate content coverage.

9. We provided five suggestions for the process of scoring essays and performance tasks. The suggestions concentrate on ensuring the reliability and validity of scores.

10. Brief constructed-response items provide an interesting means for formative evaluation at the conclusion of an instructional unit.

11. For purposes of assessment, portfolios fit within the category of constructed-response items. However, portfolios also have special characteristics, including multiple entries, self-reflection, on-going creation, student involvement, and uses with multiple audiences.

12. For purposes of assessment, portfolios present some unique issues. The teacher must decide exactly what will be evaluated, who will make the selection of materials, and who will do the judging. Otherwise, assessment of portfolios follows the suggestions made for evaluating any performance task.

KEY TERMS

alternative assessment	essay item	point system
analytic scoring	exercise	portfolio
authentic assessment	free response	primary trait scoring
automated scoring	holistic scoring	prompt
completion item	performance assessment	rubrics

EXERCISES

1. For either a unit in an area you teach or for the contents of this chapter, prepare 10 completion items. Have another student critique your items. If feasible, get three other students to supply answers to your items. Score the answers.

2. For either a unit in an area you teach or for the contents of this chapter, prepare three essay questions. Have another student critique your questions. Describe the method to be used for scoring the essays.

3. Go to the website for the National Assessment of Educational Progress: http://nces.ed.gov/nationsreportcard/. Go to the part for writing or for science. Find the *Scoring Guide/Key*. What type of scoring rubric is used?

4. Use Appendix E to find the state assessment results for your state (or a state of interest to you). See if you can find the scoring rubric used for the state's writing assessment. Also, see if you can find a scoring rubric for a performance assessment in math or science. What types of scoring rubrics do you find?

5. For either a unit in an area you teach or for the contents of this chapter, prepare three performance assessment tasks. Have another student critique the tasks. Describe the scoring rubric to be used for scoring the responses.

6. Suppose your students have been keeping a portfolio of their writing assignments, science projects, artistic productions, or a similar area. (Pick your own area.) Briefly describe how you will evaluate the portfolio contents. Consider what will be selected, who will select it, and who will judge it.

7. This is a follow-up to the Try This! exercise on page 184. Do an Internet search for "scoring rubrics." Your results will include scoring rubrics used by different states, especially for writing assessments. Pick any two states. Compare their scoring rubrics for writing. In what ways do the rubrics differ? In what ways are they similar?

8. This exercise is similar to the previous one. The following website, developed by the Chicago Public Schools (1999), is a "rubric bank": http://intranet.cps.k12.il.us/assessments/ideas_and_rubrics/rubric_bank/rubric_bank.html. It contains many scoring rubrics from states, school systems, and other sources. Access the site. Examine the scoring rubrics for any two sources. The sources may be from the same curricular area or different areas. How do the rubrics differ? In what ways are they similar?

9. The number of books and articles on portfolios is staggering. To check on some of them, use the ERIC database. Go to www.eric.ed.gov and do a search on "portfolios." You will find references to use of portfolios in specific subjects, specific grades, and for a variety of purposes. Be sure to do a boolean search using "portfolios AND education." Otherwise, most of what you get will relate to financial portfolios.

10. Recall the description of automated scoring of essays. To see one of these systems in operation, go to: http://www.vantage.com/demosite/demo.html. This site provides sample essays scored by the program IntelliMetric. Submit one of the essays and see what type of report the program yields.

Chapter 9

Interests, Creativity, and Nontest Indicators

OBJECTIVES

- List typical educational objectives related to students' interests and attitudes.
- Describe the Likert method for measuring interests and attitudes.
- List typical educational objectives related to creative thinking.
- Illustrate typical prompts used for measuring creativity.
- Describe methods for scoring responses to creative thinking items.
- Explain possible uses of nontest indicators of educational success.

What This Chapter Is About

Most teachers and schools have educational objectives beyond those related to the acquisition of knowledge and skills in the traditional content areas. Assessment techniques are needed to measure the accomplishment of these other objectives. The techniques look rather different from the assessment methods described in Chapters 7 and 8. In addition, there are some nontest methods for evaluating educational outcomes. We consider all of these matters in this chapter.

Why This Topic Is Important

We sometimes fail to specify objectives that seem important because they appear to be hard to measure. In fact, there are assessment techniques for these apparently hard-to-measure objectives. The techniques are not hard to use, but they may not come immediately to mind. Nevertheless, with a little exposure to the techniques and a little practice with them, they can be easily implemented in the classroom or for entire schools.

ASSESSING INTERESTS AND ATTITUDES

Many teachers and schools have objectives related to students' interests and attitudes. A full curricular plan should include specification of these objectives. A full assessment plan should include assessment of them. Here are examples of such objectives:

- Developing a favorable attitude toward math (or reading, science, etc.)
- Overcoming fear of speaking in public
- Developing an interest in environmental problems
- Enjoying poetry
- Developing a favorable attitude toward working cooperatively on a project

Try This!

For an area you teach or plan to teach, write an objective related to interests or attitudes such as those just listed.

Before examining methods for assessing interests and attitudes, let us consider various names for this topic. In an earlier era, knowledge and skills in the traditional content fields were called **cognitive outcomes**. In contrast, some of the outcomes covered in this chapter were called **noncognitive outcomes**. Another term of contrast with cognitive outcomes is affective outcomes. Noncognitive or affective outcomes include interests, attitudes, dispositions, behavioral matters, and, in some sources, nontraditional ways of thinking. Bloom's taxonomy was a key reference for the "cognitive versus affective" distinction. Recall from Chapter 6 that the first volume in Bloom's work was for the "cognitive domain." The second volume was for the "affective domain." In that earlier era, we might have well called this chapter "Noncognitive Measures." Some textbooks continue to use the terms noncognitive and affective. However, with the "cognitive revolution" in education and psychology, the noncognitive term is passé. Today, everything is cognitive. The cognitive realm includes how you feel as well as how you think. In keeping with this current emphasis, we prefer not to use either the noncognitive term or the affective term.

The Likert Method

Measurement experts have devised a variety of methods to assess interests and attitudes. We will examine only one of them. It is called the **Likert method**, named after Rensis Likert, who pioneered its development in the 1930s.[1] It is the most widely used method, partly because it is so simple and flexible.

Here is how the Likert method works. First, think of the target area or topic (e.g., math, environmental problems, or poetry). Second, think of different facets of the topic.

---

[1] Likert (1932) himself called it the "method of summated ratings." Today, nearly everyone calls it the Likert method.

These facets might be subtopics or different perspectives. For example, different facets of math are geometry, word problems, computing, and graphs. Different facets of environmental problems are air quality, water quality, recycling, and public policy issues. Third, translate these facets into simple statements to which students can respond.

The fourth and final step is to create the response scale for the items (i.e., the statements). The original Likert method used this 5-point scale for all items: Strongly Disagree (SD), Disagree (D), Uncertain (U), Agree (A), and Strongly Agree (SA). The responses have numerical values from 1–5 (SD = 1, . . . , SA = 5). Many Likert-type scales continue to use this 5-point response system. However, it is possible to use a considerable variety of other response scales. Even with alternative response options, people still call it a Likert-type scale. Figure 9.1 shows examples of response scales that might be used, beginning with the classic 5-point (SD . . . SA) arrangement.

Notice the variety of response formats in Figure 9.1. We could manufacture numerous other examples. The response scale can be tailored to a particular set of statements. For example, the response options may range from Dislike to Like, Disagree to Agree, or Little to Much. (If you use a standard answer sheet for responses, be sure the response options agree with the answer sheet's format.) The "smiley face" options are particularly appropriate for younger children.

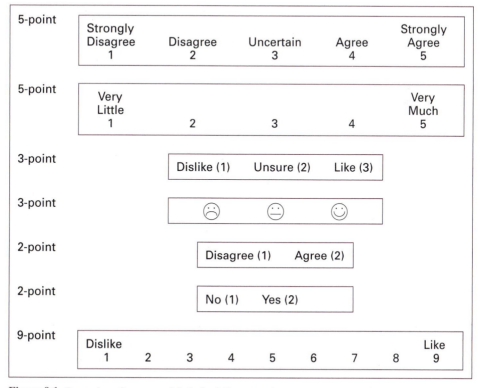

Figure 9.1 Examples of response labels for Likert-type items.

	SD	D	U	A	SA
I love geometry problems.	1[ ]	2[ ]	3[ ]	4[X]	5[ ]
Solving equations is fun.	1[ ]	2[ ]	3[ ]	4[ ]	5[X]
Making graphs is useful.	1[ ]	2[ ]	3[X]	4[ ]	5[ ]

Score = 4 + 5 + 3 = 12

Figure 9.2 Scoring Likert-type items.

To derive a score for the scale, simply add up the numerical values for the responses. Figure 9.2 shows a set of responses for a 3-item math attitude scale. The score is the sum of the response values.

Try This!

Add two more items to the statements in Figure 9.2.

Sometimes it is useful to reverse the direction of a few statements. Instead of phrasing all items in a positive direction, state some in a negative direction. This helps to keep students "on their toes." That is, students have to read each item and respond rather than marking all items routinely in one direction. If the direction of some items is reversed, remember to reverse the scale value for the responses accordingly. Consider the second item in Figure 9.3. Its direction is the opposite of that for the first and third items. Thus, we reverse the scale value of the response for the second item. Notice that the response of "5" becomes a "1" in the scoring process. The process is easy— just remember to do it.

The Problem of Faking

Assessing attitudes presents one major problem that assessing cognitive achievement does not. Students may tell you what they think you want to hear. The semitechnical term for this is **faking**. If students think you want them to express a favorable attitude, it is easy for them to do so, regardless of how they really feel. Conversely, some students might express an unfavorable attitude just to be ornery, again, regardless of how they really feel.

	SD	D	U	A	SA
Recycling is a fascinating topic.	1[ ]	2[ ]	3[ ]	4[X]	5[ ]
I hate studying air quality.	1[ ]	2[ ]	3[ ]	4[ ]	5[X]
Studying waste management is useful.	1[ ]	2[ ]	3[X]	4[ ]	5[ ]

Score = 4 + 1 + 3 = 8

Figure 9.3 Example of reversing the direction of some items.

Are there ways to deal with this problem? Yes and no. Yes, with careful research and considerable ingenuity, there are ways to detect faking or at least mitigate its effects. Some carefully constructed scales even have scores indicating the likely influence of faking. Developing such scores requires substantial research. On the other hand, for teacher-made scales, there is not much you can do about faking. The main antidote is ensuring a congenial, nonthreatening environment. In general, students don't mind letting you know how they feel about something, provided they are sure it won't hurt them to do so. For this reason, it would be imprudent to allow the score on an attitude scale to affect a student's grade.

Free-Response Measures of Interests and Attitudes

We have presented the Likert method as a simple way to assess interests and attitudes. Formally, the Likert method falls into the class of selected-response items. It is also possible to measure interests and attitudes with free-response (constructed-response) items. For example, you could ask students to write about their favorite topics in math, science, a foreign language, or another area. You could then apply a holistic or an analytic scoring rubric to the essay responses. Topics identified by the students might also be helpful in guiding instruction (e.g., in selecting instructional materials). Such guidance is a good example of using assessment for formative purposes.

Two Practical Matters

We need to raise two practical matters related to the assessment of students' interests and attitudes. They both relate to reliability, but in different ways. First, how stable are students' interests and attitudes? More specifically, are they sufficiently stable that we can get useful measures of them? Sometimes, fear that the answer may be "no" dissuades us from making the effort. However, research shows that measurement of students' interests and attitudes can be quite reliable. For the types of variables we have considered (e.g., attitudes toward various subject fields), students' attitudes are quite stable. On the other hand, students' interests and attitudes are not so rigidly fixed that they cannot be changed. If they were rigidly fixed, it would be futile to set educational objectives for them.

The second practical matter is by way of a reminder. We have noted repeatedly that reliable measurement usually requires more than just a few items. We made this point when considering different types of achievement items. The point also applies in the realm of measuring interests and attitudes. Use an adequate number of items.

Existing Measures of Interests and Attitudes

We have presented methods for creating your own measures of interests and attitudes. Are there existing measures you might use? Yes, thousands of them. However, none of them are widely used in the same way that existing measures of achievement (e.g., standardized achievement tests) are used. Hence, we do not present these existing measures of interests and attitudes in the later chapters on standardized tests (Chapters 11 and 12). One exception to this generalization is career interest measures, which Chapter 12 introduces.

Where do you find information about existing measures of interests and attitudes? There are two sources. First, you can find many of them in the ETS Test Collection (www.ets.org/testcoll). Simply search on the name of a variable, such as reading or math. You will get a mixture of achievement and attitude measures for that area. It is better to do a boolean search using AND (e.g., "science AND attitude"). That procedure limits the results to attitude measures for the area. Second, there are a few books that are collections of interest and attitude measures. Examples are Robinson, Shaver, and Wrightsman (1991) and Shaw and Wright (1967). Some of the scales in these books are relevant for educational applications. Be forewarned, however, that the research base for many of these scales is very thin. Many were used in only one study, although a few have experienced more widespread use. The ETS Test Collection and the books just cited will be particularly useful if you engage in a formal research project.

ASSESSING CREATIVITY

As noted earlier, most educational objectives relate to acquisition of knowledge and skills. Examples include decoding words, extracting meaning from printed text, correcting spelling, solving equations, knowing number facts, stating scientific principles, becoming familiar with historical trends, and so on. Generally, we want citizens to perform tasks correctly, based on sound knowledge. We want the medical doctor to prescribe the correct medicine, the accountant to keep the financial records in order, and the clerk to file the papers in the right folder.

Sometimes, however, a problem may not have a single correct answer. The knowledge base may be elusive. A task might reasonably admit of several different solutions. The job may be entirely novel, with no precedents or rules to follow. For example, the medical condition may be very unclear or an entirely new accounting system is needed. These situations call for creative thinking. When it is needed, it is a highly prized commodity.

Convergent and Divergent Thinking

Useful terms for the contrasts just outlined are **convergent thinking** and **divergent thinking**. These are wonderfully descriptive terms. In convergent thinking, the mind converges on or identifies a single correct answer. In divergent thinking, the mind casts about for a variety of answers. J. P. Guilford popularized the difference between convergent and divergent thinking in his *Structure of Intellect* model of intelligence. In its various forms (Guilford 1959, 1967, 1988), the theory postulated from 120 to 180 different facets of intelligence. Although other theories of intelligence are more popular today (see Chapter 12), the distinction between convergent and divergent thinking remains a useful legacy from Guilford's work.

So far, we have used the terms creativity and divergent thinking. Other terms describing the abilities of interest here are originality, flexibility, and innovative thinking. The professional literature uses all these terms more or less interchangeably. We also do so. The professional literature sometimes includes the term "problem solving." We have avoided that term in this section because problem solving sometimes calls for convergent thinking (e.g., solve this equation) and sometimes for divergent thinking. The most recent discussions of even creative thinking emphasize the importance of an evaluative component (see Runco, 2003).

Perhaps the first reaction upon hearing reference to creativity is to think of such fields as art, fashion design, writing, and architecture. Indeed, these fields often call for creative thinking. However, all fields call for creative thinking at some time. Thus, we hear about highly creative mathematicians, scientists, or military leaders—and teachers. The development of creative thinking skills is useful for everyone. The assessment techniques we present next have wide applicability in many different fields.

Prompts for Creative Thinking

Most of the measures of creative thinking call for constructed responses. The essential character of the methods is to present a relatively simple prompt and ask for student responses to it. We use the term "prompt" here in the same sense as in Chapter 8. It is a task or a question. Students may respond to the prompt in many different ways. The trick, as with most constructed-response items, is to score the responses meaningfully. In Chapter 8, we examined methods for scoring essays and performance tasks. For those prompts, we had some type of correct answer in mind. That is, the items called for convergent thinking. When assessing creative thinking, we still have to figure out how to score the responses, but without having a correct answer in mind. Let's first consider the nature of the prompts and then suggest methods for scoring them.

It is useful to classify the prompts for assessing creative thinking into two categories: general and field-specific. General prompts deal with everyday situations and objects. They do not call for any specialized knowledge. They may be used with any subject matter and, often, with any age level. Field-specific prompts, on the other hand, are deliberately related to specific subject matter. Their applicability may vary with the difficulty level of the subject.

Here are examples of *general prompts* for creative thinking items:

- Describe all the possible uses for a . . . brick (or pencil, or car, etc.).
- In 2 minutes, write all the words you can think of that begin with . . . B (or R, or th, etc.).
- Look at the cartoon on page 191. Write your own caption for it.
- Look at the figure on page 210. Write a title for it.
- Have students read a very short (1–2 paragraph) story. Write a funny ending for the story.

Here are examples of *field-specific prompts* for creative thinking:

- For history: How would North America be different today if the South had won the U.S. Civil War? List as many ways as you can think of.
- For science: Suppose average global temperatures increased by 10° F next year. Assume the increase lasts for at least several centuries. What would be the consequences? List as many things as you can think of.

- For literature: Consider Shakespeare's play *Romeo and Juliet*. Write a different ending for it.
- For math: Look at the graph. Tell different ways you could describe the relationship between X and Y.

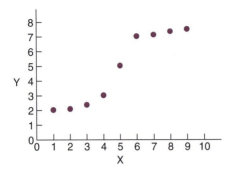

Try This!

Pick one of these areas: history, science, literature, or math. For that area, write a prompt calling for creative thinking.

Of course, we could go on listing numerous other prompts calling for creative responses. Every content field lends itself to such prompts. It works even in areas traditionally considered the exclusive province of convergent thinking, such as science and math. Areas such as literature, art, dance, music, design, and woodworking provide a ready source for other items.

Scoring Creative Responses

Prompts for creative thinking may be used strictly for instructional purposes. In that case, we do not need to worry much about scoring the responses, although we ought to have some idea about desired outcomes. To use the responses for assessment, we need a specific framework for scoring the responses.

There are *five* primary ways to score responses to the kinds of prompts just presented. Some of these ways apply to certain prompts and not to others. Let us describe each of the five ways and explore their application.

The first method calls for a *simple count*. How many responses did the student give? Just count them. With this method, there is no further reference to the nature of the responses. As a minimal quality control, one might exclude from the count obvious duplicates or utterly silly responses. However, the emphasis is on minimal control. Students get wide latitude in responding. For example, when asked to list words starting with "th," how many words are listed? Just count. When asked to list consequences of global warming, how many consequences does the student list? Just count.

Some people feel a bit squeamish about a simple count. Therefore, they apply a quality rating to each response. Then, they add up the quality ratings. This is the second method: *sum of quality ratings*. For example, apply a quality rating to each response for the global warming example. Apply a quality rating to each description of the graph. In each case, add up the ratings. In effect, this method gives credit for both quality and quantity. The quality ratings require nothing more than simple 1–2–3 or 1–5 ratings, much like the holistic ratings applied to essays in Chapter 8. Of course, it takes time to determine what constitutes quality. It also takes time to apply the quality ratings. The teacher must decide if it is worth the effort.

A third method is to score the responses for *originality*. At first, this might sound difficult. How will one define originality? In practice, it is very easy. Originality is self-defining. Specifically, we define original as uncommon. Common responses are those occurring frequently. Uncommon (original) responses are those occurring infrequently. For example, for uses of a pencil, everyone will list "writing." That will be a common response. Quite a few students may list "weapon" (or some synonym). That response has more originality, but it is still rather common. Only a rare student may list "as a lever" or "as a balance." Those are original responses. They are uncommon. For the Civil War example, common responses may refer to maps and national governments. An original response may refer to effects on sports championships or currency differences.

A fourth method is *single best* response. This method approximates the holistic rating of essays and performance tasks, as described in Chapter 8. It obviously applies to single-response items, such as the *Romeo and Juliet* example. However, it can also be used with multiple-response items. In this case, the teacher needs to scan all responses provided by a student, decide which is the best, and apply a quality rating to that best response. In some ways, this method may yield results approximating measures of convergent thinking.

A fifth method, perhaps the least obvious of them all, is to score the responses for *different perspectives*. This method works only for certain types of prompts. The history (Civil War) and science (global warming) prompts are good examples. In this method, students get points for covering different perspectives. Relevant perspectives will vary with the prompt. For example, with the Civil War example, many responses will deal with matters of political organization and identity. Other potentially relevant perspectives include economics, fashion, language, sports, and so on. The global warming prompt will elicit many responses about shorelines and agricultural productivity. Other potentially relevant responses include vacation spots, the clothing industry, and so on. After formulating some categories of perspectives, the teacher can quickly scan responses for the number of different perspectives displayed.

It should be obvious that these five methods allow for combinations. For example, a teacher might use a simple count of total responses as well as a score for most original

---

KEY POINTS SUMMARY 9.2 | *Methods for Scoring Creative Responses*

1. Simple count
2. Simple count with quality rating
3. Originality
4. Single best answer
5. Different perspectives

response for each student. Or, a teacher might use the single best response as well as the number of different perspectives.

Standardized Tests for Creative Thinking

There are several standardized tests of creative thinking. However, none of them are widely used, except for research purposes. You are not likely to find regular use of any standardized test of creativity in a regular school testing program. No state assessment programs include such tests. We do not include these tests in Chapters 11 and 12, where we treat widely used standardized tests. However, we want to acknowledge some existing tests related to creative thinking. First, to see a list of existing tests of creative thinking, go to this website: www.creativelearning.com/assess. It contains a list of some 70 tests. Second, we note that the most widely used and most thoroughly researched test of creative thinking is the Torrance Tests of Creative Thinking (TTCT). Currently, it comes in two versions: TTCT-Figural (Thinking Creatively With Pictures) and TTCT-Verbal (Thinking Creatively With Words). If you undertake program evaluation in creative thinking, we recommend that you examine the TTCT. For further information about the TTCT, go to the website for Scholastic Testing Service: www.ststesting.com/ngifted.html. These sources warrant careful attention if you undertake a formal research project involving creative thinking.

NONTEST INDICATORS

Mention "educational assessment" and the first thing that pops into mind is a test. The test might be a teacher-made quiz or a three-hour AP exam. It might be a set of multiple-choice items or a performance task. It might be norm-referenced or criterion-referenced. In whatever form, most people think of a test.

Consider, however, what we are really trying to do in educational assessment. We are trying to get information, good information, about student accomplishment. Tests are only one type of information—a very important type but still only one type. There are other sources of information about student accomplishment. We group them here under the general label **nontest indicators**. We will describe several categories of nontest indicators and make some suggestions about their use. Nontest indicators can be useful for large groups of students (e.g., an entire school system or state). Indeed, an increasing number of schools incorporate nontest indicators into a "report card" for the school. Typically, the report card contains information from tests as well as from a select number of nontest indicators. The No Child Left Behind Act specifically requires use of some nontest indicators. The act refers to typical tests as "academic assessments" and to nontest indicators as "other academic indicators." Nontest indicators can also be helpful at the classroom level, where they can be used for both summative and formative assessments.

Follow-up Activities: Jobs and College

It is a truism that the ultimate test of school outcomes occurs after students leave school. What becomes of the graduates? Answering this question provides two of the premier examples of nontest indicators of educational success: jobs and college. The questions are simple. Did the graduates get jobs? Did the graduates get into college? Here we reference the questions to the end of K–12 schooling. Interestingly, the same questions apply to the conclusion of college education, excepting only that we substitute "graduate/professional school" for "college."

Both topics, jobs and college, are of paramount importance to parents and the public at large, as well as to students and school staff. In the presence of positive evidence for these two matters, much may be forgiven even in an otherwise blemished record of schooling. In the presence of negative evidence on these two matters, much fault may be found even in an otherwise commendable record of schooling.

Obtaining information on these topics is not always easy. Of course, it is easy to get the information for a few students. Getting the information for all or nearly all students and doing so year after year presents real challenges. Many schools do not have the resources to track this information systematically. Furthermore, the questions about jobs and college are deceptively simple. At first, you expect just a "yes" or "no" answer. But there is more to a complete answer. What kinds of jobs did they get? At what pay rates? How is the job picture affected by national economic trends? What kinds of colleges did the students enter? Open-admissions or highly selective colleges? Did they perform successfully once admitted? Did they persist beyond the first year? Answering all these types of questions, all of which are quite legitimate, is a significant challenge. Nevertheless, the answers yield very useful information about the success of the educational enterprise.

Indexes From Routine Records

Schools keep a variety of records on a routine basis. Some of these records, properly summarized and analyzed over an appropriate period of time, yield useful assessment information. As one-time measures, they may be exceedingly difficult to interpret. When analyzed for successive terms or years, they can be helpful.

We will not attempt to give an exhaustive list of routine records that are relevant for assessment. The list might differ from one school to another. However, there are some obvious examples available for nearly all schools. Examples include

- Absentee rates
- Dropout rates
- Classroom discipline rates
- School-sponsored volunteer participation
- Athletic participation
- Club membership rates
- Participation in interscholastic competitions (science fairs, etc.)

Desired outcomes for these indicators should be obvious. We would like to see low rates for absenteeism, dropouts, and disciplinary cases. We would like to see high rates for volunteering, athletics, clubs, and competitions. Furthermore, we would like to see improvements in the rates over time.

Satisfaction Reports

In some ways, reports of satisfaction are the ultimate arbiters in the world of educational assessment. If people are highly satisfied with educational programs, what more need be said? If people are highly dissatisfied, all is lost. Of course, we exaggerate a bit. If people are satisfied but student achievement is demonstrably horrible, we should be concerned. If people are dissatisfied but student achievement is superb, there is work to be done to change minds. All things considered, however, reports of satisfaction rank high as nontest indicators of educational accomplishment.

Use of satisfaction reports entails three considerations. *First*, we must decide on the *target response group*. This might be parents, the public at large, students, or some other group. The choices are not mutually exclusive. For example, we could use both parents and students. The *second* decision relates to the *target categories* for the reports. Target categories range along a continuum from the very general to the very specific. Figure 9.4 shows examples of items on the very general side of the continuum. The format uses the Likert-type item presented earlier. Notice that the rating scale allows for making no rating, based on insufficient information.

On the other hand, the form may target some very specific areas. Here, the items cover details. For example, the form might target satisfaction with details of the gifted program, extracurricular activities, or parts of the instructional program. In each case, the items are specific to that area and ask for degree of satisfaction. Figure 9.5 shows an example. It takes the global statement about "quality of instruction" from Figure 9.4 and asks for separate ratings in different curricular areas.

The *third* consideration for use of satisfaction reports relates to the *method for administration*. The issue arises primarily for target audiences outside the school (e.g., parents or the public at large). Satisfaction measures for students usually involve paper-and-pencil (or web-based) forms answered by all students in the target group. The target group of students might be all students in Grade 12 or all students in Grades 7 to 9. For groups outside the school, two questions arise: (1) What will be the method of contact? It could be by telephone, mail, or personal interview. (2) Will it be a sample or the entire group? Answering these questions would take us well beyond the scope of this book. These are matters of survey methodology. The interested reader should consult books on that topic.

	Very Dissatisfied				Very Satisfied	Don't Know
Quality of instruction	1	2	3	4	5	[ ]
School administration	1	2	3	4	5	[ ]
Student achievement	1	2	3	4	5	[ ]
Quality of facilities	1	2	3	4	5	[ ]
Extracurricular activities	1	2	3	4	5	[ ]
Overall, considering everything	1	2	3	4	5	[ ]

Figure 9.4 Sample form for rating of general satisfaction.

	Very Dissatisfied				Very Satisfied	Don't Know
Rate quality of instruction in:						
Reading	1	2	3	4	5	[ ]
Mathematics	1	2	3	4	5	[ ]
Science	1	2	3	4	5	[ ]
Social studies	1	2	3	4	5	[ ]
Foreign language	1	2	3	4	5	[ ]
Music	1	2	3	4	5	[ ]
Art	1	2	3	4	5	[ ]
Physical education	1	2	3	4	5	[ ]

Figure 9.5 Sample form for rating of specific satisfaction.

Self-Reports of Achievement

Self-reports of achievement provide a potentially useful source of information about educational accomplishment. In appearance, the self-report is much like an interest measure. Students record responses on Likert-type scales. The elements rated by students are precisely the learning objectives or content outlines used to construct an achievement test. Figure 9.6 shows an example for a few topics in a junior high math course. Figure 9.7 shows an example for some of the contents of this book.

As with any rating scale like these, you need a list of items to be rated and a response scale. Base the items on the list of learning objectives. Obviously, you can create a very detailed list of objectives or a more general list. For example, each item in Figure 9.7 could be broken down into the objectives listed at the beginning of each chapter. One of the nice things about these self-report scales is that they can be made to correspond exactly to your learning objectives.

For the response scales, several possibilities suggest themselves. You could use a simple Yes-No format. Students might find it easier to use a scale with more variation.

Mark to show how much you think you have learned in each area.	Very Little				Very Much
Working with percents	1	2	3	4	5
Working with decimals	1	2	3	4	5
Graphing linear functions	1	2	3	4	5
Determining probabilities	1	2	3	4	5
Solving equations in one unknown	1	2	3	4	5

Figure 9.6 Scale for self-report of achievement in math.

Mark to show how much you think you have learned in each area.	Very Little				Very Much
Methods to determine reliability	1	2	3	4	5
Ways to demonstrate validity	1	2	3	4	5
Interpreting student performance	1	2	3	4	5
Constructing objective test items	1	2	3	4	5
Constructing essays and performance tasks	1	2	3	4	5

Figure 9.7 Scale for self-report of achievement in educational assessment.

Scales using anchor points from Very Little to Very Much or from Not at All to A Great Deal seem to work well.

Try This!

Pick an area you teach or plan to teach. Create a brief self-report of achievement in that area. You can model it after the ones in Figures 9.6 and 9.7.

Self-reports of achievement are easy to construct, administer, and score. Summaries of results consist of average ratings or percentages of students giving various responses (e.g., ratings of at least 4 on a 5-point scale). These summaries provide good information for formative evaluation at the class level. For example, consider the items in Figure 9.6. Suppose that item averages are above 4.0 except for "determining probabilities," which has an average of 2.5. This result would suggest increasing the instructional time for that topic. Of course, this is not necessarily the case. The teacher may be content with a lower average on that item. However, the data at least raise consciousness about this state of affairs.

Will students respond honestly to these items? It depends. Self-reports are fragile and must be handled with care. You would not want to use these items to assign grades to students. If students knew they were being graded on their responses, the responses would probably be useless. If students know that you are using the responses for your own feedback, they will probably respond forthrightly. The best way to avoid the implication that the responses affect grading is to collect the information anonymously. Effective use of self-reports also depends on having a positive classroom atmosphere. A sour teacher-student relationship would probably invalidate self-reports.

Provided that the self-reports are obtained in a nonthreatening atmosphere, self-reports of achievement appear to have reasonable validity. That is, the self-reports do correlate positively with actual achievement of objectives. In addition, these simple forms are an ideal method for encouraging self-assessment of learning.

Unobtrusive Measures

Social science research has a category called unobtrusive measures. These measures are used primarily for research purposes. However, they have application within the area of educational assessment. They provide good examples of nontest indicators. The key characteristics of **unobtrusive measures** are that they are naturally occurring in the normal environment and that the persons involved are oblivious to the assessment. For the latter reason, an alternate name for unobtrusive measures is nonreactive measures. In fact, if persons involved are aware of the measurement, they can easily distort it, possibly rendering it invalid.

Unobtrusive measures are highly specific to the variable being assessed. We can give some examples of them but no general rules for their development. Here are a few examples:

- A school sponsors an annual poetry contest. The number of entries is an unobtrusive measure of student interest in poetry.
- A teacher creates a web page on environmental issues (accessible only to persons with school accounts). The number of "hits" is an unobtrusive measure of student interest in environmental issues.
- A student art show is open for two days. It is difficult to post someone at the door to count attendees. However, you leave a stack of programs at the door. Count the number of programs remaining at the end of the show. The count yields an unobtrusive measure of attendance.
- The number of student winners in the local science fair is an unobtrusive measure of student success in science.

It usually takes some creative thinking to identify relevant unobtrusive measures. Furthermore, they are fragile measures. A host of environmental factors may affect them. For example, in the poetry example, if a teacher starts requiring students to submit poems, the count of entries will increase without a concomitant increase in student interest in poetry. In the web page example, if someone knows that the count is being watched, he or she may "hit" the site repeatedly, thereby destroying the value of the hit count.

Eugene Webb and colleagues (1966) popularized the notion of unobtrusive measures. The book is now available in a second edition (Webb et al., 1981) and in a reissued version of the first edition (Webb, Campbell, Schwartz, & Sechrist, 2000). All of the books provide numerous examples of unobtrusive measures, and anyone interested in developing unobtrusive measures for educational use should consult them. They will serve as a springboard for developing clever ideas for school application.

KEY POINTS SUMMARY 9.3   *Some Important Nontest Indicators*

1. Follow-up activities: Jobs and college
2. Indexes from routine records
3. Satisfaction reports
4. Self-reports of achievement
5. Unobtrusive measures

Nontest Indicators for Classroom Use

Some of the nontest indicators we have considered apply to large collections of students. The information applies to entire buildings, districts, states, or even nations. As noted previously, often schoolwide "report cards" incorporate some of these nontest indicators. However, the concept of nontest indicators also has use at the classroom level. Every teacher can keep a record of important indicators.

What types of indicators will be useful at the classroom level? The answer depends considerably on the grade level and the subject matter. One set of indicators may apply for the Grade 12 English teacher covering five sections of American literature. Another set of indicators may apply for the Grade 1 teacher who covers all subjects for a class of 25 students.

Here are a few examples for different grades and subjects:

- Number of students who volunteer for a project
- Number of students who raise their hand to answer questions in class
- Rate of completing homework assignments
- For computer-based instructional programs, number of units completed
- Number of students joining a class-related club

Obviously, each of these examples needs a more refined definition for actual application. The examples do suggest the wide range of possibilities.

Additional, potentially useful nontest indicators applicable to the classroom situation come readily to mind. Be prudent in their selection. Trying to use too many will be counterproductive. You will soon abandon all of them as being a nuisance. Start with one or two. Be wary of using more than three or four. Remember that the real value of the indicator becomes apparent only when used over a period of time. Here is an incidental benefit of using nontest indicators on a regular basis: They help remind us that we are pursuing more than high test scores.

Try This!

Think of a class you teach or plan to teach. Describe one nontest indicator of educational performance for students in this class.

Outcomes, Not Inputs

When considering nontest indicators of educational success, it is important to concentrate on outcomes, not inputs. Inputs are the resources devoted to the educational enterprise. They include such factors as student-teacher ratios, per-pupil expenditures, computer availability, number of books in the library, and so on. These inputs are usually easy to measure. Most schools have meticulous records on such matters. They are important. However, these inputs are *not* what we have in mind for nontest indicators of educational success.

The nontest indicators of success should relate to student outcomes. We want to know what is happening to students. Consider the examples introduced earlier. These are outcomes we would like to see for students. We would like them to get jobs. We would like them to get into college. We would like to see a healthy rate of participation in clubs. We would like them to enter scholastic competitions. We would like to see low absentee rates. And so on for the other examples. The key issue is not what schools put into the educational effort but what students get out of it. You will sometimes see reports of input as if they were outcomes. Do not confuse the two.

Concluding Notes on Nontest Indicators

Let us conclude this section on nontest indicators of educational success with a few caveats and a few suggestions. We begin with the caveats. Using nontest indicators of educational success is sometimes more difficult than it first appears. The difficulty arises from three sources. First, the actual collection of information can be a real nuisance. It always sounds simple. It rarely is. For example, finding out which students went to college, which ones belong to clubs, which ones do volunteer work, and so on—all these activities are difficult, if done well. Second, making sense of the information usually requires that it be collected over several time periods or across comparable schools or classes. The collection must be done consistently. This may be difficult. Third, many external factors may influence the outcomes. A school or an individual teacher may exercise little control over many of these external factors. Consider the English teacher who is keeping track of the number of students submitting entries for the local newspaper's poetry contest. The newspaper changes the entry rules. There goes the continuity in the teacher's nontest indicator. Consider the school monitoring post-high-school job placements. The national economy cools. Job placements go down. Is that the school's fault? The economy gets hot. Job placements go up. Is that to the school's credit?

A fourth caution for nontest indicators is that they vary substantially in terms of their applicability to groups versus individual students. Some of them will be very useful for tracking the status of groups. For example, surveys of parental satisfaction or rates of college attendance will be useful for entire schools, but they may not provide direct guidance in working with individual students. On the other hand, self-reports of achievement for a teacher's objectives can be very helpful at the classroom level, but such information probably does not generalize very well to an entire school.

Here are some suggestions about using nontest indicators of educational success. First, use them. They provide additional perspective on the success of the educational enterprise. They are applicable from the classroom to the district to the national level. Second, start simple. As noted earlier, they can appear deceptively simple. The temptation is to be overly ambitious. Be cautious, especially when getting started. Third, use a judicious number of indicators. Not too many, not too few. Using too many will lead to a breakdown of the entire effort. You will become overwhelmed with data collection. Using too few will narrow your vision. The temptation will be to overgeneralize from a too-thin basis. Fourth, be very explicit in defining the indicator and keeping track of it. Stating that "most students went to college" or "it seems like more students entered the contest this year" is not helpful. Be exact. Finally, do not think of nontest indicators as a substitute for test indicators. Students' performance on tests—from multiple-choice to performance assessments and from teacher-made assessments to nationally standardized tests—will continue to be the mainstay of educational assessment. However, nontest indicators provide a valuable adjunct source of information.

PRACTICAL ADVICE

1. Don't be bashful about including objectives related to interests and attitudes in your instructional objectives. And, don't neglect getting some information about changes in students' interests and attitudes in your assessment program.

2. Practice making simple scales for measuring interests and attitudes using the Likert method.

3. Gain experience in developing prompts calling for divergent thinking and in applying the methods for scoring student responses to these prompts.

4. Identify nontest indicators of student accomplishment that might help you keep track of what is happening to students. You may also want to help your school identify potentially useful nontest indicators of achievement.

SUMMARY

1. Most teachers and schools have objectives related to students' interests and attitudes. These objectives should be made explicit and they should be assessed.

2. The Likert method provides a simple procedure to develop scales for assessing interests and attitudes. We outlined steps in using this procedure.

3. "Faking" can affect the assessment of interests and attitudes. Therefore, certain precautions are in order when conducting such assessment.

4. There are many existing measures of interests and attitudes. None are routinely used in school testing programs (except career interest measures). You should investigate existing measures if you undertake a formal research program.

5. Many teachers wish to develop creative thinking abilities in their students. We illustrated the types of prompts used to assess creative (divergent) thinking with some general prompts and field-specific prompts.

6. We also outlined five approaches to scoring responses to creative thinking prompts. We labeled these: simple count, sum of quality ratings, originality, single best, and different perspectives.

7. Nontest indicators of educational success can provide useful adjuncts to the typical test indicators of performance.

8. We identified the following five categories of nontest indicators: follow-up activities (jobs and college), indexes from routine records, satisfaction reports, self-reports of achievement, and unobtrusive measures.

9. We offered several cautions about and several practical suggestions for use of nontest indicators.

KEY TERMS

cognitive outcomes
convergent thinking
divergent thinking

faking
Likert method
noncognitive outcomes

nontest indicators
unobtrusive measures

EXERCISES

1. Pick a curricular area and grade of interest to you. Develop a Likert-type scale to measure student attitude toward that area. Follow the steps in Key Points Summary 9.1.

2. Go to the ETS Test Collection (www.ets.org/testcoll). Do a boolean search on "science AND attitude" or "mathematics AND attitude" or any content area of interest to you. (Use the Advanced search feature.) Select two of the scales you find. Click on the number for each scale to get more detailed information about it. What is the target age group for each scale? If you wanted to use one of these scales, where could you get copies?

3. Consider the grade and subject(s) you teach or plan to teach. Create two field-specific prompts for creative thinking for your grade and subject. Indicate how you would score responses to each prompt.

4. Review the list of "indexes from routine records" suggested as nontest indicators on page 213. Add two more indexes to the list. Be reasonably sure that a school would have the information on hand.

5. Create a brief (10-item) satisfaction measure for use with parents. Suppose the measure applies only to your classroom. What items do you want to include? Show the response scale you would use with the items.

6. Consider the grade and subject(s) you teach or plan to teach. Create a brief self-report of achievement for that situation. For purposes of this exercise, include no more than five items. Show the response scale you will use.

Chapter 10

Administering
and Analyzing Tests

OBJECTIVES

- List suggestions for test administration in each of these areas: preparing test materials, remote preparation of students, immediate preparation of students, managing the testing environment, preparation for scoring, returning the tests, and wrapping up the assessment.
- Define the procedures for conducting an item analysis.
- Determine when to conduct a formal or an informal item analysis.
- Describe the prevalence of cheating and types of cheating.
- Outline steps that authorities recommend to prevent or, at least, reduce cheating.

What This Chapter Is About

This chapter offers a host of suggestions for the actual administration of tests and assessment exercises. The chapter presents the techniques of item analysis. These techniques help analyze the quality of a test. They are routinely applied to external tests and can be fruitfully used for classroom tests. A matter of special concern is cheating. We review the prevalence of cheating, types of cheating, and suggestions for preventing cheating.

Why This Topic Is Important

Having prepared your assessments according to the suggestions in the last four chapters, you now get ready to administer them. Naturally, you want to do a good job. The suggestions in the first part of this chapter will help you do so. After administering a test or other assessment, you may want to apply some relatively simple techniques to help examine the quality of your tests and improve future tests. Finally, because cheating has become widespread, you will want to know how to prevent it or, at least, reduce it. Therefore, you will want to see the suggestions on this topic. All these topics have very practical applications in the classroom.

ADMINISTERING TESTS

As with any type of assessment, the *purpose* of the assessment is an initial consideration. As noted in Chapter 1, assessments may be undertaken for different purposes. Some assessments are strictly for the teacher's information in guiding instruction. In such a context, student scores, in the traditional sense of that term, may not be important. Or, an assessment may be undertaken primarily for motivational purposes. Very often, however, the assessment relates to the grading of students. Results will contribute to a student's report card or other formal record. This chapter deals primarily with the treatment of assessment in this latter context. Many of the suggestions made here are not appropriate and may even be counterproductive in other contexts. It is also important to note that we assume the tests or other assessment exercises mentioned in this chapter have been prepared according to recommendations provided in Chapters 6 to 9. That is, they have resulted from use of a test blueprint and followed the suggestions for preparing selected-response and constructed-response items, including the use of scoring rubrics where appropriate.

Advice on administering tests or assessment exercises is largely a matter of common sense. But, sometimes it is useful to remind ourselves of the dictates of common sense. Such as: Drink lots of fluids if you run a 10K in 80° heat. Slow down when driving in snow. Don't wait until the night before the final exam to study your educational assessment book. All are matters of common sense, but worth gentle reminders. So, let us work through some commonsense advice about administering classroom assessments. We begin with a matter of paramount importance: fairness.

Not Fair!

Few things rank higher than fairness in students' list of virtues. Maybe nothing does. A charge of "Not fair!" rings with terrible vengeance in kid-dom. Fairness is perhaps nowhere more important to students than in the realm of assessment. Therefore, make sure your tests are fair. What does fairness mean for classroom assessment? In our consideration of validity (pp. 87–90), we examined the technical definition of fairness and how it is measured. However, students use a less technical definition. There seem to be three components to the common definition of fairness. *First*, make sure you teach what you test. This is the flip side of content validity. Under content validity, we said: Make sure your test covers what you teach. Now we say: Make sure your instruction covers what is in the test. We construe "what you teach" or "your instruction" broadly. It is not restricted to what you say in class. It includes assignments you give or topics you tell students they should cover on their own. Also, make sure you finish a topic before testing it. That includes giving students a chance to digest the material and raise questions about it before you test it.

Second, give adequate notice. Let students know when to expect a significant assessment and what it will be like. Don't leave students in the dark about your assessment procedures and schedule. Does this mean no "pop" quizzes? No, it does not mean that. But, if you are going to use pop quizzes, make sure students know they are a possibility.

Third, be fair in grading. This is especially important for essays and performance tasks. They allow for considerable latitude in judging what is acceptable. Make sure those judgments are fair. In this context, fairness has two facets. The judgments should be consistent across different students. The judgments should appear reasonable to another person, say, to another teacher.

Note that fairness does not mean being easy. Students will tolerate high standards, demanding assessment, and tough grading. Many of them even appreciate these characteristics. All in all, it is not difficult to be fair in your assessments. But, it is of the utmost importance that they be fair and be perceived as fair by students. Many of the other suggestions in this chapter relate to making the assessment process fair.

Preparing Test Materials

You have your test items or exercises on index cards, in a computer file, or perhaps on miscellaneous scraps of paper. It is now time to prepare the test document that students will receive. Here are several things to keep in mind.

1. Be sure to give *clear directions*. The task is always perfectly clear to the person who prepared the test (you). It will not necessarily be clear to the students. Include how to mark answers. If there are specific time limits on sections or exercises, note that. If supplementary materials (dictionaries, calculators, etc.) are permitted, note that.

2. Use a clean, *simple format*. Most tests—even math tests—will require reading something. Make sure the material can be easily read. Use "white space" generously. Make sure "page breaks" are sensible.

If items or exercises will appear on a computer screen, be sure the appearance on the screen is eye-pleasing. It may look fine on a printed page but not on a screen (or vice versa).

3. *Allow adequate time for producing copies*. Plan ahead. You may rely on office staff to produce materials. Be considerate of them. Or, you may produce the materials yourself. Take your time. Rush jobs invite errors.

4. *Spot check* the tests after they are reproduced. Strange things may happen as materials are being reproduced. Pages may be missing or upside down. Ink cartridges run out, copiers lose their toner, and so on. We know of one humorous (!) incident in which the correct answer key was reproduced as the last page of the test.

5. In addition to spot checking the test after it has been reproduced, *take one test and answer it* as if you were a student. This will help detect anomalies not evident elsewhere in the production process. Nonfatal mistakes can be corrected by oral instructions when tests are distributed. Fatal mistakes: Back to the copy machine (or other medium of reproduction).

Admittedly, all this cross-checking is a nuisance. No doubt, you are sick of looking at the items and exercises by now. In the long run, however, it is worth the few extra minutes of your time.

6. *Worry about security*. You will usually produce test materials a day or so before their actual use. Store them in a secure place. If the test is an especially important one, you may want to number the copies. Then, make sure all copies are accounted for when you use them, as well as when you recover them after use.

7. *For multisection courses*, prepare different but comparable forms of the test. This is another nuisance but a necessity. Using exactly the same test for five sections of a course is an invitation to chicanery.

Checklist for Preparing Test Materials

☐ 1. Give clear directions.
☐ 2. Use a simple format.
☐ 3. Allow adequate time for producing copies.
☐ 4. Spot check.
☐ 5. Take one test and answer it.
☐ 6. Worry about security.
☐ 7. For multisection courses, prepare comparable forms of the test.

Remote Preparation of Students

Of course, the most important remote preparation of students is good instruction. Without that, all else is lost. Assuming that good instruction has been provided, there are several other actions to take.

1. The first bit of advice regarding remote preparation is to *give adequate notice*. We have already covered that topic in our discussion of fairness, hence we will say no more about it here. In some high-stakes testing situations, giving adequate notice is a legal requirement; it may even mean several years' notice for such examples as high school graduation tests. However, giving adequate notice is also important for classroom tests.

2. Make *advance preparation for accommodations*. **Accommodations** is the technical term for alterations in testing conditions related to a student disability. Some students may

"Algebra class will be important to you later in life because there's going to be a test six weeks from now."

Figure 10.1 Adequate notice about upcoming assessments helps students prepare.
(With permission of Randy Glasbergen.)

require accommodations, such as large-print versions, extended time limits, and so on.[1] You may need to confer with the school psychologist or counselor about these students. Be sure you know what is required. Just as importantly, be sure you know in advance how to provide the accommodation during the testing period. That is, do not wait until you are distributing test materials to figure out how you will handle the accommodation.

Current terminology in education makes a distinction between accommodations and **modifications** in testing. Accommodations refer to changes in specific conditions for a specific test, whereas modifications refer to using some entirely different procedure to attempt measuring the same construct. For example, a student may take Test A, a traditional paper-and-pencil, multiple-choice test, as a measure of math competency but with an extended time limit. That is an accommodation. However, another student may require the use of an interview to determine math competency. That is a modification. Requirements for accommodations and modifications should be specified in the student's individualized education program (IEP). Details about IEPs are covered in Chapter 14.

3. *Consider likely circumstances.* Before you get to the actual day and period for testing, consider likely circumstances that might affect your assessment procedures. Will you need any special seating arrangements? If so, does the classroom allow for such arrangements? Are there any circumstances coinciding with your testing time that might be disruptive? A fire drill? A school rally? Will you need any special equipment or materials? A map, a projector, a computer? Try to anticipate these factors as best as you can well in advance of the testing. At the same time, be aware that you may not have control over all the details, such as an unannounced fire drill.

Checklist for Remote Preparation of Students

☐ 1. Give adequate notice.
☐ 2. Make advance preparation for accommodations.
☐ 3. Consider likely circumstances.

Immediate Preparation of Students

Immediate preparation refers to the time when you actually begin the assessment. You are ready to distribute materials and say "Go!" We offer six suggestions for this occasion.

1. If cheating is a distinct possibility, *rearrange seating as needed*. The relevance of this suggestion depends on the nature of the test, the usual seating arrangement, students' age level, and the general atmosphere in the school and classroom. Some sources suggest having students sit in alternate seats. Not many classrooms have sufficient seats to allow for this. It may be feasible to rearrange students so that likely collaborators do not sit together. If doing that, rearrange everyone so as not to single out the likely culprits or deciding who is or is not a likely culprit. Of course, none of these actions may be necessary. In fact, in a school with a strong honor code, the actions might be offensive. The main point is to think about this matter and take any needed action before distributing materials.

---

[1] For discussion of the legal context for accommodations, see Chapter 14.

2. When distributing materials, make sure *everyone gets what is needed.* Sometimes each student needs only one thing (e.g., a test booklet or a sheet of paper). That's easy to check. More frequently, each student needs two or three things (e.g., an answer sheet, a set of test questions, and a map). Take a moment to see that everyone has all needed items. Hold up a copy of each thing and ask: "Does everyone have A, B, . . .?"

3. Distributing materials is almost inevitably slightly chaotic. You do not want the chitchat and fumbling associated with distribution to continue. Therefore, once it is clear that everyone has everything, *establish order.* It is not difficult to do so, but you must be decisive about it.

4. Make sure students *get their names on everything* distributed. Nothing is quite so disconcerting as starting to score the tests and finding that you have several papers with no names. In addition, if you consider the test materials secure, it is important to have names on materials to help track down missing materials.

5. *Review directions* with students. No doubt, you have the directions on the test materials. Some students will not read them! Take a moment to walk through the directions with students. This is especially important for essays and performance tasks. The freedom of response allowed for those tasks means that students are free to go seriously awry in responding. Specific directions are also important for selected-response items if you do anything unusual in scoring those items (e.g., use a correction for guessing). Also at this time, remind students about permissible or impermissible aids (e.g., calculators).

6. Before starting students on the test, offer some quick *words of encouragement.* "Do your best." "Hundreds all around." Something along those lines will let students know you really want them to do well.

Checklist for Immediate Preparation of Students

☐ 1. Rearrange seating as needed.
☐ 2. Make sure all students get what is needed.
☐ 3. Establish order.
☐ 4. Get students' names on everything.
☐ 5. Review directions.
☐ 6. Give quick words of encouragement.

Managing the Testing Environment

Now students have started working. You need to tend to them during the testing time. There are three points to keep in mind.

1. First and foremost, *monitor the testing situation.* Don't sit at the front desk and read a magazine. That invites mischief. Occasionally circulate about the room. This is not all a matter of preventing cheating, although it is partly that. It is also a matter of seeing that students are staying at the task. Sometimes students fall asleep! Or a student may have obviously misunderstood the directions about how to record answers. Stay on top of the situation. If you are seated for part of the time, it is better to be seated in the back of the room than in full view of the students.

2. *Answer questions with fairness in mind.* Almost inevitably, one or two students will have questions about specific items or tasks. Answer the questions succinctly to provide clarification. If it seems necessary, provide the clarification for the entire class. Do not give hints about answers to individual students. That is not fair to the other students.

3. If time is important and no clock is visible, *apprise students of remaining time.* In most classrooms, a clock is easily visible. In that case, students can check for themselves. However, if no clock is visible, let students know about remaining time. For some assessments, timing will not be important.

For performance assessments completed outside the classroom, there is an important corollary to this point about time. Students may have days or even weeks to complete an assignment. Periodically remind students about the deadline for completing the work. You may want to have intermediate submissions of partially completed work to help ensure timely completion of final projects. Students are no less prone to procrastination than you are.

Checklist for Managing the Testing Environment

☐ 1. Monitor the testing situation.
☐ 2. Answer questions with fairness in mind.
☐ 3. Apprise students of remaining time, if needed.

Preparation for Scoring

You have collected the tests or projects. You are getting ready to score them. There are three points to make about preparing to score the materials. One applies to use of machine-scored answer documents. The other two apply to scoring essays and performance tasks.

1. *Clean up answer sheets* before putting them through the scanner. This will take only a few minutes per class. It is well worth the time. Make sure all answer sheets are in the same orientation. If students had to code in their names or other identifiers, make sure they did so. Sometimes students will fill in the little boxes at the top of the columns but fail to fill in the appropriate spaces in the columns. Make sure marks are sufficiently dark. Clean up smudges and stray marks. Finally, make sure your own answer key is properly completed.

2. Chapter 8 described various procedures for scoring essays and performance tasks. Now you are ready to apply one (or more) of these procedures. Before you plunge headlong into the task, here is a bit of practical advice: *Schedule appropriate time* to complete the scoring. You may be in for a long haul. Say you have five essay questions for each of 120 students. Zipping through the essays at just two minutes per essay, you have 20 hours of work ahead of you. That does not include adding up scores and preparing class summaries.

Try This!

You have a class of 25 students. Each student wrote three short essays for your test. Estimate how long it will take you to score all the essays.

It is unlikely that you can maintain consistent quality in scoring for 20 hours straight. You probably cannot do so for more than two hours at a time. You need to develop an appropriate schedule for completing such scoring efforts. You also need to build in some self-checks on consistency, as described in Chapter 8. Of course, consistency is not the only issue here. There is also your mental health.

3. Before systematically scoring all the essays or performance tasks, *spot check a few*. Although you will score the exercises anonymously (as recommended in Chapter 8), you may want to scan the responses for a few students who usually do well. If these students show confusion about an item (or a question or an exercise), it may well be that there is something wrong with the item rather than with students' knowledge of the material. You may want to take this into account when scoring the item, task, or exercise. In fact, if there is widespread confusion, you may not want to score it at all. Don't be afraid to admit to students that you had a "bum" item or task.

Checklist for Preparation for Scoring

☐ 1. Clean up answer sheets (for scannable sheets).
☐ 2. Schedule appropriate time for scoring.
☐ 3. Spot check a few tests.

Returning the Tests

A test is not complete until you have returned the scored materials to students. Students should see how they did. In addition, you should explain some things. Here are the pointers on returning materials to students.

1. *Return scored tests promptly*. The sooner, the better. If the testing experience has a chance to be a learning experience, students need to get results quickly. Scoring tests promptly is, frankly, a nuisance. It seems there are always better, more important things to do. Bite the bullet. Get into the habit of scoring and returning tests promptly. In the long run, it will simplify your life. More importantly, it may help your students.

2. When returning tests, *do not announce individual scores*. It may be embarrassing for students. It is also illegal (see p. 357). It is legal and possibly useful to publicly acknowledge particularly good performance.[2] If you "post" grades, for example, on a

---

[2] Recently, there have been legal challenges to public acknowledgment of good performance. Watch for developments on this topic.

classroom door or in an electronic database accessible to students, do so in such a way as to protect student identity. You may do so by assigning random codes known only to you and the individual student. Do not use Social Security numbers.

Although you do not reveal results for individual students, you may want to provide information about the total class performance. You may do this formally by way of a report of average or median performance. Alternatively, you may give a narrative summary of performance. For example, you may indicate that "overall, the class did very well" or "I was disappointed in class performance and we need to review some of this material."

3. When tests are returned, *explain the scoring*. This is usually easy to do for selected-response items. In most instances, it will be one point for each item. Variations on this rule will require extra explanation. For essay and performance tasks, some explanation is almost always needed. Let students know what system you used for scoring and how you applied it.

4. *Allow for student questions*, but do so judiciously. You certainly want to allow for questions about the scoring procedures. Clarify these as necessary. You may or may not want to allow for questions about individual items or exercises during class time. You should allow for such individual discussion on a personal basis outside of class time. Beginning in the middle grades, some students may use the opportunity for endless nitpicking if the situation is not managed carefully. There may not be sufficient time during class to review every question. Furthermore, some students may unwittingly put themselves in an embarrassing position by arguing an utterly silly case. On the other hand, some teachers may find it useful to review every item or exercise. It may become part of the instructional program. The main point is to know before returning test materials how you want to handle questions. If you do review each item, it will be helpful to have the results from a formal item analysis as described later in this chapter.

Checklist for Returning the Tests

☐ 1. Return scored tests promptly.
☐ 2. Do not announce individual scores.
☐ 3. Explain the scoring.
☐ 4. Allow for student questions.

Wrapping Up

After returning materials to students and reviewing results, you still have a few more steps. These steps will wrap up the assessment.

1. Here are some pointers on collecting materials. If you consider the test "secure," make sure you *recover all materials*. Collecting materials from students, like distributing the materials, is usually a bit chaotic. There is a lot of paper passing hands, some student chatter, and so on. A student may inappropriately keep a copy for later use with other students. More often, a student will inadvertently put a copy in a notebook. If possible, check immediately to see that you have all materials. If it is not possible to check immediately, do so as soon as possible later in the day. It is entirely possible that you do not consider

the materials secure. You may even allow students to keep the test. Perhaps you want students to keep it for future study, for entering it into a portfolio, or for sharing with parents.

Whenever collecting test materials, do so in such a way that students do not see other students' grades. You can do this by way of directions you give for passing papers forward. For example, direct that papers be turned upside down or some similar stratagem.

2. *Record scores.* At some point, you need to record students' scores in a grade book. This might be hardcopy or electronic, as described in Chapter 13. It is probably best to record the scores after you have reviewed the test with students. In this way, you can take account of any problems that surfaced in the review. If you recorded scores before returning the tests, be sure to make necessary corrections resulting from the review with students.

3. Finally, *make notes on changes* in items, exercises, scoring, directions, and so on. Do it while the whole experience is fresh in your mind. If you did a formal item analysis (see the next section), store this information in some way. If your test items/exercises are on index cards, record the information on the back of the card. If your items/exercises are in a computer file, enter the information there.

Checklist for Wrapping Up

☐ 1. Recover all materials.
☐ 2. Record scores.
☐ 3. Make notes on changes.

ITEM ANALYSIS

In some circumstances, administration of a test will be followed by what is called item analysis. **Item analysis** refers to a collection of techniques for examining the quality of individual test items. The techniques have developed over the years mainly in the context of selected-response items. With some simple adaptations, they can also apply to constructed-response items. We will describe them mainly in the context of multiple-choice items (a subcategory of SR items), their most frequent application.

There are two reasons to be familiar with item analysis techniques. First, they serve as a frequent point of reference for external tests, such as standardized achievement batteries and state assessments. Thus, intelligent use of these tests requires familiarity with item analysis techniques. Second, teachers can use simple versions of these techniques to

---

KEY POINTS SUMMARY 10.1 | *Master Checklist of Suggestions Related to Test Administration*

Preparing Test Materials	Preparation for Scoring
Remote Preparation of Students	Returning the Tests
Immediate Preparation of Students	Wrapping up
Managing the Testing Environment	

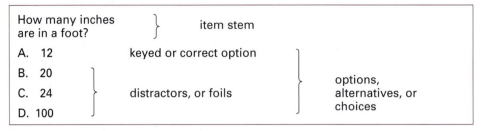

Figure 10.2   Anatomy of a multiple-choice item.

examine their own tests. This may lead to modifications in scoring a test and to improvement of future tests.

To introduce item analysis techniques, let us describe the anatomy of a test item. Figure 10.2 shows key elements in the test item.

First, we have the **item stem**. This is the question or incomplete statement presented to the student. As noted in Chapter 8, in a performance assessment, it is called the prompt or exercise. Then, in selected-response items, we have the **options**. These are the alternatives from which the student chooses an answer. The options include the **keyed response** and the **distractors**. Some sources call the distractors "foils," a rather quaint term. In an achievement or ability test, the keyed response is the correct response. In an interest or attitude measure, the keyed response indicates a response in a certain direction (e.g, a favorable attitude toward math).

Two Key Item Statistics: p and D

The typical item analysis procedure yields two key results. The first is the **item difficulty index**. It is often called the **p-value**. It expresses the percentage or proportion (hence the "p") of students who got the item right. For example, if 90% of the students answered the item correctly, the item difficulty (or p-value) is .90. If 45% of the students answered correctly, the item difficulty is .45. Notice the apparent contradiction between the name of this index and its actual meaning. The higher the item difficulty index, the easier the item. This is often a source of confusion for the novice. The item difficulty index might better be called the item ease index—but it is not called that. It is simple to calculate the item difficulty index. Simply count the number of students responding correctly and divide by the total number of students.

The second index commonly encountered in item analysis procedures is the **item discrimination index**, often abbreviated **D**. We need two sidebars at this point. First, this index has nothing to do with racial, gender, or other forms of discrimination or bias. Second, notice that we are dealing with two "D" words here: difficulty and discrimination. The D in item analysis lingo usually refers to item discrimination, not item difficulty. The item discrimination index indicates the extent to which performance on the item agrees with performance on the test as a whole.[3] Determining the item discrimination index is not as simple as determining the item difficulty index. However, it is not terribly hard to do.

---

[3] In some applications, mainly outside the field of achievement testing, item discrimination relates item performance to standing on some external criterion, not to standing on the total test.

To determine the item discrimination index, follow these steps:

1. Score the entire test. Get a total score for each student.
2. Divide students into a "high" group and a "low" group based on the total score. There are several ways to define "high" and "low" for this step. For classroom application, we recommend dividing the total group into upper and lower halves. That is, split the group at the median, giving the top 50% and bottom 50%. If several students are exactly at the median, allocate them randomly to one or the other group to get balanced groups. (It won't affect these students in terms of their actual scores on the test.)
3. Determine the percentages of students in the high and low groups who answered the item correctly.
4. Take the difference between the percentages for the high and low groups (high p minus low p). This is D, one form of the discrimination index.[4]

What is the discrimination index (D) telling us? We assume that the total score on the test is valid. Students who have higher scores (i.e., those in the high group) know more about the subject than do students with lower scores (i.e., those in the low group). We also assume that each item on the test should show this difference. The discrimination index tells us the extent to which this is true. The reasoning becomes clearer with examples. Consider the examples in Figure 10.3. It presents item analysis data for three multiple-

Item	Group	A	B*	C	D
5	High	0	90	10	0
	Low	10	50	30	10
	Total	5	70	20	5

Item Difficulty (p) = .70
Item Discrimination (D) = .40

	Group	A*	B	C	D
12	High	40	60	0	0
	Low	60	30	0	10
	Total	50	45	0	5

Item Difficulty (p) = .50
Item Discrimination (D) = −.20

	Group	A	B	C	D*
32	High	5	0	0	95
	Low	5	0	0	95
	Total	5	0	0	95

Item Difficulty (p) = .95
Item Discrimination (D) = .00

*indicates keyed, correct option

Figure 10.3 Item analysis data for three items.

[4] Be aware that different authors define D in a surprising variety of ways. Some use the upper and lower 25%, 27%, or 33% in the numerator. Some use the upper and lower 50% in the numerator but use 1/2 N in the denominator. Others use simply the difference between number of cases (not percentages) in the upper and lower groups. Although the different procedures result in numerical differences, the practical interpretations are much the same.

choice items. Each item has four options. Forty students took the test. We usually express this as N = 40. The complete test contained 50 items. The median score was 35. The high group consists of the 20 students who scored above 35 (including one student who scored exactly 35). The low group consists of the 20 students who scored below 35 (including one student who scored exactly 35). In Figure 10.3, the numbers of students in each group (high = 20, low = 20, total = 40) have all been converted to percentages.

Data in Figure 10.3 warrant slow, careful study. Let us describe what is there. On Item 5, 70% of the total group responded correctly. Therefore, p = .70. In the high group, 90% responded correctly, whereas only 50% of the low group did so. This split yields D = .40 (i.e., .90 − .50). Thus, the direction of performance on this item agrees reasonably well with performance on the total test. A good test will usually have quite a few items with data like those for Item 5.

Now look at the data for Item 12. Students in the low group actually did better than students in the high group on this item. Does that make sense? Probably not. Notice that the majority of students in the high group chose option B. Perhaps they saw something in option B that the teacher overlooked. Or—and this does happen—the teacher simply keyed the wrong answer by mistake. If that happened, the obvious remedy is to fix the scoring key.

What about Item 32? It is a very easy item. Nearly all students in both high and low groups got it right. A good classroom test will have quite a few items like this. However, the item contributes nothing to letting a teacher know about differences in levels of knowledge among the students.

Try This!

Here are the data for another item, like the data in Figure 10.3.
What is the item difficulty index (p)? ____
What is the item discrimination index (D)? ____

		A	B	C	D*
46	High	10	20	10	60
	Low	10	20	20	50
	Total	10	20	15	55

*Indicates keyed, correct option.

Some item analysis procedures concentrate only on correct/incorrect options. They do not provide separate summaries for each incorrect option. For example, the procedures would report only the 90–50–70 figures under option B for Item 5 in Figure 10.3. From these figures, you can determine p and D. You simply do not know how the incorrect responses were distributed among the three incorrect options.

How Does Item Analysis Help?

Performing item analysis on classroom tests helps in three ways. *First*, it allows you to spot "bad" or questionable items before returning test results to students. Based on the item analysis, you may modify the scoring, for example, to eliminate items that acted

| KEY POINTS SUMMARY 10.2 | *Two Main Indexes in Item Analysis* |

Item difficulty (p): Percent answering correctly
Item discrimination (D): Difference between high and low groups

strangely. It is also helpful to have the item analysis data when responding to students' questions about the items. For example, when responding to an objection that an item was "too hard," it is helpful to point out that 85% of the students got the item right. *Second*, item analysis data may help you detect misunderstandings. For example, in Item 5 in Figure 10.3, why did 20% of the total group think option C was correct? Pondering that question might suggest a slight adjustment in teaching. This use of item analysis data is a good example of formative evaluation.

Third, item analysis data may help improve future tests. Many teachers keep a personal **item bank**. The item bank contains items the teacher has used in the past or may use in the future. The item bank may be on index cards or in a computer file. The teacher will modify the file entries, periodically adding new items or deleting items as instructional content changes. Item analysis data may serve as a basis for modifying entries in the item bank. For example, data for Item 12 in Figure 10.3 suggest deleting this item.

Some sources recommend using item analysis data to modify options within items. For example, tinkering with options A and B in Item 12 might "fix" the item. Perhaps options B and C within Item 32 should be made a bit more attractive. With the exception of correcting obvious mistakes in designating correct answers, we do not recommend tinkering with options. If an item is not working satisfactorily, get rid of it and write a new item.

Especially when using item analysis techniques for classroom tests, the data will not be very stable because the number of students is small. Therefore, be cautious in the inferences you make from the data. Remember that item analysis is not a substitute for content expertise or common sense.

Item Analysis in Large-Scale Testing Programs

Let's consider item analysis techniques in large-scale testing programs. Such programs include major standardized achievement batteries and state assessment programs. Item analysis is used for two rather different purposes in such programs. First, item analysis data are used in the preparation of the tests. Large numbers of items—more than needed for the final test—are administered in research programs. Item analysis statistics are obtained and used to help select items for the final version of the test. Ordinarily, the item statistics are not the only criteria used for selection; content criteria and other considerations also enter into the selection, but the item statistics are important. Second, item statistics are presented with the final version of the test to indicate important characteristics of the test.

Item analysis techniques in these programs define item difficulty (p-value) in the same way as described already. It is the percentage of students in the total group getting the item right. The item discrimination index determined in large-scale testing programs usually differs somewhat from what we have already described in two ways. First, the high and low groups may correspond to the top and bottom one third, one quarter, or 27% of the total group. The 27% figure seems like a very strange number, but there are good technical reasons for it. We do not need to pursue that topic here. Second, in large-scale applications, the item discrimination index is actually a correlation coefficient, showing the correlation between score on the item (0 = wrong, 1 = right) and total score on the test. In this case, the discrimination index is a correlation coefficient, albeit a slightly different one than we described in Chapter 2. The correlation will have an exotic name, such as r-bis (biserial correlation) or r-pbis (point biserial correlation). However, in practice, these statistics provide much the same information as our D index.

Recall from Chapter 1 (p. 14) the distinction between classical test theory (CTT) and item response theory (IRT). Item analysis procedures provide one of the chief contrasts between these two approaches. The item analysis procedures we have described so far follow CTT. Item analysis in large-scale testing typically uses both CTT and IRT procedures. The IRT procedures require very large samples of students, hence they are not useful for classroom tests. Further, the IRT procedures are quite complex. They go well beyond what is appropriate for this book. We mention them, however, because you will see reference to IRT-based item data in large-scale testing programs. A useful source to pursue this topic is Hambleton, Swaminathan, and Rogers (1991).

Item Analysis for Interest and Attitude Measures

The item analysis procedures presented here have used achievement items, where each item had a "correct" answer. With slight modification, the same techniques work for interest and attitude measures, the types of measures covered in Chapter 9. For these measures, the "keyed" response is a response in a certain direction. The direction might be "favorable" attitude toward math or "positive interest" in science or "feeling comfortable" about public speaking. When responses are on 2-point scales (Yes-No, Agree-Disagree, Like-Dislike), the item analysis proceeds just as it did for the correct-incorrect achievement test items. When responses are on multipoint scales (e.g., a 5-point or 7-point Likert scale), there are two possible ways to proceed. First, convert the multipoint scale to a 2-point scale by grouping responses. For example, treat responses of 4 and 5 on a 5-point scale as favorable (score as 1) and responses of 1, 2, and 3 as unfavorable (score as 0). Then, proceed as described earlier to conduct the item analysis. A second alternative is to obtain the correlation between total scores and the original multipoint response. This is easily done by computer and is the more typical way to proceed. Don't try it by hand. It's too much work. The item difficulty for an item with a multipoint response is usually expressed as the average response value.

Item Analysis for Essays and Performance Items

Item analysis is useful for essays and performance items, just as it is for selected-response items. If the essay or performance task is scored simply correct/incorrect, item analysis proceeds just as it does for selected-response items. If the essay or performance task is scored on a multipoint scale, item analysis proceeds as described for interest and attitude measures. That is, you can collapse response categories to yield a 2-point scale. Or, you can determine the correlation between total scores and the multipoint scale. For the latter option, do it by computer. As for interest and attitude measures, the item difficulty for an essay or a performance task with a multipoint response is usually expressed as the average response value.

Item Analysis Computer Programs

We described how to conduct an item analysis by hand for a classroom test. A variety of computer programs are available to accomplish the analysis. Such programs are often made available with scanners for multiple-choice tests. The scanner will score the answer sheet and automatically produce the item analysis. Needless to say, this is a great boon to the teacher. Output from any of these programs will look much like the array of data in Figure 10.3. The output may also produce an estimate of test reliability. Usually this estimate uses the alpha coefficient of internal consistency described in Chapter 3 (p. 56).

When an item analysis computer program is available, we recommend its use routinely. It takes no time to get the results and only a few minutes to scan the results. On the other hand, we do not recommend routine use of item analysis if it must be done by hand. It is simply too tedious. However, even when done by hand, we do recommend conducting item analysis for especially important tests or as a periodic check on test quality.

Commercially available item analysis programs vary widely in their complexity. Some are very powerful programs that produce many kinds of analyses. Others are much simpler. Costs also vary widely from about $20 to several hundred dollars. However, at the heart of all the programs are exactly the types of analyses we described earlier: item difficulty and item discrimination indexes, usually with some analysis of options. Availability of item analysis programs is somewhat erratic. They tend to come and go. More exactly, the companies that produce them tend to come and go. Therefore, lists of vendors become quickly dated. Table 10.1 lists four sources of item analysis programs for vendors with some record of stability.

Table 10.1 Four Sources for Item Analysis Programs

Vendor	Website	Comment
Assessment Systems Corp.	www.assess.com	Offers many test analysis packages. The *Iteman* package is the simplest and most appropriate for classroom tests.
Pearson NCS	www.pearsonncs.com	The world's largest vendor of devices for scanning answer documents. Markets the *Remark* software from Principia to do item analysis.
Principia Products	www.principiaproducts.com	Offers the *Remark* software for item analysis, as well as for surveys.
Virtual Software Store	www.virtualsoftware.com	*Inter@cTest Standalone* is a relatively inexpensive package for item banking and item analysis.

Qualitative, Informal Item Analysis

We have described the quantitative approach to item analysis. This is what is normally meant by the term "item analysis." However, there are some informal, qualitative approaches to item analysis. They are easy to use and can be employed on a routine basis. Here are three simple things to do. You can use them individually or in combination. You can also use them routinely for all assessments or just occasionally for some assessments.

First, have another person read your test items and provide comments. This can be done at any time, but it is best to do so at the time you prepare the items. The other person need not have your technical expertise in the subject, although it is especially helpful if the person does have that expertise. Simply ask that person for any comments about individual items and exercises, about the directions, or about the assessment task as a whole. Comments about the assessment as a whole can be especially helpful for unusual performance tasks.

Second, you can conduct an informal item analysis after the test has been administered by approximating the formal item analysis procedures. This is especially helpful for essays and performance tasks. You may want to check responses of students who usually perform near the top of the class—students who would almost certainly be in the "high" group in a formal item analysis. Quickly scan these students' work to see how they did. This informal analysis will certainly not have the refinement or stability of the formal procedures. However, it can be done quickly and should reveal gross problems with the items or exercises.

Third, we noted earlier the advisability of discussing test results with students. This discussion has the potential to reveal especially troublesome items. If the discussion is properly handled, you will learn about unclear, tricky, or ambiguous items, without turning the session into an endless and fruitless debate.

CHEATING: PREVALENCE, PRACTICES, AND PREVENTION

Whenever assessments have significant consequences for students—for example, for grading, selection, or certification—the specter of cheating raises its ugly head. It's an unpleasant topic. Many textbooks on educational assessment avoid the topic entirely. Teachers don't particularly like to talk about it, either. However, it is unrealistic to sidestep the issue. We need to deal with it forthrightly. In this section, we summarize what is known about the frequency of cheating and suggest steps to reduce it. We include it in this chapter because it relates primarily to the administration of tests and other assessments.

Many readers will want to pursue the topic in more detail. Here are good sources for further study. Gregory Cizek (1999, 2003) has written two excellent books on cheating with special reference to elementary and high school contexts. The earlier book targets a scholarly audience, with ample citations to and analysis of original sources. The more recent book aims at a more popular level of presentation, with much practical advice for teachers. Whitley and Keith-Spiegel (2002) cover much the same territory as Cizek, but with college as the main context. Donald McCabe has written extensively on cheating and academic integrity. Any of his works are useful reference points. Two recent articles by McCabe (1999, 2001) are especially helpful. Bushweller (1999a, 1999b) has two very revealing reports. Finally, the Center for Academic Integrity (www.academicintegrity.org) provides a wealth of useful resources on this topic. We draw on all these sources for the following commentary.

Prevalence

Cheating is widespread. It is very common at the college level, even more common in high schools, and present even at the elementary school level. At the high school and college levels, the great majority of students admit to having engaged in some form of academic dishonesty on at least some occasions. A significant number of students at these levels report cheating on a regular basis. Almost universally, students report that cheating occurs routinely. Students' attitude toward cheating seems to be: "Yeah, it's wrong, but everybody does it and it's no big deal." Although the problem is most common at the high school level, cheating also happens in the elementary grades. Reported instances of cheating go down as far as Grade 2.

Practices

Cheating occurs in two main arenas. First, there is cheating on tests; that is, formal examinations usually given in a classroom setting. This category covers both teacher-made tests and standardized tests. Typical examples of cheating on tests include using crib notes, viewing another student's answers, and passing answers between students. Less common examples of cheating on tests include having another person take the test and getting an advance copy of the test. Some of the newer, high-tech methods of using crib notes or passing answers are truly amazing. For example, students can pass answers by pagers and cell phones. The latest digital-photo cell phones open up whole new worlds to cheaters.

The second main arena for cheating is assignments completed outside the classroom. The most common example is *plagiarizing* for term papers and other such written assignments. The principal mechanisms for plagiarizing are the use of Internet sites with ready-made essays and cut-and-paste papers garnered from several websites but without attribution. The old-fashioned method of simply having another student write some or all of the paper also exists. Other prime prospects in this second arena include science projects, artistic productions, and similar assignments completed outside class. The assumption, ordinarily, is that students complete this work on their own, either individually or as part of a formally constituted group. However, assistance from parents, siblings, family friends, or other students may range from incidental to complete authorship. The same holds for any homework assignment that is graded, for example, workbooks and end-of-chapter exercises.

The two categories described here—cheating on tests in the classroom and on assignments completed outside the classroom—are not the only venues for academic dishonesty. Students may also tamper with grade records, especially those in electronic files. We cover that topic in Chapter 13. There is also teacher cheating, especially by giving unauthorized assistance to students in completing standardized tests. We take up that topic in Chapter 11.

Prevention

What can a teacher do to prevent or at least reduce cheating? Experts in the field recommend proceeding on six fronts. *First*, create the right classroom atmosphere. Develop an environment emphasizing the teacher's role in helping students learn. Set reasonable standards for grading. Establish sensible workloads. Keep content interesting and meaningful. According to both experts' opinions and students' reports, the absence of a good classroom environment encourages cheating.

Second, teachers should explicitly talk to students about cheating. This teacher-talk should include defining unacceptable behavior and practices. It should convey the teacher's concern about cheating. It should identify the consequences of cheating, both immediate and longer term. Technologically savvy teachers should let students know that, just as there are term paper mills to produce papers, there are also Internet sites that check for the origin of such papers.

Third, teachers should take certain actions in immediate preparation for a test or graded assignment. Make sure the material to be covered in the test or assignment has been adequately covered in instruction. Inform students about the nature of the test or assignment (e.g., the number of questions on the test or the number of pages expected for a paper). Give advice on how to prepare for the test or assignment. Let students know what materials, if any, will be permitted (e.g., calculators, dictionaries). Uncertainty in students' minds about what will be covered and how it will be covered seems to encourage an attitude that "anything goes" to get a good grade.

Fourth, at the start of and during the administration of a test, a simple, two-word rule: Be vigilant. Pay attention to seating. If necessary and feasible, make alterations in physical arrangements. Don't sit at the front desk grading papers or reading. Perhaps occasionally move about the room. Be alert to unusual activity. Use similar care when checking assignments completed outside the classroom. Is the production consistent with the student's other work? Or, is it just "too good to be true?" Can the student answer simple questions about how the project was completed? Do the sources cited by a student accord with what was actually written? Are the sources ones that the student is likely to have consulted? Answering such questions helps to determine the authenticity of the student's work. The questions do not take very long to answer.

Related to the vigilance dictum, be aware that there are high-tech methods to help detect unusual similarities in responses to objective items. As noted earlier, there are also programs to help detect plagiarism. For a list of some of these methods, see Cizek (2003).

Fifth, when cheating does occur, confront it. Don't ignore it. Take appropriate action. Identify the cheating and impose a suitable penalty. It is hard to take such action. It is much easier to ignore it, while still lamenting its occurrence. However, be aware that, according to students, teachers' disregard of cheating is one reason students feel so free to do it.

Sixth, experts recommend that schools develop, promulgate, and enforce policies on academic dishonesty. This is beyond what an individual teacher does. But it is supportive of the individual teacher's actions. The first task is to determine if your school has such a policy. Many schools apparently do not. If your school does not have such a policy, you may want to help develop one. For sample policies, see the Center for Academic Integrity website (www.academicintegrity.org), Cizek (1999, 2003), and Whitley and Keith-Speigel

> **KEY POINTS SUMMARY 10.3**   *Some Actions to Help Prevent Cheating*
>
> 1. Create a good classroom atmosphere.
> 2. Talk to students about cheating.
> 3. Be clear about tests and assignments.
> 4. Be vigilant during a test or in reviewing outside assignments.
> 5. When cheating occurs, confront it.
> 6. Develop and promulgate a school policy on academic honesty.

(2002). If your school has a policy on academic dishonesty (assuming it is a reasonable one), review it with your students as part of the teacher-talk in the second point mentioned earlier.

PRACTICAL ADVICE

1. After you have prepared assessment materials, following the recommendations in Chapters 6 to 9, use the checklist in Key Points Summary 10.1 as a reminder of things you need to consider before, during, and after administering the assessments.

2. Learn to do a simple item analysis as outlined in this chapter. At least occasionally, apply these procedures to your tests or exercises.

3. Take cheating seriously. Use the list of actions in Key Points Summary 10.3 as a guide. For starters, establish the appropriate classroom atmosphere.

SUMMARY

1. When preparing to administer tests, make sure your tests are fair and are perceived as fair by students.

2. When preparing test materials, use clear directions and a simple format. Allow adequate time for producing copies, spot check copies, take a test yourself, and worry about security of materials. For multisection courses, develop different but comparable forms of the test.

3. For the remote preparation of students, give adequate notice, make advance preparation for accommodations, and think about the testing environment.

4. For the immediate preparation of students, rearrange seating if necessary, make sure everyone gets what they need, establish order, review directions with students, and launch them into the task with some words of encouragement.

5. Appropriately manage the environment during the test. Monitor the situation, answer questions with fairness in mind, and apprise students of time, if no clock is visible. For assessments completed outside class, keep students at the task.

6. Clean up answer sheets before submitting them for scanning. If you have a lot of essays or performance tasks to score, schedule appropriate time to complete the work and spot check a few cases before proceeding with systematic scoring.

7. Return scored tests promptly. When returning the tests, do not publicly reveal individual student's scores. Explain the scoring procedures and allow time for students' questions, but do so judiciously.

8. To wrap up the entire process, make sure you have recovered all test materials if you consider the materials secure. Record students' scores and do not forget to note any changes you want to make in the test items or exercises.

9. Item analysis is a collection of techniques for examining the quality of test items and exercises. You will see reference to these techniques for external examinations. You can also use them to analyze your own tests.

10. The two most commonly used item statistics are the item difficulty index, labeled the p-value, and the item discrimination index, labeled D. We described how to obtain both of these.

11. There are also some simple procedures to conduct informal, qualitative analyses of items and exercises.

12. Cheating occurs at all levels of education. It appears to be particularly severe at the high school level. It occurs in two main areas: formal examinations given in classrooms and assignments completed outside the classroom. The mechanisms for cheating continue to blossom, particularly those with some electronic or Internet basis.

13. Authorities offer several suggestions to prevent or, at least, reduce cheating. Every teacher should take these suggestions to heart.

KEY TERMS

accommodations	item bank	keyed response
D	item difficulty index	modifications
distractors	item discrimination index	options
item analysis	item stem	p-value

EXERCISES

1. Here are the data for three multiple-choice items. For each item, determine the item difficulty index and the item discrimination index. The numerical entries are percentages. The * marks the correct answer.

Item	Group	A	B*	C	D
15	High	30	60	10	0
	Low	30	40	20	10
	Total	30	50	15	5

Item Difficulty (p) =

Item Discrimination (D) =

Item	Group	A	B	C	D*
35	High	15	0	0	85
	Low	15	0	0	85
	Total	15	0	0	85

Item Difficulty (p) =

Item Discrimination (D) =

Item	Group	A	B*	C	D
45	High	0	70	30	0
	Low	30	50	10	10
	Total	15	60	20	5

Item Difficulty (p) =

Item Discrimination (D) =

2. Here is a complete set of student response for 10 students on five multiple-choice items. From these data, you can prepare an item analysis. Each item should have an array of data like that in Exercise 1. Complete the analysis. Determine p and D for each of the five items.

Student/Item	1	2	3	4	5
Key	A	C	B	A	D
1	A	C	B	D	D
2	B	C	B	A	D
3	A	C	C	A	D
4	B	D	B	C	C
5	D	A	B	A	C
6	A	C	C	D	D
7	A	C	B	D	C
8	A	C	B	A	D
9	C	A	B	D	D
10	B	D	B	C	D

3. Suppose you have a class of 30 students. Each student has written a five-page paper. Estimate how long it will take you to grade each paper and how long it will take to finish grading all the papers.

4. Go to one of the websites listed in Table 10.1. Each one gives examples of its item analysis reports. Examine one of the reports. What type of information does the report give about individual items? Does the report give any other type of information?

5. Go to the website for the Center for Academic Integrity (CAI): www.academicintegrity.org. Click on "CAI Research." What do you find there about research on cheating in high schools? Be careful doing this search. If you get academicintegrity.com (rather than .org) by mistake, you will have what is usually called a term paper mill.

6. If you plan to assign papers or projects for students to complete outside class, become aware of the help they can get through Internet sources (if you are not already aware). Use any search engine. Search on "term paper." Investigate some of the sites to see how they work.

Chapter 11

Standardized Tests I: Achievement

- List the major categories of standardized achievement tests.
- Identify the common characteristics of standardized achievement tests.
- Outline the major differences between teacher-made tests and standardized achievement tests.
- For each of these categories of standardized achievement tests, describe the typical features:
  a. standardized achievement batteries
  b. single-area achievement tests
  c. licensing and certification exams
  d. state assessment programs
  e. national and international testing programs
  f. individually administered achievement tests
- Identify both helpful and inappropriate practices for administering standardized tests.

What This Chapter Is About

Standardized achievement testing is surely one of the hottest topics in contemporary education. This chapter identifies common features of these tests. We explore six categories of standardized achievement tests. The major categories include achievement batteries, single-area tests, licensing and certification exams, state assessment programs, national and international testing programs, and individually administered achievement tests. For each category, we identify common features, typical uses, and a few examples of specific tests.

Why This Topic Is Important

Every teacher and school administrator will be involved in the administration and interpretation of standardized achievement tests in one form or another. All educators need to be familiar with the main features of these tests. All need to develop sensitivity to the strengths and shortcomings of such tests. All need to know how to use them intelligently. Furthermore, all need to recognize the distinctions among various types of standardized achievement tests. They serve somewhat different purposes. Finally, any intelligent understanding of educational research requires an understanding of tests covered in this chapter. Much of educational research depends on use of these tests.

STANDARDIZED ACHIEVEMENT TESTS: WHAT ARE THEY?

Contemporary reports, both in the professional literature and in the popular media, have an amazing tendency to issue generalizations about "standardized achievement tests" as if they were some monolithic entity. They are not. They come in an enormous variety of shapes, sizes, styles, and flavors. This chapter explores this diverse array of tests. To be sure, they have some characteristics in common. Yet, they also have many differences. One lesson to be learned in the chapter is: Beware of anyone making pronouncements about "standardized achievement tests" as if they were all the same.

Let us begin by recalling the distinctions made in Chapter 1 about the various uses of the term **standardized test**. There are three rather different meanings for the term. In some contexts, "standardized" simply means use of a common set of items, directions, testing conditions, and scoring procedures. In other contexts, "standardized" equates to multiple-choice testing. In still other contexts, "standardized" implies some type of national (or, at least, statewide) norms. The first meaning is the technically correct one. However, the other meanings are often used in practice. Keep these distinctions in mind when you hear reference to "standardized achievement tests."

A Broad Classification of Standardized Achievement Tests

For purposes of this chapter, we classify standardized achievement tests into six broad categories as shown in Figure 11.1. This classification is one of practical convenience rather than theoretical elegance. In practice, the boundaries between these categories are permeable. The *first* category includes achievement batteries widely used in elementary

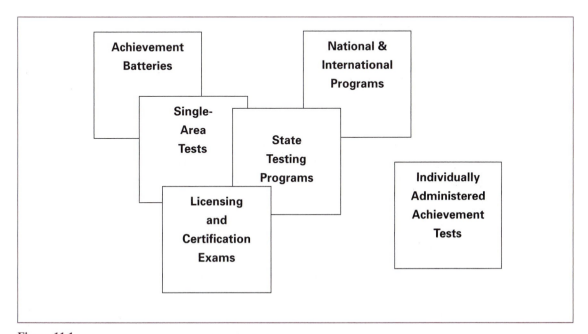

Figure 11.1 A broad classification of standardized achievement tests.

and secondary school testing programs.[1] The *second* category includes single-area achievement tests used primarily in secondary and postsecondary educational programs and in job-related contexts. The *third* category includes the numerous certification and licensing exams used by professional organizations. The *fourth* category includes tests custom-made for state testing programs, an area currently experiencing explosive growth.

The *fifth* category includes two unique testing programs: one national, the other international, each growing in importance within educational circles. The *sixth* and final category includes individually administered achievement tests, ordinarily used in conjunction with mental ability tests when diagnosing student learning problems. These are sometimes called psychoeducational batteries. In one sense, these tests could be classified as achievement batteries. However, we classify them separately because their individual administration, as well as their typical use by specially trained professionals, makes them distinctly different from the group-administered batteries in the first category.

To illustrate the permeability of the boundaries in our classification scheme, note these examples of overlap among the categories. Parts of achievement batteries can be used as single-area tests, for example in reading or science. Some state assessment programs incorporate parts of existing achievement batteries. Some certification processes utilize single-area achievement tests. Despite these areas of overlap, this organizational scheme provides useful distinctions among the types of standardized achievement tests.

Some Common Characteristics

Each of the six categories of standardized achievement tests has some distinctive features. However, they also have some common features. Before examining the individual categories, let us examine these common features that cut across all categories.

1. Most obviously, these tests aim to measure attainment of objectives in *school-based curricula*. They all explicitly try to gauge skills and knowledge developed as a result of specific instruction. This is their principal difference with "ability" tests, covered in the next chapter. From this it follows that content validity is a prime concern for these tests.

2. Most of these standardized tests use *multiple-choice items* at least to a substantial degree. Some of the tests are entirely multiple choice. Many use a mixture of multiple-choice and constructed-response items. Use of constructed-response items is increasing modestly. However, multiple-choice items still predominate in most areas. The principal exception to this generalization is in the sixth category, individually administered tests. These tests rely mostly on a free-response format.

3. Developers of standardized achievement tests typically pay considerable attention to the *technical characteristics* desired for tests. These were the characteristics we considered in Chapters 3–5. Thus, we usually have reliability data, item analysis, and other such technical information for these tests. Such information usually appears in a technical manual or other formal report for the test. In addition, the pre-

---

[1] There are a few batteries for use at the college level. We do not cover these.

publication research typically includes professional reviews for cultural, racial, ethnic, and gender bias.

4. To a significant degree, interpretation of scores on standardized achievement tests relies on use of *large-group norms*. Very often, this means national norms. In the recent past, the quality of national norming for these tests has usually been quite good. It is unusual today to find one of these tests with norms seriously askew— although there is always the possibility of that happening. When the norm is not national in scope, it is at least based on a reasonably large group considered relevant for the purposes of the test. For example, the norm may be based on all Grade 4 students in a state or all candidates for a certain type of license.

   Many standardized achievement tests also offer some type of criterion-referenced or standards-based interpretation. In particular, state assessments rely increasingly on standards-based interpretation.

CONTRASTS WITH TEACHER-MADE TESTS

As noted earlier, one of the common features of standardized achievement tests is that they aim to measure school-based learning. So do teacher-made tests, the types of tests we considered in Chapters 6–10. What is the difference between these two types of tests? There are several important differences. Perhaps the most important difference is the *level of detail* addressed by the two types of tests. The teacher-made test typically aims at a highly specific level of detail, such as the content of instruction for the past two weeks. This might be the 30 words in one chapter of a spelling book, work with multiplying fractions, analyzing one selection from an anthology, and so on. In contrast, the standardized test is likely to sample across a wide range of spelling words, math skills, or reading selections. The standardized test will not assess much detail about the ins and outs of multiplying fractions. It may have only one item or no items on this particular skill. It may not treat the particular selection in the anthology at all.

A second major difference between standardized and teacher-made tests is their respective *research bases*. Items in the standardized test will usually have an extensive research base. They will have been reviewed for content and bias, tried out with large groups of students, and subjected to various statistical analyses. Individual teachers rarely have the resources to do these things, beyond the simple analyses recommended in Chapter 10.

Third, standardized tests, as noted earlier, usually have some type of *norms*, most frequently a national or state norm. Usually, teacher-made tests will have norms based only on this teacher's previous students and then only rather informally. Availability of norms is one of the most distinctive contributions of standardized tests.

KEY POINTS SUMMARY 11.1 *Common Characteristics of Standardized Achievement Tests*

Aimed at school-based curricula	Reports on technical characteristics
Mostly selected-response format	Use of large-group norms

KEY POINTS SUMMARY 11.2 | *Main Points of Contrast Between Teacher-Made and Standardized Tests*

- Level of detail covered
- Research base
- Availability of norms
- Frequency of occurrence

A final difference between standardized tests and teacher-made tests relates to their *frequency of occurrence*. This is certainly not a theoretical difference. It is just a simple fact of life. Standardized testing occurs infrequently, perhaps once per year. Teacher-made tests occur (or should occur) frequently, many times during the year.

What do we conclude from this contrast between standardized and teacher-made achievement tests? They both have their strengths and shortcomings. They both have their place in a "best practices" approach to education. Learn to use them both intelligently. Although there are clear contrasts between standardized and teacher-made tests, the contrast should *not* be overemphasized. In many areas, the two types of assessments will yield similar, if not identical, information. In general, students who do well on one type of assessment will do well on the other type. That is, performance on the two types of assessments will usually be at least moderately correlated.

ACHIEVEMENT BATTERIES

We consider first the standardized achievement batteries used in elementary and secondary schools. The term **battery** in this context means a coordinated series of tests covering different content areas and multiple grade levels. For many of the types of tests included in this book, there are innumerable examples. However, this is not the case for the major standardized achievement batteries treated in this section. In the United States, there are five major achievement test batteries in use. Table 11.1 lists these batteries, their publishers, and dates of the most recent edition. New editions of these batteries tend to appear about every five or six years. We have not attempted to list achievement batteries used in other countries.

Try This!

Visit the website for one of the publishers listed in Table 11.1. What information is emphasized about the achievement battery listed?

Today's achievement batteries are very complex affairs. They are more like conglomerates than single tests. They include both multiple-choice and performance components. They feature vast arrays of computerized score reports. They offer both norm-referenced and criterion-referenced interpretations of student performance, including standards-based reports. Many sources, even very recent ones, describe these standardized achievement batteries as they existed 20 years ago. At that time, the tests were entirely multiple choice and almost entirely norm-referenced. That is no longer the case.

Table 11.1   Major Achievement Batteries

Battery	Publisher (web address)	Current Edition
TerraNova (CTBS)[a]	CTB/McGraw-Hill (www.ctb.com)	1996
TerraNova, Second Edition (CAT/6)	CTB/McGraw-Hill (www.ctb.com)	2000
Iowa Tests of Basic Skills[b]	Riverside Publishing (www.riverpub.com)	2001
Metropolitan Achievement Tests	Harcourt Assessment (www.harcourt.com)	2000
Stanford Achievement Test	Harcourt Assessment (www.harcourt.com)	2003

[a] CTB is the acronym for California Test Bureau, the original name of this publisher. CTB refers to the Comprehensive Test of Basic Skills (CTBS) as TerraNova and to California Achievement Tests (CAT) as TerraNova, Second Edition. Most recent references use the TerraNova tag, although references to "CAT" and "CTBS" are still common. References to California Test Bureau also remain common.

[b] Reference to the Iowa Tests of Basic Skills (ITBS) is intended to include the Iowa Tests of Educational Development and the Test of Academic Progress, both of which are designed for use in Grades 9–12 and are scaled to be continuous with the ITBS.

We present here a description of these standardized achievement tests as they exist at the beginning of the 21st century. Be wary of descriptions that are dated.

Promotional materials for each of the five major batteries emphasize their unique features. However, they are much more alike than they are different. Describing just one of them will be quite sufficient for our purposes. The others follow the same general pattern.

An Example: Stanford Achievement Test

We describe here the Stanford Achievement Test, Tenth Edition (SAT10; Harcourt Educational Measurement, 2003).[2] Other batteries listed in Table 11.2 have the same major features as SAT10. As for all of these batteries, SAT10 is a vast system of measures rather than a single test. This will become obvious in our review. SAT10 includes two levels of the Stanford Early School Achievement Test (SESAT 1 and 2), the main Stanford series, and three levels of the Test of Academic Skills (TASK 1, 2, and 3). Table 11.2 outlines the tests and levels included within this system. This table shows only the Complete Battery multiple-choice tests. There is also an Abbreviated Battery, containing shorter tests. And, there are such special editions as large-print, Braille, and Spanish editions. Consult the publisher's website or a hard-copy catalog for details on these variations.

A review of Table 11.2 reveals several features of SAT10 that are typical for the major standardized achievement batteries. Note first that there are *different levels* of the test designed for different grades. For example, Level P2 (Primary 2) is designed for use in Grades 2.5 to 3.5, that is, from the middle of Grade 2 to the middle of Grade 3. Each level contains a host of specific tests. It is this feature that gives rise to the term "battery." The *specific subtests come and go* at different levels (moving from left to right across the table). For example, sounds and letters appears at the two lowest levels but not thereafter. Separate tests in science and social studies do not appear until the Primary 3 level. Despite this come-and-go

---

[2] Notice that Stanford Achievement Test has the same initials (SAT) as the college admissions SAT, formerly known as Scholastic Assessment Test. Be careful to distinguish between these two very different SATs.

Table 11.2 Outline of Tests and Levels in SAT10

Stanford 10 Multiple Choice Scope and Sequence

Test Levels, Recommended Grade Ranges, Tests, and Administration Times

Test Levels	S1 Grade K.0–K.5 K	T	S2 Grade K.5–1.5 K	T	P1 Grade 1.5–2.5 K	T	P2 Grade 2.5–3.5 K	T	P3 Grade 3.5–4.5 K	T	I1 Grade 4.5–5.5 K	T	I2 Grade 5.5–6.5 K	T	I3 Grade 6.5–7.5 K	T	A1 Grade 7.5–8.5 K	T	A2 Grade 8.5–8.9 K	T	T1 Grade 9.0–9.9 K	T	T2 Grade 10.0–10.9 K	T	T3 Grade 11.0–12.9 K	T
Sounds and Letters	40	30	40	25																						
Word Study Skills	30	15	30	25	30	20	30	20	30	20	30	20														
Word Reading			30	30	30	25																				
Sentence Reading					30	30																				
Reading Vocabulary							30	20	30	20	30	20	30	20	30	20	30	20	30	20	30	20	30	20	30	20
Reading Comprehension					40	40	40	40	54	50	54	50	54	50	54	50	54	50	54	50	54	40	54	40	54	40
Total Reading	70	45	100	80	130	115	100	80	114	90	114	90	84	70	84	70	84	70	84	70	84	60	84	60	84	60
Mathematics	40	30	40	30																	50	50	50	50	50	50
Mathematics Problem Solving					42	50	44	50	46	50	48	50	48	50	48	50	48	50	48	50						
Mathematics Procedures					30	30	30	30	30	30	32	30	32	30	32	30	32	30	32	30						
Total Mathematics					72	80	74	80	76	80	80	80	80	80	80	80	80	80	80	80						
Language					40	40	48	45	48	45	48	45	48	45	48	45	48	45	48	45	48	40	48	40	48	40
Spelling					36	30	36	30	36	35	40	35	40	35	40	35	40	35	40	35	40	30	40	30	40	30
Listening to Words and Stories	40	30	40	30																						
Listening					40	30	40	30	40	30	40	30	40	30	40	30	40	30	40	30						
Environment	40	30	40	30	40	30	40	30																		
Science									40	25	40	25	40	25	40	25	40	25	40	25	40	25	40	25	40	25
Social Science									40	25	40	25	40	25	40	25	40	25	40	25	40	25	40	25	40	25
Basic Battery	150	105	180	140	318	295	298	265	316	280	322	280	292	260	282	260	282	260	292	250	222	180	222	180	222	180
Compare Battery	190	135	220	170	358	325	338	295	336	330	402	330	372	310	372	310	372	310	372	310	302	230	302	230	302	230
Total Testing Time	2 hrs 15 min		2 hrs 50 min		5 hrs 25 min		4 hrs 55 min		5 hrs 30 min		5 hrs 30 min		5 hrs 10 min		5 hrs 10 min		5 hrs 10 min		5 hrs 10 min		3 hrs 50 min		3 hrs 50 min		3 hrs 50 min	
Language Form D					40	40	40	40	45	45	48	45	48	45	48	45	48	45	48	45	48	40	48	40	48	40

K = No. of Items
T = Time in Minutes

phenomenon, there is a large degree of *continuity* flowing through the series. For example, some measures of reading and mathematics occur at all levels. All levels also have Basic Battery and Complete Battery scores. A typical subtest contains about 40 items and requires about 25 minutes administration time. Notice that the ratio of number of items to number of minutes of administration time tends to be in the range of 2:1 to 1:1. Subtests are aggregated into area totals (e.g., reading or mathematics) that typically have 75–100 items.

Although not noted in Table 11.2, SAT10 has a Complete Battery and an Abbreviated Battery. The Abbreviated Battery has fewer subtests, and these subtests are generally shorter than those in the Complete Battery. There is also a writing test. The writing task calls for composing a story or an essay. The result is scored by the holistic or analytic method, as described in Chapter 8.

SAT10 offers almost every type of derived score we covered in Chapter 5. It includes percentile ranks, stanines, scaled scores, grade equivalents, and normal curve equivalents. Percentile ranks and stanines appear for both individual scores and group averages. There are also ability-achievement comparisons, performance categories (below average, average, above average) on clusters of related items, and p-values for individual items.

SAT10 includes a wealth of computer-generated scoring reports. Figures 5.14 and 5.15 (pp. 123–124) introduced two such reports for SAT10, one oriented toward norm-referencing, the other oriented toward standards-based reporting. It would be useful to review those reports at this point. Teachers are the primary recipients of reports such as those in Figures 5.14 and 5.15. Teachers should be familiar with the various normed scores and the concept of a percentile band. Parents are the targets for a simpler type of report. See Chapter 13 (p. 334) for an example of a parent or "home" report. The next section shows yet another type of computer-generated report.

Recent editions of the major achievement batteries offer standards-based scores, in addition to norm-referenced scores. For example, SAT10 allows for reporting student performance in the categories of Advanced, Proficient, Basic, and Below Basic. Recall from Chapter 5 (pp. 118–119) the description of how such categories arise and see the example of such a report in Figure 5.15 (p. 124). Generally, the categories come from the judgments of teachers, administrators, and parents about appropriate or desired levels of achievement.

SAT10 research programs included almost 500,000 students. Extraordinary effort was expended to ensure representativeness of these samples in terms of racial/ethnic distribution, socioeconomic status, geographic region, and type of school control (public/nonpublic). The Technical Manual (Harcourt Educational Measurement, 2003) carefully describes the nature of these research programs and characteristics of participants.

A Class List Report for Ms. Prescott's Class

Another common type of report for standardized achievement batteries is the Class List Report. It contains scores for all students in a class on all subtests in the battery. Thus, it contains a great many scores, in a very compact format. Figure 11.2 shows part of such a report (just 10 students) for Ms. Prescott's Grade 2 class. This report is from the Iowa Tests of Basic Skills, another one of the major achievement batteries listed in Table 11.1. Notice that the list of tests across the top of the report is very similar to the list of tests for SAT10, confirming the point made earlier that these achievement batteries tend to be very similar. Such class list reports are available for all the major achievement batteries.

THE IOWA TESTS

LIST OF STUDENT SCORES
Iowa Tests of Basic Skills® (ITBS®)

Class: Prescott
Building: Lockwood Elementary
District: Port Charles CSD

Form/Level: A/ 8
Test Date: 09/2003
Norms: Fall 2000
Order No.: 000000000
Page: 2
Grade: 2

STUDENT NAME / I.D. Number / Birth Date / Age / Level / Form / (Gender)
Calculator Code: F-1 F-2 F-3 — Program: A B C D E F G H I J K L M N O P Z

Student	Measure	Reading Vocabulary	Reading Comprehension	Reading TOTAL	Word Analysis	Listening	Language Spelling	Language TOTAL	Math Concepts	Math Problems	Math Computation*	Math TOTAL	CORE TOTAL	Social Studies	Science	Sources of Information	COMPOSITE
Grant, Martin (M) 12/94, Age 08-09, Level 8, Form A	SS	162	160	161	159	159	172	170	169	170	167	170	167	168	175	173	167
	GE	2.4	2.3	2.4	2.3	2.3	3.0	2.9	2.9	2.9	2.8	2.9	2.7	2.8	3.2	3.1	2.7
	NS	6	5	6	5	5	8	7	7	7	8	7	6	6	7	7	7
	NPR	62	59	60	54	57	90	81	81	78	91	81	75	74	84	85	77
Hardy, Paula (F) 06/95, Age 08-03, Level 8, Form A	SS	172	172	172	203	168	176	184	166	161	156	164	173	160	162	166	172
	GE	3.0	3.0	3.0	5.0	2.8	3.2	3.6	2.7	2.4	2.3	2.5	3.0	2.4	2.5	2.7	3.0
	NS	7	7	7	9	7	8	8	6	6	5	6	7	5	6	6	7
	NPR	79	82	83	98	79	94	93	74	61	58	68	85	58	62	72	86
Hassle, Jasmine (F) 03/95, Age 08-06, Level 8, Form A	SS	182	169	176	185	179	169	194	169	170	169	170	180	164	171	175	177
	GE	3.6	2.9	3.2	3.8	3.4	2.8	4.2	2.9	2.9	2.9	2.9	3.4	2.6	2.9	3.2	3.2
	NS	8	7	7	7	8	7	9	7	7	8	7	8	6	7	7	8
	NPR	91	77	87	88	92	84	98	81	78	93	81	93	67	78	88	91
Jenkins, Humprey (M) 06/95, Age 08-03, Level 8, Form A	SS	162	160	161	162	165	156	161	163	151	158	157	160	168	157	164	162
	GE	2.4	2.3	2.4	2.5	2.6	2.1	2.4	2.5	1.9	2.4	2.1	2.4	2.8	2.0	2.6	2.4
	NS	6	5	6	6	6	5	6	6	4	6	5	5	6	5	6	6
	NPR	62	59	60	60	73	48	62	67	36	64	50	59	74	51	67	65
Kerrigan, Will (M) 06/95, Age 08-03, Level 8, Form TIL	SS	170	160	165	153	162	167	170	176	173	167	164	166	184	171	162	166
	GE	2.9	2.3	2.6	2.0	2.5	2.7	2.9	3.3	3.0	2.8	2.5	2.7	3.8	2.9	2.4	2.7
	NS	6	5	6	5	6	7	7	8	7	8	6	6	8	7	6	6
	NPR	76	59	69	41	66	79	81	91	82	91	68	73	93	78	62	75
McFadden, Eugene (M) 05/95, Age 08-04, Level 8, Form A	SS	188	193	190	208	196	176	174	176	173	167	174	179	189	202	193	191
	GE	4.0	4.3	4.1	5.4	4.5	3.2	3.1	3.3	3.0	2.8	3.1	3.4	4.1	5.0	4.3	4.1
	NS	8	8	8	9	9	8	8	8	8	8	7	7	9	9	9	9
	NPR	94	95	95	99	99	94	85	91	82	91	87	92	96	99	98	99
Ochi, Jiro (M) 06/95, Age 08-03, Level 8, Form TIL	SS	154	145	150	153	162	154	159	156	164	154	160	156	173	153	155	158
	GE	2.0	1.5	1.8	2.0	2.5	2.0	2.3	2.1	2.6	2.2	2.3	2.1	3.1	2.0	2.1	2.2
	NS	5	3	4	5	6	4	5	5	6	5	5	5	7	5	5	5
	NPR	44	20	33	41	66	40	56	48	67	50	58	47	82	42	46	54
Ornelas, Jorge (M) 09/95, Age 08-00, Level 8, Form A	SS	178	202	190	208	179	176	174	183	183	174	183	182	195	180	186	187
	GE	3.4	5.0	4.1	5.4	3.4	3.2	3.1	3.7	3.7	3.3	3.6	3.6	4.4	3.5	3.8	3.9
	NS	7	9	8	9	8	8	7	8	8	9	8	8	9	8	9	9
	NPR	86	98	95	99	92	94	85	97	92	97	96	95	99	89	96	99
Peck, Stephan (M) 07/95, Age 08-02, Level 8, Form A	SS	194	181	188	203	162	162	159	153	173	160	163	170	164	153	164	170
	GE	4.4	3.5	4.0	5.0	2.5	2.4	2.3	2.0	3.0	2.5	2.4	2.9	2.6	2.0	2.6	2.9
	NS	9	8	8	9	6	6	5	5	7	6	6	7	6	6	6	7
	NPR	96	91	95	98	66	67	56	41	82	71	66	81	67	42	67	82

SS=Standard Score, GE=Grade Equivalent, NS=National Stanine, NPR=National Percentile Rank

For further information on the interpretation of this report, please visit www.riversidepublishing.com or refer to the Interpretive Guide.

* = Math Computation is not included in the Math Total or in any score that includes the Math Total.

Riverside Publishing A HOUGHTON MIFFLIN COMPANY

Figure 11.2 A sample class list report for an achievement battery.

The Class List Report facilitates identifying patterns in the achievement levels of students within a class. To read the Class List Report efficiently, concentrate on one type of score (e.g., just percentile ranks or stanines). Then, scan the report horizontally for each student and vertically for each test area. The horizontal scan will help identify strengths and weaknesses for each student. The vertical scan will help identify the range of achievement levels among students.

Let's illustrate the process with several students (horizontal scans) and test areas (vertical scans). We will use national stanines (NS) as the means of interpretation, letting all other scores fade into the background. Begin with Stephan Peck, the last student on the list. Stephan shows an interesting pattern of scores. He is especially strong in reading: stanine 9 in Vocabulary, stanine 8 in Comprehension, and stanine 9 in Word Analysis. He is above average in most other areas, but not as strong as in reading. His performance in mathematics is of some concern. Although somewhat above average in Problems and Computation, he is only at stanine 5 in Concepts, a relative low point in his profile. This is surprising in the light of his excellent performance in reading. Ms. Prescott may want to conduct some follow-up evaluation of Stephan's grasp of math concepts. Next, scan the row for Jiro. This student hovers around the national average (stanine 5) in most areas. However, there is a relative weakness in Reading Comprehension (but not Vocabulary), which may merit follow-up evaluation.

Now let's scan vertically to examine the array of scores within test areas. We will examine only two areas to illustrate how to proceed. Consider first the Word Analysis test. Among the students shown here, there is considerable range in performance. Four of the nine students are at stanine 9 and three students are at stanine 5, with one each at stanines 6 and 7. Considering how word analysis skills develop in the primary grades, the four students at stanine 9 have probably mastered most of the essential word analysis skills. The other students are progressing satisfactorily but still need development in this area. Now look at the Mathematics Concepts area. Although no students are below average in this area, only one student reaches stanine 9. As a group, these students are not quite as strong in Math Concepts as in Word Analysis.

Try This!

From Figure 11.2, pick one student, other than one treated in the text. Scan the row for that student. What conclusions do you draw about that student?

Now, pick a test area, other than one treated in the text. Scan the column for that test. What conclusions do you draw about that test area?

Typical Uses and Special Features

Achievement batteries are used for a great variety of purposes. Sometimes the diversity of purposes becomes problematic, as the different purposes are not always entirely compatible. The original intent for these tests was to monitor the progress of individual students in the major areas of the school curriculum, with the teacher being the primary recipient of the test information. This is still a major purpose and probably the most common application of these tests. However, other uses have also become common. School buildings and school districts, for example, now use summaries of test scores for groups of students to evaluate the curriculum. In some instances, these summaries are also used to evaluate the effectiveness of school personnel: teachers, principals, and superintendents. Such usage, of course, is very different from the originally intended purpose.

Scores from achievement batteries are now routinely reported to parents. Further, group summaries are reported to school boards and local communities as measures of school effectiveness. Finally, achievement batteries (or parts of them) are employed in many research projects as dependent variables. For example, the SAT10 reading and mathematics test results for the primary grades might be used as measures of the effect of participation in a prekindergarten program. These diverse uses put extraordinary strain on the developmental requirements and interpretive materials for these tests.

Materials from the publishers of the achievement batteries understandably emphasize their unique characteristics. However, even casual observation reveals that the similarities among these batteries far outnumber the dissimilarities. Let us identify some of these common features.

First, although one of these batteries may be referred to as "a" test (e.g., the Stanford test or the Iowa test), each is actually *a system of many interrelated tests*. There are a dozen or more separate tests at each level, multiple levels, and multiple forms. Increasingly, there are long versions and short versions, multiple-choice and open-ended versions, and editions in different languages or other such variations. Further, there may be item banks, customized versions, and secure editions for the series. The modern versions of these batteries actually consist of well over a hundred identifiably separate tests. However, all of these tests are related to one another, not just in name but also in terms of developmental procedures, normative structures, and interpretive systems. The direct comparability of normed scores across content areas and grade levels is one of the greatest values of these achievement batteries. These batteries are probably the only source of directly comparable information about students' relative strengths and weaknesses in relation to an external standard. Teacher-assigned marks differ in difficulty level by subject area and grade. Ms. Vasquez is known as a tough grader. Mr. Norcross gives almost all "A" grades. The standardized achievement battery allows for direct comparability across subject areas and grades. Similarly, a classroom test score of 80 in science may be relatively much better or worse than a score of 80 in mathematics.

Second, quite apart from the number of identifiably separate tests, the array of *supplementary materials* and scoring reports for these batteries is staggering. There may be separate interpretive booklets for students, parents, teachers, and school administrators. There are numerous options for computer-generated scoring reports. There are practice tests, locator tests, detailed lists of objectives, and a host of other ancillary materials.

Third, the *norming procedures and other research programs* for these achievement batteries are, in general, exemplary. They employ the latest, most sophisticated methodologies. Samples are well in excess of what is required for statistical stability. Extraordinary measures are taken to ensure representativeness by gender, race, ethnic group, geographic region, socioeconomic status, and other demographic characteristics. The technical manuals for these batteries are usually very extensive.

Fourth, many of the major achievement batteries now employ *methods of assessment in addition to multiple-choice items*. The publishers and the achievement batteries themselves have long been criticized for their exclusive reliance on multiple-choice methodology. Such reliance is no longer true. For example, all of the batteries now have some form of free-writing exercise for the evaluation of the quality of writing. Recent editions of some major batteries have extensive arrays of open-ended and performance measures.

There is still some question about the extent to which these forms of assessment will be used, since they are considerably more expensive than multiple-choice tests, especially with respect to scoring costs. There are also significant other questions about the technical quality of some of these alternative methods.

Fifth, all of the achievement batteries depend heavily on the *same sources of information for their content*. Included within these sources are (a) statements of curricular goals from professional organizations, such as the National Council of Teachers of Mathematics (NCTM), the National Council of Teachers of English (NCTE), and similar organizations; (b) major textbook series; (c) outlines prepared for projects, such as the National Assessment of Educational Progress (see p. 266 later in this chapter); and (d) curricular guides from state departments of education, the more populous states being particularly influential in this regard. In establishing the content for these tests, for better or for worse, you will not find "mavericks" striking out in new directions.

SINGLE-AREA ACHIEVEMENT TESTS

There is a wide variety of achievement tests that cover a single content domain. These tests are generally designed for use in high school or college, often for use at the end of a course or an entire program of study. Such tests are also available as occupational competency tests. The classification scheme adopted in this chapter excludes from this category the parts of achievement batteries (e.g., the mathematics test from Stanford Achievement Test) that could be used as a stand-alone test. Also excluded are occupation-related tests that lead to certification or licensing; we cover those tests in the next category.

Try This!

To illustrate the vast number of tests in the category of single-area achievement tests, go to www.ets.org/testcollection. Enter the name of a subject field, such as biology, psychology, Spanish, or mathematics. Scan the list of results. Note, in addition to achievement tests related to the area, you will find measures of attitude toward the area.

Examples

Let us consider several examples to illustrate this huge, seemingly endless category of tests. The Degrees of Reading Power (DRP) provides an interesting example of a single-area achievement test. As suggested by its title, it focuses exclusively on reading. It purports to measure only reading comprehension. It yields a single score. DRP spans the grade range from 1 to 12. It has Primary, Standard, and Advanced levels, with several forms at each level.

DRP has two distinctive features. First, its test items use what is called a modified cloze procedure. The classic *cloze procedure* involves presentation of text with every "nth" word deleted. Usually, "n" is 6 or 7; for example, every 6th or 7th word is deleted. The student's task is to supply the missing words. Getting them correct signals understanding of the text. The modified cloze procedure deletes selected words, not every nth word. Further, the modified procedure uses multiple-choice options to fill in the missing words rather than using free response. Figure 11.3 illustrates the cloze procedure. It shows original text (from the first paragraph in this section), the classic cloze procedure, and the modified cloze procedure.

Original Text

The Degrees of Reading Power (DRP) provides an interesting example of a single-area achievement test. As suggested by its title, it focuses exclusively on reading. It purports to measure only reading comprehension. It yields a single score. DRP spans the grade range from 1 to 12. It has Primary, Standard, and Advanced levels, with several forms at each level.

Classic Cloze Procedure (supply the missing words)

The Degrees of Reading Power (DRP) _____ an interesting example of a single-_____ achievement test. As suggested by _____ title, it focuses exclusively on _____. It purports to measure only reading _____. It yields a single score. DRP _____ the grade range from 1 to 12. _____ has Primary, Standard, and Advanced levels, _____ several forms at each level.

Modified Cloze Procedure (select the word to go in each space)

The Degrees of Reading Power (DRP) provides an interesting ___1___ of a single-area achievement test. As suggested by its title, it ___2___ exclusively on reading. It purports to measure only reading comprehension. It yields a single ___3___. DRP spans the grade range from 1 to 12. It has Primary, Standard, and Advanced levels, with several forms at each level.

1. thing	example	dozen	helpful
2. hurts	tells	focuses	reads
3. score	top	bottom	book

Figure 11.3 Examples of Cloze-type reading items.

A second distinctive feature of DRP relates to score interpretation. DRP raw scores convert to a DRP scale based on the readability level of the test material. In turn, the DRP scale points to the readability level of numerous books. Thus, it is hoped that a student's DRP score will aid in selecting reading material appropriate for that student.

Try This!

To see how the DRP score scale relates to the readability level of a wide variety of books, go to the DRP website (www.tasaliteracy.com/drp/drp-main.html).

DRP also provides norms, for example, percentiles. Thus, it is a very good example of using both criterion-referenced and norm-referenced interpretation. As noted elsewhere in this book, it is not the test itself that is criterion-referenced or norm-referenced. It is the method of interpreting scores on the test.

Here is a second interesting example of a single-area achievement test: the STAR Math test (Renaissance Learning, 2003). This is a computer-adaptive test for use in grades 1–12. The item pool consists of approximately 2,400 multiple-choice items, ranging from simple addition problems to high school algebra and geometry problems. An individual student completes only 24 items, with items selected by a computerized branching routine. We described such branching routines in Chapter 1 (p. 17). The initial item is selected according to the student's grade. Thereafter, a correct answer branches the student to a more difficult item, while an incorrect answer branches to an easier item. In the end, it is expected that the student's placement will be accurately determined.

Figure 11.4 shows a copy of the computer-generated report for this test. National normative data for STAR Math yield grade equivalents, NCEs, and percentile ranks. Notice the use of a percentile band. The report also provides a criterion-referenced instructional placement recommendation. Thus, this is another example of a standardized achievement test providing both criterion-referenced and norm-referenced interpretation. Many

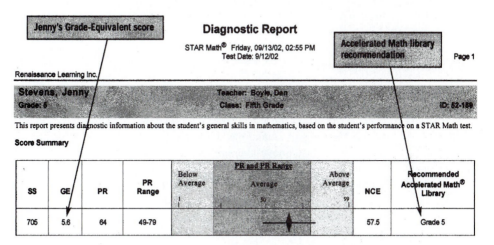

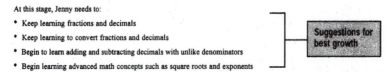

Figure 11.4 Computer-generated report for STAR Math.

(Reproduced with permission of the publisher Renaissance Learning, Inc. STAR Math® is a registered trademark of Renaissance Learning, Inc.)

computer-administered tests, such as STAR Math, are now becoming available for use in schools.

Try This!

To see examples of test items and score reports for STAR Math, visit this website: renlearn. com/starmath.

Looking at Jenny's Report

What can be learned from looking at a report such as Jenny's in Figure 11.4? As with the ITBS report examined earlier, one must focus on certain scores, go slowly, and remember that the scores are not perfectly reliable. Let's focus on the percentile score. On this STAR Math report, Jenny has a percentile rank of 64. That is, her overall math performance is slightly above average for her grade. Below the box with the normed scores, the report provides a criterion-referenced interpretation, with instructional suggestions. Jenny shows reasonable mastery of numeration concepts and basic operations with whole numbers. The instructional suggestions emphasize work with fractions and decimals, both in terms of numeration concepts and computations. It is important to coordinate this information with other information the teacher has about Jenny's performance in math.

Diagnostic Tests

Diagnostic tests in reading and mathematics constitute a special case of single-area achievement tests. Most of the single-area tests emphasize a total score, although a few subscores may be given. In contrast, diagnostic tests, while concentrating on one area, yield many scores. For example, a diagnostic reading test may yield scores for word knowledge, comprehension, speed, blending, and syllabication. A diagnostic math test may yield separate scores for computing in addition, subtraction, multiplication, and division with whole numbers, fractions, and decimals. Whereas the typical single-area test may have 50–100 items and take about 40 minutes, a diagnostic test may have several hundred items and require 2–3 hours. Thus, there is the usual trade-off between amount of information and testing time. If you want detailed information, it takes a lot of time. If you do not want to spend too much time, resulting information will be limited.

Diagnostic achievement tests are generally limited to reading and math and to the elementary grades. However, the tests may be used with high school students experiencing difficulty with the subject matter. Diagnostic tests are particularly popular in Title I programs. Table 11.3 lists several diagnostic tests in current use.

Many sources equate standardized achievement tests with *summative* assessment. Diagnostic tests, such as those listed in Table 11.3, provide clear examples of standardized tests that are used almost exclusively for *formative* assessment, specifically for planning instruction based on students' strengths and weaknesses. In this regard, the DIBELS measures warrant special mention. DIBELS concentrates on prereading and early reading skills in the primary grades. The materials are unusual in that they do not have to be purchased

Table 11.3 Examples of Diagnostic Tests

Test	For More Information
California Diagnostic Mathematics Test	http://www.ctb.com
California Diagnostic Reading Test	http://www.ctb.com
Dynamic Indicators of Basic Early Literacy Skills (DIBELS)	http://dibels.uoregon.edu
Group Reading Assessment and Diagnostic Evaluation (GRADE)	http://www.agsnet.com
Group Mathematics Assessment and Diagnostic Evaluation (GMADE)	http://www.agsnet.com
Stanford Diagnostic Mathematics Test	http://www.harcourt.com
Stanford Diagnostic Reading Test	http://www.harcourt.com

from a commercial publisher. Master copies can be downloaded (free) directly from the DIBELS website (see Table 11.3), then copied for classroom use. Another unusual feature of the DIBELS tests is that they tend to be very brief. Several require only one-to-three minutes per subtest, with many alternative forms available, thus encouraging repeated use throughout the year. In effect, they follow the pattern for self-referencing on repeated measures described in Chapter 5 (p. 125). The series also provides both criterion-referenced and norm-referenced interpretation of scores. The DIBELS tests must be individually administered. All other diagnostic tests listed in Table 11.3 can be group administered.

Try This!

Access the DIBELS website: http://dibels.uoregon.edu. What tests do you find for First Grade? Download one of the test forms. Also, examine one of the sample score reports. Do you see evidence of both criterion-referenced and norm-referenced interpretation?

As final examples in this category of single-area achievement tests, we should mention that the SAT II: Subject Tests, the GRE Subject Exams, and the Advanced Placement (AP) Exams are all good examples of single-area achievement tests. Some states also offer single-area tests. The most notable example is the New York State Regents Examinations. All of these examples have useful websites for further exploration.

Typical Uses and Special Features

There are two typical uses for single-area achievement tests. First, they are used to determine a student's performance in a highly focused area, such as a body of knowledge or skill. Second, they may be used to evaluate the adequacy of an instructional program. In this second use, it is assumed not only that the test has content validity, but also that individuals are making a reasonable effort to acquire the knowledge or skill tested.

What generalizations can we develop about single-area achievement tests? There is such a vast array of these tests that generalizations are somewhat hazardous. However, at least if we limit the list to typical examples offered by major publishers, we can discern some common characteristics.

Most of the tests in this category are group-administered, paper-and-pencil, multiple-choice tests. Some occupationally related tests also have a performance component. Test length tends to be in the range of about 50–200 items, with many of the tests having more than 100 items. Computer-adaptive tests have large item pools but examinees actually complete only a relatively small number of items. Most of the tests in this category emphasize use of a single, total score, while still giving a few subscores. The diagnostic tests, which are actually minibatteries, are an exception to this generalization. The total scores tend to be highly reliable—usually .90 or higher. This is not surprising. An individual's knowledge of a well-defined body of information, concepts, and skills is a pretty stable phenomenon when measured with a large sample of items. Reliability of subscores on these tests is almost entirely a function of the number of items in the subtest. Of course, the test manual should report reliability data for subscores as well as the total score. As a general rule, one should be wary of the reliability of any score based on fewer than about 20 items.

To indicate validity, tests in this category depend almost exclusively on content validity. Test content is matched with a course of study, whether an individual course or an entire program, or with a systematic job description. There are occasional attempts to gather other types of validity evidence for these tests, but content validity predominates. You must carefully check the publication dates on the tests in this category. Some of the tests are quite thoroughly out-of-date but continue to be referenced in the standard sources of information about tests. Tests in all of the other categories tend to be updated regularly. However, that is not true for many of the tests in this category of single-area tests.

LICENSING AND CERTIFICATION TESTS

We consider next tests used for purposes of licensing and certification. There are numerous tests in this category. In some ways, they are like single-area achievement tests. Tests in both categories concentrate on one area, usually focusing on a total score. However, licensing and certification exams have a distinctive purpose. They also feature considerable concern with the cut-off score for defining acceptable performance. We group licensing and certification exams together here because they tend to be very similar in purpose, structure, development, and usage. However, there is a technical distinction between licensing and certification. See Impara (1995) for an excellent orientation to these tests. **Licensing** involves a legal grant by a government agency to practice. States control most licensing procedures, although the federal government controls a few of them. The principal concern in licensing is determination that the minimal level of knowledge and/or skill is present in order to protect the public. **Certification** involves a statement that a level of proficiency has been attained but it does not necessarily imply a right to do anything. Certification may aim at a minimal level or a higher level of knowledge/skill, depending on the particular purpose.

Examples

Here is a simple example of a licensing exam: The examination for a private pilot license. This exam is administered by the Federal Aviation Administration (FAA), which is responsible for licensing all U.S. pilots. The exam consists of three parts: a written exam containing 60 multiple-choice questions, an oral exam, and a flight exam. The examinee must also have a total of 40 hours of flight instruction and solo flight time. A person must pass all parts of the exam to receive a pilot's license. State-administered exams used to obtain a driver's license also fall into this category. Licensing involves passing a written exam (usually multiple choice), a road test (performance exam), and meeting certain age and residency requirements.

The Praxis Exams

The Praxis exams provide an interesting example of certification tests. The Praxis series is a descendent of the National Teacher Exams (NTEs). The call for "highly qualified" teachers in the No Child Left Behind Act has obviously stimulated use of the Praxis exams. They are an unusual example of certification and licensing exams in several respects. First, most certification or licensing exams are single tests. Praxis, in contrast, is an umbrella title for a host of different tests. We describe the variety of specific tests later. Second, even within the Praxis series, there are notable differences among the tests. For example, some of the tests have score ranges of 100–200, while others have ranges of 150–190 or 250–990. Some of the tests are strictly multiple-choice, while others are a mixture of multiple-choice and essay tests. The performance database for various tests ranges from thousands of cases to a mere handful. In addition, different states establish their own cut-off scores. Further, a state may use some of the tests but not others. All in all, interpreting Praxis scores is an uncommonly complex affair.

The Praxis series includes three major components. The first part is Praxis I: Academic Skills Assessment. This part has three tests: reading, writing, and mathematics. Each test requires one hour. The reading and math exams each have 40 multiple-choice items. Writing has 38 multiple-choice items and one essay, scored on a 6-point holistic scale. Praxis I exams are available in both traditional paper-and-pencil format and in computer-administered format. Praxis I exams are typically taken by prospective teachers about midway through their educational program or before formal acceptance into the program.

The content orientation of the Praxis I exams differs from that for the Praxis II exams. The Praxis II exams, described next, can trace their origins to specific college (or graduate) courses. The Praxis I exams are much more general in nature. They cover skills in reading, writing, and mathematics that one would expect to find in the typical high school graduate.

Praxis II: Subject Assessments include more than 100 tests in specific subject areas. Some of the tests are in content areas for classroom teachers (e.g., Latin, geography, and theater). Some tests cover teaching skills (e.g., Spanish pedagogy, principles of learning and teaching, and introduction to the teaching of reading). Other exams cover nonclassroom specialist areas (e.g., library media specialist, school psychologist, and speech-language pathology). Most of the Praxis II exams require two hours. The Praxis website (www.ets.org/praxis) provides detailed content outlines and sample items for each test. Some of the tests consist entirely of multiple-choice items. Others are a mixture of multiple-choice and essay items. Human judges rate the essay items, using procedures described in Chapter 8.

Norms and Cut-off Scores.   Praxis norms provide a classic example of "user norms." The norms are based on whatever individuals took the exams in the most recent three-year period. For Praxis I exams, this means approximately 90,000 cases. For Praxis II exams,

---

KEY POINTS SUMMARY 11.3 *The Praxis Series*

Praxis I: Academic Skills Assessments
(Reading, Writing, Mathematics)

Praxis II: Subject Assessments
(More than 100 tests related to content areas,
teaching skills, and specialist areas)

Praxis III: Classroom Performance Assessments
(For practicing teachers)

• **Go to www.ets.org/praxis for details**

---

the numbers range from about 75,000 to fewer than 10 cases per test. Scaled scores, as mentioned earlier, differ from test to test. The Praxis materials (ETS, 2002) do not provide the usual full range of percentiles. The materials give the median score and "average performance range" (i.e., the middle 50% of scores) for each test. From these data, assuming a roughly normal distribution of scores, we can estimate what the various state cut-off scores mean. On the widely used Praxis I exams, the estimation indicates that most states set their cut-off scores at approximately the 10th to 20th percentile.

Praxis III is quite different from Praxis I and II. Praxis III aims to assess the skills of practicing teachers rather than those in training. It does not involve a test in the usual sense of that term. Praxis III involves direct observation of classroom practice, preparation and evaluation of a teaching portfolio, and a semistructured interview. We provide additional details on Praxis III in Chapter 15.

Typical Uses and Special Features

Little needs to be said to describe typical uses of licensing and certifying tests. They are used to document, in a very official manner, the competency of examinees in relevant skills and knowledge. However, there is a secondary use when examinees are products of a clearly identifiable educational program. In such cases, the administrators of the program use results of the test as a measure of the program's adequacy. We should note that various types of professional associations generally govern the use of tests in this category, but these associations often contract with professional testing organizations for preparation of the tests.

The distinctive features of licensing and certifying tests arise from the crucial consequences they have for examinees. First, in order to yield very reliable scores, these tests tend to be quite lengthy. Tests having several hundred items and requiring several hours for administration are common. As a result, total scores on these tests tend to be highly reliable, usually in the neighborhood of .95. Second, the tests typically have very clear, explicit content outlines. Examinees usually have access to these outlines well in advance of the test. Third, there is extraordinary security surrounding these tests. They may be administered only once or a few times each year at carefully controlled testing sites. Further, to protect the security of test content, test items are changed frequently. For some types of testing, it may be a virtue to use exactly the same test items repeatedly. It would be very imprudent to use exactly the same items repeatedly for a certification exam. Fourth, both test developers and test-takers, understandably, have a preoccupation with cut-off scores and how these are derived. As described in Chapter 5 (pp. 118–120), there is a large element of judgment involved in setting the cut-off scores, although the judgments generally take into account examinees' actual performance.

STATE ASSESSMENT PROGRAMS

Recent years have witnessed explosive growth in the scope and influence of state assessment programs. The No Child Left Behind (NCLB) Act is the principal source of the increase. NCLB requires each state to have a testing program (if it wants to receive federal funds). Some states have had testing programs for many years. Now all do. Further, NCLB dictates important features of the state assessment programs. We mention some of those features in this chapter. Chapter 14 on legal issues also identifies some of these features.

The current situation is exceptionally fluid. The status of state assessment programs is changing rapidly in response to NCLB. Attempting to describe these programs is a frightening prospect. A description today will surely be out-of-date tomorrow—even five minutes from now. How will we handle this hazardous task? We take two approaches. First, we will describe general characteristics of most state programs. Second, we direct the reader to current sources of information about these programs. These sources provide the most up-to-date descriptions. Each reader will surely want to check the information for his or her own state program.

General Characteristics

In many respects, the state assessment programs are quite diverse. However, surveys of all of the state programs reveal that they have several common characteristics. There are a few exceptions to these generalizations, but they are just that—exceptions.

1. The typical state assessment program concentrates on basic skill areas. Basic skills include reading, math, writing, and, increasingly, science. The programs typically do not include such areas as social studies, art, music, physical education, and so on. We repeat: There are exceptions.

2. State assessment programs concentrate on Grades 3–8 and one or two grades in the Grade 9–12 range. For the most part, NCLB dictates the grade selection.

3. Many state assessment programs use some combination of custom-made tests and one of the standardized achievement batteries described earlier in this chapter. The standardized batteries provide national, norm-referenced information. The custom-made tests ordinarily yield a state norm or, more typically, standards-based interpretation.

4. The custom-made tests are developed either directly by the state or by an outside contractor. In either case, the tests aim to measure the specific objectives (content standards) established by the state. It follows that content validity reigns supreme. The test must match the state-specified curriculum objectives.

5. Most state programs employ some combination of objective, multiple-choice testing, and performance (constructed-response) measures. We described the essential

features of each type of measure in Chapters 7 and 8, respectively. However, the final result for each student is a single score in each content area (reading, math, etc.). It is particularly noteworthy that most states use a free-writing exercise, scored by one of the methods described in Chapter 8.

6. According to NCLB, states must provide public reports of the results from the assessment program. These reports provide information for each school district and building, as well as for the entire state. Reports must give information for certain subgroups of students (e.g., by racial/ethnic group). Typically, all these reports are Internet accessible. See the state websites in Appendix E to access the reports.

7. As also dictated by NCLB, the reports must utilize the "proficient" definition. We described development of such definitions in Chapter 5 (see p. 118). The reports listed in the previous point must give percentages of students reaching the "proficient or better" level. Further, the reports must give information on year-to-year changes in the percentages of students in the proficient category.

8. Some states use a test for high school graduation. At present, about one quarter of the states have such a requirement. Another one quarter awaits implementation of such legislation. The exact result of the requirement is rather diverse. In some cases, receipt of a high school diploma is contingent on passing the test. In other cases, everyone receives a diploma, but the diploma gets a notation if the test was passed. There are always multiple opportunities to pass the test and remedial activities for those who fail. In virtually all cases, passing the test is only one of several requirements for graduation. Other requirements might include minimum attendance, completing certain courses, and so on. However, the testing requirement tends to be the lightning rod, receiving most of the public's attention.

9. Finally, in most states, nonpublic school students, including the home schooled, do not participate in the state-assessment program. In some states, this is a sizable fraction of students, and in some districts a very sizable fraction. In other states, the fraction is small.

KEY POINTS SUMMARY 11.4 *General Characteristics of State Testing Programs*

- Concentrate on basic skills
- Grades 3–8 plus one high school grade
- Use custom-made and existing achievement batteries
- Aimed at state content standards
- Combination of multiple-choice and performance items
- Reports to the public
- Proficiency basis for reporting
- Some use of high school graduation tests
- Includes public school students

Sources of Information about State Assessment Programs

Several sources provide information about state testing programs. The first source is the Council of Chief State School Officers (CCSSO), headquartered in Washington, D.C. CCSSO is a coordinating body for state education systems[3] at the pre-K–12 grade level. CCSSO regularly collects and disseminates information about state assessment practices. Its website (www.ccsso.org) is a prime source of information about state assessment programs. At the CCSSO website, most of the relevant information occurs under the headings "assessment," "assessment systems," or "accountability." For the most part, the CCSSO site presents summary information about state assessment practices. Obviously, it takes time to collect and summarize information from the states. Consequently, the most recent information from CCSSO is always one or two years out-of-date.

Two sources introduced in Chapter 6 (see pp. 139–140) provide convenient links to state assessment Internet sites. These are the Align to Achieve project (www.align-toachieve.org) and the Mid-continent Research for Education and Learning Center (www.mcrel.org). These two sources are useful primarily for rapid access to information about different states.

Finally, of course, a key source of information about state assessment programs is each state's education department. Appendix E contains the current URLs for these departments. As with any list of URLs, some of these will change. However, even when an old site does not provide a link to a new site, it is never difficult to search for a state education department's site. The state sites, understandably, offer details. The typical state site presents (a) the state content standards (objectives); (b) an outline of the state's assessment program, sometimes including sample items or even complete forms of previously used tests; and (c) reports of results. As noted earlier, these reports typically include statewide summaries and reports for school districts and buildings. Many of the reports also contain nontest indicators, such as attendance and graduation rates.

Try This!

Using Appendix E, access the website for your state (or a state of interest to you). Make sure you can find the information about the state's assessment program. What content areas does your state's program cover? What grades are included?

A NATIONAL AND AN INTERNATIONAL TESTING PROGRAM

We include in this category two very distinctive projects operated through national governmental or quasi-governmental bodies. One operates for the entire United States. The other covers many countries. The two projects are very similar in overall design. This makes it convenient to describe them in a single section. Both projects have assumed increased importance in recent years. Everyone in today's educational world should be familiar with these two programs.

---

[3] CCSSO also covers certain territories and other entities. We confine our references to states.

A National Testing Program: NAEP

Many tests, such as the SAT, ACT, and Stanford series may legitimately be called "national" tests. But there is one testing enterprise that merits this appellation in a special way. This is the *National Assessment of Educational Progress* (**NAEP**). It is not a single test but a federally funded testing project. NAEP was formulated in the 1960s specifically to provide a set of benchmarks regarding the educational attainments of Americans. In its earliest years, it included both students in school and out-of-school adult samples. In more recent years it has been confined entirely to in-school samples, specifically in Grades 4, 8, and 12. Each testing phase concentrates on just one or a few curricular areas, such as reading, mathematics, writing, or geography. For example, the arts were treated in 1997 and are not scheduled for assessment again until 2008. Reading and math are now covered every other year: 2005, 2007, etc. Foreign language is on the docket for 2012. (See the NAEP website referenced in Try This! for the full schedule of projected assessments.)

Special efforts are made to secure representative samples of students for nationwide and, more recently, state-level reporting. Reports also give results by gender and ethnic groups. NAEP does not report scores for individual students. It includes both multiple-choice (selected-response) and open-ended (constructed-response) test items. Some of its open-ended items have become models for other testing efforts that refer to the use of "NAEP-like" items. NAEP reports sometimes refer to themselves, perhaps somewhat pretentiously, as the "nation's report card," a term incorporated into its website within the National Center for Education Statistics website: (nces.ed.gov/nationsreportcard). The website provides a wealth of information about trends in achievement, group contrasts in performance, outlines of test content, sample items, and so on. NCLB legislation has mandated periodic participation in NAEP by states. Thus, from a rather sleepy, academic beginning in the 1960s, NAEP has risen to be a significant element in the national educational scene. For a trenchant critique of many of NAEP's practices, see Pelligrino, Jones, and Mitchell (1999).

Try This!

Access the NAEP website (www.nces.ed.gov/nationsreportcard). Then access sample items for one of the curricular areas assessed. What kinds of items do you find? Also, note the methods used for reporting results for national samples and for subgroups.

An International Testing Program: TIMSS

In 1995, students in selected grades in 40 countries took achievement tests in mathematics and science. Known as the *Trends in International Mathematics and Science Study* (**TIMSS**),[4] the project resulted in numerous reports in the public media about the relative

---

[4] The TIMSS acronym came into common usage when the project was in its third phase: thus, the Third International Mathematics and Science Study. As the project moved beyond that point, its new tag became Trends in International Mathematics and Science Study with the same acronym. However, many sources still refer to the project as the Third International Mathematics and Science Study. The first international study was for mathematics in 1964. Science was first studied in 1980–1982, with a second science study in 1983–1984. The third study, covering math and science, occurred in 1995, with follow-ups in 1999 and 2003.

levels of achievement in the various countries. Earliest reports of this project, dating back to 1964, received little attention. However, the public rhetoric of the 1990s and 2000s included reference to "world-class standards" and being "first in the world." Such phrases were prominent in the Goals 2000 federal law, enacted in 1994 (see Chapter 14 for further discussion of this law). Naturally, such references imply comparisons among nations. Thus, what began as a little noticed, research-oriented exercise suddenly assumed enormous importance. Like NAEP, TIMSS does not report results for individual students; rather, it concentrates on group summaries. A partial replication of the 1995 testing but only with students in Grade 8 occurred in 1999 with release of results in 2001. Another round of testing occurred in 2003. TIMSS currently projects a four-year cycle for testing. These projects occur under the aegis of the International Association for the Evaluation of Educational Achievement, using the rather abbreviated acronym of IEA. TIMSS maintains a comprehensive website (www.timss.org or www.ustimes.org) with descriptions of the scope of the project, sample items, and results for participating countries. Results from both NAEP and TIMSS are conveniently summarized in an annual publication titled *The Condition of Education* (followed by the year designation) from the National Center for Education Statistics (see www.nces.ed.gov).

NAEP and TIMSS have attained considerable visibility. However, there are some lesser known educational assessment programs that are, in many ways, similar to NAEP and TIMSS. For example, a spinoff from the TIMSS project is the Program for International Student Assessment (PISA). It undertook its initial assessment of 15-year-olds in reading, mathematics, and science in two dozen countries in 2000. A second example is the National Assessment of Adult Literacy (NAAL). NAAL targets the English language literacy of Americans age 16 and older. Although concentrating on language literacy, the project also includes a health literacy survey. Further information on PISA and NAAL may be found on their respective websites listed in Key Points Summary 11.5.

Special Features

The NAEP and TIMSS projects share some distinctive characteristics. First, the emphasis for these programs is on group performance. Second, each wave of testing typically addresses only one or a few areas. Even when more than one area is covered within a single year, they are treated as largely independent projects. In contrast, an achievement battery yields scores in a dozen different areas and does so for each student. Third, the national and international testing programs concentrate on a small number of grade or age cohorts. Finally, these programs attempt to collect extensive information about a wide variety of

KEY POINTS SUMMARY 11.5	*Major National and International Assessment Programs*
• NAEP	www.nces.ed/gov/nationsreportcard
• TIMSS	www.nces.ed.gov/timss or www.timss.org
• PISA	www.nces.ed.gov/surveys/pisa
• NAAL	www.nces.ed.gov/naal

educational practices (amount of homework, instructional time, etc.) that might help to interpret test results.

INDIVIDUALLY ADMINISTERED ACHIEVEMENT TESTS

All of the achievement tests introduced thus far in this chapter are group administered. However, there are some achievement tests deliberately designed for individual administration in much the same manner as individually administered ability tests covered in Chapter 12.

Examples

We illustrate individually administered achievement tests with two examples. First, there is the Wechsler Individual Achievement Test, Second Edition (WIAT–II). It includes subtests for oral language, listening comprehension, written expression, spelling, word reading, pseudoword decoding, reading comprehension, numerical operations, and mathematics reasoning. In addition, for a brief assessment, three subtests may be used to yield a Screener Composite score. The first edition was designed for use with children in the age range 5–19 years, but the second edition has expanded age coverage to include ages 4 through adults, including norms for college students. A principal goal of the WIAT is to investigate **ability-achievement discrepancies**. For this purpose, the WIAT is linked to all three of the Wechsler intelligence scales (see Chapter 12 for additional information on these scales).

Administration of these individual achievement tests is quite different from the previously described achievement tests, almost all of which are group administered. For a test such as the WIAT, only one student is tested at a time. The examiner is seated across from the examinee, with the stimulus booklet laid out on a table. The examiner establishes rapport and proceeds through the administration in what seems like a conversational tone but is actually a well-practiced presentation of the standardized directions. The examiner must be thoroughly trained in the use of the WIAT to ensure valid administration. Typical administration time is about 50 minutes.

A second example of tests in this category is the third edition of the Woodcock-Johnson (WJ III; Woodcock, McGrew & Mather, 2001). In its previous editions, the test was known as the Woodcock-Johnson Psychoeducational Battery. The WJ III is actually a system of two tests: the Woodcock-Johnson III, Tests of Cognitive Abilities (WJ III Cog) and the Woodcock-Johnson III, Tests of Achievement (WJ III Ach). Table 11.4 lists the tests in WJ III Ach.

Examination of Table 11.4 reveals that WJ III Ach is quite a complex series. It includes a total of 22 different tests. Some of these are in the Standard Battery. Others occur in the Extended Battery. Further, both the Standard Battery and the Extended Battery contain supplemental tests. Some of the tests use audio recordings. Some tests are timed, others are not.

The cognitive battery, based on Cattell's theory of fluid and crystallized intelligence, has 10 tests in a Standard Battery and an additional 10 tests in an Extended Battery. All together, the WJ III system has 42 tests and numerous composites derived from combinations of these tests, making for a dizzying array of information. Administration and scor-

Table 11.4   Tests in the Woodcock-Johnson III Achievement Battery

Reading	Written Language
Basic Reading Skills	Spelling
Reading Fluency	Writing Fluency
Reading Comprehension	Writing Samples
*Word Attack	*Editing
*Reading Vocabulary	*Academic Knowledge
Oral Language	Supplemental Tests
Story Recall	Story Recall-Delayed
Understanding Directions	Handwriting Legibility Scale
*Picture Vocabulary	Writing Evaluation Scale
*Oral Comprehension	*Spelling of Sounds
Mathematics	*Sound Awareness
Calculation	*Punctuation & Capitalization
Math Fluency	
Applied Problems	
*Quantitative Concepts	

*These tests appear in the Extended Battery.

ing of a test like WJ III requires specialized training. The WJ III manuals make this perfectly clear. Test interpretation, as with the WIAT, depends heavily on contrasting performance levels among this multiplicity of tests. The WJ III is normed for ages 2–90 on samples considered representative of the national population for those ages.

Typical Uses and Special Features

In typical applications of these individually administered achievement tests, there is an interest in diagnosing discrepancies among various achievement levels or between achievement and mental ability. Hence, these tests usually entail joint administration with some measure of mental ability. Determination of specific learning disabilities is a frequent objective of such analyses. Because of the special emphases of tests in this category, these tests are sometimes referred to as **psychoeducational batteries**. Many of the applications of these individually administered achievement tests are tied closely to federal and state laws regarding identification and treatment of various disabilities. We examine these laws in Chapter 14.

Obviously, the most distinctive feature of tests in this category is the fact that they are individually administered. Perhaps more importantly, their purpose is somewhat different from that of the typical group-administered achievement test in at least four ways. First, while group summaries are important for nearly all of the group-administered tests, group summaries are largely irrelevant for the individually administered tests, except possibly in some research projects. Second, the focus of attention for group-administered tests is often the curriculum or program of study as much as it is the individual student. In fact, as noted earlier, individual scores may not even be reported in some circumstances for group-administered tests. Curriculum evaluation is not an issue for individually administered tests.

Third, individually administered achievement tests focus intensively on analysis of intra-individual differences in performance among different achievement areas and between achievement and mental ability. This type of analysis occurs for some group-administered tests but even where it does occur, it is typically less crucial than for the individually administered achievement test. (An exception to these generalizations is the Wide Range Achievement Test, Third Edition (WRAT–III) that is used almost exclusively as a quick screening device.) A final important difference is that these individually administered achievement tests are ordinarily used by school psychologists and other such specialists. In contrast, classroom teachers administer and receive reports for most of the other types of achievement tests described in this chapter.

ADMINISTERING STANDARDIZED TESTS

In Chapter 10, we reviewed suggestions for administering teacher-made tests. The suggestions covered remote and immediate preparation of students, managing the testing environment, and concluding the testing. Many of the same suggestions apply to the administration of standardized tests. However, there are a few special concerns for these tests. We need to introduce these special points. At the same time, we will reiterate some of the earlier points.

Before Testing

1. We repeat here the key point about remote preparation of students: *Provide good instruction* in relevant knowledge and skills. It is easy to get lost in the swirl of recommendations about test-taking skills, the testing environment, and so on. Let's not forget the over-riding importance of good instruction. That having been said, we can proceed to the following more specific suggestions.

2. *Attend to students' test-taking skills.* The relevance of this suggestion varies widely with the previous experience of students. The majority of students in Grades 4 and higher in developed countries have plenty of experience with standardized tests. They know how to mark answer sheets. They know how multiple-choice items work. They know that these tests usually have time limits. And so on. However, younger children, students who are recent immigrants, and other students may need special help. Be alert to these students. Provide additional work on test-taking skills as needed.

All standardized tests begin with a few practice items. You will work through these as part of the test administration. In addition, many standardized tests have entirely separate practice tests. If possible, use these. They will help to ensure a uniform starting point for students in terms of familiarity with item types and methods of responding.

Many textbooks also have "tips for taking tests." You may find it helpful to use these tips. Be aware, however, that many of the favorite tips—for example, looking for grammatical inconsistencies or unusual options—are virtually worthless. The people preparing standardized tests know how to write and edit items. The tests will not contain these types of clues. Don't waste students' time on such "hot tips."

3. *Read the test directions to yourself in advance.* It is standard advice to emphasize the importance of reading the test directions accurately. We will give this advice below.

However, from a practical viewpoint, it is also important for the teacher (or whoever is administering the test) to look over the directions before actually beginning the test administration. Do this a day or two before, if possible. If test materials are not delivered to you until just before the testing session, take a few minutes to scan the directions before launching into the administration. It is important to see how the directions are set up. Which parts do you read to yourself? Which parts do you read to students? How do the directions handle time limits? What do the directions say about getting students ready? Are students permitted to use calculators, dictionaries, and so on? If permissible, mark the booklet of directions to facilitate your later use of the booklet. You should know about these matters before you start the actual testing session.

4. *Ensure availability of materials.* Make sure you will have available everything you and the students need. Knowing what you need is part of the reason for advance reading of directions. Of course, it is usually someone else's responsibility to make sure you have what you need for a standardized test. The principal, assistant principal, a counselor, or someone ordinarily tends to this. But, it can be helpful to take some initiative on this point.

5. *Talk to students about the test.* Let the students know you want them to do well. Make sure they have some idea about what the test covers, for example, reading and math or math and writing. Using practice tests will obviously help with this point. Give students some idea of what will happen with the results.

During the Test

1. *Ensure proper environment.* Just before starting the administration, ensure a proper environment for testing. Make sure the lighting is adequate, students have acceptable working space, desks are cleared, and so on. It may be helpful to post a "Testing—Do Not Disturb" sign on the classroom door. Rearrange seating, if necessary.

2. *Follow the directions.* The key point here is that the test has been standardized with a certain set of directions. You need to follow these directions meticulously in order to actually have a standardized test. This is not an occasion for creative approaches!

Directions for standardized tests usually come in two parts. The first part contains general directions. These directions deal with such matters as how to handle students' questions, use of different languages to clarify directions, seating arrangements, and so on. The general directions usually apply to all tests in a battery or an assessment program.

The second part of the directions contains wording for each test. Read these specific directions exactly as they are presented. In some cases, you need to read directions even for individual items or exercises. For example, in the primary grades, every item may be dictated to students, at least in some tests. However, you need to rely on the general directions to know how to handle student questions or other unanticipated circumstances.

3. *Time accurately.* Most standardized tests have time limits. Learn to time accurately from the time you say "Go" until the time you say "Stop." Then, make sure students really do stop. You may need a stopwatch. Make sure you know how it works. At the beginning of each timed test, record the time or make sure you have started the stopwatch. Note what the ending time should be.

Some tests do not have strict time limits, but they have a general direction to allow sufficient time for "nearly all students to finish." When faced with this direction, you need some discretion in deciding when "enough is enough."

4. *Monitor the situation.* After students have started a test, circulate about the room. Make sure students are working on correct sections of the test and are recording answers appropriately. Circulating should also discourage cheating.

One especially important part of monitoring the situation comes at the end of each timed section. Some students will finish early. The folklore is that many standardized tests put a premium on speed. That is generally not the case. In fact, test constructors usually set very generous time limits. Hence, many students will finish well before the time limit. Keeping order in a classroom under these circumstances presents a real challenge. Be ready for it.

5. *Make notes* on unusual circumstances that might influence the scores of the entire class or individual students. For example, note that a test was interrupted by substantial construction noise outside. Note that Ned seemed really ill; the poor little guy's eyes were watering and he had trouble reading the items. The battery in Tom's calculator went dead. Such notes will prove helpful when you (or someone else) wants to interpret the scores later.

After the Test

1. *Retrieve all materials.* Your teacher-made tests may or may not be considered secure. In contrast, standardized tests are virtually always considered secure. Therefore, take special pains to retrieve all materials at the conclusion of each testing session. Then store the materials securely until you can deliver them to the school's central office.

2. *File your notes.* File the notes you made during test administration in a convenient place. Make sure you can find them several weeks later when the test results arrive.

3. *Clean up answer documents as needed.* It is entirely possible that you are expected to do nothing with answer documents other than return them to a central office. However, you may be expected to do some cleaning up. This is particularly true for scannable answer sheets. Check that names and other identifiers have been properly coded, that answer marks are sufficiently dark, and that smudges and stray marks are cleaned up. On essays or projects, make sure names (or other identifiers) are properly recorded; if there are multiple sheets, ensure that they all have identifiers.

Clearly Unethical Practices

In the preceding sections, we identified what are generally considered "principles of good practice" for administering standardized tests. Now we must identify some reprehensible practices that are clearly unethical. Do not do any of these things.

1. *Do not change students' answers.* This is a simple, unambiguous dictum. The temptation will come for the student who, perhaps, was obviously having a bad day. Leave the answer document as is and record the "bad day" in your notes. A difficult case comes when you are "cleaning up" answer documents. What should you do if the situa-

| KEY POINTS SUMMARY 11.6 | *Checklist for Principles of Good Practice in Administering Standardized Tests* |

Before Testing

1. Provide good instruction.
2. Attend to students' test-taking skills.
3. Read the test directions to yourself in advance.
4. Ensure availability of materials.
5. Talk to students about the test.

During the Test

1. Ensure proper environment.
2. Follow the directions.
3. Time accurately.
4. Monitor the situation.
5. Make notes.

After the Test

1. Retrieve all materials.
2. File your notes.
3. Clean up answer documents as needed.

tion could go either way, such as when you could read the answer as either this mark or that—and one of them is correct? In such circumstances, we recommend consulting with another professional (e.g, the school principal).

2. *Deliberately not following directions* is unethical. We call attention specifically to two objectionable practices. The first is extending the time limit. Do not do it, except when this is a preapproved accommodation for a particular student. Second, follow the test directions regarding how to handle student questions. Most frequently, the directions allow for clarification of procedural matters (e.g., how to mark answers), but do not allow for help with the meaning of test items. Some directions may allow for clarifying items. However, the main point is to follow the test directions.

3. *Do not give the actual test items in advance to students.* This is the most difficult point to cover. On the one hand, it is clearly unethical to give students the actual test items and, of course, coach them on the correct answers. This is the rawest, most egregious form of "teaching to the test." In the form just described, everyone agrees that it is entirely unprofessional. On the other hand, if there is a good match between test content and the instructional program, then, in a way, you are always teaching to the test. In addition, we have already recommended that you let students know something about what the test will cover, its format, and so on. Where is the dividing line between acceptable and unacceptable practice? At the extremes, the question is easily answered. There is, however, a gray area. (That does not mean that the whole answer is gray.) The profession has good agreement on the *general principle* to use in answering the question. Any practice that improves scores on the test *without* a concomitant increase in the underlying abilities, knowledge, and skills covered by the test is objectionable. Practices that improve test scores *with* a concomitant increase in the underlying abilities, knowledge, and skills covered by the test is acceptable. In fact, they are commendable. It is what we call education!

PRACTICAL ADVICE

1. When you encounter reference to "standardized tests," remember to make the distinctions introduced at the beginning of this chapter. There are many types of "standardized tests." What is true for one type may not be true for other types.

2. Keep in mind the special strengths of both teacher-made and standardized tests. Both types contribute to a full assessment program.

3. When using one of the standardized achievement tests, be very cautious about interpreting scores based on small clusters of test items. Many of the tests provide reports on these clusters, but they are usually not very reliable.

4. When using any standardized test, be sure you know the basis for the norms or proficiency categories.

5. If you will be taking a licensing or certification exam, check the content outline for it. The content outline will almost certainly be web-accessible. Also, determine how cut-off scores were established for the exam. It is useful to determine the passing rate for groups that recently completed the exam.

6. Become familiar with the variety of information provided about assessment on your state's website. Appendix E lists the state websites.

7. You will have no immediate practical use for information provided by NAEP and TIMSS. However, reports from these programs are being used in an increasing number of contexts. Spend some time studying the NAEP and TIMSS websites so that you can access information from them.

8. Before administering a standardized test, review the principles of good practice in Key Points Summary 11.6.

SUMMARY

1. In the popular media and in everyday conversation, the term "standardized test" has several different meanings. It is important to distinguish among these meanings.

2. We identified six major categories of achievement tests: achievement batteries, single-area tests, licensing and certification exams, state testing programs, national and international testing programs, and individually administered achievement tests.

3. Four characteristics are common to most standardized achievement tests. They all concentrate on assessing outcomes of instruction. They rely mostly on selected-response formats, although they may also incorporate constructed-response items. They nearly always have norms based on large samples and usually have detailed reports of technical characteristics.

4. Teacher-made achievement tests contrast with standardized tests principally in four ways. Teacher-made tests typically aim at greater detail. They do not ordinarily

have an extensive research base or any norm beyond the teacher's own previous students. Teacher-made tests occur with much greater frequency than standardized tests.

5. Achievement batteries are series of tests covering many content areas and a wide range of grades. Today's batteries are conglomerates, utilizing both selected-response and constructed-response items, offering both norm-referenced and criterion-referenced interpretation, appearing in both long and short versions, and featuring a multitude of score reports. There are five major achievement batteries in use in the United States.

6. There are numerous single-area achievement tests. They are available for virtually every curricular field. Some are single-score tests applicable to a single course, such as biology or American history. Others (e.g., diagnostic reading tests) are minibatteries providing several scores and spanning multiple grades.

7. Licensing and certification exams aim to establish a person's competence in a well-defined area usually related to job qualifications. There is special concern about establishing cut-off scores for these types of exams. The Praxis series illustrates some of the issues in this category.

8. Recent years have witnessed explosive growth in state assessment programs, motivated in large part by provisions of the No Child Left Behind Act. State programs currently concentrate on reading and math in Grades 3–8 and one high school grade. Science must be tested beginning in 2007–2008. Some state programs go well beyond these content areas and grades. Score interpretation for these programs relies mainly on standards-based proficiency categories.

9. NAEP and TIMSS are, respectively, national and international assessment programs. They each concentrate on providing group summaries of performance in selected content areas for a few ages or grades. With increasing frequency in recent years, NAEP and TIMSS data have been used as benchmarks for other testing programs.

10. Individually administered achievement tests are used by school psychologists and other specialists mainly for evaluation of special education, learning disability, and other such cases. Results from these tests are often compared with results from mental ability tests to examine achievement-ability discrepancies.

11. We identified several "principles of good practice" related to the administration of standardized tests. We also reviewed clearly unethical practices.

KEY TERMS

ability-achievement discrepancies	licensing	standardized test
battery	NAEP	TIMSS
certification	psychoeducational batteries	

EXERCISES

1. For one of the publishers listed in Table 11.1, access the website. What does the publisher emphasize about the achievement battery?

2. To make sure you can use the information in Table 11.2, answer these questions:

• What are the names of the math tests at the Primary 3 level?

• How many items are in the Intermediate 2 Complete Battery?

• What is the administration time for the Advanced 1 Science test?

• What test level is recommended for the beginning of Grade 6?

3. To make sure you can use the information in Figure 11.2, answer these questions for Jasmine:

• What was her stanine score for Vocabulary?

• What was her grade equivalent (GE) for Reading Comprehension?

• What was her percentile rank (NPR) for the Composite?

4. If you have access to a test booklet for any level of the batteries listed in Table 11.1, answer these questions:

• For multiple-choice questions, how many options are used?

• Are sample items used at the beginning of each test?

• How long is each test?

5. Using the ets.org/testcollection website, find examples of single-area achievement tests. Pick a content area of interest to you. Click on "'DescriptorSearch" in the left-hand box, then type the content area of interest to you in the next box. Click on "Search." What tests do you find?

6. Access the NAEP website: www.nces.ed.gov/nationsreportcard; or find a hardcopy of a NAEP report. What group comparisons are made? What trends over time are reported?

7. Repeat Exercise 6 for the TIMSS website: www.nces.ed.gov/timss or www.timss.org.

8. To learn about the use of achievement batteries in research projects, if you have access to the Education Resources Information Center (ERIC) database (www.eric.ed.gov), enter as a keyword in the query box the name of any of the major achievement batteries listed in Table 11.1. You will obtain a selection of research studies employing the test. You may also obtain a variety of reports of test results for school systems or entire states. Examine a selection of results to see what types of research use the tests.

9. Using Appendix E, access the website for your state testing program (or for a state of interest to you). Compare the state's program to the list of characteristics listed on pages 263–264.

Characteristics	Your State
Content areas	_____
Grades	_____
Standardized test used	_____
Proficiency levels	_____
Public reports	_____
Objectives listed	_____
Performance levels listed	_____

10. If you have a specimen set for a standardized achievement test, find the *Directions for Administering*. Read the directions to a class or even to a few friends as if you were the teacher administering the test in your classroom. Ask for a critique of your reading. For example, were the directions audible? Was the pace appropriate?

11. Return to Figure 11.2. Scan the scores for Martin Grant. What conclusions do you reach? Now scan the scores for the Mathematics Computation column. What conclusions do you reach? Compare your conclusions in both instances with conclusions reached by another person.

Chapter 12

Standardized Tests II: Ability, Interests, and Personality

OBJECTIVES

- Identify the purposes served by mental ability tests.
- Describe the variety of structures used for mental ability tests and the types of items used to represent these structures.
- Describe the method for administering individual mental ability tests and give examples of such tests.
- Outline the major characteristics of group-administered mental ability tests and give examples of such tests.
- Identify the role tests play in the definition of mental retardation and learning disabilities.
- Outline the major distinctions among personality tests and give examples of each category.
- Describe the typical uses of personality tests and behavior rating scales in the school context.
- State the purpose and typical structure of career interest inventories.

What This Chapter Is About

In addition to standardized achievement tests, as covered in Chapter 11, a variety of other standardized tests are used in schools. This chapter provides an overview of these other types of tests. We cover three main categories: mental ability, personality tests (including behavior rating scales), and career interest inventories. For each category, we identify the general purpose of the tests, outline the approaches used, and give examples of a few tests. The intent is to provide an overview, not a detailed analysis, of each category.

Why This Topic Is Important

Teachers will administer and receive reports of scores for some of the tests in this chapter. Many of the tests will be administered by professionals with specialized training in tests (e.g., school psychologists and school counselors). However, teachers will see reports of the scores and are expected to have some familiarity with the nature of the tests. Thus, everyone in the educational enterprise needs an introduction to these other standardized tests.

MENTAL ABILITY TESTS

Human beings possess and display a wide range of abilities. Cataloging all of these abilities presents an interesting challenge. Some are easy to identify. For example, there is athletic ability, musical talent, and artistic flair—or lack thereof—in each case. Some abilities are more difficult to recognize. Traditionally, the type of ability of most interest in educational circles has been mental ability. (We leave aside our near obsession with athletic ability.) Most people believe that mental ability has something to do with success in school. To be sure, it is not the only important factor in school success. Effort, motivation, concentration, and a host of other variables are also important. But, it seems that human beings have a level of mental ability that makes school learning more or less difficult. That is, students with high mental ability find it easier to learn academic subjects. Students with less of this mental ability find it more difficult to learn academic subjects.

For more than 100 years, researchers have tried to measure this thing called mental ability. The earliest attempts were rather clumsy and not very successful. That is, the measures did not seem to relate to success in academic learning. Newer developments led to measures that did seem to relate to school learning. In subsequent sections, we will examine what some of these tests look like. Before doing that, we need to examine two preliminary topics: names and theories for mental ability.

A Profusion of Names

Over the years, a variety of names have been used for what we are here calling mental ability. The names come and go, some quickly, some lingering over decades. Among the names, in addition to mental ability, are intelligence, aptitude, learning ability, academic potential, cognitive ability, and a veritable profusion of other terms. In subsequent sections, we use these terms more or less interchangeably. All of the terms assume that there is a relatively important human trait that is at least somewhat independent of specific school learning. They also assume that this human trait has some importance, specifically for school learning.

Discussions of mental ability almost inevitably involve reference to "**IQ**." IQ is an abbreviation for intelligence quotient. Let us sketch the meaning of this term, which has achieved the status of a household term in our culture. The 1916 edition of the Stanford-Binet introduced the notion of the IQ. In its original form, it *was* a quotient. Specifically, it was mental age (MA) in months divided by chronological age (CA) in months, multiplied by 100 to remove the decimal point. (Recall the definition of mental age from page 108.) For example, Kim has a mental age of 120 months (10 years) and chronological age of 132 months (11 years), giving an IQ of $(120/132) \times 100 = 91$. This is the classic definition of IQ. However, current tests do *not* use this definition. Rather, current tests use a standard score system with a mean of 100 and standard deviation of 15 or 16. (Recall the nature of standard scores from page 104.) On some current tests, this standard score (with M = 100, SD = 15) is specifically identified as an "IQ." Other tests use the same standard score system but call the resulting score by some other name (e.g., cognitive ability index or school ability index).

Theories About Mental Ability

Debates about the nature of human mental ability constitute one of the great sagas in the behavioral sciences. What exactly do we mean by "mental ability" or "intelligence?" For many years, the main contestants in this debate were the unitary theory and the multiple-factor theory. According to the unitary theory, an overall mental ability was dominant. This was general intelligence or, simply, "g." The antagonist theory maintained that there were several relatively independent mental abilities, including verbal, numerical, spatial, perceptual, and several other abilities. Currently, the most widely held position is a **hierarchical theory**. This theory says that both the unitary theory and the multiple-factor theory are partly correct (and partly incorrect). The hierarchical theory allows for several partly independent abilities but also maintains that these abilities are related to one another; and they combine to form an overall or general mental ability.

Figure 12.1 outlines the hierarchical conception of human intelligence. We portray it with three levels. At the lowest level are some very specific skills or abilities. At the intermediate level, some of these more specific skills combine into more general abilities (verbal, spatial, etc.). At the highest level, the intermediate abilities coalesce into an overall, general mental ability. For example, very specific (Level 1) abilities might include memory for digits, memory for words, and memory for geometric figures. They are somewhat discrete abilities, but also related to one another. As a group, they form the Level 2 ability of short-term memory. Short-term memory, in turn, is one component of overall, general mental ability.

There are actually several different hierarchical theories of intelligence. Although Figure 12.1 uses three levels, some theories may use more than three levels. The theories also differ somewhat in the list of intermediate abilities. However, all the hierarchical theories follow approximately the pattern shown in Figure 12.1. Most of the current tests of mental ability reflect the hierarchical theory of intelligence. Consequently, most mental ability tests yield an overall score, as well as several subscores. We will see how this works out for sample tests in the following sections.

Gardner's theory of multiple intelligences (MI theory) has been very popular in educational circles. In its earlier version, Gardner (1983, 1986, 1993) postulated seven intelligences: linguistic, musical, logico-mathematical, spatial, bodily-kinesthetic, intrapersonal, and interpersonal. More recently, Gardner (1999) announced the addition of naturalist, spiritual, existential, and moral intelligences to the array. The full array seems to be some mixture of partially separate factors of intelligence, other types of talent, and personality variables. In any case, Gardner's theory, despite its popularity, has had negligible influence on the practical measurement of mental ability.

There are many fascinating questions about the concept of mental ability. For example, how closely related are the Level 2 abilities, such as verbal and numerical abilities? Is

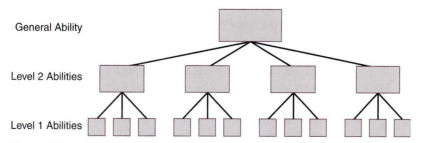

Figure 12.1 Outline of the hierarchical theory of mental ability.

mental ability rather stable or quite malleable? What is the magnitude of group differences in mental ability? As tempting as it is to pursue these questions here, we will not do so. Rather, we focus on the very practical task of describing the tests of mental ability in actual use. These are the tests a teacher will use or hear about in ordinary school settings. The reader interested in the questions raised in this paragraph can consult such sources as Brody (1992); Flanagan, Genshaft, and Harrison (1997); Lubinski (2004); Sternberg (1994a); and Wolman (1985). For an excellent, brief summary, see Neisser et al. (1996).

The mental ability tests used in schools fall into two general classifications: individually administered tests and group-administered tests. The tests share certain common features, but they are also different in important ways. In the following sections, we describe each of these types of tests.

INDIVIDUALLY ADMINISTERED MENTAL ABILITY TESTS

The first category of mental ability tests includes individually administered tests. A teacher would not ordinarily administer such tests. However, teachers will encounter reports of scores from these tests. Thus, teachers need to be familiar with them. It is expensive and time-consuming to give these tests. Usually, they are administered only to students with special needs. These tests play a key role in the identification of learning disabilities, mental retardation, and other such conditions. They may also be used in the selection of students for gifted programs. Most students will complete school without ever taking one of these tests. In this section, we describe the general nature of such tests and then give examples of them.

General Features of Individually Administered Mental Ability Tests

The most obvious feature of individually administered mental ability tests is that they are given to one individual at a time. Figure 12.2 shows the typical arrangement. The person administering the test, typically a school psychologist, sits at a table with the student. The test contains a variety of materials arrayed on the table. The test examiner presents each question or task to the student. Most responses require an oral answer or the completion of some task, such as manipulating blocks. The examiner scores each response as it is given, asking for clarification if necessary. The complete set of test items covers a wide range of difficulty levels. However, the examiner presents only those items appropriate for the student's ability level. The test usually requires about one hour to complete. In addition to presenting the items and scoring them immediately, the examiner makes observations about the student's approach to the tasks. For example, the examiner may observe that the student is easily distracted or seems very slow in responding.

Administration of these tests requires advanced training. Professionals such as school psychologists, counselors, and clinical psychologists take entire courses in their graduate programs to learn about administration of these tests.

Table 12.1 shows examples of items that might appear in an individually administered intelligence test. The test items cover a host of mental functions. A common criticism of mental ability tests is that they rely exclusively on verbal skills. However, most contemporary mental ability tests contain about an even mixture of verbal and nonverbal material. It is true that the verbal parts of the tests tend to be better predictors of school success. This is entirely understandable: By and large, school is a highly verbal affair.

Figure 12.2 Typical arrangement for individually administered intelligence test. (© Bob Daemmrich/The Image Works.)

In accordance with the hierarchical theory of intelligence adopted by most contemporary tests, these categories sum up to several subscores (e.g., verbal comprehension, spatial reasoning, and short-term memory). Then, all of the categories sum up to a total score indicating overall level of intelligence. On most intelligence tests, this total score is an IQ. As noted earlier, some tests call the total score an IQ. Other tests use a different name, but it has the same connotation as IQ.

Try This!

Pick a category in Table 12.1. For that category, write one question you think would be a good measure for a student in Grade 2. Then write one question for a student in Grade 10.

Examples of Individually Administered Mental Ability Tests

The most widely used individual intelligence test for school-aged children is the Wechsler Intelligence Scale for Children, Fourth Edition (WISC-IV). The "Wechsler" name is renowned in the field of intelligence testing. Wechsler originated several widely used tests, in addition to the WISC. Others include the Wechsler Adult Intelligence Scale (WAIS), the Wechsler Memory Scale, and the Wechsler Preschool and Primary Scale of

Table 12.1 Examples of Items Included in Individual Intelligence Tests

Category	Examples	Comment
Vocabulary	• What does angry mean? • What does arrogant mean?	Vocabulary items are very common in intelligence tests. Vocabulary usually correlates highly with total scores based on many kinds of items. Some tests consist entirely of vocabulary items.
Verbal Relations	• What is the opposite of tardy? • How are a bus and a car alike? • Father is to son as mother is to what?	This category includes antonyms, similarities, analogies, and other items dealing with the relationships between words and concepts.
Information	• Show me your elbow. • How many days are there in a week?	It is important to get items that are not too culturally bound or overly dependent on formal schooling. The emphasis is on common, everyday information.
Meaning, Comprehension	• Make a sentence from these words: the, Ed, car, drove. • Why do we have speed limits on highways? • Examiner reads a paragraph, then asks for a summary of its main point.	These items deal with meaning other than single words. The items emphasize connections, concepts, and relationships, usually of a verbal nature
Arithmetic	• Jim bought 2 pencils for 10 cents each. How much did he pay? • Jim bought 5 pencils for 12 cents each and 2 notebooks for 80 cents each. How much did he pay?	These are good, old-fashioned word problems. The items avoid very complicated computations (e.g., $1\frac{3}{4} \times \frac{2}{3}$). The items concentrate on mental manipulation of fairly simple numbers.
Short-term Memory	• Listen, then repeat the numbers I say: 9–4–7–2–6. • Listen: dog, house, cow, table. (Pause.) What was the second word I said?	The first item is called digit span. It can employ any number of digits. It can also be used with digits repeated backward. Obviously, the lists can become very long. Some items call for immediate repetition; for other items, there may be a delay of several minutes.
Form Patterns	Use the blocks to make a building like this picture.	There are a great variety of items using puzzles, form boards, and blocks. Many of these items are modeled on entire tests developed in the early days of testing (e.g., Kohs Block Design, Porteus Mazes, and Seguin Form Board).
Psychomotor	Fill in as quickly as possible: 	1	2	3
X	T	O | | 3	1	2	3	1		These items are usually speed tests. The example here requires only one row but actual tests might have 20 such rows. The basic tasks are simple. The tasks require eye-hand coordination and concentration. Another example is comparing columns of numbers.

Table 12.2 List of Subtests and Index Scores in the WISC-IV

Index Score	Core Subtests	Supplementary Subtests
Verbal Comprehension	Similarities Comprehension Vocabulary	Information Word Reasoning
Perceptual Reasoning	Block Design Matrix Reasoning Picture Concepts	Picture Completion
Working Memory	Digit Span Letter Number Sequencing	Arithmetic
Processing Speed	Coding Symbol Search	Cancellation
Full-Scale IQ (FSIQ)	Sum of the four Index scores	

Intelligence (WPPSI). We also encountered the Wechsler Individual Achievement Test (WIAT) in the last chapter.

Table 12.2 outlines the structure of the WISC-IV. The full array contains 15 subtests. The usual administration employs 10 of these subtests (the core subtests). Sometimes the examiner will use one or more of the supplementary subtests. WISC-IV yields three types of scores. First, each subtest has a score. Second, highly related subtests combine to yield Index scores. There are four Index scores: Verbal Comprehension, Perceptual Reasoning, Working Memory, and Processing Speed. Finally, the four Index scores combine to yield a Full-Scale IQ. Notice that this structure corresponds closely to the three levels shown in the hierarchy in Figure 12.1. Earlier editions of the WISC had Verbal and Performance IQs. The fourth edition abandons this structure. Interpretation of the WISC-IV uses the Full-Scale IQ, as well as the Index scores and subtest scores. Differences among the Index scores—for example, the difference between Verbal Comprehension and Perceptual Reasoning—often play a prominent role in interpretation.

Although the WISC-IV is the most widely used individually administered intelligence test, it is by no means the only one. The second most popular test in this category for use in schools is the Woodcock-Johnson III, Tests of Cognitive Abilities (WJ-Cog). It is especially popular among school psychologists. We encountered the Woodcock-Johnson III, Tests of Achievement (WJ-Ach) in the previous chapter. Like the WISC, WJ-Cog consists of a series of subtests, requiring about one hour for administration. As jointly normed tests, WJ-Cog and WJ-Ach are particularly attractive for conducting **discrepancy analysis** in the identification of learning disabilities. Discrepancy analysis involves comparing a person's achievement levels and ability levels. Achievement levels significantly below measured ability contribute to the definition of a learning disability. Because the WJ series has both cognitive (mental ability) and achievement measures, it facilitates this type of analysis. In a similar way, the WISC and Wechsler Individual Achievement Test (WIAT) are jointly normed, thus providing a basis for discrepancy analysis.

The oldest of the individually administered intelligence tests is the Stanford-Binet Intelligence Scale, now in its fifth edition, referred to as SB5. For many years, the Stanford-Binet was the premier measure of intelligence. It originated from the pioneering work of

Table 12.3 Outline of the Structure of Stanford-Binet, Fifth Edition (SB5)

Organization of the Stanford-Binet, Fifth Edition

Factors	Domain	
	Nonverbal (NV)	**Verbal (V)**
Fluid Reasoning (FR)	*Nonverbal Fluid Reasoning** Activities: Object Series/Matrices (Routing)	*Verbal Fluid Reasoning* Activities: Early Reasoning (2–3), Verbal Absurdities (4), Verbal Analogies (5–6)
Knowledge (KN)	*Nonverbal Knowledge* Activities: Procedural Knowledge (2–3), Picture Absurdities (4–6)	*Verbal Knowledge** Activities: Vocabulary (Routing)
Quantitative Reasoning (QR)	*Nonverbal Quantitative Reasoning* Activities: Quantitative Reasoning (2–6)	*Verbal Quantitative Reasoning* Activities: Quantitative Reasoning (2–6)
Visual-Spatial Processing (VS)	*Nonverbal Visual-Spatial Processing* Activities: Form Board (1–2), Form Patterns (3–6)	*Verbal Visual-Spatial Processing* Activities: Position and Direction (2–6)
Working Memory (WM)	*Nonverbal Working Memory* Activities: Delayed Response (1), Block Span (2–6)	*Verbal Working Memory* Activities: Memory for Sentences (2–3) Last Word (4–6)

Note: Names of the 10 Subtests are in *italic*. Activities are shown with the levels at which they appear. *Routing Subtests

(Reproduced with permission of the publisher, Riverside Publishing.)

Alfred Binet in the public schools of Paris, France, in the early 1900s. Binet's task was to identify children not likely to benefit from regular classroom instruction. This effort foreshadowed the origin of special education. This is still one of the main uses of these types of tests. The earlier editions of the Stanford-Binet featured a single, total score and gave rise to the term "IQ." The current edition, SB5, follows the hierarchical theory of intelligence. That is, it consists of a number of subtests and yields intermediate level scores, as well as a total score. Table 12.3 outlines the structure of SB5. The Stanford-Binet is still widely used, but it has fallen from its once lofty position as *the* measure of intelligence. It is now clearly eclipsed by the WISC. Here is another seemingly trivial but actually very important change in SB5. Previous editions used a standard deviation of 16 for the IQ, but the new edition uses 15, the same as the Wechsler scales.

Not all individually administered intelligence tests have multiple subtests and a one-hour administration time. A good example of a much simpler approach is the Peabody Picture Vocabulary Test, now in its third edition (PPVT-III). It requires only about 15 minutes to administer. Not only is it much shorter than the typical individually administered test, all of its items are multiple choice. Each item consists of a single word. The student selects one of four pictures that illustrates that word. The PPVT yields only one score. Interestingly, this score correlates highly with the total score on the much more complex tests such as the WISC and Stanford-Binet.

GROUP-ADMINISTERED MENTAL ABILITY TESTS

We turn now to description of group-administered mental ability tests. As we did for individually administered tests, we will first describe the general features of these tests, and then give a few examples. We will find that the group tests are similar to the individual tests in some ways, but different in other ways.

General Features of Group-Administered Mental Ability Tests

The most obvious feature of the group test is that, as suggested by the name of this category, it can be administered to a group all at one time. The most typical arrangement would be administration to a classroom of students. However, with appropriate spacing and proctoring, these tests can be administered to hundreds of people at once. Administration of these tests does not require the specialized training needed to administer the individual tests. Many teachers will administer one of these group tests to their students.

Items appearing in group tests are very similar in many ways to the items appearing in individually administered tests. This is entirely understandable considering the origin of the group tests. The earliest group tests were developed after the individual tests were already in widespread use. The group tests essentially tried to duplicate, as far as possible, the individual tests but in a format suitable for group administration. The primary adaptation was to convert the free-response format of the individual test into a multiple-choice format.[1] Thus, we find in group-administered tests many of the same types of items found in individually administered tests, but with a multiple-choice format. Table 12.4 shows examples of the types of items often found in group tests of mental ability. These are not the only types of items in such tests. However, this sampling of items gives an idea of the types of items commonly encountered.

Try This!

Pick one of the categories of items in Table 12.4. Write one additional item you think would be appropriate for students in Grade 3 and one item for students in Grade 10. Have someone else critique your items.

---

[1] In the earliest group-administered tests, most but not all items were multiple choice. A few items were free response, but the responses could be objectively scored. For example, inserting the next number in a number series (3, 6, 9, ___) is easily scored, although no options are given.

Table 12.4   Examples of Items Often Found in Group-Administered Mental Ability Tests

Verbal

Definitions

1. Arrogant means   A. gigantic   B. haughty   C. salubrious   D. humble

Opposites

2. The *opposite* of generous is   A. costly   B. stingy   C. short   D. nice

Analogies

3. Father is to son as mother is to ___   A. wife   B. sister   C. daughter   D. brother

Categories

4. Which does not belong?   A. hot   B. cold   C. fast   D. cool

Figural

Sequences (Complete the Pattern)

5. ○ ○ △ □ ○ ○ △ □ ○   ___ ___   ○ △   ○ □   △ □   △ ○

                                               A.   B.   C.   D.

Matrix

6.

        + □ +   ○ +   □ +   + ○ +

                 A.   B.   C.   D.

Quantitative

Series, Patterns

7. What comes next?   3, 7, 11, 15 _____   A. 16   B. 14   C. 19   D. 20

Word Problems

8. Jim is six years older than Sue. Sue is two years older than Kim. Kim is how many years younger than Jim?

                A. 8   B. 4   C. 12   D. 7

       A second adaptation of the individually administered format to the group format was to use a fixed number of items for all examinees and, at least approximately, a uniform time for administration. Many of the group-administered tests used in elementary and secondary schools have 50–100 items and can be completed in about 45 minutes. Interestingly, this feature of the tests—fixed number of items and time limit—is changing as some of these tests convert to a computer-adaptive mode.

       Most of the group-administered mental ability tests try to predict success in school, from the primary grades through graduate and professional school. Outside the school context, the tests try to predict success in various types of jobs. Thus, the main way of validating these tests is to show their correlation with success in school or on the job. All of the tests start with the assumption that there is an underlying ability (or a number of mental abilities) that is (a) somewhat independent of specific previous learning and (b) important for future performance.

Examples of Group-Administered Mental Ability Tests

Let us examine examples of group-administered mental ability tests in two major categories. The first category includes those used in elementary and secondary schools in conjunction with standardized achievement batteries. The second category includes tests used to predict success in college, graduate, and professional schools.

Recall that we reviewed achievement batteries in Chapter 11 (pp. 248–255). Each of these batteries has a companion group-administered mental ability test. The achievement battery was normed with and features joint reports with its companion mental ability test. Table 12.5 shows the names of the mental ability tests and the corresponding achievement batteries. Notice that two of the mental ability tests are paired with two different achievement batteries. A school that uses one of the achievement batteries will often use the corresponding mental ability test in selected grades. For example, a school may use one of the achievement batteries in each of Grades 3–10 and the mental ability test in Grades 4, 7, and 10. When a school uses a group mental ability test, it usually does so only in a few grades.

All three of these mental ability tests operate from the early primary grades through high school. Each has a series of levels, graduated in difficulty to accommodate the increasing mental ability of students, while still having a fixed number of items. All three of the tests also espouse a hierarchical structure, yielding several subscores and a total score. Table 12.6 outlines the general structure of the three tests. Exact structures may vary somewhat from level to level. Some of the tests also give cluster scores. For example, in the Nonverbal area, OLSAT gives cluster scores for figural reasoning and quantitative reasoning. In general, the structure of the three tests is much more similar than dissimilar.

As was true for their corresponding achievement batteries, norms for these tests are based on very large, nationally representative samples. Their total scores tend to be very reliable, usually in the neighborhood of .95. Reliability of subscores is largely a function of numbers of items in the subtest. As with any test, beware of scores based on a small number of items. Clusters of 10 or fewer items are usually not very reliable and probably should not be reported.

Table 12.5   Group-Administered Mental Ability Tests Paired With Achievement Batteries

Group Mental Ability Test	Achievement Battery
Cognitive Abilities Test (CogAT)	Iowa Test of Basic Skills
Otis-Lennon School Ability Test (OLSAT)	Metropolitan Achievement Test and Stanford Achievement Test
Test of Cognitive Skills (TCS)	Terra Nova (CTBS) and Terra Nova Second Edition (CAT/6)

Table 12.6 Structure of Three Group-Administered
Mental Ability Tests

Test	Scores
CogAT	Total, Verbal, Quantitative, Nonverbal
OLSAT	Total, Verbal, Nonverbal
TCS	Total, Verbal, Nonverbal, Memory

All of these tests yield the full panoply of normed scores: percentiles, stanines, NCEs, and standard scores. Usually they provide a standard score with a mean of 100 and standard deviation of 15 or 16. Obviously, this type of score looks very much like an IQ, although the test manuals studiously avoid use of that term—while still using the metric associated with it. All of the tests also yield some type of comparison of scores with scores on the corresponding achievement battery. The exact methods for constructing these comparisons differ, but the essential purpose is the same: to indicate whether the achievement scores are consistent with the mental ability scores. Of particular concern are students whose achievement scores fall well below what is predicted by their mental ability scores. This is like the discrepancy analysis mentioned under individually administered mental ability tests earlier in this chapter. The group test results are not used for any formal diagnosis. However, they may suggest the need for follow-up evaluation.

Figure 12.3 provides an example of how group-administered mental ability test scores are reported, including one method for showing the comparison of mental ability and achievement scores. This is the same report as introduced in Chapter 5 (Figure 5.14) to illustrate different types of normed scores for an achievement test. Here, however, we concentrate on the mental ability scores, specifically, those for the Otis-Lennon School Ability Test (OLSAT), administered in conjunction with Stanford Achievement Test. Notice that the report presents scaled scores, percentile ranks and stanines for the OLSAT total score, as well as verbal and nonverbal subtests. Notice the SAI column. SAI stands for School Ability Index. This is a standard score with a mean of 100 and standard deviation of 16. The right side of the report presents the percentile scores in the form of bands, based on the standard error of measurement for each score. Dora's scores are generally in the middle of the range, with the verbal score slightly higher than the nonverbal score. The fact that the percentile bands for the verbal and nonverbal scores overlap almost entirely indicates that we should not try to make much out of the difference between these two subtest scores.

Notice the column labeled AAC Range. "AAC" means "achievement/ability comparison." Based on performance of students in the norming program, the OLSAT is used to predict how well students will do on each of the achievement tests. Students are then divided into three groups. *High* means the student performed higher than predicted. *Low* means the student performed lower than predicted. *Middle* means the student performed about as predicted; that is, in the middle of the predicted range. Most of Dora's achievement test scores are in the middle range. In several subtest area, she performed at a higher level than predicted by her OLSAT scores.

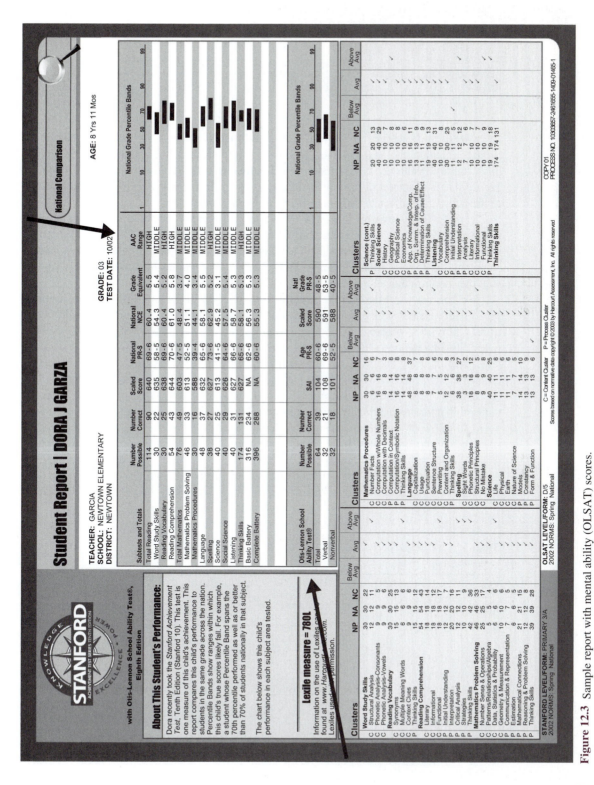

Figure 12.3 Sample report with mental ability (OLSAT) scores.

(From *Stanford Achievement Test Series—Tenth Edition*. Copyright © 2003 by Harcourt Assessment, Inc. Reproduced by permission. All rights reserved.)

289

Try This!

Look at the AAC column in Figure 12.3. Do you see a pattern to the "High" areas for Dora's scores? In what types of subtests does she tend to have a high ability-achievement comparison?

The second category of group-administered mental ability tests includes those designed to predict success in college, graduate, or professional school. Based on the predictions, the test results are often used to select individuals for admission to a school. Table 12.7 lists nine examples of these tests. Many readers of this book have already taken some of these tests. Some readers will take others of them in the future.

Most of these tests operate with the same assumptions identified earlier for other group mental ability tests. They assume that there is some basic ability (or abilities) somewhat independent of school learning. They assume that this basic ability (or abilities) has something to do with future learning. Predictive validity studies for the tests show how well they confirm this assumption.

We will not work through the structure and other details of any of these tests. Table 12.7 gives websites where more information can be obtained about them. The websites usually provide a generous number of sample items. However, we will add these brief notes. The first two tests listed in Table 12.7 are easily recognized as the widely used college selection tests. The ACT has always maintained that it is a measure of what has been learned in high school. We include it in this list because its primary purpose is to predict success in college. The SAT I (formerly Scholastic Assessment Test) traditionally maintained that it was measuring basic abilities rather independent of specific schooling. However, it is now changing its philosophy, maintaining that it wishes to be a measure of specific school achievement—an interesting change in stance. For example, the College Board (2004) reported: "In January 2003, the College Board conducted a survey of reading and writing curricula. The results of the survey are being used by test development committees to set specifications for the new SAT, ensuring that the new test will accu-

Table 12.7   Examples of Mental Ability Tests Used to Predict Success in Postsecondary Schooling

Test	Website
ACT	www.act.org
SAT I: Reasoning Test	www.collegeboard.com/student/testing/sat/
Graduate Record Exam (GRE)	www.gre.org
Miller Analogies Test	www.milleranalogies.com
Graduate Management Admission Test (GMAT)	www.gmac.com/gmac
Law School Admission Test (LSAT)	www.lsac.org
Dental Admission Test (DAT)	www.ada.org/prof/ed/testing/dat
Medical College Admission Test (MCAT)	www.aamc.org/students/mcat
Armed Services Vocational Aptitude Battery (ASVAB)	www.asvabprogram.com

Figure 12.4 Some tests in Table 12.7 are widely recognized symbols in society.

Hoping to impress the chicks, Daryl had his SAT scores tattooed on his right arm.

rately reflect high school and college curricula and classroom practice." That certainly sounds like building an achievement test.

Some of the tests listed in Table 12.7 have companion measures of achievement. For example, paralleling the SAT I are the SAT II Subject tests aimed at specific subject areas. Similarly, the GRE has Subject exams in different areas. Some of the entries in Table 12.7 are hybrid mixtures of straightforward achievement and presumed ability. This is particularly true for the MCAT and DAT. For example, the MCAT includes a subtest on physical sciences (PS) and another on verbal reasoning (VR). Most people would consider PS a pure achievement measure and VR a measure of general mental ability. The LSAT and GMAT, on the other hand, do not test anything about knowledge of the law or management. We have included the ASVAB because its most important purpose is to predict success in military schooling programs. Despite the diversity of audiences for the tests listed in Table 12.7, there are remarkable similarities in their types of items (e.g., vocabulary, analogy, and numerical sequence items).

In this and the previous section, we outlined features of the more widely used mental ability tests, both individual and group tests. Each year brings revisions of established tests or entirely new tests. Each revision or new test promises to be a better, purer measure of intelligence. It's like the search for the Holy Grail. Will we ever get a definitive measure of mental ability? Probably not. But, the pursuit goes on. Meanwhile, take the claims about "new and better" with a grain of salt.

INTELLIGENCE TESTS AND THE DEFINITION
OF MENTAL RETARDATION

Intelligence tests, especially the individually administered tests, play a crucial role in the definition of **mental retardation**. In earlier days, mental retardation was defined almost exclusively in terms of intelligence test scores. Specifically, a score below 70 on the traditional IQ scale defined mental retardation. Today, mental retardation is defined by three criteria. Two organizations provide definitions of these criteria: the American Association on Mental Retardation (AAMR, 2002) and the American Psychiatric Association through its *Diagnostic and Statistical Manual of Mental Disorders*, Fourth Edition (APA, 2000). The definitions from AAMR and APA are very similar but not identical. The three criteria are substantially subaverage intellectual ability, limitations in adaptive behavior, and onset before the age of 18. All three criteria must be met to result in a classification of mental retardation.

The *first* criterion is almost universally defined by performance on an individually administered intelligence test. Subaverage is usually defined as at least two standard deviations below the mean (national norm). On most of the tests, this translates into an IQ of 70 or below (see Figure 12.5). Some definitions go one standard error of measurement—usually 3–5 points—above the cut-off of 70.

As a sidebar, we note the importance of understanding such notions as "two standard deviations below the mean" and "standard error of measurement." We covered these terms in earlier chapters. At the time, they may have seemed very abstract and possibly useless. However, the professional educator needs to know these concepts and terms to understand how the very practical matter of defining mental retardation occurs.

The *third* criterion requires that the onset of the condition occur during the developmental years. AAMR uses age 18 as the operational cut-off point. Some other sources use age 22 or age 25. The point remains the same: By definition, MR is something that develops early in life. Consider a 35-year-old who had normal development during her school years, then sustains brain injury in an accident. She may meet the first two criteria, but would not be considered MR.

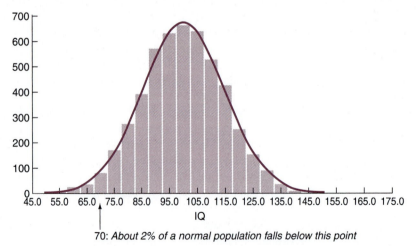

70: *About 2% of a normal population falls below this point*

Figure 12.5 The usual cut-off score for defining mental retardation is an IQ of 70.

Significantly subaverage intellectual functioning
Limitations in adaptive behaviors
Onset before age 18

What about the *second* criterion? What is adaptive behavior? This is a concept we have not encountered elsewhere. **Adaptive behavior** refers to skills required for coping in everyday life. Alternative terms are functional skills, coping skills, and social maturity. Examples of adaptive behavior include feeding and dressing oneself, purchasing items at a grocery store, and making sense out of weather forecasts. The basic question is this: Can this person get along in normal daily life? Obviously, appropriate adaptive behavior varies by age. For example, we expect a 9-year-old to be able to tie his shoes. We expect a 20-year-old to make purchases at a grocery store, but we do not expect that of a 6-year-old.

The AAMR definition of mental retardation refers to adaptive behaviors in three areas: conceptual, social, and practical. Conceptual skills include such areas as reading, writing, and handling money. Social skills include such areas as ability to follow rules, obey laws, and avoid victimization. Practical skills include such areas as eating, dressing, and using a telephone. According to the AAMR definition, significant limitations in adaptive behavior mean being at least two standard deviations below the mean in at least one of these areas *or* on an overall score combining the three areas.

How do we measure adaptive behavior? Just as there are tests for intellectual functioning, there are tests for adaptive behavior. These tests attempt to measure performance on the types of everyday skills listed earlier. The tests were developed specifically to define mental retardation more holistically than just in terms of IQ. Most adaptive behavior scales yield separate scores in several domains as well as a total score. Table 12.8 outlines some of the typical domains and provides examples of items within the domains.

Table 12.8 Examples of Content Domains Covered in Typical Adaptive Behavior Scales

Domain	Sample Content
Communication	Writes own name
	Makes local telephone call
Personal Care	Uses eating utensils (knife, fork, spoon)
	Dresses self
Money and Time	Makes small purchases at store
	Knows days of the week
Social Skills	Plays with other children
	Entertains self with electronic game
Motor Skills	Draws circle and square
	Hops over a line

Adaptive behavior tests differ from intelligence tests in two important ways. First, an intelligence test tries to elicit maximum performance—the best a person can do. An adaptive behavior test tries to measure typical performance—how a person normally functions in everyday life. Second, although the person being evaluated answers the items in an intelligence test, some other person answers the questions on an adaptive behavior test. Most frequently, this other person would be a parent or primary caregiver. Some adaptive behavior tests have versions for teachers. For example, there might be questions about the student's behavior in the classroom. Can Ned follow simple directions? Can he consistently write his full name?

At present, the premier measure of adaptive skills is the Vineland Adaptive Behavior Scales (VABS; Sparrow, Balla, & Cicchetti, 1984). It has a standard interview version, an expanded version, and a classroom version. Teachers complete the classroom version, which has 244 items and takes about 20 minutes to finish. Some items are the same as those answered by a parent/caregiver, plus items related to academic functioning. For each item, the teacher indicates whether the student "usually," "sometimes," or "never" does the activity. From these responses, total scores are developed and then converted into norms for the student's age or grade group.

The VABS, although the most widely used measure of adaptive functioning, is not the only one. There are several others that a teacher might encounter. However, they all ask about how a child or student typically functions in everyday life. The test results are used not only to identify the student's typical level of functioning (and possibly classification as mentally retarded), but also to plan an educational program for the student.

Try This!

Think of children in Grade 6. Identify three adaptive behaviors (everyday functional skills) you think are needed by these children. Compare your list with someone else's.

INTELLIGENCE TESTS AND THE DEFINITION OF LEARNING DISABILITIES

Just as intelligence tests play a significant role in the definition of mental retardation, they also play a role in the definition of learning disabilities. At present, the prevailing definition of a learning disability relates to a discrepancy between intelligence and achievement. There is some effort to change this approach (see Bailey, 2003; Dombrowski, Kamphaus, & Reynolds, 2004; Kersting, 2004), but it is the dominant approach today. Typically, both intelligence and achievement are defined by test performance. **Discrepancy analysis** is the official term used for contrasting intelligence and achievement for identifying learning disabilities; the term also sometimes indicates discrepancies for different facets of intelligence or of achievement. We referred to this term earlier when describing individual mental ability tests. It must be admitted that there are substantial problems with the discrepancy analysis approach (see Flanagan, Andrews, & Genshaft, 1997; Reschly, 1997; and Watkins & Canivez, 2004).

We need to distinguish between legal requirements for handling learning disabilities and the official definitions of such disabilities. Laws indicate what must be done with

Table 12.9   Selected List of Conditions in DSM-IV

Learning Disorders: Reading Disorder, Mathematics Disorder, Disorder of Written Expression, Learning Disorder NOS[a]

Motor Skills Disorder: Developmental Coordination Disorder

Communication Disorders: Expressive Language Disorder, Mixed Receptive-Expressive Language Disorder, Phonological Disorder, Stuttering, Communication Disorder NOS[a]

---

[a] In DSM-IV, NOS is the abbreviation for Not Otherwise Specified.

learning disabled students, such as providing accommodations or developing an individualized education program (IEP). Laws may also indicate which specific types of disabilities require such actions. However, laws do not always say how such cases are identified. (We take up the matter of specific laws in Chapter 14.) The most authoritative source for the definition of learning disabilities is the American Psychiatric Association's *Diagnostic and Statistical Manual of Mental Disorders*, Fourth Edition (APA, 2000). It is usually abbreviated **DSM-IV**. This source provides the official definitions of conditions such as schizophrenia, bipolar disorder, depression, and so on. We referred to it earlier in the definition of mental retardation. It is also the source for defining attention deficit/hyperactivity disorder (ADHD) and a variety of other conditions relevant for school contexts. Thus, the teacher may consider a publication from the American Psychiatric Association marginally relevant, but selected sections are crucial for anyone in education.

Thorough treatment of DSM-IV goes well beyond the scope of this book. However, we can note some of the conditions included within DSM-IV and generally how it describes conditions. Table 12.9 shows the specific conditions listed under Learning Disorders, Motor Skills Disorder, and Communication Disorders. (These sections immediately follow the section on mental retardation.)

For each condition, DSM-IV gives a description of symptoms, indicates prevalence rates, distinguishes the condition from related conditions (differential diagnosis), and discusses possible etiology (causes). In some cases, DSM-IV also indicates what kinds of tests are to be used for diagnosis. Professionals, such as school psychologists and clinical psychologists, rely heavily on this classification system. Some of the assessment instruments discussed later (e.g., self-report inventories and behavior rating scales) tie their reporting systems to the DSM-IV classifications.

Both mental ability tests and achievement tests play crucial roles in the identification of learning disabilities. Other conditions commonly encountered in schools also depend on the use of personality tests and behavior rating scales. We describe these in the next section.

PERSONALITY AND BEHAVIOR RATING SCALES

The next category of tests to consider in this chapter includes several types of personality measures. We review three types: self-report inventories, projective techniques, and behavior rating scales. Many of these tests concentrate on clinical applications that fall outside the realm of ordinary educational assessment. Therefore, we provide here just an overview of these categories, with special reference to the types of measures a teacher might encounter. For more detailed descriptions of clinical applications, refer to books on psychological testing (e.g., Anastasi & Urbina, 1997; Groth-Marnat, 2003; and Hogan, 2003.)

Self-Report Inventories

The most widely used type of personality measure is the **self-report inventory**. This type of test consists of simple statements to which a person responds True or False, Yes or No, or some similarly simple options. Table 12.10 shows examples of the types of statements contained in typical self-report inventories. The table also illustrates the types of responses. Notice that the statements are very simple. The response is also simple. It is easy to add up the responses on these inventories. Hence, they are sometimes called **objective inventories**, because they can be objectively scored. In contrast, scoring the responses to projective tests, described in the next section, requires considerable judgment.

Try This!

Add one statement to those in Table 12.10 that might tell something about a student's self-esteem.

Topics covered by the statements depend on what the inventory is trying to measure. A comprehensive inventory will include many topics. A more focused inventory—for example, one concentrating on depression or hyperactivity—will cover fewer topics. Accordingly, it will have fewer items and take less time to complete. Some inventories include statements to check on honesty of responses. For example, look at Item 5 in the first group of statements in Table 12.10. Can anyone honestly respond "Yes" to this statement? An inventory may include several such statements. Responses to the statements

Table 12.10   Examples of Statements in Self-Report Inventories

	Yes	No
1. I often feel sad	O	O
2. People don't like me.	O	O
3. I have a lot of friends.	O	O
4. My family is unhappy.	O	O
5. I like everybody.	O	O

	True	False
1. People make fun of me.	O	O
2. I have trouble sitting still.	O	O
3. Reading is hard.	O	O
4. I'm good at sports.	O	O
5. I usually study hard.	O	O

yield a score about the probable honesty of responses. These scores are called "validity indexes." This is obviously a different use of the term "validity" from the usual reference to this term.

The most common application of self-report personality inventories is in clinical practice. They are also widely used in research on personality. However, some self-report inventories are used in school contexts for assessing such variables as self-concept, depression, and social adjustment. A school psychologist might use one of these inventories to help diagnose a child's problem. Teachers would not ordinarily use these inventories. However, teachers will hear reference to them when working as part of a team.

There is an enormous variety of self-report personality inventories. They range from comprehensive inventories with several hundred items and yielding dozens of scores to very short inventories with only 10 items and yielding one score. They also vary in terms of their target audiences. Some aim at a particular age group. Some aim only at people with one suspected kind of problem. We briefly describe here four inventories that are among the more popular for use with school-age groups. Our intent is to give an overview of a few inventories rather than give a detailed analysis of each one. For critiques of any of these inventories, see the sources listed in Appendix A.

Table 12.11 lists the titles and key features of the four inventories we describe here. Notice the tremendous range in numbers of items and numbers of scores. The Children's Depression Inventory (CDI), the most widely used measure of depression in children, has only 27 items; it even has a 10-item short form for quick screening. At the other extreme in length is the Minnesota Multiphasic Personality Inventory—Adolescent (MMPI-A), weighing in at a hefty 478 items and yielding 68 scores. The MMPI-A is an adaptation for youth of the Minnesota Multiphasic Personality Inventory, Second Edition (MMPI-2), the most widely used personality inventory in clinical practice for adults.

The Eating Disorder Inventory (EDI-2; Garner, 1991) is a good example of a very targeted instrument. As suggested by its title, it is used with persons suspected of eating difficulties. Its 91 items cover body image, eating habits, self-perception, and so on. Scores can be interpreted in terms of norms based on persons already diagnosed with several eating disorders. The Piers-Harris Children's Self-Concept Scale, Second Edition

Table 12.11   Examples of Self-Report Inventories

Scale	Target Ages	Number Items	Number Scores[a]	Examples of Scores
Children's Depression Inventory	7–17	27	6	Negative Mood, Ineffectiveness, Interpersonal Problems, Total
Eating Disorder Inventory	12+	91	11	Drive for Thinness, Perfectionism, Body Dissatisfaction
Minnesota Multiphasic Personality Inventory—Adolescent (MMPI-A)	14–18	478	68	Schizophrenia, Brooding, Social Introversion, Alienation
Piers-Harris Children's Self-Concept Scale	7–18	60	9	Popularity, Behavioral Adjustment, Total Self-Concept

[a]The number of scores includes subscores, totals, validity indexes, and, in some cases, provisional scores.

(Piers-Harris 2; Piers & Herzberg, 2002) is the most widely used measure of self-concept in school settings. It yields separate scores for behavioral adjustment, intellectual and school status, physical appearance and attributes, freedom from anxiety, popularity, happiness and satisfaction, and a total score that sums up the six subscores. It also has two "validity scales" to check on honesty of responding.

The latter four examples illustrate the nature of self-report inventories. There are hundreds of other such inventories. They vary in their targeted constructs, length, age ranges, and quality of development. As noted earlier, teachers would not ordinarily administer one of these inventories, except perhaps in a research project. However, teachers will hear reference to these inventories, especially for students experiencing difficulties.

Try This!

To get an idea of the vast number of self-report inventories, try this. Access the ETS Test Collection (www.ets.org/testcoll). Insert as a search term "self-concept" or "depression" or another term of interest to you. Search by major descriptor. How many entries do you get?

Projective Techniques

Projective techniques present a person with an ambiguous or innocuous stimulus and a simple instruction about how to respond. The person constructs a response with near maximum freedom. Presumably, the response reveals something about the individual's personality, motivations, and inner dynamics.

The apparent simplicity of projectives can be deceiving. Intelligent use of these techniques requires advanced training and supervised experience. Even then their value is controversial. Nevertheless, projective techniques are widely used by professionals such as school psychologists. Therefore, although teachers would never administer these instruments, teachers do need to have some familiarity with them. For contrasting points of view about the value of projective techniques, see Lilienfeld, Wood, and Garb (2000, 2001); and Meyer (1999, 2001). For an overview of several of the more widely used techniques, see Groth-Marnat (2003).

The classic, most well-known projective technique is the Rorschach inkblot test. Its standard version consists of 10 inkblots. Some are black and gray, others contain a bit of red or a mixture of pastel colors. Figure 12.6 shows a sample inkblot. The examiner shows an inkblot and says, "Tell me what you see." There are additional directions, but the latter statement gives the essence of the technique. The Rorschach is a favorite of clinical psychologists. However, it is not as widely used in school contexts. We mention the technique here mainly because it is so thoroughly identified in the popular consciousness with projective methodology.

Another classic example of projective techniques is the Thematic Apperception Test (TAT). It consists of 30 cards, each containing a picture, most frequently with one or two people. (One card is entirely blank!) Only a selection of the 30 cards is presented to an individual. The examiner asks the person to tell a story about what is happening and how the story will end. Again, the specific directions are somewhat more elaborate, but the latter description gives the essence of the task. The TAT is aimed at adults. There is also a

Figure 12.6 Example of a Rorschach-like inkblot: What do you see?

Children's Apperception Test (CAT). Although widely referenced in the professional literature, neither the TAT nor the CAT receive much use in school contexts.

The most widely used projective technique in school contexts is some version of the human figure drawing (HFD) technique. There are some specific versions of this technique. They go by such names as the Draw-A-Man or Draw-A-Person (DAP) test. We will describe the generic version of the test. The student is given a pencil (with eraser) and a blank piece of paper. The student is asked to draw a picture of himself or herself. See the sample drawing in Figure 12.7. After that is completed, the person is asked to draw a person of the opposite sex. The student may also be asked to draw another person, say, a parent. Interestingly, the original Draw-A-Man test was developed not as a personality test but as a nonverbal intelligence test. It still receives some use for this purpose.

Two other drawing techniques widely used in school contexts are the House-Tree-Person (HTP) test and the Kinetic Family Drawing (KFD) test. Each title gives the essence of the task. In the HTP, the child draws a house, a tree, and a person. In the KFD,

Figure 12.7 Example of self-drawing by an 8-year-old boy.

the child draws a picture of a family doing something. You can get information about these projective techniques using the sources of information in Appendix A.

There are many other projective techniques. They include sentence completions (e.g., I like to _____, My family _____), word associations (e.g., I say "hot," you say _____; I say "Mother," you say _____), and some perceptual-motor tasks. They all present a relatively simple stimulus to which the person responds freely.

The scoring and interpretation of projective techniques go well beyond the scope of this book. However, the teacher needs to be aware of four points. First, as noted earlier, these techniques are not for use by persons untrained in their administration and scoring. Teachers should not try to use them. Second, even those trained in their use often employ them only informally to help "open up" a difficult child or to suggest avenues for further exploration. Third, even when used formally with elaborate scoring by professionals trained in their application, results from these tests rarely yield definitive conclusions. They do not lead to sudden flashes of insight about a person's deepest self. Finally, be wary of extreme positions, in either direction, about the value of these techniques. They are not worthless, when used by trained professionals. On the other hand, they do not work magic in understanding a person.

Behavior Rating Scales

Behavior rating scales (BRSs) are now used routinely in schools for determination of such conditions as attention disorders, hyperactivity, depression, and assorted emotional problems. The BRS has two essential features. First, someone other than the person being evaluated completes the rating. Typically, the "someone else" is a teacher, parent, or other caregiver. In this way, a BRS is much like the adaptive behavior scales covered earlier. The basic difference is that the adaptive scale aims at functional skills, whereas the BRS aims at problem behaviors, such as hyperactivity.

The second essential feature is that the BRS, as suggested by the title, lists specific behaviors. The person completing the form indicates the frequency of observing the behavior. The descriptors are usually short: 1–3 words. Table 12.12 shows typical descriptors that might appear in a BRS. Notice that the items try to concentrate on specific, observable behaviors. This is in contrast to the self-report inventories, which tend to concentrate on feelings or perceptions. The BRS ratings are made on 3- to 5-point scales, typ-

Table 12.12 Examples of Items and Ratings Typical of Behavior Rating Scales

This child . . .	0 Never	1 Sometimes	2 Often	3 Always
1. Hits other kids.	0	1	2	3
2. Fidgets.	0	1	2	3
3. Does sloppy work.	0	1	2	3
4. Cries.	0	1	2	3
5. Screams at others.	0	1	2	3
6. Completes work late.	0	1	2	3
7. Makes strange noises.	0	1	2	3
8. Squirms when seated.	0	1	2	3

Table 12.13   The Three Widely Used Multiscore Behavior
Rating Scales

Title	Acronym
Behavior Assessment System for Children	BASC
Child Behavior Checklist	CBCL
Conners' Rating Scale	CRS

ically ranging from "Never" to "Always" or "Definitely Not True" to "Definitely True."
The right part of Table 12.12 shows such a rating scheme.

There are two broad groups of BRSs. The first group includes several multiscore systems. These systems attempt to cover a multitude of conditions, typically yielding a dozen or more scores. The second group includes instruments that target just one area. Let us briefly describe examples from each category.

Multiscore Systems

There are three widely used multiscore behavior rating scales. Table 12.13 lists them. There are additional multiscore systems, but these three get most of the action. We sketch here the common features of these scales rather than giving detailed descriptions of any one of them. For detailed treatment of any of these scales, see Ramsay, Reynolds, and Kamphaus (2002); and Andrews, Saklofske, and Janzen (2001). Also see the manuals for the separate scales (Achenbach, 1991; Conners, 2001; and Reynolds & Kamphaus, 2004). Consult Buros' Mental Measurements Yearbooks for reviews (see Appendix A for description of this source).

Each of the multiscore systems is actually a collection of several instruments. Typically, the system has separate scales to be completed by parents, teachers, and the student. The student forms are actually like the self-report instruments treated earlier. That is, the student is describing himself or herself. The parent and teacher forms call for rating the student's behavior. In addition, some of these multiscore systems have long forms and short forms or levels for younger and older children. Thus, reference to using "the Conners" or "the BASC" can be ambiguous. It could mean a parent's long form or short form, a teacher's long form or short form, or a student self-report. We need to be careful about such references.

The most important feature of the multiscore systems is that they try to cover many problem areas. Some of the forms yield several dozen scores. Table 12.14 lists areas commonly covered by these multiscore systems. Of course, each system has its own unique set of scores. However, the areas listed in Table 12.14 give the flavor of these multiscore systems.

Table 12.14   Examples of Areas Covered in
Multiscore Behavior Rating Scales

Aggression	Anger
Anxiety	Depression
Hyperactivity	Inattention
Opposition	Withdrawal

Single-area Scales

There are numerous single-area behavior rating scales. The nature of their items and response scales are the same as those listed in Table 12.14. However, as suggested by the term "single-area," they concentrate on just one problem area (e.g., inattention). Thus, they tend to be much shorter than the multiscore systems. Whereas a multiscore instrument may have about 100 items, a single-area scale may have only 20 items. Although each of these single-area scales concentrates on just one area, the scale may actually yield several scores. However, the scores are closely related (e.g., covering different aspects of hyperactivity or depression). Like the multiscore systems, the single-area scales are typically completed by a teacher, parent, or other caregiver.

Among the most widely used single-area scales are the ADHD Rating Scale IV (DuPaul, Power, Anastopoulos, & Reid, 1998) and the ADHD Symptom Checklist-4 (Gadow & Sprafkin, 1997). As suggested by their titles, these scales focus on attention deficit/hyperactivity disorder. Each requires only about 10 minutes to complete. The types of items are like those in Table 12.12, but limited to behaviors in the ADHD syndrome. For useful, brief descriptions of single-area behavior rating scales, see Volpe and DuPaul (2001).

Behavior rating scales, both multiscore systems and single-area scales, are now widely used in educational settings. They are used to help identify students with special problems, to quantify the extent of the problem, and as a follow-up measure to show progress in alleviating the problem. The decision to use one of these scales will usually be made by a school psychologist or similarly trained professional. Once the decision is made, completion of the forms will often involve classroom teachers and parents. Results will often be referenced in an individualized education program (IEP).

CAREER INTEREST INVENTORIES

Career interest inventories, also known as vocational interest tests, form a distinctive category of standardized tests. Many high school and college students take these tests. Their purpose is to help in choosing a specific job or general occupational area. Because jobs often presume specific educational preparation, these inventories help students select an educational program, such as a college major, leading to a job.

General Characteristics

Career interest inventories typically include a large number of items, approximately 100–300. Each item is a simple statement or activity. The student indicates a liking or a disliking, an agreement or a disagreement with each item. The student usually completes the inventory in about 30–40 minutes. Although there are many items, each item requires only a quick reaction. Thus, many items are completed in a relatively short time. Figure 12.8 shows examples of items that might appear in a career interest inventory. Notice the simplicity of response. The figure shows only a few items. Imagine an inventory containing, say, 200 such items.

There are two main ways for scoring responses to career interest inventories. The first way concentrates on broad interest areas. Examples of such broad areas are mechanical, artistic, scientific, management, and so on. See Figure 12.9. With this approach, the student gets a profile of scores in these broad interest areas. For example, a student's profile may show me-

---

Mark whether you like (L), dislike (D), or are indifferent (I) to each activity.

	L	I	D
1. Fixing things	0	0	0
2. Reading books	0	0	0
3. Playing with children	0	0	0
4. Solving puzzles	0	0	0
5. Working by myself	0	0	0
6. Writing stories	0	0	0

In each group of three statements, mark the thing you like to do Most (M) and the thing you like to do Least (L). Make no mark for the other thing.

	M	L
a. Working with tools	0	0
b. Reading to children	0	0
c. Working in a garden	0	0
a. Writing poems	0	0
b. Reading adventure stories	0	0
c. Telling jokes	0	0

Figure 12.8 Sample items for a career interest inventory.

chanical as highest, scientific next, and so on. Another student's profile may show artistic as highest, followed by communication. The broad interest areas are cross-referenced to lists of specific jobs, such as those found in the *Dictionary of Occupational Titles* (*DOT*)[2] or the *Occupational Outlook Handbook* (*OOH*). The U.S. Department of Labor maintains and periodically updates the *DOT* and *OOH*. (For websites, see Exercise 9 at the end of this chapter.)

Try This!

Think of your own interests and those of your friends. Can you think of one additional broad interest area that might be added to those in Figure 12.9?

Scientific	Mechanical
Communications	Persuasive
Business	Arts
Social Services	Outdoor

Figure 12.9 Examples of broad interest areas used with career interest inventories.

---

[2] The *Dictionary of Occupational Titles* (*DOT*) was recently renamed *O*Net*, but the traditional *DOT* title will certainly be used in various publications for many years to come.

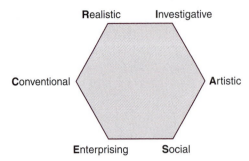

Figure 12.10 The RIASEC hexagon.

One application of this broad-interest approach to scoring career interest inventories is the Holland hexagon system (Holland, 1997). This system uses the six points of a hexagon to describe areas of interest. Points diagonally opposite are very dissimilar. Points closer together are more similar. We sometimes describe the system with the initials for the six points: RIASEC. Figure 12.10 shows Holland's hexagonal RIASEC system. Reports that use the RIASEC system usually list the two or three letters that are the highest for a person's profile. For example, a person who scores highest in Social and Enterprising would be listed as SE.

The second main approach to scoring career interest inventories is **criterion-keying**. In this approach, preliminary research identifies items that people in a particular occupation select, agree with, or like. Those items then go in a scale for that occupation. The resulting scale essentially measures the extent to which a student expresses agreement with people already in an occupation. For example, for the items in Figure 12.8, suppose we find that elementary school teachers say they like "solving puzzles" and "writing stories." Then, those two items would go in the elementary teacher scale. Note that it does not make any difference why elementary teachers like these items. The simple fact is that they say they do. It's an empirical fact. Hence, criterion-keying is sometimes called "empirical keying." Under this approach, the final scores from the inventory tell how well the respondent's answers agree with the responses from a variety of occupational groups. The assumption is that a person with interests similar to those of people already in an occupation might be a good match with that occupation.

Typical Uses and Users

Career interest inventories are used most widely with high school students. The most common grades for their administration are Grades 9 and 10, although some schools may use them as early as Grade 8 or as late as Grade 12. The inventories also experience some use among lower division college students, especially for students who are having trouble deciding about a major. Persons thinking about a midlife career change may also take one of these inventories.

Counselors, especially high school counselors, are key individuals deciding what inventory to use, when to use it, and how to communicate the results. That makes sense, because initial decisions about jobs and career tracks tend to be made in the high school years. Of course, the student completing the inventory is the primary user of the information. Increasingly, the career interest inventories described later can be taken on-line (for a fee) by anyone. (To take one, go to the websites listed in Key Points Summary 12.3.) Thus, those persons taking the inventory may be interpreting the scores themselves rather than with the help of a counselor. This circumstance places a special burden on the publishers of the inventories.

Widely Used Career Interest Inventories

There are three widely used career interest inventories. They all have the same general purpose. They are quite similar in the types of scores they report. However, they do have some differences. We provide a thumbnail sketch of each of these inventories here. For additional details on any of these inventories, see their respective websites, as given in Key Points Summary 12.3.

Strong Interest Inventory

According to a number of surveys, the Strong Interest Inventory (SII) is the most widely used career interest inventory. Often referred to simply as "the Strong," the earliest versions of this inventory appeared in the 1920s. Over the years, its successive editions have been known as the Strong Vocational Interest Blank, the Strong-Campbell Interest Inventory, and the current Strong Interest Inventory. The names for the successive editions are often used interchangeably. The inventory's author, E. K. Strong, pioneered the criterion-keying approach described earlier. Scores based on criterion-keying are still a prominent part of the reports on the Strong. However, the current edition also yields scores based on broad interest areas and on the RIASEC system.

Kuder Career Planning System

The Kuder Career Search With Person Matching (KCS) is another widely used career interest inventory. It is part of the overall Kuder Career Planning System, which also includes the Kuder Skills Assessment. Like the Strong name, the Kuder name (after J. Frederick Kuder, the original author of this and other interest inventories) is famous in the field. The KCS provides scores in broad interest areas. As suggested by the full title of the inventory, it also provides a match of the person's profile of interests with the profiles of 2000 individuals already working in various occupations. Specifically, a report presents occupational biographies for 14 individuals with the best match to a person's profile.

Self-Directed Search

A third widely used career interest inventory is the Self-Directed Search (SDS). The SDS bases its organization and reporting system directly on the RIASEC scheme shown in Figure 12.10. The inventory consists of 228 items, requiring about 30 minutes to complete. Items cover activities a person might like to do, occupations, competencies, and self-ratings of abilities. Scores are translated into the RIASEC codes. Then, these codes are cross-referenced to the *Dictionary of Occupational Titles*. The SDS emphasizes that it is self-administered, self-scored, and self-interpreted.

KEY POINTS SUMMARY 12.3   *Three Widely Used Career Interest Inventories*

Strong Interest Inventory (SII)
  www.cpp-db.com/products/strong

Kuder Career Search With Person Matching (KCS)
  www.kuder.com/common/kcs.htm

Self-Directed Search (SDS)
  www.self-directed-search.com

Scores obtained from the various career interest inventories tend to be quite reliable. This is not surprising. For students in the age range where these inventories are used, interest patterns have become fairly stable. At least for the more widely used inventories, research shows that the scores have a reasonable degree of validity. That is, people who enter an occupation compatible with their measured interests tend to be satisfied with their career choice. Interestingly, the research also shows that people who go into an occupation incompatible with their interests tend to switch careers later into an occupation that is more compatible with their interests. Of course, the validity is by no means perfect. There are exceptions to the general patterns established in the research.

PRACTICAL ADVICE

1. When working on an IEP team or in a similar situation, you may encounter reports of scores for unfamiliar tests. (A report may even limit itself to acronyms for the test, such as VABS or PPVT.) Become proficient in using the sources of information in Appendix A to learn about the tests. By themselves these sources will not make you an expert in interpretation of the tests. However, with a little practice, you can participate intelligently in discussions about the tests.

2. Be very wary of any all-or-none interpretations of mental ability. Specifically, be wary of interpretations that suggest it is all due to either hereditary or environmental influences. The best evidence we have at present is that a student's current mental ability results from some combination of hereditary and environmental factors. Be wary of interpretations suggesting that there is no such thing as general mental ability or of interpretations suggesting that there are no separate factors. Our best understanding at present is the hierarchical theory.

3. Remember to apply to the tests covered in this chapter what you learned about reliability and validity. Most of the tests you encounter will have a reasonable degree of reliability—but not perfect reliability. Most of the tests will have some degree of validity—but far from perfect validity. Think of the tests as providing some useful information, but be cautious about generalizing too much. Always seek additional information.

SUMMARY

1. Tests of mental ability appear under a variety of titles. Most of these tests reflect a hierarchical theory of mental ability. In general, these tests attempt to predict school performance based on items that are not highly dependent on in-school learning.

2. Individually administered mental ability tests are used mostly with students needing special attention. Administration of these tests requires advanced training. Examples of these tests include the WISC-IV, SB-5, WJ-Cog, and PPVT. The VABS illustrates the concept of adaptive functioning, especially important in the definition of mental retardation.

3. Group-administered mental ability tests at the elementary and secondary school levels are often used in conjunction with a standardized achievement battery. Tests such as the SAT, ACT, and GRE try to predict success in college or graduate school.

4. We use the term "personality test" to include a great variety of tests with widely differing characteristics. One common distinction is between objective and projective tests. Personality tests also include measures of such traits as self-concept, depression, hyperactivity, and attention deficit.

5. Behavior rating scales call for a teacher or parent to rate the occurrence of very specific behaviors. These scales are widely used for the identification of such conditions as attention deficit and hyperactivity.

6. Career interest inventories are widely used in secondary schools to help students choose a career and/or college major. Scores on such tests may be based on broad interest areas tied to lists of occupational titles or on matching a student's interest profile with the interests of people already in an occupation.

KEY TERMS

adaptive behavior	DSM-IV	objective inventories
behavior rating scales	hierarchical theory	projective techniques
criterion-keying	IQ	self-report inventory
discrepancy analysis	mental retardation	

EXERCISES

1. Refer to Table 12.1. Pick three categories. Prepare two test questions for each category. Make one question appropriate for Grade 2 students and one for Grade 10 students. Be sure to indicate what are acceptable answers. Have another person critique your items.

2. Refer to Table 12.4. Follow the same instructions as for Exercise 1. However, use a multiple-choice format for answers. Again, have someone else critique your items.

3. Consider the four Index scores on the WISC-IV (see p. 283 for descriptions). Which Index score do you think is *most* important for success in school? Which do you think is *least* important? Compare your answers with someone else's answers.

4. Go to Figure 12.3. Find the part of the report that gives scores on the Otis-Lennon School Ability Test. What types of scores appear there? Can you explain each type of score? Then, find the "AAC Range." Can you explain these results?

5. Access the website for one of the tests listed in Table 12.7 (mental ability tests to predict success in postsecondary schooling). Try to find examples of the types of items in the test. What kind of items do you find?

6. To see summaries of the AAMR definition of mental retardation, as well as the range of issues of interest to the organization, visit this website: www.aamr.org. Can you find the criteria for defining mental retardation? What does the site say about adaptive behavior?

7. Refer to Table 12.12. Add five items to the list. Each item must be a specific behavior that a teacher could observe.

8. Here are the websites for the three career interest inventories described in this chapter.

Strong   www.cpp-db.com/products/strong

Kuder: www.kuder.com/common/kcs.htm

SDS: www.self-directed-search.com

Each site allows you to access sample reports. Find the sample reports for each inventory. See if you can tell which parts of the reports use the broad-area approach and which parts use the criterion-keying approach to giving scores.

9. Check out the *Dictionary of Occupational Titles* at this webiste: http://www.dictionary-occupationaltitles.net/

Check out the *Occupational Outlook Handbook* at this website: http://www.bls.gov/oco/

What can you learn about jobs for teachers at these sites?

Chapter 13

Grading and Reporting

OBJECTIVES

- List the major *purposes* served by assigning grades.
- Explain five major *rationales* used for developing grades and identify their strengths and weaknesses.
- Identify the types of *coding schemes* used for grading.
- Explain the *effect of variability*, *zero scores,* and *regression to the mean* when combining elements to form a composite grade.
- Identify typical formats for *report cards*.
- Outline suggestions for conducting a *parent-teacher conference*, including communication about standardized test results.
- Describe the position courts have taken regarding teachers' assignment of grades.

What This Chapter Is About

Every teacher needs to assign grades. These grades are ordinarily based on combinations of individual assessments: tests, quizzes, projects, and so on. Then the grades are reported, usually in the form of a report card. The grades are a primary vehicle for communicating with other people about students' progress. There are also several other mechanisms for reporting student progress. In this chapter, we examine the factors that go into grading and reporting. Specifically, we examine the diverse purposes served by grades and the various rationales for assigning grades. Then we look at the mechanics of developing grades from separate elements. Finally, we describe several methods for reporting grades and other indicators of student progress.

Why This Chapter Is Important

Assigning grades is one of the most important things a teacher does. Grades have a finality not present in a lesson plan or daily conduct of class—both of which can be modified "on the fly." Grades become part of a student's permanent record. They are a matter of keen interest to students and their parents.[1] Hence, teachers need competence in the grading

---

[1] All references to "parents" here and in other sections include guardians.

"Those are my test results, and here is my
position paper questioning the entire testing process."

(With permission of Cartoon Resource.)

process. They need to know the options for grading and reporting. They need to be able to complete the process efficiently. They need to avoid certain pitfalls. They need to develop finesse in communicating about grades and other indicators of student progress.

DEFINITION OF GRADING

In previous chapters, we considered scoring a *single* assessment, such as an essay, a multiple-choice test, or a science project. In this chapter, we consider grading. **Grading**, as we use the term here, implies (a) combining several assessments, (b) translating the result into some type of scale that has evaluative meaning, and (c) reporting the results in a formal way. For example, three tests, each scored as percent right, are combined with homework assignments and an extra credit project into a final letter grade on the familiar A–F scale. Then, these letter grades for several different content areas and perhaps from several different teachers appear on a report card. Figure 13.1 depicts the entire process. We start with different pieces of information. We combine these in some way. The combination is translated into some type of scale. Then, there is a final reporting mechanism. We use the single term "grading" for this entire process. Another common term for the process, although now used less frequently, is *marking*.

Figure 13.1 suggests the topics we need to consider in this chapter. How do we combine the separate pieces of information? What are the common scales used for the combined information? What are the reporting mechanisms? In each case we want to consider the advantages and disadvantages of various alternatives. Before considering these practical matters, we need to review two more general topics: (1) the purposes of grading and

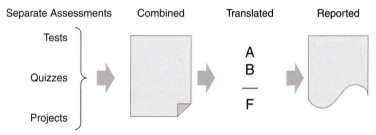

Figure 13.1 Summary of steps in the grading process.

(2) rationales for grading schemes. These two topics will set the stage for the more practical topics. They will also serve as guides for judging the suitability of alternatives.

PURPOSES OF GRADES

Grading serves a variety of purposes. To do a good job of grading, we need to have these purposes clearly in mind. As we describe various purposes, note that particular methods of reporting may be more appropriate for one purpose, less so for another purpose.

Feedback

Recall from Chapter 1 (p. 7) that providing feedback is one of the purposes of assessment. Perhaps nowhere is this more important than in the grading process. In fact, providing feedback is important to at least three distinct groups: parents, students, and teachers. We treat each group separately here, beginning with parents.

Feedback to Parents. Grades, especially as communicated on a report card, provide crucial feedback to parents about their child's progress in school. The other main sources of feedback are results from standardized tests and teachers' comments. We treat these other two sources elsewhere in this chapter.

At a general level, grades tell parents whether or not their child's progress is satisfactory. Grades also give parents an indication of particular strengths and weaknesses of the child. Depending on the type of report card used, parents may receive feedback on behavior, effort, and other such variables, in addition to grades in subject areas.

Parents may be only dimly aware of their children's performance on the multitude of assessments that comprise a grade. Parents may see some but not all of the scores on quizzes, tests, and projects. Some parents may see none of them—or only those on which the student did particularly well. Grades, formally communicated, ensure that parents are getting an overall summary of performance. The formal communication of grades often serves as an ideal opportunity for other types of communication between teacher and parent. We take up examples of such other communication later in the chapter.

Feedback to Students. Grades also serve as important feedback to the student. It seems likely that the value of this feedback increases with the child's age. Grades may not be very meaningful to the Grade 1 student. But certainly by middle school, students are aware of the meaning of grades. And, in the high school years, students are keenly aware of grades.

Grades help students keep track of their progress. Grades help identify strengths and weaknesses, and changes in performance (up or down), and they may even influence choice of careers or college majors. The student who consistently gets good grades in science may be drawn to pursue further work in that field.

Feedback to Teachers. Grades can also be important feedback to the very teachers who assign the grades. This is especially true when the assessments underlying the grades are reasonably consistent across time. Changes in the distribution of grades may help to indicate the relative effectiveness of different instructional approaches. Changes in grades may also indicate variations in the nature of the student groups being served. Of course, such changes are not resulting from elegant experimental designs. However, in a way, every teacher's classroom is like a mini action research project. Every teacher should be alert to changes occurring in this project. Grades are one source of information for the project.

Administrative Purposes

Grades often serve administrative purposes. These purposes can be quite different in their intent and effect than any of the feedback purposes just described. Some of these administrative purposes use single grades. Most of the purposes depend on combinations of grades, such as grade point averages or rank in class that arise from combinations of grades in separate subjects. Grades may be one factor in determining promotion or retention in grade level. This is especially true in the primary and elementary grades. Grades may also enter into qualification for high school graduation. At both middle school and high school, grades may affect eligibility for participation in athletic and other extracurricular activities. Some regulations regarding grades may originate outside the school (e.g., from an athletic conference). Other regulations may arise from internal school policies. Failing grades may prohibit a student from playing football, being in the school band, or running for class officer.

Grades often serve as the basis for academic awards. Many schools have an honor roll or similarly named record based on grades. Grades usually determine awards at graduation for overall achievement or excellence in a single subject.

A variety of organizations external to the school use the school's grades. Most colleges use grades as one of the most important criteria for admission, as well as for scholarship awards. Employers may use grades for job selection. Even some car insurance companies use grades to give discounts in insurance rates.

Teachers have little role in affecting these many administrative uses of grades (except for promotion/retention decisions). However, it is important for teachers to be aware of these many administrative uses of grades, all of which originate with the grading practices implemented by individual teachers.

Motivation

A final purpose of grades is to provide motivation. In an ideal world, all students would study to their utmost for the sheer joy of learning. Alas, we do not live in that ideal world. Most students like to get good grades. They work harder to get good grades. Thus, quite

KEY POINTS SUMMARY 13.1	*Main Purposes of Grading*
Feedback To parents To students To the teacher	**Administrative Purposes** Internal to the school External organizations **Motivation**

apart from feedback to parents, staying eligible for the basketball team, and other such purposes, grades may serve as motivators for students.

RATIONALES FOR ASSIGNING GRADES

What basis shall we use to assign grades? We refer here not to the specific tests, projects, quizzes, exams, and so on that go into the grade. Rather, we refer to the general approach to assigning grades. We can identify five different rationales for assigning grades. Some sources call these approaches "philosophies of grading." Let us define each of these rationales and then examine their strengths and weaknesses.

Achievement relative to fixed standard. We can assign grades based on a student's achievement in relation to a fixed standard. Ordinarily, the fixed standard is some well-defined body of content or set of skills. A simple example of a well-defined body of content is "the 300 words in the Grade 4 spelling book." A simple example of a set of skills is "can replace the spark plugs, air filter, and oil filter in a V-6 internal combustion engine in 60 minutes." If a student correctly spells nearly all of the 300 words, say 290 or more, that's terrific. If a student gets more than 50 of the words wrong, that's awful. If the student makes all of the engine replacements in 45 minutes, that's good. The perceptive reader will spot these as classic examples of criterion-referenced interpretations. There is a clear external standard. We determine how the student stacks up with respect to this standard.

Achievement relative to group performance. The norm-referenced alternative to the latter rationale is to grade a student relative to performance within the group. Thus, the student who spells the most words correctly—whether that is 75% right or 90% right—gets a high grade. The student who spells the fewest words correctly—be that 50% right or 75% right—gets a low grade. Notice that in this example 75% could warrant a high grade or a low grade depending on how other students perform. This example uses just one test but the same principle applies if we are using the combination of several tests in determining a final grade. That, of course, is the essence of the norm-referenced approach. The more popular name for this approach is "grading on the curve."

Achievement relative to ability. A third rationale is to grade each student in relation to that student's ability. In this context, "ability" usually means mental ability, intelligence, academic aptitude, or some similar construct. The basic idea here is that a student's achievement should be judged according to potential. The very bright student is expected to achieve at a superior level. If he or she doesn't do so, this should be reflected in the grade. Conversely, the student of more limited ability should be rewarded with high grades if the student exceeds expectations.

Achievement relative to effort. A rationale similar to that of achievement relative to ability is to grade achievement relative to effort. According to this rationale, a student's grade depends, at least in part, on effort expended. The student who is working really hard—diligently completing all assignments, perhaps doing extra credit projects, and so on—should get a high grade even if the quality of the work is mediocre. Conversely, mediocre work resulting from meager effort warrants a low grade. Notice, by comparison, that according to the first rationale described earlier, mediocre work gets a mediocre grade regardless of the effort exerted.

Achievement as improvement. A fifth rationale is to assign grades based on degree of improvement. In effect, we base the grade on the difference between final performance and some measure of initial status in the area. A student who shows great progress during the marking period gets a high grade, regardless of the absolute level of the final performance. A student who shows little progress, or perhaps even gets worse, merits a low grade, again regardless of the final level of performance. Notice that this method requires that we have a measure of initial status, the starting point for each student.

Pros and Cons of the Various Rationales

All of the five rationales for grading are legitimate, reasonable positions. They all have a certain degree of appeal. Yet they all have certain drawbacks. Let us examine their comparative strengths and weaknesses.

Using achievement in relation to a fixed standard is probably the most common rationale. It is appealing because it focuses exclusively on achievement, which is usually the goal of the educational enterprise. At least in appearance, it avoids the relativism of all the other rationales. However, this approach is not without its own difficulties. There are two main problems with this rationale. First, it does not, within itself, say what is a reasonable standard of performance. Is spelling 90% of the words correctly the standard for acceptable performance? Is 70% inadequate? What if in the past 10 years no student in Grade 4 has ever correctly spelled 90% of the words? Would we still use 90% as the definition of good performance? What if even experienced auto mechanics require more than 60 minutes to make the three engine replacements? Would we still expect a shop student in

---

KEY POINTS SUMMARY 13.2 *Rationales for Grading*

Achievement relative to fixed standard

Achievement relative to group performance

Achievement relative to ability

Achievement relative to effort

Achievement as improvement

Grade 11 to do so in order to pass? Referring to achievement relative to a fixed standard sounds definitive. However, in practice, what constitutes the standard is someone's opinion. It may be a panel of people or a single individual, typically a teacher. But it's still just an opinion.

A second difficulty with the rationale of achievement in relation to a fixed standard is the problem of getting a well-defined body of content or set of skills. We used examples that are quite simple: Grade 4 spelling words and a few mechanic's skills. What is the appropriate body of content for reading comprehension? For algebra? For French? We can give some arbitrary definitions, such as "everything in the textbook." But that's not very helpful and not very precise. Clear specification of learning outcomes, as recommended in Chapter 6, is the best solution to this difficulty. However, it does not eliminate the difficulty.

Achievement relative to other students is nicely empirical. It ensures a level of realism sometimes lacking in the first rationale. It avoids the problem of setting unrealistically high (or low) standards. You will not have the situation where everyone fails. In addition, it's pretty easy to rank students, and then draw lines to assign grades. Grading students in relation to other students has two main drawbacks. The first, and the more severe of the two, is that an individual's grade depends in part on other people. This seems unfair. A student may have done a great job, but gets a low grade because other students did better, perhaps only marginally so. Or the student may get a high grade when the student's performance was really rather mediocre, but marginally better than other students'. Of course, this is only to describe the inherent characteristics of a norm-referenced system.

The second difficulty with the rationale of achievement relative to other students is the definition of "other students." What is the relevant group of other students? Students in one class? This teacher's students in the past 10 years? Students in this school system? Students in the state? To use the rationale of achievement in relation to other students, the teacher needs to have a reasonably clear answer to this question. Another difficulty with this approach is that it has the potential to encourage unhealthy competition if the group is simply a single class. In that case, students are competing only against their classmates. Unhealthy competition is not a practical difficulty if the comparison group is a national or statewide group.

We can treat the last three rationales—achievement in relation to ability, effort, and improvement—together. They have similar strengths and weaknesses. Their principal strength is their concentration on the individual student. In a sense, we are using the individual to define the standard and the norm. That is appealing. All three of these approaches have two drawbacks. First, they can lead to conclusions that most people find awkward, if not abhorrent. The point is most easily illustrated at the extremes of the achievement continuum: very high and very low. For example, one student tries very hard and therefore gets an A, although the student's performance was substantially lower than that of another student who performed quite well but without much effort and therefore got a B−. Kelly, with an IQ of 150, gets a C, whereas Matt, with an IQ of 80, gets a B+. Why? Because Kelly should have done much better, whereas we were pleasantly surprised by Matt's performance. Of course, Kelly's performance was world's better than Matt's in an absolute sense. Jen, starting with little knowledge of Spanish, makes great progress during the year. Abby, already quite proficient, makes only modest progress. Jen gets a higher grade because of her greater progress, although Abby is clearly better than Jen. One can easily multiply examples like these that result from use of any of the last three rationales. Most people are uncomfortable with such conclusions.

The second difficulty with the last three rationales is not so obvious. It is a technical difficulty. We must mention it but we will not attempt to work out the details here. Recall from Chapter 4 the matter of reliability. We considered the importance of getting reliable measures of achievement. It's not easy to do so. There are many sources of unreliability. In the grading process, we hope to get very reliable grades for achievement partly by combining many specific measures. That should work. Combining several moderately reliable measures (tests, quizzes, projects, etc.) should make the final grade quite reliable. However, in each of the last three rationales, we are introducing another type of measure: ability, effort, or initial status. We then get the *difference* between this other measure and our measure of achievement. The *difference* becomes the basis for grading. Such differences are nearly always *less reliable* than either of the original measures, often substantially so. The problem may be particularly severe for the effort variable because we usually do not have a reliable measure of effort. The judgment about effort is often based on informal observations. When this unreliable measure is combined with achievement to formulate a grade, the resulting grade may be quite unreliable. The problem may be particularly severe when using ability or initial status for a very different reason. For ability or initial status, we may have quite reliable measures. However, these variables are usually highly correlated with the measure of final achievement. When that is the case, the reliability of the difference deteriorates.

Research Results and Conclusions

Although measurement experts quite uniformly endorse use of achievement alone—uninfluenced by effort or ability—as a basis for grading, research shows that many teachers allow ability and/or effort to modify grades to varying degrees, thus rendering the meaning of grades ambiguous or positively misleading for parents, students, and other teachers (Brookhart, 1993; Cizek, Fitzgerald, & Rachor, 1996; Cross & Frary, 1999; McMillan, 2001; Plake & Impara, 1993; Stiggins, Frisbie, & Griswold, 1989).

What can we conclude from this discussion of various rationales for grading? We should note first that a school district may have an explicit policy statement regarding these issues. If that is the case, obviously the teacher needs to conform to that policy. In the absence of such a policy, we recommend the following. To the extent possible, adopt the first rationale: Assign grades based on achievement in relation to a fixed standard. In doing so, be as clear as possible in formulating the standard. Communicate the standard to students, parents, and other stakeholders. In addition, make sure the standard is realistic in terms of actual student performance. In effect, we are suggesting use of the first rationale tempered by the second rationale.

What about taking into account ability, effort, and improvement? We recommend against use of these rationales as a basis for grading. The perspectives provided by these rationales are important. Use these additional perspectives in formulating comments, written or oral, to students and parents. But do not use them as a basis for assigning formal grades. Some reporting systems will also allow for *separate* marks for effort or progress. That is an ideal way to account for these other perspectives.

KEY POINTS SUMMARY 13.3	*Pros and Cons of the Various Rationales for Grading*	
Rationale	**Pros**	**Cons**
Fixed Standard	Focuses exclusively on achievement	Standard is just opinion
		Difficulty getting clear definition
Group Performance	Ensures realism	Individual's grade depends on others
	Always clear how to determine	Choosing relevant group
Ability, Effort, Improvement	Concentration on individual	Awkward conclusions
		Problems with reliability

CODING SYSTEMS: THE ACTUAL GRADES

The various elements entering into a grade will ultimately be translated into some type of coding system. These are what we think of as "the grades." In this section, we examine the more widely used coding systems. At least in upper grades, the first two categories (letter and percentage grades) clearly predominate (Camara, 1998).

Letter Grades

The letter grade system, no doubt, is the most widely used coding system in the United States. Its use has even spread beyond the schools into the general culture. Thus, we see cities graded A, C−, and so on. Businesses adopt the system, as in "A+ Used Cars." We use letter grades in ordinary conversation: "I'd rate that play an F." It's really quite amazing.

Actual implementation of the letter grade system obviously has some variations. The most basic system includes these grades A, B, C, D, and F. This is essentially a 5-point scale, often translated as 4, 3, 2, 1, and 0. In fact, that is the most common set of numerical values used to develop a grade point average (GPA). Of course, + or − may be attached to any of the letters. Depending on how many such attachments we use, the scale may expand to 15 points. It is rare to attach + or − to the F grade. The F grade seems to have such a purity of meaning that it is not susceptible to refinement. Figure 13.2 shows three variations of the letter grade scale, along with commonly used numerical equivalents. Obviously, other variations are possible for both the number of scale points and the numerical equivalents of the letter grades.

Percentage Grades

Another coding system is the percentage system. Values in the system range from 0 to 100. It is very common to encounter this system for single tests, especially those consisting of items each scored right or wrong. It is less common to encounter the scale as an overall grading system. However, its use for single tests seems to lead to its conversion to an overall grading system. To think of it in terms similar to those for letter grades, the percentage system is essentially a 100-point system (or more exactly, a 101-point system).

5 points

A	B	C	D	F
4.0	3.0	2.0	1.0	0.0

9 points

A	A−	B+	B	B−	C+	C	D	F
4.0	3.7	3.3	3.0	2.7	2.3	2.0	1.0	0.0

13 points

A+	A	A−	B+	B	B−	C+	C	C−	D+	D	D−	F
4.33	4.0	3.67	3.33	3.0	2.67	2.33	2.0	1.67	1.33	1.0	.67	0.0

Figure 13.2 Three versions of the letter grade coding system with sample numerical equivalents.

It is not unusual to see tables showing conversions between the letter grade and percentage grade systems. Unfortunately, there is no universal standard for the conversions. Figure 13.3 shows two common conversion schemes. However, one can find nearly infinite variations for these conversions.

Verbal Descriptors

Some reporting systems use verbal descriptors, such as Excellent, Good, Fair, and Needs Improvement or a similar set of labels. The labels usually correspond, at least approximately, to letter grade variations. In fact, both letter grades and percentages often carry some type of verbal description. However, verbal descriptions can be employed without

A	B	C	D	F
90–100	80–89	70–79	60–69	Below 60

A+	A	A−	B+	B	B−	C+	C	C−	D+	D	D−	F
97+	93–96	90–92	87–89	83–86	80–82	77–79	73–76	70–72	67–69	63–66	60–62	<60

Figure 13. 3 Two common conversion schemes for percentages and letter grades.

reference to letter or percentage grades. Verbal descriptions may be used for achievement levels in the usual school subjects. One obvious example is the Pass/Fail grading system.

Verbal labels are used more frequently for such variables as behavior, effort, and attendance. In this use, the verbal labels have the advantage of being easily adapted to a particular variable. For example, "effort" may be described as Always Tries Hard, Usually Tries Hard, Needs to Work Harder. Class participation may be described as Often Makes Excellent Contributions, Sometimes Contributes Effectively, Rarely or Never Contributes. Thus, the labels arise from the nature of the variable.

Try This!

Suppose you have letter grades for students, but you want to report in terms of verbal descriptors. What *verbal labels* would you give for these letter grades?

A _____   B _____   C _____   D _____   F _____

Checklists

When the area being assessed consists of highly specific skills, the report can take the form of **checklist grading**. The list contains the skills. Each skill that is mastered or satisfactorily completed gets a check mark. In most instances, this amounts to a "yes" or "no" decision for each entry. In some applications there may be an additional level of distinction (e.g., Mastered, Partially Mastered, or Not Mastered). Figure 13.4 shows an example for primary level math skills. A checklist can provide excellent information about what a student has achieved. At the same time, the list suggests specific areas where the student needs additional work. Checklist reporting has three potential limitations. First, it may be difficult to construct such a list for many areas of the curriculum. As Haladyna (1999a) notes, checklist grading is largely limited to simple behaviors. Second, such lists may become too long to be manageable. Third, many users still want some type of summary information (e.g., a letter grade) to indicate overall standing in the area. For example, for the student described in Figure 13.4, is that superior, average, or substandard performance?

Skill	Mastered	Partial Mastery	Not Mastered
Counts objects to 10	✔		
Counts objects to 100		✔	
Identifies basic shapes	✔		
Knows basic addition facts		✔	
Knows basic subtraction facts			✔

Figure 13.4 Sample checklist for primary math skills.

Narrative Reports

Yet another grading system uses **narrative reports**. These reports can range from a single paragraph to several pages. Often, there will be one or two paragraphs for each subject area. The report may refer to grades on specific tests and projects but it allows for infinite flexibility in expressing the level of performance. The report will usually incorporate comments about effort, special strengths, areas needing development, and so on. In reaction against the apparent sterility of simple letter or percentage grades, some schools have attempted to convert entirely to narrative reporting formats. However, this format is very labor-intensive for teachers, hence it ordinarily works only in small schools. In addition, because of the many administrative uses of grades, as described earlier in this chapter, schools must usually maintain some type of summary grading system (letters, percentages, ranks, etc.) even if they are also using narrative reports. We refer in this section to reporting systems that are primarily narrative in nature. Of course, many reports that use letter grades or percentages also allow for (but do not require) brief written comments by the teacher.

Before leaving the coding systems, we should reflect for a moment on the trade-offs made by using fewer or more categories. For example, let us contrast the 5-point and 13-point systems shown in Figure 13.2. With fewer categories, there are fewer decisions required. With five categories, there are only four decision points. With more categories, there are more decision points; a 13-category system yields 12 decision points. Thus, with fewer categories, fewer students will be borderline cases; that is, sitting on the edge between adjacent categories. This should lead to fewer errors in classification. On the other hand, the consequences of error are much greater with fewer categories. There is a much greater difference between the adjacent categories B and C in the 5-point system than between the adjacent categories of B and B- in the 13-point system. Using fewer categories leads to more dissimilarity within categories. For example, the B category in the 5-point system covers a much wider range of achievement than the B category in the 13-point system. Thus, paradoxically, using more categories leads to greater precision but also more errors, although most of the errors are less serious.

Is there an optimal number of categories? There is probably no good answer to this question. However, it is useful to be aware of the trade-offs made by using more or fewer categories.

COMBINING INFORMATION TO GET A FINAL GRADE

Most teachers will base a grade on several sources of information: exams, quizzes, projects, daily work, and so on. It is conceivable that a final grade in, say, science, will result from just one test. Indeed, some educational systems use this one test-one grade approach.

KEY POINTS SUMMARY 13.4 *Main Coding Systems*

Letters	Checklists
Percentages	Narratives
Verbal descriptors	

Also, many certification and licensing exams operate this way. However, the typical grading system in U.S. schools depends on combining several sources of information to arrive at a final grade. Regarding this process, there are four points to consider. The first is how to record all this information. The second is how to weight the various sources appropriately to form a composite. The third is how to convert the composite into a common scale, the common scale being what we usually think of as the final grade. Finally, the composite on a common scale must be converted to a grade. Let us examine each of these issues.

Record Keeping

We want record keeping to be accurate and efficient. The key to achieving these goals is organization. Organization, in turn, depends on two factors. First, we must clearly specify what information will be used. Second, we must record this information in such a way that the combining operation works efficiently. The first step—clearly specifying what information will be used—is almost entirely a matter of judgment. What tests will be used? What projects? Will homework assignments count? What about seatwork, workbook pages, and so on? Decisions must also be made about how much each of these elements will count; that is, what weight each element will have in determining a final grade. At the beginning of each year, term, or grading period, the teacher must decide *what* elements will count and what their *weights* will be. Deciding what will count is a significant task for the new teacher. After some experience, the teacher will tend to use the same elements in successive grading periods, perhaps revising the list of elements and their weights modestly with additional experience. After making the decisions about what will count and how much it will count, the information must be recorded in some manner.

The traditional way to record information is in a **grade book**. The teacher records each test, quiz, and assignment in the grade book. At report card time, the teacher weights the various entries, adds them up, divides by some factor, and converts the result to a final grade.

Electronic Spreadsheets

Today, many teachers do almost all the recording, weighting, adding, dividing, and so on electronically. The teacher has a choice of using (a) a generic spreadsheet or (b) a software package specifically designed for grading. Let us examine each option briefly.

Generic Spreadsheets. Every teacher will have access to a standard electronic **spreadsheet**, such as Microsoft's Excel. Although the most frequent application of such tools is in the world of accounting, they are easily adapted to the grading function. Figure 13.5 shows an Excel spreadsheet for a (very small) class. Each row is a student. Each column is a test, quiz, or other assessment element. Use the first row to enter "headers"; that is, labels for each column. The first column will be headed "Student." If desired, enter other identifying information in adjacent columns before entering test information. In these respects, the layout is very much like the handwritten grade book. The difference comes in ease of manipulating the entries and making calculations. We do not intend to teach how to use Excel or any other spreadsheet here. Most readers will already know how to do this. If you don't, take a workshop on it. You can learn the basics in an hour.

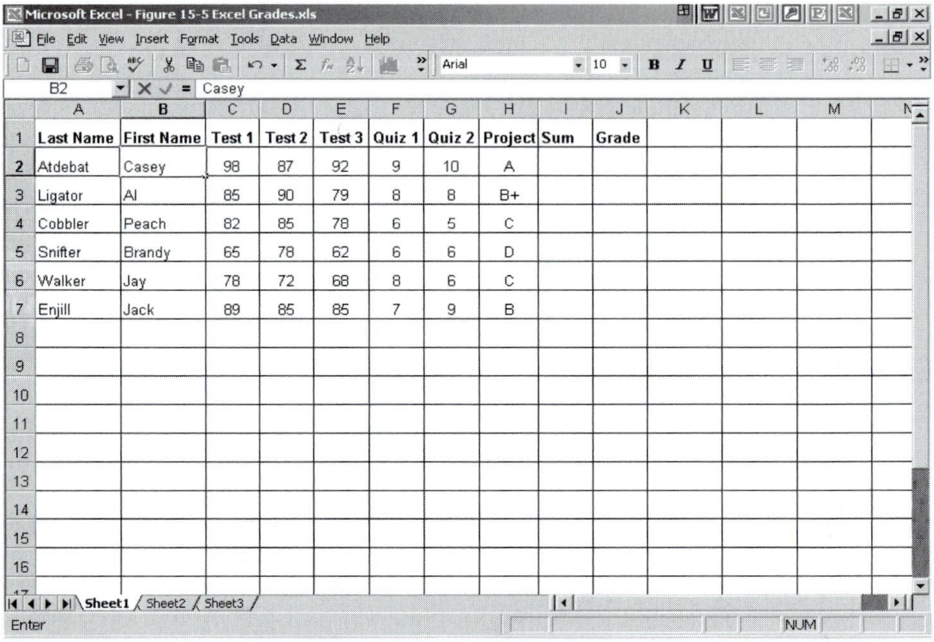

Microsoft Excel - Figure 15-5 Excel Grades.xls

Last Name	First Name	Test 1	Test 2	Test 3	Quiz 1	Quiz 2	Project	Sum	Grade
Atdebat	Casey	98	87	92	9	10	A		
Ligator	Al	85	90	79	8	8	B+		
Cobbler	Peach	82	85	78	6	5	C		
Snifter	Brandy	65	78	62	6	6	D		
Walker	Jay	78	72	68	8	6	C		
Enjill	Jack	89	85	85	7	9	B		

Figure 13.5 An Excel spreadsheet used in the grading process.

Specialized Software Packages. Teachers can also choose from an incredible variety of software packages specifically designed for the grading process. It is hazardous to list the many packages available for this purpose. More appear every day. Established ones issue new versions. Some are no longer available. The packages vary in cost and utility. Some are free, downloadable from the World Wide Web. Many of the packages range in cost from $30 to $100 for individual copies but also have site licensing arrangements for schools. Most of the packages allow recording grades on specific assignments, combining these grades into a final grade with weights assigned to the specific assignments, and reporting to both parents and students. Once learned, a package can be a blessing for the teacher.

Try This!

To see the variety of software packages available for grading, enter "gradebook" as a search term in any search engine for the World Wide Web. Note the variety of packages available. Pick one or two of the sites identified and check what the software will do. Follow up this search with Exercise 4 at the end of the chapter.

Figure 13.6 shows sample screens from one specialized software package for grading. The top screen contains grades entered. The middle screen shows just a few of the options for using the package. The bottom screen shows a sample report of student grades and a summary distribution of those grades.

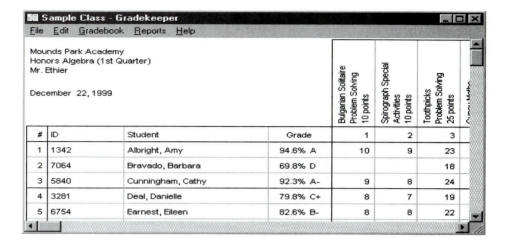

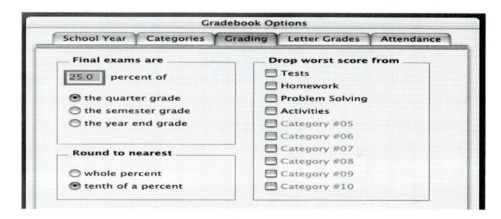

Mounds Park Academy

December 22, 1999
Honors Algebra (1st Quarter)
Mr. Ethier

Student	Exam	Quarter
Albright, Amy	92.0% A-	94.6% A
Bravado, Barbara	81.0% B-	69.8% D+
Cunningham, Cathy	93.0% A	92.3% A-
Deal, Danielle	82.0% B-	79.8% C+
Earnest, Eileen	83.0% B	82.6% B-
Average	86.2% B	83.8% B

0	A+	0	B+	1	C+	1	D+	0	F
1	A	0	B	0	C	0	D		
1	A-	1	B-	0	C-	0	D-		

Figure 13.6 Sample screens from a "gradebook" software package.

(Reproduced with permission of Gradekeeper.com.)

Security

Be sure to use commonsense security measures with any electronic spreadsheet. Have a backup copy of the work. The backup may be a handwritten record or an alternative electronic record. If you have only one copy on a hard drive, floppy, CD, or any other medium, and something happens to that one copy, well . . . no more need be said. Also, be cautious about storing records exclusively on a mainframe, central server, or even your own hard drive. Students have been known to "hack" into a school's computer system and change grades (Bushweller, 1999a).

Applying Weights to the Elements

In a typical grading situation, the teacher will combine several elements to get a final grade. The elements will be exams, quizzes, projects, and so on. Usually, the teacher wants these various elements to have different weights. For example, tests may count more than quizzes, a major project (while being represented by only one grade) gets significant weight, and so on. When all grades have been entered into a spreadsheet, applying weights is quite easy. Table 13.1 shows a simple example. Here there are five elements: three tests and two quizzes. We add up the three tests and give the sum a weight of 2. We gave a weight of 2 to the test sum because we judge the tests to be much more important than the quizzes. We also add the quizzes. Then, the weighted sum of tests and the sum of quizzes gives a total.

Applying weights to scores entered in a spreadsheet is quite simple. However, there are two additional steps that are often required. Let us examine each of them.

Converting All Scores to a Common Scale

First, it is not unusual to have elements on different types of scales. For example, test and quiz scores may be in percent-right form: 80%, 92%, and so on. Project grades may be in letter grades: A, C+, and so on. Other elements (e.g., homework assignments) may be in the form of check marks. The trick is to get all this material combined in some manner.

The most common problem is converting letter grades into numerical form for combining with test scores that are already in numerical form. For this purpose, the teacher must have handy a letter grade to number grade conversion chart. Figure 13.7 shows several versions of such charts. These are not the only possible conversions. The numerical conversions to a GPA-like scale (see Figure 13.2) would also serve the purpose. In any case, the teacher needs to have some such conversion.

If the teacher assigns grades in a school that uses verbal labels (Excellent, Good, etc.), then it will be useful to have a conversion system like those in Figure 13.3 but substituting labels for the letter grades.

Table 13.1   Scores on Five Elements to Be Combined Into a Total

Student	Test 1	Test 2	Test 3	Quiz 1	Quiz 2	Test Sumx2	Quiz Sum	Total
Dan	86	92	80	7	9	516	16	532
Ned	78	67	82	6	6	454	12	466
Matt	98	90	92	9	10	560	19	579

A	B	C	D	F				
95	85	75	65	50				
A	B+	B	B−	C+	C	C−	D	F
95	87	85	82	77	75	72	65	50

Figure 13.7 Sample conversions of letter grade to numerical form.

Converting the Composite to a Grade

After getting the composite score on a common scale, the result must be converted to a final grade. The type of final grade desired (letter, percent, etc.) will be dictated by the school's grading system. Ordinarily, it will be whatever system is used for report cards. There are several ways to accomplish this goal, depending on how the composite was formed. (In the examples used in this section, we assume that elements enter the composite without weights. We also assume that the problems identified in the next section are adequately handled.)

The composite may have been formed so that it is already in percentage form. This occurs when each element has been expressed as a percentage and these percentages are averaged. Table 13.2 gives an example. In this example, the quiz was originally 10 points but it was converted to percentage form.

If the final grade is to be in percentage form, we have it. If it needs to be converted to a letter grade or verbal label, we will use a conversion system, such as those shown in Figure 13.3.

The composite may be in the form of total points. This occurs when elements entering the composite are on different types of scales. For example, there may be a 50-point test, two 25-point tests, three 10-point quizzes, and a project worth 30 points. The maximum number of possible points is 160. The distribution of students' total points, based on this maximum of 160, must be converted to a grade. It would be possible to convert students' totals to percentage form, using 160 as a divisor. Then the teacher would proceed as in the previous example, either working directly with percents or converting percents to letter grades.

Another common scenario is to have grades for all elements expressed as letter grades: A, B+, and so on. In this case, convert each letter grade to numerical form. To do so, use a scheme like those shown in Figure 13.3 or Figure 13.7. Then average the numerical grades and convert the average back into a letter grade.

Table 13.2 Combining Percentage Grades by Averaging

Student	Test 1	Test 2	Quiz 3	Average
Joe	90	88	74	84
Jim	80	90	90	87
Sue	76	62	88	75
Sid	62	80	62	68

THREE SPECIAL PROBLEMS

Throughout the entire process of developing final grades from separate assessments, there are three special problems requiring attention. They may seem like mere technicalities, but they can have major consequences. Specifically, if not properly handled, they can surreptitiously undermine what the teacher really intends to happen in the grading process. Many teachers appear to be unaware of these difficulties and their effects (Plake & Impara, 1993). Let us examine the nature of each of these problems and offer suggestions for controlling them.

The Effect of Variability on Weights

Here is a curious, counterintuitive effect when combining elements to form a composite. The elements here are tests, quizzes, projects, and so on. The composite is the combination of these elements that will serve as the basis for the final grade. Let us state the general principle and then illustrate it. The principle is this: *The effective weight of an element depends on its variability, not on its absolute numerical value.* Table 13.3 provides a simple illustration for five students. The example combines a 100-point test with a 10-point quiz. Scores on the test cluster narrowly in a 4-point range around 80. Scores on the quiz scatter widely from 2 to 10.

The teacher intends the 100-point test to be the main determinant of the final grade. After all, it has 100 points. The quiz, with just 10 points, should play a minor role. However, as illustrated in Table 13.3, the final grade is determined primarily by the quiz. Why? Because the quiz has much greater variability (a range of 8 points) than does the test (a range of only 4 points). Examine the scores in the table to verify this.

What can be done to avoid this troublesome turn of events? The solution proceeds with the following steps. First, determine the degree of variability for each element that will enter the composite. A quick visual check of the ranges (the difference between highest and lowest scores) for each variable will often be sufficient. The more technical approach—easy to do with most spreadsheets—is to calculate the standard deviation for each variable. Then make the variabilities equal by multiplying or dividing as needed. Multiplying will increase variability. Dividing will decrease variability. Once the variabilities are equal, apply weights according to your intentions, giving greater weight to those elements judged more important, less weight to those items judged less important.

Table 13.4 shows the result when we take two steps. First, divide the quiz grade by 2, thus giving it the same 4-point spread as the test. Second, apply a weight of 5 to the test

Table 13.3 Illustration of the Effect of Variability in Forming a Composite

	100-point Test	10-point Quiz	Composite
Kelly	82	2	84
Kim	81	4	85
Jill	80	10	90
Meg	79	8	87
Sue	78	6	84

Table 13.4   Applying Weights to Scores in Table 13.3

Student	100-point Test $\times$ 5	10-point Quiz $\times$ $\frac{1}{2}$	Composite
Kelly	410	1	411
Kim	405	2	407
Jill	400	5	405
Meg	395	4	399
Sue	390	3	393

(because we think the test is five times more important than the quiz). Now the test is the main determinant of the composite.

If all elements are considered equally important, just add them together without weights. But be sure to check on the equivalence of variabilities first. Otherwise, you may inadvertently weight an element simply because it has greater variability.

The mathematically inclined reader will note that it is possible to weight an element by increasing its variability and not formally applying a weight to the element. Indeed, that is so. However, it takes some mental gymnastics to keep track of that way of proceeding. In addition, it may not make sense to students and parents. Therefore, we recommend first adjusting the variabilities and then applying the rational weights. The mathematically inclined will also note that there are many ways to accomplish the goal of differential weighting. For example, one could convert all scores to T-scores (see Chapter 5) or use roots and powers. In the examples used here, we have employed simple multiplication and division of scores.

We have illustrated this point with just two elements in the composite. That was to keep matters simple. However, the principle holds no matter how many elements enter the composite. In fact, the more elements entering the composite, the more opportunities for this effect to influence the final grade in unintended ways.

The Effect of Zero Scores

In a gradebook spreadsheet, it is not unusual to have a few zero scores. Most frequently, they result from a student's absence or failure to turn in an assignment. Occasionally, the student may have actually scored zero. Zero scores merit special scrutiny because of the huge consequences they have for a student's composite or total score. Sometimes the teacher may not intend for the zero score to have such an effect—but it does.

Consider the sample data in Table 13.5. In this example, the composite is simply the average of the four test scores, with no weighting. Joe's zero score on Test 2 has a devastating effect on his average. Even though he was an A-level student on Tests 1 and 3, his final average is near a failure level. Is this reasonable? Does the teacher intend that this one grade have such momentous consequences? Joe's zero stands out like a sore thumb in the small data set in Table 13.5. However, it might easily be overlooked in a spreadsheet of 30 or 130 students.

What should be done about zero entries? When constructing final grades, the teacher must make a decision about these entries. Three possibilities suggest themselves. First, disregard the zero. Base the grade (the average in this example) on only the other tests.

Table 13.5   Sample Data Set Illustrating Effect of a Zero Score

Student	Test 1	Test 2	Test 3	Test 4	Average
Joe	96	0	90	94	62
Kim	85	90	80	84	85
Siobhan	65	70	75	71	70

This should not be done routinely, lest it encourage students to skip tests and assignments. However, this course of action might be advisable when a student misses a test or an assignment with good reason and there is no opportunity for makeup. A second course of action is to assign the lowest grade that might have occurred if the student had completed the test or assignment but did so at a low level of performance. This would virtually never sink to zero. In the example used in Table 13.5, the score might be 50 or 60. Or the rule might be to assign a grade that is 10 points lower than the lowest score in the class. This method would certainly penalize the student but it would not have the cataclysmic effect of a zero. A third option, of course, is to leave the score at zero and let it have its full effect. The important point here is that the teacher should be alert to the effect of zero scores and make a conscious decision about how to handle them.

Try This!

In Table 13.5, assign Joe a score of 60 for Test 2. Calculate his new average. What do you conclude? Should his score on Test 2 stay at zero?

The Effect of Regression to the Mean

Here is a subtle but potentially pernicious problem that occurs when combining elements to form a composite. The composite will show *less variability* than the elements entering it. This will occur whenever the elements are not perfectly correlated. In practice, the elements are almost never perfectly correlated. The technical name for the phenomenon is **regression to the mean**. We do not need to explain fully why this occurs—but it really does occur. The problem is especially noticeable when each element is in letter grade or percentage form and the composite is expressed as an average in the same coding system. Table 13.6 illustrates the problem for a group of students. The table shows the distribution of letter grades on three tests and on the composite based on the three tests. Notice that the composite has fewer extreme grades (A and B+ at the higher extreme, D and F at the lower extreme) than any of the individual tests.

Table 13.2, introduced earlier, illustrates the problem in terms of individual cases. Notice that there each test ranges from 62 to 90 but the averages range from 68 to 87. For these data, we might have required a score of 90 to get an A. There is an A on each test, but there are no As for the average grade. To avoid this odd happening, simply create a new distribution of grades for the composite, in this case the average. For example, while requiring a 90 to get an A on any test, we might require an 85 to get an A for the composite. A similar adjustment may be made at the lower end of the distribution.

Table 13.6 Illustration of the Effect of Regression to the Mean on a Distribution of Grades for a Group

	Percent of Grades			
Grade	Test 1	Test 2	Test 3	Composite
A	5	10	5	2
B+	15	10	15	8
B	15	20	20	25
C+	25	20	20	30
C	20	25	20	25
D	20	15	5	10
F	5	5	5	0

GRADES FOR NONACADEMIC AREAS

Many report cards call for ratings of nonacademic areas, such as classroom behavior and effort. (Some report cards do *not* provide for such ratings.) The areas rated and the coding systems vary so enormously that it is difficult to formulate advice regarding these matters. Nevertheless, many teachers will complete such ratings, so let us introduce the topic.

Behavioral areas usually appear in the form of a list of specific behaviors. Teachers make ratings with verbal labels. Figure 13.8 shows typical lists of behaviors. Entries in the left column concentrate on interpersonal relations. Entries in the right column concentrate on work habits. Figure 13.9 shows typical systems of verbal labels differing in numbers of categories, used for ratings of behavior and effort. Any of these systems of verbal labels could apply to the statements contained in Figure 13.8.

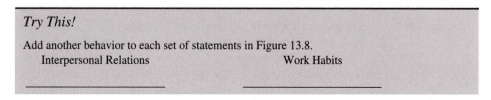

Try This!

Add another behavior to each set of statements in Figure 13.8.

Interpersonal Relations   Work Habits

_____   _____

Rating categories such as those in Figure 13.8 are very common in the early grades, where one teacher usually completes them for all the students in a class. In the upper grades, ratings, if any, are usually limited to effort. The subject area teacher who assigns a grade for academic work in the subject area assigns the rating of effort.

KEY POINTS SUMMARY 13.5   *Three Special Problems in Combining Scores*

Effect of variability on weights
Effect of zero scores on the composite
Effect of regression to the mean

[ ] Cooperates with other students	[ ] Pays attention in class
[ ] Respects others' rights	[ ] Completes homework
[ ] Participates in group activities	[ ] Asks for help when needed
[ ] Is courteous in conversation	[ ] Completes seat work

Figure 13.8 Sample statements for rating behavior and work habits.

How should a teacher rate the behavioral areas? Just as for measures of achievement, ratings of behavioral areas should be reliable and valid. Chapter 10 described some methods for developing reliable and valid methods for assessing behavior. Some of those methods are applicable to ratings of behavioral areas appearing on report cards. In addition, it is useful to recall some of the general principles developed in the chapters on reliability and validity. For example, making the observations more objective, using multiple measurements, and employing a variety of techniques to arrive at the ratings will tend to increase the reliability and validity of the ratings.

REPORT CARDS

Like running shoes, report cards come in a great variety of styles. Some are very basic, some more elaborate. As with the coding systems used by a school, the individual teacher has little to say about the form of the report card. In fact, the teacher may not even see the full report card. The teacher may input grades, and perhaps comments, into an electronic system and the computer prepares the actual report card. The key feature of the report card is that it brings together in one place the grades from different subject areas and, in the upper grades, from different teachers. It may also bring together grades from academic areas and indicators for nonacademic areas, such as behavior, attendance, and so on.

The report card serves an important communication function in education. It is the primary vehicle for communicating with parents. As students progress in grade level, they also become intensely interested in the report card. Hence, it is important that teachers have clear policies for grading and that these policies are understood by parents, students, and other teachers. There appears to be room for significant improvement regarding this aspect of assessment (Cizek et al., 1996; Waltman & Frisbie, 1994).

Figures 13.10 and 13.11 show examples of typical report cards. The first is a very simple one, giving only letter grades in the academic subjects and a count of absences.

Two categories	*Three categories*	*Four categories*
Satisfactory (S)	Excellent (E)	Excellent (E)
Unsatisfactory (U)	Improving (I)	Good (G)
	Unsatisfactory (U)	Passable (P)
		Weak (W)

Figure 13.9 Sample systems of verbal labels used for behavior ratings.

Northwest Area High School   Academic Report

Student Name: _____   ID:_____

Subject	Term 1	2	3	4
English	——	——	——	——
Math	——	——	——	——
Biology	——	——	——	——
History	——	——	——	——
Phys Ed	——	——	——	——
Spanish	——	——	——	——

Days Absent ___

Code

A	Excellent
B	Good
C	Fair
D	Substandard
F	Failure
NG	No Grade

Figure 13.10 A very simple report card.

Southeast Middle School Report Card

Student Name: _____   ID:_____

Subject	Term 1	2	3	4
Reading	——	——	——	——
Language	——	——	——	——
Spelling	——	——	——	——
Science	——	——	——	——
Phys Ed	——	——	——	——
Social Studies	——	——	——	——
Spanish	——	——	——	——
Music/Art	——	——	——	——

Code

90–100	Excellent
80–89	Good
70–79	Fair
60–69	Substandard
Below 60	Failure
NG	No Grade

	Term 1	2	3	4
Respect for authority	——	——	——	——
Cooperation with peers	——	——	——	——
Attention during class	——	——	——	——
Completion of homework	——	——	——	——
Apparent effort	——	——	——	——
Neatness	——	——	——	——

Code

S: Satisfactory

N: Needs Improvement

U: Unsatisfactory

Days   Absent ___   Tardy ___

Figure 13.11 A more elaborate report card.

The second is more elaborate. It contains grades in the academic subjects as well as a variety of behavioral ratings and reports of absence and tardiness.

OTHER PROCEDURES FOR REPORTING TO PARENTS

The report card is only one mechanism for providing feedback to parents. There are several other mechanisms. Let us examine three of them. As is true for report cards, these other mechanisms will vary from one school system to another. Even within a school system, the mechanisms may vary by grade level (e.g., from elementary to high school levels).

Parent-Teacher Conference

Many schools hold **parent-teacher conferences**. The typical scenario is that a teacher meets with one or both parents of a child for about 15 minutes. Very often, the conference occurs shortly after a report card period. The conference allows for a face-to-face exchange, as opposed to the more impersonal, one-way communication provided by the report card. The teacher can elaborate on the basis for grades, discuss behavioral observations, and suggest ways the parents might help the child's progress. The parents, in turn, can raise questions about the child's progress, express concerns about a teacher's approach, and perhaps add perspective about factors that might be affecting the child's performance.

Practices regarding parent-teacher conferences vary widely. In some schools, parents are expected to participate and most do. In other schools, the conferences may be optional. A teacher and parent may meet only at the expressed request of one or the other. The usual context for such a request is either low academic grades or a behavioral problem.

No doubt, the parent-teacher conference may cause anxiety: for both teacher and parent. It can be a particularly anxious experience for new teachers. (It can be equally daunting for parents new to the process.) With experience, both teachers and parents become

Figure 13.12 Parent-teacher conferences may cause anxiety.

(STONE SOUP © 2004 Jan Eliot. Reprinted with permission of UNIVERSAL PRESS SYNDICATE. All rights reserved.)

more proficient and less anxious in using this reporting mechanism. Here are 10 suggestions for teachers when conducting a parent-teacher conference.

1. Organize your materials before beginning the conferences. Have a folder or other set of documents for each student. If possible, have them in the order that parents will appear. It may be helpful to have examples of the student's work in addition to the student's grades. Also, have a brief but formal agenda you intend to follow with each visit. The agenda might be as follows: review grades, summarize special strengths, suggest areas needing improvement, comment on behavior, solicit questions, answer questions, conclude with notes about upcoming topics and assignments.

2. Focus first on the student's achievement. That should be the main topic. If there are behavioral problems, discuss these after treating achievement.

3. Be ready to explain your rationale for grading and your methods for assessment. Very often, the parent will not know how a grade was determined.

4. If you have given behavioral ratings—for example, about effort or conduct—try to be as explicit as possible about the basis for the ratings.

5. The child's behavior may not be the same at home as in your classroom. Some children who misbehave in your classroom may be perfect angels at home. Some children who are terrors at home may behave wonderfully in your classroom. Thus, don't be completely surprised if your perception of the child differs from that of the parents. You may both be right.

6. Be honest in reporting. Don't sugarcoat your oral report. Specifically, don't tell the parent the child is doing fine if the child is not.

7. Be ready with specific suggestions for ways the parents can help. For example, alert the parents to topics that will be coming up in the near future. For lower grade students, it may be helpful to provide parents with worksheets and exercises that the parents can use with the child.

8. Some parents may refer to or ask questions about students other than their child. For example, a parent may ask, "Did Jan (the parent's child) do worse than Josie (Jan's friend) on that science test?" It is not appropriate to refer to any other student's performance during a conference.

9. Make sure you know whom to call upon if you encounter a particularly obnoxious parent. The appropriate person may be the principal, assistant principal, or counselor. Find this out before beginning a round of parent-teacher conferences.

10. If the conference includes reference to standardized test results, see the suggestions in the next section on that topic.

Reporting Standardized Test Results to Parents

Another type of feedback to parents is a report of results from standardized tests. Parents ordinarily receive results from standardized tests administered in the schools. In most schools, such tests are administered once per year. The tests may be commercially available test batteries or state-prepared tests. Publishers of standardized tests, those described in Chapter 11, have reports specifically designed for parents. These reports are usually less detailed than the reports designed for teachers. Whereas the teacher report will often contain three or four different types of scores (e.g., percentiles, stanines, grade equivalents,

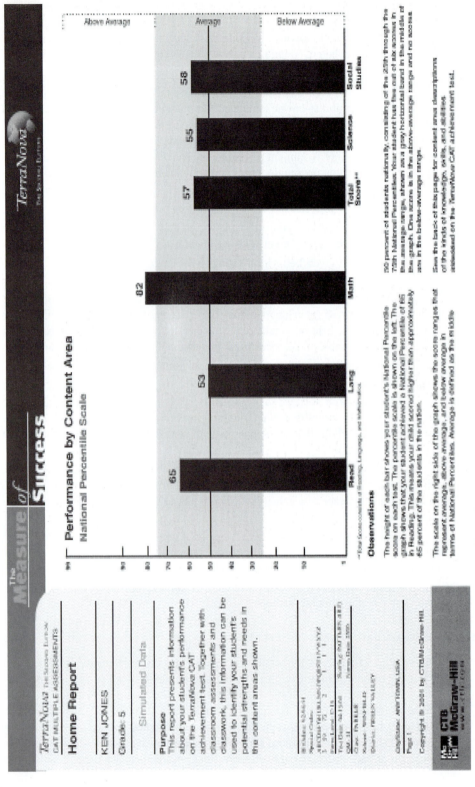

Figure 13.13 Sample parent report, called a Home Report, for the Terra Nova test battery. (Sample Home Report from TerraNova The 2nd Edition (CAT); reproduced with permission of The McGraw-Hill Companies, Inc.)

and standard scores), the parent report will usually have only one type of score. Percentiles and stanines are the common scores for parent reports. The parent reports usually contain brief descriptions of the tests, too. Increasingly, the parent reports incorporate some type of narrative; that is, translation of the numerical scores into verbal descriptions.

Figure 13.13 shows an example of a parent report from a standardized test. The report uses percentile scores (only) presented in a graphic format. Notice the verbal descriptors (along the right side of the report) for different ranges in the percentile scale. Compare this with a sample report for a teacher in Chapter 11 (p. 252). Notice how simple the parent report is in comparison with the teacher report.

Some schools may prepare their own reports of test scores for parents rather than using a report format prepared by a publisher or state. These locally prepared reports may not have the same elegance of commercially prepared reports. However, a locally prepared report can be effective. It should contain the following elements:

- Child's name and grade
- Date of administration
- Name of the test, using the full name rather than an abbreviation (e.g., Stanford Achievement Test rather than SAT, an abbreviation that could be particularly confusing)
- Full titles of specific tests being reported (e.g., Reading Comprehension rather than RC)
- Brief description of the type of score used for the report (e.g., percentile or stanine, such as those given in the Glossary for this book)

It is useful, although not required, to have a profile of scores rather than just a list of scores. As is the case for commercially prepared reports, we recommend use of only one type of score rather than the multiplicity of scores provided on a teacher's report. Figure 13.14

Report of Scores on the New York Test of Basic Skills

For ___Kelly L___   Grade__6__   Tested___1-10-05___

	Stanine*	Profile
Word Analysis Skills	6	1 2 3 4 5 6 7 8 9
Reading Comprehension	7	1 2 3 4 5 6 7 8 9
Spelling	4	1 2 3 4 5 6 7 8 9
Math Computation	5	1 2 3 4 5 6 7 8 9
Math Concepts	7	1 2 3 4 5 6 7 8 9
Science	4	1 2 3 4 5 6 7 8 9
Social Studies	7	1 2 3 4 5 6 7 8 9
Total Battery Score	6	1 2 3 4 5 6 7 8 9

*The stanine is a simple 9-point scale ranging from 1 (low) to 9 (high), with 5 being average. These stanines are based on the national norms for this test battery. Thus, your child is compared with a national group of students at this grade level.

Figure 13.14 Sample of locally prepared report of standardized test scores.

shows an example of a simple, locally prepared report of standardized test scores using stanines. For a useful summary of the great variety of reports sent to parents, along with recommendations for such reports, see Goodman and Hambleton (2004).

Here are eight suggestions for conversing with parents about reports of standardized test scores.

1. Be sure you understand the type of score used in the report to parents. If necessary, review the definitions of scores in Chapter 5.

2. Be sure you understand the nature of the norm group used for the report (e.g., national, state, or local norm).

3. Give the parent a brief explanation of both the type of score and the norm group. Do not assume the parent already knows about these matters.

4. Do not dismiss the results as unimportant. They are important to the parent.

5. If the results are highly suspect for a student, for example, well below how the student usually performs—try to investigate this before talking to the parent.

6. Refer to the degree of congruence between the test results and other information (e.g., classroom work) for the student. In most cases, the different sources of information will be reasonably consistent and will reinforce one another. If the sources of information are discrepant, try to explain why this might be so. Try to present an integrated picture.

7. Use the conversation about the test results to elicit the parent's help with the child's schoolwork and overall development.

8. Some parents may raise questions that you cannot answer (e.g., about the technical characteristics of the test). Before meeting with parents, find out to whom you should refer such questions. It may be the principal, counselor, or school psychologist. Don't try to go beyond your competence in answering questions. It is a mark of a professional to know when to seek outside help or make a referral.

Some schools may not routinely provide results of standardized tests to parents. In that case, please be aware that parents have a legal right to the information if they ask for it. The relevant law is the **Family Educational Rights and Privacy Act (FERPA)** of 1994, sometimes called the Buckley amendment. FERPA has two main thrusts. First, the individual (or, in the case of minors, a parent or guardian) has a right of access to information about the individual. Second, institutions (e.g., schools) may not reveal to a third-party information about the individual without the individual's consent. Of course, the law has many details about the exact meaning of these provisions, but the two principles just identified are the main ideas. Here's the practical application to the current topic: Parents have a right to see test scores for their children.

Other Communications

The report card, the parent-teacher conference, and reports of standardized test results are the primary means of communicating with parents about students' progress. However, there are other mechanisms. Particularly in the lower grades, it is not unusual to send home a regular stream of completed assignments. Of course, students know how they have done on major tests, projects, and so on. Some of these may find their way into the hands of parents. Some will not. Even when a teacher specifically sends something home by way of the student, there is no guarantee that the item will reach its destination. Many a communication finds its fate crumpled at the bottom of a book bag or locker, only to surface at the beginning of summer vacation: a bit late. In ideal situations, teachers and parents will interact on a regular basis at school events or other informal venues. Every teacher needs to be alert to opportunities for communication beyond the formal ones outlined earlier.

LEGAL CONSIDERATIONS

In today's litigious society, some teachers may worry about the legal ramifications of their grading practices. Indeed suits have been brought over grades. A parent may feel that a grade has been unfairly assigned and bring suit, hoping that the court will overturn the grade. Can we provide any guidance to teachers about this matter? Yes. Based on analysis of how the courts have dealt with such cases, we formulate the following two generalizations.

First, the courts give great deference to the judgments of educators. Judges are very reluctant to substitute their opinions for those of teachers about the grading of students' work. This deference to educators includes both what should be taught—the content of instruction—and how it should be graded—the assessment.

Second, while deferring to educators' judgments regarding methods of assessment, the courts do have some minimal criteria for what is acceptable. To put it positively, the grading procedures should be rational and evenhanded. To put it negatively, the procedures cannot be arbitrary, capricious, or bad-faith efforts. Within these broad guidelines, great discretion is afforded to educators. Let us give some examples. Assigning grades by lottery would be unacceptable. That is not a rational procedure. It is arbitrary. Using one set of criteria for boys and another set for girls would be unacceptable. That is hardly evenhanded. However, any of the rationales we discussed earlier—for example, grading in relation to ability or grading by reference to other students' performance—would be acceptable. They are all rational procedures. We might debate which is the best rationale, but none of them are arbitrary, capricious, illogical, or just plain stupid. Suppose a teacher weights one test 20% and another test 80% to arrive at a final grade. In the teacher's judgment, the second test is far more important than the first. The courts are loath to meddle with such judgments.

Here is advice from a practical perspective. Be sure to have a rationale for your grading and apply your procedures fairly. If you do so, someone may still file suit. In our judicial system, it is easy to file suit. However, it is unlikely that the suit will be successful if your grading is rational and evenhanded. For review of court cases illustrating the principles outlined here, see Alexander and Alexander (2001); and Fischer, Schimmel, and Kelly (1999).

Now, here is a separate legal consideration. Final responsibility for awarding grades that become part of a student's official school record rests with the school administration, not the individual teacher. Of course, the individual teacher is expected to assign grades. However, a superintendent or principal has the legal authority to change the grade assigned by a teacher. School administrators are very reluctant to take such action. They rarely do so. It can cause considerable friction between teachers and administrators. In addition, administrators generally do not have the time and informational resources to be assigning grades. Nevertheless, in rare circumstances, an administrator may change a grade and has a legal right to do so.

This section refers to the grades assigned in ordinary classroom situations. Somewhat different principles and precedents apply to such matters as state-mandated minimal competency tests for graduation and the use of tests for placing students in special education classes. Chapter 14 treats these other cases.

PRACTICAL ADVICE

1. The most important prelude to assigning grades competently is having good assessments. The most important prelude to having good assessments is having a good assessment plan. Therefore, before worrying about grades, make sure you have good assessments and an assessment plan.

2. Find out if your school has an explicit rationale for grading. If it does, study it carefully and implement it. If it does not, clarify your own thinking about the rationale you will adopt.

3. Study the details of the grade coding system used by your school (e.g., letter grades, percentages). Before attempting to assign your own grades, make sure you understand the school's system.

4. Learn to use an electronic spreadsheet to record and manipulate your grades. It may take a bit of time to become proficient with one of these spreadsheets, but it will save you an enormous amount of time in the long run.

5. When determining grades, carefully consider the effects of weights, variability, and zero scores on the final grade.

6. For conducting parent-teacher conferences, review the specific suggestions made on pages 332–333.

7. Use the report card, reports of standardized tests, and other means of communication to provide feedback to parents and to elicit parents' help with their child's progress.

SUMMARY

1. Grading refers to combining a number of specific assessments into a composite or total, translating the composite into a coding system, and reporting the results in a formal way.

2. Grades serve a variety of purposes. Most importantly, they serve as feedback to students, parents, and teachers. Grades also serve a host of administrative purposes. And grades serve as motivators.

3. There are five major rationales for grading, sometimes referred to as philosophies of grading. They are grading relative to a fixed standard, to group performance, to ability, to effort, and to improvement. All are legitimate positions, each with advantages and disadvantages. The most suitable position seems to be grading in relation to a fixed standard tempered by reference to group performance.

4. Grades can be expressed as letters, percentages, verbal labels, checklists, or in the form of narrative reports.

5. For purposes of combining scores on separate assessments, it is helpful to use an electronic spreadsheet.

6. When combining separate assessments to arrive at a final grade, be alert to the effect of differential variability, zero scores, and the regression phenomenon.

7. Report cards are a primary mechanism for reporting grades to students and, more especially, to parents. Report cards come in an enormous variety of formats. Many call for behavioral ratings as well as grades in academic subjects.

8. Parent-teacher conferences are another mechanism for communicating student progress. Careful planning for the conference can make it an effective means of communication.

9. Parents usually receive reports of standardized test results for their children. Teachers may need to help parents interpret the reports.

10. In a legal context, the courts defer to educators' judgments about student grades, requiring only that the grading process is not arbitrary, capricious, or done in bad faith.

KEY TERMS

checklist grading
FERPA (Family Educational Rights and Privacy Act)

grade book
grading
narrative reports

parent-teacher conferences
regression to the mean
spreadsheet

EXERCISES

1. List appropriate verbal labels for the following percentage grades. Compare your labels with those developed by another person.

Percent	Verbal label
95–100	_____
80–85	_____
60–65	_____

2. Here are composite scores for several students. They are averages of percentages on three tests. What letter grades would you assign to the averages? Decide for yourself what letter grading system to use, such as 5-point, 10-point, 13-point, etc.

Average Score: 98   95   92   87   84   77   70   69   58

Letter Grade: __ __ __ __ __ __ __ __ __

3. This is a follow-up to an earlier TRY THIS! exercise. Download one of the free or free trial copies of a gradebook from the Web. Enter your own sample data (use the data in the next exercise or devise your own sample). Try out different features of the gradebook.

4. Enter the scores listed below into a spreadsheet. Use a generic spreadsheet, such as Excel, or download a free trial copy of a gradebook from the Web. Then complete steps a–e.

Student	Test 1	Test 2	Quiz 1	Quiz 2	Quiz 3	Project	Total	Grade
Matt	98	85	10	8	8	A−	___	___
Ned	90	78	7	6	0	B−	___	___
Abby	72	83	9	6	7	B+	___	___
Kelly	68	84	9	8	6	C+	___	___

   a. Convert the letter grades to percents. Devise your own system for doing so. See Figure 13.2 for suggestions.

b. Decide what to do about Ned's 0 score on Quiz 3. (He was absent for a week with chicken pox.)

c. Give Tests 1 and 2 weights of 2.

d. Using the newly weighted scores, add the scores together to get the Total.

e. Assign a final letter grade to the Total scores. Devise your own system for assigning final letter grades. See Figure 13.3 for suggestions.

5. Here is a set of behavioral ratings from a report card. What observations might serve as a basis for the ratings? Compare your notes with another person's.

Area Rated	Basis for the Rating
Completes homework	_____
Works cooperatively	_____
Pays attention in class	_____
Respects others' rights	_____
Effort	_____

6. Get a report card from any school. Use one of your old report cards, if convenient.

   a. What type of grade *coding system* does it use?

   b. Does it give any indication of the *rationale* for grading?

   c. Are there any *behavioral ratings*?

Chapter 14

Educational Assessment and the Law

OBJECTIVES

- Distinguish among the three meanings of "the law."
- Identify basic terms used to identify laws.
- For each of the following laws, describe the main implications for assessment:
  - 14th Amendment
  - Civil Rights Act
  - Elementary and Secondary Education Act (ESEA)
  - Rehabilitation Act, and the Americans With Disabilities Act (ADA)
  - Individuals With Disabilities Education Act (IDEA)
  - No Child Left Behind (NCLB) Act
  - Family Educational Rights and Privacy Act (FERPA)
- Summarize key court decisions about the uses of assessment.

What This Chapter Is About

This chapter begins by describing what is meant by the term "the law," including some of the specialized language used in the law. Then, attention focuses on major laws in which assessment plays a prominent role. Finally, several famous court cases are summarized to illustrate how the laws are applied in particular situations.

Why This Topic Is Important

Laws significantly influence the way education is conducted today. For example, the No Child Left Behind (NCLB) Act and the Individuals With Disabilities Education Act influence numerous aspects of everyday educational activities. Assessment issues are crucial in implementing these laws. Everyone in education needs familiarity with the origin of these laws and their implications for educational practice.

DEFINITION OF LAWS

In ordinary conversation, the word "law" refers to a written rule originating with some legislative body. For instance, in most states, there is a law that the speed limit on rural interstate highways is 65 miles per hour. There is a law that one must be 21 years old to purchase alcoholic beverages. However, this common meaning of the word law is not sufficient for our purposes. To discuss the interface of assessment and the law requires an expanded conception of the source of laws. Specifically, laws originate from three sources.

The first type of law is **statutory law** or **legislation**. This is the common meaning of the term law. These laws originate with a legislative body, such as the U.S. Congress, state legislature, or local governing body. Typically, the legislature's action must be endorsed by an executive (e.g., the president or governor) before becoming law. For simplicity, we include the U.S. Constitution in this first category; more technically, it is in a category by itself. The second type of law is **administrative law** or **regulations**. An administrative agency, ordinarily in the executive branch of government, prepares these regulations. Very often, they provide the details on implementing a particular law. Although not passed by a legislature, these regulations usually have the force of law. The third type of law is **case law**; that is, court decisions. Courts interpret the meaning of laws when applied in particular circumstances. A court's decision, once rendered, has the force of law, at least within the jurisdiction of the court. Included within our definition of court decisions are consent decrees and consent orders. In these instances, the court does not render a decision in favor of one of the contesting parties, but in the process of contesting the issue, the parties reach agreement as to how the issue will be resolved. It is important to note that the force of the law is much the same regardless of its origin: statutory, administrative, or case. That is, all these sources give rise to laws that must be obeyed.

BASIC TERMINOLOGY

Most of the laws relevant to assessment are federal in origin. There are a few state laws and even, occasionally, a local law related to testing. Further, states usually have specific laws and regulations designed to implement federal laws within the state's organizational structure. However, we concentrate here on federal laws because they are the dominant forces related to testing. Reference to laws brings with it a blizzard of numbers and initials. To assist with later review of specific laws, we identify the following special terms and abbreviations.

U.S.C. stands for United States Code. This means a law passed by the U.S. Congress. A title number, identifying the general area of law, precedes the initials U.S.C. and a section number follows the initials. For example, 29 U.S.C. §791 (Title 29, United States

---

KEY POINTS SUMMARY 14.1 *Three Sources of Laws*

- Statutory law; legislation
- Administrative law; regulations
- Case law; court cases

Code, Section 791) designates part of the Rehabilitation Act described later. (The symbol § is read as "section.")

C.F.R. stands for Code of Federal Regulations. This is administrative law, whereas U.S.C. is statutory law. Numbers preceding and following "C.F.R." identify the particular regulation. For example, 34 C.F.R. Part 200 contains the regulations for NCLB.

P.L. stands for public law. A specific P.L. (e.g., P.L. 94–142) has two parts. The first part (94) indicates the congressional year, here the 94th Congress. The second part indicates the numbered law within that congressional year, here the 142nd law enacted by the 94th Congress. The P.L. number is unrelated to the U.S.C. number. The P.L. number for some laws—including our example here, P.L. 94–142—becomes the popular method for referencing the law. In other instances, the popular name for a law comes from the law's title—for example, No Child Left Behind or an acronym, such as IDEA: the Individuals With Disabilities Education Act. IDEA is actually a successor to P.L. 94–142. One goes by an acronym, the other by a P.L. number.

We list the major laws related to testing in Figure 14.1 roughly in historical sequence. However, several points must be emphasized about this order. First, many of these laws are under continual revision. This most often occurs by amendment, where the name and number of the law remain the same but amendments are attached. At other times, the revision is so sweeping as to merit a new name and number, but many of the basic ideas for the new law come from the earlier version. Tracing the lineage of a particular law can be very challenging. Second, partly because of these changes, what once was legal may now be illegal and vice versa. Third, among the laws we consider, there is much cross-referencing. The laws listed in Figure 14.1 form a web or network. They are not isolated, entirely independent entities. For example, one law may indicate that it incorporates a definition from another law. In such a case, in order to interpret one law the reader must consult the other law. Here is an important related point: Names change without change in meaning. For example, earlier laws referred to "handicapped" but more recent laws use the term "disabled" or "persons with disabilities" to identify the same category; see Data Research (1994) as well as the preamble to 42 U.S.C. §2000 for this particular change. Earlier documents also referred to Negroes, whereas the term African-Americans now prevails. Fourth, most "laws" have both statutory and administrative versions. One needs to consult both sources for a full understanding of "the law."

For readers interested in pursuing the full text of laws or court cases, Table 14.1 lists several useful sources. United States laws (U.S.C.s) and regulations (C.F.R.s) are available on general websites. In addition, various government agencies maintain their own websites, including the laws and regulations the agencies oversee. Good examples are the

Table 14.1 Useful Sources of Information on Laws and Court Cases

For the full text of U.S. laws (codes), go to: http://uscode.house.gov/search/criteria.php

For the full text of U.S. regulations, go to: http://www.gpoaccess.gov/nara/index.html

For Individuals With Disabilities Education Act, go to: http://www.ed.gov/offices/OSERS/IDEA/

For No Child Left Behind Act of 2001, go to: http://www.ed.gov/nclb

For court cases, access: LexisNexis or Westlaw, which also contain laws and regulations.

For court cases, laws, and regulations, as well as a variety of legal services, go to FindLaw.com websites for IDEA and NCLB. Often, these websites also include ancillary materials, such as simplified versions of the laws and training programs related to implementing the laws. For court cases, there are two standard databases: LexisNexis and Westlaw. Each database maintains a comprehensive and cross-referenced list of court decisions. These are essential tools for lawyers. They are very useful, although not essential, sources for educators interested in the interface of assessment and the law. Most major academic libraries subscribe to at least one of these databases.

Be aware that traditions for recording and citing matters in the law are quite different than they are in the fields of education, psychology, and other social sciences. To begin searching in the law, we recommend reading "For Social Scientists: How to Find the Law," which is Appendix C in Monahan and Walker (2002). In addition, try Exercise 5 at the end of this chapter.

Try This!

Access the website for either IDEA or NCLB, as given in Table 14.1. Find out how to download a copy of the entire law. To verify that you have successfully accessed the law, indicate here how many pages the law has.

IDEA _____   NCLB _____

Why Is It So Confusing?

Why does the material on legal issues related to assessment, indeed to all of education, seem so confusing? You would think that legal matters would be crystal clear. Consider the law that the posted speed limit is 65 miles per hour. That is very clear. The fact is that many legal matters related to education are not so clear. There are several reasons for this lack of clarity. It should help our understanding of the whole area to make these reasons explicit.

First, a given law may go by several different names. Every federal law has a P.L. number, as described earlier (e.g., P.L. 94–142). Every federal law also has a "U.S.C." number (e.g., 20 U.S.C. §1400). Many laws also go by their official, verbal titles (e.g., Individuals With Disabilities Education Act). Many laws go by their abbreviated titles (e.g., IDEA or ADA). Thus, four different sources may all refer to the same law but with different "tags."

Second, the legislative bodies responsible for laws frequently revise them. Some of the laws are under almost continual revision. For example, the well-known No Child Left Behind (NCLB) Act is technically a revision of the Elementary and Secondary Education Act (ESEA) of 1965. The original IDEA law from 1990 turned into IDEA-97 and then IDEA 2004 (technically, Individuals With Disabilities Education Improvement Act of 2004, but still known as IDEA). Such revisions are common. Hence, reference to IDEA or to ESEA becomes ambiguous. In addition, revisions of the laws sometimes carry a new P.L. number or title and sometimes they do not.

Third, as indicated earlier, there are statutory laws and administrative laws (regulations). Regulations appear for almost every statutory law. Often, the regulations do not appear until more than a year after the statutory law has been enacted. For example, IDEA-97 was signed by President Clinton on June 4, 1997. The "final regs" did not appear until

March 12, 1999, nearly two years later. IDEA 2004 was signed into law by President Bush in December 2004; final regulations will probably appear in 2006. Also, the regulations may change without the statutory law changing. Further, the way that regulations actually implement the statutory law is sometimes surprising. Complaints about a particular law may not apply to the (statutory) law but may really be about the regulations.

Fourth, court rulings may affect interpretation of laws. Thus, when someone says "According to the law, you must do this," what this may mean is "A court's interpretation of the law is that you must do this." Adding to confusion on this point is the fact that court rulings differ in their applicability. This occurs in two rather different ways. On the one hand, courts rule in specific cases, with all their surrounding circumstances. A change in circumstances might result in a change in how the court would apply the law. On the other hand, rulings of district and circuit courts apply, strictly, only within their respective jurisdictions. Thus, a court in one district may interpret the law one way, while a court in another district may conclude differently.

For all of these reasons, understanding the applicability of laws to educational assessment presents a real challenge. Nevertheless, some understanding of these matters is necessary. The following sections identify the major laws relevant to assessment, with an emphasis on the practical implications. In general, these laws have many provisions beyond those related to assessment. We concentrate on the assessment issues, with just occasional reference to other aspects of the laws.

LAWS RELATED TO ASSESSMENT

Figure 14.1 lists the statutory laws of primary importance in the field of educational assessment. The laws appear approximately in chronological order. Lines show major connections between the laws (e.g., revisions or significant amendments). However, there is much cross-referencing among many of the laws. For example, one law may specifically adopt the definitions originally given in another law. After describing these laws, we will examine some relevant court decisions (case law).

The 14th Amendment

The first law relevant to assessment is the 14th amendment to the U.S. Constitution, specifically, Section 1. One part of Section 1 is the "due process" clause. Another part is the "equal protection" clause. Table 14.2 presents Section 1 of the 14th amendment, with key words marked in boldface. The **equal protection clause** is the most important part for testing. The 14th amendment was ratified in 1868. Its principal intent was to prevent states (mainly the Confederate states) from enacting laws restricting the rights of former slaves. Who would have thought that a constitutional amendment enacted in 1868, in the aftermath of the U.S. Civil War, would relate to the use of tests today? It does. Here is the key notion: If a test (or anything else) operates to arbitrarily restrict the rights (including opportunities) of some individuals (citizens), then the equal protection clause of the 14th amendment becomes relevant.[1]

---

[1] The 5th amendment also has a "due process" clause. It deals with matters such as double jeopardy, self-incrimination, and other items not relevant to our considerations here.

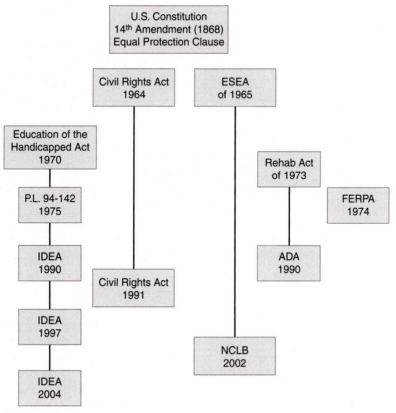

Figure 14.1 Major laws related to educational assessment.

When developing laws reviewed here, the U.S. Congress has frequently referenced the 14th amendment. Occasionally, Congress has also used two other reference points. The first is the power to regulate interstate commerce, given to Congress in Article I, Section 8(3) of the U.S. Constitution: "To regulate commerce with foreign nations, and among the several states, and with the Indian tribes." The second reference point is controlling purse strings related to federal programs. If a state or other agency does not take certain actions, Congress withholds federal funds from that state or agency. Controlling the purse strings is an enormously powerful mechanism. For example, states are not required to participate in all the testing mandated by No Child Left Behind. However, if they do not participate, they do not receive any Title I funds from the federal government: a powerful incentive to participate.

Table 14.2   Section 1 of the 14th Amendment of the U.S. Constitution

All persons born or naturalized in the United States, and subject to the jurisdiction thereof, are citizens of the United States and of the state wherein they reside. No state shall make or enforce any law which shall abridge the privileges or immunities of citizens of the United States; nor shall any state deprive any person of life, liberty, or property, without **due process** of law; nor deny to any person within its jurisdiction the **equal protection** of the laws. [Emphasis added.]

The Civil Rights Acts of 1964 and 1991

The mid-1960s, the era of the civil rights movement in the United States, witnessed passage of one of the most influential pieces of legislation relevant to assessment in modern times: the Civil Rights Act of 1964. Specifically, Title VII of this act dealt with employment discrimination. In fact, one popular name of the Civil Rights Act was the Equal Employment Opportunity Act. The principal concern was that employers might arrange their employment procedures, including tests, to exclude African-Americans. The resulting laws ultimately covered other minority groups, including women, but the primary target group was African-Americans. The Civil Rights Act of 1964 created the Equal Employment Opportunity Commission (EEOC). The EEOC, in turn, created the Uniform Guidelines on Employee Selection (EEOC, 1978), a prime example of administrative law. Congress enacted a major revision of the Civil Rights Act in 1991. Most of the 1964 provisions remained intact. However, there was one major change relevant to employment testing, namely the prohibition of what was called subgroup norming.

Although the principal thrust of the Civil Rights Acts was in the area of employment, the laws have relevance to educational assessment. Specifically, the legality of high school graduation tests has been challenged under the Civil Rights Acts. The core argument goes like this: It is common on such tests for minority group students to score lower than majority group students. The tests prevent the minority students from receiving a high school diploma. Therefore, the argument goes, use of the tests violates the Civil Rights Acts (as well as the 14th amendment). In several court cases described later, we will see how this argument has fared in the courts.

Elementary and Secondary Education Act of 1965

The Elementary and Secondary Education Act (ESEA) of 1965 was enacted in the same era as the first Civil Rights Act. ESEA represented a major increase in the federal government's activity in education. Alexander and Alexander (2001, p. 65) called ESEA "the most important elementary and secondary program ever enacted by Congress." Previously, education was considered a local matter. Local schools, governed by locally elected or appointed school boards, had principal responsibility for educational decisions. To be sure, states had some authority to establish broad policies. However, the emphasis was on local control. For many of the same reasons underlying the Civil Rights Act, the U.S. Congress became active in education. Primary target groups were minority students, the disadvantaged, and students performing at substantially below average levels.

ESEA had two primary implications for assessment and testing. First, the act required that newly established programs be evaluated. Typically, this meant the use of standardized tests. Hence, ESEA resulted in substantial increases in the use of the types of tests we described in Chapter 11 (e.g., standardized achievement batteries and diagnostic tests in reading and math). Second, this emphasis on evaluation helped fuel the emerging accountability movement. Not only were the new federally funded programs subject to evaluation, but everything was to be evaluated. Furthermore, there was a new emphasis on public reporting of the results of evaluations. The No Child Left Behind Act, described later in this chapter, is truly the offspring of the original ESEA.

Rehabilitation Act of 1973, and the Americans With Disabilities Act of 1990

Two closely related laws are the Rehabilitation Act of 1973 (29 U.S.C. §701; P.L. 93–112) and the Americans With Disabilities Act of 1990 (ADA; 42 U.S.C. §12101; P.L. 101–336). In many ways, the ADA is a revision and expansion of the Rehabilitation Act, although the latter remains in effect. Section 504 is the particularly relevant part of the Rehabilitation Act. The primary purpose of these laws was to provide access for the handicapped, with initial focus on such items as architectural barriers. Could a person in a wheelchair use the local public library? Thus, the international symbol for "handicapped accessible" is a wheelchair. However, these laws construe the terms handicapped or disabled very broadly to include not only physical handicaps but also psychological or mental disabilities. The definition includes "specific learning disabilities," which has led to an explosive growth in the number of persons and types of "barriers" covered by the laws.

Environmental adjustments for the persons with disabilities are often called **accommodations**. Ramps and elevators are obvious accommodations for persons in wheelchairs. Accommodations in testing conditions may involve large-print editions of tests for people with visual handicaps. A particularly controversial accommodation is extending the time limits on tests. The crucial question is whether an accommodation "levels the playing field" for the person with a disability or gives that person an unfair advantage over others who do not receive the accommodation. More technically, an accommodation in testing should render the test's validity and norms equally applicable to disabled and nondisabled examinees. Consider a reading comprehension test. Its purpose is to determine understanding of the printed word. A person with limited vision may need a large-print version of the test. For such a person, a normal-print version is a test of vision, not reading comprehension. A person with normal vision will perform no better on the large-print version than on the normal-print version. Thus, the large-print version seems an entirely reasonable accommodation. Now consider use of a reader for the test; that is, someone who reads the test to the person with a visual disability. This accommodation may very well change the nature of what is being measured. The test may now measure listening comprehension rather than reading comprehension. Further, everyone—both visually disabled and nondisabled persons—may do better with a reader.

Consider also the question of extending the time limit on a test, an accommodation often proposed for certain learning disability cases. If the test is a pure power test (see p. 20 in Chapter 1), giving additional time to someone who wants more time should be acceptable. However, very few tests are pure power tests. The student with a learning disability may do better with more time, but so might other examinees (or they may not).

Numerous studies are currently being directed at the effects of various accommodations on test performance. Clearly, we have much to learn about this topic. Several sources have provided useful summaries of practices, regulations, and research on accommodations for various types of assessments and groups of students, such as students with learning disabilities, English language learners, etc. (Abedi, Hofstetter, & Lord, 2004; Camara, 2001; Nester, 1994; Pitoniak & Royer, 2001; Thurlow, Elliott, & Ysseldyke, 1998; Thurlow & Ysseldyke, 2002; Willingham et al., 1988). Among the important points made in these sources are the following. First, practices and regulations are in continual flux, making it difficult to develop generalizations. Second, the anticipated effects of an accommodation may not be realized. For example, extended time (or any other change) may

Table 14.3 Purposes of the Americans With Disabilities Act

(1) to provide a clear and comprehensive national mandate for the elimination of discrimination against individuals with disabilities;

(2) to provide clear, strong, consistent, enforceable standards addressing discrimination against individuals with disabilities;

(3) to ensure that the Federal government plays a central role in enforcing the standards . . . and

(4) to invoke the sweep of congressional authority, including the power to enforce the fourteenth amendment and to regulate commerce, in order to address the major areas of discrimination faced day-to-day by people with disabilities.

not improve scores for the target group; or, the change may improve scores for all students, not just for those in the target group. In the latter circumstance, the change does not "level the playing field" but actually gives an unfair advantage. Some accommodations work as intended, but not all do so. Third, there is the question of whether scores derived from a test administered with accommodations should be "flagged"; that is, marked to indicate the nonstandard administration. This is a policy issue on which testing professionals have no consensus position.

Current practice makes a distinction between an *accommodation* and a *modification* of an assessment. In an accommodation, the student is taking essentially the same test as other students but with some change in testing conditions (e.g., with a large-print edition or with an extended time limit). A modification involves an attempt to assess a given skill or trait but with an essentially different methodology.

Table 14.3 gives the statement of purpose for the ADA.[2] Notice the reference to the 14th amendment and to Congress's power to regulate commerce. Basic definitions covered by the ADA are essentially the same as those for IDEA shown in Table 14.4.

Individuals With Disabilities Education Act: IDEA 2004 and Its Predecessors

A succession of laws beginning in 1970 treated individuals with disabilities in educational settings. For a history of earlier laws and court cases dealing with the disabled, see Alexander and Alexander (2001). We list here the major landmarks, omitting the many intermediate revisions and amendments. The first law was Education of the Handicapped Act (EHA) enacted in 1970. A major revision was entitled Education for All Handicapped Children, enacted in 1975. This was P.L. 94–142, a tag that stuck and is still used today. This law was amended at least four times (each time receiving a new P.L. number). With the amendments in 1990, the law was renamed Individuals With Disabilities Education Act, yielding the well-recognized acronym **IDEA**. There was a major revision in 1997 and another in 2004, officially entitled Individuals With Disabilities Education Improvement Act of 2004 (IDEA; 20 U.S.C. §1400; P.L. 108–446). Popularly the law is known as

---

[2] In Table 14.3, as well as in Tables 14.4 to 14.9, we quote directly from the laws but present only excerpts in order to illustrate certain points. For ease of reading, we have omitted section numbers and have reformatted the text.

Table 14.4   IDEA's Definitions of Disability

The term '**child with a disability**' means a child—

- with mental retardation, hearing impairments (including deafness), speech or language impairments, visual impairments (including blindness), serious emotional disturbance (referred to in this title as 'emotional disturbance'), orthopedic impairments, autism, traumatic brain injury, other health impairments, or specific learning disabilities; and
- who, by reason thereof, needs special education and related services.

CHILD AGED 3 THROUGH 9—The term 'child with a disability' for a child aged 3 through 9 (or any subset of that age range, including ages 3 through 5), may, at the discretion of the State and the local educational agency, include a child—

- experiencing developmental delays, as defined by the State and as measured by appropriate diagnostic instruments and procedures, in 1 or more of the following areas: physical development; cognitive development; communication development; social or emotional development; or adaptive development; and
- who, by reason thereof, needs special education and related services.

The term '**specific learning disability**' means a disorder in 1 or more of the basic psychological processes involved in understanding or in using language, spoken or written, which disorder may manifest itself in the imperfect ability to listen, think, speak, read, write, spell, or do mathematical calculations.

(B) DISORDERS INCLUDED—Such term includes such conditions as perceptual disabilities, brain injury, minimal brain dysfunction, dyslexia, and developmental aphasia.

(C) DISORDERS NOT INCLUDED—Such term does not include a learning problem that is primarily the result of visual, hearing, or motor disabilities, of mental retardation, of emotional disturbance, or of environmental, cultural, or economic disadvantage.

either IDEA or IDEA 2004. Table 14.4 contains the definitions of **child with a disability** and **specific learning disability** from IDEA. The excerpts in Tables 14.4 to 14.7 omit most of the cumbersome outlining in the original law, as well as the numerous cross-references to other parts of the law. We try to give the flavor of the original law, especially the emphasis on numerous specific provisions, without pretending to give an exhaustive treatment. For a more detailed description of various disabilities than that contained directly in the law, as well as data on prevalence rates, see Smith, Polloway, Patton, and Dowdy (2004).

The essential point of all these laws was to provide a "free appropriate public education" for all children, with special attention to those with a handicap/disability. The phrase "free appropriate public education" is used so frequently in these laws and associated documents that it receives its own acronym: **FAPE**. The key word in the phrase is "appropriate." What will be appropriate? Is it appropriate to place the disabled in separate classrooms? What are appropriate ways to assess the needs of the student with a disability? Notice in the definitions contained in Table 14.4 reference to specific conditions and the probable causes of those conditions. Assessments nearly always enter into these diagnostic functions.

The Individualized Education Program (IEP)

IDEA calls for development of an **individualized education program**, popularly known as an **IEP**.[3] Each child with a disability must have an IEP. The law specifies who is to be involved in preparation and execution of the IEP, procedures for updating the IEP, and the role of assessment in the IEP. Table 14.5 presents excerpts from the IDEA law regarding the IEP. These are only excerpts presented to give the flavor of the law. The law contains many other provisions, beyond those presented here, with further definitions, requirements, and exceptions. IDEA is quite explicit about the composition of the IEP team. Table 14.5 presents excerpts from the law regarding the team. Each IEP team must include a regular classroom teacher and a special education teacher. Typically, a school psychologist would also be included because such a person has special training in assessment. We reiterate the earlier caution that these are only excerpts and one must consult the entire law for a full understanding of requirements.

The Role of Assessment in the IEP

At the heart of an IEP is the provision of instruction for students with disabilities, especially instruction within the general education curriculum. However, assessment plays a key role in the IEP. We concentrate here on these assessment issues. Table 14.6 identifies

---

Table 14.5   Excerpts From IDEA on the IEP Team

The term 'individualized education program team' or 'IEP Team' means a group of individuals composed of—

- the parents of a child with a disability;
- not less than 1 regular education teacher of such child (if the child is, or may be, participating in the regular education environment);
- not less than 1 special education teacher, or where appropriate, not less than 1 special education provider of such child;
- a representative of the local educational agency who—
  is qualified to provide, or supervise the provision of, specially designed instruction to meet the unique needs of children with disabilities; is knowledgeable about the general education curriculum; and is knowledgeable about the availability of resources of the local educational agency;
- an individual who can interpret the instructional implications of evaluation results, who may be a member of the team described in clauses (ii) through (vi);
- at the discretion of the parent or the agency, other individuals who have knowledge or special expertise regarding the child, including related services personnel as appropriate; and
- whenever appropriate, the child with a disability.

---

[3] For the acronym IEP, the professional literature uses every combination of these words: individual or individualized, education or educational, and program or plan. The official wording in the IDEA law is "individualized education program." Fortunately, nearly all references are simply to IEP.

Table 14.6   Excerpts From IDEA on the IEP

The term 'individualized education program' or 'IEP' means a written statement for each child with a disability that is developed, reviewed, and revised in accordance with this section and that includes—

(I) a statement of the child's present levels of academic achievement and functional performance, including—

- how the child's disability affects the child's involvement and progress in the general education curriculum;
- for preschool children, as appropriate, how the disability affects the child's participation in appropriate activities; and
- for children with disabilities who take alternate assessments aligned to alternate achievement standards, a description of benchmarks or short-term objectives;

(II) a statement of measurable annual goals, including academic and functional goals, designed to—

- meet the child's needs that result from the child's disability to enable the child to be involved in and make progress in the general education curriculum; and
- meet each of the child's other educational needs that result from the child's disability;

(III) a description of how the child's progress toward meeting the annual goals . . . will be measured and when periodic reports on the progress the child is making toward meeting the annual goals (such as through the use of quarterly or other periodic reports, concurrent with the issuance of report cards) will be provided;

(IV) a statement of the special education and related services and supplementary aids and services, based on peer-reviewed research to the extent practicable, to be provided to the child, or on behalf of the child, and a statement of the program modifications or supports for school personnel that will be provided for the child—

- to advance appropriately toward attaining the annual goals;
- to be involved in and make progress in the general education curriculum . . . and to participate in extracurricular and other nonacademic activities; and
- to be educated and participate with other children with disabilities and nondisabled children in the activities described in this subparagraph;

(V) an explanation of the extent, if any, to which the child will not participate with nondisabled children in the regular class and in [other] activities . . . ;

(VI) a statement of any individual appropriate accommodations that are necessary to measure the academic achievement and functional performance of the child on State and districtwide assessments . . . ; and

- if the IEP Team determines that the child shall take an alternate assessment on a particular State or districtwide assessment of student achievement, a statement of why—
- the child cannot participate in the regular assessment; and
- the particular alternate assessment selected is appropriate for the child;

(VII) the projected date for the beginning of the services and modifications . . . , and the anticipated frequency, location, and duration of those services and modifications . . . .

the essential elements of an IEP. Appendix D provides a sample form for an IEP, with references to the appropriate federal regulations. This form is only an example. The companion website (http://www.ed.gov/about/offices/list/OSERS) provides additional detail about the regulations (U.S. Department of Education, 2000). Individual states or even school districts may have their own forms. Assessment enters the IEP picture in four principal ways. Examination of the form in Appendix D will help identify these ways. First, assessment contributes to the original identification of a student with a disability. This includes the basis for statements about the child's "present levels of educational performance." The definition of "present levels" would ordinarily include results from standardized tests as well as classroom assessments. Often, a crucial part of the definition will use the "discrepancy model" described in Chapter 12 (p. 283); that is, a discrepancy between measured achievement and measured mental ability. Second, the IEP calls for specification of "measurable annual goals." When the emphasis is on the word "goals," this is an instructional matter. When the emphasis is on "measurable," this is an assessment matter. Of course, in practice, these are inseparable. The important point is that goals must be specified in such a way that progress toward them can be assessed in some meaningful way. Third, as implied by the second condition, there must be follow-up assessment in order to determine if progress has been made. Finally, the student's participation in district and state assessments must be treated. The student may need accommodations or modifications in order to participate. If the IEP team determines that the student will not participate, reasons must be given for this determination.

Table 14.7 shows some of the IDEA provisions related to assessment. Teachers play a central role in both the identification of disabilities and the execution of an IEP. School psychologists and administrators must be thoroughly familiar with these provisions.

Table 14.7 Sample Statements Related to Evaluation Procedures From IDEA

In conducting the evaluation, the local educational agency shall—

use a variety of assessment tools and strategies to gather relevant functional, developmental, and academic information, including information provided by the parent, that may assist in determining—

- whether the child is a child with a disability; and
- the content of the child's individualized education program, including information related to enabling the child to be involved in and progress in the general education curriculum, or, for preschool children, to participate in appropriate activities;

(B) not use any single measure or assessment as the sole criterion for determining whether a child is a child with a disability or determining an appropriate educational program for the child; and

(C) use technically sound instruments that may assess the relative contribution of cognitive and behavioral factors, in addition to physical or developmental factors.

(3) Each local educational agency shall ensure that—

assessments and other evaluation materials used to assess a child under this section—

- are selected and administered so as not to be discriminatory on a racial or cultural basis;
- are provided and administered in the language and form most likely to yield accurate information on what the child knows and can do academically, developmentally, and functionally, unless it is not feasible to so provide or administer;
- are used for purposes for which the assessments or measures are valid and reliable;
- are administered by trained and knowledgeable personnel; and are administered in accordance with any instructions provided by the producer of such assessments. . . .

| KEY POINTS SUMMARY 14.2 | *The Role of Assessment in the IEP* |

- Identification
- Setting measurable goals
- Follow-up evaluation
- Inclusion in state and district assessments

Examination of the excerpts in Table 14.4 to 14.7 reveals two main points. First, the statements are consistent with the professional standards emphasized throughout this book about technical quality of tests. Second, the statements are highly specific regarding selection and administration of assessments. Hence, a general understanding of professional standards for tests is not sufficient to comply with all the legal requirements. One must read the law itself and the relevant regulatory declarations.

Another provision in these laws calls for educating the disabled in the "least restrictive environment." In practice, this means **mainstreaming** or **inclusion**; that is, including students with disabilities in regular classrooms rather than in separate special education classrooms. As with many aspects of the law, there are exceptions to this principle.

Most of the provisions in IDEA 2004 are the same as those in IDEA-97. However, there are some new provisions plus subtle changes in wording throughout. One of the new elements is reference to use of "universal design principles." These principles emphasize designing materials that are usable by people with a wide range of functional capabilities. IDEA 2004 cross-references this topic to the Assistive Technologies Act of 1998, again illustrating the interconnectedness of many federal laws related to persons with disabilities. IDEA 2004 also gives increased emphasis to reporting "disproportionality"; that is, differential rates of identification of persons with disabilities by racial and ethnic categories.

No Child Left Behind Act

Although officially titled the No Child Left Behind Act of 2001 (**NCLB**; P.L. 107–110), this new federal law was not adopted until 2002. It is a blockbuster: nearly 1,000 pages. Technically, NCLB is a revision of the ESEA law of 1965 described earlier. However, the changes are so sweeping that NCLB usually goes by its own name and acronym.

NCLB has generated political controversy. However, it was adopted with overwhelming bipartisan support. The legislation passed the U.S. House of Representatives by a vote of 381–41 and the U.S. Senate by a vote of 87–10 (with three not voting). Senator Edward (Ted) Kennedy, an influential member of the Democratic party, was head of the Senate Education Committee partly responsible for developing NCLB. And, of course, President Bush, a Republican, signed the bill into law.

Before examining details of NCLB, let us describe its background. Recall from Chapter 1 the basic tenets of standards-based education. It has these key features:

1. Clearly specifying instructional objectives
2. Establishing student performance standards
3. Setting the standards at a rigorous level
4. Applying the standards to all students
5. Public reporting of assessment results

Figure 14.2 President Bush, with Senator Ted Kennedy, at the signing of NCLB.
(U.S. Department of Education.)

On their own, these five features simply characterize an approach to education. NCLB essentially translates these features into legislative mandates. That is, it makes this approach to education the "law of the land." And, NCLB adds a *sixth* feature: It sets a 12-year timetable for accomplishing all this.

Let us comment briefly on each of the six features. Clear specification of educational objectives is hardly new with NCLB. This approach has characterized most of education for the past 50 years. Clearly specifying performance standards is relatively new in education. It takes the criterion-referenced approach to test interpretation to a new level. Use of terms such as below basic, basic, proficient, and advanced, as reviewed in Chapter 5, are an outgrowth of this development. The field of educational assessment had been inching in this direction for some time. However, NCLB institutionalized the approach. The third feature (setting high standards) is the one that demands performance at the "proficient" level. The fourth feature (applicability to all students) gives the origin of the law's title. That is, all of the features apply to all students: *No child* can be excluded. In particular, students with disabilities, students from low socioeconomic levels, minority students, and so on—all are supposed to achieve the high standards. The fifth feature calls for the assessment results to be reported regularly and in detail. An important aspect of the required reporting is presenting results for various subgroups of students.

Sometimes it seems that a new federal law appears "out of nowhere." Ordinarily, however, new laws have a discernible history. Such is the case with NCLB. Its origin is generally traced to publication of *A Nation at Risk: The Imperative for Educational Reform* (National Commission on Excellence in Education, 1983). This report, issued in the heat of the "cold war," was highly critical of U.S. education. It provided a stimulus for increased federal involvement in education. That increased involvement took flesh in two federal initiatives: Improving America's Schools Act (IASA) of 1994 and, even more so, in Goals 2000: Educate America First (popularly known as Goals 2000). Both of these

Table 14.8   Excerpts From the No Child Left Behind Act

Each State plan shall demonstrate that the State has adopted challenging academic content standards and challenging student academic achievement standards . . .

The academic standards . . . shall be the same academic standards that the State applies to all schools and children in the State.

Standards under this paragraph shall include—

• challenging academic content standards in academic subjects that —
  • specify what children are expected to know and be able to do;
  • contain coherent and rigorous content; and
  • encourage the teaching of advanced skills; and

• challenging student academic achievement standards that—
  • are aligned with the State's academic content standards;
  • describe two levels of high achievement (proficient and advanced)
  • describe a third level of achievement (basic) to provide complete information

Each State plan shall demonstrate that the State has developed and is implementing a single, statewide State accountability system . . .

Each State accountability system shall—
  include sanctions and rewards, such as bonuses and recognition, the State will use to hold local educational agencies and public elementary schools and secondary schools accountable for student achievement and for ensuring that they make adequate yearly progress

Each State shall establish statewide annual measurable objectives . . . which—
  • shall be set separately for the assessments of mathematics and reading or language arts
  • shall identify a single minimum percentage of students who are required to meet or exceed the proficient level on the academic assessments that applies separately to each group of students
  • shall ensure that all students will meet or exceed the State's proficient level of academic achievement on the State assessments within the State's timeline

federal laws were seen as extensions of the ESEA of 1965, described earlier in this chapter. Both emphasized a standards-based approach to education, high standards, and serving *all* students. Both had strong bipartisan support. Who wants to be against high standards for everyone? For a history of the laws leading up to NCLB, see Boston (2002) and Jorgensen and Hoffmann (2003).

NCLB has obvious implications for educational assessment. The law is shot through with references to assessment, standards, accountability, and related terms. Let us outline the main points. NCLB excerpts in Table 14.8 supplement the following narrative description. NCLB calls for:

• Each state to establish challenging academic standards
  • at least in mathematics and reading or language arts by 2002–2003
  • and in science by 2005–2006; other curricular areas remain optional

- Each state to measure student progress toward meeting the standards:
  - in mathematics and reading or language arts by 2005–2006
  - annual assessment in each of Grades 3–8 and one grade in the Grade 10–12 span
  - and in science (selected grades) by 2006–2007; other areas are optional
  - annual assessments in selected grades before the above referenced dates
- Use of "proficient" as the required level of achievement
- Use of one indicator of success other than the tests
- Meeting the proficient level by *all* students
- Special assessment provisions for students with:
  - limited English proficiency, or
  - with disabilities
- Public reporting of results (adequate yearly progress reports)
- State participation in the National Assessment of Educational Progress (NAEP)

NCLB gives individual states the responsibility for developing objectives and assessments. In the years immediately preceding passage of NCLB, the United States came very close to adopting a single, national set of standards and assessments. (See Boston, 2002, for a useful history on this point.) The states balked at such nationalization. This state-based feature of the law has spawned explosive growth in these activities (setting objectives and devising assessments) among the states. One result of this feature is that it is difficult to make comparisons across state lines. Every state has a different set of objectives and a different way of assessing those objectives. However, the required participation in NAEP may ultimately allow for some comparisons among states. To facilitate examination of the activities within each state, we provide in Appendix E a list of websites for state assessment programs.

Try This!

Carefully read the text in Table 14.7. How many references to "proficient" do you find?

NCLB established a 12-year timetable for accomplishing the goal of bringing all children to the proficient level in basic academic subjects. The target year is 2014. States must report annually until that time about the progress of students, including specified subgroups, toward the goal. The relevant technical term is **adequate yearly progress** (AYP). Schools that do not demonstrate adequate yearly progress are subject to penalties and corrective action. Upon first failing to show adequate yearly progress, a school is labeled "in need of improvement." If the school continues to fail the adequate-yearly-progress standard, other sanctions come into play.

We have outlined here the main features of the assessment-related provisions of NCLB. This law has many other provisions. For example, it indicates how funds will be allocated to states. It creates a number of special grant programs. In addition, one of the more widely cited sections is the one on "highly qualified teachers." The law defines this term, identifies national targets for bringing all teachers to this level, and sets a timeline for reaching the targets.

IDEA makes explicit reference to the regular classroom teacher. NCLB does not do so. However, it is clear that NCLB has implications for regular classroom teachers. Teachers will be involved in the administration of the state assessments. Many teachers will also help to develop state standards, assessment items, and, perhaps, even the definition of proficient. Earlier chapters in this book treated all of these topics. We hope readers of the earlier chapters have developed the skills to contribute meaningfully to these activities.

Family Educational Rights and Privacy Act

The Family Educational Rights and Privacy Act of 1974 (**FERPA**) is also known as the "Buckley amendment," after its chief sponsor, Senator James Buckley of New York. In comparison with laws such as IDEA and NCLB, FERPA has a very modest scope. The principal purposes of FERPA are to guarantee that individuals have open access to information about themselves, that individuals can challenge the validity of information in agency files, and that unwarranted other parties do not have access to personal information. FERPA's special relevance for assessment deals primarily with test scores. Records in school files, including test information, have to be available to the student or, in the case of minors, to parents or guardians. Although it may be hard to believe today, in pre-FERPA days it was common for schools and other agencies to prohibit parents from seeing the test results for their children.

Further, the law states specific restrictions on the release of information to other parties without the individual's (or guardian's) consent. Teachers and other school personnel may not reveal a student's educational record, including assessment results, without permission. There are exceptions to this prohibition (e.g., in connection with accreditation processes and health emergencies). It is also permissible to share information with school personnel having a "legitimate educational interest." For example, a school psychologist obviously has a legitimate interest in examining a child's school record; teachers often need to share information about a student's performance in order to plan effectively for the student.

FERPA defines a category of "directory information." This category includes such information as name, address, birthdate, honors, and awards. Directory information may be made public without the individual's (or parents'/guardians') consent. However, schools must notify the parties annually of their right to *not* make such information public. FERPA's inclusion of honors and awards in the category of directory information means that schools may publish such lists as honor rolls, winners of athletic and academic competitions, and so on. More recent than FERPA, the Gramm-Leach-Bliley Act of 1999, although aimed principally at financial institutions, also has implications for schools' use of student information.

KEY POINTS SUMMARY 14.3   *Frequently Used Acronyms for Laws Related to Educational Assessment*

ADA	Americans with Disabilities Act
ESEA	Elementary and Secondary Education Act
FERPA	Family Educational Rights and Privacy Act
IDEA	Individuals with Disabilities Education Act
NCLB	No Child Left Behind Act

Gifted and Talented Students

What about the gifted and talented?[4] From a legal perspective, the picture for these students is quite different than for legally defined minorities and students with disabilities. The reason for the difference is simple. There are no *federal* laws, at present, regarding gifted students. The matter is in the hands of the states. This circumstance has two important consequences. *First*, it is not feasible in this brief section to summarize the great variety of state practices. Approximately 30 states make some legally mandated provision for gifted students (Karnes & Marquardt, 1997). That means about 30 different sets of laws. The other states have no laws regarding gifted students.

A second consequence of this state-based situation is that court cases regarding gifted students arise solely in state courts, not federal courts. Recall our earlier observation that cases related to such laws as IDEA and ADA arise in the federal courts. That happens because IDEA and ADA are federal laws, not state laws. Because any laws related to gifted education are state laws, cases regarding these laws arise in state courts. A very practical result of this circumstance is the difficulty in tracking cases in the state courts. Further, cases in one state are not legally controlling precedent for courts in other states.

Despite these peculiar circumstances for gifted education, we can outline two broad areas related to assessment of gifted students. First, in contemporary practice, the term "gifted and talented" is broadly construed. We recognize many gifts, many talents. Therefore, the assessment methods used to identify students for gifted programs are correspondingly diverse.

Programs that emphasize excellence in traditional academic areas tend to use traditional intelligence and achievement tests. For example, standardized achievement tests, as described in Chapter 11, or tests of mental ability, as described in Chapter 12, might be used. A common cut-off score for selecting students is two standard deviations above the mean. Refer back to Figure 5.3 (p. 98) to place this cut-off in context.

There are many programs for gifted students outside of traditional academic areas. Obvious examples are programs in the fine arts, including, music, dance, and painting. Assessment methods for selection of students in these programs tend to emphasize evaluation of products, performances, and portfolios. We reviewed use of these assessment methods in Chapter 8. Thus, the generalization is this: The assessment method varies with the type of gifted program.

Here is a second common feature of gifted programs with relevance to assessment. Many gifted programs mimic the procedures and terminology used with disabled students. Thus, there may be a multidisciplinary team (MDT) responsible for identifying gifted students. An IEP may be developed for a gifted student, with attendant progress reports, and so on. Assessment techniques would apply to all these situations just as they do for disability cases. A good example of this pattern is the program mandated in the state of Pennsylvania. However, we hasten to reiterate that states differ in their laws and procedures, and some states have no laws or procedures related to gifted students.

---

[4] The term "gifted and talented" is the most common designation for these students. For simplicity, we will refer to "gifted" from this point on.

Try This!

Access the website for the Pennsylvania Association for Gifted Education (PAGE): www.penngifted.org. See if you can find the procedures and terms paralleling those for disability cases.

ILLUSTRATIVE COURT CASES

Recall from our definition of "laws" that court decisions constitute the third type of law: case law. The courts deal with application of statutory and administrative laws, as well as previous court decisions, to particular cases. There is a plaintiff who claims that someone (a person, corporation, school, etc.) violated a law. There is a defendant (the person, corporation, etc.) who asserts compliance with the law. Legal counsel usually represents each side: plaintiff and defendant. The court hears the case and decides in favor of one side. For the types of cases of interest here, judges—not juries—make the rulings. When first filed, the cases are usually identified by the names of the plaintiff and defendant, in that order, for example, *Hogan v. City of Scranton*. Here, someone named Hogan, the plaintiff, claims that the City of Scranton, the defendant, violated the law. Often, there are multiple plaintiffs and defendants in a particular case, but the practice is to reduce the title to single names.

As noted earlier, most of the laws related to testing are federal in origin. Hence, federal courts hear the cases. The local district justice deals with your parking ticket, because this relates to a local ordinance. But the local district justice does not hear a case involving a federal law. The federal judiciary has 94 *district* courts, 12 *circuit* courts, and, of course, one *supreme court*. Suits originate in district courts. District decisions may be appealed to a circuit court (whose full name is circuit court of appeals). Circuit court decisions may be appealed to the U.S. Supreme Court. Upon appeal, the higher court first decides whether to hear the appeal, leave the decision stand, or send the case back (remand) to the lower court for further consideration.

Try This!

For a more detailed description of U.S. federal courts, go to: www.uscourts.gov. What is the district and circuit for your hometown?

There are literally thousands of cases brought before the courts involving tests and the laws outlined earlier. For example, Data Research (1997) lists more than 400 cases related just to IDEA. We will not attempt a comprehensive review of the cases arising from any one of the laws. Rather, we outline below a few cases that illustrate how the courts deal with the interface of testing and the law.[5]

---

[5] When citing court cases in this section we have generally cited the final disposition of the case and have not included all the original filings, appeals, and remands. Referencing the final disposition will lead the reader to earlier steps in the process.

Debra P. v. Turlington and *GI Forum v. TEA*

A state requires students to pass a test in order to graduate from high school. Pass rates on the test are substantially different for minority and white students. Does the test requirement violate any federal laws? More specifically, does use of the test in this way violate the 14th amendment, the Civil Rights Act of 1964, or any related law? Two similar cases, *Debra P. v. Turlington* (1984) and *GI Forum v. TEA* (2000), illustrate how the courts have dealt with this question.

Debra P. v. Turlington

This case arose in Florida in 1979. Debra P. was one student serving as lead plaintiff in a class action filed on behalf of all African-American students in Florida.[6] Ralph Turlington was the state's Commissioner of Education, administratively responsible for enforcing the state's testing program. In 1976, the Florida legislature, through the state's Department of Education, began requiring that students pass a functional literacy test, the State Student Assessment Test, Part 2 (SSAT-II), in order to receive a high school diploma. The test was administered in fall 1977, 1978, and 1979. Black students were failing the test at a rate of about 10 times higher than white students.

Debra P. et al. brought suit in the district court in 1979. The legal proceedings bounced between the district court and circuit court for five years, concluding in 1984. This case did not go to the U.S. Supreme Court. The case is important not only for its final decision but also for the reasoning applied by the courts. In fact, the circuit court reversed the district court's initial ruling not because of the conclusion but because of the reasoning used to reach the conclusion.

Here are the important points about the *Debra P.* case. First, the state was permitted to use the test as a diploma requirement. Second, the state had to delay implementation of the requirement until 1982–1983 in order to provide adequate notice (this is part of due process) about the requirement. Third, a crucial part of the case turned on adequate demonstration of the "instructional validity" of the test. Recall our description of this concept in Chapter 4. The state contracted for extensive empirical studies to demonstrate instructional validity. Provision for remedial work for those failing the test was also an important consideration. Fourth, in the court's opinion, mere disproportionate impact of the test on one group did not render the test illegal. Fifth, there was no clear demonstration of a causal link between the vestiges of previous segregated schooling and current pass rates on the test. The remedial programs were important on this point. Further, in the court's view, imposition of the test requirement may have actually helped to remedy any remaining effects of segregated schooling. This is an interesting application of the concept of consequential validity, although neither the court nor the defendants used this term.

---

[6] As the case progressed, three classes were formed, but this point is unimportant for our summary. Numerous officials in addition to Turlington were named as defendants, but this fact, too, is unimportant here.

GI Forum v. TEA

In a case very similar to *Debra P.*—but much more recent—a group of minority students, with GI Forum as lead plaintiff, brought suit against the Texas Education Agency (TEA) in the federal district court at San Antonio. Beginning in the 1980s, Texas required students to pass the Texas Assessment of Academic Skills (TAAS) test, as well as meet other criteria, in order to graduate from high school. African-American and Hispanic students failed the tests (reading, math, and writing) at substantially higher rates than whites.

In January 2000, Judge Edward Pardo ruled the TAAS test permissible despite the disparities in pass rates. There were several important points in the court opinion. First, the judge used concepts from the EEOC regulations (arising from the Civil Rights Act), originally intended for employment tests. He transformed the concept of "business necessity" into "educational necessity." Second, much was made of the technical quality of the tests: their development, especially steps taken to detect item bias; reliability; and curricular validity, including "opportunity to learn." Curricular validity in this case is the same as instructional validity in the *Debra P.* case. Third, and perhaps most significantly, the judge referenced the impact of the test. Specifically, he noted that the test helps to (a) identify and remediate weaknesses and (b) motivate students, teachers, and schools. Again, these reasons are very good examples of consequential validity, although the term is not used in the court opinion. See Phillips (2000) for detailed treatment of the *GI Forum* case and its lessons.

Larry P. v. Riles, *PASE v. Hannon*, and *Crawford v. Honig*

We consider these three cases together because, in combination, they illustrate the complexity of understanding court decisions. The cases take us on a fascinating journey through the courts. As with the case of *Debra P.*, these cases involved multiple plaintiffs and defendants, appeals, remands, and other legal proceedings. We outline here only the major conclusions.

Larry P. v. Riles

This case originated in San Francisco (Northern District of California) in 1971 and concluded in 1984. Larry P. was an African-American child assigned to a class for the educable mentally retarded (EMR) based mainly on an individually administered intelligence test. Court records cite a list of tests approved by the state for EMR placement, but most attention focused on the WISC and Stanford-Binet. (We described these tests in Chapter 12.) Wilson Riles was the superintendent of public instruction for California. Plaintiffs claimed violations of the Civil Rights Act of 1964, the Rehabilitation Act of 1973, the Education for All Handicapped Children Act of 1975, and the equal protection clauses of the federal and state constitutions.

The district court (Judge Robert Peckham) concluded that the tests were discriminatory and banned their further use. This ruling, perhaps more than any other, gave rise to headlines such as "IQ Tests Found Illegal" and "Intelligence Tests Unconstitutional." However, note the following points in the full decision and in the court's reasoning. First, the ruling applied only to African-American students, not to other minority (or white) students. Second, the ruling applied only to assignment to EMR classes or their substantial equivalents. The ruling did not prohibit use of the tests for other purposes (e.g., selection for gifted classes). Third, an important element in the court's reasoning was the conclusion that EMR classes were "dead-end" classes. In some ways, the ruling was more an indictment of the EMR program than of the tests. Finally, the court concluded that the IQ tests carried more weight than justified in the light of state statutes.

PASE v. Hannon

Meanwhile, over in Chicago (Northern District of Illinois), a highly similar case arose: *PASE v. Hannon*. Parents in Action on Special Education (PASE) filed suit against Joseph Hannon, superintendent of the Chicago Public Schools, on behalf of African-American students assigned to educable mentally handicapped (EMH) classes based in part on individual intelligence tests. In this instance, the district court ruled the tests were not culturally biased, except for a few items, which would not significantly influence final placement of students. Hence, the tests were permissible. Amazingly, the judge in this case commented item by item on the WISC, WAIS, and Stanford-Binet, thereby seriously compromising the security of these tests. There were several other important points in this case, according to the final opinion. The professionals involved in the placement seemed to have appropriate professional training and were using good professional judgment. Information besides intelligence tests played a significant role in the placement. Potential value of the EMH classes for the students assigned to them also seemed important. Did the judge in this case know about the ruling in the *Larry P.* case? Yes. The judge cited the *Larry P.* case, but explicitly disagreed with that ruling.

Crawford v. Honig

We return now to California and even to Judge Peckham's courtroom to hear *Crawford v. Honig*. Demond Crawford, lead plaintiff, was an African-American student diagnosed as learning disabled. Bill Honig was now superintendent of California's public schools. Crawford's parents wanted to have an IQ test administered to her. The state declined, citing the decision in the *Larry P.* case. However, Judge Peckham reversed (vacated) his earlier ruling, thus allowing use of an IQ test for Crawford and, in effect, for all other African-American students. An interesting sideline of this case, noted by Kaplan and Saccuzzo (2001), is that Crawford was of mixed African-American and Hispanic parentage. Thus, the parents could have secured administration of the IQ test simply by switching the child's racial/ethnic identification, but the parents refused to do so.

Careful reading of the court proceedings in these cases reveals four important points not treated in the final rulings but partially determinative of the rulings. First, the difference between a diagnosis of mental retardation and learning disabilities was crucial. Tests may be especially helpful in making this distinction. Second, the quality of the final educational program or treatment following diagnosis was very important. Third, current understanding of the nature of intelligence and its determinants arose repeatedly in testimony. We touched on some of these matters in Chapter 12 under theories of intelligence. Theories sometimes seem very dry. However, theoretical developments have important practical implications in the real world—such as in courtrooms. Finally, the methods used to analyze item bias in

KEY POINTS SUMMARY 14.4	*Examples of Court Cases Related to Assessment*

Debra P. v. Turlington	*GI Forum v. TEA*
Larry P. v. Riles	*PASE v. Hannon*
	Crawford v. Honig	

these cases—very much an armchair analysis—seem primitive by today's standards. Recall that we described contemporary approaches to the study of item bias in Chapter 4.

The most typical way in which a court acts is by rendering a decision. The decision concludes in favor of either the plaintiff or the defendant, perhaps not in every detail, but on the whole. However, court decisions are not the only way in which the courts act. There are also **consent decrees**, or consent orders. In these instances, the court does not render a decision in favor of one of the contesting parties. Rather in the process of contesting the issue, the parties reach agreement as to how the issue will be resolved. The court then gives force to the agreement and makes it binding. *Lee v. Butler County Board of Education* (2000) illustrates a consent decree. Table 14.9 contains selections from the decree. Although the

Table 14.9 Excerpts From a Consent Decree on Evaluation Procedures in *Lee v. Butler County Board of Education*

Accordingly, it is ORDERED that the proposed consent decree on the special education issue is approved.

The Alabama State Department of Education [DOE] agrees to implement the commitments outlined below to resolve the issue of racial disparities observed in certain special education exceptionalities (*mental retardation, emotional disturbance, and specific learning disabilities*) at the local district level.

The severity/duration of the problem with subsequent prereferral interventions, including *functional assessment of the classroom environment*, must now be a part of the information collected and attached to the referral form.

If said student is found in need of being administered *a non-traditional intelligence test*, such non-traditional intelligence test will be administered.

. . . eligibility criteria for emotional disturbance includes: (1) parents as a possible rater for one of the three required *behavior rating scales*, and (2) the requirement of *observations in two or more educational settings*.

. . . eligibility criteria for specific learning disabilities to use a *predicted achievement model*, based on regression to the mean, to determine whether or not there is a *severe discrepancy between a student's ability and achievement*.

Total score on an adaptive behavior scale or two subcomposite scores of an *adaptive behavior scale* must be at least *two standard deviations below the mean* (usually 70 or below). A school version of an adaptive behavior assessment is required.

It is so ORDERED.

From 2000 WL 33680483 (M.D. Ala). Emphasis added.

decree arose from a case involving the Butler County Board of Education, the decree binds the Alabama Department of Education. Excerpts in Table 14.9 cover only a few of the provisions of the agreement. However, these excerpts illustrate how concepts covered in earlier chapters enter the legal arena. The consent decree makes very specific demands for assessment procedures. For example, the decree requires functional assessment of the classroom environment and use of adaptive behavior assessments, among other requirements. (Notice also the reference to "two standard deviations below the mean." This citation emphasizes that you need to know your statistics even to understand court actions!) The decree required annual reports on progress in implementing the agreement in each year from 2001 to 2005.

A Concluding Reminder on Grading

We conclude this section on court cases related to assessment with a reminder about a point made in Chapter 13. The point relates to educators' assignment of grades. The courts generally defer to the judgment of educators in the assignment of grades. The courts are reluctant to intervene in such matters. The minimum standard is that the basis for the grading be rational and nonarbitrary. Otherwise, the courts give wide latitude to educators' judgments about grading.

PRACTICAL ADVICE

1. Every school system will have legal counsel with expertise in the matters covered in this chapter. You need to rely on that expertise. Nevertheless, every teacher needs familiarity with the laws we have covered. Use the websites listed in this chapter to gain that familiarity.

2. Be careful not to overgeneralize from single court decisions. Often, a court decision turns on very special circumstances or applies only to a limited geographical region. Further, initial decisions are often appealed and overturned. This caution is not an invitation to disregard court decisions. It simply alerts you to the realities of legal proceedings.

3. When consulting laws, be sure to check also on administrative regulations. The "regs," as they are called, often contain much more specific directions than do the (statutory) laws.

SUMMARY

1. Laws come in three major forms: statutory laws enacted by legislative bodies, administrative laws (regulations) promulgated by government agencies, and case law created by court decisions.

2. Many specialized terms and initials are used to label laws. Among the more frequent initials are U.S.C., P.L., and C.F.R. Various sources may use any of these tags, or the full name of the law, or commonly recognized acronyms, such as IDEA or NCLB.

3. The 14th amendment to the U.S. Constitution includes an "equal protection clause" and a "due process clause"

frequently used in legislation and in court cases related to use of tests.

4. The Civil Rights Acts of 1964 and 1991 relate primarily to discrimination in employment. However, they also apply to assessment when the assessment relates to fairness either in employment or education.

5. The Rehabilitation Act and ADA relate primarily to access to facilities for the physically handicapped. However, these laws also extend to access for the mentally disabled, including those with learning disabilities. These laws call for accommodations in testing the disabled.

6. IDEA 2004 is the most recent law related to the treatment of the disabled in education. This law had several important predecessors, stretching back to 1970. The principal thrust of these laws is to provide an appropriate mainstreamed or inclusionary education for students with disabilities. The law requires an IEP for each such student.

7. The No Child Left Behind (NCLB) Act requires states to establish challenging academic standards and to bring *all* students to a *proficient* level on these standards. The law also requires detailed reporting of results for the assessments.

8. FERPA requires that individuals know about their test results and that the results not be revealed to other parties without the individual's permission.

9. There are no federal laws applicable to gifted students. Some states do have laws about the gifted. Assessment relates mainly to selection of students for gifted programs. The nature of the assessment varies in accord with the nature of the gifted program.

10. In the *Debra P.* and *GI Forum* cases, courts concluded that high school graduation tests were acceptable provided that they had instructional validity and that students received adequate notice about the tests. Differential passing rates for different groups did not render the tests unacceptable.

11. The *Larry P.*, *PASE*, and *Crawford* cases dealt with a complex set of issues related to the use of tests for placing students in special education classes. The quality of the special education classes became part of the issue.

12. The courts usually act by rendering a decision in favor of one of the contesting parties. However, the courts may also act by enforcing a consent decree in which the contesting parties reach agreement on how they will handle some matter.

13. The courts generally defer to educators regarding assignment of grades, requiring only that the process be rational and nonarbitrary.

KEY TERMS

accommodations
ADA (Americans With Disabilities Act)
adequate yearly progress (AYP)
administrative law
case law
consent decrees
C.F.R. (Code of Federal Regulations)
disability

equal protection clause
ESEA (Elementary and Secondary Education Act)
FAPE (free and appropriate education)
FERPA (Family Educational Rights and Privacy Act)
IDEA (Individuals With Disabilities Education Act)
IEP (individualized education program)

inclusion
legislation
mainstreaming
NCLB (No Child Left Behind) Act
P.L. (public law)
regulations
specific learning disability
statutory law
U.S.C. (United States Code)

EXERCISES

1. You are the regular classroom teacher on an IEP team for a 10-year-old boy with a reading disability. The boy is reading at a Grade 1 level. What would you include in this student's IEP?

2. Access the website for IDEA (http://www.ed.gov/ offices/OSERS/IDEA). Download the text of the law. Try to find the full text of the law for any of the excerpts contained in Tables 14.4 to 14.7.

3. Access the website for NCLB (http://www.ed.gov/ nclb). Download the text of the law at http://www.ed. gov/policy/elsec/leg/esea02/index.html. Try to find the full text of the law for the excerpts contained in Table 14.8. If you can download the law into a word processing system, do a word search on "proficient." How many times does the word appear in the law?

4. Access the website for the National Association for the Gifted (http://www.nagc.org). What information about *your state* can you obtain from the association?

5. Determine if your library allows access to the Lexis-Nexis or Westlaw databases. If it does, access the database. Or use the FindLaw.com website. Enter the name of any of the court cases treated in this chapter (e.g., *Debra P.* or one of the other cases). Enter the name of the case to do a search. Try to find the exact expression of the court's final ruling on the case.

6. The Learning First Alliance is an association of 12 leading educational associations. The alliance's website (www.learningfirst.org) allows downloading several excellent descriptions of the No Child Left Behind law. Access this website. What resources for parents does the site contain?

7. Identify a type of disability with which you are most familiar (e.g., visual disability or learning disability). Go to the sample IEP form in Appendix D. What type of assessment information would you include under "Present Levels of Educational Performance" in the second section of the report? What type of "Measurable Annual Goals" might you include in the next section?

8. If you have access to forms used by a local school, obtain the IEP form used by the school. Compare it with the sections in Appendix D. How do the forms differ? How are they the same?

Chapter 15

Evaluating Teaching: Applying Assessment to Yourself

OBJECTIVES

- Distinguish between evaluation for purposes of looking your best and for purposes of seeking improvement.
- Identify key reasons why evaluating teacher effectiveness is difficult.
- For each of the following sources of information, identify potential uses for your own self-evaluation.
  - Administrator ratings
  - Mentor/colleague ratings
  - Videotaping and audio recordings
  - Portfolios
  - Student test scores
  - Student ratings
  - Parent ratings
  - Student self-reports of achievement
  - Unobtrusive measures
  - Teacher competency tests and additional certifications
- Describe the purpose of reflection for self-assessment and list several aids to reflecting on your own teaching.

What This Chapter Is About

Most of educational assessment deals with assessing students. However, it also applies to assessing yourself as a teacher. This chapter suggests approaches to evaluating your own teaching, strictly for your own self-improvement. The chapter presents several sources of information to use for self-evaluation and comments on practical aspects of using each source. It also identifies sources of evaluation you will encounter on which you simply want to perform your best. The importance of reflection about the information garnered from these sources is emphasized.

Why This Topic Is Important

Every teacher will undergo mandated, administrative evaluations. These are necessary. Some teachers will also seek additional teaching certifications. These may have personal value. However, it is also useful to undertake your own evaluation. Self-evaluation requires a somewhat different approach than mandatory evaluation, although there may be some overlap in procedures. We hope that reading this chapter will clarify the difference in approaches and that you will adopt some of the procedures recommended here for your own self-evaluation.

OUR FOCUS OF ATTENTION

This chapter focuses on techniques that might be useful for self-evaluation and self-improvement. It does *not* suggest a comprehensive, administratively required system for evaluating teachers. That topic goes well beyond what we want to cover. There are other books devoted to that topic, and interested readers may consult such sources as Millman and Darling-Hammond (1990), Nolan and Hoover (2004), Stronge (1997), and the *personnel evaluation standards* from the Joint Committee on Standards for Educational Evaluation (1988). Administratively required systems of teacher evaluation must take into account such matters as record keeping, legal requirements, employment decisions, and so on. Such systems may be a matter of contract. In contrast, the following sections focus on procedures that you may use to analyze and improve your own performance as a teacher. Of course, these personal procedures overlap to some extent with administratively required evaluation. However, there are important differences in how the information gets used. The difference is most evident in what you, as the teacher, want to present. For purposes of self-evaluation, you want to obtain a balanced picture of normal performance, including weaknesses, chinks in the armor, and areas for improvement. You want to readily admit the need for changing some approach. In contrast, for your administrative evaluation, you want to put your best foot forward and make yourself look just terrific. This difference between evaluation for administrative purposes and for self-analysis is an important perspective. Keep it in mind as you proceed through this chapter. In addition, be aware that some of the techniques or sources of information suggested here for use in self-analysis would have little use in a formal, administrative evaluation system.

The essential foundation for self-evaluating your own teaching is your *attitude* toward the task. If you think you are the world's greatest teacher and there is no room for improvement, then you can skip this chapter. It won't do you any good. Or, if you are a mediocre teacher and don't really care about improving because your job is secure, then you, too, can skip this chapter. You have to start with an attitude that you do want to improve and that you are interested in examining information that might lead to such improvement. Then, you have to examine the information in a process of *self-reflection*. You have to make sense of the information in order for it to be useful.

Remember, too, that you are always being evaluated, whether or not you know it. Students, parents, colleagues, and administrators are always noticing how you perform. They are forming judgments about your performance. Some of this information gets translated into formal evaluation, as when a principal completes an annual evaluation for you. Some of it never gets used. It simply becomes part of the general, noisy background of the job situation. For purposes of your self-evaluation, the trick is to use various sources of information wisely. Using the information wisely implies self-reflection. The information will do you no good if you do not think about it. The remainder of this chapter suggests what these various sources of information are and how you might use them.

Let's Remember Basic Principles

Earlier chapters introduced basic principles of assessment. These principles included reliability, validity, methods for interpreting performance, fairness, and practical matters, such as cost and efficiency. We applied these principles throughout subsequent chapters to procedures for assessing students. These same principles apply to evaluating your own teaching. The information should be reliable. Information sources should be valid indicators of teaching skill. Recall, too, that low reliability limits validity. Original data need to be interpreted. This may involve norm-referenced or criterion-referenced interpretation. We want the indicators to be fair, economical, and efficient. All these points are simply reminders of topics covered earlier in the book.

Why Is It So Difficult?

Why is it so difficult to evaluate teaching? Consider this comparison. In basketball, the rim is exactly 10 feet above the floor. The rim itself has a diameter of 18 inches. The free-throw line is exactly 15 feet from the plane of the backboard. These circumstances are the same in every gymnasium. It is not difficult to determine who the best free-throw shooter is, regardless of where people shoot. In contrast, the circumstances prevailing in a teacher's classroom may change substantially. There is a different group of students every year. One year seems to bring a bumper crop of budding geniuses. Another year brings a different group of students. In fact, groups of students change, at least moderately and perhaps substantially, from the beginning to the end of a single year. The teacher may not teach the same subjects every year. The grade levels taught may change. The school system and the state are always tinkering with the curriculum standards, requiring changes in teaching materials and strategies. Thus, drawing conclusions about the quality of teaching gets quite complicated. However, the fact that the task is difficult does not mean that it is impossible or meaningless. It only suggests proceeding cautiously. Our common observation is that teachers differ in quality. Everyone knows teachers who are simply great, year after year, with different subjects and other changes in circumstances. Everyone knows teachers who are horrible, year after year, with different subjects and other changes in circumstances. Apparently, there is some generality to the concept of "good teaching." Certain types of information will help to get at this concept.

ADMINISTRATOR RATINGS

Administrator ratings are the most common method for evaluating teachers. Virtually all teachers, at least in the early years of their careers, will undergo administrator ratings. The building principal is the usual evaluator, although other school administrators may

Central School District
Teacher Rating Form

Teacher: _____   Grade/Subject: _____

Administrator: _____   Date of Rating: _____

Describe the Class: _____

Comments:

Overall rating:
[ ] Very Good   [ ] Satisfactory   [ ] Needs Improvement   [ ] Unsatisfactory

Figure 15.1 Example of a very general administrator rating form.

contribute. The administrator will usually visit the class for perhaps half an hour. The visit may be announced or unannounced. In your first year of teaching in a building or under a new principal, you should determine what the local practice is. A teacher contract may spell out the conditions.

What do administrator rating forms look like? They come in two formats. Some forms are very general, leaving room for lots of free-response comments, and perhaps one overall rating. Figure 15.1 shows such a form. The second type of form calls for ratings of specific behaviors. The form may allow for an overall rating, but the emphasis is on specific items. Figure 15.2 shows an example of this second type of form.

Try This!

Examine the items in Figure 15.2. What behaviors seem to be missing from the six items presented there? List two or three items that might be added to the form. It may be helpful to think of characteristics of really good (or bad) teachers you have had.

One of the most consistent criticisms in the field of teacher evaluation is that administrator ratings are seriously flawed. They have very limited reliability and are subject to a host of distortions. This is not entirely the fault of the administrators themselves. Very often, the observations and ratings are made with insufficient frequency to yield reliable results. To increase the frequency of classroom visitations to a

Southwest School District
Teacher Rating Form

Teacher: _____   Grade/Subject: _____

Administrator: _____   Date of Rating: _____

Behavior	Rating (1 = low, 5 = high)				
1. Classroom management Comment:	1	2	3	4	5
2. Clarity of objectives Comment:	1	2	3	4	5
3. Interaction with students Comment:	1	2	3	4	5
4. Use of voice Comment:	1	2	3	4	5
5. Use of technology Comment:	1	2	3	4	5
6. Apparent preparation Comment:	1	2	3	4	5

Overall rating: [ ] Very Good   [ ] Satisfactory
                  [ ] Needs Improvement   [ ] Unsatisfactory

Figure 15.2 Example of an administrator rating form focusing on specific behaviors.

level that would yield adequate reliability may not be practical. Consider the building with 20 teachers. To visit each teacher six times during the year for, say, 45 minutes would mean about three weeks worth of work—not counting the possible meetings with teachers after the visits. Despite the importance of teacher evaluation, principals have a lot of other things to worry about. Furthermore, some principals tend to be too lenient in their ratings. After all, they are often cheerleaders, as well as evaluators, for the teachers. But this leniency, or other response distortions, hurts the reliability and validity of the ratings.

What should you do about administrator ratings for purposes of your self-evaluation? Probably nothing. Try to look your absolute best on these administrator ratings and hope they come out nicely. If you have any choice in the matter, arrange for more rather than fewer of these ratings. It will improve reliability. Also, try to get ratings on specific teaching behaviors rather than just global evaluations. And, of course, take the advice from your administrator seriously.

MENTOR/COLLEAGUE RATINGS

Quite apart from the official administrator ratings you receive, you may want to arrange for ratings by a mentor or colleague. Observations and ratings by a mentor or colleague are not common. However, they can be useful. We encourage their use.

Whom should you choose for this task? It is not an easy choice. You want someone whose judgment you trust, someone who will be objective and frank. Do *not* choose a spouse or best friend. It puts that person (and you) in an awkward position. The spouse or friend may not be willing to tell you how awful your presentation was. If they do, you may be terribly hurt. Choose someone with whom you have a strictly professional relationship.

Assuming you secure a wise and trusted colleague for the task, follow the same two bits of advice given earlier for administrative ratings. First, more is better. One visit probably will not give reliable information. Try to arrange for several visits. A half-dozen would be ideal, although it may be difficult to get that many. From a practical viewpoint, it may be impossible to arrange for any visits. However, you can ask your colleague to view a videotape. Second, have the person focus on specific behaviors, such as classroom management, students' time-on-task, and so on. Of course, you will be open to all comments, but having specific behaviors in mind should help the process.

VIDEOTAPING AND AUDIO RECORDING

Some evaluation systems require the use of videotapes. Someone will videotape you in your classroom. The completed videotape may be entered into a portfolio. In fact, most recommendations for portfolio development suggest inclusion of videotapes. For example, advanced certification by the National Board for Professional Teaching Standards (NBPTS) requires videotapes.

Viewing a videotape of your teaching can be a useful exercise. Most people are startled to see how they appear to others. Mannerisms to which you were oblivious become painfully obvious. What you thought was a coherent explanation actually sounds like a word salad. Your intention to have a highly interactive class turns out to be 90% teacher-talk. Directions are unclear. Students can't see the print on the overhead projector. And so on. All teachers should view themselves occasionally on videotape.

When submitting a videotape for administrative evaluation or advanced certification, you want to be at your very best. You want a flawless presentation, clear attention to students, and a model of time-on-task learning. When preparing a videotape for your own self-evaluation, you want to see a typical, normal classroom situation.

(© Syracuse Newspapers/The Image Works)

Videotapes can be very useful. However, they present some practical problems. The required equipment may not be readily available. For the tape to be really useful, someone should be pointing the camera at you and periodically panning the classroom. That requires an operator. Further, the camera and the operator may be a distraction in the classroom. Thus, videotaping can be inconvenient and expensive. It is no wonder that videotaping is used rather infrequently.

As with virtually any assessment tool, more is better for getting reliable results from videotapes. Using a single videotape for 30 minutes of class time is like having one 30-item quiz for a student. You would not want to base a final grade on one 30-item quiz. Similarly, you would not want to draw definitive conclusions about teaching performance from one 30-minute tape. On the other hand, a stellar (or miserable) performance on the 30-item quiz tells you something about the student. In the same way, a stellar (or miserable) performance on the videotape tells you something. Remember the general principle: More information means greater reliability. Hence, if you are using videotapes, try to get several.

There is a very practical alternative to the videotape: an audio recording. An audio recording is very easy to obtain. Nearly everyone has a simple audio recording device. It can be used inconspicuously in a classroom. Just place it on the front desk and flip it on for 60 minutes. An audio recording certainly does not provide the rich detail of a videotape. However, an audio recording does capture important features of classroom activities. Because it is so easy to use, we recommend use of audio recording several times each year for your own self-evaluation.

When using either videotapes or audio recordings, be sure to focus on specific variables. Upon first seeing or hearing yourself, you are likely to be utterly fascinated. Get beyond that. Try to identify such variables as use of voice, interaction with students, time management, nonverbal communication, and specification of learning goals. You may need to look at these variables at different times; that is, by reviewing the video or audio tape several times. At least once when viewing a videotape, do so with the sound off. This will help you focus on nonverbal communication as one important feature of the classroom environment. It may also be helpful to view the tape several weeks after it was completed; you may be a bit more objective when reviewing it later.

PORTFOLIOS

Chapter 8 described the use of portfolios for assessing students' work. Portfolios can also be used for assessing a teacher's work. The teaching **portfolio** will contain samples of the teacher's work (e.g., lesson plans, exams, and student projects). An increasing number of schools allow for, encourage, or require the submission of a portfolio for purposes of teacher evaluation. Numerous books and websites describe the development of a teaching portfolio. See, for example, Bullock and Hawk (2001), Campbell, Cignetti, Melenyzer, Nettles, and Wyman (2004), and Tucker, Stronge, and Gareis (2002). Certification by the NBPTS depends heavily on use of a teacher's portfolio.

Preparation of a portfolio can be very time-consuming. Bullock and Hawk (2001) estimated that preparing the portfolio for NBPTS requires about 120 hours. That's a lot of time. Peterson (2001) distinguished between a portfolio and a **dossier**. The portfolio may be very large, sprinkled generously with actual samples of work. In contrast, the dossier has only 10 to 12 pages. The dossier "boils down" the essential points. It summarizes what is in the portfolio. Peterson maintains that the dossier is much more useful than the portfolio for purposes of evaluation. For development of an electronic portfolio, see Montgomery and Wiley (2004).

For most uses of a portfolio or dossier you are trying to look your very best. You are trying to impress the principal, the superintendent, or an external board. If you admit to any faults, they will be small matters just to give the impression that you are being totally frank. We wish you luck in putting the package together. However, this sort of thing is *not* very helpful for your self-evaluation. If you want to use a portfolio for self-evaluation, it is probably best to keep a separate one for your personal use, one that may even contain information about your worst performances.

STUDENT TEST SCORES

Common sense suggests that students' performance on tests should tell us something about teaching effectiveness. A teacher's main responsibility is to get students to learn. Good teaching should lead to good student performance. Similarly, ineffective teaching will lead to poor student performance. The basic rationale here is quite simple. Everyone agrees on it.

Translating this simple rationale into practice becomes very complicated. At the root of the difficulty is the varying nature of the student groups for whom the teacher is responsible. The simplest design for evaluating teachers is to look at students' test scores at the end of the year. Whoever has the highest average test scores is the best teacher. There is great intuitive appeal to this simple design. However, it fails to account for initial differences in students' previous learning, general cognitive ability, family circumstances, and so on. Winning this game is easy: Just start with the brightest students. They will probably have the top scores at the end of the year.

The end-of-year design improves substantially by dealing with gain scores; that is, changes from the beginning to end of the year (or other unit of time). This is sometimes called the **value-added approach**. However, there are still difficulties. Do we expect the same degree of gain for all types of students? And, do we have a test that legitimately measures the variable of interest at both the beginning and the end of the year? Would we give an end-of-year algebra test to students at the beginning of the algebra course in order to measure gain? That would border on being inhumane. Nevertheless, students would differ in their initial preparation for algebra, so we could not assume that they were all starting at the same point. Lingering in the background of these efforts to use test scores is the fear of excessive teaching-to-the-test.

All of these difficulties have led some authors to abandon the effort to use students' test scores as an index of teaching effectiveness, despite the idea's initial appeal. In a frequently cited article, Glass (1990), a highly respected researcher, recommended against any use of test scores for teacher evaluation. However, one needs to consider Glass's context. He was examining the possible use of test scores for the high-stakes matter of determining teacher pay. For that purpose, the use of test scores is hazardous because of the problems already mentioned. However, the hazards do not beset other uses. If you want to see if Meg just set a school record in the 100-meter butterfly, you had better have a very good timing device, one that measures accurately to the hundredths of a second. If you need to determine only whether Meg can swim reasonably well or is likely to drown, you can stand at the side of the pool and watch her without any sophisticated timing device.

Several projects have made a frontal attack on the technical problems involved in using test scores as an index of teaching effectiveness. At least in theory, the problems are

2-21   © LaughingStock International Inc./dist. by United Media, 2004

"I think my test results are a pretty good indication of your abilities as a teacher."

Figure 15.3 Do you think this student scored high or low on the test?

(HERMAN© by Jim Unger; reprinted by permission of United Features Syndicate, Inc.)

solvable, although it takes Herculean effort to solve them. The most well-known effort is the Tennessee Value-Added Assessment System (TVAAS). The TVAAS project is very large-scale and very complex. It has won high praise in some quarters. At a minimum, it deserves credit for accepting the commonsense notion that teachers and schools should make a difference in students' learning and then trying to solve the technical problems of acting on this notion.

Try This!

To get an idea of what the TVAAS project does, check one of these websites:
   http://www.shearonforschools.com/TVAAS_index.html
   or
   http://www.state.tn.us/education/tstvaas.htm

However, these types of efforts go well beyond what an individual teacher can undertake. What advice is there for purposes of your self-evaluation? There are three points. *First*, examine whatever information you can find about your students' test performance to see what it might suggest about your teaching. See the example to follow in connection with Table 15.1. This examination includes students' performance on nationally standardized tests, state assessments, and your own tests. It also includes any results for externally prepared measures of interests and attitudes. *Second*, be cautious in drawing definitive conclusions, either positive or negative, from these sources of information. Note that

Table 15.1   Summary of Students' Standardized Test Scores at the End of Two Years

	Reading		Math		Language	
Student	Gr 3	Gr 4	Gr 3	Gr 4	Gr 3	Gr 4
Erin	52	62	60	50	48	50
Devon	38	40	50	52	36	52
Ian	42	40	48	40	40	40
Cynthia	50	65	62	62	55	60
Jen	68	76	54	44	60	64
Libby	54	52	48	46	50	62
Lindsey	80	85	90	80	82	86
Megan	25	30	35	35	30	35
Jess	40	56	54	50	55	58
Jenny	84	86	78	75	66	80
Katie	45	55	48	48	52	58

being cautious does not mean disregarding the information. It simply means being tentative in drawing conclusions from any one source. You should look at multiple sources across several time periods. *Third*, identify a few key sources of test information that are entirely under your own control. Use these from year to year or term to term in order to track your students' learning. These sources may include a few end-of-unit tests, projects, essays, or subsets of your own test items that you use on a regular basis. You certainly do not want to use exactly the same tests for all assessments every year. However, you can use a few items or exercises on a continuing basis. Comparing student performance on these repeated items or exercises should suggest something about your success. This procedure does not eliminate the problem of the changing nature of the students you have. You still need to take those changes into account. However, you also need to continually focus on student learning when examining your performance.

What test information might you examine? The answer will depend on the grade level and content area you teach. High school teachers might have an Advanced Placement (AP) exam or a state-prepared exam in algebra or American history. These teachers should examine their students' performance each year or term. Will the results provide a definitive index of teaching effectiveness? No. Will the results have some relevance for examining teaching effectiveness? Yes. Most elementary school teachers will have results from nationally standardized tests, such as those examined in Chapter 11, or state-prepared tests in basic skill areas. Such results may be available for the students at the end of last year and at the end of the current year; that is, the year when you taught the students.

Laying out the results as in Table 15.1 will help detect patterns. The table shows scores in percentiles at the end of Grade 3 (last year) and end of Grade 4 (this year). Notice that the students showed good progress in reading and language arts but lagged somewhat in math. The pattern does not hold for all students, but it is definitely a trend for the group. We raise the same questions for this example as for the high school example. Will the results provide a definitive index of teaching effectiveness? No. Will the results have some relevance for examining teaching effectiveness? Yes.

STUDENT RATINGS OF TEACHERS

Virtually every reader of this book has completed student ratings of college instructors. Such ratings are very widely used at the college level. The amount of research completed on student ratings of college instructors is nothing short of breathtaking. For summaries of this research, see Cashin (1995), Marsh (1987), Marsh and Dunkin (1997), and Perry and Smart (1997). Are student ratings applicable to elementary and secondary teachers? Apparently, yes. Student ratings are not used as often at the elementary and secondary levels as at the college level. However, the ratings seem to perform in much the same way across all educational levels. Of course, some adjustments are needed in the types of forms, particularly for the primary grades. However, student ratings at the precollege level seem to yield reasonably reliable and valid information about teaching performance. Peterson (2000a, 2000b) has summarized much of the research on this precollege use; see also Danielson and McGreal (2000) for recommendations on this topic.

At the college level, there are several widely used forms for student ratings and an untold number of locally prepared forms; see Hogan (2003) for a summary on this matter. At the precollege level, there are no widely used forms. However, you may draw on sev-

---

Metro School District
Students' Form for
Grade: 7 Teacher: Ms. Monahan

Please rate each of these items for your class.

In this class . . .	Not True		Unsure		Very True
I understand what I'm supposed to do.	[ ]	[ ]	[ ]	[ ]	[ ]
I can get help if I need it.	[ ]	[ ]	[ ]	[ ]	[ ]
Directions for homework assignments are clear.	[ ]	[ ]	[ ]	[ ]	[ ]
Tests are fair.	[ ]	[ ]	[ ]	[ ]	[ ]
Classes are boring.	[ ]	[ ]	[ ]	[ ]	[ ]
Our science projects are fun.	[ ]	[ ]	[ ]	[ ]	[ ]

Figure 15.4 Sample student rating form for use in a Grade 7 class.

eral existing sources for appropriate forms. Alternatively, you may make up your own form. It is not difficult to do. Kenneth Peterson has developed several student-rating forms that he has made available (free) for teachers to use. His website (www. teacherevaluation.net) contains the forms. The site has a variety of other forms and suggestions for teacher evaluation. You can make up a form for your own use. Figure 15.4 shows an example. Keep it simple. Use only 5 to 10 items. Ask students to rate items that they have experience with, such as use of class time, nature of tests and feedback, clarity of assignments, and so on. Do not ask students to rate items such as your level of knowledge of material. Have students complete the forms anonymously. You are more likely to get honest responses that way.

Try This!

Examine the items in Figure 15.4. List two or three items that might be added to the form to cover aspects of teaching that seem to be missing.

There are several points to keep in mind about the use of student ratings. First, as with other sources of information, make sure you have a sufficient base to draw conclusions. You should have results from at least four or five groups of students; more is even better. Do not try to draw definitive conclusions based on one group of students. Second, you probably will not have any comparative norm to help your interpretation, unless many teachers in your school are using the same form. Thus, you are faced with the question: What is a good (or bad) average rating? This question is not easy to answer. It is important to note that students tend to be lenient in their ratings. Thus, on a 5-point scale (1–5), an average rating of about 4.0 is rather normal. By looking at your ratings over several years, you can develop your own norm. This will at least allow you to determine if your averages are moving up or down.

PARENT RATINGS

Paralleling the use of student ratings of teachers is parent ratings of teachers. This is not a widely used source of information, but it does seem to be growing in use. That makes some sense. After students, parents are probably the next most important stakeholders in the educational enterprise. The process for parent ratings of teachers is very similar to that for student ratings. Parents will complete a simple form indicating their degree of satisfaction with several items. There are two major differences between student ratings and parent ratings. First, the items should be different. Parents should be asked to rate items about which they have first-hand knowledge. They will not know about how you manage the classroom (except by way of hearsay from their child). However, they should know whether homework assignments are clearly communicated. They should know whether they are receiving adequate feedback about their child's progress. Figure 15.5 shows an example of a parent rating form. Notice how its items differ from those for students in Figure 15.4.

The second major difference between student and parent forms relates to procedures for obtaining the information. It is easy to administer the student form. In contrast, getting the form to the parent and then getting it back is not easy. You may get a poor response. That will limit your ability to draw conclusions. If only 25% of the parents return the form, you have a real problem. You do not know whether the 25% who returned the form are representative of the entire group. It may be that they are. On the other hand, it could be that the 75% who did not return the form differ substantially in their level of satisfaction (either more positive or more negative) than the 25% who did return the form. You must be prudent in dealing with this matter.

Beltway District
Parents' Form for
Grade: 4 Teacher: Ms. Vasquez

Please rate each of these items for your child's class.
Have your child return the form in the envelope provided.

	Not True	Unsure	Very True
I get clear information about my child's progress.	[ ] [ ]	[ ] [ ]	[ ]
My child understands homework assignments.	[ ] [ ]	[ ] [ ]	[ ]
My child seems to enjoy going to school.	[ ] [ ]	[ ] [ ]	[ ]
I know what my child is studying.	[ ] [ ]	[ ] [ ]	[ ]

Other comments:

Figure 15.5 Sample form for parent rating of teacher.

Interpretation of results from parent rating forms presents the same problem as interpreting results from student rating forms. Very often, you will not have any norm. On a 5-point scale, what constitutes an acceptable level of satisfaction: 3.5, 4.0, 4.5, . . . ? It is not an easy question to answer. As with student ratings, if you have information from parent ratings over several terms or years, you can at least note increases or decreases in average ratings.

Peterson (2000b) and Stronge and Ostrander (1997) provide useful discussions of both parent and student ratings. They give examples of forms that have been used for these purposes. See also Airasian and Gullickson (1997) for examples of teacher self-evaluation forms.

STUDENT SELF-REPORTS OF ACHIEVEMENT

Chapter 9 contained recommendations for using students' self-ratings of achievement as a measure of student progress. Such ratings are particularly helpful for assessing student progress in areas that may be difficult to assess by conventional tests or exercises. An incidental benefit of student self-ratings of achievement is that they can be a valuable source of information about your own teaching. We recommend their use for that purpose.

Consider the self-reports in Figure 15.6, reintroduced here from Chapter 9. The topics might come from a junior high math class. Of course, the teacher might have an additional 10–20 topics in the list. Analysis of students' responses may provide valuable information about your teaching. The responses may suggest changes in your teaching. For example, suppose that average ratings are above 4.0 for all items except "determining probabilities," which has an average of 2.5. That might suggest increased emphasis or changing the approach to that topic.

It is very easy to make up forms to secure students' self-reports of learning. The forms can be tailored exactly to your instructional program. They are simple for students to complete. Students should complete the forms anonymously. The results are easily summarized.

Self-reports of student achievement may not have a high degree of credibility with external audiences. Other people may well object that the reports do not *really* get at student learning and that the reports can easily be influenced by the teacher's directions. This source of information may not be useful for external audiences. The information is strictly for your purposes. However, research shows that self-reports of achievement do correlate

Mark to show how much you think you have learned in each area.	Very Little				Very Much
Working with percents	1	2	3	4	5
Working with decimals	1	2	3	4	5
Graphing linear functions	1	2	3	4	5
Determining probabilities	1	2	3	4	5
Solving equations in one unknown	1	2	3	4	5

Figure 15.6 Scale for self-report of achievement in math.

moderately well with actual measured achievement. Thus, self-reports are a valid, although not perfect, source of information. This conclusion, combined with their ease of use, makes self-reports a recommended source for your self-evaluation.

UNOBTRUSIVE MEASURES

Recall another topic from Chapter 9: unobtrusive measures. These are naturally occurring sources of information. In Chapter 9, we treated them as indicators of student accomplishment. They can also be used as indicators of your success as a teacher.

The nature of unobtrusive measures is that they are highly peculiar to a particular topic; that is, for a particular grade level and content area. Therefore, it is difficult to provide a convenient list of such measures. Consider some of the examples introduced in Chapter 9. The Grade 9 English teacher may keep track of how many students submit entries for a poetry contest. The Algebra I teacher may note how many students elect to take Algebra II. The Grade 2 teacher may observe how many students read a book during a 15-minute "quiet time" in class. The possibilities are endless. It takes some creative thinking to identify useful unobtrusive measures. Once identified, they are often very easy to record and compare from year to year. We recommend that you try to identify a few unobtrusive measures that will give you feedback about your teaching effectiveness.

Like student self-reports of achievement, unobtrusive measures will not have great weight in the public forum. They are highly contextualized. It is easy to dismiss them as unimportant or only tangentially relevant. Thus, restrict their use to your own self-evaluation. Appropriate unobtrusive measures can be very meaningful for your own information.

TEACHER COMPETENCY TESTS AND ADDITIONAL CERTIFICATIONS

Every list of teacher evaluation methods includes teacher competency tests and additional certifications. Teacher competency tests include those in the Praxis series as well as tests that might be developed by a particular state or professional association. Recall that the Praxis series appeared in Chapter 11. Specifically, the Praxis I and II series illustrated standardized tests used for certification. The **Praxis III** series carries the subtitle "Classroom Performance Assessment." It includes some conventional tests of knowledge. More importantly, Praxis III includes assessment of your in-class performance by trained assessors.

The most visible advanced certification program is the **National Board for Professional Teaching Standards** (**NBPTS**) system. Like Praxis III, NBPTS involves examination of in-class performance and portfolio development, including videotapes. The entire process takes about one full year of effort. At present, Praxis III and NBPTS are not widely used. However, their use is likely to increase, as the emphasis on "highly qualified teachers" in the No Child Left Behind Act continues to develop.

Try This!

To get more detailed information about Praxis III and the NBPTS system, go to these websites:
   http://www.ets.org/praxis/
   http://www.nbpts.org/

We do not recommend use of teacher competency exams and advanced certifications as part of your self-evaluation. These methods of evaluation may be very useful for their own purposes. We do not think they serve a useful purpose for self-evaluation. Of course, the procedures will give you some insights into yourself. However, your approach to these assessments is to do your very best. You want to "pass the test" or get a new certification. They are like the administrator ratings treated earlier in this chapter. They do not provide a good context for frank admission of areas needing improvement. Furthermore, these tests and certifications are one-time events. Your self-evaluation needs to be continuous.

DON'T FORGET THE "OTHER STUFF"

Procedures for evaluating teachers tend to concentrate on classroom performance. This is understandable. The classroom is the main venue for performing as a teacher. However, classroom performance is not everything. Most teachers have other responsibilities, too. Exact responsibilities will usually be spelled out in a contract or handbook. Very often, teacher responsibilities extend to such matters as serving on school committees, developing new skills (e.g., computer and Internet skills), and pursuing professional development (e.g., by attendance at meetings of professional associations).

Your administratively mandated evaluation may or may not cover these other responsibilities. Regardless of whether or not they are included, you should include these other areas in your self-evaluation. Simple indicators will cover some of these areas. Did you attend some professional meetings? Did you present a session at one of these meetings? Did you learn to use Power Point or video streaming? Did you adopt a new electronic gradebook? You should be able to note such accomplishments or lack thereof.

Evaluating your performance on school committees and other such group activities is considerably more difficult. Of course, it is easy to determine whether you attended meetings. It is not easy to determine whether you contributed constructively. The main point is that you should be examining your role in these non-classroom-based areas of a teacher's responsibilities.

THE IMPORTANCE OF CONTENT

Discussions of teaching effectiveness usually focus on what a teacher does and on sources of information about the teacher. In fact, most of this chapter focuses on these topics. In the midst of these discussions, it is important to remember the content of teaching. And, as part of self-evaluation, it is important to emphasize keeping yourself up-to-date on content. What are the new developments in science? What is going on in world politics? Are there new trends in business? A good self-analysis of teaching should include reference to efforts to stay current in the area of teaching competence. You may be doing a good job of teaching students that the world is flat. Nice job teaching, but wrong content.

Here is a simple checklist that will give you clues about whether you are keeping up-to-date regarding content. In the last year, have you . . .

- ☐ Read any journal articles related to your field?
- ☐ Read any full-length books in your field?
- ☐ Attended any professional meetings in your field?

☐ Participated in professional meetings as a presenter, discussant, or chair?

☐ Served as a judge for student contests in your field?

☐ Served as an advisor to student contestants in your field?

☐ Taken any formal courses (e.g., graduate courses) in your field?

In each case, reference to "your field" means the content of what you teach, not the methodology of teaching. Of course, this checklist is not definitive, but it provides at least some key indicators of keeping up-to-date in a field.

FROM INFORMATION TO REFLECTION TO ACTION

Reflection is the process of thinking about your own work as a teacher, then drawing conclusions that lead to improvements. There is an increasing consensus among educators that reflection is a vital part of competent professional practice. McEwan (2002) identifies reflection as one part of the 10 traits of highly effective teachers. Jay (2003) refers to reflection as the heart of practice for quality teaching. Nearly all writers on the subject of reflection emphasize two characteristics of reflection. First, it involves raising difficult questions. Second, its purpose is action. Moore (1998), for example, states: "Reflective teaching means you must ask basic, but often difficult questions about the appropriateness and success of your teaching" (p. 7). McEwan (2002) notes: "Reflection is the examination of one's teaching practice in a thoughtful and even critical way, learning from the process, and then using what has been learned to affect one's future action" (p. 117). Ghaye and Ghaye (1998) emphasize: "It is a deliberate, conscious and public activity principally designed to improve future action" (p. 5). The importance of reflection is by no means confined to the field of teaching. It has been stressed by philosophers (e.g., Socrates's famous dictum: *Know thyself*) and religious leaders, as well as by contemporary gurus of business management (Lowney, 2003).

The preceding sections of this chapter have identified sources of information that might be useful for looking at your teaching. However, all the information in the world will not be helpful unless you think about the information and try to draw conclusions from it regarding possible improvements. Simply collecting information will not help.

Figure 15.7 Hoping, as well as reflection, needs to be followed by action.

You have to think about—reflect on—the information and try to draw conclusions from it. Having drawn conclusions, you need to take action. Although good information about your teaching is useless without reflection, reflection by itself in the absence of good information can also be useless. You need both. And both must be translated into specific actions aimed at improvement.

Several mechanisms will aid the reflection process. Personal journals are often recommended. Martin, Majesky, and Eckler (2003) provide useful examples of entries from

---

The Top 10 Things I've Learned About Teacher Evaluation

I first started observing student teachers about 40 years ago. Since that time, I have run workshops on analyzing one's own teaching, looked at innumerable videotapes of teachers, and visited countless classrooms. I have interviewed prospective teachers (and administrators), written evaluations of hundreds of teachers, and operated institutional systems for rating teachers (and administrators). I have served on school boards, wrestling in part with matters of teaching quality. And, I have myself been evaluated as a teacher. From all of these experiences, I think I have learned some basic principles about evaluating teachers. I offer them here, with the hope that they will be of some help to aspiring, new, and perhaps even veteran teachers.

1. *The starting point is attitude.* This point was made at the beginning of the chapter. If you are not open to change, nothing else matters.
2. *It is difficult to evaluate teaching, but it is not impossible.* There are complexities, but they are not insurmountable. Further, for most purposes, you do not need an impeccable method, just a useful one.
3. *Focus on student learning.* In the business of teacher evaluation, it is easy to get caught up in matters of "style." Keep your focus on student learning. Let matters of style take care of themselves. (This is not an invitation to be a grouch.) In connection with this point, make sure you keep up-to-date in your teaching area(s).
4. *Use multiple sources of information.* Using multiple sources should increase both the reliability and the validity of self-evaluation. You may not use all of the sources recommended in this chapter, but use more than one.
5. *Accept criticism.* This is hard to do. Human nature resists criticism. It's unpleasant. If you find yourself continually explaining away unflattering results, you have a real problem. Learn to accept criticism and reflect on it.
6. While accepting criticism, *do not overreact to isolated criticism.* You may be a fine teacher, but not all students, parents, and administrators will like you. Balancing this point with the last one is a delicate act.
7. *Student background makes a difference.* It makes a difference in level of learning. It may well make a difference in your approach. Make adjustments.
8. *Be self-reflective.* All the information in the world is not going to be helpful unless you reflect on it. Use simple mechanisms to help your self-reflection. And, plan to follow up your reflections with action aimed at improvement.
9. *There is research on these topics.* Find out what the research says. Don't be content to operate with populist rhetoric on these matters of teacher evaluation.
10. *Finally, for heaven's sake, if your evaluations are continually negative, even after you have tried to improve, get out.* Get a different job. In the long run, you will probably be happier, as will your potential students.

reflective journals. A personal portfolio, other than the one used for administrative evaluations or advanced certification, may be helpful, too. Another very simple mechanism is recording brief but explicit notes on any of the sources of information treated earlier in this chapter. For example, after obtaining students' self-reports of learning, make brief notes regarding your conclusions about the results. After analyzing students' gain scores on some test, record your observations about what you learned from the analysis. In fact, such brief notes can become part of a journal or personal portfolio. The very process of recording the notes should aid the reflection process.

PRACTICAL ADVICE

1. Construct your own system of self-evaluation. Obviously, you do not want to disregard the administratively required evaluation in your school. However, you want to have your own system, one that is strictly for your personal feedback.

2. Use multiple sources of information. We presented several possible sources for you to use. Do not make your system so elaborate that it collapses. However, do not limit yourself to just one source.

3. Be cautious in your interpretation of information—but do try to reach conclusions about your teaching effectiveness.

4. Reflect on the information you get and keep trying to find ways to improve.

SUMMARY

1. In some types of evaluation you want to look your very best. This is the case for administratively required evaluations and for new certifications. However, you should also attempt to develop honest self-evaluation, in which you readily admit deficiencies and areas needing improvement.

2. When considering procedures for teacher evaluation, it is important to remember that the fundamental principles of assessment—for example, reliability and validity—still apply.

3. The evaluation of teaching presents some special problems. Chief among these is the varying nature of student groups that a teacher encounters. Differences among student groups must be taken into account. However, that does not mean that no conclusions can be drawn. It simply suggests proceeding cautiously. It is especially important to use multiple sources of information and multiple time frames.

4. Every teacher will undergo administrator evaluations. Do your best on these. However, they are not particularly useful for your self-evaluation.

5. Ratings by mentors or colleagues can be very useful. However, it may be difficult to arrange for them.

6. All teachers can profit from viewing themselves on videotape. Videotapes are usually inconvenient to obtain. A practical alternative is an audio recording. It is not as rich as a videotape, but its convenience recommends it.

7. A teaching portfolio may be required by your school or for a special certification. If so, do a good job on it. You may want to keep a separate portfolio strictly for your own self-analysis.

8. Student test scores, properly used, can provide useful information. It is very difficult to use them for high-stakes purposes. For your own analysis of your teaching, they should always be part of the picture.

9. Student ratings of your instruction provide you with useful information. As with other types of information, make sure you have a sufficient base of such ratings to draw meaningful inferences.

10. Parent ratings can also be useful, although they are more difficult to obtain than are student ratings. If you use parent ratings, be sure to ask about areas with which parents will be familiar.

11. Student self-reports of achievement are easy to obtain and very flexible. They allow you to cover areas that may be difficult to tease out in other ways. Although you will not have an external norm for interpreting the general level of results, you can at least compare ratings on different items.

12. Some areas allow for the use of unobtrusive measures. You need to think creatively about possible indicators. If you can identify some relevant indicators, they can be very useful for your self-evaluation.

13. You may need to or want to pursue teacher competency tests or additional certifications. You want to perform at your maximum level on such measures. Ordinarily, they are not useful for your self-evaluation.

14. Most procedures for teacher evaluation concentrate on classroom performance and elements closely connected with classroom activities. However, teacher responsibilities usually extend to such other areas as serving on school committees, participating in professional associations, and so on. Be sure to cover these other areas in the scope of your self-evaluation.

15. Reflection on the information obtained from various sources is crucial. Several mechanisms may be used to help with the reflection process.

KEY TERMS

dossier	portfolio	reflection
NBPTS (National Board for Professional Teaching Standards)	Praxis III	value-added approach

EXERCISES

1. Pick a content field and grade level you teach or might teach. Construct a *self-report of achievement* for your students to use. Use no more than 10 statements. Use either a 3-point or 5-point response scale for the statements. Let the end points be "Very Little" and "Very Much."

2. Pick a grade level (the content area does not make any difference) and build a simple rating form *for students to rate teaching effectiveness*. Use language appropriate for the grade level. Use no more than five statements. Be sure to designate the response scale that students will use.

3. For the same grade level, build a *parent rating form*. Use five statements. Be sure to concentrate on matters that parents would know about.

4. Go to the website for the National Board for Professional Standards (http://www.nbpts.org). Write a brief (one paragraph) description of what you would need to do to undergo the NBPTS evaluation.

5. Go to this website: http://www.teacherevaluation.net. Briefly describe at least three types of teacher evaluation procedures you find there.

Appendix A

Sources of Information About Tests

At one time or another, you may need to get information about an existing test. There are two rather different contexts for this need. First, you may have a *specific purpose* in mind and you want to know what tests are available for that purpose. Here are examples of that purpose:

- You are a high school biology teacher. You would like to use an end-of-year biology test that has national norms. What tests are available for you to consider?
- You are doing your master's thesis on a technique to improve students' interests in math. Are there existing tests you could use for your project?
- You are part of a school's test committee to select a standardized achievement test. What tests should the committee review?

In each of these cases, you want to search for a number of possibilities, review them, and select one for use.

Here is a second type of need. You hear reference to a *specific test* but you are not familiar with it. You want to get some basic information about the test. Here are examples:

- Juanita has just transferred to your school. In her records, you see reference to her scores on the ABC Inventory. You want to get some information about what this inventory measures.
- You are reading a research report that refers to the North Coast Math Test. Can you quickly find some information about this test? Are there any professional reviews of this test?
- You know that you want to use the Stanford Diagnostic Reading Test. Can you find the latest edition and who publishes it?

In each of these cases, you have the name of a specific test. You need to get some information about the test.

There are three principal sources of information about tests. They help to answer the kinds of questions in the examples just listed. You should become familiar with each of these sources. In addition, we will mention three other sources of information about tests for more specialized uses: professional journals, specialized books on particular topics, and colleagues in the field.

COMPREHENSIVE LISTS OF TESTS

The first major source of information is comprehensive lists of tests. How many tests are "out there" for possible use? The short answer is: More than you can possibly imagine. Some sources include as many as 20,000 tests. How can you keep track of all that? Fortunately, there are comprehensive lists of tests to help with the task. Some of these lists are available in book form (hard copy). Some are available in electronic form, specifically on searchable websites. Let's examine each of these forms.

In Book Form

There are two comprehensive lists of tests in book form. They are:

- *Tests in Print* (TIP) and
- *Tests: A comprehensive reference for assessments in psychology, education, and business*, referred to here simply as *Tests*.

TIP is now in its sixth edition, called TIP VI (Murphy, Plake, Impara, & Spies, 2002). New editions appear approximately every four years. TIP attempts to list all tests that are commercially available in English. The current edition lists more than 4,000 tests. Each entry in TIP provides a brief description of the test, including scores, publisher, target population, and cost. Figure A.1 shows a sample entry from TIP. Note the important information provided in the entry, such as the test's purpose, target audience, publisher, and so on. Note also, however, the absence of information about the test's quality. The "cross

---

[2547]
Test of Mathematical Abilities for Gifted Students.
Purpose: "Designed to identify students who have talent or giftedness in mathematics."
Population: Ages 6–12.
Publication Date: 1988.
Acronym: TOMAGS.
Scores: Total score only.
Administration: Group or individual.
Levels, 2: Primary, Intermediate.
Price Data, 2001: $149 per complete kit including manual (53 pages), 25 each Primary Level and Intermediate Level student booklets, and 25 each Primary Level and Intermediate Level profile/scoring sheets; $39 per 25 student booklets (specify level); $14 per 25 profile/scoring sheets (specify level); $49 per manual.
Time: (30–60) minutes.
Authors: Gail R. Ryser and Susan K. Johnsen.
Publisher: PRO-ED.
Cross References: For reviews by Robert B. Frary and Delwyn L. Harnisch, see 14:391.

Figure A.1 Sample entry from *Tests in Print*.

(From Murphy, L. L., Plake, B. S., Impara, J. C., & Spies, R. A. (Eds.). (2002). *Tests in Print VI* (p. 670). Lincoln, NE: Buros Institute of Mental Measurements. With permission of the publisher and the Board of Regents of the University of Nebraska-Lincoln.)

references" at the bottom of the entry tell whether there are reviews of the test's quality. We discuss these reviews in the next section.

Tests, now in its fifth edition (Maddox, 2003), is similar to TIP. It attempts to list all tests that are commercially available in English and in any way related to business, education, or psychology. Also like TIP, new editions of *Tests* appear every three-to-five years.

Both TIP and *Tests* have several useful indexes. For example, they each include an index of key words. Thus, if you have an interest in a certain construct—for example, attitude toward math or self-concept—you can identify tests referencing these key words. Each source also has a list of test publishers.

TIP and *Tests* only include regularly published tests; that is, ones you can buy from a publisher. There are also "unpublished" tests. They are unpublished in the sense that you cannot buy them from a publisher. However, they are published in the sense that they appear in a journal article. The main source for these "unpublished" tests is the *Directory of Unpublished Experimental Mental Measures*, referred to here as the *Directory*. The *Directory* is now available in its eighth edition, called volumes. Thus the most recent issue is volume 8 (Goldman & Mitchell, 2003). The *Directory*'s authors monitor the appearance of unpublished tests in more than 30 professional journals (e.g., the *Journal of Educational Psychology*, the *Journal of Experimental Education*, and the *Journal of School Psychology*). Entries in the *Directory* provide simple descriptive information about the test, including the journal in which it appeared. Of course, because the test is "unpublished," there is no publisher or cost information.

Most college and university libraries, as well as larger public libraries, have copies of TIP, *Tests*, and the *Directory*. They are usually in the reference section of the library.

Try This!

Find each of these sources in your college/university library. Note the call letters for your own use.

Source   Call Letters

TIP   _____

Tests   _____

Directory   _____

In Electronic Form

Probably the most useful source of basic information about tests currently available is the Internet-accessible ETS Test Collection. It is available at:

http://www.ets.org/testcoll

Like TIP and *Tests*, this site provides only basic information about a test. For example, it includes the test's purpose, target audience, scores, and publisher. The ETS Test Collection includes approximately 20,000 entries. You can search it based on test title, author, or key word (descriptor). Refer back to our two basic situations: (1) You have the name of a test and you need information about it. (2) You need to find tests available for a certain purpose. For the first situation, you can enter the name of a test. The website returns basic information about it. (Be sure to use the exact test title. The search is unforgiving about minor variations in titles.) For the second situation, you can enter key words (e.g., math attitude or biology). You will get a list of tests related to the key word(s). Then, you can link to the basic information about specific entries.

Try This!

Go to: http://www.ets.org/testcoll. Click on "Database Search," then on the drop-down menu for "Search for," click on "Descriptor Search." Enter key words for an area of interest to you (e.g., chemistry or self-concept). You will get a list of tests. Click on one of the tests. This will take you to basic information about that test.

The great strength of all the comprehensive lists is precisely the fact that they are comprehensive. They cast a very broad net. They are useful for getting a quick, general idea of what tests may be available for a specific purpose. And, they are useful for getting simple, basic information about a particular test. The biggest shortcoming of the comprehensive lists is that they contain little information about the quality of the test. Some of the tests are worthless. Some are very good. The good and the bad get equal treatment. How do you know whether an entry is any good? You cannot tell from the entries in the comprehensive lists. To get an idea about the quality of a test, we turn to the next source: test reviews.

TEST REVIEWS

As suggested by the title, sources in this category provide a review of the test. Professionals in relevant fields write the reviews. They give their professional opinion about the quality of the test, using the criteria for test quality we have emphasized throughout this book. For example, they comment on the reliability and validity of the test, the nature of the norm group, the ease of using the materials, and so on.

There are two principal sources of these test reviews:

- Buros' *Mental Measurements Yearbook*, and
- *Test Critiques*

These two sources are very similar, but they do have some differences. Let us briefly describe each of them.

Buros's *Mental Measurements Yearbook* is a classic reference source in the field of testing and assessment. It is often abbreviated as " Buros" or simply "MMY." First published in 1938, MMY is now in its 15th edition (Plake, Impara, & Spies, 2003). New editions appear about every three years. Each of the recent volumes has contained reviews of approximately 300 tests. For most entries, there are two independent reviewers. For example, a reading test might be reviewed by a testing specialist and a reading specialist. Each review in MMY is about 1,000 words, the equivalent of four double-spaced typed pages of text. The review covers the test's purpose, reliability, norms, validity, development procedures, and recommendations for or against its use.

In purpose, *Test Critiques* (TC) is very similar to MMY. Volumes of TC appear about every five years. The most recent edition is volume XI (Keyser, 2004). Although very similar to MMY in purpose and the structure of reviews, TC differs from MMY in several ways. The TC reviews tend to be longer. TC has only one reviewer per test. TC covers fewer tests than does MMY. TC tends to cover only the more widely used tests, whereas MMY casts a broader net. There is one other important difference between MMY and TC. MMY reviews are available online for libraries that subscribe to that service or, absent that service, to anyone for a fee. TC reviews are not currently available online.

The great strength of MMY and TC is that they provide professional opinions about the quality of a test. The comprehensive lists referred to earlier do not; they provide only basic, descriptive information. There are two main shortcomings to the test review sources. First, it takes quite a bit of time to complete a review. From the time a test first appears to the time a review of it appears may be three or more years. Meanwhile, people are trying to decide whether to use the test. Second, it must be admitted that the reviews are only opinions. It is not unusual, when two reviews are available, to find one reviewer recommending use of the test and the other reviewer recommending against its use. Of course, in many instances the two reviewers agree. However, contrary conclusions remind us that the reviews are only opinions.

Try This!

Check your college/university library for availability of the hard copies of MMY and Test Critiques. Note their call letters for future use. Also, check the availability of MMY reviews online. Note its access site.

Source	Call letters/Access site
Buros's MMY (hard copy)	_____
Test Critiques	_____
Buros's MMY online	_____

PUBLISHERS' CATALOGS

The third major source of information about tests is publishers' catalogs. Of course, this information is available only for published tests. All of the major test publishers issue a catalog at least annually. Today, these catalogs are available in hard copy as well as online. Appendix B lists the major test publishers. The list has contact information, including websites. Sources such as TIP and *Tests* list approximately 200 test publishers. However, a relatively small number of publishers, as given in Appendix B, produce the great majority of tests used in education.

The publisher's catalog is the key source of information for practical details about a test. For example, the catalog tells about different forms of a test, types of answer media, the most recent norms, and current costs. Information about such practical details is often very dated in such sources as TIP, *Tests*, MMY, and TC.

The great shortcoming of the publisher's catalog is that it is, obviously, not an unbiased source of information. The publisher is in the business of selling tests. Thus, claims in the catalog about the test's reliability, the quality of norms, and so on must be taken with a grain of salt.

Larger test publishers have employees who can be very helpful. Many publishers have technical experts in their home offices. These experts have conducted research on the tests. The largest publishers also have field representatives (salespersons) who travel to schools to help sell the tests. All of these people can be enormously helpful in getting practical information about a test. For example, they will know if a new edition of a test is scheduled to appear next year. Of course, like the publisher's catalog, these people are not an unbiased source of information about a test's quality.

Try This!

Go to the website for one of the publishers listed in Appendix B. Find one of the publisher's tests. What information is displayed for the test?

OTHER SOURCES OF INFORMATION

The comprehensive lists, test reviews, and publishers' catalogs are the most important sources of information about tests. There are several other sources that we will describe just briefly. First, some *professional journals* regularly provide information about tests and other assessment methods. Examples are the *Journal of Educational Measurement*, *Educational and Psychological Measurement*, and *Applied Measurement in Education*. The journals tend to have advanced, often very technical treatment of topics. Journals may be an important source for someone conducting a research project. They are not usually helpful for ordinary classroom applications. Another alternative source of information is *specialized books*, ones concentrating on tests in a specific field or even on just one test. For example, there are books on tests just for self-concept or just for social attitudes. For someone interested in a specialized topic, a relevant book can be a gold mine. However, there are not many such books. And, at least in more active fields, they tend to become outdated quickly. Finally, *professional colleagues* can be an important source of information. Suppose you want to use a diagnostic reading test or an algebra test. A call or an e-mail to some trusted, experienced colleagues will quickly identify several possibilities. Of course, you need to use your own judgment to make a decision, but knowing what colleagues currently use can be a very helpful first step.

Appendix B

Major Test Publishers

Publisher	Address	Telephone	Website
ACT, Inc.	Iowa City, IA 52243-1008	800-645-1992	www.act.org
American Guidance Service	4201 Woodland Rd., Circle Pines, MN 55014-1796	800-328-2560	www.agsnet.com
College Board, The	45 Columbus Ave., New York, NY 10023-6992	212-713-8000	www.collegeboard.com
CTB/McGraw-Hill	20 Ryan Ranch Rd., Monterey, CA 93940	800-538-9547	www.ctb.com
Educational & Industrial Testing Service (EdITS)	P.O. Box 7234, San Diego, CA 92167	800-416-1666	www.edits.net
Educational Testing Service	Rosedale Rd., Princeton, NJ 08541	609-921-9000	www.ets.org
Harcourt Assessment	555 Academic Court, San Antonio, TX 78204-2498	800-211-8378	www.harcourtassessment.com
NCS Pearson	11000 Prairie Lakes Dr., Eden Prairie, MN 55344	800-627-0365	www.ncspearson.com
National Career Assessment Services	601 Visions Parkway, P.O. Box 277, Adel, IA 50003	800-314-8972	www.ncasi.com
PRO-ED	8700 Shoal Creek Blvd., Austin, TX 78757-6897	800-897-3202	www.proedinc.com
Psychological Assessment Resources	P.O. Box 998, Odessa, FL 33556	800-331-8378	www.parinc.com
Psychological Corporation, The	19500 Bulverde Rd., San Antonio, TX 78259	800-211-8378	www.psychcorp.com
Riverside Publishing	425 Spring Lake Dr., Itasca, IL 60143-2079	800-323-9540	www.riverpub.com
Sigma Assessment Systems	P.O. Box 610984, Port Huron, MI 48061-0984	800-265-1285	www.sigmaassessmentsystems.com
Slosson Educational Publications	538 Buffalo Rd., East Aurora, NY 14052-0280	888-SLOSSON (756-7766)	www.slosson.com
Wide Range, Inc.	P.O. Box 3410, Wilmington, DE 19804	800-221-9728	www.widerange.com

Appendix C

Useful Formulas

COMPUTING FORMULA FOR THE STANDARD DEVIATION

Chapter 2 gives the basic definition for the standard deviation as follows:

$$SD = \sqrt{\frac{\Sigma(X - M)^2}{N}}$$

In most instances, we use a software package to calculate SD. However, if one must calculate it by hand, the formula given above is very cumbersome. Although the following formula looks harder, it is actually much easier to use

$$SD = \sqrt{\frac{\Sigma X^2 - \frac{(\Sigma X)^2}{N}}{N}}$$

In this formula, ΣX^2 says, square each score, then add up these squared scores. $(\Sigma X)^2$ says add up all the scores, then square that sum. Here is an example using the data in Figure 2.6.

Scores (X):	6	9	4	5	5	1
X^2	36	81	16	25	25	1

$\Sigma X^2 = 184$ $(\Sigma X) = 30$ $(\Sigma X)^2 = 900$ N = 6

$$SD = \sqrt{\frac{184 - \frac{900}{6}}{6}} = \sqrt{\frac{184 - 150}{6}} = \sqrt{5.66} = 2.38$$

If you want to estimate the standard deviation in the population, use N − 1 rather than N in the denominator of these formulas.

CORRELATION COEFFICIENT

Chapter 2 introduced the correlation coefficient (r). The chapter did not contain any formulas for r. The formulas give little insight into what the correlation means. For the sake of completeness in presentation, we provide several formulas here. First, there are two versions of the basic definition of r. The first version uses deviation scores (e.g., X minus the mean of X). The version also employs the standard deviations of the X and Y variables. The second version converts both X and Y scores into their respective z-scores. The last formula uses raw scores; that is, the original X and Y scores. The formula appears quite forbidding, but it is easy to use. It's just rather tedious. We give an example using this formula. For virtually any practical work, you will use a computer program to calculate r.

Calculating r with deviation scores:

$$r = \frac{\Sigma(X - \bar{X})(Y - \bar{Y})}{NS_X S_Y}$$

Calculating r with z-scores:

$$r = \frac{\Sigma Z_x Z_y}{N}$$

Calculating r from raw scores:

$$r = \frac{N\Sigma XY - (\Sigma X)(\Sigma Y)}{\sqrt{[N\Sigma X^2 - (\Sigma X)^2][N\Sigma Y^2 - (\Sigma Y)^2]}}$$

Example of calculating r from raw scores

X	Y	X^2	Y^2	XY
2	3	4	9	6
5	4	25	16	20
6	7	36	49	42
4	5	16	25	20
8	9	64	81	72

$\Sigma X = 25$ $\Sigma Y = 28$ $\Sigma X^2 = 145$ $\Sigma Y^2\ 180$ $\Sigma XY = 160$

$(\Sigma X)^2 = 625$ $(\Sigma Y)^2 = 784$

$r = $ 0.93

SPEARMAN-BROWN CORRECTION FOR SPLIT-HALF RELIABILITY

$$r_c = \frac{2r_h}{1 + r_h}$$

where

r_c = the corrected , full-length reliability

r_h = the correlation between the two half-length tests

The Spearman-Brown formula has a more general form that allows one to determine the estimated effect on internal consistency reliability of any change in test length. The more general form is:

$$r_c = \frac{nr_o}{1 + (n - 1)r_o}$$

where

n is the factor by which test length is changed

r_c is the corrected reliability

r_o is the original reliability

In this formula, *n* may be a fraction. For example, one may estimate a corrected reliability for a test one fourth ($n = .25$) the length of the original test. Or one may estimate the effect of tripling ($n = 3$) the length of the test. One may also set r_c at some desired value, then solve for *n* to determine what change in test length is required to obtain r_c, given a starting value of r_o. For all these changes in test length, the Spearman-Brown formula assumes that the items added (or lost, in the case of shortening the test) are equivalent to other items in the test.

DISTINGUISHING AMONG THREE TYPES OF STANDARD ERRORS

The standard error of measurement:

$$SEM = SD_X \sqrt{1-r_{XX}}$$

where

SD_X = the standard deviation of the test whose reliability has been determined

r_{XX} = the reliability of the test

The standard error of the mean:

$$S_{\bar{X}} = \frac{SD_X}{\sqrt{N}}$$

where

SD_X = the standard deviation of scores

N = the sample size

The standard error of estimate:

$$SE_{Y'} = SD_Y \sqrt{1 - r_{XY}^2}$$

where

SD_Y = SD of the test for which a score is being predicted from the X variable

r_{XY} = the correlation between the X and Y variables

STANDARD ERROR OF MEASUREMENT FOR A DIFFERENCE

The standard error of measurement for the difference between two scores (score 1 and score 2) is the square root of the sum of the squares of the standard errors for each score. For example, if SEM for test 1 is 5 points and SEM for test 2 is 8 points, the standard error of the difference is 9.4 points: SQRT ($5^2 + 8^2$)

$$SEM_{diff} = \sqrt{SEM_1^2 + SEM_2^2}$$

CORRECTION FOR GUESSING

To correct for guessing, the following formula is applied:

$$RS_c = RS_o - \frac{W}{K - 1}$$

where

RS$_c$ = corrected raw score

RS$_o$ = original raw score

W   = number of wrong answers

K   = number of options in multiple-choice items

Note: Omitted items are not counted as wrong.

Here are some examples to illustrate how the formula works:

- On a 50 item test composed of multiple-choice items with five options, Tom got 40 right and 10 wrong. What is his score when the correction for guessing is applied?

$$[40 - (10/(5-1)) = 40 - 2.5 = 37.5]$$

- Suppose Tom got 40 right and omitted the remaining 10 items. What is his corrected score?

$$[40 - 0 = 40]$$

- On a 50 item True-False test, Jen got 25 items right and 25 wrong. What is her corrected score?

$$[25 - (25/(2-1)) = 25 - 25 = 0]$$

Appendix D

Sample IEP

(With References to Federal Regulations[1])

Sample Form

Individualized Education Program (IEP)

_____   _____
Student Name   Date of Meeting to Develop or Review IEP

Note: For each student with a disability beginning at age 14 (or younger, if appropriate), a statement of the student's **transition service needs** must be included under the applicable parts of the IEP. The statement must focus on the courses the student needs to take to reach his or her post-school goals.

Statement of Transition Service Needs—
34 CFR §300.347(b)(1)

"The IEP must include...[f]or each student with a disability beginning at age 14 (or younger, if determined appropriate by the IEP team), and updated annually, a statement of the transition service needs of the student under the applicable components of the student's IEP that focuses on the student's courses of study (such as participation in advanced- placement courses or a vocational education program);"

Present Levels of Educational Performance

Statement of Present Levels of Educational Performance—
34 CFR §300.347(b)(1)

"The IEP for each child with a disability must include . . . a statement of the child's present levels of educational performance, including—

"(i) How the child's disability affects the child's involvement and progress in the general curriculum (i.e., the same curriculum as for nondisabled children); or

"(ii) For preschool children, as appropriate, how the disability affects the child's participation in appropriate activities;"

1 of 5

---

[1] Extracted from http://www.ed.gov/about/offices/list/OSERS/index.html (U.S. Department of Education).

Measurable Annual Goals (Including Benchmarks or Short-Term Objectives)

Statement of Measurable Annual Goals, Including Benchmarks or Short-Term Objectives—34 CFR §300.347(a)(2)

"The IEP for each child with a disability must include . . . a statement of measurable annual goals, including benchmarks or short-term objectives, related to—

"(i) Meeting the child's needs that result from the child's disability to enable the child to be involved in and progress in the general curriculum (i.e., the same curriculum as for nondisabled children), or for preschool children, as appropriate, to participate in appropriate activities; and

"(ii) Meeting each of the child's other educational needs that result from the child's disability;"

Special Education and Related Services	Start Date	Frequency	Location	Duration
Supplementary Aids and Services	Start Date	Frequency	Location	Duration
Program Modifications or Supports for School Personnel	Start Date	Frequency	Location	Duration

Statement of the Special Education and Related Services, Supplementary Aids and Services, Program Modifications, and Supports For School Personnel—34 CFR §300.347(a)(3)

"The IEP for each child with a disability must include... a statement of the special education and related services and supplementary aids and services to be provided to the child, or on behalf of the child, and a statement of the program modifications or supports for school personnel that will be provided for the child—

"(i) To advance appropriately toward attaining the annual goals;

"(ii) To be involved and progress in the general curriculum in accordance with 34 CFR §300.347(a)(1) and to participate in extracurricular and other nonacademic activities; and

" (iii) To be educated and participate with other children with disabilities and nondisabled children in the activities described in this section;"

Beginning Date, Frequency, Location, and Duration of Services and Modifications—34 CFR §300.347(a)(3)

"The IEP for each child with a disability must include . . . the projected date for the beginning of the services and modifications described in 34 CFR §300.347(a)(3), and the anticipated frequency, location, and duration of those services and modifications;"

2 of 5

Explanation of Extent, if Any, to Which Child Will Not Participate with Nondisabled Children

Explanation of Extent, if any, to Which Child will Not Participate with Nondisabled Children—34 CFR §300.347(a)(4)

"The IEP for each child with a disability must include ... an explanation of the extent, if any, to which the child will not participate with nondisabled children in the regular class and in the activities described in 34 CFR §300.347(a)(3);"

ADMINISTRATION OF STATE AND DISTRICT-WIDE ASSESSMENTS OF STUDENT ACHIEVEMENT

Any Individual Modifications In Administration Needed For Child To Participate In State Or District-wide Assessment(s)

Statement Of Any Individual Modifications in Administration of State or District-wide Assesments—34 CFR §300.347(a)(5)(i)

"The IEP for each child with a disability must include ... a statement of any individual modifications in the administration of State or district-wide assessments of student achievement that are needed in order for the child to participate in the assessment;"

If IEP Team Determines That Child Will Not Participate In A Particular State Or District-Wide Assessment

• Why isn't the assessment appropriate for the child?

• How will the child be assessed?

If Child Will Not Participate in State or District-wide Assesment—34 CFR §300.347(a)(5)(ii)

"If the IEP team determines that a child with a disability will not participate in a particular State or district-wide assessment of student achievement (or part of an assessment), the IEP must include a statement of—

"(A) Why that assessment is not appropriate for the child; and

" (B) How the child will be assessed;"

How Child's Progress Toward Annual Goals Will Be Measured

How Child's Progress Will Be Measured—
34 CFR §300.347(a)(7)(i)

"The IEP for each child with a disability must include …
a statement of how the child's progress toward the annual
goals described in 34 CFR §300.347(a)(2) will be
measured;"

How Child's Parents Will Be Regularly Informed Of Child's Progress Toward Annual Goals And Extent To Which Child's Progress Is Sufficient To Meet Goals By End of Year

How Parents Will Be Informed of Their Child's
Progress—34 CFR §300.347(a)(7)(ii)

"The IEP for each child with a disability must include …
a statement of how the child's parents will be regularly
informed (through such means as periodic report cards),
at least as often as parents are informed of their
nondisabled children's progress, of—

"(A) Their child's progress toward the annual goals;
and

"(B) The extent to which that progress is sufficient to
enable the child to achieve the goals by the end of the
year."

[Beginning at age 16 or younger if determined appropriate by IEP team]

Statement of Needed Transition Services, Including, If Appropriate, Statement Of Interagency Responsibilities Or Any Needed Linkages

Statement of Needed Transition Services— 34 CFR §300.347(b)(2)

"The IEP must include ... for each student with a disability beginning at age 16 (or younger, if determined appropriate by the IEP team), a statement of needed transition services for the student, including, if appropriate, a statement of the interagency responsibilities or any needed linkages."

Definition of "Transition Services"— 34 CFR §300.29

"(a) As used in [Part B], "transition services" means a coordinated set of activities for a student with a disability that:

"(1) Is designed within an outcome-oriented process, that promotes movement from school to post-school activities, including post-secondary education, vocational training, integrated employment (including supported employment), continuing and adult education, adult services, independent living, or community participation;

"(2) Is based on the individual student's needs, taking into account the student's preferences and interests; and

"(3) Includes: (i) Instruction; (ii) Related services; (iii) Community experiences; (iv) The development of employment and other post-school adult living objectives; and (v) If appropriate, acquisition of daily living skills and functional vocational evaluation.

"(b) Transition services for students with disabilities may be special education, if provided as specially designed instruction or related services, if required to assist a student with a disability tod benefit from special education."

[In a state that transfers rights to the student at the age of majority, the following information must be included beginning at least one year before the student reaches the age of majority]

The student has been informed of the rights under Part B of IDEA, if any, that will transfer to the student on reaching the age of majority.   Yes ☐

Age of Majority—34 CFR §300.347(c)

"In a State that transfers rights at the age majority, beginning at least one year before a student reaches the age of majority under State law, the student's IEP must include a statement that the student has been informed of his or her rights under Part B of the Act, if any, that will transfer to the student on reaching the age of majority, consistent with 34 CFR §300.517."

5 of 5

Appendix E

State Web Sites

Alabama http://www.alsde.edu

Alaska http://www.educ.state.ak.us/

Arizona http://www.ade.az.gov

Arkansas http://arkedu.state.ar.us/

California http://www.cde.ca.gov

Colorado http://www.cde.state.co.us

Connecticut http://www.state.ct.us

Delaware http://www.doe.state.de.us

District of Columbia http://www.k12.dc.us

Florida http://info.doe.state.fl.us

Georgia http://www.doe.k12.ga.us

Hawaii http://arch.k12.hi.us

Idaho http://www.sde.state.id.us

Illinois http://www.isbe.state.il.us

Indiana http://ideanet.doe.state.in.us

Iowa http://www.state.ia.us

Kansas http://www.ksbe.state.ks.us

Kentucky http://www.kentuckyschools.org

Louisiana http://www.doe.state.la.us

Maine http://janus.state.me.us/education

Maryland http://www.msp.msde.state.md.us

Massachusetts http://www.doe.mass.edu

Michigan http://www.mde.state.mi.us

Minnesota http://cfl.state.mn.us

Mississippi http://www.mde.k12.ms.us

Missouri http://www.dese.state.mo.us

Montana http://www.metnet.state.mt.us

Nebraska http://www.nde.state.ne.us

Nevada http://www.nde.state.nv.us

New Hampshire http://www.ed.state.nh.us

New Jersey http://www.state.nj.us

New Mexico http://www.ped.state.nm.us

New York http://www.emsc.nysed.gov

North Carolina http://www.dpi.state.nc.us

North Dakota http://www.dpi.state.nd.us

Ohio http://www.ode.state.oh.us

Oklahoma http://www.sde.state.ok.us

Oregon http://www.ode.state.or.us

Pennsylvania http://www.pde.psu.edu

Rhode Island http://www.ridoe.net/

South Carolina http://www.sde.state.sc.us

South Dakota http://www.state.sd.us

Tennessee http://www.state.tn.us/

Texas http://www.tea.state.tx.us

Utah http://www.usoe.k12.ut.us

Vermont http://www.state.vt.us

Virginia http://www.pen.k12.va.us

Washington http://www.k12.wa.us

West Virginia http://oepa.state.WV.us

Wisconsin http://www.dpi.state.wi.us

Wyoming http://www.k12.wy.us

Glossary

ability-achievement discrepancy A substantial difference between measured ability and measured achievement used in defining learning disabilities.

accommodation An adjustment in the environment or testing conditions designed to eliminate the effects on test performance of a disability.

accountability A movement in education requiring schools and public officials to demonstrate the success of educational programs, often with the use of tests.

ADA Americans With Disabilities Act, a federal law enacted in 1990 requiring various accommodations for persons with disabilities, including reference to such areas as architectural barriers and learning disabilities.

adaptive behavior Behavior related to functioning in everyday life; used as part of the definition of mental retardation.

adequate yearly progress (AYP) Part of the No Child Left Behind Act requiring schools to report progress annually in the percentage of students meeting the "proficient" level of achievement.

administrative law Law resulting from administrative governmental agencies; often called regulations; contrasted with statutory law and case law.

affective domain Outcomes related to feelings, emotions, attitudes, interests, and dispositions; contrasted with cognitive domain.

age equivalent A type of norm in which a person's score is referenced to scores typical for other persons at various age levels.

alignment analysis A formal method for matching test content to curriculum standards; a specific application of content validity studies.

alternate form reliability Reliability determined by correlating two forms of a test.

alternative One of the options in a multiple-choice item.

alternative assessment Assessment techniques other than the usual methods; often contrasted with objectively scored items (e.g., multiple-choice items); examples are projects and portfolios used for assessment.

analytic scoring Scoring a test exercise for several presumably different traits or characteristics.

assessment Methods for obtaining information about students for determining status, achievement, or levels of performance.

authentic assessment Assessment techniques that attempt to use realistic questions, projects, and methods of responding.

automated scoring Scoring or grading of written materials or other products by way of computer programs that attempt to simulate human judgment.

battery A set of tests typically covering different areas or traits and different grade or age levels but coordinated in terms of overall structure and methods of interpretation.

behavior rating scale A set of questions or items about a child's specific behaviors (e.g., neatness, paying attention, aggressive acts), usually completed by a teacher, parent, or other caregiver.

bias Tendency of a measure to yield systematically different scores for certain types of individuals for reasons other than real differences in the trait being measured.

bivariate distribution Representation of the relationship between two variables on a Cartesian (X, Y) coordinate system; also called a scatterplot or scattergram.

Bloom's taxonomy Any one of three classification systems (cognitive, affective, psychomotor) usually attributed to Benjamin Bloom and colleagues; most references are to the cognitive taxonomy.

blueprint An outline of the content of a test, especially in relation to the curricular content the test is intended to cover.

case law Law based on precedents set by court decisions.

central tendency The statistics that describe the middle or typical scores in a distribution; the usual measures of central tendency are the mean, median, and mode.

certification A procedure for demonstrating that a person has met the qualifications for some job or other type of position; the indicator that the demonstration has taken place.

C.F.R. Code of Federal Regulations; the comprehensive list of regulations emanating from the federal government.

checklist grading Assigning grades to students by checking off level of performance (e.g., Met or Not Met; Advanced or Basic) for lists of objectives, behaviors, or areas.

chronological age A person's age, usually given in years and months (e.g., 8–4 means 8 years and 4 months).

classical test theory (CTT) The traditional theory about the construction and reliability of tests, incorporating true score theory.

coefficient alpha A measure of the internal consistency of items on a test; often called Cronbach's alpha.

cognitive domain Areas of development related to knowledge or thinking; often contrasted with the affective and psychomotor domains.

cognitive outcomes Educational outcomes or objectives related to knowledge and thinking; often contrasted with the affective and psychomotor outcomes.

completion item A test item requiring the student to complete a statement, often in the fill-in-the-blank format.

computer-adaptive testing (CAT) A method of testing in which items presented to an examinee are determined by the examinee's responses to earlier items.

concurrent validity Test validity demonstrated by the relationship between a test and some other criterion measured at approximately the same time.

confidence band A band placed around a test score based on the standard error of measurement.

consent decree An agreement between contesting parties about how an issue will be resolved, with the agreement sanctioned by a court of law.

consequential validity Test validity defined by the consequences of using the test for a particular purpose.

construct A trait or variable, such as reading ability, creativity, or attentiveness.

construct irrelevant variance Variance in test scores associated with variables other than those we want to measure.

construct underrepresentation Failure to fully measure the construct we want to measure; measuring only part of the construct of interest.

construct validity A broad array of methods used to support the proposition that a test is measuring its target construct.

constructed-response (CR) item A test item requiring the examinee to construct an answer rather than select an answer from given alternatives.

content standards Lists of objectives that students are expected to learn; sometimes include expected levels of performance.

content validity Test validity defined by the match between test content and some well-defined body of material, such as a curriculum or a set of job skills.

contrasted groups A method for demonstrating the validity of an assessment by showing that groups differ in scores in the expected direction; usually classified as a type of criterion-related validity.

convenience group A group obtained because it is conveniently available rather than being drawn according to a rational sampling plan, usually with reference to test norms.

convergent thinking Mental operations that require a person to develop one correct answer to a problem.

correction for guessing Deducting a certain amount of credit when scoring selected-response items on the assumption that the person guessed at a fraction of items, thus getting some right by chance.

correlation coefficient The numerical expression, ranging from -1.00 to $+1.00$, of the relationship between two variables.

criterion-keying Selecting items based entirely on whether they discriminate between groups; used especially with career interest inventories and some personality tests.

criterion-referenced Interpreting test performance in relation to some well-defined external criterion rather than in relation to norms; contrasted with norm-referenced interpretation.

criterion-related validity Demonstrating test validity by showing the relationship between test scores and some external criterion.

Cronbach's alpha See coefficient alpha.

cut-score A score on a test or criterion indicating passing vs. failing, proficient vs. less than proficient, or some other such division.

D   Abbreviation for the item discrimination index.

descriptive statistics   The branch of statistics devoted to describing characteristics of raw data, including such measures as central tendency, variability, and correlation.

developmental norm   A test norm based on level of development within the trait or characteristic being measured.

deviation IQ   Norms for IQs based on standard scores.

differential item functioning (DIF)   Procedures for determining if test items are performing differently for different groups of examinees (e.g., by gender or racial/ethnic group).

disability   A condition limiting a person's ability to perform under normal circumstances; includes physical, mental, and emotional conditions.

discrepancy analysis   Analyzing differences in various areas of performance (e.g., achievement and ability or different types of abilities); often used for identification of learning disabilities.

distractor   Option in a multiple-choice item other than the correct, or keyed, option.

divergent thinking   Mental operations that require a person to develop many different answers to a problem, especially novel or unique answers.

dossier   An abbreviated or condensed portfolio, especially as applied to a teacher's portfolio of accomplishments.

DSM-IV   *Diagnostic and Statistical Manual of Mental Disorders*, Fourth Edition; the American Psychiatric Association's official classification system for mental and emotional disorders.

equal protection clause   A clause in the 14th amendment to the U.S. Constitution guaranteeing all citizens the right to equal protection under the law.

error score   The hypothetical difference between a person's obtained score and true score.

ESEA   Elementary and Secondary Education Act, a set of federal laws related to education originally enacted in 1965; the No Child Left Behind Act is officially a revision of the ESEA.

essay item (or test)   A test requiring the writing of an essay in response to a prompt or a question; often applied to any type of test other than multiple-choice tests.

exercise   An assessment item or question, often one requiring a constructed response.

expectancy table   A method for displaying criterion-related validity data by indicating expected standing on the criterion for various levels of test performance.

external criterion   The criterion—for example, performance in school or on the job—used to demonstrate test validity.

face validity   The appearance that a test measures its intended target, especially unaccompanied by any empirical evidence.

factor analysis   A class of statistical methods for identifying dimensions underlying many scores or other indicators of performance by examining the relationships among the scores.

fairness   Lack of bias in an assessment.

faking   Answering test items in such a way as to appear in an especially favorable or unfavorable light.

FAPE   Free and appropriate education. A phrase often appearing in federal laws to emphasize that students with disabilities must be served with a free and, especially, an education environment appropriate for the disabilities.

FERPA   Family Educational Rights and Privacy Act, a federal law specifying how information about individuals must be handled; also known as the Buckley amendment.

foils   Another term for the distractors in multiple-choice items.

formative evaluation   Evaluation or assessment that emphasizes use of the information for guiding instruction; contrasted with summative evaluation.

free response   A method of responding to assessment items or exercises in which the student is "free" to respond as seen fit; another term for constructed response.

free-response item   A test item calling for a free response.

frequency distribution   A distribution of raw scores, usually presented in grouped intervals arranged from high to low.

goals   General or global types of educational outcomes; sometimes contrasted with more detailed, specific objectives.

grade book   The book in which a teacher records student scores and grades; sometimes the term designates just an electronic version.

grade equivalent   A type of test norm expressing a person's performance in comparison with the performance of students in various grades in school.

grading   The process of evaluating students' performance and assigning some designation for levels of performance (e.g., a letter, number, percentage, or verbal label).

hierarchical theory   A theory or model of intelligence that postulates a tree-like arrangement of specific abilities aggregated into higher, successively more general abilities.

high-stakes testing   Testing that has very important consequences for individuals, such as certification and licensing tests, admissions tests, or tests required for passing courses.

histogram   A graphic representation of a frequency distribution with vertical columns erected to the level of frequencies for score intervals in the distribution.

holistic scoring   Assigning a single score to an essay (or a similar task) based on the overall impression of its quality; contrasted with analytic scoring.

IDEA   Individuals With Disabilities Education Act, a federal law related to identification and treatment of individuals with disabilities, including learning disabilities; the most recent version is known as IDEA 2004.

IEP   Individualized education program, which must be provided for each student identified as having a disability.

inclusion   The practice of including students with disabilities in the regular (general) curriculum to the extent feasible.

inferential statistics   The branch of statistics dealing with drawing inferences about total populations based on analysis of data in samples.

institutional norm   Norms based on the average (or median) performance of entire institutions rather than on individual persons.

instructional validity   Demonstration that persons taking an achievement test were exposed to material on the test or had an opportunity to learn the material.

internal consistency reliability   Items that, for the most part, are measuring the same trait or characteristic as indicated by the intercorrelations among the items; a type of reliability.

interrater reliability   The degree of agreement about individuals' performance among different raters of a test, response, or product.

intraclass correlation coefficient (ICC)   A type of correlation expressing the degree of agreement among more than two raters or judges.

intrarater reliability   The degree of agreement about individuals' performance when the same rater or judge rates the performance on different occasions.

IQ   Intelligence quotient. In its original form IQ = (mental age)/(chronological age) x 100. In current tests, the IQ is a standard score. Also sometimes used simply to mean intelligence.

item   A single assessment question or exercise; a test typically consists of a number of items.

item analysis   Statistical analysis of individual test items, especially to determine their difficulty level and discriminating power.

item bank   A large group of test items, especially when organized in some systematic manner and/or available electronically.

item difficulty index   Percent right (or in a specified direction) on a test item; usually abbreviated "p" (for percent).

item discrimination index   An index of the degree of separation between high and low groups on a test item.

item response theory (IRT)   A method of test construction using item characteristic curves.

item stem   The question or opening part of a test item to which the examinee must supply an answer.

kappa   A measure of association for categorical data (i.e., data on nominal scales).

keyed response   The correct or desired answer for a selected-response item.

KR-20   Kuder-Richardson Formula No. 20; an index of internal consistency.

KR-21   Kuder-Richardson Formula No. 21; an index of internal consistency which assumes that all items have equivalent difficulty values.

kurtosis   The peakedness or flatness of a frequency distribution.

legislation   Law that originates with an elected legislative body.

licensing   The legal procedure for allowing someone to practice an art or a profession.

Likert method   A format for attitude items in which an examinee expresses a degree of agreement or disagreement with a statement.

local norm   A norm based on a local group of individuals; usually contrasted with a national norm.

mainstreaming   The practice of placing students with disabilities in regular classrooms rather than in separate classrooms; inclusion is the more current term.

mean   The average; one of the measures of central tendency.

measurement   The process of determining the quantity of something; often used as a substitute for the term test or assessment.

median   The middle score, when scores are arranged in numerical order; one of the measures of central tendency.

mental age (MA)   The typical score on a test for persons of a given age; a type of test norm utilizing these typical scores.

mental retardation   A condition of substantially subaverage intellectual ability accompanied by difficulty in adaptive functioning and with onset during the developmental years.

metacognition   Thinking about, analyzing, or evaluating one's own thought processes.

mode   The most frequently occurring score in a distribution of scores; one of the measures of central tendency.

modifications   Use of an alternative assessment methodology when the existing one is not feasible for a person with a certain disability; modification calls for a different assessment rather than the existing assessment administered with accommodations.

multiple-choice item   A test item that presents several choices from which a person selects an answer; often used to designate any type of selected-response item.

NAEP   National Assessment of Educational Progress, a program for surveying knowledge and skills in several content domains in the United States.

narrative reports   Reporting of test performance in ordinary words rather than in numerical scores.

national norm   A norm based on a group intended to be representative of the entire nation at least at selected age or grade levels.

NBPTS   National Board for Professional Teaching Standards, an organization that provides for assessment and certification of teachers beyond regular state requirements.

NCLB   No Child Left Behind Act of 2001, technically a revision of ESEA, a federal law with extensive requirements for specifying content standards, performance levels, and public reporting of results. Actually enacted in 2002, hence sometimes referenced as NCLB 2002, other times as NCLB 2001.

noncognitive outcomes   Outcomes or objectives falling outside the cognitive domain (e.g., development of interests, attitudes, and dispositions).

nontest indicator   An indicator of student accomplishment obtained without directly testing or assessing students on their level of accomplishment.

norm group   Any group whose performance on a test is used as a basis for interpreting the scores of other individuals.

normal curve   A density curve that is symmetrical and unimodal with asymptotic tails; often called the bell curve.

normal curve equivalent (NCE)   A type of test norm that is equivalent to percentile norms at the 1st, 50th, and 99th percentiles, but has equal intervals throughout the scale.

normed score   Any score interpreted in the framework of a set of norms.

norm-referenced   Interpretation of test scores in relation to how groups of people have actually performed on the test; contrasted with criterion-referenced interpretation.

objective inventory   A test of interests or personality that can be scored in a simple, clerical-like manner (e.g., by counting responses to multiple-choice or true-false items).

objective item   Any test item or exercise that can be scored "objectively" (i.e., by simple inspection of the response); responses to such items are often "machine scored."

objectives   Specific learning targets for students; the elements of content standards; usually more specific than goals.

observed score   A person's actual score on a test; contrasted with true score.

odd-even reliability   Method for determining reliability by separately scoring odd-numbered and even-numbered items on the test.

opportunity to learn   Used in connection with the concept of content validity (*see*), showing not only that an assessment covers the curriculum but also that students were actually exposed to or taught the material.

options   The possible answers presented in a selected-response item.

parent-teacher conference   The formal meeting of a teacher with parents (or guardians) regarding a student's progress in school, often including report of assessments.

percentage-right score   Expressing test performance as the percentage of items answered correctly or in a certain direction out of the total number of test items; to be distinguished from percentile score.

percentile   A type of norm giving a point on a scale below which a specified percent of the cases in the norm group falls.

percentile rank (PR)   The percentage of cases in the norm group falling below a given raw score; often used interchangeably with the term percentile.

performance assessment   An assessment requiring people to perform some action, especially an action that simulates a real-life situation; usually contrasted with a paper-and-pencil test.

performance standards   The levels of performance or scores expected or required on an assessment; often given as advanced, proficient, basic, and below basic.

P.L.   Public law; each law enacted by the U.S. Congress has a P.L. number indicating the session of Congress and the number of that law within that session.

point system   A method for scoring tests in which points are awarded for items or parts of items; points are then added to yield a total score.

portfolio   A collection of work, usually completed over some lengthy period of time.

portfolio assessment   Assessment based on examination of the contents of a portfolio.

Praxis III   The third part of the Praxis series of exams; this part is designed for use with practicing teachers.

precision of measurement   An index of reliability derived from the item response theory, showing how well a score was estimated from the model and the items.

predictive validity   Validity demonstrated by showing the extent to which a test can predict performance on some external criterion when the test is administered well in advance.

primary trait scoring   A method for scoring essays or similar products in terms of the extent to which a particular purpose is accomplished.

projective technique   A method of testing where the test stimuli are relatively ambiguous and there is substantial freedom in how the person responds.

prompt   A term used with performance assessments, especially writing assignments, to indicate the task or question to which a student responds.

psychoeducational battery   A set of individually administered tests designed to assess mental abilities and achievement in a coordinated manner, especially related to learning disabilities, ADHD, etc.

psychomotor domain   The area of educational objectives dealing with movement of body parts, including small-muscle and large-muscle movements; contrasted with cognitive domain and affective domain.

p-value   The percentage right or scored in a certain direction for a test item; also presented simply as "p."

range   A measure of variability in data indicating the distance from the lowest to highest score in the set of data.

ratio IQ   (MA/CA) x 100. Mental age divided by chronological age with the result multiplied by 100. The old-fashioned way of determining IQs.

raw score   The original result of scoring a test (e.g., number right or marked in a certain direction) before reference to some type of norm or criterion.

reflection   The process of thinking about information, procedures, and records, especially about one's own performance or practices.

regression to the mean   The tendency for extreme scores (either high or low) to move toward the group mean when tested at another time; occurs when scores on the two occasions are not perfectly correlated.

regulations   Administrative laws, originating with a government agency to supplement legislation.

reliability   The consistency or dependability of test performance across occasions, scorers, and specific content.

reliability coefficient   The numerical index, almost always a correlation coefficient, indicating the reliability of a measure.

rubric   A set of guidelines for scoring or grading responses to a performance assessment.

scaled scores   A type of standard score used to link various levels of a multilevel test.

scattergram   See bivariate distribution.

selected-response (SR) item   Test items in which the examinee selects a response from given alternatives (e.g., multiple-choice or true-false items).

self-report inventory   An interest, a personality, or a behavioral test in which the person responds to a set of items (usually very brief statements) descriptive of self.

skewness   Asymmetry in a frequency distribution; may be to the left or to the right, as indicated by the "long" tail.

Spearman-Brown correction   A formula allowing estimation of the effect on reliability of lengthening or shortening a test.

specific learning disability   One of several types of learning disabilities defined in law.

split-half reliability   A measure of reliability based on splitting the test into two halves, then correlating performance on the two halves.

spreadsheet   The form and format used for entering data into electronic systems, such as Excel and SPSS, often used for recording students performance on tests, etc.

stability coefficient   A correlation coefficient showing the relationship between performance on two different occasions; see also test-retest reliability coefficient.

standard deviation   The square root of the sum of the deviates about the mean (squared), divided by N; the most common measure of variability.

standard error of measurement (SEM)   An index of the degree of variability in test scores resulting from imperfect reliability.

standard score   A type of norm in which raw scores are converted to a scale with a new mean and standard deviation, both usually selected to be nice, memorable numbers.

standardization   May refer to having fixed directions for a test or to the process of developing norms for a test.

standardized   Most frequently refers to use of uniform conditions for administering and scoring a test; sometimes also means having norms for the test.

standardized test   A test having uniform conditions for administering and scoring and often having some type of norms; in popular usage, may refer to such a test that is entirely multiple choice.

standards-based education (SBE)   An approach to education, arising out of the accountability movement, that emphasizes clear identification of content to be learned, specification of required levels of performance, application of the same standards for all students, and assurance of the opportunity to learn.

stanine   A standard score system with a mean of 5 and standard deviation of approximately 2, designed to contain the entire distribution in the range of 1–9, with equal intervals except at the tails of the distribution.

statutory law   Law resulting from action of a legislature; same as legislation; contrasted with administrative law (regulations) and case law.

subgroup norms   Separate norms for each of several subgroups (e.g., different racial/ethnic or gender groups).

summative evaluation   Evaluation emphasizing final level of performance; often used for grading or determining the success of a program; contrasted with formative evaluation.

table of specifications   An outline of the content of a test especially in relation to the curricular content the test is intended to cover; also known as the test "blueprint."

taxonomy   A classification system; in education, usually refers to systems for classifying objectives or levels in areas, such as the cognitive domain.

test   A standardized process or device that yields information about a sample of behavior or cognitive processes in a quantified manner; the set of items a person answers to yield a score.

test-retest reliability coefficient   Reliability determined by correlating performance on a test administered on two different occasions.

theta   The score derived from application of item response theory to test performance.

TIMSS   Trends in International Mathematics and Science Study, a program for testing math and science in many countries at a few age or grade levels; formerly known as Third International Mathematics and Science Study.

true score   The score a person would theoretically get if all sources of unreliable variance were removed or cancelled out; contrasted with observed score.

T-score   A standard score system with $M = 50$ and $SD = 10$.

two-way table   The format for doing a table of specifications using elements of content for rows and elements of processes for columns.

unobtrusive measure   A measure of behavior obtained without direct contact with an individual and without the individual being aware of the measurement.

U.S.C.   Abbreviation for United States Code; that is, federal statutory law.

user norms   Norms based on all cases that completed a test, at least within some specified period of time.

validity   An indication of the extent to which a test measures what it is intended to measure.

validity coefficient   Validity indicated by a correlation coefficient; test scores are correlated with some other criterion.

value-added approach   Assessment based on gain or change from initial status in contrast to assessment based only on final status.

variability   The degree of scatter, or difference, among scores in a data set.

variable   A construct or dimension along which objects vary.

z-score   The score resulting from subtracting from a raw score the mean, then dividing by the standard deviation, thus $z = (X - M)/SD$; sometimes called the normal deviate score.

References

Abedi, J., Hofstetter, C. H., & Lord, C. (2004). Assessment accommodations for English language learners: Implications for policy-based empirical research. *Review of Educational Research, 74*(1), 1–28.

Achenbach, T. M. (1991). *Child Behavior Checklist.* Burlington, VT: University Associates in Psychiatry.

Airaisian, P. W., & Gullickson, A. R. (1997). *Teacher self-evaluation tool kit.* Thousand Oaks, CA: Corwin.

Alexander, K., & Alexander, M. D. (2001). *American public school law* (5th ed.). Belmont, CA: West.

American Association on Mental Retardation. (2002). *Mental retardation: Definition, classification, and systems of supports* (10th ed.). Washington, DC: Author.

American Educational Research Association, American Psychological Association, & National Council on Measurement in Education. (1999). *Standards for educational and psychological testing.* Washington, DC: American Educational Research Association.

American Federation of Teachers, National Council on Measurement in Education, & National Education Association. (1990). *Standards for teacher competence in educational assessment of students.* Washington, DC: Author.

American Psychiatric Association. (2000). *Diagnostic and statistical manual of mental disorders*, (4th ed., text rev.). Washington, DC: Author.

Anastasi, A., & Urbina, S. (1997). *Psychological testing* (7th ed.). Upper Saddle River, NJ: Prentice Hall.

Anderson, L. W., Krathwohl, D. R., Airaisian, P. W., Cruikshank, K. A., Mayer, R. E., Pintrich, P. R., Raths, J., & Wittrock, M. C. (2001). *A taxonomy of learning, teaching, and assessing: A revision of Bloom's taxonomy of educational objectives.* New York: Longman.

Andrews, J. J. W., Saklofske, D. H., & Janzen, H. L. (Eds.). (2001). *Handbook of psychoeducational assessment: Ability, achievement, and behavior in children.* San Diego, CA: Academic Press.

Angelo, T. A., & Cross, K. P. (1993). *Classroom assessment techniques: A handbook for college teachers* (2nd ed.). San Francisco: Jossey-Bass.

Attali, Y., & Bar-Hillel, M. (2003). Guess where: The position of correct answers in multiple-choice test items as a psychometric variable. *Journal of Educational Measurement, 40*, 109–128.

Bailey, D. S. (2003). Who is learning disabled? *APA Monitor on Psychology, 34*(8), 58–60.

Barr, M. A., Craig, D. A., Fisette, D., & Syverson, M. (1999). *Assessing literacy with the learning record: A handbook for teachers, grades K–6.* Portsmouth, NH: Heinemann.

Barr, M. A., & Syverson, M. (1999). *Assessing literacy with the learning record: A handbook for teachers, grades 6–12.* Portsmouth, NH: Heinemann.

Barton, J., & Collins, A. (Eds.). (1997). *Portfolio assessment: A handbook for educators.* Menlo Park, CA: Addison-Wesley.

Beck, M. D. (2003, April). *What are panelists really thinking when they set performance standards?* Paper presented at the meeting of the National Council on Measurement in Education, Chicago, IL.

Bennett, R. E. (1993). On the meanings of constructed response. In R. E. Bennett & W. C. Ward (Eds.), *Construction versus choice in cognitive measurement: Issues in constructed response, performance testing, and portfolio assessment* (pp. 1–27). Hillsdale, NJ: Erlbaum.

Bennett, R. E., & Ward, W. C. (1993). (Eds.). *Construction versus choice in cognitive measurement: Issues in constructed response, performance testing, and portfolio assessment.* Hillsdale, NJ: Erlbaum.

Benson, B., & Barnett, S. (1999). *Student-led conferencing using showcase portfolios.* Thousand Oaks, CA: Corwin.

Berk, R. A. (Ed.). (1984). *A guide to criterion-referenced test construction.* Baltimore: Johns Hopkins University Press.

Black, P., & William, D. (1998a). Assessment and classroom learning. *Assessment in Education, 5*(1), 7–74.

Black, P., & William, D. (1998b). Inside the black box: Raising standards through classroom assessment. *Phi Delta Kappan, 80*(2), 139–144.

Bloom, B. S. (Ed.). (1956). *Taxonomy of educational objectives, handbook 1: Cognitive domain.* New York: Longman.

Borman, W. C., Hanson, M. A., & Hedge, J. W. (1997). Personnel selection. *Annual Review of Psychology, 48,* 299–337.

Boston, C. (2002). The politics of national testing. In L. M. Rudner (Ed.), *What teachers need to know about assessment* (pp. 49–55). Washington, DC: National Education Association.

Brody, N. (1992). *Intelligence* (2nd ed.). San Diego: Academic Press.

Brookhart, S. M. (1993). Teachers' grading practices: Meaning and values. *Journal of Educational Measurement, 30,* 123–142.

Bryant, F. B., & Yarnold, P. R. (1995). Principal-components analysis and exploratory and confirmatory factor analysis. In L. G. Grimm and P. R. Yarnold, *Reading and understanding multivariate statistics* (pp. 99–136). Washington, DC: American Psychological Association.

Bullock, A. A., & Hawk, P. P. (2001). *Developing a teaching portfolio: A guide for preservice and practicing teachers.* Upper Saddle River, NJ: Prentice-Hall.

Burstein, J., Kukich, K., Wolff, A., Lu, C., & Chodorow, M. (1998). *Computer analysis of essays.* Paper presented at the annual meeting of the National Council on Measurement in Education, San Diego, CA. Retrieved January 6, 2004, from http://www.ets.org/research/dload/ncmefinal.pdf.

Bushweller, K. (1999a). Digital deception. *American School Board Journal, 186*(3), 18–23.

Bushweller, K. (1999b). Generation of cheaters. *American School Board Journal, 186*(4), 24–32.

Camara, W. J. (1998). *High school grading policies (RN–04).* New York: College Board.

Camara, W. J. (2001). Do accommodations improve or hinder psychometric qualities of assessment? *The Score Newsletter, 23*(4), 4–6.

Campbell, D. M., Cignetti, P. B., Melenyzer, B. J., Nettles, D. H., & Wyman, R. M., Jr. (2004). *How to develop a professional portfolio: A manual for teachers* (3rd ed.). Boston: Allyn Bacon.

Cashin, W. E. (1995). *Student ratings of teaching: The research revisited* (IDEA Paper No. 32). Manhattan, KS: Center for Faculty Evaluation and Development.

Cizek, G. J. (1999). *Cheating on tests: How to do it, detect it, and prevent it.* Mahwah, NJ: Erlbaum.

Cizek, G. J. (2003). *Detecting and preventing classroom cheating: promoting integrity in assessment.* Thousand Oaks, CA: Corwin.

Cizek, G. J. (Ed.). (2001). *Setting performance standards: Concepts, methods, and perspectives.* Mahwah, NJ: Erlbaum.

Cizek, G. J., Bunch, M. B., & Koons, H. (2004). Setting performance standards: Contemporary methods. *Educational Measurement: Issues and Practice, 23*(4), 31–50.

Cizek, G. J., Fitzgerald, S. M., & Rachor, R. E. (1996). Teachers' assessment practices: Preparation, isolation, and the kitchen sink. *Educational Assessment, 3*(2), 159–179.

Cohen, J. (1960). A coefficient of agreement for nominal scales. *Educational and Psychological Measurement, 20,* 37–46.

College Board. (2004). *The new SAT 2005.* Retrieved October 29, 2004, from http://www.collegeboard.com/newsat/colleges/research.html

Conners, C. K. (2001). *Conners' Rating Scales—Revised: Technical manual.* North Tonawanda, NY: Multi-health Systems.

Council of Chief State School Officers. (2002). Models for alignment analysis and assistance to states. Washington, DC: Author. Retrieved December 10, 2004, from http://www.ccsso.org/projects/alignment_analysis/Models/

Crawford v. Honig, 37 F.3d 485 (9th Cir. 1994).

Crocker, L., & Algina, J. (1986). *Introduction to classical and modern test theory.* New York: Holt, Rinehart & Winston.

Crocker, L. (Ed.). (1997). Editorial: The great validity debate. *Educational Measurement: Issues and Practices, 16*(2), 4.

Cronbach, L. J. (1951). Coefficient alpha and the internal structure of tests. *Psychometrika, 16,* 297–334.

Cross, L. H., & Frary, R. B. (1999). Hodgepodge grading: Endorsed by students and teachers alike. *Applied Measurement in Education, 12,* 53–72.

Danielson, C., & McGreal, T. L. (2000). *Teacher evaluation to enhance professional practice.* Alexandria, VA: Association for Supervision and Curriculum Development.

Data Research (1994). *Statutes, regulations, and case law protecting individuals with disabilities.* Rosemont, MN: Author.

Data Research (1997). *Students with disabilities and special education* (14th ed.). Rosemont, MN: Author.

Debra P. ex rel. Irene P. v. Turlington, 730 F.2d 1405 (11th Cir. 1984).

Dombrowski, S. C., Kamphaus, R. W., & Reynolds, C. R. (2004). After the demise of the discrepancy: Proposed learning disabilities diagnostic criteria. *Professional Psychology: Rsearch and Practice, 35,* 364–372.

Dodd, A. W. (1997). Issues to consider when scoring student portfolios. In S. Tchudi (Ed.), *Alternatives to grading student writing* (pp. 265–273). Urbana, IL: National Council of Teachers of English.

DuPaul, G. J., Power, T. J., Anastopoulos, A. D., & Reid, R. (1998). *ADHD Rating Scale IV.* Los Angeles: Western Psychological Services.

Early Office Museum (2004). *History of the Lead Pencil.* Retrieved December 10, 2004, from www.earlyofficemuseum.com/pencil_history

Ebel, R. L., & Frisbie, D. A. (1991). *Essentials of educational measurement* (5th ed.). Englewood Cliffs, NJ: Prentice Hall.

Educational Testing Service. (2002). *The Praxis series: Understanding your Praxis scores 2002–03.* Princeton, NJ: Author.

Educational Testing Service. (2003). *The Praxis series: Professional assessments for beginning teachers.* Princeton, NJ: Author.

Farr, R., & Beck, M. D. (2003). Evaluating language development. In J. Flood, D. Lapp, & J. M. Jensen (Eds.), *Handbook of research on teaching English language arts* (2nd ed., pp. 590–599). Mahwah, NJ: Erlbaum.

Farr, R., & Tone, B. (1994). *Portfolio and performance assessment: Helping students evaluate their progress as readers and writers.* Fort Worth, TX: Harcourt Brace.

Feldt, L. S., & Brennan, R. L. (1989). Reliability. In R. L. Linn, *Educational measurement,* (3rd ed.). Washington, DC: American Council on Education/Oryx.

Fischer, L., Schimmel, D., & Kelly, C. (1999). *Teachers and the law* (5th ed.). New York: Longman.

Flanagan, D. P., Andrews, T. J., & Genshaft, J. L. (1997). The functional utility of intelligence test with special education populations. In D. P. Flanagan, J. L. Genshaft, & P. L. Harrison (Eds.), *Contemporary intellectual assessment: Theories, tests, and issues* (pp. 457–483). New York: Guilford.

Flanagan, D. P., Genshaft, J. L., & Harrison, P. L. (Eds.). (1997). *Contemporary intellectual assessment: Theories, tests, and issues.* New York: Guilford.

Frey, N., & Hiebert, E. H. (2003). Teacher-based assessment of literacy learning. In J. Flood, D. Lapp, & J. M. Jensen (Eds.), *Handbook of research on teaching English language arts* (2nd ed., pp. 608–618). Mahwah, NJ: Erlbaum.

Frisbie, D. A. (1973). Multiple-choice versus true-false: A comparison of reliabilities and concurrent validities. *Journal of Educational Measurement, 10,* 297–304.

Frisbie, D. A. (1974). The effect of item format on reliability and validity: A study of multiple choice and true-false achievement tests. *Educational and Psychological Measurement, 34,* 885–892.

Gadow, K. D., & Sprafkin, J. (1997). *Attention Deficit Hyperactivity Disorder Symptom Checklist–4* (ADHD-SC4). Stony Brook, NY: Checkmate Plus.

Gardner, H. (1983). *Frames of mind: The theory of multiple intelligences.* New York: Basic Books.

Gardner, H. (1986). The waning of intelligence tests. In R. J. Sternberg & D. K. Detterman (Eds.) *What is intelligence?* (pp. 73–76). Norwood, NJ: Ablex Publishing.

Gardner, H. (1993). *Multiple intelligences: The theory in practice.* New York: Basic Books.

Gardner, H. (1999). *Intelligence reframed: Multiple intelligences for the 21st century.* New York: Basic Books.

Garner, D. M. (1991). *Eating Disorder Inventory-2 professional manual.* Odessa, FL: Psychological Assessment Resources.

Ghaye, A., & Ghaye, K. (1998). *Teaching and learning through critical reflective practice.* London: David Fulton.

GI Forum Images de Tejas v. Texas Educ. Agency, 87 F. Supp.2d 667 (W.D. Tex 2000).

Glass, G. V. (1990). Using student test scores to evaluate teachers. In J. Millman and L. Darling-Hammond (Eds.), *The new handbook of teacher evaluation: Assessing elementary and secondary school teachers* (pp. 229–240). Newbury Park, CA: Sage.

Glass, G. V., & Hopkins, K. D. (1996). *Statistical methods in education and psychology,* (3rd ed.). Boston: Allyn & Bacon.

Goldman, B. A., & Mitchell, D. F. (2003). *Directory of unpublished experimental mental measures* (Vol. 8). Washington, DC: American Psychological Association.

Goodman, D. P., & Hambleton, R. K. (2004). Student test score reports and interpretive guides: Review of current practices and suggestions for future research. *Applied Measurement in Education, 17,* 145–220.

Gronlund, N. E. (1993). *How to make achievement tests and assessments* (5th ed.). Boston: Allyn & Bacon.

Gronlund, N. E. (2000). *How to write and use instructional objectives* (6th ed.). Upper Saddle River, NJ: Prentice Hall.

Groth-Marnat, G. (2003). *Handbook of psychological assessment* (4th ed.). New York: Wiley.

Guilford, J. P. (1959). Three faces of intellect. *American Psychologist, 14,* 469–479.

Guilford, J. P. (1967). *The nature of human intelligence.* New York: McGraw-Hill.

Guilford, J. P. (1988). Some changes in the structure-of-intellect model. *Educational and Psychological Measurement, 48,* 1–4.

Haladyna, T. M. (1994). *Developing and validating multiple-choice test items.* Mahwah, NJ: Erlbaum.

Haladyna, T. M. (1999a). *A complete guide to student grading.* Boston: Allyn & Bacon.

Haladyna, T. M. (1999b). *Developing and validating multiple-choice test items* (2nd ed.). Mahwah, NJ: Erlbaum.

Haladyna, T. M. (2004). *Developing and validating multiple-choice test items* (3rd ed.). Mahwah, NJ: Erlbaum.

Haladyna, T. M., & Downing, S. M. (1989a). A taxonomy of multiple-choice item-writing rules. *Applied Measurement in Education, 1,* 37–50.

Haladyna, T. M., & Downing, S. M. (1989b). The validity of a taxonomy of multiple-choice item-writing rules. *Applied Measurement in Education, 1,* 71–78.

Haladyna, T. M., & Downing, S. M. (2004). Construct-irrelevant variance in high-stakes testing. *Educational Measurement: Issues and Practice, 23*(1), 17–27.

Haladyna, T. M., Downing, S. M., & Rodriguez, M. C. (2002). A review of multiple-choice item-writing guidelines for classroom assessment. *Applied Measurement in Education, 15,* 309–334.

Hambleton, R. K., Swaminathan, H., & Rogers, H. J. (1991). *Fundamentals of item response theory.* Newbury Park, NJ: Sage.

Harcourt Educational Measurement. (2003). *Stanford Achievement Test Series Tenth Edition: Spring technical data report.* San Antonio, TX: Author.

Harrow, A. J. (1972). *A taxonomy of the psychomotor domain.* New York: David McKay.

Hebert, E. A. (2001). *The power of portfolios: What children can teach us about learning and assessment.* San Francisco: Jossey-Bass.

Hewitt, G. (1995). *A portfolio primer: Teaching, collecting, and assessing student writing.* Portsmouth, NH: Heinemann.

Hogan, T. P. (1981). Relationship between free-response and choice-type tests of achievement: A review of the literature. Green Bay, WI: University of Wisconsin. (ERIC Document Reproduction Service No. ED 224 811.)

Hogan, T. P. (2003). *Psychological testing: A practical introduction.* New York: Wiley.

Hogan, T. P. (2005). Types of test scores and their percentile equivalents. In G. P. Koocher, J. C. Norcross, & S. S. Hill (Eds.) *Psychologists' desk reference* (2nd ed., pp. 111–116). New York: Oxford.

Hogan, T. P., & Agnello, J. (2004). An empirical study of reporting practices concerning measurement validity. *Educational and Psychological Measurement, 64,* 802–812.

Hogan, T. P., Benjamin, A., & Brezinski, K. L. (2000). Reliability methods: A note on the frequency of use of various types. *Educational and Psychological Measurement, 60,* 523–531.

Holland, J. L. (1997). *Making vocational choices: A theory of vocational personalities and work environments* (3rd ed.). Odessa, FL: Psychological Assessment Resources.

Impara, J. C. (Ed.). (1995). *Licensure testing: Purposes, procedures, and practices.* Lincoln, NE: Buros Institute of Mental Measurements.

Interstate New Teacher Assessment and Support Consortium. (1992). *Model standards for beginning teacher licensing and development: A resource for state dialogue.* Washington, DC: Council of Chief State School Officers.

Jay, J. K. (2003). *Quality teaching: Reflection as the heart of practice.* Lanham, MD: Scarecrow.

Jenkins, C. B. (1996). *Inside the writing portfolio: What we need to know to assess children's writing.* Portsmouth, NH: Heinemann.

Joint Committee on Standards for Educational Evaluation. (1988). *The personnel evaluation standards: How to assess systems for evaluating educators.* Thousand Oaks, CA: Corwin.

Joint Committee on Standards for Educational Evaluation. (2003). *The student evaluation standards: How to improve evaluations of students.* Thousand Oaks, CA: Corwin.

Joint Committee on Testing Practices. (2004). *Code of fair testing practices in education.* Washington, DC: Author.

Jones, K. (1997). Portfolio assessment as an alternative to grading student writing. In S. Tchudi (Ed.), *Alternatives to grading student writing* (pp. 255–263). Urbana, IL: National Council of Teachers of English.

Jorgensen, M. A., & Hoffmann, J. (2003). *History of the No Child Left Behind Act of 2001 (NCLB).* San Antonio, TX: Harcourt Assessment.

Kaplan, R. M., & Saccuzzo, D. P. (2001). *Psychological testing: Principles, applications, and issues* (5th ed.). Belmont, CA: Wadsworth/Thomson Learning.

Karnes, F. A., & Marquardt, R. G. (1997). Legal issues in gifted education. In. N. Colangelo and G. A. Davis (Eds.), *Handbook of gifted education* (pp. 536–546). Boston: Allyn & Bacon.

Kersting, K. (2004). Debating learning-disability identification. *APA Monitor on Psychology, 39*(9), 54–55.

Keyser, D. J. (Ed.). (2004). *Test critiques* (Vol. XI). Austin, TX: Pro-Ed.

King, B. M., & Minium, E. M. (2003). *Statistical reasoning in psychology and education* (4th ed.). New York: Wiley.

Koretz, D., Stecher, B., Klein, S., & McCaffrey, D. (1994). The Vermont portfolio assessment program: Findings and implications. *Educational Measurement: Issues and Practice, 13*(3), 5–16.

Kramer, J. J. (Ed.). (1993). *Curriculum-based measurement.* Lincoln, NE: Buros Institute of Mental Measurements.

Krathwohl, D. R., Bloom, B. S., & Masia, B. B. (1964). *Taxonomy of educational objectives, handbook II: Affective domain.* New York: Longman.

Kreitzer, A. E., & Madaus, G. F. (1994). Empirical investigations of the hierarchical structure of the taxonomy. In L. W. Anderson & L. A. Sosniak (Eds.), *Bloom's taxonomy: A forty-year retrospective* (pp. 64–81). Chicago: University of Chicago Press.

Kuder, G. F., & Richardson, M. W. (1937). The theory of estimation of test reliability. *Psychometrika, 2,* 151–160.

Lane, S. (2004). Validity of high-stakes assessment: Are students engaged in complex thinking? *Educational Measurement: Issues and Practices, 23*(3), 6–14.

Larry P. ex rel. Lucille P. v. Riles, 793 F.2d 969 (9th Cir. 1984).

Lee v. Butler County Board of Educ., 2000 WL 33680483 (M.D. Ala.).

Lescher, M. L. (1995). *Portfolios: Assessing learning in the primary grades.* Washington, DC: National Education Association.

Likert, R. A. (1932). A technique for the measurement of attitudes. *Archives of Psychology, 140,* 1–55.

Lilienfeld, S. O., Wood, J. M., & Garb, H. N. (2000). The scientific status of projective techniques. *Psychological Science in the Public Interest, 1,* 27–66.

Lilienfeld, S. O., Wood, J. M., & Garb, H. N. (2001). What's wrong with this picture? *Scientific American, 284*(5), 80–87.

Lowney, C. (2003). *Heroic leadership: Best practices from a 450-year-old company that changed the world.* Chicago: Loyola.

Lubinski, D. (2004). Introduction to the special section on cognitive abilities: 100 years after Spearman's (1904) " 'general intelligence,' objectively determined and measured." *Journal of Personality and Social Psychology, 86,* 96–111.

Maddox, T. (2003). *Tests: A comprehensive reference for assessments in psychology, education, and business* (5th ed.). Austin, TX: Pro-Ed.

Mager, R. F. (1984). *Preparing instructional objectives.* Belmont, CA: Pitman Learning.

Marsh, H. W. (1987). Students' evaluations of university teaching: Research findings, methodological issues, and directions for future research. *International Journal of Educational Research, 11,* 253–388.

Marsh, H. W., & Dunkin, M. J. (1997). Students' evaluations of university teaching: A multidimensional perspective. In R. P. Perry & J. C. Smart (Eds.), *Effective teaching in higher education: Research and practice* (pp. 241–320). New York: Agathon.

Martin, W. R., Majesky, J. J., & Eckler, K. (2003). *Handbook of teaching reflectively in grades K–12.* Lanham, MD: Scarecrow.

Marzano, R. J. (2001). *Designing a new taxonomy of educational objectives.* Thousand Oaks, CA: Corwin.

Marzano, R. J., Brandt, R. S., Hughes, C. S., Jones, B. F., Presseisen, B. Z., Rankin, S. C., & Suhor, C. (1988). *Dimensions of thinking: A framework for curriculum and instruction.* Alexandria, VA: Association for Curriculum and Development.

Marzano, R. J., Pickering, D., & McTighe, J. (1993). *Assessing student outcomes: Performance assessment using the dimensions of learning model.* Alexandria, VA: Association for Curriculum and Development.

McCabe, D. L. (1999). Academic dishonesty among high school students. *Adolescence, 34*(136), 681–687.

McCabe, D. L. (2001). Cheating: Why students do it and how we can help them stop. *American Educator, 25*(4), 38–43.

McEwan, E. K. (2002). *10 traits of highly effective teachers: How to hire, coach, and mentor successful teachers.* Thousand Oaks, CA: Corwin.

McMillan, J. H. (2001). Secondary teachers' classroom assessment and grading practices. *Educational Measurement: Issues and Practices, 20*(1), 20–32.

Mehrens, W. A. (2002). Consequences of assessment: What is the evidence? In G. Tindal & T. M. Haladyna (Eds.), *Large-scale assessment programs for all students: Validity, technical adequacy, and implications* (pp. 149–177). Mahwah, NJ: Erlbaum.

MetaMetrics. (2004). MetaMetrics launches the Quantile framework for mathematics. Retrieved October 10, 2004, from http://www.lexile.com/news/9-13-2004.html

Meyer, G. (Ed.). (1999). The utility of the Rorschach in clinical assessment [Special section: I]. *Psychological Assessment, 11,* 235–302.

Meyer, G. (Ed.). (2001). The utility of the Rorschach in clinical assessment [Special section: II]. *Psychological Assessment, 13,* 419–502.

Millman, J., & Darling-Hammond, L. (Eds.). (1990). *The new handbook of teacher evaluation: Assessing elementary and secondary school teachers.* Newbury Park, CA: Sage.

Monahan, J., & Walker, L. (2002). *Social science in law: Cases and materials* (5th ed.). New York: Foundation Press.

Montgomery, K. L. (2001). *Authentic assessment: A guide for elementary teachers.* New York: Longman.

Montgomery, K., & Wiley, D. (2004). *Creating e-portfolios using PowerPoint: A guide for educators.* Thousand Oaks, CA: Sage.

Moore, K. D. (1998). *Classroom teaching skills* (4th ed.). Boston: McGraw Hill.

Murphy, L. L., Plake, B. S., Impara, J. C., & Spies, R. A. (Eds.). (2002). *Tests in Print VI.* Lincoln, NE: University of Nebraska Press.

National Assessment Governing Board. (2001). *Geography framework for the 1994 and 2001 National Assessment of Educational Progress.* Washington, DC: Author. (Available at www.nagb.org/pubs/gframework2001.pdf)

National Commission on Excellence in Education. (1983). *A nation at risk: The imperative for educational reform.* Washington, DC: U.S. Government Printing Office.

National Council of Teachers of English, & International Reading Association. (1996). *Standards for the English language arts.* Urbana, IL: Author.

National Council of Teachers of Mathematics. (2000). *Principles and standards for school mathematics.* Reston, VA: Author.

Neisser, U., Boodoo, G., Bouchard, T. J., Boykin, A. W., Brody, N., Ceci, S. J., Halpern, D. F., Loehlin, J. C., Perloff, R., Sternberg, R. J., & Urbina, S. (1996). Intelligence: Knowns and unknowns. *American Psychologist, 51,* 77–101.

Nester, M. A. (1994). Psychometric testing and reasonable accommodation for persons with disabilities. In S. M. Bruyére & J. O'Keefe (Eds.), *Implications of the Americans With Disabilities Act for psychology* (pp. 25–36). New York: Springer.

Nolan, J., Jr., & Hoover, L. A. (2004). *Teacher supervision and evaluation.* Hoboken, NJ: Wiley/Jossey-Bass.

Nunnally, J. C., & Bernstein, I. H. (1994). *Psychometric theory,* (3rd ed.). New York: McGraw-Hill.

Page, E. B., & Petersen, N. S. (1995). The computer moves into essay grading: Updating the ancient test. *Phi Delta Kappan, 76,* 561–565.

Parents in Action on Special Educ. v. Hannon, 506 F. Supp. 831 (E.D. Ill. 1980).

Parshall, C. G., Spray, J. A., Kalohn, J. C., & Davey, T. (2002). *Practical considerations in computer-based testing.* New York: Springer.

Pellegrino, J. W., Jones, L. R., & Mitchell, K. J. (Eds.). (1999). *Grading the nation's report card: Evaluating NAEP and transforming the assessment of educational progress.* Washington, DC: National Academy Press.

Perry, R. P., & Smart, J. C. (Eds.). (1997). *Effective teaching in higher education: Research and practice.* New York: Agathon.

Peterson, K. D. (2000a). Student surveys for school teacher evaluation. *Journal of Personnel Evaluation in Education, 14,* 135–153.

Peterson, K. D. (2000b). *Teacher evaluation: A comprehensive guide to new directions and practices.* Thousand Oaks, CA: Corwin.

Peterson, K. D. (2001). Presenting complex teacher evaluation data: Advantages of dossier organization techniques over portfolios. *Journal of Personnel Evaluation in Education, 15,* 121–133.

Phillips, S. E. (Ed.). (2000). Defending a high school graduation test: *GI Forum v. Texas Education Agency* [Special issue]. *Applied Measurement in Education, 13*(4).

Piers, E. V., & Herzberg, D. S. (2002). *Piers-Harris Children's Self-Concept Scale* (2nd ed.). Los Angeles: Western Psychological Services.

Pitoniak, M. J., & Royer, J. M. (2001). Testing accommodations for examinees with disabilities: A review of psychometric, legal, and social policy issues. *Review of Educational Research, 71*(1), 53–104.

Plake, B. S., & Impara, J. C. (1993). Assessment competencies of teachers: A national survey. *Educational Measurement: Issues and Practices, 12*(4), 10–12, 39.

Plake, B. S., Impara, J. C., & Spies, R. A. (Eds.). (2003). *The fifteenth mental measurements yearbook.* Lincoln, NE: University of Nebraska Press.

Ramsay, M. C., Reynolds, C. R., & Kamphaus, R. W. (2002). *Essentials of behavioral assessment.* New York: Wiley.

Raymond, M. R. (2001). Job analysis and the specification of content for licensure and certification examinations. *Applied Measurement in Education, 14,* 369–415.

Renaissance Learning. (2003). STAR Math CS Technical manual. Wisconsin Rapids, WI: Author.

Reschly, D. J. (1997). Diagnostic and treatment utility of intelligence tests. In D. P. Flanagan, J. L. Genshaft, & P. L. Harrison (Eds.), *Contemporary intellectual assessment: Theories, tests, and issues* (pp. 437–456). New York: Guilford.

Reynolds, C. R., & Kamphaus, R. W. (2004). *Behavior Assessment System for Children* (2nd ed.). Circle Pines, MN: American Guidance Service.

Robinson, J. P., Shaver, P. R., & Wrightsman, L.S. (Eds.) (1991). *Measures of personality and social psychological attitudes.* San Diego: Academic Press.

Rodriguez, M. C. (2002). Choosing an item format. In G. Tindal & T. M. Haladyna (Eds.), *Large-scale assessment programs for all students: Validity, technical adequacy, and implications* (pp. 213–231). Mahwah, NJ: Erlbaum.

Rodriguez, M. C. (2003). Construct equivalence of multiple-choice and constructed-response items: A random effects synthesis of correlations. *Journal of Educational Measurement, 40,* 163–184.

Runco, M. A. (Ed.). (2003). *Critical creative processes.* Cresskill, NJ: Hampton.

Ryan, J. M., & DeMark, S. (2002). Variation in achievement scores related to gender, item format, and content area tested. In G. Tindal & T. M. Haladyna (Eds.), *Large-scale assessment programs for all students: Validity, technical adequacy, and implementation* (pp. 67–88). Mahwah, NJ: Erlbaum.

Sackett, P. R., & Yang, H. (2000). Correction for range restriction: An expanded typology. *Journal of Applied Psychology, 85,* 112–118.

Sands, W. A., Waters, B. K., & McBride, J. R. (1997). *Computer-adaptive testing: From inquiry to operation.* Washington, DC: American Psychological Association.

Schmidt, F. L., Ones, D. S., & Hunter, J. E. (1992). Personnel selection. *Annual Review of Psychology, 43,* 627–670.

Seashore, H. G. (n.d.). *Test service notebook 148: Methods of expressing test scores.* San Antonio, TX: Harcourt Assessment.

Seddon, G. M. (1978). The properties of Bloom's taxonomy of educational objectives for the cognitive domain. *Review of Educational Research, 48*(2), 303–323.

Seidel, S., Walters, J., Kirby, E., Olff, N., Powell, K., Scripp, L., & Veenema, S. (1997). *Portfolio practices: Thinking through the assessment of children's work.* Washington, DC: National Education Association.

Shaklee, B. D., Barbour, N. E., Ambrose, R., & Hansford, S. J. (1997). *Designing and using portfolios.* Boston: Allyn & Bacon.

Shapiro, E. S. (1989). *Academic skills problems: Direct assessment and intervention.* New York: Guilford Press.

Shaw, M. E., & Wright, J. M. (1967). *Scales for the measurement of attitudes.* New York: McGraw-Hill.

Shermis, M. D., & Daniels, K. E. (2003). Norming and scoring for automated essay scoring. In J. Burstein & M. D. Shermis (Eds.), *Automated essay scoring: A cross-disciplinary perspective* (pp. 169–180). Mahwah, NJ: Erlbaum.

Shinn, M. R. (Ed.). (1989). *Curriculum-based measurement: Assessing special children.* New York: Guilford.

Shinn, M. R. (Ed.). (1998). *Advanced applications of curriculum-based measurement.* New York: Guilford.

Simmons, J., & Carroll, P. S. (2003). Today's middle grades: Different structures, students, and classrooms. In J. Flood, D. Lapp, & J. M. Jensen (Eds.), *Handbook of research on teaching English language arts* (2nd ed., pp. 357–392). Mahwah, NJ: Erlbaum.

Smith, J. K. (Ed.). (1998). Editorial. *Educational Measurement: Issues and Practices, 17*(2).

Smith, T. E. C., Polloway, E. A., Patton, J. R., & Dowdy, C. A. (2004). *Teaching students with special needs in inclusive settings* (4th ed.). Boston: Pearson.

Snow, R. E. (1993). Construct validity and constructed-response tests. In R. E. Bennett and W. C. Ward (Eds.), *Construction versus choice in cognitive measurement: Issues in constructed response, performance testing, and portfolio assessment* (pp. 45–60). Hillsdale, NJ: Erlbaum.

Sparrow, S. S., Balla, D. A., & Cicchetti, D. V. (1984). *Vineland Adaptive Behavior Scales, Interview Edition Expanded Form Manual.* Circle Pines, MN: American Guidance Service.

Sternberg, R. J. (1994b). Triarchic theory of human intelligence. In R. J. Sternberg (Ed.), *Encyclopedia of human intelligence*, pp. 1087–1091. New York: Macmillan.

Sternberg, R. J. (Ed.). (1994a). *Encyclopedia of human intelligence.* New York: Macmillan.

Stiggins, R. J., Arter, J. A., Chappuis, J., & Chappuis, S. (2004). *Classroom assessment for student learning: Doing it right—using it well.* Portland, OR: Assessment Training Institute.

Stiggins, R. J., Frisbie, D. A., & Griswold, P. A. (1989). Inside high school grading practices: Building a research agenda. *Educational Measurement: Issues and Practices, 8*(2), 5–14.

Stiggins, R. J., Rubel, E., & Quellmalz, E. (1988). *Measuring thinking skills in the classroom* (Rev. ed.). West Haven, CT: NEA Professional Library.

Stronge, J. H. (Ed.). (1997). *Evaluating teaching: A guide to current thinking and best practice.* Thousand Oaks, CA: Corwin.

Stronge, J. H., & Ostrander, L. P. (1997). Client surveys in teacher evaluation. In J. H. Stronge (Ed.), *Evaluating teaching: A guide to current thinking and best practice* (pp. 129–161). Thousand Oaks, CA: Corwin.

Sunstein, B. S., & Lovell, J. H. (Eds.). (2000). *The portfolio standard: How students can show us what they know and are able to do.* Portsmouth, NH: Heinemann.

Tabachnik, B. G., & Fidell, L. S. (2001). *Using multivariate statistics* (4th ed.). New York: HarperCollins.

Thurlow, M. L., Elliott, J. L., & Ysseldyke, J. E. (1998). *Testing students with disabilities: Practical strategies for complying with district and state requirements.* Thousand Oaks, CA: Corwin.

Thurlow, M. L., & Ysseldyke, J. E. (2002). *Including students with disabilities in assessments.* Washington, DC: National Education Association.

Tucker, P. D., Stronge, J. H., & Gareis, C. R. (2002). *Handbook on teacher portfolios for evaluation and professional development.* Larchmont, NY: Eye on Education.

Traub, R. E. (1993). On the equivalence of the traits assessed by multiple-choice and constructed-response tests. In R. E. Bennett & C. W. Ward (Eds.), *Construction versus choice in cognitive measurement: Issues in constructed response, performance testing, and portfolio assessment* (pp. 29–44). Hillsdale, NJ: Erlbaum.

United States Department of Education. (2000). *A guide to the individualized education program.* Jessup, MD: ED Pubs. Retrieved November 9, 2004, from http://www.ed.gov/parents/needs/speced/iepguide/index.html

Volpe, R. J., & DuPaul, G. J. (2001). Assessment with brief behavior rating scales. In J. J. W. Andrews, D. H. Saklofske, & H. L. Janzen (Eds.), *Handbook of psychoeducational assessment: Ability, achievement, and behavior in children* (pp. 357–385). San Diego, CA: Academic Press.

Waltman, K. K., & Frisbie, D. A. (1994). Parents' understanding of their children's report card grades. *Applied Measurement in Education, 7,* 223–240.

Watkins, M. W., & Canivez, G. L. (2004). Temporal stability of WISC-III subtest composite: Strengths and weaknesses. *Psychological Assessment, 16,* 133–138.

Webb, E. J., et al. (1966). *Unobtrusive measures: Nonreactive research in the social sciences.* Chicago: Rand McNally.

Webb, E. J., et al. (1981). *Nonreactive measures in the social sciences* (2nd ed.). Chicago: Rand McNally.

Webb, E. J., Campbell, D. T., Schwartz, R. D., & Sechrist, L. (2000). *Unobtrusive measures* (Rev. ed.). Thousand Oaks, CA: Sage.

Whitley, B. E., & Keith-Spiegel, P. (2002). *Academic dishonesty: An educator's guide.* Mahwah, NJ: Erlbaum.

Williams, J. D. (2000). Identity and reliability in portfolio assessment. In B. S. Sunstein & J. H. Lovell (Eds.), *The portfolio standard: How students can show us what they know and are able to do* (pp. 135–148). Portsmouth, NH: Heinemann.

Williamson, D. M., Bejar, I. I., & Sax, A. (2004). Automated tools for subject matter expert evaluation of automated scoring. *Applied Measurement in Education, 17,* 323–357.

Willingham, W. W., Ragosta, M., Bennett, R. E., Braun, H., Rock, D. A., & Powers, D. E. (1988). *Testing handicapped people.* Needham Heights, MA: Allyn & Bacon.

Wolman, B. B. (Ed.). (1985). *Handbook of intelligence: Theories, measurements, and applications.* New York: Wiley.

Woodcock, R. W., McGrew, K. S., & Mather, N. (2001). *Woodcock-Johnson III.* Itasca, IL: Riverside.

Yang, Y., Buckendahl, C. W., Juszkiewicz, P. J., & Bhola, D. S. (2002). A review of strategies for validating computer-automated scoring. *Applied Measurement in Education, 15,* 391–412.

Name Index

Subject Index